Chaucer and Langland

Chaucer
and Langland

The Antagonistic Tradition

JOHN M. BOWERS

University of Notre Dame Press

Notre Dame, Indiana

Library of Congress Cataloging-in-Publication Data

Bowers, John M., 1949–

Chaucer and Langland : the antagonistic tradition / John M. Bowers.

   p. cm.

Includes bibliographical references and index.

1. English literature—Middle English, 1100–1500—History and criticism.

2. English literature—Middle English, 1100–1500—Criticism, Textual.

3. Chaucer, Geoffrey, d. 1400—Appreciation. 4. Langland, William,

1330?–1400?—Appreciation. 5. Chaucer, Geoffrey, d. 1400—Influence.

6. Langland, William, 1330?–1400?—Influence. 7. Manuscripts, English (Middle)

8. England—Intellectual life—1066–1485. I. Title.

PR255.B69   2007

821'.1—dc22

                                  2006039806

For

Lee Cagley
Kate and Steve McKenna
Elaine Zerga and Vince Felgar
Douglas Unger

The Culture Club

Contents

Acknowledgments

INITIAL RESEARCH FOR THIS VOLUME BEGAN MORE THAN TWO DECADES ago with a Fellowship for College Teachers from the National Endowment for the Humanities. Many new ideas emerged during the 1995 NEH Summer Institute on "Chaucer and Langland" organized by C. David Benson and Elizabeth Robertson at the University of Colorado, Boulder. This unusually accomplished fellowship of medievalists emerged with new resolve to bring these two great poets of the late fourteenth century back into a single historical frame in our future research as well as our classrooms.

Work on this book gained momentum during a 2000–2001 sabbatical from the University of Nevada, Las Vegas, supplemented by the generous award of a Guggenheim Fellowship. An invitation from the Rockefeller Foundation permitted a four-week residency at the Bellagio Study Center where Gianna Celli and the staff at the Villa Serbelloni afforded gorgeous seclusion, while other residents, including Alastair Minnis, offered lively intellectual companionship. I wish to express my deep gratitude to Warden Dame Jessica Rawson and the Fellows of Merton College, Oxford, for hosting me as a Visiting Research Fellow for the Trinity term 2001. A note in the Bodleian MS Bodley 619 of *Treatise on the Astrolabe*—"secundum Astrolabium Collegii de Merton"—serves as a reminder of Chaucer's own connection with Oxford's oldest collegiate foundation. Finally, the Fletcher Jones Trust provided a much-valued residence at the Huntington Library during the summer of 2002.

I have profited from gestures of assistance, large and small, from colleagues who made the work more correct and the enterprise more lively.

x   Acknowledgments

They have included John Alford, Denise Baker, Helen Barr, Caroline Barron, Charles Blyth, Michael Calabrese, David Carlson, Jeffrey Jerome Cohen, Andrew Cole, Helen Cooper, Carolyn Dinshaw, A. I. Doyle, Hoyt Duggan, Carol Everest, John H. Fisher, Andrew Galloway, Linda Georgianna, Alex-andra Gillespie, Richard Firth Green, Ralph Hanna III, Roger Highfield, Anne Hudson, Andrew James Johnston, Terry Jones, Henry Ansgar Kelly, V. A. Kolve, Steven Kruger, Kathryn Lynch, Anne Middleton, Jenni Nuttall, Charles Owen, Lee Patterson, Derek Pearsall, Thomas A. Prendergast, Pa-mela Robinson, Philip Rusche, Wendy Scase, R. Allen Shoaf, James Simpson, Paul Strohm, Penn Szittya, Stephanie Trigg, and Karl Wilcox. During the past dozen years my book *The Politics of "Pearl": Court Poetry in the Age of Rich-ard II*, as well as articles in *Studies in the Age of Chaucer* and *Yearbook of Langland Studies*, became adjunct projects as I learned much from historians with lit-erary interests such as Michael J. Bennett and Nigel Saul and especially the latest pioneers in paleography such as Linne Mooney, Simon Horobin, and Kathryn Kerby-Fulton. Derrick G. Pitard kindly sent an advance copy of his "Selected Bibliography for Lollard Studies" from *Lollards and Their Influence*. The University of Notre Dame Press's outside reader Bruce Holsinger pro-vided many pages of comments so careful, thoughtful, and detailed that I can hardly estimate my debt of gratitude.

Certainly I have failed to name other scholars who have contributed to this enterprise, so I wish to thank them anonymously. This is fitting, since the whole issue of named and anonymous figures remains central to the discus-sions that follow. Trial sections of this volume have previously appeared as book chapters in *Inscribing the Hundred Years' War in French and English Cultures*, *Rewriting Chaucer: Culture, Authority and the Idea of the Authentic Text, 1400–1602*, and *Speaking Images: Essays in Honor of V. A. Kolve;* and as journal articles in *Chaucer Review, Chaucer Yearbook, Medieval Perspectives,* and *Yearbook of Langland Studies*. I am grateful to editors and presses for permission to publish ma-terials revised from these prior studies.

Abbreviations

BJRL	*Bulletin of the John Rylands Library*
CT	*The Canterbury Tales*
ChauR	*Chaucer Review*
EETS e.s.	Early English Text Society, extra series
EETS o.s.	Early English Text Society, original series
EHR	*English Historical Review*
ELN	*English Language Notes*
ES	*English Studies*
ELH	*English Literary History*
FCS	*Fifteenth-Century Studies*
HLB	*Huntington Library Bulletin*
HLQ	*Huntington Library Quarterly*
JEGP	*Journal of English and Germanic Philology*
JMEMS	*Journal of Medieval and Early Modern Studies*
JMH	*Journal of Medieval History*
LSE	*Leeds Studies in English*

M&H	*Medievalia et Humanistica*
MÆ	*Medium Ævum*
MLN	*Modern Language Notes*
MLQ	*Modern Language Quarterly*
MLR	*Modern Language Review*
MP	*Modern Philology*
MS	*Mediaeval Studies*
N&Q	*Notes and Queries*
NLH	*New Literary History*
NM	*Neuphilologische Mitteilungen*
NML	*New Medieval Literatures*
P&P	*Past and Present*
PBA	*Proceedings of the British Academy*
PL	*Patrologia Latina*
PMLA	*Publications of the Modern Language Association*
REL	*Review of English Literature*
RES	*Review of English Studies*
SAC	*Studies in the Age of Chaucer*
SB	*Studies in Bibliography*
SCH	*Studies in Church History*
SP	*Studies in Philology*
STC	*Short Title Catalogue*
TLS	*Times Literary Supplement (London)*
TRHS	*Transactions of the Royal Historical Society*
YES	*Yearbook of English Studies*
YLS	*Yearbook of Langland Studies*

CHAPTER ONE

Introduction

The Antagonistic Tradition

ONE WELL-REGARDED HISTORY OF MEDIEVAL ENGLISH LITERATURE claims the fatherhood of Chaucer as the constitutive idea for the entire tradition. Another survey of fifteenth-century poetry assesses Chaucerian fatherhood as the disabling dynamic to account for the shortcomings of his literary progeny. And yet another book critiques the English brotherhood of writers and readers looking back to "congenial" Chaucer to find their own family resemblances.[1] Different as their approaches are, each book accepts the historical fact of Chaucer as the father of English literature. My enquiry begins with the simple question why Geoffrey Chaucer—not William Langland—was granted the patriarchal position not described in exactly these words until John Dryden's Preface to the *Fables* (1700): "he is the Father of English Poetry."[2] Although Chaucer's own concept of literary tradition suggests that he considered himself primarily an heir, not a begetter, the notion of a patrilineal inheritance deriving from him as a father figure was already formulated within a generation of his death when Thomas Hoccleve acknowledged Chaucer's fatherhood in the famous commendation in *The Regiment of Princes* (c. 1412): "Allas, my fadir from the world is go, / My worthy maistir Chaucer—him I meene."[3]

An explosion of English-language writings during the later fourteenth century can be attributed to a diversity of cultural and intellectual forces,[4] and A. I. Doyle's legendary doctoral thesis, *A Survey of the Origins and Circulation of Theological Writings in English,* provides a magisterial appraisal of vernacular book-production exactly contemporary with Chaucer's career but almost completely separate from his literary activities.[5] Nonetheless, Hoccleve's insistence upon Chaucer's foundational position was continued throughout the fifteenth century by a series of literary heirs, most notably John Lydgate, who repeatedly named the poet and left no doubt that Chaucer—and Chaucer alone—originated the English poetic practices which these later writers worked to fortify as a self-conscious tradition.

Schooled by Nietzsche, Foucault, and Derrida, we recognize that literary genealogies necessarily depend upon stable origins that are not always fixed, unitary, or even factually real.[6] Christopher Cannon provides one of the most theoretically informed accounts describing how the myth of the Chaucerian origin made itself true: "I think that Middle English written tradition existed in the plural and that this plurality profoundly qualifies Chaucer's claim to have started anything."[7] Although the two fourteenth-century poets were roughly contemporary and their works have been valuably studied within a shared historical context, all evidence points to Langland holding the senior position with a poem rapidly disseminated and immediately influential.[8] Helen Cooper has confirmed Coghill's long-standing view that Chaucer himself read *Piers Plowman* during the 1380s and Langland's poem informed his estate satire in the General Prologue of the *Canterbury Tales,* specifically his portrait of the Plowman.[9] Frank Grady suggests that the intertextual relationship went back even further when Langland's dream-poetry gave impetus to Chaucer's own strange and unpredictable *House of Fame,* with its non-narrative discourse and formal habits of literary development that might otherwise have become normative.[10]

A. C. Spearing corrects Harold Bloom's historically short-sighted view that early authors such as Shakespeare belonged "to the giant age before the flood, before the anxiety of influence became central to poetic consciousness," in order to trace the dynamics of the family romance in the fifteenth-century tradition following Chaucer.[11] But the author of *The Book of the Duchess* had his own rebellions to stage. Since Langland shows no signs of reading Chaucer's works, the direction of influence was entirely one way, with the anxiety felt exclusively on Chaucer's part.[12] Any dialogue that might have emerged between the two contemporary London poets devolved into a Chaucerian monologue.[13] While Chaucer shows a half-humorous sense of competitiveness with his older colleague John Gower, his struggles with Langland come closer to Bloom's sense that "strong poets make that history by misreading one another so as to clear imaginative space for themselves"; real *agon* resides at the heart of this antagonism between "major figures with the persistence to wrestle with their strong precursors, even to the death."[14]

Along with *Piers Plowman,* Chaucer's *Troilus* had entered circulation among London's reading circles during the mid-1380s—the text was quoted extensively by Thomas Usk in his *Testament of Love* about 1385[15]—and *Troilus* somehow remained yoked with Langland's work into the fifteenth century when the two long poems were copied together in HM 114 and both works were mentioned in the wills by Thomas Stotevyle (1459) and Sir Thomas Charleton (1465).[16] As a result, the *Canterbury Tales* in the 1390s became Chaucer's last best chance for engaging with Langland's literary achievements and topical challenges while also rebelling against Langland's kind of literature. Even Chaucer's representation of himself as small and pudgy (*CT,* VII, 700–704) may have been meant to distinguish him from "long lean Will" Langland. The entire Chaucerian tradition would carry forward this burden of anxiety, repressed and neurotically expressed, into the fifteenth century.

My investigations suggest some important rewriting of the history of English literature at the close of the Middle Ages and the beginning of the Renaissance as well as a revised sense of the origins of "English literature" as a cultural category inherited and then fixed by early print editors. Departing from prevailing accounts that privilege the Chaucerian tradition, my version of this story begins and ends with *Piers Plowman.* Langland's work not only encouraged parallel underground practices but also established itself as a textual presence, really a cultural presence with practical social and political challenges, steadily affecting the development of the official and highly visible Chaucerian tradition in works such as Hoccleve's *Regiment of Princes* and Lydgate's *Troy Book.* In the literary firmament, Langland became the adjacent black hole whose gravitational field consistently determined the shape and luminosity of the bright star Chaucer.

Though his ascendancy as the father of English literature has established itself as the official story since the sixteenth century, Chaucer's preeminence in this fabricated genealogy of national poets was by no means automatic or guaranteed.[17] In terms of the literary timeline, the earliest complete version of Langland's *Piers Plowman* in the B-text (1378–81) predates the composition *Troilus and Criseyde* (early 1380s) and the *Canterbury Tales* (1390–1400). Anticipating these achievements, Langland had already challenged the dominance of Latin and French writings by composing a long, serious, and widely read English poem—Middleton estimates that copies must have numbered in the hundreds by 1400[18]—some years before Chaucer pursued similar ambitions and more than a decade before their contemporary, Gower, composed his *Confessio Amantis* in English reportedly at the prompting of Richard II.[19] Langland achieved historical priority since his work was actually read, quoted, copied, and imitated throughout the last decades of the fourteenth century, whereas there is little hard evidence that Chaucer's works had any wide readership even at court during his lifetime. Langland's first nineteenth-century editor staked this claim firmly: "As the aera of these Visions is now ascertained to have preceded the great work of Chaucer by twenty years, the author must be considered the first English poet."[20] But this claim did not prevail in the history of English literature institutionalized later during the Victorian era.

As many as twenty manuscripts of *Piers Plowman* can be dated paleographically to the fourteenth century. This crude statistic by itself indicates that Langland's poem was copied and read by his contemporaries.[21] On the other hand, the fact that no *Canterbury Tales* manuscript, with the possible exception of Hengwrt, can be confidently dated to the poet's lifetime suggests that his compositions did not circulate in significant numbers among his immediate contemporaries.[22] The copies of *Troilus* and *Boece* mentioned in Chaucer's playful "Adam Scriveyn" were probably executed by the professional scribe now identified as Adam Pinkhurst, but these seem to have been private commissions as the poet's fair copies, not for presentation or circulation.[23] Beverly Boyd has described what was probably also the piecemeal and confusing status of the *Canterbury Tales* when the work did enter circulation: "not known as a unit by Chaucer's public or by his friends, the materials existing separately or in clusters, sometimes in more than one version, borrowed back and forth by individuals in more than one attempt to put together a unified work."[24] If manuscripts provided the sole evidence for dating his literary career, Chaucer might today be classified as a fifteenth-century poet. Recent critical assessments confirm the implications of early work by Aage Brusendorff leading to the conclusion that Geoffrey Chaucer, as an English author, was very much manufactured as a cultural presence early during the century after his death.[25] Recent attention to the "Ellesmere Chaucer" confirms the notion of a poetic identity constructed from later redactions of the *Canterbury Tales*.[26]

The fundamental terms of the Chaucer tradition required structures that were linear, interlocking, and continuous. "Only continuity can guarantee that nature repeats itself," Michel Foucault observed, "and that structure can, in consequence, become character."[27] Biblical commentators arguing with each other as they did in early fifteenth-century England, for example, become part of the character of a culture, because these differences of opinion take place within the bounds of cultural identity and indeed define the strict borders of that identity. Secular literary tradition formulates itself on the same template. Its scriptures are literary classics such as the *Canterbury Tales,* its exegetes are the professional readers such as Adam Pinkhurst, and its saints are the canonized authors such as Chaucer, Gower, and Lydgate. Such a tradition's continuity and cohesiveness also exercised an exclusionary force.

The word *tradition* actually entered the English language in a largely pejorative sense during the later fourteenth century at almost exactly the moment when Langland and Chaucer were producing substantial poetic works that would contest the beginnings of an English literary tradition. The online *Middle English Dictionary* produces its earliest attestation from the Wycliffite Bible's translation of Mark 7:3 ("Pharisees waisschen ofte her hondis, holdinge the *tradiciouns* or statutis of eldere men") and Colossians 2:8 ("Se þe that no man diseyue þou by philosofye and veyn fallace, or gilouse falshede, vp the *tradicioun* of men"). The *OED* offers further insights into the term's earliest semantic valence by citing two passages from other Lollard writings as its first attestations, each protesting the claims of customary practice to justify self-serving ambitions.[28] As critics of religious houses, John Wyclif's followers proposed a return to original practices based upon scriptural authority as opposed to prevailing traditions that were clearly man-made. One Wycliffite tract complained how monasteries defended the practice of owning property on the basis of *tradition*—"a tradycion þat þei han hem-sijlfe made."[29] The Carmelites, for example, had developed an elaborate historical fiction tracing their origins back to the prophets Elijah and Elisha, when they had in fact begun as hermits who settled on Mount Carmel only at the end of the twelfth century.[30] Thus the word's earliest appearance in vernacular writings came loaded with a sense of fictitious origins, artificial construction, and self-serving motives. It is therefore significant that the *MED*'s second attestation comes from the Chaucerian poet John Lydgate, himself a member of a religious order, whose *Troy Book* (1412–20) offers a wholly positive sense in support of long-established practices:

> For by techyng of al holy chirche,
> Þe holy doctryne and *tradiciouns,*
> We schal dispise swiche oppiniouns
> Whiche of þe fende wer founde nat of late.[31]

T. S. Eliot's "Tradition and the Individual Talent" (1919) made the now famous argument that a literary tradition repeatedly underwent revisions whenever a new talent came upon the scene.[32] In the opening sentence of *The Chaucer Tradition* (1925), Brusendorff offered a similar notion of the malleability of cultural inheritance: "Tradition means the handing down of information in such a way that it is laid open to the influence of the successive generations through which it passes."[33] This view that authors were constantly subject to revaluation was memorably mocked by Northrop Frye when describing how literary reputations rise and fall on an imaginary stock exchange.[34] "To say that Chaucer 'started a tradition' is to create that 'start' and that 'tradition' at a blow."[35] Championed by agents who included fifteenth-century Lancastrians deeply anxious about instability and change, the great fiction about *tradition* became its existence as a stable and unchanging fixture. Later Chaucerian poets committed their enterprises to continuing this Chaucer tradition in large part to exclude any competing founder such as Langland, much as Chaucer explicitly claimed the classical tradition of "Virgile, Ovide, Omer, Lucan and Stace" (*Troilus* 5.1792) to obscure and elude his real debt to Boccaccio.[36]

The basic operation of any tradition involves transmitting something to the next generation, and this process enlists that power of patriarchal succession, literally from father to son, with heavy obligation imposed upon each new generation to respect what was handed down. Chaucer himself had an almost instinctive response to this structure of social regulation. The two pilgrims placed prominently at the beginning of his General Prologue are the Knight and the Squire, father and son, who graphically represent the social mechanism by which power and status are transmitted lineally.[37] Near the conclusion of the Knight's Tale, Duke Theseus imposes his own authoritative sense of well-regulated succession ordained by the First Mover.[38] Central to this orderly worldview is the somber reminder that all things progressively decay from their original integrity—"Descendyng so til it be corrumpable" (*CT,* I, 3010)—so that the best, the strongest, and the most authoritative "thyng" is located at the beginning of the sequence. True greatness resides in firstness.

Tradition's strongest defense resides in its deeply conservative faith that everything was better in the distant past. As the prime beneficiary of this retrospective scheme in literary history, Chaucer himself undercut this proposition in his somberly witty lyric *The Former Age.* His ironic vision of primeval perfection entailed a whole host of privations such as no wine, no bread, no spices, no housing, no bedding, no metalwork, and no consumer goods—

since there was no money and there were no merchants. This "blissed folk" lived in caves, slept on the bare earth, drank cold water, and contented themselves with a diet of nuts and berries.[39]

Cultural agents who invoke tradition invariably rely upon the fiction of venerable age and time-tested authority. Eric Hobsbawm focuses on traditions such as those surrounding the British monarchy that attempt to establish continuity with a usable historical past: "'Invented tradition' is taken to mean a set of practices, normally governed by overtly or tacitly accepted rules and of a ritual or symbolic nature, which seek to inculcate certain values and norms of behavior by repetition, which automatically implies continuity with the past."[40] His prime example is the use of Gothic style for the nineteenth-century rebuilding of Parliament. Anthropologists investigating traditional societies tell much the same story. "Over and over, researchers in such societies have been told, 'That is the way we have always done it,' even when the specific custom may in some cases be shown to have been very recent in origin."[41] It takes only two generations to make anything *traditional*.[42]

Much more rapidly, Chaucer's poetry was being promoted as traditional within two decades of his death. While seemingly hostile to change, tradition can therefore become an engine for innovation. For those constructing a vernacular tradition in the early fifteenth century, Chaucer would become installed as the literary "first mover" meant to generate succession and guarantee cultural continuity for the English nation. Because such traditions are constructed most frequently when rapid social and political transformations undercut the patterns for which prior traditions were designed—here the metropolitan literary traditions of romances, biblical texts, Anglo-French writings, and Langlandian poetry described by Ralph Hanna in *London Literature, 1300–1380*—Geoffrey Chaucer, however much honored as an innovator, became immediately more useful when viewed as the stable source of time-honored customs securely anchored in the Plantagenet past of John of Gaunt.

George Kane's conjunction of Langland and Chaucer as the two dominant poets from fourteenth-century England found much to distinguish them: "Of the two Chaucer appears cosmopolitan, international, a time-spanner. By contrast Langland's focus may seem narrow: no classical furniture or Roman ruins or hillsides in Lombardy here, but a bristling complex of theological and moral and spiritual cruces."[43] Viewing Chaucer's differences from Langland as intentional, self-styled, and even strategic on the part of the author of the *Canterbury Tales,* I wish to examine their overlapping careers and particularly the later histories of manuscript production in order to suggest dual posterities deriving from two writers who occupied the same geographical space (London) and the same historical span (1370s–90s). By retracing the well-worn paths from Medieval to Renaissance, I give ample regard to the Langlandian role in shaping this double tradition by tracking the public life of *Piers Plowman* from the text's latest datable reference to the Normandy Campaign of 1360, to allusions in letters to the rebels of 1381, to anonymous works such as *Pierce the Ploughman's Crede* and *Mum and the Sothsegger* inspired by Langland's poem, and finally to Robert Crowley's first printed edition as Protestant propaganda in 1550.[44]

While the general outline of Langlandian history has become familiar from the work of many recent scholars,[45] my investigation draws upon a wide variety of cultural materials—especially the numerous *Piers* manuscripts produced over the course of two centuries—to suggest that Langland's poem retained much of its controversial potential, offering its title character for appropriation by Lollard sympathizers and, at other moments, becoming the target of antireformist suppression in the form of various literary police-actions. At a time when ecclesiastical authorities were rallying the loyalties of laymen, vernacular texts were also forced to choose sides, and Chaucer, whose jobs included various forms of civil service, had already produced literary texts that admirably served the orthodox ends of the traditionalists against the reformers.[46]

James Simpson's *Oxford English Literary History* has proposed a retrospective narrative that simplified and narrowed the category of "literature" as part of a sixteenth-century revolutionary campaign intent upon demolishing the prior order. Langland the reformist becomes Langland the cultural revolutionary in this extended Tudor narrative, although the ultimate advantage went (again) to the Chaucerian heritage with its coherent genealogy and cleanness of design.[47] Instead of delineating the Chaucerian and Langlandian traditions separately so that the advantage would always automatically revert to the author of the *Canterbury Tales,* I propose studying the two in their mutual relationship, each necessary to configure the other, like the double helix of the DNA molecule. There is counterpose as well as intertwining, convergence as well as rivalry, redundancy as well as parts without apparent purpose in this double-track tradition. Chaucer and his followers such as Hoccleve were clearly aware of *Piers Plowman,* while Langland and his nameless successors seem largely innocent of Chaucer's literary achievements until the Protestant era. Since the B-text of *Piers Plowman* was apparently composed in London and as many as a third of all manuscripts were copied in London, the two traditions of English literature competed in the same arena of literary production, not region against region.[48] As Ralph Hanna has described Langland's antagonist presence, "this Otherness essentially occupies a space of consciousness, not of geography."[49]

Across this terrain of religious controversy and textual contests, the history of *Piers Plowman* proceeds not as a continuous strand but as a succession of isolated episodes, moments of contestation and accommodation in which the work operated in a number of ways under shifting conditions of disciplinary moves and countermoves. Sometimes subject to clerical franchise, sometimes resisting all manner of factional appropriation, and at still other times open to seizure by Lollard sympathizers, Langland's poem was read, it was glossed, it was copied and recopied, and it offered itself as a model for religious and political satires such as *Pierce the Ploughman's Crede* (c. 1393) and *Richard the Redeless* (c. 1400) far more incendiary than the original work. Largely prosaic in its vernacular program of translation and tract production, Lollardy produced only a small body of English verse, nearly all of it Langlandian.

CHAPTER 2, "Beginnings," establishes the year 1360 as the common starting point for my double narrative with a historical episode that linked both poets.[50] The most recent datable event in *Piers Plowman* is the Normandy Campaign of 1360. Collapse of this military expedition brought a dispiriting end to the series of England's military successes with famous victories at Crécy (1346) and Poitiers (1356). Retreat into an insular isolationism provoked displeasure among the warriors who fought these battles, always with the expectation of personal renown and reward, while offering hope of solace to taxpayers who funded these expeditions without the prospect of direct personal gain. Langland's poem reflects this withdrawal into narrower concerns with strictly English social and religious causes. These domestic themes would permanently mire his work in controversies over the abuses of pilgrimage, the corruption of the mendicant orders, the theology of salvation, and the mercenary motives for religious vocations—that is, those same issues increasingly associated with Lollard activists committed to "þe reformaciun of holi chirche of Yngelond."[51]

As a fluke of history, young Geoffrey Chaucer actually participated in the Normandy Campaign of 1360. One of the earliest life-records indicates he was taken prisoner and Edward III contributed £16 to his ransom. Like his subsequent career as a diplomat, Chaucer's literary activities remained steadily internationalist in outlook. He vigorously engaged with French

cultural models from the outset of his poetic career, and from the 1380s onward he explored Italian literary works by Dante, Petrarch, and particularly
Boccaccio in order to create an entirely new kind of English literature. As a
result, his poetry cannily evaded direct comment upon the domestic controversies that became the hallmark of Langlandian poets. By casting himself as
a player on the European stage, Chaucer also became available as the official
literary representative of a newly emergent English nationalism that could be
recognized only in this larger international context.[52] Creation of the *idea* of
a national culture became one of the preconditions for the exercise of state
authority at home and Lancastrian ambitions for dominion overseas, specifically in Normandy.[53]

In his touchstone study *Beginnings,* Edward Said reminds us that no neat
narrative continuity automatically emerges amid the jumbled events of national history: "A beginning immediately establishes relationships with works
already existing, relationships of either continuity or antagonism or some
mixture of both."[54] Recognition of this counterfeit deployment of Aristote-
lean cause-and-effect removes the privileged authority of an origin and repo-
sitions this power, as a written act, at an intentionally assigned *fons et origo.*
Instead of describing some natural starting point, this historical account con-
trives some event as a point of departure that makes sense specifically in
terms of its conclusion. Great explanatory power resides in the designation
of a beginning.[55]

Erich Auerbach had anticipated this critique when considering Modernism's rejection of plot as the complete representation of any total chronological continuum. "Life has always long since begun," he wrote, "and it is
always still going on."[56] Therefore even a pristine origin, which seems as absolute as God's creation or an individual's birth, can be recognized as part of
an artificial pattern, like the system of primogeniture, designed to justify certain ends in the grand scheme of dispersal and recovery. When Chaucer has
the Nun's Priest rewrite the biblical text from the opening of Genesis—"In
principio / Mulier est hominis confusio" (*CT,* VII, 3163–64)—he rewrites
human history as a vast chronicle of male downfalls through female contriv-
ances. In the absence of an authentic origin, an author's narrative demands
some fictional consolidation. Every act of creation contains its own beginning in the intentional production of meaning. However random and contrived, a good beginning makes good narrative sense.

A story may lack an ending and even a middle, but it never lacks a beginning. "Call me Ishmael." "It was the best of times, it was the worst of times."
"All happy families are happy in the same way." Nonetheless, Langland es-

tablished his problematic sense of a beginning in the well-known but deeply puzzling opening lines of *Piers Plowman*:

> In a somer sesoun, whanne softe was the sonne,
> I shop me into shroudes as I a shep were,
> In abite as an ermyte vnholy of werkis,
> Wente wyde in þis world wondris to here.

These lines begin the A version. These lines also begin the B version without rewriting to resolve the issues that prompted continuing the poem. These lines are still used to begin the C version, again without major clarification.[57] The omission of an expository prologue with formal instructions for negotiating the poem's conceptual syntax (*forma tractatus*) established a troubling absence that Langland chose never to remedy, or rather tried to remedy only with the C-text *apologia* some five passus into the text.[58] However brief in its lyric, antiromance mode, the prologue of a true *chanson d'aventure* goes somewhere because the author knows where he is heading, while Langland kept coming back to the same starting point as if constantly changing his mind about his poem's contents without changing its opening lines.

After a first line so formulaic that it sounds like a cliché, Langland's second line poses an immediate challenge on the basic level of meaning. What is a *shep*—a sheep or a shepherd? Is the narrator a hermit or only dressed like one? Is the protagonist "unholy of works" or would be unholy only if he really were a hermit?[59] Circumstances prior to the first lines are required to understand these first lines, contrary to Aristotle's declaration "a beginning is that which itself does not of necessity follow something else" (*Poetics* 7). Langland's poem is immediately hobbled by the problem of "the lyf that ys lowable and leel to the soule" as one of the most hotly debated issues in late medieval culture. The ideal life preached by the Franciscans remained one of the central organizing discourses even while corrupt practices, such as Will's vagabond existence, rendered this ideal livelihood as an absence marked by intense nostalgic longing.[60]

D. Vance Smith's *Book of the Incipit* offers perhaps the most sophisticated and insightful elaboration of Nietzsche, Foucault, Habermas, Derrida, and Said himself in a highly theorized interrogation of Langland's compulsive practice of beginning again. Focusing upon institutional and dynastic needs for stable starting points, his chapter "Origo: Genealogy, Engenderment and Digression" epitomizes the argument that *Piers Plowman*, rather than showing a careless attitude toward its beginnings, becomes obsessed with rehearsing these initiative gestures in its ten separate dream episodes.[61] Since Langland's injunctions to ethical action refuse to impose finality upon temporal priorities, any one of his dramatic ending-episodes such as Piers's tearing of the Pardon immediately offers itself as a major new point of departure. As Middleton has suggested, the C-text *apologia* represents a late-career attempt at beginning all over again, five passus deep into his revised text, as a "primary confrontation with his powers and talents that formed and articulated the first intentions of the work" in an interpolated episode that also declares *"his work finished—as finished as it will ever be."*[62] By challenging the violence and divisiveness enacted by genealogical formation, Langland forfeited the obvious benefits that might have fallen to his work as patrimony within any later literary tradition deployed as continuity and lineal power.

This recursiveness is reflected in the internal movements of the poem throughout. Because Langland's thinking is ruminative rather than narrative as Aristotelian cause-and-effect, his thoughts are structured by associative rather than architectural designs. *"Piers* has no plot not because nothing happens," Mary Carruthers has observed, "but because nothing that does happen seems very much to affect anything else that happens."[63] Organization is modular instead of sequential or even spiral. The disrupted episode becomes Langland's signature.[64] There is little sense of narrative direction and almost no novelistic sense that things need to happen where they do, not earlier or later. The narrator Will remains as clueless about the direction of events as the reader. Despite an apparatus that divides the text into passus, spiritual progress becomes very much a matter of three steps forward, two steps back. Derek Pearsall has pointed out that nothing so much distinguishes Langland from his Lollard successors than this characteristic method of groping after the truth, qualifying, circling around, and returning again and again to difficult questions: "Lollards do not seek the truth—they know the truth."[65]

Speaking through the character Imaginatyf later in his career, Langland expresses ongoing skepticism about the knowability of any true beginning— "Was neuere creature vnder Crist þat knewe wel þe bygynnyng" (C.14.159)— as the precondition for a coherent deployment of materials in his unending search for truth. Revising extensively in the middle stretches of the text, the poet could transpose sections so readily from B to different positions in C because these materials were seldom securely anchored. Over and over, Langland's poem seems motivated by thematic repetitions that cause events— never fully "cause" and never exactly "events"—to circle back upon themselves for further examination rather than moving forward to some clear conclusion. This circularity frustrates any sense of logical concatenation and can create instead a sense of intellectual motion sickness.

Like his wayward series of eight disjointed dream-sequences, with two baffling dreams-within-dreams in B, the chronologies in all three standard versions of *Piers* are disrupted by a neglect of linear development. Anything could happen almost anywhere—or not. The retelling of the Crucifixion and Harrowing of Hell in B.18 assimilates the characters and events of sacred history, but then the account moves beyond narrative solidity into apocalyptic time. The poem ends *in medias res* at some vague midpoint where Christian history stops unfolding. The narrator himself remains in a liminal state of conscious—"til I gan awake"—neither continuing his visionary experience nor re-entering the waking world to practice the lessons learned while dreaming. Not open-ended as an explicit invitation for future writers to continue the enterprise, the poem's final action in which Conscience has been lulled into a state of complacency by Friar Flattery represents a great leap backward spiritually to the action of the second vision, where the penitential process went further and achieved more.[66]

The poem's relentless synchronicity has its counterpart in its treatment of literary history, as if the only antecedent that Langland could imagine was himself, the author of the previous version of *Piers*. He shows none of Chaucer's or Gower's fascination with pagan mythology just as he demonstrates little acquaintance with classical literature as a learned syllabus. Of course he did have his poetic predecessors. *Piers* is affiliated with the native tradition of other alliterative poems such as *Wynnere and Wastoure* and Harley 2253's "Song of the Husbandman,"[67] yet the keenest anxiety of influence that Langland felt came from the influence of his own previous versions. Though intensely nostalgic for some imaginary past before the "pestilence tyme" (B.Pro.84), the poet infused *Piers* with a sense of literary history so nebulous about national history, so careless of its literary precedents, and so lacking in concern for its own posterity—reflected in the poet's astonishing indifference to the vicissitudes of his work's dispersal in a scribal culture—that his own position within the English tradition became a permanent problem. "Langland stands quite against the Chaucerian projective," Hanna notes, "the imagination of a literary future."[68] Though his poem was included in CUL Dd.1.17's enormous assemblage of historical writings, *Piers Plowman* represents what might now be termed contemporary history, maybe even a forerunner of "gonzo journalism," with its outraged chronicling of a corrupt Christian community during the reader's own day.

Like the text itself, its characters lack the discursive integrity of real beings with past lives and future ambitions. What did Lady Mede do as a girl? How will she live after her marriage plans have been thwarted? We can pose questions such as these about the Wife of Bath but not about Lady Mede. Like his allegorical characters, Langland constantly revised his own image as a vernacular writer, further destabilizing his position as an author with any firm placement in this nascent tradition. The distinction between poet and dream-narrator remains insoluble. As a literary figure, Langland had a career that also defies any clear charting of artistic development. The existence of the Z-text raises questions about the stability and boundaries of his canon.[69] Recent studies have even questioned the basic order of his revisions, whether A then B and then C—*or* B then C and then A.[70]

Rather than providing clarity, a modern parallel-text edition is more likely to bewilder the reader while actually misrepresenting the fluidity of the author's revisions. It becomes impossible to grasp any consistent reasons for the poet's additions, deletions, and transpositions of materials, as well as his obsessive fussiness with rewriting certain passages while leaving others untouched. Almost like Walsingham's revisions of his monastic chronicles, each version of Langland's poem can be viewed as an effort to keep pace with the rapidly changing drama of national life, while also attempting to avoid misprision and forestall misappropriation. He was constantly "spinning" the text in response to these events, taking particular care in the C-text to adjust theological notions banned as erroneous by the Blackfriars Council of 1382.[71] Permanently embedded in contemporary controversies, *Piers Plowman* became a text pulled along by national events as they unfolded.[72] Constantly renewing itself as a living text—so different from its exact contemporary *Troilus and Criseyde,* with its pleas for stability and constancy—*Piers Plowman* could never stake its claim as the stable starting point for any historical tradition.

By contrast, Chaucer was a master of beginnings that consistently demonstrated a clear sense of where the writer wanted to start, how he wished to present his characters and materials, and in what direction he intended each story to proceed. The importance of beginnings was reinforced by rhetorical treatises such as the *Poetria Nova,* by Geoffrey of Vinsauf, whose advice Chaucer paraphrases when he describes the start of Pandarus's plotting in *Troilus and Criseyde* (1:1065–69).[73] But Chaucer employed an instructional manual only to confirm his own appreciation of a story's clear beginning. His habitual use of the opening word *Whilom* proclaims the starting point that confidently implies *in the beginning* as much as it expresses the sense of *once upon a time*. The Knight's Tale begins "Whilom as olde stores tellen us" (*CT,* I, 859), the Miller's Tale begins "Whilom ther was dwellynge at Oxenford" (I, 3187)—and so forth. Never does the poet show uncertainty in his opening lines even when playfully prattling at the start of *Parliament of Fowls*. To this day, one of the most famous beginnings in English literature remains the Chaucerian passage that high school students still memorize: "Whan that Aprill with his shoures soote."

Chaucer displays a similar sense of craftsmanship in shaping his literary career. When he wrote the *Book of the Duchess* and attached his first major poem to the occasion of the Duchess of Lancaster's death around 1368, Chaucer initiated a whole series of "new beginnings" anchored in precise moments in English history. He began adapting his literary genres from the French tradition of Guillaume de Machaut. He rendered the Latin legend of Ceyx and Halcyon derived ultimately from Ovid's *Metamorphoses*. And he began writing in an English poetic diction that self-consciously broke with the native tradition of "rum ram ruf," disdained along with the alliterative poets, such as Langland, who are never even acknowledged in Chaucer's works. His neglect of these alliterative writers can no longer be attributed to their provincial isolation. Strong evidence indicates that both Langland and the *Pearl* Poet resided in the metropolis and their works circulated in London during Chaucer's lifetime.[74]

Storytelling and career planning are both related to a sense of narrative construction. Although translated from Deguileville's vast *Pèlerinage de la vie humaine*—perhaps very early as stated by Thomas Speght, perhaps very late as suggested by Terry Jones—Chaucer composes his *ABC to the Virgin* as a prayer with its stanzas arranged according to the order of the alphabet.[75] Here the poet signaled his deep-down awareness of the artificial imposition of a sequence based upon some predetermined sense of how to begin: A, then B, then C, and so on. Many of Chaucer's narratives proceed upon the assumption that historical beginnings are similarly artificial in their determinations. The Knight narrates the opening chapter in the history of Western civilization in his account of the reign of Theseus. The chronicle of conflict between Athens and Thebes is connected through Diomede to the history of the Trojan War. The destruction of Troy and the escape of its refugees from Carthage connect not only with the foundation of Rome under Aeneas but also with the foundation of Britain under Brutus.[76] The Man of Law's new beginning actually represents a continuation of this narrative in which the old Britons have their secret Christian practices legitimized by the arrival of Custance. And so on. Chaucer did more than write an abecedarian lyric to the Virgin Mary. Through the course of his career, he constructed an abecedarian history of Western civilization leading to the emergence of British culture: A is for Athens, B is for Brutus, C is for Custance, and so on.[77]

Chaucer was haunted by an almost crushing sense of prior literary history but not narrowly *native* literary history.[78] His gestures toward the past become remembrances tinged with mourning over the loss of books including those whose existence he himself suppressed.[79] He acknowledged the Greek foundations of Homer, even though he had never seen a Greek text of *The Iliad* and could not have read it if shown a codex during his travels in northern Italy.[80] He was intensely aware of the Latin tradition stemming from Virgil and Ovid, even though he routinely used French adaptations to assist his understanding of these classical works. His dream lore was derived explicitly from the late Roman writer Macrobius (fl. c. 400), and he translated *De Consolatio Philosophiae* by Boethius (d. 524). He acknowledged the authority of the later Latin writer Alanus de Insulis (d. c. 1202) and used materials derived from Guido delle Colonne's *Historia Destructionis Troiae* (1287). He took the lead among Englishmen in venerating the works of the trecento Italian authors Dante and Petrarch. As a parallel phenomenon, the extraordinary compilation *Chaucer Life-Records* tells us that his own family history perfectly represented the pattern of transmitting inheritance from son to son, with only one heir in each generation.[81] John Chaucer bequeathed to Geoffrey Chaucer, who bequeathed to Thomas Chaucer. In the cultivated London circles of the late fourteenth century, the poet Chaucer similarly positioned himself as the sole heir of the European literary legacy and hence the sole progenitor for an English tradition.[82]

Near the end of *Troilus,* Chaucer places himself in the succession of the great poets of antiquity (5:1792). In the *House of Fame,* he provided a similar roster of the six great writers who upheld the fame of Troy: Homer, Dares Phrygius, Dictys Cretensis, Lollius, Guido delle Colonne, and "Englyssh Gaufride" (1464–70). Osbern Bokenham referred to Chaucer as "Galfryd of Ynglond" and "Galfridus Anglicus" when commending his predecessor in his *Legendys of Hooly Wummen,*[83] and E. K. Rand long ago suggested that Chaucer was naming himself as the author of *Troilus*. Redating *House of Fame* to the late 1380s, Helen Cooper has revived this view of an authorial signature when the English Geoffrey Chaucer claimed his rightful place along with its weighty obligations.[84] The dubious rewards of literary renown are chillingly dramatized in the Prologue to the *Legend of Good Women,* however, where Chaucer is accused on charges of "heresy" for what he had written in his Trojan epic *Troilus.*

When literature as a cultural category is defined in terms of dynastic inheritance, literary careers become no longer freestanding but understood in terms of succession and continuity. Each new writer constitutes a link in the chain of historical transmission, but only if he makes an effort to associate himself with past writers and to reach out to future ones. Chaucer's obsession with constructing a literary genealogy in which he figured as heir to prior achievements became one of his most strategic acts of history making. His literary allusions create a sense of adjacency that placed him next in line. He conceived of a continuum, then entered it. Jockeying for position in a race when Langland did not even recognize the nature of the competition, Chaucer cunningly situated himself to become patriarch for the English branch of that larger Continental family tree. Casting himself as sole English heir of European literature, Chaucer re-enacted the Trojan settlement of "Brutes Albyon" to become the first inhabitant of an unpopulated literary realm. Like Geoffrey of Monmouth's barren Britain open for colonization, Chaucer's literary Britain had also been emptied of any native inhabitants.[85] Along with the accumulated wealth of his clan, he also inherited the obligation of managing the family's holdings, which included many far-flung properties handed on from generation to generation. By making constant recourse to a usable past, his own works in turn became a poetic archive available to later writers. In nearly all of his major works, however, he depicted the founder's obligation as burdensome, time consuming, and even dangerous.

Masterful in his invention of beginnings, Chaucer created notorious problems with his endings. The Parson's Tale was not the conclusion that readers expected for the *Canterbury Tales,* for example. Many works simply have no endings, or they are left unfinished, or they show other signs of incompleteness.[86] *The Romaunt of the Rose, The House of Fame, Anelida and Arcite, A Treatise on the Astrolabe, The Legend of Good Women,* and most famously the *Canterbury Tales* are unfinished. Within the *Canterbury Tales* itself, the Cook's Tale, the Squire's Tale, the Monk's Tale, and Chaucer's own Tale of Sir Thopas lack proper conclusions. Vinsauf's *Poetria Nova* offered no support for this neglect of endings: "Let the conclusion, like a herald when the race is over, dismiss it honorably" (18). In a sense, nothing so clearly indicates the poet's sense of himself as founder of an ongoing tradition than his refusal to impose closure upon his literary projects.[87] These unfinished works provided an open invitation for literary heirs to perform their filial duties by continuing the family business. It was a ploy that actually solidified Chaucer's executive position. The activities of a whole series of continuators such as John Lydgate, the *Beryn* Poet, Robert Henryson, and even William Shakespeare attest to the success of this strategy.[88] Chaucer's primacy as "the firste fyn-dere of our fair langage"—to recall the precise terms of Hoccleve's com-mendation—became the beginning of the ongoing story written by his suc-cessors. Endings became Lydgate's peculiar strength,[89] because he so clearly cast himself as the last surviving heir to this tradition in the fifteenth century.

CHAPTER 3, "Naming Names," looks at the processes by which the En-glish tradition formulated itself around a named author and did not—and could not as a genealogical program—accommodate an author whose name was withheld, suppressed, forgotten, and eventually unrecoverable by future generations of readers wanting to reconstruct that lost legacy. Since Chaucer is credited with doing so much to create a sense of personal selfhood in lit-erature,[90] one of my questions in this book asks why his invention as an En-glish writer, along with the making of his literary canon, took place during the century after his death rather than during his lifetime.

The nineteenth-century French historian Ernest Renan long ago identi-fied the twin processes for creating national self-consciousness: "The es-sence of a nation is that all individuals have many things in common, and also that they have forgotten many things!"[91] Like national history, literary tradition also defines itself partly by what it forgets. Strategic amnesia con-stantly operates in the process of canon-formation by forcibly excluding au-thors and works in a process nicely described by Vance Smith: "The fiction that is implicit in the authoritative beginning is thus most crucially an act of forgetting, an obliterating of the extrinsic features that really authorize it or that undermine it, of the dispersed motives and unnatural violence that must be forgotten in creating a pure origin."[92] Though now viewed as founders, Langland and Chaucer actually arrived on the literary scene midway in a chronology stretching back to the eighth century when Cædmon was desig-nated as the first-named English poet in Bede's *Ecclesiastical History*.[93] The monks who collected and preserved these books in their libraries continued to play a significant role in the creation of literary history as a legitimate cul-tural category, and monastic writers such as Ormm, Robert of Gloucester, Robert Mannyng, Dan Michael of Northgate, and Walter Hilton made signal contributions to the production of vernacular texts.[94] Self-conscious of their own English-language tradition, alliterative poets almost always declared their reliance upon pre-existing accounts with phrases like "as þe boke telles."[95] These writers operated with a sense of continuity soon to be permanently disrupted.

English literary history suffered two major episodes of self-induced amnesia for periods prior to its now official foundation in the later fourteenth century. First, the cultural dislocations following the Norman Conquest had resulted in a massive forgetting of the Anglo-Saxon poetic tradition so that Bede's first-named poet Cædmon, the self-naming Cynewulf, and the anonymous author of *Beowulf*—as well as the uncountable writers and texts lost through centuries of neglect—were denied their places in some continuous tradition of English poetry.[96] Second, earlier works in Middle English such as *Havelok the Dane, King Horn, Sir Orfeo,* and *The Owl and the Nightingale* look to us like productions of scattered provincial locations such as Grimsby, Southampton, Winchester, and Guildford and therefore examples of a cottage industry that never cohered into an authentic literary movement.[97] The *Ormulum, Cursor Mundi, Northern Homilies, South English Legendary,* Robert Mannyng's *Handlyng Synne,* Michael of Northgate's *Ayenbite of Inwit* and even the *Prick of Conscience,* along with the *Ancrene Wisse* and the Katherine Group, also look like the inconsequential experiments of isolated clergymen. Even the poetical achievements of Harley 2253, Digby 86, and BL Add. 46919 (William Herebert's religious verses) can be viewed as dead-end efforts because they found no obvious posterity.[98] Since works such as the *Short Metrical Chronicle,* Laȝamon's *Brut,* and Robert Mannyng's *Chronicle* made effective claims upon English language and English history, this earlier period was not necessarily destined for cultural oblivion. Recent books by Thorlac Turville-Petre, Christopher Cannon, and Ralph Hanna attempt to resuscitate this earlier episode in Middle English literary history by acknowledging and then challenging the official start-up enterprise during the second half of the fourteenth century.[99]

Nor was the author of the *Canterbury Tales* entirely innocent of a neglect that verges upon suppression. The durability of this traditional beginning around 1350, accepted once again in the new *Oxford English Literary History,*[100] can be attributed partly to Chaucer's own refusal to acknowledge any Middle English poetry or any named poet prior to his own inaugural career. Although *Sir Orfeo* and the generous, wide-ranging contents of the Auchinleck manuscript were likely produced in London and known directly by Chaucer himself, he nonetheless failed to make explicit claims upon such works as native antecedents.[101] Similarly, while aware of *Piers Plowman* and perhaps also *Sir Gawain and the Green Knight* as vernacular poems read by other Londoners, even by courtiers within the household of Richard II, Chaucer scrupulously avoided acknowledging the contributions of any contemporary poet to the exuberant literary life of the metropolis, neglecting even his friend "moral Gower" except as a recipient charged with correcting *Troilus*.[102] Before making a grand entrance, it was necessary for him to clear the stage.

While Chaucer was famous for preferring French and Italian sources, Langland was nearly as delinquent of prior English poetry except for passing allusions to popular works such as "rymes of Robyn Hood and Randolf Erl of Chestre" (B.5.396).[103] His alliterative versification could have claimed descent from venerable Anglo-Saxon practices, even if fourteenth-century readers would have struggled with understanding the Old English language.[104] Kerby-Fulton notes that the poet of the A-text casts himself in the role of a Saxon *scop*,[105] and Langland himself makes an appeal to some venerable form of English when he argues for an earlier, more authentic meaning of the word *lollares:* "As by þe Engelisch of oure eldres, of olde mennes techynge" (C.9.214). Though he was also aware of Anglo-Saxon history when alluding to the famous episode of Pope Gregory sending missionaries led by St. Augustine of Canterbury (B.15.442–50), the poet did not assert this prestigious national lineage or even reflect upon this distinctive versification, as did the *Gawain* Poet with his "lel letteres loken."[106] A large enough body of fourteenth-century alliterative poetry survives for the distinction of an English School,[107] but Langland behaves as if he were the only writer pursuing a poetic craft so singular that he could hardly justify it as a legitimate occupation.[108] He was the first English poet to compose a substantial work that achieved a truly nationwide readership, very different from the regional audiences achieved by other fourteenth-century alliterative works, but he gave no indication of appreciating his own exclusive position. While Chaucer wrote about, rewrote, wrote over, and wrote back to other literary works, Langland undertook a form of writing about the *process* of writing, writing as justification for writing, and writing as the pretext for further writing in his neverending process of revising his one and only work.

Langland seems interested less in named poets than in the snatches of learned Latin texts that he gathered into his macaronic poem. The non-English accretions are not marginal glosses that have somehow intruded into the body of the text but really constitute main structural elements for organizing intellectually the allegory of the dream-narrative.[109] While his relentless citation of learned authorities worked at justifying the status of this bilingual project, his addiction to Latin quotations had the side effect of compromising the Englishness of his poem while blurring the distinction between text and gloss, between the center and the margins. Morton Bloomfield's famous assessment deserves citation one more time: "It is like reading a commentary on an unknown text."[110] If Chaucer shows symptoms of Bloomian anxiety of influence when acknowledging his predecessors Virgil, Statius, and Dante—and especially when *not* acknowledging Boccaccio— Langland's anxiety is largely self-contained in his struggles with the prior versions of his own poem, B coping with the inadequacies of A, and C wrestling with the seismic implications of B.[111] Instead of affiliating his poem with other literary texts, Langland consistently appropriated the discursive forms of legal documents such as Mede's charter, Piers's pardon, Hawkyn's acquittance, Moses's maundement, and Peace's patent.[112] This centrality of documentary forms serves as important evidence of the poem's immediate readership and perhaps even the poet's own professional activities in London.[113] Since the text of *Piers Plowman* is so conspicuously interlarded with Latin citations, its scholastic language made a credible bid for aligning the poem with the authoritative tradition of Latin writings and its author with the prestigious pedigree of *auctores*.[114] As a writer, however, Langland almost entirely lacked Chaucer's sense of the bookishness of any literary works, including his own.[115] By absorbing so many textual ingredients while acknowledging so few, the proliferating versions of *Piers Plowman* had the power to saturate all available textual space and fill every textual niche—as evidenced by the wide variety of manuscript anthologies in which it survives—while losing much of the distinctiveness of its own literary identity in the process.

Seemingly oblivious to literary forebears such as Richard Rolle (d. 1349) with right of precedence as an English religious author,[116] Langland appears equally delinquent about his own claims as a named author upon subsequent literary history. His concentration upon the events of contemporary England excluded any abiding concern for posterity. Even the prophetic features in his writings disregard continuity with future events while urgently addressing the needs of his own present moment when he envisioned, as Wyclif did, the forces of the Antichrist already unleashed and requiring urgent measures for spiritual renewal.[117] He made no effective attempts at connecting his name to the work and may have actively obstructed efforts at identifying him as the writer responsible for *Piers Plowman*. When the figure Kynde awakens the dream narrator by calling his name—"And nempned me by my name" (B.11.321)—the poet teasingly omits including the name itself.

If not for a brief biographical note added to Trinity College Dublin MS 212 (D.4.1), we would have no concrete evidence for Langland's full name, place of birth, and paternal connections.[118] The authorial inscriptions and anagrammatic wordplays so brilliantly discussed by Anne Middleton—

"I haue lyued in lond," quod I, "my name is Longe Wille" (B.15.152)—look more like inside jokes intended for coterie readers, somewhat like the jibes that James le Palmer playfully directed at his fellow Exchequer clerks in *Omne Bonum*. These inscriptions probably contributed to some sophisticated program of self-personification lost upon the reading public after the poet's death and the disappearance of his initial audience. To the extent that these signatures attested to Langland's authorship, they were conspicuous failures.[119]

Five C-text manuscripts contain the following notation at the end of Passus 10: *Explicit visio Willielmi . W. de Petro le Plouhman*.[120] Otherwise the great majority of *Piers* manuscripts contain no attempt at authorial naming, and almost no effort was made at retrieving Langland's full name before the sixteenth century. The blankness of the poet's identity means that he could not be associated with prominent patrons, such as the Despensers perhaps, who occupied their own highly visible niches in national history. When copying a text that lacked the stabilizing force of a named author, scribes often felt free from the sort of authority that prevented their transcriptions from becoming acts of collaborative rewriting.[121] Each copying job became a personalized effort at adjusting the poem's contents to current circumstances and target audiences. To the frustration of modern editors, these textwriters went about the business of producing their own D-texts, E-texts, and F-texts of *Piers Plowman*, while the stabilizing authority of the author, always vague at best, exercised less control over their various combinations and permutations.

Hanna focuses upon a London readership as Langland's first audience, simultaneously metropolitan and provincial, with legal interests understood specifically as royal legal service or parliamentary service and located in one of the great houses of the Strand.[122] This readership sometimes overlapped with Chaucer's audience during their lifetimes and into the middle of the next century, when their works appear together in wills drawn up for the Lincoln's Inn lawyer Thomas Stotevyle in 1459 and Sir Thomas Charleton, a speaker of the House of Commons (d. 1465), who owned "an engelysche boke the whiche was called Troles . . . j of perse plowman, a nodr of Cauntrbury tales."[123] The elusive name "Will Langland" was in all likelihood a pseudonym recognized as such by the original coterie who knew his real name, perhaps William Rochelle as indicated by the Dublin manuscript or William Wychwood as suggested by the five C manuscripts including HM 143 and Ilchester. The poem's author therefore remained almost totally anonymous throughout subsequent generations and unavailable for acknowledgment even by his poetic followers, who were also nameless as they extended his legacy in a long but spottily attested lineage of works such as *Pierce the Ploughman's Crede, The Plowman's Tale,* and *The Banckett of Iohan the Reve vnto Pers Ploughman*.[124] It was the title character Piers the Plowman whose name bestowed coherence to a literary heritage begun ominously with John Ball's letters to the rebels in 1381.

While Langland left a single anonymous poem in at least three unstable versions famously characterized as snapshots of a work forever in progress,[125] Chaucer crafted solid literary monuments upon which he made sure his name would be inscribed, even if he felt no guarantee that his name would remain legible, like those names carved in ice and melted away in the *House of Fame* (1136–64). Deeply aware of prior European traditions and even the Petrarchan notion of a modern author's address to posterity,[126] Chaucer expressed ambivalence about his own role in serving the needs of any English posterity. Yet his concerns over a future readership steadily drew attention to issues that hardly registered with Langland. Near the end of *Troilus,* Chaucer launches his poem upon these uncertain paths of literary appreciation—"Go, litel bok, go, litel myn tragedye"—where it would follow in the tracks of great epic poets such as Homer and Virgil. This is a bracing moment when a single writer parts company with the anonymous enterprise of earlier English poetry (rendered even more anonymous by Chaucer's own steady neglect) and attempts inserting himself into the great tradition of *named* European authors.

But in the very next stanza of *Troilus,* the poet anguishes about the fortunes of a work composed in a national language so unstable that a future audience's understandings could not be assured: "And for ther is so gret diversite / In Englissh and in writyng of oure tonge" (*TC,* 5.1793–94). This rhetorical address to the book itself rather than to future readers signals the poet's concerns for a work that he must surely have considered his masterpiece, substantial, serious, complete, and firmly linked to the centuries-long tradition of epic as well as tragic poetry. Yet when he comes to consider his own position in that tradition toward the end of the *House of Fame,* he professes a desire for anonymity: "Sufficeth me, as I were ded / That no wight have my name in honde" (*HF,* 1876–77). His plea for oblivion represents disingenuous posturing, of course, coming in a highly sophisticated reflection upon the question of literary fame and featuring a storyteller who explicitly names himself first as "Geffrey" (729) and even more grandly as "Englyssh Gaufride" (1464–70).[127]

By contrast to Langland's role as the perennial outsider, Chaucer's Prologue to the *Legend of Good Women* represents the dreamer explicitly as a court poet and lists those titles that constituted the syllabus of a royal readership. As an early effort at securing this status, Chaucer's translation of the *Roman de la Rose* brought into courtly English the full sensibility of French poetry along with the psychology and value-laden imagery of aristocratic love. *The Book of the Duchess* commemorated the death of John of Gaunt's first wife, who was the source of the Lancastrian title as well as the family's enormous wealth. *The Parliament of Fowls* recalled the international negotiations leading to the marriage of Richard II with Anne of Bohemia. *Troilus and Criseyde* celebrated the youthful excesses as well as the intellectual pretensions of the Ricardian court during the 1380s, while these philosophical and antiquarian interests were also reflected in the poem's companion piece, *Boece*. Before they were converted into the Second Nun's Tale and the Knight's Tale, his *Seynt Cecile* provided a model for wedded virginity and *The Love of Palamon and Arcite* offered a paradigm for chivalric brotherhood. The chamber knight Sir John Clanvowe quoted from this latter work in his own *The Boke of Cupide*—which perhaps in turn provided Chaucer with the model for the God of Love as Richard II's fictional alter ego in the Prologue to the *Legend*—in a gesture that Steven Justice finds rich in significance: "Clanvowe's poem in effect renders Chaucer a classic, a body of work recognized as normative and publicly available, and it thereby, for the first time, implicitly identified a *vernacular English tradition* of literature."[128]

The fall of Richard II spelled the neglect, disintegration, and outright destruction of a great deal of the court culture that the king had fostered and Chaucer had contributed to. The *Pearl* Poet's work may represent a signal instance of this suppression, surviving in a single modest manuscript unrecognized for its literary importance before the nineteenth century, while its author remains shrouded in an anonymity unlikely to be dispelled.[129] It is important to recognize that Chaucer's output, also linked to the Ricardian court, might have suffered a similar fate. There is a puzzling delay between Chaucer's death and the publication of his minor works, especially the shorter courtly works, and the scattered survival of the lyrics and dream-poems suggests precarious resources for preservation.[130] Lost are *The Book of the Lion*, his translations of *De Maria Magdalena* and Innocent III's *De Miseria Condicionis Humane*, and the "many a song and many a leccherous lay" mentioned in Chaucer's Retraction and confirmed by Gower in his *Confessio Amantis*.[131] The G Prologue of *The Legend of Good Women*, probably the version closest to the Ricardian court after 1394, survives in only a single manuscript.[132] Copied around 1420, this sole surviving copy in Cambridge CUL Gg was produced during the same period when Henry V's official reconciliation with the dead

Richard II was dramatized by reburial of the deposed monarch in Westminster Abbey.[133] As part of a larger program of cultural reclamation and dynastic legitimation, King Henry's public respect for Richard II's legacy contributed to reviving interest in the London-dialect poets whose careers had flourished in the last decades of the fourteenth century.[134]

Having one's name remembered after death had become one of the central obsessions of Christian culture at the end of the medieval period.[135] Unlike the renunciation of funeral pomp expressed in the wills of his friends the Lollard knights—famously compared to the instructions for a humble burial in Piers the Plowman's will[136]—Chaucer's burial in Westminster Abbey represented a clear bid for posthumous remembrance in a place of prime national visibility near the royal mausoleum of St. Edward the Confessor, Edward III, and Richard II. The tombs of his son Thomas and granddaughter Alice in the village church at Ewelme carry forward the family enterprise for ensuring remembrance of their names and persons.[137] In 1437 Alice Chaucer and her husband, William de la Pole, went further, founding the Ewelme almshouse whose community served a chantry chapel offering prayers for the founders.[138] As a pervasive cultural principle, this religious impulse could only have intensified a writer's desire for posthumous remembrance of his literary identity. Meant to recall and retrace his career as a man of letters, Chaucer's Retraction to the *Canterbury Tales* brilliantly fuses this double concern for the salvation of the soul through penance *and* the remembrance of his literary works catalogued in the manner of a bibliography. Gower's tomb displays a similar doubleness of concern by including pious prayers for his soul, while the supine effigy's head is pillowed by three books with their Latin titles clearly labeled in order of composition—*Speculum Meditantis, Vox Clamantis,* and *Confessio Amantis*—so that his burial site also served to advertise his identity as an author.[139]

CHAPTER 4, *"Piers Plowman* and the Impulse to Antagonism," examines how the fervent reformist intentions of Langland's poem rendered the work subject to repeated appropriation during its author's lifetime and for the two centuries afterwards, within cultural contexts in which the impulse for reform remained the single constant. Anne Middleton concluded her review of my book *The Crisis of Will in "Piers Plowman"* (1986) with a challenge for tracing this reception history: "In what climate, under what local and intense pressures, does such commonplace organic matter of moral culture transform itself into a new substance, seemingly more durable, brilliant, and transparent than its constituents, and lending itself to different uses?"[140] I hope now to address these questions on behalf of *Piers Plowman* while bring- ing also into this antagonistic dynamic the more visible and apparently more stable textual presence of the *Canterbury Tales*. In doing so, my work shows its clear debt to the cultural poetics of New Historicism in its insistence that medieval meaning is inseparable from medieval usage.[141] Critical interest in "bad" manuscripts such as Ilchester and HM 114 of *Piers* often stands in in- verse proportion to their editorial utility.[142] A literary history that discloses cultural conflicts also alters the status of "minor" authors such as Thomas Hoccleve and John Lydgate, as well as anonymous writers such as the author of *Richard the Redeless* and *Mum and the Sothsegger*, while their textual produc- tions achieve new meaning in diachronic relationship with "major" literary works such as *Piers Plowman*.

Thomas Tyrwhitt's landmark edition of the *Canterbury Tales* in the 1770s made available a literary masterpiece that conformed to the aesthetic stan- dards famously expressed by Dr. Johnson in his *Preface to Shakespeare*: "The end of poetry is to instruct by pleasing."[143] Frank Kermode has gone further in suggesting that canonic figures induce a peculiar pleasure for the reader, the sort of pleasure readily apparent in the *solaas* of Chaucer's work, entirely apart from any political or ideological factors.[144] But if the prosaic Lollards and other late medieval puritan readers were suspicious of the sorts of aes- thetic pleasures embodied in Chaucer's poetry, Langland provided different resources for attracting and holding an audience. Evidence indicates that *Piers Plowman* had become a national bestseller by the 1380s for reasons al- most entirely political and ideological. Modern readers seldom admit great enjoyment from reading this work, and probably no undergraduate has wished it longer or extant in more versions.[145] Yet it was a vernacular work read widely enough by 1381 for its title character's name to be recognized and have a range of meaningful connotations. Quoted by organizers of the En- glish Rising, Langland's poem defined what it meant for a vernacular text to achieve this literary status on a national level. *Piers* also discovered for the first time the drawbacks of national visibility.

During the so-called Peasants' Revolt, two letters or broadsides urged rebellion by invoking the name of "Peres plouȝman" as a representative of rural labor.[146] After the crushing of this revolt and execution of its leaders, the Benedictine historian Thomas Walsingham and the Augustinian canon Henry Knighton published these texts and cast the clerical ringleader John Ball as the agent of John Wyclif, who therefore stood as the ultimate instiga- tor of the rebellion.[147] Despite disclaimers in *De Blasphemia*, the Oxford theologian may not have been so innocent of involvement: "Wyclif's public rhetoric proclaimed that the lords had a responsibility to ease the oppressions of the poor; that their failure to do so sprang from a complacent enjoyment of their wealth, which was meant for the common good; that this irresponsibility increased the burdens of taxation in the countryside; that the nobility was therefore as blameworthy as the clergy."[148] Much as they differed in their attitudes toward friars, for example, Wyclif's followers and the rebels of 1381 had one thing permanently in common from the viewpoint of the religious chroniclers: they were disturbers of the peace. Adam Usk perpetuated the official view that Wyclif's followers "most wickedly incited numerous massacres, plots, disputes, quarrels, and rebellions, which continue to this day and will result, I fear, in the ruin of the kingdom."[149] Tarred with the same brush of heresy and sedition, *Piers Plowman* remained implicated in the later upheavals surrounding Lollardy as an actual reform movement and as a perceived threat to ecclesiastical and governmental stability of England.[150]

In the first decades of the fifteenth century, Lancastrian initiatives at literary promotion ran parallel to efforts by Archbishop Thomas Arundel to burn dangerous books along with a few heretics as a reactive strategy against the Lollard threat. Aptly described as the most important figure in Lollard history since Wyclif himself,[151] the autocratic and politically astute Arundel called in his marker for supporting Henry IV over Richard II. Some bargain must have been struck when the two men met in Paris, in violation of the terms of their exiles specifically *not* to communicate with each other, so that they had already committed treason before returning together to England in order to seize royal and ecclesiastical control of the kingdom.[152] Arundel took back from Roger Walden the title and power as archbishop of Canterbury even more boldly than Bolingbroke usurped the throne of England. King Henry's own doctrinal loyalties were not entirely clear at the beginning of his rule, since he restored Robert Lychlade and William James to the university from which they had been expelled as Wycliffites,[153] but the ecclesiastical strategy's advantages, under Arundel's ruthless determination, became basic to the defense of Henry's insecure regime. "The Lancastrians viewed the Lollards as an opportunity rather than a threat."[154] Making the doctrine of the Eucharist into the litmus test for orthodoxy, Arundel's war on heresy simultaneously countered criticism of ecclesiastical wealth and Caesarian clergy that he himself so clearly represented.[155]

Though often exaggerated, the Lollard specter was not altogether a political fiction or paranoid fantasy. Clandestine biblical translations, home-based education in religion, and the secret exchange of English theological writings became potent ingredients in this textual demimonde. "We can be sure that there was a network of Lollard households, linked by itinerant preachers, and its vigor is confirmed by the recruiting drive through the midlands of Oldcastle's agent Thomas Ile."[156] Even Wyclif's own Latin works were still professionally copied at Oxford around 1400.[157] Though biblical translations produced since Wyclif's time were declared illegal in 1409, the 230-plus surviving Wycliffite Bibles and thirty-one Lollard Sermon Cycles represent mostly high-quality manuscripts—large, written in book hands, rubricated and illuminated in a costly fashion—that might have been produced at Oxford, London, or a well-supported private scriptorium such as the one suggested for Sir Thomas Latimer's manor at Braybrooke.[158] The material affluence as well as spiritual vitality of this homemade heresy promoted the vernacular as a sacred language and fostered an awareness of a unique English identity with expressions such as the "Englische nacioun" and "þe pepel of Englond."[159] Such a challenge could not go unanswered.

Despite the high-level sponsorship of Chaucerian manuscripts, including productions by Chaucer's successors, the Langlandian tradition did not go extinct between the poet's death in the early 1390s and the first printing of *Piers Plowman* by Crowley in 1550. Manuscript copies continued to be manufactured throughout the fifteenth and early sixteenth centuries, including the Sion College manuscript (now Toshiyuki Takamiya MS 23) produced in the same year as Crowley's printed edition. No scribal copy of *Piers* rivals the expensive, elegantly decorated Chaucerian manuscripts such as the Ellesmere *Canterbury Tales,* although Chancery copying in at least five B manuscripts, along with highly personalized editing in manuscripts such as HM 114 and Corpus Christi MS 201, suggests that Langland had the brightest if not the best readers.[160] Evidence of gentry owners remains sketchy but suggestive: BL Harley MS 6041 with the arms of the Hoo family of Bedfordshire; University of London Library V.17 with the escutcheon of Sir William Clopton, a landowner in Worcestershire; and the late Bodleian MS Digby 145 copied out by Sir Adrian Fortescue in 1532.[161]

The Langlandian tradition established itself within a community of readers not entirely segregated from Chaucer's audience in the fourteenth century, but more distant and further down the social scale into the fifteenth century. The professional Scribe D who copied the Ilchester manuscript of *Piers* around 1400 later produced the two landmark manuscripts Corpus 198 and Harley 7334 of the *Canterbury Tales* as well as an astonishing series of eight copies of Gower's *Confessio Amantis.* As evidence of aristocratic patronage, Scribe D's Oxford Christ Church 148 of *Confessio Amantis* has an original shield of arms indicating the volume was completed for one of Henry IV's sons, probably Thomas, Duke of Clarence, while another of his productions, Oxford Bodley 294 of the *Confessio Amantis,* bears the erased motto of Humphrey, Duke of Gloucester.[162] Treating the *Confessio* as the classic cornerstone of a new vernacular canon, these high-quality royal productions attest that Gower lived long enough (d. 1408) and worked diligently enough as a promoter of the Lancastrians to become temporarily their most-favored poet during the first decade after Chaucer's death.[163]

Scribe D's colleague Adam Pinkhurst copied the Hengwrt and Ellesmere manuscripts of the *Tales* probably after he had already produced the highly regarded Trinity College, Cambridge, MS B.15.17 of Langland's B-text.[164] In addition to the crucial oath and signature in the Scriveners' Company Common Paper for 1391–92 that led to his identification, the nonliterary documents discovered by Linne Mooney place Pinkhurst's professional career between 1385 and 1427. If also the "Adam Scriveyn" to whom Chaucer addressed a witty one-stanza poem chiding his carelessness while also teasing him for his youthful long hair, Adam Pinkhurst started working as the poet's copyist probably in the 1380s with fair copies of *Troilus* and *Boece.* The fragmentary Peniarth MS 393D of *Boece,* with handwriting belonging to Pinkhurst, may actually be this commissioned copy preserving Chaucer's own corrections: "So ofte adaye I mot thy werk renewe / It to correct and eke to rubbe and scrape."[165] In addition to the two complete copies of the *Canterbury Tales,* Pinkhurst also executed Cambridge CUL Kk.1.3/20's single-leaf fragment preserving portions of the Prioress's Prologue and Tale. He also copied the fragment of *Troilus* preserved in Hatfield House's Cecil Papers, which appears late and therefore not the error-plagued copy mentioned in "Adam Scriveyn." Somewhat different from Scribe D, then, Pinkhurst worked earlier in his career on Chaucer's works of the 1380s, took a detour to copy *Piers* in the Trinity manuscript, but then abandoned Langland to concentrate upon high-quality manuscripts of Chaucer.[166]

Thus the shadow presence of *Piers* figured in the material development of the Chaucerian legacy in ways traceable in the career of Pinkhurst as well as Scribe D. With a total of five Chaucer copy jobs that survive complete or as fragments, plus the lost fair copy of *Troilus,* Pinkhurst emerges as the premier Chaucer specialist among this group of professional textwriters.[167] His Cambridge Trinity B.15.17 of the *Piers* B-text begins to look more and more like the exception that proves the rule. If the author Chaucer emerges as the founding hero of English literary history, his eventual triumph in this *grand récit* owes something to Langland's role as the antagonistic foil in this historical drama.

CHAPTER 5, "Political Corrections: *The Canterbury Tales*," explores ways that Chaucer began responding to the shadow presence of Langland by a variety of evasions and provocations still legible in the accomplished text of his last major work of the 1390s. While Lollards set the intellectual agenda for the closing decades of the fourteenth century, *Piers Plowman* had set the literary agenda. When Langland's poem began circulating among his London readers of civil servants, government scribes, and lesser clergy, Chaucer had completed only his *Book of the Duchess* and perhaps *Parliament of Fowls* while just making headway on *Troilus and Criseyde*. Thereafter if an English poet wanted to write literature that did *not* look Langlandian—a project that I believe Chaucer pursued after 1381 when inaugurating this double-track tradition for English literature—what would he write?

To make himself hard to recognize as Langlandian, such a poet would abandon dream-vision for straightforward narrative. He would exchange the first-person for the third-person narrator. He would entirely reject alliterative poetics by developing the stanzaic form of rhyme-royal. He would translate vernacular masterpieces by near-contemporaries such as Boccaccio rather than confect a network of borrowings from Latin religious sources. In short, he would write *Troilus and Criseyde, The Love of Palamon and Arcite,* and finally the *Canterbury Tales*. His authorial personality would be modest, good-natured, and self-effacing. The poet would find ways of joking about the most serious issues of his day such as plague, revolt, heresy, war, and royal tyranny.[168] Always the survivor, Chaucer had learned the advantage of mocking himself instead of showing disrespect to others, as Langland so readily admitted (B.15.5–6). While not making enemies, the affable writer attracted friends during his lifetime and admirers thereafter. His ability at rendering himself lovable succeeded at securing a posterity of affectionate readers. Evidenced in the *Canterbury Interlude* and Lydgate's Prologue to the *Siege of Thebes,* Chaucerian humor became almost genetically encoded so that Chaucer's kind of literature continued from writer to writer throughout subsequent centuries.

Chaucer's famous merriness belies a worried caution that can be read in decisions to drop various pilgrims from the tale-telling scheme, notably the Plowman. Other gaps and omissions invite further speculations. Why did the Five Guildsmen, the principal representatives of London's political life, disappear after the General Prologue even when Chaucer needed the Carpenter to take offense at the Miller's Tale? Why did Chaucer leave the Cook's Tale incomplete? Why did he apparently cancel the Man of Law's Endlink with its accusations that the Plowman's brother, the Parson, sounded like a Lollard? Is his unfinished pilgrimage narrative related in any sense to the unfinished pilgrimage to St. Truth in *Piers Plowman*? For all of Chaucer's cheerfulness in the *Canterbury Tales* during the 1390s, the Chaucerian tradition of the fifteenth century would inherit these embedded anxieties while remaining reactive to the persistence of *Piers Plowman* as a largely unacknowledged adversarial presence.

CHAPTER 6, "The House of Chaucer & Son," starts with a highly speculative account envisioning the use of the poet's Westminster tenement as a repository for his literary papers and center for early editing, copying, and circulation especially for the *Canterbury Tales*. The discussion continues with a more factual account tracing efforts at appropriating this literary legacy by the competing heirs Thomas Hoccleve and John Lydgate.

The most powerful and enduring creation of the Langlandian tradition—never really a coherent "tradition" since its contributors worked in isolation and never even knew the name of the founding author[169]—came in the formation of a fifteenth-century Chaucerian tradition that *was* coherent, self-conscious, and practically addicted to naming its founding father. As part of an effort to deny a textual pluralism with *Piers Plowman* as part of a large body of vernacular theological writings increasingly associated with Lollards, Chaucer's status at the head of a literary genealogy was artificially formulated as a quasi-official project of manuscript production with masterpieces such as the Ellesmere *Canterbury Tales* as well as the lesser-known landmarks BL Lansdowne 851, Petworth MS 7, and BL Add. 35286. The cultural value of these art books was further enhanced because Chaucer was advertised as author of their contents.[170]

This textual project was apparently begun among the proponents of the future Henry V, a group wittily characterized by Pearsall as the "Lancastrian Society for the Advancement of English."[171] Luxury book production as a means for promoting dynastic prestige and claiming family connections had already been established by the Bohuns, the family of Henry IV's first wife, Mary de Bohun, who was the mother of Henry V.[172] The cultural business of book making had many advantages. Since the Lancastrian government was notoriously short on money, for example, manuscript production even for the exquisite Ellesmere *Canterbury Tales* was much less costly than Richard II's architectural projects, such the £10,000–£12,000 contributed to the expansion of Westminster Abbey, and his jewelry purchases, such as the £20,000 spent on a golden robe decorated with precious gemstones.[173]

Who these book-commissioning agents were and how exactly this project was carried forward remain matters of speculation. Although no substantial evidence for an English royal library exists until the reign of Edward IV, more than three hundred books and unbound quires were already stored in the Tower by the end of Edward II's reign, with the presumption that largely undocumented collections continued throughout the reigns of Edward III, Richard II, and Henry IV.[174] Clearly there was some sense that books mattered, if only as valuable commodities that could be confiscated, used as collateral for loans, and bestowed as gifts to guests and favorites. Nearly all of Richard II's surviving books look like presentation volumes of the sort that Froissart describes personally giving to the monarch, who accepted the gesture with evident pleasure and generous reward later.[175] Jenny Stratford has recently suggested that the *novum studium* commissioned at Eltham Palace in 1401–2 functioned as a luxurious study for Henry IV's books.[176] The chance survival of the richly illustrated Lichtenthal Psalter provides a useful instance of a deluxe volume commissioned by the Bohun family at Pleshey Castle during the early 1380s, moving with Joan FitzAlan's daughter Mary de Bohun into the household of her husband, Henry Bolingbroke, and then traveling to Bavaria with their elder daughter, Blanche, in 1402 when she married Ludwig III, Count of the Rhine Palatinate.[177] The last will of Henry V shows an extensive inventory of his religious and scholarly books as well as other unnamed volumes bequeathed to his infant son with the significant phrase "pro libraria sua." These scattered bits of evidence suggest that Henry IV and Henry V had indeed assembled a royal collection, including some grandly executed manuscripts such as the Corpus Christi *Troilus* with its famous frontispiece, subsequently ravaged by dispersals during the last years of Henry VI's reign.[178]

Early in the fifteenth century when so many resources were mobilized for native book manufacture, including masterful illuminations by the miniaturist called "Johannes" and the immigrant artist Hermann Scheere,[179] the agents for luxury manuscript production must have included Thomas Chaucer (d. 1434), the poet's son and sole heir. As a member of the house of Lancaster and especially the inner circle of Prince Henry, Thomas has been described as "a self-made man of great wealth, acquisitive yet circumspect, politic and *affairé*, well-versed in all branches of administration and diplomacy, a practiced chairman and envoy, influential and respected" and overall "the most important commoner in English politics in the early decades of the century."[180] As part of a larger project of fostering specific literary practices throughout the institutions of London's documentary culture, the business of Lancastrian canon-formation was not some spontaneous or naturally occurring phenomenon. The Ellesmere *Canterbury Tales* and Campsall *Troilus*—which bears the arms of Henry V while he was still Prince of Wales between 1399 and 1413[181]—did not simply happen, and the ongoing productions of high-quality manuscripts such as Corpus 198 and Harley 7334 did not perpetuate themselves by aesthetic appeal alone through some agentless marketplace.[182] There were promoters, and more than anyone else on the scene, Thomas Chaucer had both motive and opportunity to oversee the copying of his father's works.

Always adroit at safeguarding his life and livelihood, Chaucer ensured a degree of artistic immunity by composing the *Canterbury Tales* as a closet work meant for posthumous publication. This wide-ranging anthology with its raucous frame-narrative had no associations with the Ricardian court and actually contained elements distinctly anticourtly and explicitly satirical of Ricardian excesses.[183] As a result, the compilation represented a "collected works" immediately available for appropriation by supporters of the new Lancastrian regime. The poet's literary papers would have passed to his son Thomas Chaucer, who continued to lease the poet's Westminster house until his own death in 1434. "The scribe of the Hengwrt and Ellesmere *Canterbury Tales* presumably worked for Chaucer's literary executors, perhaps his son Thomas and friends within the ambience of the court."[184]

The eighteenth-century editor Thomas Tyrwhitt had already established the same inference: "When we recollect that Chaucer's papers must in all probability have fallen into the hands of his son Thomas, who, at the time of his father's death, was of such age and discretion as to be made Speaker of the House of Commons in the very next year, we can hardly doubt that all proper care was taken of them."[185] Situated strategically between the cultural activity of Westminster Palace and the relative safety of Westminster Abbey, the poet's last known residence probably doubled as a manuscript archive— really the first Center for Chaucer Studies—where the poet's literary remains were preserved, fair copies and foul papers were sorted out, and exemplars were prepared for professional copying by the most accomplished local scribes such as Adam Pinkhurst and the prolific Scribe D, who shared training and perhaps employment in government service locally at Westminster.

Since Thomas Chaucer became instrumental in securing some measure of stability for the new Lancastrian monarchy especially in Parliament, despite some wavering in his allegiance between Henry IV and Prince Henry,[186] the energetic production of Chaucerian works occurred within a complex political network involving Thomas with the mainstays of the ruling dynasty.

They were all members of the same clan, it should be remembered, since Thomas's mother was the sister of John of Gaunt's longtime mistress and third wife, Katherine Swynford, whose children were legitimized by Richard II as the formidable Beaufort branch of the family. Royal documents dignified Thomas Chaucer with the phrase "our beloved kinsman" (*dilecto consanguineo nostro*), and letters between the Beauforts and the Lancastrian kings referred to the poet's son as "cousin Chaucer."[187] Their sponsorship of the *Canterbury Tales* preempted the work's potentially subversive contents, as well its racier satires of characters such as the Pardoner, and instead invested the hefty work with a cultural prestige and textual presence that established its author—their kinsman—as the founding father of a particular kind of poetry conceived as courtly, moral, and steadily committed to political and religious orthodoxies.

One survey of book-owning trends concludes that possessing a Chaucer volume became one visible gauge of an individual's fashionable tastes during these early Lancastrian decades.[188] "Chaucer was made the father of English poetry because he was servile, doing useful work serving dominant social interests, materially and ideologically, in both his poetic and other employments."[189] The author's patriarchal status thus operated in two mutually supportive genealogies—Chaucer the father of English poetry *and* Geoffrey the father of Thomas Chaucer—eventually made explicit in Speght's edition of 1598.[190] The late Tudor editor's engraved frontispiece, labeled "The Progenie of Geffrey Chaucer," makes this point graphically by reproducing on the right side the family tree of Chaucer, based on armorial evidence from the tomb of Thomas Chaucer reproduced at the bottom of the page, and then extrapolating the genealogy to its last male member, Edmund de la Pole (d. 1513). In heavy-handed parallel, Speght traced the genealogy of the Lancastrian line on the frontispiece's left-hand side from John of Gaunt to the first Tudor monarch, Henry VII (d. 1509).[191]

Fifteenth-century praise for Chaucer as a philosopher and rhetorician strongly indicated this newfound role of respectability. The poet had been redeemed from his own malicious humor, scathing irony, and wicked charm. With the pious personality concocted by Hoccleve in his *Regiment of Princes,* Chaucer the poet underwent a makeover in order to become an acceptable founder of a literary dynasty constructed in tandem with the new royal dynasty. Thus installed as the patriarch of English letters, Chaucer first defined the role later imposed upon Shakespeare as the official National Poet expressing the kingdom's priorities, shaping class consciousness, and fostering new respect for the dignity and beauty of England's national language.[192] In service to the *OED* project, the nineteenth-century Chaucer Society provided printed editions that encouraged the view of Chaucer as founder of the lexicon as well as the literature of England.[193]

These efforts at canon-formation and author creation can be studied through surviving prestige manuscripts such as the Ellesmere *Canterbury Tales*, whose format resembles official London books such as the *Liber Albus* and whose early history is associated with the De Vere family, the Earls of Oxford.[194] Clifford Geertz has famously compared practicing ethnography to studying a manuscript "foreign, faded, full of ellipses, incoherences, suspicious emendations, and tendentious commentaries, but written not in conventionalized graphs of sound but in transient examples of shaped behavior."[195] For a student of the later Middle Ages, this analogy has an appealing reversibility. Studying manuscripts constitutes a form of ethnography in which the traces of medieval literary culture assume greater legibility and social meaning when we invest critical authority in the early manuscripts of Langland and Chaucer beyond the needs of academic editorship to produce modern printed texts.[196] Like anthropologists, we start interpreting the activities of the medieval scribes such as Adam Pinkhurst as professional readers "whose job it was to make decisions on behalf of the medieval reader about how the text should go down on the page—*conscious* decisions, that is, about editing, annotating, correcting, rubricating, or illustrating a text."[197]

Evidence for other early owners of Chaucer manuscripts indicates that readers such as the Chancery clerks Richard Sotheworth and John Stopyndon were urban in their placement, secular in their interests, and fully invested as bookmen who read and copied manuscripts as well as owning them. Sotheworth and Stopyndon are also noteworthy because they had connections with Thomas Chaucer in his capacity as Chief Butler of England.[198] After Hoccleve's short-lived success with his *Regiment of Princes*—and after Henry V's death in 1422—Lancastrian stalwarts such as the Duke of Suffolk and the Duke of Gloucester transferred their active patronage to John Lydgate as the poet principally charged with carrying forward this Chaucerian tradition into the middle of the fifteenth century.[199] As owner of the best-surviving manuscript of Lydgate's *Siege of Thebes* (BL Arundel 119), Suffolk had interests that were further served since he was the husband of Alice Chaucer, the poet's only known grandchild.

CHAPTER 7, "*Piers Plowman*, Print, and Protestantism," revisits the now familiar episode in literary history when Chaucer was embraced as a forerunner of the Henrician Reformation and Langland resurfaced to become the fourteenth-century literary prophet for the more radical Edwardian

Protestants. Robert Crowley's edition of *The Vision of Pierce Plowman* included
a preface that announced the poet's full name as Robert Langland, identified
his birthplace in Shropshire not far from the Malvern Hills, and placed his
career during Edward III's reign when he shared John Wyclif's insights into
the reforms necessary for the English Church.[200] Crowley's edition appeared
"cum priuilegio" with royal permission, it went through three printings during its first year, and the humanist editor corrected his text as new manuscripts became available. As signal tribute, he bestowed upon Langland the
title *autour* that became basic to his literary-historical identity thereafter.

By the later fifteenth century, Chaucer's central status had already been
given important affirmation by William Caxton's decision to print his major
works *The Parliament of Fowls, The House of Fame,* and *Troilus and Criseyde.*[201] Caxton's "first folio" edition of the *Canterbury Tales* in 1476 was followed six
years later by a second edition revised by comparing the text with a better
manuscript after the publisher was informed that his first printing was "not
accordyng in many places unto the book that Gefferey Chaucer had made."[202]
Spurred by the new humanist philology with its concerns for authenticity,
Caxton also began representing Chaucer as a classical author, even dubbing
him "laureate poete" as a recollection of the honor accorded to Petrarch in
Italy.[203] The conspicuous absence in Caxton's print project was *Piers Plowman,*
whose nameless author continued to be consigned to a largely invisible fringe
existence.

Tracing any underground tradition offers a particular challenge because
political writings addressing the topics of the day, whether John Ball's bill-
casting letters, the *Twelve Conclusions of the Lollards,* or Langland's own combat-
ive poem, were ephemeral texts anonymously circulated and therefore most
likely to become part of the lost literature of the Middle Ages.[204] Documentary evidence nonetheless indicates that *Piers Plowman* transcended its political moment (actually three or four different moments in its three or four
different versions) and retained its active reading public throughout the fifteenth century and well into the period of Reformation controversies. As
continuing Protestant propaganda, a compiler around 1554 included lines
from a B-text of *Piers Plowman* in an eccentric hodgepodge of prophecies
and diatribes directed against the Catholic practices being reintroduced by
Queen Mary.[205]

Protestant reformers had already claimed Chaucer by the time William
Thynne appended the *Plowman's Tale*—a Lollard tract with an explicitly Langlandian title—to the conclusion of his 1542 edition of the *Canterbury Tales*
and dedicated the entire work to his patron, Henry VIII.[206] Chaucer's cen-

trality gained further strength through a series of collected works published with royal privilege during the Tudor period in a process of print canonization never extended to his contemporary Gower and actually withdrawn from his successor Lydgate.[207] Since Thynne dedicated his edition to Henry VIII, who was said to have exercised direct oversight on its contents, Chaucer's modern identity was animated and legitimated by the king himself.[208] The wording of this omnibus collection's title—*The Workes of Geffray Chaucer*—reflects the special status of the first vernacular author to have his literary works assembled in a single volume, invoking the English equivalent of the Latin *Opera* as the term employed for classical authors such as Aristotle and Virgil. Even the imposing physical size of these volumes from Ellesmere to Speght parallels the impulse toward greater centralization of royal authority as part of an English nationalism dependent upon notions of historical origin and genealogical descent traceable to Ranulph Higden's early fourteenth-century *Polychronicon* and its later continuations.[209]

But there were limits on how harshly the Tudor Chaucer could condemn ecclesiastical corruption. Francis Thynne recalled how his father had been obliged to exclude a savagely anticlerical piece entitled "The Pilgrim's Tale" (c. 1537–39) from his *Workes of Geffray Chaucer*:

> This tale, when Kinge Henrye the Eighte had redde, he called my father unto hym, sayinge, "Williame Thynne! I dobte this will not be allowed; for I suspecte the Byshoppes will call thee in questione for yt." To whome my father, beinge in great fauore with his prince (as manye yet lyvinge canne testyfye,) sayed, "yf your grace be not offended, I hoope to be protected by you." Wherevppon the kinge bydd hym goo his waye, and feare not. All which not withstandinge, my father was called in questione by the Bysshoppes, and heaved at by cardinall Wolseye, his olde enymye . . . the Cardinall caused the kinge so muche to myslyke of that tale, that Chaucer must be newe printed, and that discourse of the *Pilgrymes Tale* lefte oute.[210]

As a result, "The Pilgrim's Tale" survives separately as a printed fragment without authorial attribution.[211] John Bale's *Index Britanniae Scriptorum* (1548) nonetheless attributed the *Curia Veneris* to Chaucer as further indication of the ways that the poet's religious allegiance had been rigorously stipulated as Protestant.[212]

Sketched in these broad strokes, the two literary legacies led to a crowning irony at their point of convergence. The same Protestant movement that bestowed official status upon Langland also redefined Chaucer, in ways perhaps more faithful to his true identity, as a poet exhibiting Wycliffite sympathies. The Lollard knights John Clanvowe, William Neville, Lewis Clifford, and Richard Stury had been his friends, professional associates, and probably members of his first audience.[213] In context of these shifting political valences and valuations, I trace the literary fortunes of *Piers Plowman* and the parallel trajectory of the Chaucer tradition, particularly the formidable textual presence of the *Canterbury Tales*. While Langland's didactic poem attracted a wide spectrum of nonacademic readers with all manner of political interests and religious causes, I am particularly interested in the "Teflon-like" quality of Chaucer's crowning literary achievement, its resistance to fatal controversy, its steady refusal to be segregated as some maverick masterpiece, and especially its resilience during the decade following the poet's death when his reputation as a Ricardian loyalist and author of Lollard-like translations placed survival of his work in real jeopardy. Stephen Greenblatt and Catherine Gallagher could be speaking specifically about the *Canterbury Tales* when they describe this trait in particular literary works: "We are fascinated by the ways in which certain texts come to possess some limited immunity from the policing functions of their society, how they lay claim to special status, and how they contrive to move from one time period to another without losing all meaning."[214]

The convergence of the Langland and Chaucer traditions during the early Reformation meant that works such as the *Canterbury Tales* were subjected to political constructions curiously lacking during the preceding century. So highly charged had the *Tales* become that Francis Thynne reported only the fictional mode of Chaucer's narratives kept them from being officially banned: "In one open parliamente (as I haue herde Sir Johne Thynne reporte, beinge then a member of the howse) when talke was had of bookes to be forbidden, Chaucer had there for euer byn condempned, had yt not byn that his woorkes had byn counted but fables."[215] Although the Elizabethan Settlement would again banish *Piers Plowman* along with the extreme Protestantism of Edward VI's reign (1547–53),[216] Chaucer was granted a reprieve because of his craft as a fiction writer. Richard Edwards dramatized *Palamon and Arcyte* in a version played over two nights before Queen Elizabeth at Oxford in 1566,[217] and Shakespeare made his own adaptation of the Knight's Tale in *Midsummer Night's Dream* and again in *The Two Noble Kinsmen*.[218] Thomas Speght's 1598 edition clearly established Chaucer's reputation as a genial storyteller and universal moralist—"he was a man of rare conceit and of great reading"—while also linking the poet with the Lancastrian dynasty that provided historical legitimacy for Tudor monarchs.[219]

Previously suspected for its lurking Lollard heresies, *Piers Plowman* suddenly looked obsessively Catholic after the 1550s, and its political fortunes waned during the Elizabethan period when Catholicism became the new religious threat in England.[220] George Puttenham's *Arte of English Poesie* (1589) classified Langland as a social malcontent and further denigrated his abilities as a poet. There had been a fleeting reference in the *Mirror for Magistrates* in 1559—"the sentence of the Rat of renoune / Which Pierce the plowman discribes in his dreame"—and Edmund Spenser showed some admiration for Langland's antiquarian verse and rustic settings.[221] But otherwise *Piers Plowman* attracted no coherent literary posterity during the later Tudor period or for over two centuries thereafter.

This is the story that I want to investigate. I do so fully aware that literary history as a category of critical inquiry has suffered under withering critiques such as Jean-François Lyotard's famous indictment of the *grand récit*: "The grand narrative has lost its credibility, regardless of what mode of unification it uses, regardless of whether it is a speculative narrative or a narrative of emancipation."[222] Confidence in the validity of any historical master narrative has been further eroded by postmodern skepticism concerning storytelling itself. Hayden White has been widely persuasive in his view that "real life can never be truthfully represented as having the kind of formal coherency met with in the conventional, well-made or fabulistic story."[223] As an alternative hermeneutic, Joel Fineman recommended exploring the explanatory power of the anecdote or isolated episode.[224] This redirection of interpretative attention to "anecdotal evidence" comes naturally to British and American academics taught by New Criticism to focus upon isolated crux passages. Erich Auerbach's *Mimesis* also demonstrated the value of concentrating upon representative episodes such as "Odysseus' Scar" in Homer's *Odyssey,* and he concluded his sweeping chronological survey rather paradoxically with endorsement of Modernism's regard for the random occurrence—"to exploit it not in the service of a planned continuity of action but in itself."[225] The view that diachronic history represents an artificial narrative of selective events, forged into a logical connection with contrived heroes and type-cast adversaries, raises fewer theoretical objections when discussing a literary tradition because (I hope) everyone now understands that *tradition* means nothing other than the artificial manufacture of a narrative made and remade by successive generations. The value resides in uncovering the special interests and half-explicit intentions vested in constructing this story of Great Authors and Great Books across artificially demarcated Periods.

Late medieval literary production in England nonetheless renders itself remarkably discursive. Rivalries were real. Divisions became stark. Contests had recognizable players resorting to a full arsenal of weaponry. My own formulation of this literary-historical narrative maps a veritable *antagonistic tradition* across two centuries of manuscript productions and stylistic influences. Lollard/Langlandian efforts at contestation ran parallel to early Lancastrian/ Chaucerian capacities for resisting those gestures and persisting in these efforts as the ground of authority, even when the political threat was effectively neutralized after the crushing of Sir John Oldcastle's 1414 revolt.[226]

Within this symbiotic relationship, the official tradition drew disproportionate energy from fringe practices. The overdetermination of this reactive dynamic generated by the sheer number of named successors and quality manuscripts, as well as the new print technology starting with Caxton's two printings of the *Canterbury Tales,* established the hegemony of the Chaucerian tradition and sharpened its discursive asymmetry with the Langlandian antagonist. In this dynamic counterpoise, however, the minority challenge never had its collective identity entirely neutralized or its sense of community negated.[227] Constructed from an aggregate of textual agents over time, this underground tradition was instead domesticated during the early Tudor period by writers such as Skelton and Spenser.[228] Thereafter the Langlandian project was made official with Crowley's printing in 1550, while its urgent topics were discovered already also represented in the writings of Chaucer in Thynne's edition of 1542. As editors, Thynne and Crowley embodied the two impulses of John Leland (c. 1503–52), the civic humanist committed to serving the state, and of John Bale (1445–1563), the radical Protestant committed to reforming the official Church. The antiquarian efforts of these two proto-medievalists were already formulating *tradition* in terms of British literary identity extending over periods of dramatic cultural change.[229]

Historiography has drawn upon this protagonist-antagonist dynamic for its basic emplotment since Thucydides' *Peloponnesian War*. While some Marxist critics have raised suspicions that social antagonism exists only as a fantasy construction that cannot be objectified, the dynamic has otherwise been acknowledged as a real opposition most readily detectable in its resistance to closure.[230] The presence of the Other prevents the Official from coming fully into being. The presence of Langland, that is, kept Chaucer from becoming fully Chaucerian and eventually compelling his *Canterbury Tales* to disclose what had long been repressed.[231]

This diachronic narrative begins in the fourteenth century and ends in the sixteenth century. Though I refer to medieval and Renaissance as categories that typically organize academic discussions, I prefer the terms Lancas-

trian and Reformation when discussing periods with usable dating and veri-
fiable consequences, even though a sizable lacuna interrupts the continuity
of the chronological record. Pearsall remarks upon this later fifteenth-
century hiatus that separates these two discrete periods: "By the end of the
century, it is hard to see where the vigorous early Lancastrian promotion of
English as a high-status literary language in the early part of the century has
got to. . . . The idea of England too seems to be in abeyance, awaiting the release of one of those historical triggers that will impel it forward once again
into prominence. When decisive change came, it was the product of a completely different set of circumstances, historically contingent, altogether not
inevitable, namely, the Henrician Reformation."[232] As separate Lancastrian
and Reformation time spans, not components in a dialectic or coherent trajectory of national events, my history remains resolutely non-Hegelian as a
series of contingent rather than logical episodes organically connected.

Most literary critics today have fully assimilated the author-centered em-
piricism that drove Ernst Gombrich's bold opening statement in his 1950
classic *The Story of Art*—"There really is no such thing as Art. There are only
artists."[233] Yet I resist individualizing my two literary artists Langland and
Chaucer so that they occupy nonoverlapping historical spaces and become
segregated on either side of the great divide imposed by the still influential
literary history of Bernard Ten Brink. His *History of English Literature* placed
Langland with Richard Rolle among the backward-looking figures of volume 1 (late medieval) while positioning Chaucer with Wyclif among the
forward-looking writers in his volume 2 (early Renaissance).[234] Instead, I en-
visage the two poets as contemporaries in late fourteenth-century London
and persistent literary rivals throughout the next two centuries of literary
production. Nicholas Watson has shrewdly identified the instincts that moti-
vate this recuperative process: "Historical scholarship—the kind that seeks
to build stories out of textual and material remains and even the kind that
critiques this storytelling—tends to find itself paraphrasing or repeating the
past, as its language and assumptions are pulled magnetically toward those of
the subject under discussion."[235] My double-strand historical fiction operates
self-consciously in the original sense of a *fictio* or a made-up story, very much
paraphrasing the story elaborated by Hoccleve and Lydgate about Chaucer,
then the story made up by Bale and Crowley about Langland.

Stanley Fish has observed that historicist criticism must have some practical confidence in a "substratum of unmediated fact" underlying any self-
conscious construction.[236] Though admittedly fabricated, my narrative derives from an archive of factual evidence in an effort to connect the dots
and expose the broad outlines of this antagonistic tradition in early English

literature. Surprisingly perhaps, my discussions regularly engage with the mass-marketed *Who Murdered Chaucer? A Medieval Mystery,* because its authors, led by Terry Jones, also offer a speculative master-narrative for the beginning of the Chaucer tradition, often in agreement with my own about Henry IV, Archbishop Arundel, and Henry V, often not about Chaucer and Richard II, but always deserving serious notice as a well-informed attempt at putting the pieces together to make a good story.

CHAPTER TWO

Beginnings

SOME DATES ARE MORE PROPITIOUS THAN OTHERS FOR BEGINNINGS. Everything depends upon what story is going to be told. I have chosen the year 1360 for my fiction of origination because it included major international events that involved both Langland as commentator and Chaucer as minor player while releasing cultural energies that would help shape the directions of their separate careers.[1] The Normandy Campaign of 1359–60 is the latest datable event in *Piers Plowman,* and the mercenary motives of the men who undertook this foreign expedition provided Langland with the starting point for his lifelong concern with the corruptive power of Mede as financial reward. By an accident of history, the young Geoffrey Chaucer actually participated in this campaign and was taken prisoner by the French. The year 1360 also witnessed the arrival in England of forty French noblemen as hostages guaranteed by the Treaty of Brétigny. Their lengthy English captivity posed a potent challenge to an emergent English culture, which included the creation of an English national literature.[2]

Langland and 1360

In contrast to Langland's own slipperiness as a historical entity, *Piers Plowman* makes reference to datable events and engages in topical allusions of the sort cautiously avoided by Chaucer. A prime example is also our best evidence for the beginning of Langland's poetic project. All three canonic versions of the poem include a lengthy reference to the Normandy Campaign of 1359–60.[3] Lady Mede defends herself against Conscience's accusation that she exercised a corruptive influence upon the king's conduct in waging war (A.3.176–95). In lines that appear almost the same in the B-text (3.185–208), Lady Mede asserts that if she had been marshal of England, she would have ensured a conquest of the entirety of France.

Lady Mede's argument reflected the pro-war sentiments of other sources such as the *Anonimalle Chronicle,* which was compiled for the period 1333–81 by a Benedictine monk of St. Mary's, York.[4] This contemporary historian lamented Edward III's weakness and claimed that the "captains and their men could easily have conquered the kingdom of France to the advantage of the king of England and his heirs, if he had allowed them."[5] Sir Thomas Gray's *Scalacronica* (c. 1369) also condemned the abandonment of the war effort and the disadvantages of the treaty. Specifically, Gray warned that the cessation of fighting would erase the profit motive that sustained the chivalric enterprise: "The hand shall be liberal in rewarding those who deserve it, for the encouragement of others to do the like—the one thing in the world most helpful in waging war."[6]

All contemporary testimony indicates that the war's early phase after the victories at Crécy and Poitiers proved highly profitable for the Englishmen who had fought. Avesbury's chronicle preserves letters from Edward III's captains telling the same enthusiastic story of lucrative pillage.[7] The greatest rewards went to the military leaders among the nobility: plunder, profits from ransom, charges for capitulation, bribes to leave towns unharmed, and revenue from French fiefs in English possession.[8] New wealth took the form of conspicuous consumption such as grand residences in the country and townhouses in London. The Savoy Palace in London was built by Henry of Grosmont, Duke of Lancaster, with income from the captured town and castle of Bergerac.[9]

There was also a large increase in the acquisition of luxury goods, such as the jewelry that Lady Mede is wearing in profusion as an example of this outrageous display (A.2.10–14). When Langland compares her rich ornaments to the sumptuous jewelry of a king—"Icorounid wiþ a coroune, þe King haþ non bettere!"—he is criticizing the fact that many *nouveaux riches* overstepped bounds by ornamenting themselves like royalty.[10] The Sumptuary Law of 1363 was designed to combat these excesses. Overall, however, the financial advantages went principally to the earls and larger landowners. The rich got richer.[11] The Treaty of Brétigny confirmed the terms for ransoming King Jean II of France with 3 million gold crowns going directly to the king of England.[12] Only after 1360 did Edward III possess enough treasure to require the construction of a special stronghold in 1365, the moated Jewel House, which remains today one of the few surviving remnants of Westminster Palace.

Charles Tilly's maxim "War made the state" highlights the fact that wartime revenue gathering accelerated the formation of a large, well-organized, stationary bureaucracy in Westminster as an essential phase in creating an English state.[13] Much of this process must have been invisible even to those fostering it. When Edward III announced the resumption of hostilities in 1369, he understood simply that the prospect of financial gain motivated English political culture, particularly those in the chivalric classes, with little regard for those footing the bill or keeping the records. Jean Froissart did little to idealize English chivalry when he described their campaigns against prosperous neighbors: "Their land is more fulfilled of riches and all manner of goods when they are at war than in times of peace."[14] Although Langland understood that the lure of financial gain motivated knights to wage war, he condemned this motivation by placing its defense in the mouth of Lady Mede.

The period of peace guaranteed by the Treaty of Brétigny did not last long after the arrival of the French hostages in England. When Louis of Anjou broke parole, King Jean II took it as a point of honor to return to London, where he died in 1364. The war commenced again in 1369 when his son Charles V violated English sovereignty by summoning Edward the Black Prince as a vassal to Paris, and Edward III responded by formally reasserting his claim to the French throne.[15] The best scholarly guesses have dated the A-text of *Piers Plowman* to the period between 1368 and 1374, and so the poet's original allusion to the Normandy Campaign remained topical after the failure of the Treaty of Brétigny and the resumption of hostilities. Langland had been lucky. His discussion remained relevant just as his pinpointing of the source of corruption remained consistent.

In his influential *De Re Militari,* Vegetius formulated the view that war could be justified by the need to establish peace. Drawing upon antecedents such as Gratian's *Decretum,* Thomas Aquinas was incisive in his rationale for fighting: "All who make war seek through war to arrive at a peace more perfect than existed before war."[16] Royal profit-making was never numbered among these legitimate motives. Denise Baker has finely registered the contents of these passages in *Piers*: "Langland implicitly contests Edward III's official declaration that the war was being fought to pursue his legitimate claim to the French throne."[17] The English king's willingness to relinquish his claim to the crown of France under the Treaty of Brétigny clearly contradicted the official reasons for pursuing armed conflict in the first place.

The chronicle versions of the Normandy Campaign read quite differently. A week after Easter 1360, the English army had been overtaken by a terrible storm that devastated the troops with wind, rain, hail, and snow. While Lady Mede belittled this natural disaster as a "dym cloud" (A.3.180), all other witnesses testified to a major disaster for the English with extensive loss of baggage, vehicles, horses, and human life. *The Brut* even suggested divine retribution: "þousandeȝ of our men & of her horses in her iourneying (as it were þorugh vangeaunce) sodenly were slayn & perisshed."[18] The English used this calamity to good purpose as rationale for extricating themselves from a failed mission. Jean de Venette even connected the peace negotiations with piety for the Easter season,[19] while Jean Froissart offers an account of the king's motivation closely aligned with Langland's:

> Storms, tempests and lightning so great and so horrible descended from the heavens upon the host of the king of England that it seemed very probable to all those who attended that the age was about to end—because there fell from the air hailstones so large that they killed men and horses, and the most hardy of them were terrified. And then the king of England gazed toward the church of Notre Dame de Chartres, and he himself vowed and yielded devoutly to Our Lady, and he promised, as he said and confessed afterwards, that he would be accorded to peace.[20]

Writing much nearer the actual events, Langland has Lady Mede blame the humiliating withdrawal upon Conscience—the King's conscience—as an early indication of the official version eventually transmitted by Froissart. Langland's irony of having Lady Mede seize the upper hand in mocking Conscience provides further support for Baker's reading of this passage as "an indictment of the economics of chivalry."[21]

The first dream-sequence in *Piers Plowman* shows how aristocratic self-interest had determined the course of military policy, while expenditures upon the war shifted resources away from the domestic sphere, specifically from the administration of justice.[22] Langland's objection to further hostilities with France focuses upon the fact that corruption at court meant a breakdown of the legal system protecting him and his nonchivalric readers (B.4.113–48). Often missing from national discussion until the 1370s was the realization that wartime taxation took money out of the pockets of those who profited least from these victories, particularly the clergy, prosperous peasants, and tradesmen outside the military economy.[23] Overseas failures exasperated these discontents.[24] The situation reached a crisis in 1377–80 when the innovative poll tax was introduced as a more efficient means for financing the fighting. The widespread unpopularity of this revenue-gathering scheme led directly to the English Rising of 1381, in which Langland's poem became notoriously implicated as historical events overtook its concerns with labor and the rural economy.[25]

Richard II's Anglo-French truce of 1389 provided hope for a more peaceful future even as it sowed the seeds of discontent among the warrior elite.[26] The royal truce may have prompted Langland to remove from his C-revision a pessimistic passage in which Clergie despaired of peace ever being concluded (B.13.173–76). Omission of this passage signals a strengthening of Langland's pacificist sentiments, as well as providing further evidence for a later dating of the C-text. Anna Baldwin has detected a growing hostility to the war throughout the C-text, suggesting that the twenty-five new lines added for describing overseas campaigns express the poet's growing abhorrence of war.[27] In this late revision, Lady Mede's speech does indeed contain harsher self-condemnation as she harangues Conscience (C.3.233–56). Too remote historically from the C-text of the 1380s, the Normandy Campaign has disappeared as a topical reference, replaced by this more open-ended critique of war. "Mede's argument is now more generalized in its reference to the French wars," Pearsall has noted. "She argues that a king has a responsibility to fight imperialistic wars of conquest and distribute the plunder among his men."[28]

The C-text's more intense opposition to the French wars aligned itself with the radical pacifism that arose throughout the middle strata of English society at the end of the fourteenth century. John Wyclif had defended the "just war" but departed from the interests of his aristocratic patrons, notably John of Gaunt, by condemning the sort of personal profit seeking that he equated with the sin of avarice.[29] The Wycliffite theologian John Coryngham of Merton College, Oxford, preached a wide range of pacifist views, including his belief that it was sinful to kill even in self-defense. His sermons were directed specifically against Bishop Despenser's "crusade" of 1383. This ecclesiastical *chevauchée* attracted an unusual amount of clerical comment while also strengthening the pacifist resolve of Lollard critics such as Walter Brut and William Swinderby.[30] As an extreme gesture, Coryngham threatened excommunication to any parishioner paying a subsidy to the king for pursuing wars outside the realm.[31]

Langland's opposition to the war became one further element that allied *Piers Plowman* with the radical Lollard agenda most notoriously expressed in the *Twelve Conclusions of the Lollards* posted on the door of Westminster Hall during the 1395 Parliament. This provocative document condemned manslaughter in battle as an act contrary to Christ, who "taute for to loue and to haue mercy on his enemys, and nout for to slen hem." While making no exception even for crusades against non-Christians, Lollard objections focused specifically upon the wrongness of the mercenary motives for slaying fellow Christians.[32] Waging war for temporal profit, it should be noted, had been Langland's consistent complaint since inventing the warmonger Lady Mede in the 1370s.

In the midst of the Lollard crisis of 1395 that prompted Richard II to hurry home from his Irish campaign,[33] the Dominican Roger Dymmok wrote his rebuttal *Liber contra XII Errores et Hereses Lollardorum* preserving in both Latin and English the original text of the *Conclusions*. He argued that war, like capital punishment, preserved the kingdom and safeguarded its people. Yet Dymmok summoned the authority of St. Augustine to emphasize that the horrors of war sprang specifically from human avarice, almost as if to acknowledge the legitimacy of objections such as Langland's to the greed of the men fighting these wars.[34]

Dymmok later waded into an entirely different area of contention, not actually raised by the Lollard document, when he considered the means for financing the king's wars. He wrote several chapters arguing that the protection of the kingdom far outweighed the burdens of taxes upon private persons, concluding that the king had a duty to secure the economic means necessary to fulfill his sacred duties as defender of the realm (260–67). In the midst of this discussion, Dymmok inserted a defense of royal magnificence as visible expression of the king's authority. The prestige of the king extended to the prestige of the kingdom (264–66). Here the Dominican theologian revealed an awareness, absent from the Lollard accusations on this score, of the linkage between the French wars and English affluence. Again Langland had anticipated this insight in his depiction of Lady Mede's extravagant jewelry representing the economic nexus of war profits and expenditures on luxury goods.

Like iconoclasm, pacifism became another aspect of vernacular reformism simply waiting to be adopted by Lollardy.[35] It remained one of the defining features for more extreme Lollard communities such as the conventicle investigated in East Anglia during the fifteenth century. At the diocesan synod at Norwich in 1428, William White confessed that he had written against the principle of fighting for one's country—*pro patria pugnare*.[36] A question on the just war became thereafter a standard feature in interrogating suspected Lollards. As late as 1527, it remained one of the incriminating questions at the trial of the Cambridge theologian Thomas Bilney.[37]

Langland's reference to the Normandy Campaign and his criticism of English concessions came very much after the fact. He wrote after the expedition had failed, after the king had bargained away his claim for the French throne, after England had lost its advantage on the field of battle, and even (in the C-text) after Richard II had concluded a truce in 1389. Warfare and chivalry faded from the poem's consciousness. The metaphorical depiction of Christ as a knight jousting at Jerusalem in *Piers* B.18 preserves some vestige of this vanished ideal of chivalry.[38] Though this knightly imagery was informed by crusader ideologies, the poet seemed immune to contemporary propaganda most persistently generated by Philippe de Mézières for an actual crusade to liberate Jerusalem.[39]

Langland became so focused upon domestic issues that Du Boulay's *The England of "Piers Plowman"* never mentions hostilities with France.[40] While Chaucer situated his narratives in foreign locations such as Brittany, Flanders, Lombardy, Syria, and even the faraway reaches of the Mongol Empire, Langland narrowed his concerns to contemporary England. When Truth sends the pardon to Piers and his followers, knights were obliged to protect the community at home—"And bad hym holde hym at home"—while Langland made no allowance for foreign wars (B.7.9–12). Picked up by later imitations such as *The Crowned King*, with its concern for the king solving day-to-day problems at home, this focus upon domestic issues ensured the ongoing topicality of Langland's poem and its ever-present potential to stir controversy.

Chaucer and 1360

The year 1360 was important for Geoffrey Chaucer in his personal life. This event is documented inconspicuously in the account of William de Farley, Keeper of the King's Wardrobe. On 1 March of that year, Edward III contributed £16 toward the ransom of Geoffrey Chaucer, who had been captured by the enemy on French territory.[41] Years later in 1386, Chaucer testified at the Scrope-Grosvenor trial that he had witnessed the Scropes armed before the town of Réthel about twenty miles northeast of Reims.[42] These two bits of evidence have allowed conjecture that the young Chaucer served under Prince Lionel in the division that took this route to Reims, which was then besieged from early December 1359 until January 1360. Speculation runs that Chaucer was taken prisoner during the siege or the unsteady advance of English forces into Burgundy which concluded with a truce in March 1360.

The expeditionary force in which Chaucer served was the largest ever sent to France, but the campaign itself was entirely lacking in battlefield glories. Knighton reported that the French even refused to mount an active defense of Paris.[43] The Chandos Herald gave this episode only the scantest notice in his *Vie du Prince Noir*: "Both the king and the prince encamped there, ready for battle, but no battle took place."[44] Two questions follow. If there were no battles, under what circumstances did young Geoffrey Chaucer fall into French hands? And what were the conditions of his imprisonment following his capture?

Though the English did not know it, they were encountering Charles V's new strategy for avoiding full-scale battles of the sort that the English tended to win. Instead, the English were forced to engage in a series of expensive, time-consuming sieges upon fortified towns such as Reims and Paris, while the French used their army at a distance to pick off stragglers and foragers.[45] Sir Thomas Gray described how unarmed English esquires were taken prisoner while gathering corn to feed the horses.[46] As one minor casualty of this strategy under circumstances like those described by Gray, Chaucer's capture became as inglorious as the expedition itself.

The entire campaign was brought to a humiliating close by the peace of Brétigny. Edward III and his sons departed for England in the middle of May.[47] In all probability Chaucer went with them, at about the same time that the forty French hostages were gathering at Calais in compliance with the newly concluded treaty. Also present at Calais, England's foothold in French territory, Jean Froissart readied himself to follow this dazzling array of noblemen to England where he would gain employment with Queen Philippa. Froissart's presence in England for most of the 1360s would epitomize a French cultural incursion that undercut, in terms of courtly prestige, England's military and diplomatic achievements.[48]

The possibility that Chaucer was captured near Reims has prompted speculation that the young would-be writer had opportunity to meet the great French poet Guillaume de Machaut, who was a canon of the cathedral and endured the siege inside the city walls. Donald Howard painted a very cheerful picture of Chaucer's captivity as "a pleasant respite, a time to converse and read, hear songs and stories." He further speculated that the young Englishman might also have met Eustache Deschamps, who was perhaps with his uncle Machaut inside Reims during the siege.[49] It is attractive to imagine this serendipitous gathering of three men who would later be remembered as the great poets of the age. But it is better to consider what we know for certain: the teenage Chaucer was captured by Frenchmen on enemy territory. While Froissart's *Chronicles* correctly reported how kings and princes were entertained with lavish courtesy,[50] prisoners who ranked farther down the social scale could not have counted upon such careful hospitality. Some years after the fact, Sir John Strother received a letter from his man Walter Ferrefort, still in captivity, begging to be ransomed from a French prison where he remained bound with iron fetters.[51]

Chaucer languished in French captivity for several weeks, even months, before and after the ransom was agreed upon. Even though he ranked as a yeoman to a royal prince, he had good reason to fear the brutality of his captors as well as the vengefulness of civilians. Fourteenth-century warfare was largely a matter of inflicting damage upon the general population.[52] Knighton described the English advance in terms of its destructiveness: "And then the king led his army toward Paris, burning, slaying, and laying waste all around him."[53] In a noteworthy departure from his source material, Chaucer's *Melibee* later recalled war's sufferings visited upon the common people: "ther is ful many a man that crieth 'Werre, werre!' that woot ful litel what werre amounteth" (*CT,* VII, 1038–42).[54] In retaliation, peasants sometimes massacred English troops as well as knights captured by French noblemen. As one of the prime witnesses to the 1359–60 campaign, Jean de Venette reported how a peasant force at Longueil cut down a band of English prisoners without giving thought to possible ransom.[55] Indeed, some contemporary writers urged that the war's end would be hastened if hostages were killed rather than ransomed.[56] Targeting the noblemen who made war, the Jacquerie of 1358 was largely a violent reaction by the civilians who endured war's hardships.[57]

In addition to the threat of violence, Chaucer would have shared the widespread privations of the French themselves, especially inside the besieged city of Reims where supplies ran dangerously low.[58] And the weather was horrible, with steady autumn rains turning to snow as the temperatures plummeted. Several accounts describe the ferocious storm that hit the English troops outside Chartres. Knighton adds detail to the devastating event: "A terrible storm burst upon them, with thunder and hail, and killed men beyond number, and more than 6,000 horses, so that the army's supply train was almost entirely destroyed, and they had to return to England."[59] The psychic trauma of Chaucer's wartime experience has sometimes been discerned in his later reluctance to glorify warfare or give chivalric exploits much heroic notice.[60] Chaucer's own description of Criseyde's fears about violent abuse if she is taken captive by the Greeks (*TC,* 5.701–7)—a passage without parallel in Boccaccio's *Filostrato*—may owe some of its intensity to the anxieties that Chaucer himself suffered while a prisoner of the French.

Besides encouraging pacifist sentiments comparable to Langland's, Chaucer's captivity provided grounds for his career-long antipathy toward the French and all things French. This point has never been properly considered. Even if he was not brutalized and physically mistreated, he had reason to feel humiliated. When he had his first opportunity to distinguish himself on the field of battle, he ended up a captive. Since the young Chaucer as a French-speaker probably sounded as provincial as his Prioress (*CT,* I, 126),[61] his captors had cause to mock his outlandish pronunciation of their language. They may even have insulted his very humanity. A ballade by Eustache Deschamps, describing his encounter with English troops in Calais, uses as its refrain "Oil, je voy vo queue"—"Yes, I see your tail." This taunt played upon the long-standing slander that Englishmen had tails like animals or devils.[62] Chaucer's French captors could have ridiculed his mother-tongue as well, mocking him with English words pronounced like bestial grunts such as those recorded by Deschamps:

L'un me dist *dogue,* l'autre *ride;*
Lors me devint la coulour bleue:
Goday fait l'un, l'autre *commidre.*

One said to me "dog," the other "ride";
My coloring then turned pale:
"Good day," said one, the other, "come hither."[63]

While Deschamps felt threatened by the English troops at Calais,[64] Chaucer would have been at the mercy of the French majority inland. The poet Jean Régnier left a moving account of an unlucky English prisoner who spoke no French at all, surrounded by Frenchmen who did not understand his cries for help in English.[65]

The point of this historical speculation is not simply to fill a minor lacuna in the early biography of Geoffrey Chaucer.[66] Yet I believe that a great deal depends upon revising the fanciful account of the young would-be poet sitting around the dinner table with Machaut, enjoying fine wine while discussing *dits* and *ballades*. Nobody in France in 1360 would have recognized the adolescent Chaucer as a future literary genius, probably not even the adolescent Chaucer himself. The far more likely account of the yeoman's experience accords with the documented horrors of other English captives. They suffered the common misery of freezing weather and scarce food. They were mocked and humiliated by their French captors. And they lived with the constant threat of chains, long-term imprisonment, and quick, violent death—or slow, miserable death—far from home and family. Donald Howard's version of events provides a cheerful beginning for Chaucer's career as a man of letters, one characterized by Machaut's friendship, collegiality, and fatherly support. This other version provides a very different beginning for Chaucer's career, one marked by emotional trauma, personal antagonism, and a clear set of reasons for starting a life-long project of resentment and retaliation against the French, not by force of the sword—where he had already failed miserably—but by force of the pen. The critical commonplace that Chaucer's entire oeuvre can be seen as antifrancophone, in the larger context of the Hundred Years' War, can be traced more specifically to his personal experiences in 1360.

Queen Philippa's death in 1369 deprived many of the French-speaking members of her household of a source of patronage. Jean Froissart, who entered the queen's service in 1360, had left England by the time of her death and remained away for more than a quarter-century. His absence signaled a cultural vacuum made more pronounced by worsening relations between England and France. The year 1369 signaled the renewal of official hostilities when Charles V violated English sovereignty. A year earlier, John of Gaunt suffered the loss of his first wife, Duchess Blanche of Lancaster, and his quick search for a new wife was clearly designed to win advantage over the French. In 1370 the Duke of Lancaster launched a military assault that landed at Calais, crossed Artois and Picardy, and then advanced into Normandy.[67] Documentary evidence suggests that Chaucer was again present on this incursion into Normandy,[68] while the death of Blanche would provide the occasion for his first major English poem. *The Book of the Duchess* represented the opening salvo in his own personal campaign against the French motivated by antagonisms that can be traced back to his bitter experiences during the Normandy Campaign of 1360.[69]

CHAPTER THREE

Naming Names
"Langland" and "Chaucer"

MICHEL FOUCAULT'S ESSAY "WHAT IS AN AUTHOR?" (1969) RECOGNIZED
the problematic linkage between a writer's name and the works that he wrote
or was credited with writing. The cultural operation of an author's name
functioned by classification, specifically its power to group together certain
texts as authorial, to discuss the relationship of these texts with each other,
and to contrast them with texts by other authors.[1] Which texts are authentic
and which are spurious? In what order were they written? What influences
did they absorb from the author's earlier texts, and how did they in turn influence works later in the author's career? Since these determinations have
typically been assigned to scholars establishing a canon by sorting out authorial from nonauthorial works, we should not be surprised that frequently the
complicated task of establishing an author's name has also fallen to editors.

The scholarly traditions for fixing the names of "Geoffrey Chaucer" and
"William Langland" indicate a sharp contrast in the resources of evidence.
Chaucer established his own name as a literary figure during his lifetime, and
his reputation as a named poet grew steadily in the decades after his death.
This claim applies mostly to the longer and later works such as the *Canterbury
Tales,* less so to the shorter and earlier works. Surprisingly, manuscript an-
thologies such as Bodley 638 and Tanner 346 neglect authorial attribution for
the dream-visions, perhaps reflecting Chaucer's own carelessness with his

more courtly works, and these poems were jumbled together with pieces by Hoccleve and Lydgate in compilations such as Huntington HM 140 and John Shirley's book EL 26.A.13 without any attempt at authorial naming.[2] Shirley's Ellesmere anthology actually attributes its brief *Troilus* extract to Gower.[3] But the self-conscious successors Hoccleve and Lydgate worked much more diligently at naming their predecessor, and the authorship of the *Canterbury Tales* was carefully established by internal attribution. The name "Chaucer" typically recurs in these manuscripts as a running-header, page after page, for the Tale of Sir Thopas and the Tale of Melibee.

A century later, these practices changed from underattribution to over-attribution with a growing body of apocryphal works. Folio editions of Chaucer during the Tudor period welcomed a large number of these spurious works, even works known to have been written by other poets. For modern editors beginning with Tyrwhitt, the challenge became removing apocryphal works such as *The Testament of Love* which had attached themselves to the strong authorial presence materializing under the name of Geoffrey Chaucer and shaping his authorial identity for later readers from Sydney and Shakespeare forward to Keats and Wordsworth.[4] Although Skeat's *Chaucerian and Other Pieces* expelled spurious works, this much-cited volume created an official apocrypha solidly buttressing the institutional canon.[5]

The Chaucerian poet Osbern Bokenham expressed a desire to avoid the malicious criticism of Cambridge scholars by publishing anonymously— "Wherfore hyr malyhs to represse / My name I wil not here expresse"— but still his name came to be readily attached as a note at the end of his *Legendys of Hooly Wummen* in BL Arundel 327.[6] By contrast, William Langland is a "poet nearly anonymous" in more than fifty surviving manuscripts.[7] Nor did the author of *Piers Plowman* hazard naming patrons or members of his immediate coterie audience: "The kind of literary wares Langland is dealing in—interclerical polemics, reformist prophecy, and theological controversy—are not such as one would openly advertise in connection with named contemporaries."[8] Because Langland's name was not firmly attached to his works during his lifetime, he created almost insurmountable obstacles for later readers trying to determine his identity. Writers in the subsequent *Piers Plowman* tradition, who remained ignorant or deeply confused over what name to attach to the work, usually made no attempts whatsoever at naming its author. Consequently Langland provided no model for literary authorship, no impetus for the stable formation of a canon, no potential for family or institutional endorsement, and no fixed origin for deriving a literary posterity. Before Skeat, only the HM 114 scribe even recognized that there were three different versions of *Piers*. Robert Crowley erred in placing Langland's career during the reign of Edward III, and even Skeat wrongly attributed *Richard the Redeless* to Langland and therefore extended his career to 1399. At the heart of these muddles, lack of a name became one decisive factor in disqualifying the author of *Piers Plowman* from any effective claim as Father of English Poetry.

Naming William Langland

George Kane's rigorous evaluation of the external evidence demonstrates the difficulty of making an open-and-shut case for "William Langland" as the poet's name.[9] Few as they are, the facts bear repeating. The Trinity College Dublin MS 212 contains on its last leaf an inscription in a later hand (c. 1400–1412) stating that Stacy de Rokayle of Shipton-under-Wychwood in Oxfordshire was the father of William Langland (*pater willielmi de Langlond*) and that William made the book called *Piers Plowman* (*willielmus fecit librum qui vocatur Perys ploughman*).[10] George Russell has suggested that the localized production of C-text manuscripts such as TCD 212 in the West Country may have provided privileged information about the author not available to copyists in London and other parts of England.[11]

Even if the accuracy of the Dublin manuscript's information is accepted at face value, the fact that the poet bore a surname different from his father's has caused some difficulty. Kane wondered whether the poet was a bastard or merely lived during a period when the determination of last names was still in flux. What he does not allow is that Stacy de Rokayle's son may have used a *nom de plume* for the same reason as authors in later generations—to shield himself, his family, his supporters.[12] While Kane briefly considers the possibility that the ascription deliberately offered disinformation, he quickly rejects it: "For such a falsification I can by speculation find no motive that stands up to scrutiny except conceivably a conspiracy to conceal the true identity of the author of *Piers Plowman*."[13] Yet such efforts at concealment, encouraged by the poet himself, may afford the best explanation for adopting a last name different from his reputed father's. The controversial contents of *Piers Plowman* would fully justify the author's desire for concealment, first by assuming a pen name to dodge responsibility for the text, and then by dissociating even his pseudonym from the poem in its earliest copies.

The state of the texts suggests the troubled circumstances of the poem's publication. Working on the traditional view that the A-text was the first version of *Piers Plowman,* Doyle has remarked that it does not survive in the earliest manuscripts but is preserved instead in manuscripts that, as a group, are the latest in dating and the furthest removed in dialect from the poet's original.[14] Never formally published because unfinished, the A-text had escaped. Earlier copies of all three versions must have existed, and their disappearance might be explained in terms of an active campaign of suppression, the result of a backlash that also prompted the revisions of the C-text as well as possibly revisions within the B-text itself. Steven Justice has put forward suggestions about variant passages that might constitute evidence of authorial changes prompted by concerns over hostile public reception:

> Maybe he thought those things too dangerous to say to the whole world. Or maybe he wrote the more diffident version first and then attached himself to more radical possibilities. Or maybe he wrote the more radical version first and then recoiled from his own radicalism. Or maybe he wrote the different versions for circulation among different audiences, a more audacious one for patrons and intimates, a bowdlerized one for public release.[15]

Justice comments specifically upon a passage concerning the disendowment of Church property, which was quickly becoming a signature theme for John Wyclif and his followers.[16]

The Athlone editors conclude that the earliest copies of the B-text derived from an archetype "at least two and possibly more removes from the authorially sanctioned B exemplar,"[17] and this editorial view encourages further speculation that the poet, acutely concerned over reactions to his poem, did not actively encourage or carefully oversee transmission of this text beyond his patron and immediate coterie. George Russell speculates about the circumstances for unsupervised release and circulation: "Our B-text is a chance survivor of a shape of the poem which was the product of a massive and intense revision of the first stage—that is, A—but which, for various reasons, mostly political, religious and ideological, was either called in by the author or was suppressed by others, and the existing manuscripts are descendants of a single manuscript that escaped this suppression."[18] Unauthorized manuscripts were copied informally and moved rapidly beyond the poet's control and supervision as evidenced by appropriation in 1381:

> But at the moment John Ball cites *Piers,* one must recognize the existence of a general vernacular literary public and a general vernacular

literary culture. In these circumstances, anyone so inclined can acquire the poem without the author's say-so, can read it without supervision, can absorb it and subject it to interpretation—even an interpretation the author would reject. In short, the author loses control of the text—here of its themes, but analogously, Langland had invariably lost control of the text in the stages of its social production.[19]

Late in his career Langland himself reflected upon the risky consequences of publishing when Leaute cautions Will against truth-telling (C.12.38–40):

Ac be neueremore þe furste the defaute to blame;
Thouh thowe se, say nat sum tyme, þat is treuthe.
Thyng þat wolde be pryué, publische thow hit neuere.

The unfinished look of the C-text, with some passages untouched and others hastily composed, suggests that the poet may have kept this version private until he was safely in his grave. Only then was this large-scale revision, available in the poet's drafts or "foul papers," copied by scribes familiar enough with the Worcestershire dialect to take their own liberties even in the authoritative HM 143. Some variations in the earliest C manuscripts again suggest that drafts may have been leaked prior to the poet's death.[20] Even the proposition that the A-text was a late abbreviation of the poem would fit this scenario of acute caution in the face of hostile reception. According to this alternative account, the poet sought to sanitize its contents at the end of his life, while simplifying its style, but he died before getting much further than Passus 11. In the posthumous continuation of the A-text reporting Will's death, John But took pains to include his own last name, but he was unable or unwilling to provide the poet's.[21]

Skeat was deeply troubled by the scarcity of Langlands in late medieval documents. "This is a difficulty which I can hardly get over," he wrote in his introductory section "The Author's Name."[22] As a pen name invented for protection, however, *William Langland* provided the poet with abundant opportunities for exploring various puns and semantic possibilities. By clearly establishing "Will" as the narrator's name, for example, the poet was able to draw upon the centuries-old theology of the will (*voluntas*) to deploy an allegory in which the faculty of the human volition, even when properly advised by reason, was not able to perform good works (Dowel) in a manner guaranteed to win salvation.[23]

Defined as a long strip of plowland, *Langland* connotes a rustic, upland narrator befitting a poem about a plowman while also providing further opportunities for meaningful punning. Accordingly, Middleton has explored the dreamer's exploits into the "lond of longynge" (B.11.8) to show how the cryptographic signature invokes the mirroring of Langland and *lond/long*.[24] Anagrammatic wordplay with the dreamer's name was more obvious later in the B-text: "I haue lyued in lond," quod I, "my name is Longe Wille" (B.15.152). This passage attracted the attentions of a few early readers. In the late fourteenth-century Rawlinson Poet. 38, a fifteenth-century hand wrote beside this line the only red-ink sidenote in the entire manuscript: "Longe Wylle" (fol. 74a). In Laud Misc. 581, a notation probably from the early sixteenth century was more confident of the line's significance: "nota the name of thauctour" (fol. 64a). Skeat relied heavily upon this line in reaching his own conclusions about the author's name—William instead of Robert Langland[25]—but he noted with some discomfort that the line disappeared from the C-text, replaced by a reference to the poet's long residency in London (C.16.286–88). The C-text performs a protective revision by deleting reference to the poet's name and canceling this identity even as a pen name. Furthermore, the C-text advertizes the poet's London address only after he had perhaps removed himself from the metropolis for a more secure livelihood back in Worcestershire.

The narrator of the C-text states that he was recognized as a writer unfriendly to the "lollares of Londone." This claim may have masked the opposite reality that the poet had brought upon himself suspicion of offering support for London's "Lollards" as the term came to be identified with Wycliffites.[26] Hadn't John Ball borrowed from *Piers Plowman* in his seditious broadsides? Hadn't Ball later confessed that he was in league with the heretic John Wyclif?[27] If Langland spent a great deal of his career in London in the same Cornhill district where he places himself in the C.5 autobiography, he risked becoming a visible public figure at precisely the time during the 1380s when discussing radical theological issues became risky business. "Subverters of all kinds became suspect at a time of general subversion."[28]

Langland had already shown restraint in the B-text about 1378–81. He never specifically named Richard II, any magnate such as John of Gaunt, or any prelate such as the bishop of Norwich. When Lady Mede is brought to trial in London, Langland even refuses to name the royal clerk to whom she is entrusted: "The kyng called a clerk—I kan noȝt his name" (B.3.3). He could have said more about the court but chose not to: "Forþe I kan and kan nauȝt of court speke moore" (B.Prol.11).[29] Though clearly alluding to the Duke of Lancaster's interference in London politics at the end of the 1370s, his Belling of the Cat fable avoided any overt name-calling.[30] Because the realm's powerful men were sensitive to public criticism, especially around the time of the Appellants, the Cambridge Parliament of 1388 took steps to expand laws against defamation in order to give the council power to punish any man "so bold as to speak ill or spread false report, or lies, or any false matter" about prelates, dukes, earls, barons, and other members of the nobility, as well as officers of the king's household and justices of the realm. "It is agreed and assented in this parliament that any such should be taken and imprisoned," Knighton reported in his record of the statutes.[31] By the first decade of the next century, *Mum and the Sothsegger* employed Langlandian language for lamenting an even harsher atmosphere of intolerance:

> And yf a burne bolde hym to bable the sothe
> And mynne hum of mischief that misse-reule asketh,
> He may lose his life and laugh here no more,
> Or y-putte into prisone or y-pyned to deeth,
> Or y-brent or y-shent or sum sorowe haue
> That fro scorne other scathe scape shal he neure.[32]

In the immediate aftermath of the Cambridge Parliament of 1388, the C-text responded not only to the aggressive new statutes for punishing labor abuses but also the penalties for those who criticized the noblemen and ecclesiasts of the kingdom.[33] Englishmen in general demonstrated violent reactions to all possible forms of harmful speech. "The contemporary records are rife with punishments accorded to speech," one recent investigation of the period has concluded, "whether it be slander, false rumor, lies, deceptions, falsehoods, vulgarity, or simply the language of a 'common scold.'"[34] This hypersensitivity only increased during the early years of Lancastrian rule, when the unfortunate John Sparrowhawk was executed in the most extreme manner of drawing, hanging, and beheading simply for blaming the rainy weather on Henry IV.[35]

Dialect analysis of the manuscripts induced Skeat and later scholars such as Samuels to speculate about the poet's whereabouts late in his career. "Such a concentration of C-MSS in dialects of the south-west Midlands is unlikely to have come about without an authorial presence in the area," but Horobin has recently argued that Worcester dialect does not preclude London copying.[36] Based on the older view, the Athlone editors suspected that the poet had left London at the end of his career when the final revision of the C-text began circulating.[37] Pearsall has suggested that the turmoil of 1381 may have prompted Langland to leave London "when the author of the poem that had been so inflammatorily used and alluded to by the spokesmen of the Revolt may have believed himself to be about to become extremely unpopular with the authorities."[38] No prosperous retirement to the countryside of his boy-hood days such as Shakespeare's return to Stratford, Langland's relocation to the Worcester area would have been a retreat to a friendlier provincial loca-tion where revision of the C-text could proceed without posing a clear and present danger for its author. Langland might even have sought safety under the protection of local patrons. Hanley Castle has been identified as a Des-penser stronghold and administrative center recently connected with the Ro-kayle memorandum; in 1341, a man by the name of William Rokayle had been ordained by the bishop of Worcester at Bredon, near Hanley Castle.[39]

Much evidence suggests local support for other dissident voices. Origi-nally a Worcester man, Wyclif's Oxford disciple John Aston was welcomed back by a local conventicle in 1387. William Swinderby followed his example in the 1390s. Walsingham reported that Oldcastle went into hiding in the Mal-vern area in 1415. Worcester remained "a favorite area into which a number of men accused of Lollardy and threatened with the sanctions of the law had chosen to 'retire' or 'disappear' from the late 1380s onward."[40] Perhaps di-rectly influenced by *Piers Plowman,* an important collection of Lollard ser-mons was written sometime after 1387 by scribes trained in the Worcestershire dialect.[41] More than a hideout for Wyclif's early followers and other suspi-cious characters, Worcestershire emerges as a provincial battlefield where the terminology of heresy itself was fought out. Probably the earliest surviving instance of the word *Lollardi* as "Wycliffites" appears in a 1387 letter by the bishop of Worcester prohibiting Wyclif's followers, such as Aston and Swin-derby, from preaching in his diocese.[42]

Langland is now believed to have continued his C-revisions after 1388,[43] and so he was positioned historically and geographically to have engaged in these contests over terms of condemnation. He responded to the anti-Wycliffite definition of "Lollard" by pressing instead a self-consciously con-servative sense of *lollares* as fraudulent friars, and indeed the entire class of gyrovagues who pursued irregular lives of vagrancy and false begging ac-cording to a longstanding tradition of Christian complaint.[44] Early in his ca-reer around 1400, Scribe D's work on the Ilchester *Piers* showed a similar willingness to enter into these same Lollard/Wycliffite controversies, pro-ducing a unique Prologue that gave immediate attention to Langland's ver-sion of *lolleres lif* and bolstering the poet's efforts at neutralizing any conno-tation of heresy.[45] Like Langland himself, Scribe D was not "worried about offending anti-Wycliffite readers with all these 'lollares' prominently featured in C."[46]

The author's efforts at keeping his identity secret may have been abetted by his earliest scribes. While copyists of Hilton's *Scale of Perfection* and Love's

Mirror of the Life of Christ routinely omitted the names of their authors, the strong personality of Langland's first-person narrator seems to require an authorial name in the manner of *Sir John Mandeville's Travels,* a work that appears as a companion piece with *Piers Plowman* in five manuscript collections.[47] Though now largely regarded as a complete fabrication, Mandeville's name gained international currency while Langland's name failed to achieve easy recognition even in London.[48] Whereas the anonymity of poems such as *William of Palerne* and *Wynnere and Wastoure,* surviving in single manuscripts, may represent the ignorance, carelessness, or indifference of the copyists, the almost complete anonymity of *Piers Plowman,* surviving in over fifty copies, some datable to the poet's lifetime, invites wider speculation.[49]

The blankness of the early C-text manuscripts produced in such close proximity to the poet's final location, whether Worcester or London, suggests intention rather than ignorance as the reason for the consistent omission of the poet's name. In his brief study "The Anonymity of Langland," Allan Bright long ago pointed to collusion between poet and audience: "The times were such, and the risks were so great, that it was prudent for Langland to conceal his identity as far as possible, though the name of the author may have been generally, if not openly, known."[50] Certainly when compared with the consistent attribution of the *Canterbury Tales* to Chaucer during the fifteenth century, the failure of the fourteenth-century *Piers* scribes to name their author is a phenomenon of real significance. If Langland remained resident in London throughout the 1380s and the Trinity MS B.15.17 manuscript of the B-text was copied by Adam Pinkhurst, the question arises why this professional textwriter, who readily included Chaucer's name in Hengwrt and Ellesmere, did not know and include his author's name when producing his copy of *Piers Plowman.*

More evidence suggesting authorial obfuscation surfaces in a series of notations made by copyists who wanted to identify their author but apparently had incomplete or unclear information. Five C manuscripts, including the early and authoritative HM 143, contain the following notation at the end of Passus 10: *Explicit visio Willielmi .W. de Petro le Plouhman.* Skeat speculated that the abbreviation stood for William of Wychwood, the last name deriving from the poet's birthplace according to the testimony of the Dublin manuscript.[51] Insisting upon William Langland as the author's name, George Kane took pains to discount this testimony, arguing that the five scribes merely reproduce a wrong guess in their common source. Yet Kane remained baffled by these false leads as well as the overall difficulty at establishing the poet's true name, unless there was a conspiracy to conceal the author's identity.[52] This possibility remains suggestive. While not deleting this nearly worthless notation or concocting a complete surname by guesswork, these five scribes continued obscuring the author's full name. Specifically, the failure of the well-placed HM 143 scribe and his corrector to include any more than the initial of the poet's last name in the Passus 10 explicit, not even in an opening title or concluding colophon, suggests some covert operations at a time when the poem's controversial contents were becoming more inflammatory.[53] In the long run, these five copyists endorsed the practice of attributing *Piers Plowman* to an entity rendered effectively anonymous for the lack of a full surname.[54]

By the sixteenth century, the consensus had evolved that the poet's name was Robert Langlande. The first name was perhaps based on a confused reading of B.8.1: "Thus y robed in russet I romed aboute." Perhaps working from information provided by Nicholas Brigham (d. 1558), John Bale provided accounts of the Langland's name and background twice in his *Index Britanniae Scriptorum*:

> Robertus Langlande, natus in comitatu Salopie in villa Mortymers
> Clyberi in the cleyelande within viij. myles of Malborne hylles,
> scripsit,
> Peers ploughman,   li. i. "In a somer sonday whan sote was þe sunne."
> *Ex collectis Nicolai Brigan.*[55]

The editor Robert Crowley accepted Bale's ascription along with biographical information in the preface to his edition's three printings in 1550: "the authour was named Roberte langelande, a Shropeshere man borne in Cleybirie, about viii myles from Maluerne hilles."[56] The name was inscribed by sixteenth-century hands in two other manuscripts, Society of Antiquaries MS 687 (p. 470) and Bodleian Laud Misc. 581: "Robart Langeland / borne by malverne hilles" (fol. 1a). A note was also squeezed at the bottom of the paste-down in the Huntington manuscript HM 128: "Robertus Langlande natus in comitatu Salopie in villa Mortymers Clybery in the claylande, within viij myles of Malborne hylles, scripsit, peers ploughman." Apparently the common source for all these attributions, Bale's testimony deserves serious consideration because his researches turned up biographical information found nowhere else. While not accepting Robert as the poet's first name, Skeat was sufficiently impressed by the specificity of the information to include it in his author's biography: "He was born at Cleobury Mortimer, in Shropshire."[57]

Langland's Editorial Lives

Skeat's inclusion of an "Author's Life" among his edition's supporting materials can be traced back to the thirteenth-century *accessus ad auctores*.[58] Moving from the medieval to the modern, these practices assumed greater significance in the larger editorial enterprise. More than providing biographical information for the curious reader, this narrative exposes what have already served the editor as assumptions enabling the preparation of the text itself. George Kane has been quite candid about this process: "What the editor of *Piers Plowman* does when he edits is to create, out of textual detail, an hypothesis of original readings based ultimately on an assumption (however well or ill founded) about authorship."[59]

Therefore the editor no less than the literary historian forms a conception for the discursive frame of the author's life, which includes his social circumstances, prevailing literary practices, political engagements, the age's intellectual and religious climate, and the audience's expectations and responses. This authorial biography comes to operate as a dominant instance of the "explanatory categories by which to account for the text."[60] The temptation to force surviving evidence to fit a biographical outline that supports an editorial viewpoint remains strong even when dealing with a modern writer whose life is generously documented. When a medieval writer such as Langland has his historical identity constituted only by a fragile tissue of internal and external evidence,[61] the ways in which different editors have conceived his biography serve almost as reactions to a Rorschach test. Some version of authorial biography, explicit or implicit, has invariably been devised as an editorial fantasy. The author did not merely compose the poem. In a very real sense, the poem as it is edited, annotated, and prefaced comes to compose the author.

In the first printed edition of *The Vision of Pierce Plowman* in 1550, Robert Crowley embodied the humanist zeal to recover a maximum knowledge about his author.[62] This is how his brief introduction begins: "Beynge desyerous to knowe the name of the Autoure of this most worthy worke . . ." Knowing the writer's name became a matter of primary importance so that motives and intentions could be ascribed to the person who materialized under this label. Probably on the basis of information from John Bale, Crowley announced that "the Autour was named Roberte langelande, a Shropshere man borne in Cleybirie, about viii. myles from Maluerne hille." Since Crowley himself was born only a few miles from the Malvern Hills at Tetbury in Gloucestershire, we may also glimpse an early indication of the ways an editor begins to identify personally with his author. This subliminal recognition of kinship invites a blurring of distinctions between authorial agency and editorial enterprise. The editor's literary, religious, and political values come to represent the author's. Inevitably the editor's reconstructed text and to some extent his personality are superimposed upon the author's.

While conscientious to emend *Piers Plowman* in the second and third printings as new manuscripts became available to him,[63] Crowley steadily positioned Langland as a contemporary of John Wyclif, linking the poet and the theologian as twin precursors of the Protestant Reformation that he himself championed. Insisting upon the distinction of this venerable precedent, he generally avoided modernizing vocabulary in the manner of sixteenth-century manuscripts such as Sion College.[64] The more ideologically motivated a scholar, the less likely he was to update older texts so that they would appear in their original native dress.[65] As a propagandist, Crowley was deeply committed to the more radical movement during the first years of Edward VI's reign under the protectorate of Edward Seymour, Duke of Somerset, when the various treason laws of Henry VIII were repealed along with the Act of Six Articles. Protestantism proved a very useful policy in 1550, since it guaranteed the backing of Londoners and provided justification for further confiscation of Church property.[66] Little wonder that the year 1550 serves as a conventional starting point in the history of aggressive nation-formation in England and the extension of state authority into local affairs.[67]

Crowley's second printing added marginal notes that further emphasized the religious contents of *Piers Plowman*. These editorial comments harmonized the poem's contents with the religious views of the day. The Prologue "declareth the greate wyckednes of the byshoppes," Passus 3 "what abuse was in auriculer confession," Passus 5 "that Abbayes shoulde be suppressed," and so forth. While these attacks on traditional religion targeted the same corrupt practices that figured in Langland's poem, the Edwardine reforms sought destruction rather than correction. Their extremist agenda included removing images from churches, disbanding parish fraternities, abolishing processions, dissolving chantries, banning the veneration of local saints, and destroying the pilgrimage trade.[68] In the same year 1550, altars were exchanged for Communion tables, Protestant pastors replaced Catholic priests, and Nicholas Ridley became bishop of London. Amid these religious tumults, Crowley constructed his editorial image of Langland as a prophetic proto-Protestant. Invention of an author always included factors other than artistic merit, in this case Reformation values.[69] Langland's authorial integrity relied specifically upon his Christian beliefs that diverged from Catholic uniformity.

So the author's status became contingent upon the correctness of his religious commitments. This standard had been employed since the time of St. Jerome and was already evident when Bede certified Cædmon as the first-named poet in English precisely because he was inspired to versify the Christian Scriptures. The procedure for canonizing an author assumed recognizable analogy with canonization of a saint, since each procedure exemplified the orthodoxies of the culture conferring official status. Both the saint and the author rely upon a substantial dossier of documents for the construction of this prestigious identity. In Langland's own day, for example, Richard II invested considerable energy compiling a dossier to support canonization of his grandfather Edward II, petitioning Pope Boniface IX with a book of the royal martyr's miracles, which Richard himself took pains to investigate for authenticity.[70]

For Crowley, a specific ideological formation asserted the legitimacy of Langland's authorial status and, consequently, justified editorial alterations wherever old Catholic doctrines were detected. Such passages could no longer be considered authorial, as Crowley defined his author, and therefore they needed to be emended just as prophetic passages needed to be rejected as spurious: "prophecye is lyke to be a thinge added of some other man than the fyrste autour." Doctrinal errors became textual errors. Thus the Protestant editor altered *body* to *bread* in Langland's account of the sacrament of the Eucharist (B.12.85–86). He changed *scrifte* to *Christe* in order to make the line more doctrinally sound (B.5.76). He substituted the name of Christ for Mary (B.7.202). He deleted a reference to purgatory (B.15.346) since Protestants eliminated this theology in order to abolish the costly practice of remembering the dead. His edition also lacks a passage praising the monastic life (B.10.297–308) since destruction of the monasteries had been under way since 1535.[71]

Crowley's third issue was reprinted by Owen Rogers with the addition of *Pierce the Ploughman's Crede* in 1561—the same year as John Stow's expanded edition of *The Workes of Geffrey Chaucer*—but the text of *Piers Plowman* was not newly edited and not printed again for more than a century and a half. After such a considerable gap of time, nineteenth-century editions redefined Langland's authorial image in ways that have steadily influenced literary history until the present day.

Printed by Lord Byron's publisher John Murray, Thomas Dunham Whitaker's 1813 edition conceived Langland according to the image of his own
historical period as a Romantic wanderer and dreamer.[72] Whitaker himself
was a Lancashire vicar, and he decided that his poet too was an "obscure
country priest, much addicted to solitary contemplation." Despite the text's
familiarity with London and Westminster, the poet was pictured in a rustic
setting where he pursued the almost Wordsworthian practice of rambling
through the countryside, then returning to his study to recollect in tranquility.
This is how Whitaker describes the poet in his "Introductory Discourse":

> I can conceive him (like his own visionary William) to have been some-
> times occupied in contemplative wanderings on the Malvern Hills,
> and dozing away a summer's noon among the bushes, while his wak-
> ing thoughts were distorted into all the misshapen forms created by a
> dreaming fancy. Sometimes I can descry him taking his staff, and
> roaming far and wide in search of manners and characters; mingling
> with men of every accessible rank, and storing his memory with hints
> for future use. I next pursue him to his study, sedate and thoughtful,
> yet wildly inventive, digesting the first rude drafts of his Visions;
> and in successive transcriptions, as judgement matured, or invention
> declined, or as his observations were more extended, expanding or
> contracting, improving and sometimes perhaps debasing his original
> text.[73]

It is interesting to note that the image of the wandering poet and even some
of Whitaker's phrases—"dozing away a summer's noon" and "sometimes I
can descry him"—would find their way into Matthew Arnold's *Scholar Gypsy*
and *Thyrsis* as later formulations of the alienated intellectual and poetic vagabond.

This concoction of an authorial biography informs Whitaker's assessment of the poem for editorial purposes. *Piers Plowman* needed to be obscure
in order to safeguard the poet who exposed corruption among the high and
mighty: "Above all, the great ecclesiastics were as vindictive as they were corrupt: and hence the satirist was compelled to shelter himself under the distant generalities of personification."[74] His view of the poem's protective
obscurities meant that Whitaker was inclined to accept various corruptions
and garbled readings as they stood, because these dark passages accorded
with his understanding of the poet's general procedure for sheltering beneath obscure and evasive language.[75] What Annabel Patterson describes

as "functional ambiguity," Quintillian had originally recommended for the writer to avoid giving offense to hostile powers: "If danger can be avoided by some ambiguity of expression, everyone will admire its cunning."[76]

Whitaker made an important contribution by puzzling over the obscurity of the author's identity and making Langland's anonymity into a subject for scholarly speculation. Since the editor imagined a writer whose satirical subjects necessitated a strategy of self-concealment, he pictured Langland as a Romantic rebel who masked his true identity to avoid the consequences of his fierce social commentary: "From his subordinate station in the church, this free reprover of the higher ranks was exposed to all the severities of ecclesiastical discipline: and from the aristocratical temper of the times he was liable to be crushed by the civil power. Everything, therefore, of a personal nature was in common prudence to be avoided."[77] The editor was even skeptical that the author could have published under his own name. His prefatory discussion refers to Langland—"if such were really the author's name"—as a writer whose personal obscurity mirrored the obscurity of his poetry: "To the same necessity of reserve and concealment, which dictated the vehicle of allegory, is to be ascribed the uncertainty which must now for ever remain as to the name of the writer."[78]

Whitaker himself operated in a literary culture in which authorial anonymity and the use of pen names were common for a variety of reasons, from social decorum to legal discretion. At the same time that Whitaker was editing, Jane Austen's novels were being published without her name attached. Appearing in the same year of 1813, *Pride and Prejudice* had a title page that read simply "by the Author of *Sense and Sensibility*." Because he readily appreciated the reasons why a writer concealed his or her true identity, Whitaker was more willing to suppose that "Langland" was not the poet's real name. He was also willing to appreciate the relationship between authorial obscurity and textual obscurity, with the result he printed passages that later editors emended according to the more exacting standards of modern print culture. "The Visions concerning Piers Plouhman are, beyond comparison, the most obscure work in the English tongue," Whitaker concluded, so that the elucidation of many passages must "be abandoned as hopeless."[79]

Thomas Wright's 1842 edition of *The Vision and Creed of Piers Ploughman* is best understood in context of his other scholarly projects.[80] Work on *Three Chapters of Letters Relating to the Suppression of the Monasteries* had furnished his intellectual imagination with a detailed knowledge of monastic foundations as well as the assaults launched upon these religious institutions by agents of the Reformation. In the years following, though it was already under way as an ancillary project, he produced the two-volume collection *Political Poems and Songs,* which contained verses addressing a variety of historical topics—war and peace, rebellion and civil war, the deposition and the deaths of kings, heresies of the Lollards, and corruption of religious institutions—written from the reign of Edward II to the accession of Richard III.[81] Taken together, these two other scholarly projects help to explain why he situated *Piers Plowman* in the context of "a series of great consecutive political movements co-existent with a similar series of intellectual revolutions in the mass of the people."[82]

Wright detected the allusion to the Normandy Campaign of 1360 as evidence for dating the poem to the reign of Edward III. While he showed a typical Protestant prejudice against monastic corruption, the editor nonetheless concluded that the poem faithfully reflected its age:

> The history of England during the fourteenth century is a stirring picture; its dark side is the increasing corruption of the popish church; its bright side, the general spread of popular intelligence, and the first stand made by the commons in the defence of their liberties, and in the determination to obtain a redress of grievances.
>
> Under these circumstances appeared *Piers Ploughman.*[83]

Though he did not perform an exhaustive search for the manuscripts, Wright found eight copies in the British Museum and nearly a dozen each in Oxford and Cambridge libraries. He was struck by the remarkable degree of variation that Skeat would later resolve into his three canonic versions. He noted the relatively early production of these manuscripts, with approximately two-thirds dating from the fourteenth century, and he chose for his copy-text Cambridge Trinity College B.15.17, the same B manuscript later selected as the copy-text by Kane and Donaldson.[84] Mostly he was impressed by the ordinariness of these books produced in what he considered the new democratic spirit of the age: "That the manuscripts are seldom executed in a superior style of writing, and scarcely ever ornamented with painted initial letters, may perhaps be taken as a proof that they were not written for the higher classes of society."[85]

Aware that the poet's criticism of religious corruption associated *Piers* with the radical reforms of John Wyclif and his followers, Wright discerned no outright attack on Catholic doctrine and no questioning of traditional governance. "The writer of Piers Ploughman was neither a sower of sedition, nor one who would be characterized by his contemporaries as a heretic," although *Piers Plowman*'s attacks upon Church corruption "must have helped in no small degree the cause of the Reformation."[86]

The author emerges from these editorial speculations as a religious writer deeply schooled in monastic theology, perhaps at Oxford, but he responded with a powerful sense of individual commitment, offering his poem for an eventual correction on the national level during the sixteenth century. Impressed by the poet's knowledge of the Bible and the Church Fathers, Wright decided that he was a member of a monastic foundation, and therefore the editor loaded his explanatory notes with references to England's monasteries. He called his poet simply the Monk of Malvern.[87] Following the longstanding practice of naming the author Robert, Wright disallowed any direct identification of the poet with the dreamer Will. Sir Frederick Madden had recently discovered the memorandum in the Trinity Dublin manuscript, but Wright was not persuaded.[88]

Walter W. Skeat's 1886 parallel-text edition of *Piers Plowman* represents a magnificent example of the Victorian obsession with imposing order and elucidating the truth. His second volume included a fully elaborated "Author's Life" in which Skeat drew together evidence from a variety of sources in order to devise his own version of William Langland as a hugely energetic poet always on the move.[89] On the testimony of John Bale, the poet was born in Cleobury Mortimer in Shropshire. The note on the Dublin manuscript suggested that Langland then moved to Shipton-under-Wychwood in Oxfordshire, where his father, Stacy de Rokayle, held a farm under the Despensers. But the opening lines of the poem indicated a relocation to Malvern to receive his early education, perhaps at the priory of Great Malvern. Then Langland settled in London during his mature career as indicated by the Cornhill reference in the autobiographical passage of the C-text. Finally, the poet retired to the West Country where the poem's final version was completed and the early C-text manuscripts were copied for a local readership.

Langland emerges from these biographical speculations as a hard worker who embodied Skeat's own standards for Victorian industriousness. His "Author's Life" ends on this rousing note of approbation: "The man who composed *Piers Plowman,* and wrote it out himself, and subsequently revised it with great care, making numerous additions to it, and again wrote it out at least twice, not only proved his industry, but has left an enduring monument of a useful life."[90] According to this conception of a hyperactive writer, Skeat perceived in the surviving manuscripts ten different forms of the poem, not including the possibility of an eleventh version in the Z-text.[91] In 1909 Skeat sent the aspiring *Piers* editor R. W. Chambers a letter in which he renewed his confidence in the poet's ability to serve as his own copyist:

There is a presumption that Wille was *himself* a scrivener: & one reason why he took so readily to rewriting things was precisely because he had no need to be beholden to any one for making his rough drafts. He could alter his work easily enough, because he *could do it himself!*

Then his friends would borrow his rough-drafts which were not on loose sheets, but in regular quires and probably loosely (or well) bound. And his friends would copy them out (& a nice mess they sometimes made): & if any of them liked to add lines on his own account, there was nothing to prevent him.[92]

This bold but well-informed speculation not only stipulates a profession for Langland as a professional textwriter but also specifies a coterie readership of similarly trained scribes in the sorts of government offices such as Chancery now being proposed by Steven Justice and Kathryn Kerby-Fulton.[93]

Bolstering his notion of Langland as a supremely industrious poet, Skeat detected four varieties of the A-text, two of the B-text, two of the C-text, and two mixed texts combining A+C and B+C. He decided that BL MS Harley 875 preserved the *"earliest* form of the A-text," and he described the Ilchester manuscript as an early draft of the C-text. As the most tangible evidence of the poet's diligence as copyist, Skeat accepted Bodleian MS Laud Misc. 581 as probably an autograph or a fair copy from an autograph, which the author himself had supervised and corrected. Skeat thought that the numerous crosses in the margins indicated lines that Langland wanted to change and *did* change in his C-revision.[94] The Laud manuscript does inspire confidence. It was written in the fourteenth century, and its language includes southwest Worcestershire relict forms. The text is clearly written, its Latin lines are boxed in red for easier identification, and blanks are left to mark off blocks of text, each introduced by a ¶ sign colored in blue. The scribe had a real feel for *Piers Plowman* and produced one of the most "user-friendly" copies. Skeat's presumption that Langland was a truly hands-on writer, whose diligence was represented not abstractly by a transcendent text but concretely by an actual transcription, encouraged the high degree of editorial confidence that he invested in readings offered by the Laud manuscript.[95]

In 1906 John M. Manly's article "The Lost Leaf" muddled this confident narrative and started a controversy over multiple authorship that complicated the editorial history of *Piers Plowman* throughout the twentieth century.[96] Abandoning Skeat's view of a restless writer constantly on the move and tirelessly revising his work, Manly reckoned five separate writers contributing to this long-term project, including John But's continuation in the

A-text's Passus 12. Manly was so confident about multiple authorship—really serial authorship—that he published his views in *"Piers Plowman* and Its Sequence" in the second volume of the authoritative *Cambridge History of English Literature*. In this formulation, the B-poet is harshly criticized as a writer with "no skill in composition, no control of his materials or thought," and the C-reviser is disparaged as a "man of much learning, of true piety and of genuine interest in the welfare of the nation, but unimaginative, cautious and a very pronounced pedant."[97] Manly's harsh judgments do not accommodate the possibility that a single author could behave differently at different periods during a long career.

After Manly's authoritative pronouncements, editors could no longer take for granted the singleness of authorship, the consistency of poetic practice across all three versions, or even the steady excellence of the poet's literary achievement. For Manly's student Thomas A. Knott, the obvious course was to isolate the work of a single anonymous contributor.[98] For him, this became the A1 poet, who composed the section of the A-text through Passus 8 (126) based on the manuscript Trinity College Cambridge R.3.14.[99] Though Knott's edition, which was advertised in 1915, remained unpublished, David Fowler continued this project in a 1949 Chicago dissertation, which he subsequently combined with Knott's A1 and published in 1952 as *A Critical Edition of the A-Version* with an introduction reasserting Manly's views on multiple authorship.[100]

As one casualty of these controversies, R. W. Chambers was diverted from his editorial work on a new A-text in order to defend the single-author view against scholars such as Mabel Day who marshaled great masses of textual evidence in support of Manly.[101] Central to the case of unitary authorship was the argument for the poet's consistent excellence—really an assumption necessary for Chambers's proposed new edition—which Lee Patterson has very incisively characterized as "the logic of textual criticism and the way of genius."[102] It had been Skeat's contention that there was little likelihood two or more poets of such great powers would have brought their talents to bear upon a collaborative project. Proceeding upon this sensible hypothesis, Chambers and his collaborator J. H. G. Grattan sought to rescue this original talent by shifting blame onto corrupt archetypal manuscripts and faulty copyists.

Oddly enough, the real culprit in this scenario became Langland himself. Chambers saw the poet in the A-text growing confused in his artistic ambitions and daunted by the complexity of his theological questions. The poet remained stymied for some period of years until he could advance with fuller

confidence and artistic vision in the B-continuation. Many years later, working as the C reviser, Langland became a quirky old curmudgeon with flagging
energy and spotty judgment, too often willing to allow scribal corruptions to
stand in the B copy from which he worked and, in the end, failing to complete his revision.

Several paradoxes attend the Athlone editions of *Piers Plowman,* completed after many decades by Chambers's pupil George Kane in collaboration with E. Talbot Donaldson and George H. Russell.[103] One of these internal contradictions has been the absolute necessity for assuming single
authorship *and* the absolute irrelevancy of considering any particulars of the
poet's life. The curious reader searches vainly throughout the vast introductions to the three Athlone volumes for any section headed "The Author's
Life." It is a telling fact that Langland's name does not occur a single time in
the 172-page introduction to Kane's *A Version.* Even more tellingly, the author's name does not appear on the title pages of the *A Version* (1960), the
B Version (1975), or the long-awaited *C Version* (1997). As an official supplement to these editions, Kane's *The Evidence for Authorship* (1965) is astonishing
in both the rigor of its argumentation and the narrowness of its three conclusions: a single poet wrote all three versions, his name was William Langland, and the title of the poem in all three versions was *Piers Plowman.* The
severe limits of these historical investigations remain pervasive throughout
the massive editorial undertaking.

Resisting the corrosive effects of an older literary historicism that would
dissolve the author into his general cultural setting, New Criticism encouraged the Athlone editors to isolate Langland's art upon a pedestal so high, as
it were, that nobody could discern his work clearly except for the editors
themselves.[104] Although his biography is minimized, Langland assumes the
strongest version of the author function described by Foucault: "The author
is therefore the ideological figure by which one marks the manner in which
we fear the proliferation of meaning."[105] Katherine O'Keeffe puts the question this way when dealing with earlier medieval texts whose originary moment has receded historically beyond the reach of documentary recuperation:
"What does it mean to speak of the *Beowulf* poet, for example, save to long
for an origin which ensures (by definition) 'authority' for a reading of which
we approve?"[106]

The radical split between man and writer was already apparent in E. Talbot Donaldson's *The C-Text and Its Poet* (1949). Four chapters are devoted
to "the C Reviser" without any reference to the poet's life, while the final
chapter, "The Poet: Biographical Material," explores Langland's professional

livelihood in London without direct reference to his activities as a writer.[107] Donaldson portrays Langland very much as a literary loner without ecclesiastical employment, without institutional affiliation, without consistent patronage, and without a stable and supportive coterie. The poet's self-described isolation gives no sense of an immediate audience for commenting upon his writings or offering suggestions for revision. Standing outside any professional group or institutional environment, Langland was unswayed by social allegiances or factional commitments. Thus the author could be understood solely as a text-producing entity. His work comes to represent a particular aesthetic doctrine: "The art object, ideally self-enclosed, is freed not only from the necessities of the surrounding world (necessities that it transforms miraculously into play) but also from the intention of the maker."[108] According to this view, Langland was the great poet who produced the great poem—period. To the extent that any authorial identity emerges, it becomes interchangeable with his existential function as a writer. He is what he did, and what he did was produce the three versions of *Piers Plowman*.

Because Kane formally disavowed the reconstruction of a biography for the poet,[109] his views on Langland's life need to be gleaned from publications outside the Athlone project. His 1951 book *Middle English Literature* with its substantial discussion of *Piers Plowman* had already abandoned the quest for retrieving any historical identity for the poet. The book's index did not include a single entry for the name "Langland" but offered instead these suggestive subheadings under *Piers Plowman*: "artistic impulse of the author," "conflicting tendencies of the author," "effect of the author's moral impulse," "fluency of author," and so forth.[110] His influential essay "The Autobiographical Fallacy in Chaucer and Langland Studies" (1965) worked hard at debunking biographical speculations of the sort traceable to Whitaker's 1813 edition. These speculations had maintained that Langland bore some real-life resemblance to the distressed dreamer and befuddled religious thinker inside his poem. Kane caricatured the portrait of "a lanky, embittered malcontent in rusty cassock, striding arrogantly about the Malvern Hills."[111] Yet as much as he recoiled from the Romantic image of the artist, Kane elsewhere invoked his own made-up portrait of Langland:

> He was clearly writing for readers united in the concerns registered in his poem, probably educated clergy anxious for ecclesiastical reform, and I would guess that he wrote from within that group. There is little chance that his audience, recognizing how the author writes all the parts and manipulates all the puppets, would unthinkingly impute to

him the Dreamer Will's recurrent spiral of anxieties about grace and
works, predestination, original sin and divine justice to the poet in any
simple way, or read the poem as a record of the poet's own search for
salvation, as a *Bildungsroman*.[112]

Langland is understood as a writer who produced a text for an audience of
educated readers. Rather than some messy personal copy used as a prompt-
text for oral performances, this published text for a literate readership must
be postulated in order to rationalize specific editorial methods. Langland
"writes all the parts and manipulates all the puppets" as an author fully in
command of his thoughts, his beliefs, his words, and finally—emphatically—
his text.

   Any lingering suspicion that the poet himself was uncertain, confused,
fuzzy-headed, or halting in his conception of his work needed to be banished. Even Chambers's views cannot co-exist with Kane's editorial assumption of Langland as an expert craftsman certain of his intentions and fully
capable of realizing those intentions in his finished text. Nowhere is this
conception most succinctly stated than in "Conjectural Emendation" (1966):
"The editor of a major poet must begin with the presumption of the excellence of his author."[113] This presumption obliged Kane-Donaldson to reject
any possibility that their author "experienced a frequently recurrent falling-
off of taste, judgment, imagination and technical powers with respect to
detail during the major creative process of composing a whole, fulfilled
poem."[114]

   Working almost exclusively from the C-text's autobiography (5.1–108),
Donaldson's 1949 depiction of Langland as a London poet had followed
Skeat's view while ignoring Skeat's use of internal references to Malvern and
external references to Shipton-under-Wychwood, as well as the poet's Worcestershire residence suggested by the dialect of the earliest C-text manuscripts. For Donaldson and his coeditor Kane, Langland became firmly
established as a London-based writer, so much so that they chose as their
copy-text Trinity College Cambridge MS B.15.17, a London manuscript with
writing that resembled the hand of the Ellesmere *Canterbury Tales,* both now
demonstrated to have been the work of Adam Pinkhurst.[115] Though conced-
ing that Langland's native dialect did not perfectly match the London-tainted
dialect of the Trinity manuscript, the editors nonetheless argue that the manuscript represents "the closest dialectal and chronological approximation to
the poet's language." They were especially impressed by the conformity of its
grammar with standard usage instanced in the best manuscripts of Chaucer

and Gower.[116] Defending Trinity B.15.17 against Skeat's preferred manuscript, Laud Misc. 581, Kane-Donaldson selected the product of a London
workshop because they had come to believe that Langland's language mostly
accorded with the London English of his time.[117] As the work of London's
professional textwriters, *Piers* looks less and less like the homemade artifact
described by Skeat.

The year 1978 saw the publication of two new editions, Carl Schmidt's
B-text and Derek Pearsall's C-text.[118] Though dealing with different versions
of the poem, their introductions expressed a common desire to return Langland's work to a wider social context. The poem did not simply mirror its social background as Wright and Skeat imagined, but the three versions energetically interacted with national events over the course of the poet's long
career. In these implicit definitions of authorship, one detects the salutary influence of Raymond Williams's "social formation" from *Marxism and Literature* published only a year earlier as an expression of a particular moment in
critical history.[119] Pearsall insists that *Piers Plowman* was not a guarded personal document but rather a social text participating in "close relation to the
political and religious upheavals of his day." Following Russell's view that the
C revision was undertaken partly as an act of self-censorship, Pearsall proposes that authorial revision should be considered as a response to current
events, particularly the Wycliffite controversies: "Maybe even one of the motives that prompted him to make the revision is to clarify his thinking and his
position in relation to those matters of ideology that the Lollards had made
peculiarly their own."[120]

Focusing specifically on John Ball's appropriation of *Piers Plowman* in
1381, Schmidt accounts for the blankness of the poet's public identity in a
manner that harkens back to Whitaker's view of intentional evasion: "It may
indeed have been dangerous to be known as the author of a work the name
of whose hero was used as a slogan by dangerous revolutionary preachers,
no matter what the real intentions of the writer himself. This may be one reason why virtually nothing is known about the poet except what can be de-
duced from the text itself."[121] Schmidt could have gone further. While Skeat
remained baffled that Stacy de Rokayle's son should have assumed for himself the rare and improbable name "Langland," Whitaker had suggested the
poet had produced a work so inflammatory that he could not risk using his
real family name. Ralph Hanna has suggested that Rokayle's son chose to
write under his mother's maiden name, with "Langelond" put forward as
a prominent Somerset family,[122] although Lister Matheson confirms that

"Langland" appeared as a common field-name throughout England.[123] Instead of the French-sounding patronym Rochelle, this stout English pen name with upland connotations then made possible the poem's punning inscriptions of authorial identity.

The messiness of the poem's textual condition no longer needs to be explained exclusively in terms of the absurd circumstances that bedeviled the creative process. The poet's involvement in the disruptive circumstances of the 1380s provides its own plausible account. For Pearsall, this meant not reaching aggressively beyond the manuscript testimony to retrieve the lost purity of the author's original. Restoring the archetype of the best textual tradition, he has reconstituted a literary work with a more empirical social reality based upon a particularly authoritative manuscript. Huntington HM 143 was produced in the poet's dialect at the end of the fourteenth century by a London professional with a hand resembling Adam Pinkhurst's. Its ambitious program of decoration suggests a conscientious first edition. Evidence of privileged insider information, with its reference to William W. at the end of Passus 10, complements the superior textual authority of this manuscript to suggest some direct connection to the author. And yet "corrections" in the text by the supervisor, who also added a running commentary on the text's contents, indicate a reform-minded reader alert to the heated religious debates of the day.[124]

Langland's work had established a variety of metropolitan agents—friends, patrons, colleagues, eager and astute readers—who were able to facilitate this sort of professional manufacture of *Piers*. "Langland's public was not of the market place or inn-yard; from its character, his poem was directed to persons of education and therefore of some standing. This implies a patron or patrons, and the presumption is that one of these will have paid for making a necessarily postulated first, clean, scribal copy."[125] A sophisticated textual sociology allows Ralph Hanna to sketch his own scenario for early *Piers* circulation by analogy with John Trevisa's better documented career. Interaction between a writer and his patron would explain many textual circumstances assumed by the Athlone editors.[126] According to Hanna's account of textual transmission, the patron took the best copy of the B-text, leaving the poet himself with a somewhat poorer copy from which to revise the C-text, while an even poorer copy served as the exemplar for the version represented by all the surviving B manuscripts. If patron and coterie are factored as editorial ingredients, then simplification and added emphasis—which Kane denigrates as scribal activity—might be reinterpreted as accommodations made by the author himself to this immediate audience. A different understanding of the author-scribe distinction will have important implications for future attempts at editing *Piers Plowman*.[127]

Foucault insisted that the idea of the author "does not refer purely and simply to a real individual, since it can give rise simultaneously to several selves, to several subjects—positions that can be occupied by different classes of individuals."[128] My survey of the print tradition suggests how different editors have used the almost total blankness of Langland's biography as a screen upon which to project their own cultural values, sometimes even their own personalities. Crowley saw Langland as a precursor of the Protestant Reformation, Whitaker imagined him as the rustic bard of the Romantics, and Skeat praised him as an industrious Victorian. For Manly and the advocates of multiple authorship, *Piers Plowman* became a Pre-Raphaelite artifact exemplifying the communal creativity of the Middle Ages. This anonymous collaboration preserves the brilliant achievement of a lone genius. Their vivid A1 poet stands out against the extravagant B poet and prosaic C reviser much as the dramatic brilliance of the Wakefield Master blazes forth among the mediocre talents of the Towneley Cycle.

Throughout the second half of the twentieth century, the joint efforts of the Athlone editors reformulated Langland almost as a character out of Samuel Beckett. He becomes the writer sealed in an empty room, the dimly heard genius producing a brilliant poem in three distinct versions, each of them ruined almost the instant that it left his hands. He is absurdity itself—a voice without an audience, a laborer without rewards, an author without control over his own texts. The A version was snatched unfinished and abandoned from his work desk. The B-text was published in such a slapdash manner that a corrupt archetype served as the exemplar for all surviving copies. He was forced to settle for a defective B copy as the basis for revising his C version, which was posthumously disseminated, unfinished and unpolished, among the uncomprehending provincials of the western shires. These textual shambles remain the sad testament of a master poet whose hand was stilled, almost in mid-tinker, by the untimely death described by the doggerel-scribbling John But. Then the scribes set to work defacing the magnificence of *Piers Plowman*.[129]

The task for the editors Kane, Donaldson, and Russell became retrieving the poem not only from the typical carelessness of the copyists but also from the adverse circumstances of the poet's own unfortunate career. They reconstruct the masterpiece that Langland would have intended if, for example, he had possessed a perfect copy of the A-text from which to expand the B-text *and* if he had retained a perfect B-text copy from which to revise his C-text. As much as retrieving the pristine purity of the text, their mission became restoring the dignity of human creativity itself. Kane's own herculean achievement for more than five decades matches the poet's life-long perseverance as conceived by his teacher R. W. Chambers. Published in 1939 on the eve of World War II, *Man's Unconquerable Mind* made this appeal to the reader: "In time of danger and responsibility many people of many nations have drawn comfort from their great writers." His survey of the great English authors placed *Piers Plowman* in this heroic tradition going back to *Beowulf* and looking forward to the philologists at University College, London—where Kane himself was trained and launched upon his career as an editor.[130] The description of Langland's end sounds this note most distinctly:

> He has spent his life in the search of St. Truth: he has achieved neither wealth, nor honor, nor depth of learning. But he will not give in. He passes out of our sight.
> Still nursing the unconquerable hope,
> Still clutching the inviolable shade.

Even the unfinished status of Langland's drafts and revisions are granted special dignity: "They end, not with the victory of the cause, but with the individual human soul refusing to accept defeat."[131]

This insistence upon the heroic dimension of Langland's enterprise invites comparison with the work of another English medievalist also commencing his own long, difficult project in the 1930s. Actually quoted by Chambers as author of "Beowulf: The Monster and the Critics" (1936), J. R. R. Tolkien depicted in *Lord of the Rings* a protagonist with many of the same heroic qualities, which included persistence against legions of dark adversaries and courage in the face of almost certain failure.[132] Against all odds, Frodo the Hobbit completed his epic undertaking only to have the story of his achievement distorted and slowly forgotten, even as his name was lost to the memory of his people. Tolkien surely had the example of Beowulf more clearly in mind. But this paradigm of a specific brand of English heroism, valuing humility and tenacity despite repeated setbacks, becomes equally legible in the profile of Langland sketched by Chambers and realized by Kane himself in his hard-won victory with the completion of the three-volume Athlone editions in 1997.

Definitely Geoffrey Chaucer

The business of naming Geoffrey Chaucer began with Geoffrey Chaucer. Starting with *The Book of the Duchess,* he projected his own image as an interesting individual into his dream-visions, and he continued to invest later works such as *Troilus* and the *Canterbury Tales* with the sense of an engaging if elusive personality. He virtually ensured that later readers would echo Harry Bailey's curiosity: "What man artow?" In addition to the titles of the courtly works listed in the Prologue to the *Legend of Good Women,* Chaucer elaborated a second catalogue in his Retraction and affixed this prose postscript to the *Canterbury Tales* as a whole. This appendix cataloguing his prior free-standing literary productions, particularly the four dream-visions and *Troilus and Criseyde,* appears in all twenty-eight manuscripts that contain complete copies of the Parson's Tale.[133] Probably authorial, the Ellesmere colophon firmly attached the poet's name to the work: "Heere is ended the book of the tales of Caunterbury, compiled by Geffrey Chaucer." His name is even more securely preserved in the titles and running-headers for the Sir Thopas and Melibee, positioned at the collection's center where pages were less likely to be lost. Thus Chaucer's name was attached to his masterpiece with the apparatus as well as with the Man of Law's condescending reference to "Chaucer, thogh he kan but lewedly / On metres and on rymyng craftily" (*CT,* II, 47–48).

Prior to the 1390s, the poet had become known as the author of *Troilus* among literate Londoners such as Thomas Usk as well as the two associates named near the poem's end, John Gower and Ralph Strode, whose careers included work as lawyers in the English capital.[134] The Man of Law inhabits the same metropolitan circles and is likely formulated from an amalgam of the poet's two friends. Moreover, the Man of Law represents exactly the sort of educated sergeants and justices presumed to have formed Chaucer's earliest readership.[135] He names Chaucer as a writer and provides a list of his main love stories. The harshness of his remarks about Chaucer's poetic skills bespeaks the intimacy of a local readership (*CT,* II, 46–54). Yet the limits of the Man of Law's familiarity are carefully circumscribed. He knows the quality of the writing well enough to offer a derogatory assessment, he knows the poet's typical subject matter, and he identifies an important affiliation with Ovid. But he knows Chaucer by reputation only as the writer of books, but not as a man. Physically present, the poet is one of the pilgrims listening when the Man of Law makes these cutting remarks. The opinionated Man of Law, who speaks so expertly about Chaucer's literary output, does not recognize the presence of the author himself. Unlike Usk, Strode, and Gower, the lawyer is strictly a member of a reading audience who knows Chaucer through his literary notoriety—"as knoweth many a man"—but *only* as a name.

While those who knew the name did not necessarily know the man, those who knew the man did not always acknowledge him as an innovative writer. Around 1385 Eustache Deschamps sent a ballade praising him by name as a translator, not an original poetic talent—"Grand translateur, noble Geffroy Chaucier."[136] But the French poet's specificity of including both first and last names makes a noteworthy contrast with Chaucer's English contemporaries. Written around 1376–79, John Gower's *Mirour de l'Omme* makes a reference to *Troilus* but does not actually include the poet's name.[137] Thomas Usk even more clearly alludes to *Troilus* and intends for his readers to catch his homage to Chaucer as a philosophical poet, but his *Testament of Love* omits actual mention of the poet's name:

> the noble philosophical poete in Englissh whiche evermore hym be-syeth and travayleth right sore my name to encrease. [Love says.] In wytte and in good reason of sentence he passeth al other makers. In the *Boke of Troylus* the answere to thy questyon mayste thou lerne.[138]

Later adapted as the Knight's Tale, the original *The Love of Palamon and Arcite* catalogued in the Prologue to the *Legend of Good Women* (F. 420) was also quoted in the opening two lines of *The Boke of Cupide* by Sir John Clanvowe (d. 1391). But again Chaucer's name is not invoked in connection with these lines borrowed by the poet's most prominent chivalric reader.[139]

John Gower makes a commendation to Chaucer by name in his first version of the *Confessio Amantis,* completed around 1390 supposedly at the request of Richard II. Like Usk, Gower uses his character Venus to praise Chaucer's special achievements as a love poet—"And gret wel Chaucer whan ye mete / As mi disciple and mi poete"[140]—but this passage disappears in the Lancastrian version produced later in the 1390s as a commendation to Henry of Derby, the future Henry IV.[141] Scholars have long suspected some witty exchange between Chaucer and Gower as friends, colleagues, and literary rivals, notably in the Prologue to the Man of Law's Tale where Gower's tales of rape and incest become targets of ridicule.[142] The fictional London lawyer can recite a short bibliography of actual titles while Gower himself, who knew Chaucer well enough to act as his attorney,[143] alludes only vaguely to juvenile lyrics that do not survive. One further ingredient can be added to the inside jokes. The Man of Law exploited Chaucer for the purposes of name dropping but did not recognize the man himself; Gower knew the man personally but deleted his name from the second version of his *Confessio Amantis*.

Chaucer's contacts with Italy have long been identified as a major influence upon his innovative sense of vernacular authorship.[144] Dante was already revered as a literary figure, with deluxe editions of his *Commedia,* a hagiographic biography by Boccaccio, and a series of public lectures devoted to his works. Petrarch provided the living example of a writer who had achieved the status of an international celebrity with all of the rewards and obligations that attended upon it. Possibly Chaucer traveled among the 457 Englishmen who accompanied Prince Lionel to Italy in 1368 for his wedding to Violante, the daughter of Galeazzo Visconti. Petrarch was an honored guest at the wedding feast, and Thomas Speght's edition of 1598 gave support to the tradition that the two poets met on that occasion: "Some write that he with Petrarke was present at the marriage of Lionell Duke of Clarence with Violant daughter of Galeasius Duke of Millaine." Donald Howard goes further in dramatizing the encounter: "Chaucer may have gazed at him from afar: someone must have pointed him out, told of his works, answered Chaucer's questions."[145]

Still in his twenties, Chaucer would have been impressed by this literary luminary. He may also have been deeply disturbed by what else he heard while at the Lombard court. Though suffering from an infected leg injury, Petrarch was obliged to present himself at the Visconti household in order to serve as an intermediary with the pope. He was also obliged to attend the wedding festivities despite the fact that his own grandson had died in Pavia on the very same day. Years later when Chaucer invoked the image of Petrarch as "the lauriat poete" in the Clerk's Prologue, he conceived of a posthumous fame when the author was "deed and nayled in his cheste" (*CT,* IV, 26–38) and therefore safely beyond the demands of patron and public. Whether or not witnessed firsthand in Lombardy, Petrarch provided an enduring example of literary celebrity both attractive and cautionary.

Though David Wallace does not follow Howard in placing Chaucer at Pavia for a personal encounter with "FrAunceys Petrark," he does detect the sinister side of Petrarchan poetics assimilated from his political patrons "to announce and embellish the will of the state as embodied in the person of a single masculine ruler."[146] Chaucer dramatized this princely willfulness in his narrative of Walter as a Lombard tyrant reminiscent Bernabò Visconti, who is featured among the modern instances in his Monk's Tale: "God of delit and scourge of Lumbardye" (*CT,* VII, 2400). As a domestic despot, Walter also served as a literary figuration of the "tirauntz of Lumbardye" (*LGW* F 374), whose example Richard II was accused of following during the later 1390s. Philippe de Mézières, who had translated Petrarch's version of the story of Patient Griselda into French during the 1380s, issued his *Letter to Richard II* (1395), which urged a marriage to young Isabelle of France by recommending Griselda, the wife of the Marquis of Saluzzo, as the model of a pliable bride to the English king.[147] Thus the sinister equation of Richard II with a Lombard tyrant became another grim aspect of Chaucer's Petrarchan legacy.

More certainly present at the Visconti wedding in 1368, Jean Froissart later embarked upon a career that combined the dual roles of court poet and chivalric chronicler. His career proved hugely successful. By comparison, Chaucer's professional achievements appear more guarded and nowhere clearly reliant upon his literary efforts. As a poet who wrote exclusively in English, Chaucer lacked mobility. He was permanently committed to his livelihood in London and did not have Froissart's options to move from one French-speaking court to the next.[148] The events of 1381 may also have played some part in confirming this strategy of discretion. The rebels who attacked London were determined to kill any man identified as a writer. "Everyone who could write a writ or a letter should be beheaded," the *Anonimalle Chronicle* reported. Walsingham added this terrifying report: "It was dangerous enough to be known as a clerk, but especially dangerous if an ink-pot should be found at one's elbow: such men scarcely or ever escaped from the hands of the rebels."[149] Since Chaucer resided at Aldgate and was employed as controller of the custom, he had every reason to fear for his life in 1381.

John of Gaunt was a particular target of the mob's rampage, and his Savoy Palace was vandalized and burned, with the destruction of its jewels, plate, wine stores, vestments, expensive bedding, silk hangings, and other valuable contents.[150] Among what the Monk of Westminster described as "priceless objects" would have been the Duke of Lancaster's books,[151] and among these books was perhaps a presentation manuscript of Chaucer's *Book of the Duchess*. This aristocratic elegy may have been copied as a beautifully ornamented volume, such as the *ABC to the Virgin* that Howard pictures in this way: "Each page elaborately decorated with paintings and gold leaf, the margins overflowing with floriations and drolleries."[152] The outburst of public violence served to dramatize the vulnerability of courtly books and governmental documents, as well as the courtly and bureaucratic writers themselves, which could hardly have left Chaucer unaffected. He furthermore witnessed how a literary work such as *Piers Plowman* could be appropriated in ways beyond the writer's control. Far too publically committed to national events, Langland provided a continuing example that completed the lessons of 1381.

Probably written after *Troilus* as a literary masterpiece with legitimate claims upon posterity, Chaucer's *House of Fame* engages in a very sophisticated but troubled reflection upon the implications of literary fame. The poet envisions fame's crushing burden, which resembles the torments inflicted upon the prideful in Dante's *Purgatorio* (Canto X). In an announcement nothing short of shocking, the dreamer Geffrey says that he seeks no name recognition and wants no remembrance after his death: "Sufficeth me, as I were ded, / That no wight have my name in honde" (*HF* 1876–77). This was clearly a pose contradicted by Chaucer's assiduous efforts at constructing an authorial identity beckoning to later generations of readers. Indeed, his plea for oblivion ran counter to the central obsession of late medieval culture when Christians invested tremendous effort and expense so that they might be remembered when dead.[153] English culture in all locations, urban and rural, had been mobilized for memorializing the dead in order to help these souls escape purgatory more quickly. Chaucer's allusion to Dante provides a rueful contrast (*HF* 450).[154] Christian remembrance shortened the pains of purgatory, whereas literary fame imposed its own counterpart to purgatory's long-term obligations. George Kane believes that Chaucer would have found much of Dante in Langland's poem, not least of which would have been its legitimate bid as the founding literary masterpiece of a vernacular tradition.[155] But *Piers Plowman* had also earned a dubious notoriety for its author while alive—and Chaucer's encounter with the B-text during the 1380s brought these lessons home[156]—while his *House of Fame* anticipated the popular model for the Romantic poet whose fame was bestowed posthumously, after some time lag, when posterity's judgment finally recognized his artistic genius.

As further reflection upon the consequences of literary fame, the Prologue to *The Legend of Good Women* dramatizes the writer's worst fears by staging a terrifying trial, partly Kafkaesque and partly *Alice in Wonderland,* in which the poet stands accused of some ludicrous form of heresy.[157] After the Merciless Parliament of 1388 approved commissions for the suppression of heretical writings under the directions of the King's Council, the poet's friends the Lollard knights were summoned for examination.[158] Chaucer's dreamvision internalizes this anxiety over being interrogated by royal authorities for the books that he had written. The dreamer had produced important works only to have these poems deeply misunderstood when the writer's intentions were trumped by the king's more powerful authority. Chaucer had already anticipated the problem of an audience's misprision at the end of *Troilus* (5.1797–98). Here the royal audience has misjudged the poet's meaning and, what is more, rejected the poet's right to stipulate his own meaning.

As the result of these misreadings of the *Romaunt* and *Troilus,* the dreamer is condemned to perform literary penance by producing a certain kind of poetry and thereby losing, too, his freedom to determine the future course of his literary career.[159] Chaucer's fears of royal displeasure were not misplaced. By the end of the 1390s, Richard II's sensitivity showed itself in his order to the sheriffs to arrest anyone speaking evil publicly or privately to the dishonor of the monarch, with the result that many were accused of saying something "which could turn to the slander, disgrace or dishonor of the king's person." Those accused of slander needed to acquit themselves in single combat. "This was not only a great destruction of the realm," Walsingham wrote, "but struck fear into all members of the community."[160]

When the Man of Law fails to recognize Chaucer riding beside him on the road to Canterbury, the episode dramatizes the security that the poet imagined himself to have achieved. He had become an author with public reputation and an established body of works, *and* he managed to remain a private man with the luxury of moving anonymously throughout society. Thus he evaded the harsher aspects of authorial accountability represented in the *Legend,* which was significantly the work cited at length by the Man of Law. The image of the author within the frame-narrative of the *Canterbury Tales* reflects what we can guess about Chaucer's conduct as a writer abroad in the world—silent, observant, secretive, and closely guarded about his name and occupation. Nobody knew who he was or even *what* he was professionally. When Harry Bailey presses him to identify himself, the mysterious pilgrim adroitly dodges the question (*CT,* VII, 707–9).

As capstone to this strategy of evasion, the Retraction of the *Canterbury Tales* exploits the contradiction between Christian humility and literary self-promotion.[161] By denigrating the corpus of his literary works, the poet echoes the language of pious contemporaries and court colleagues whose wills employed the contemptuous language of "wretched body" about their earthly remains. Alice Chaucer's own two-tier tomb at Ewelme gives graphic representation to this doubleness of future prospects, the upper effigy resplendent and the lower effigy cadaverlike.[162] The Retraction's confession of authorial wrongdoing and its plea for his audience's forgiveness complete the penitential role that Chaucer already imagined for himself in the *Legend* Prologue. His appeal follows the pattern of Christian remembrance deeply embedded in orthodox penitential practices. But this prayer functions also as his appeal for a posterity of future readers who will continue to enjoy his poetry with all of its dubious values and mixed morality. Like the recantations of Lollards such as his long-time friend Sir Lewis Clifford in 1402, Chaucer's Retraction turned into a cunning restatement of his basic beliefs.[163]

Chaucer's literary career apparently did not boost his material earnings, certainly not on the scale achieved by Jean Froissart as a professional writer. During Froissart's return to England in 1395, his *Chronicles* reported how he was generously rewarded by Richard II after presenting the king with an ornate book of his love poetry: "He gave me through one of his knights, called Sir John Golafre, a goblet of silver gilt, weighing well over a pound, with a hundred nobles inside it, which has made me a richer man for the rest of my life."[164] Though the extant record does not indicate Chaucer benefited from literary patronage, he succeeded in safeguarding his career from the repercussions that might otherwise have befallen him. Froissart had the advantage of residing abroad when his patron Richard II was deposed, while Chaucer remained in London to weather the turbulence of the Lancastrian revolution.[165]

Yet Chaucer's sense of national history and his steady regard for literary tradition indicate his keen sense of the continuity leading forward to future generations of English readers. Edmund Burke described exactly this sense of a contractual *partnership* across generations for political, scientific, and cultural enterprises: "As the ends of such a partnership cannot be obtained in many generations, it becomes a partnership not only between those who are living, but between those who are living, those who are dead, and those who are to be born."[166] After he was dead, Chaucer's name was indeed remembered because he had so successfully fostered this sense of partnership. Specifically he had been savvy enough about naming his readers, not his employers, and did not obviously pursue aristocratic favor through his writings. The cryptic references at the end of *The Book of the Duchess* (1318–19) indicate that the work was obliquely *about* John of Gaunt but not addressed directly *to* John of Gaunt. Though works such as *The Parliament of Fowls* can be connected with royal affairs,[167] the poet did not emulate his French contemporaries such as Machaut and Froissart, nor did he set a precedent for English successors such as Hoccleve and Lydgate, by addressing his works to noblemen or including their names as showy compliments.[168] Even his address to Henry IV in his late *Complaint to His Purse* does not actually name the new king, and the envoy itself survives in only five of the eleven manuscripts as evidence of something makeshift.[169]

Why such a reluctance to name dukes and kings? Chaucer's reading of history had emphasized the lesson that princely houses come and go, but readers endured. When Eustache Deschamps sent a ballade praising Chaucer by name, the French poet stipulated that their intermediary had been Sir Lewis Clifford, the courtier and diplomat.[170] The *Chaucer Life-Records* suggest Richard II's household knight was a member of the poet's circle and provided an important link between the royal court and the civil service.[171] Identification of "Lewys" in the *Treatise on the Astrolabe* as Sir Lewis's son has fueled speculation of a more intimate connection between the families.[172] The ballade entitled *Truth* was probably addressed to Clifford's son-in-law Sir Philip la Vache; the fact that the envoy survives in only one of the twenty-four witnesses of the poem (BL Add. 10340) again suggests a special adaptation or redaction for some private occasion typical of a small, closely knit coterie.[173] These "new men" were driven to seek renown—to make names for themselves—and the poet furthered their pursuit of name recognition to the point where it would include his own.[174]

Chaucer could have dedicated *Troilus* to King Richard as the obvious model for the Trojan prince—hence Maidstone's praise of the monarch "handsome as Troilus" in 1392[175]—but instead he chose to direct his masterpiece to John Gower and Ralph Strode. He addressed a single-stanza poem to his scribe Adam—probably the textwriter Adam Pinkhurst—with the reprimand for more careful copying in the future, clearly indicating the exacting standards that he placed upon professional readers and their correct transmission of his works.[176] His *Complaint of Venus* was adapted from ballades by the Savoyard poet Oton de Grandson, who is mentioned by name as "flour of hem that make in Fraunce."[177] He wrote an envoy to Robert Bukton—or Peter Bukton—with an allusion to the Wife of Bath, a witty reference clearly designed for a coterie reader with privileged knowledge of the *Canterbury Tales* during the 1390s. "It does not greatly matter which Bukton was the recipient of the poem," the *Chaucer Variorum* editors have noted. "What *is* significant is that Bukton belonged to the same class as Chaucer himself, a class that found rapid advancement in the service of the high nobility."[178]

Lenvoy de Chaucer a Scogan was addressed to an educated, well-placed individual—named seven times in forty-nine lines—who entered the poet's circle as a newcomer in the 1390s. Henry Scogan served as a squire of Richard II's household and accompanied the king on his Irish expedition in 1394, when he had the opportunity to make the acquaintance of Bolingbroke's eleven-year-old son, Henry. Like Chaucer, Scogan successfully negotiated the transition to the new regime, serving as tutor to Henry IV's four sons.[179] There were expectations built into the rhetoric of reciprocity in Chaucer's *Lenvoy,* and sometime after Chaucer's death in 1400 and before his own around 1407, Scogan had occasion to write his *Moral Ballade* fulfilling this sense of invitation, clearly intent upon preserving the older poet's name while also addressing the special interests of those attending his poem's original presentation.[180]

While continuing the conversational tone of *Lenvoy*, Scogan also continues Chaucer's practice of producing *literature* in the strict sense of poetry designed to be read as a physical document: "Sende un-to you this litel tretys here / Writen with myn owne hand ful rudely."[181] Intending his poem for presentation before an audience that included the four royals headed by Prince Henry, Scogan used the occasion to make probably the earliest attempt at establishing Chaucer as a national literary figure, praising him grandly as "this noble poete of Bretayne" (126). Later poets would echo this phrase so frequently that the innovative concept of an author representing the entire British Isles soon became a commonplace, one completely at odds with the historical reality of a poet not known much beyond a small London audience during his lifetime. But Chaucer had positioned himself to best advantage with the new dynasty in his *Complaint to His Purse*, and Scogan continued fashioning him as the primary model for clerkly wisdom and courtly accomplishment for the entire realm.

John Shirley's headnote in Ashmole MS 59 indicates the *Moral Ballade* was presented at a supper in the London Vintry organized by some merchants and attended by the royal princes.[182] We have scattered evidence of the role that poetry played on such social occasions. Hoccleve wrote a jocular piece for the Temple dining club described in the author's headnote as *la Court de Bone Conpaignie*—"the Court of Good Company."[183] As reconstructed from Scogan's poetic offering, the intersection of the royal court and the merchant elite perfectly reflected the social terrain where Chaucer had found his favorite literary opportunities. The Vintry audience also raises some intriguing questions about Chaucer's ongoing connections with the wine merchant neighborhood where he grew up in the household of his father, the prosperous London vintner John Chaucer.[184]

This particular supper took place at the house of Lewis John. The prominent Welshman was appointed deputy in the port of London to the king's chief butler, Thomas Chaucer, who was also responsible for having John elected to Parliament in 1413.[185] Knighted in 1439, Sir Lewis John maintained government employment under three successive Lancastrian monarchs with the special favor of Henry V. His first wife was the daughter of Aubrey de Vere, Earl of Oxford, whose family is connected with the early history of the

Ellesmere *Canterbury Tales*.[186] Since the *Moral Ballade* was designed to be read aloud by a third party rather than Scogan himself, it is intriguing to imagine how its themes of fatherhood and generational succession—concepts that became essential ingredients for configuring a patriarchal structure of literary history—would have been even more strongly emphasized if the reciter of the poem had been Geoffrey's own son, Thomas.[187]

In addition to naming Chaucer as a poet, Scogan emphasizes three times Chaucer's title as "maister" in terms less conventional than such epithets usually appear (65–69):

> My mayster Chaucer—God his soule have!—
> That in his langage was so curious,
> He sayde, the fader whiche is deed and grave,
> Bequath nothing his vertue with his hous
> Unto his sone . . .[188]

The reference to Chaucer bequeathing his house to his son represents perhaps a knowing allusion to the Westminster tenement, leased for the last months of the poet's life and then leased again by his son Thomas.[189] Lee Patterson's remarks upon Chaucer as *master* of a craft deserve careful notice: "Scogan's Chaucer provides instances of verbal mastery and moral perspicuity whose values can be learned only through diligent application and careful imitation."[190] Although fifteenth-century followers tended to praise Chaucer as an improver of the language rather than the inventor of any new art, Scogan and other disciples such as Lydgate named no English poetic masters whose expertise predated their fraternity's. Not merely an earlier master, Chaucer was the *only* earlier master.

If Shirley's note can be credited, the social context of the guild supper strongly implied the senior poet's craft authority as a "maister," and this professional lexicon invokes a strong sense of guild solidarity as well as the sense of craft identity that membership afforded.[191] Furthermore, the adjective *curious* as applied to Chaucer's language connotes a sense of workmanship that is skillful, elaborate, ingenious, and intricately wrought.[192] Scogan's language of craftsmanship and the concepts of guild hierarchy, however, need to be read back into the controversies of the last two decades of the fourteenth century.

During the entire careers of Chaucer and Scogan, the craft guilds became such aggressive civic associations that London's political history played out in the conflict between the rich victualer merchants and a coalition of nonvictual crafts.[193] In response, the Cambridge Parliament of 1388 had launched an assault upon all liveried companies, including the urban craft guilds.[194] The Commons had been badly shaken by the Rising of 1381 and remained deeply suspicious of all forms of voluntary associations that might conspire as urban *covens* fostering sedition. Throughout the charters mandated after 1388, one key self-defense offered by many guilds specified their care for preserving the memory of deceased members. Here is the ordinance from the Carpenters' Guild of London: "Also is ordeined þat what tyme þat any of þe bretheren or of þe sostren dyeþ, þey schul haue a trental of messes out of þe comune box of þe forseid fraternite þat her soules mowe þe better be holpen."[195] In context of the guild supper described by John Shirley, the practice of recalling the names of dead members provides a social as well as a religious gloss for Henry Scogan's *Moral Ballade* with its solemn commemoration of the dead "maister" Chaucer.

Taken together with Chaucer's reference to the Wife of Bath in his *Lenvoy a Bukton*,[196] Scogan's own quotation of the Wife of Bath (97–104) indicates which sections from the *Canterbury Tales* were actually known among the poet's immediate audience. Thomas Hoccleve's *Dialogue* also alluded directly to the Wife of Bath:

> The Wyf of Bathe take I for auctrice
> Þat wommen han no ioie ne dyntee
> Þat men sholde vpon hem putte any vice;
> I woot wel so / or lyk to þat seith shee.[197]

John Lydgate, too, summoned Chaucer's feminist authority figure in *A Mumming at Hertford* when his indignant wives cite the Wife of Bath's arguments:

> And for oure partye þe worthy Wyff of Bathe
> Cane shewe statutes moo þan six or seven,
> Howe wyves make hir housbandes wynne heven,
> Maugre þe feonde and al his vyolence.[198]

Skeat's edition of the *Moral Ballade* used quotation marks to signal these lines from the Loathly Lady's lecture on *gentillesse* (*CT*, III, 1131–32) as if Scogan expected his audience to recognize this literary borrowing. Scogan then quotes the entirety of Chaucer's poem *Gentilesse* (105–25) with a sense of admiration largely lacking among modern readers but very influential in the fifteenth century.[199] Charles of Orleans and his custodian, the Duke of Suffolk, husband of Alice Chaucer, show their mutual fondness for the lyric genre that came to dominate much of the early Chaucerian tradition. Following their master's example already endorsed by Scogan, these noble *ditteurs* became active participants in a specialized sort of love poetry that mixed morality with advice-giving to princes.[200]

Scogan's reference to *Boece*—"Boece the clerk, as men may rede and see" (150)—suggests the continuing influence of Chaucer's translation as philosophical reading matter. The royal prisoner James I of Scotland begins his *Kingis Quair* with a reading of this text.[201] When John Walton, a canon of Osney Abbey outside Oxford, came to write his verse translation of *The Consolation of Philosophy* around 1410 for Elizabeth Berkeley, daughter of John Trevisa's patron, he acknowledged Chaucer as the unsurpassed model for English poetry.[202] And the Monk's Tale, which Scogan cited for its examples of Nero, Belshazzar, and Antiochus (174–81), enjoyed a considerable afterlife by fostering collections of *de casibus* tragedies as a powerful later medieval genre. Though not much favored among modern readers, the Monk's Tale was singled out for anonymous inclusion with the running title "The Falle of Princis" in the pious Augustinian compilation Huntington HM 144.[203] John Lydgate paid the ultimate homage to Chaucer's tragedy collection in his own vast panorama of royal misfortunes, *The Fall of Princes*.[204]

Though neglected by modern readers, Scogan's *Moral Ballade* serves Terry Jones and his colleagues as evidence that a princely conspiracy to wrest power from Henry IV had begun by 1407, with Chaucer's son Thomas and his old friend Scogan working behind the scenes as instigators.[205] Unhappy with Arundel's appointment as chancellor in that same year, these young supporters of baronial interests were encouraged by the king's declining health and constant rumors of his imminent death. Scogan's poem bolstered their optimism with its bold claim, attributed to Chaucer in the passage quoted above (65–69), that a dead father bequeathed to his son nothing of his moral character. As he approached the throne, Prince Henry sought more and more to distance himself from his father's criminal usurpation. In this historical context, Chaucer's *Gentilesse*, seemingly so formulaic and innocuous, proves provocative with its allegation that the authority of king (crown) and archbishop (mitre) was invalidated by their vicious conduct (109–11):

For unto vertu longeth dignitee
And nought the revers, saufly dar I deme,
Al were he mytre, croune, or diademe.

The claim that earthly authority needed to be based upon moral worth also boldly recalls Wycliffite arguments from thirty years earlier.

As a Welshman during the years following Owain Glyn Dŵr's revolt, Lewis John had suffered in his business life, and only during Henry V's first year in 1414 did he succeed in securing parliamentary exemption from the ban on Welshmen owning property in London. So this little "souper" in John's home looks very much like a power dinner: "Certainly every guest we know about, or can guess at, had larger agendas, none of them favorable to either the authority of the ailing king or of the ambitious archbishop-cum-chancellor. And right in the middle of that wheeling-and-dealing, almost like a centerpiece, is a poem by Chaucer."[206] Whatever maneuvering took place behind the scenes, the poetry of Chaucer, his reputation as the founding master of the English tradition, and his work's connection with Prince Henry and his circle appear firmly established in Scogan's *Moral Ballade* by 1407 and poised for a continuing political trajectory during the decades immediately following.

The notation in the Hengwrt manuscript recording the unfinished state of the Cook's Tale—"Of this Cokes tale / maked Chaucer na moore"—indicates both an awareness of a named author at an early date *and* an acute self-consciousness of the work's incomplete execution.[207] The unfinished status of so many of Chaucer's works made an open-ended appeal to later writers as well as copyists, such as the scribe who added the missing Adam stanza to the Monk's Tale in Hengwrt perhaps ten years after the manuscript's original production.[208] What proved one of the most decisive installments to the fifteenth-century continuation of the *Canterbury Tales* was the construction of the one pilgrim most notably absent from the General Prologue—Chaucer himself. Within a decade of the poet's death, the Ellesmere manuscript supplied this deficiency by providing a painted portrait with precise, realistic details found nowhere in the text.[209] Ellesmere's various headnotes repeat what had been so carefully kept secret within the frame-narrative, the uncommunicative pilgrim's name:

> Bihoold the murye wordes of the Hoost to Chaucer (fol. 151a)
> Heere bigynneth Chaucers tale of Thopas (fol. 151b)
> Heere the hoost stynteth Chaucer of his tale of Thopas (fol. 153a)
> Heere bigynneth Chaucers tale of Melibee (fol. 153b)
> Heere is ended Chaucers tale of Melibee and of dame Prudence
> (fol. 167b)

The manuscript's running-headers include Chaucer's name an additional fifteen times at the tops of fols. 151a–166b. An almost identical pictorial likeness, probably based on a common model, appears in the BL Harley 4866 manuscript of Hoccleve's *Regiment of Princes,* a work composed for Prince Henry in 1412–14. This handsome portrait was occasioned by Hoccleve's stanzas praising Chaucer's devout service to the Virgin and a defense of images against unnamed antagonists certainly understood as Lollards.[210] If the famous *Troilus* frontispiece from the Corpus Christi Cambridge manuscript (c. 1415) advertised the poet's identity in terms of his aristocratic following—with Richard II shown sitting in the front row of listeners—Hoccleve's portrait contributed to the business of "Chaucer-fashioning" by conscripting him to the clerkly campaign for fostering orthodox practices.[211]

A distinct circle of courtiers had supported Wycliffite preachers and very likely provided material backing for the production of Wycliffite sermon cycles and translations of the Bible.[212] The Merciless Parliament of 1388 moved against this royal inner circle, ordering Sir Thomas Latimer to bring his heretical writings to London for inspection, but none of this group was harmed and most of its members survived and prospered, including Sir John Cheyne who served as speaker in Henry IV's first Parliament.[213] Chaucer had longstanding associations with the Lollard knights Sir Richard Stury, Sir John Clanvowe, and Sir Lewis Clifford,[214] and his Prologue to the *Treatise on the Astrolabe* entered the fray as a self-conscious response to the Wycliffite translation project of the 1390s with its use of sect vocabulary such as "naked wordes in Englissh."[215] Clanvowe's puritanical tract *The Two Ways* actually embraced the title Lollard by claiming solidarity with "swich folke þe world scoorneth and hooldeþ hem *lolleris.*"[216] Some of his writings such as the Wife of Bath's Prologue cleverly incorporated a wide range of Lollard issues, including laywomen discussing the Scriptures in English.[217] Opposition to war, which had already become a hallmark Wycliffite theme, finds an intriguing Chaucerian counterpart in the Manciple's Tale with its lengthy consideration of whether any real difference exists between a military commander and a murderer (*CT,* IX, 227–34). Chaucer most likely wrote this final narrative of the *Canterbury Tales* after the 1395 posting of the *Twelve Conclusions of the Lollards* concerning a full range of Wycliffite topics, including pacifism.

Even more specifically, the frame-narrative of the *Canterbury Tales* itself incorporates a large number of satiric themes identical to the complaints against pilgrimage voiced by Lollards such as William Thorpe.[218] What Hoccleve was doing—and doing decisively—was denying Chaucer's disruptive relationship with Wycliffism and revising his image to become an opponent of radical reformers. He explicitly named Chaucer and described him as a man who had been devoted to rosaries, pilgrimages, and Marian piety, all features that stood in stark contrast to the practices of the heretics. Addressing Death, Hoccleve made the far-reaching claim that Chaucer's name, because it was preserved in books, had already achieved artistic immortality:

> But nathelees, yit hastow [Deth] no power
> His name slee; his hy vertu astertith
> Unslayn from thee, which ay us lyfly hertith
> With bookes of his ornat endytyng.[219]

By equating Chaucer's image in his book with images in churches, Hoccleve invoked religious controversy only to resolve it wholly in his author's favor.[220] As a named author *and* a pious Christian, Chaucer materializes as an adversary to threats against traditional practices. Like an image, a name conjured the person into being as a powerful historical and political reality. Denial of a name, as Hoccleve rendered anonymous the Lollard iconoclasts, made a whole unwanted group of religious dissidents disappear.[221]

As speaker of the Commons in 1410, Thomas Chaucer demonstrated his parliamentary skills by mustering support for Henry IV's taxation with an alacrity that impressed even McFarlane, and he remained Prince Henry's parliamentary agent responsible for orchestrating the business of the Commons.[222] So when the Lollard Disendowment Bill proposed the confiscation of the temporalities from the bishops and abbots in that same 1410 session, Prince Henry was naturally suspected as its silent sponsor.[223] In order to fashion the image of a strong nationalist monarch when he became king, Henry V needed to refute suspicions that he had previously been a supporter of Lollardy. Possibly the new king commissioned Lydgate to write his *Defence of Holy Church* when he came to the throne because he needed to advertise his orthodoxy. As an ancillary component of this Lancastrian policy, Geoffrey Chaucer's reputation as an author also needed to be cleansed of controversy in order for him to be installed as the great National Poet.[224]

It mattered more what cultural values Chaucer represented, less what sort of poetry he actually wrote. Once this sanitation of the poet's identity was completed, the fiction of the author's official status became the precondition for poets such as John Lydgate and the anonymous *Beryn* Poet taking him as their model. An expanding national public received his work as "always already read" in ways intended to efface and render illegible the inflammatory topics that the poet had so cunningly embedded in his writings.[225] Almost immediately attempts were made at domesticating the *Canterbury Tales* as an expensive, handsome, and prestigious "coffee-table book" in Ellesmere, Corpus Christi 198, Harley 7334, Lansdowne 851, Petworth 7, and Cambridge CUL Dd.iv.24. Efforts to pre-empt its classification as a dissident book guaranteed that its author might serve other cultural and political ends.[226] Hobsbawm made exactly this observation for an invented tradition "quite unspecific and vague as to the nature of the values, rights and obligations of the group membership they inculcate."[227]

The *Beryn* Poet empowered Chaucer by burying him. Instead of praising the dead master in the manner of Hoccleve and Lydgate, this continuator around 1420 named him nowhere. His refusal to invoke the original author makes the *Canterbury Interlude* into a forgery designed to be accepted as an authentic part of the literary work.[228] Assigned to the central position of the Northumberland manuscript where it was less likely to be detected as spurious, this lengthy supplement not only restructures and redefines the essential nature of the *Canterbury Tales* as a round-trip journey,[229] but also reforms the essential nature of Chaucer himself as a writer fully endorsing the practice of pilgrimage and the veneration of holy relics. Chaucer became an author for whom the literality of pilgrimage and the veneration of Becket's shrine posed no problems.[230] This rollicking expansion of the frame-narrative spelled business as usual for pilgrims representing the robust, entirely orthodox majority of English society.

In his Prologue to *The Siege of Thebes* from around 1420–22, Lydgate also distances Chaucer from controversies dangerous to his cultural status. With Chaucer's name placed boldly in the margin of the authoritative Arundel 119 manuscript, Lydgate includes a twenty-line commendation to the "Floure of poetes thorghout al Breteyne" and thus grants him greater prominence than the original poet-narrator had claimed for himself anywhere in the *Canterbury Tales*.[231] The text's most recent editor observes how homage is doubly inscribed: "Lydgate praises Chaucer in the language of Chaucer's poetry."[232] Yet the act of honoring the author as a monumental figure has the paradoxical effect of rendering him an absence, a memory, a dropout from the frame-narrative, and a voice silenced in the process of being transformed into a text. Despite the specificity of literary citation, Chaucer's name too has vanished from this passage as part of a larger cultural process aptly described as "the memorialization of Chaucer's absence."[233] Somewhat like the saint venerated inside the cathedral itself, the Canterbury poet has been translated by death into something more valuable for becoming unseen and inaccessible—a literary relic. Chaucer becomes an entity whose transcendent power restores poetical vitality in the way St. Thomas's relics were believed to restore physical health.

Near the end of *The Siege of Thebes,* Lydgate's account of Creon's tyranny overlaps with the military ascendancy of Theseus as his narrative begins drawing heavily upon the Knight's Tale. Lydgate finally satisfies the long-deferred expectation by naming the original author when he describes the desperate plight of the Theban widows: "And as my mayster Chaucer list en-dite . . ."[234] As the chronologies of the two narratives dovetail, Lydgate makes even more explicit reference to the Knight's Tale as well as the stretch of the Canterbury roadway where the tale had been originally told:

> But yif ye list to se the gentyllesse
> Of Theseus how he hath hym born,
> Yif ye remembre ye han herde it to forn
> Wel rehersyd at Depforth in the vale,
> In the bygynnyng of the *Knyghtys Tale* . . .[235]

Though he prompts the reader to recall where the story was originally told, Lydgate himself has not remembered correctly where the reference to Dept-ford occurred within Chaucer's frame-narrative. Mention of the town five miles outside London actually came in the Reeve's Prologue (*CT,* I, 3906). How did Lydgate become confused? A copy of *The Serpent of Division,* c. 1420–22, refers to "the large writings and golden vollums of that woorthye Chaucer"[236] which indicates Lydgate knew the poet's works in deluxe manu-scripts such as Ellesmere. Lydgate's faulty recollection of textual details sug-gests that he did not own, and did not have ready access to, one of these ex-pensive copies of Chaucer's works. When Lydgate urges his audience to learn more about Hypsipyle, he directs his readers not to Chaucer's *Legend of Good Women* (F 1396–1579) but rather to Boccaccio's *Genealogie Deorum Gentilium*— "Lok on the book that John Bochas made"—as further indication that the monk-poet was not intimately familiar with all of Chaucer's works.[237]

In *The Master of Game,* by contrast, the Duke of York's reference to Chau-cer's *Legend of Good Women* suggests a real insider's tribute: "ffor as Chaucer saiþ in this prologe of the xxv. good wymmen. Be wryteng haue men of ymages passed for writyng is þe keye of alle good remembraunce."[238] This aristocrat had operated within the courts of Richard II, Henry IV, and Henry V, where Chaucer's works found their first high-status readership. Be-cause Edward of York was a prisoner for several years after the fall of Richard II, it is also worth recalling that several of Chaucer's early aristocratic readers such as Charles d'Orléans, his brother Jean d'Angoulême, and James I of Scotland were also prisoners and constituted Chaucer's "captive audience" during the Lancastrian regime.[239] Found guilty of treason but later granted clemency, Duke Edward had been remembering the poet's own account of being prosecuted on charges of heresy and then granted mercy on condition of future good service. York died fighting for Henry V at Agincourt.

At some geographical as well as social remove from these primary Chaucer materials, the Monk of Bury St. Edmunds never admits to an outsider's estrangement from the literary enterprise. He actually worked harder and more effectively than Hoccleve to perpetuate Chaucer's name and secure his canon, in the meantime rendering himself as the most deserving heir-apparent. Written perhaps not long after 1400, Lydgate's *Floure of Curtesye* very specifically includes the dead poet's name: "Chaucer is deed, that had suche a name / Of fayre makyng."[240] Usually dated prior to 1412, Lydgate's adaptation of the *House of Fame* as *The Temple of Glas* presents a large cast of Chaucerian lovers including Griselda, Canacee, May, Dorigen, and Emelye— "as Chaucer telliþ us."[241] The reference to Canacee reminds us that the Squire's Tale was not then considered an artistic failure, and Lydgate alludes to this story again in his *Debate of the Horse, Goose, and Sheep*: "Chaunser remembrith the swerd, the ryng, the glas / Presentid wern vpon a stede of bras."[242] Judged by the forty-two extant manuscripts, *The Life of Our Lady* was Lydgate's most successful poem, and it includes a commendation to Chaucer notable for its length as well as its piety. It begins: "And eke my maister Chauser is ygrave . . ."[243]

Composed during the same period 1412–20, *The Troy Book* repeatedly names "my maister Chaucer." Lydgate also refers to him as "my maister Galfride" in order to provide a classicized version of his name befitting the classical story of the Trojan War. Another passage not only names Chaucer but also invokes something of the writer's personality, which Lydgate describes as kind and generous:

> For he þat was gronde of wel seying
> In al hys lyf hyndred no makyng
> My maister Chaucer þat founde ful many spot
> Hym liste not pinche nor pruche at euery blot
> Nor meue hym silf to perturbe his reste
> *I haue herde telle* but seide alweie þe best.[244]

This portrait comes not from firsthand acquaintance but from hearsay testimony: "I haue herde telle." Even if not fact based, the description of Chaucer's paternal kindness becomes a cultural truth establishing him as a teacher who never hindered the writing of poetry by other hands. According to Lydgate, then, Chaucer himself made these earliest efforts at encouraging the creation of the Chaucerian tradition.

In his miniature *de casibus* poem entitled "A Thoroughfare of Woe," Lydgate recalls Egeus's speech from the Knight's Tale (*CT,* I, 2847) and alludes specifically to the Monk's Tale: "My mayster Chaucier, chief poete of Bretayne / Which in his tragedyes made ful yore agoo."[245] Thus he yokes the two pilgrims originally put at odds with each other's values when the Knight cut short the Monk's Tale (*CT,* VII, 2767–2807), just as he aligns monastic and chivalric values again in the *Siege of Thebes* where Monk Lydgate serves as narrator for a vast prequel to the Knight's Tale. But certainly Lydgate's most extensive act of Chaucerian commemoration comes in *The Fall of Princes* (1431–38) where the Prologue recalls how the tragedies of the Monk's Tale had figured among the comedies of the *Canterbury Tales.* The grandiose title King of Poetry ("of makyng souereyne") clearly implies the structures of dynastic descent that became a primary feature of Chaucer's Lancastrian identity:

> My maistir Chaucer, with his fresh comedies,
> Is ded, allas, cheeff poete off Breteyne,
> That whilom made ful pitous tragedies;
> The fall of pryncis he dede also compleyne,
> As he that was *of makyng souereyne.*[246]

A monarch needs a realm, and Lydgate bolsters Chaucer's status as the founder not just of English but of British literature—"cheeff poete off Breteyne"—by providing one of the fullest and most important lists of his literary productions.

As an adjunct to the enterprise of naming the chief national poet, Lydgate ensures that his works also have their own proper names. Chaucer made a translation from Italian and gave it an English title, "the name off Troilus & Cresseide." Chaucer is credited with a complete translation of Boethius's *Consolation of Philosophy* as well as the *Treatise on the Astrolabe.* The puzzling reference to "Dante in Inglissh" has usually been taken to mean *The House of Fame.*[247] *The Book of the Duchess* is recollected twice separately as the "pitous story off Ceix and Alcione" and "the deth eek of Blaunche the Duchesse."

Lydgate lapses into a monklike defense of writing as remedy against sloth when he says that Chaucer "dede his bisynesse" to translate *The Romance of the Rose* and was eschewing idleness when he wrote *The Parliament of Fowls*. He records the lost works *The Book of the Lion* and "Origen vpon the Maudeleyne," as well as the missing lyric productions of ballades and roundels, while bestowing considerable praise upon the fragmentary work not much valued by modern critics, *Anelida and Arcite*.[248] He established the tradition that *The Legend of Good Women* was written "at request off the queen" and thus provides early testimony for connecting Chaucer with Queen Anne of Bohemia.[249] When finally reaching Chaucer's last major literary work, "the book off Cantirburi Talis," Lydgate exposes his moralistic preferences in terms of which specific tales he chooses to name:

> In prose he wrot the Tale off Melibe,
> And off his wiff, that callid was Prudence,
> And off Grisildis parfit pacience,
> And how the Monk off stories newe & olde
> Pitous tragedies be the weie tolde.[250]

He omits modern favorites such as the Miller's Tale, the Wife of Bath's Tale, and the Pardoner's Tale, which might have detracted from Chaucer's reputation as a moralist. By ending his bibliographical catalogue with the Monk's Tale, Lydgate signals his solidarity with his fictional alter ego and literary precursor, the Monk in the *Canterbury Tales,* while further validating his preference for the tragic genre at the beginning of his own *De Casibus Virorum Illustrium*. Later in Book I of his *Fall of Princes,* Lydgate repeats his admiration for the Monk's Tale and alludes also to the *Legend of Good Women,* which he took as yet another collection of tragic tales devoted specifically to Cupid's martyrs.[251]

In Book III of the *Fall of Princes,* Lydgate represents the literary tradition of named authors as a project closely interconnected with nations and rulers. Princes support writers with their wealth, and writers glorify kingdoms with their poetry. But notice how Lydgate names the poets but not the princes:

> Daunt in Itaille, Virgile in Rome toun,
> Petrak in Florence hadde al his plesaunce,
> And prudent Chaucer in Brutis Albioun
> Lik his desir fond vertuous suffisance,
> Fredam of lordshepe weied in ther ballaunce,

Because thei flourede in wisdam and science,
Support of princis fond hem ther dispence.[252]

Nothing of this princely patronage is evident in the *Chaucer Life-Records,* however, where Chaucer's enterprises as a poet are never mentioned and his official incomes came from a range of government offices and high-level services. The allusion to Brutus's Albion suggests that Lydgate had perhaps read Chaucer's *Complaint to His Purse*—"O conquerour of Brutes Albyon"—and inferred from its five-line envoy some longstanding mutuality of support between writer and royalty.[253] But this is a very late poem, perhaps the last lines that Chaucer ever penned, written in the immediate aftermath of Richard II's deposition and Henry IV's seizure of the throne.

More than three decades into the Lancastrian regime, Lydgate imagined some sort of collusion between rulers and writers in which he himself, quite unlike Chaucer, played an energetic and profitable role. Bodleian MS Rawlinson C.446 of Lydgate's *Siege of Thebes* is prefaced by a sumptuous opening page that includes a picture of the monastic poet presenting his book to an enthroned king. If not an actual event, the picture depicts a cultural process new in England during the first decades of the fifteenth century. No comparable evidence suggests Chaucer ever presented his work to a royal patron. The *Troilus* frontispiece in Cambridge Corpus Christi MS 61, which shows Chaucer reciting his poetry to a king, represents a fifteenth-century fiction imposing this courtly role upon the poet many years after the fact.[254]

Chaucer's revolutionary notion of competitive kingship in which a qualified candidate could be elected—"by lyne and free eleccion"[255]—found its parallel in the construction of a genealogy of poetic tradition in which rival claimants were tested in order to determine the winners. Begun in the 1320s, the Chaworth Roll demonstrates how the genealogy of English kings from Egbert to Edward II was continued to include Henry IV and his children in order to confirm continuity and the authority of lineal descent.[256] As a literary counterpart, Lydgate's "Title and Pedigree of Henry VI" encouraged the notion of empowering patrilinage.[257] In Fairfax 16, the collection of Chaucer and his literary kinsmen Clanvowe, Hoccleve, Richard Roos, and Charles of Orleans ends with Lydgate's verse-rendering of royal genealogy added by a later fifteenth-century hand: "The regnynge of kynges after the conquest by the monke of bury" (fols. 330b–32b).[258]

In his *Siege of Thebes,* Lydgate cites the *Genealogie Deorum Gentilium* in order to argue the unifying strength of family trees, and then, almost by process of mental association, he elides this notion of kinship bonds in order to describe the succession of Italian poets "lineally" from Petrarch to Boccaccio:

Rede *Of Goddes the Genologye,*
Lynealy her kynrede be degrees,
Ibraunched out upon twelve trees,
Mad by Bochas de Certaldo called,
Among poetys in Ytaille stalled
Next Fraunceys Petrak swyng in certeyn.[259]

Later in his Epilogue to the *Fall of Princes,* Lydgate imposes a similar configu-
ration of the succession of English writers when he considers the credentials
of John Gower, Ralph Strode, and Richard Rolle as the presumed author of
Prick of Conscience:[260]

In moral mateer ful notable was Goweer,
And so was Stroode in his philosophye,
In parfyt lyvyng, which passith poysye,
Richard Hermyte, contemplatyff of sentence,
Drowh in Ynglyssh the Prykke of Conscience.[261]

These references to moral Gower and philosophical Strode suggest that Lydgate knew their names from the conclusion to *Troilus* (5.1856–57). But even
as mere names, they needed to be judged and quickly dismissed in order to
clear space in the fourteenth century for only one legitimate English founder.
When claiming literary predecessors, Lydgate follows Chaucer's practice by
aligning himself with the Continental authors:

The Fal of Prynces gan pitously compleyne,
As Petrark did, and also Iohn Bochas;
Laureat Fraunceys, poetys bothe tweyne,
Toold how prynces for ther greet trespace
Wer ovirthrowe, rehersyng al the caas,
As Chauceer dide in the Monkys Tale.[262]

Deeply schooled in the archival sensibilities of monastic culture, Lydgate invoked more consistently and more persuasively the notion of poetic succession as "*the* conception of the history of English writing."[263]

While positioning himself as the legitimate heir of Chaucer, Petrarch,
and Boccaccio, Lydgate nonetheless imbues these final lines with a sense of
decline and fall befitting the *de casibus* genre. He places himself inside English
geography as a man born in the village of Lydgate, and he places his native
village in English history as a casualty of warfare and destruction. It had

once been a famous castle town, but it was burned down during the same Danish invasions that led to the martyrdom of St. Edmund of Anglia, patron of Lydgate's monastery.[264] Though ostensibly written at the prompting of the Duke of Gloucester, the entire *Fall of Princes* dramatizes the same harsh reality that had provoked Chaucer's Knight to interrupt the Monk— namely, his insistence that the great men of the realm were most vulnerable to reversals of fortune. This relentless tragic pattern presaged Gloucester's own sudden fall in 1447.[265]

Consolation comes in the form of historical remembrance, and these historical writers rely in turn upon literary descendants to keep their own names alive in human memory. Lydgate followed Chaucer's example by carefully attaching his name to his works and linking his career with famous poetic predecessors as well as aristocratic patrons. By constructing a literary genealogy and enforcing the practice of "naming names," Lydgate had reason to expect that his successors would honor their partnership and preserve his memory. Careful investments in the production of manuscripts assisted this long-term goal. Evidence suggests a distinct group of scribes, miniaturists, and illuminators operating in his neighborhood for three decades chiefly on Lydgate's poems.[266] This program of literary production proved instrumental in securing Lydgate's position in the triumvirate of early canonic writers.

The solidity of this formulation of literary history descending from Chaucer, based upon named and self-naming writers, serves as further reminder of the profound obscurity surrounding Langland during the first half of the fifteenth century after his work had outlasted his original coterie readership. While the anonymous *Prick of Conscience* was sometimes attributed to Richard Rolle, *Piers Plowman* remained resolutely the achievement of a poet who had failed to make a name for himself as a vernacular author. As a telling contrast, at the very threshold of his literary career Lydgate had left an autograph signature, grandly phrased, in one of his student books which indicated his own drive for future name recognition: *Sciant presentes et futuri quod ego Johannis Lydgate*—"Let those present and those future know that I am John Lydgate."[267]

CHAPTER FOUR

Piers Plowman and the Impulse to Antagonism

John Ball, John Wyclif, and "Peres Ploughman"

THE YEAR 1360 PROVIDED THE MOST IMMEDIATE HISTORICAL EVENT that *Piers Plowman* took notice of, but the year 1381 affords the first notice that history took of *Piers Plowman*. As part of his well-known account of the English Rising, Thomas Walsingham's *Historia Anglicana* records one of rebel leader John Ball's letters with its unmistakable references to Langland's poem:

> John Schep, som tyme Seynt Marie prest of York, and nowe of Colchestre, greteth welle Johan Nameles, and Johan the Mullere, and Johan Cartere, and biddeth hem that thei war of gyle in borugh, and stondeth togiddir in Goddis name, *and biddeth Peres Plouʒman go to his werke,* and chastise welle Hobbe the Robbere, and taketh with ʒou Johan Trewman, and alle his felaws . . .[1]

Such knowledge came only from the poem's circulation as a public document, though we cannot know to what degree. "Was *Piers Plowman* (at one absurd extreme) the bedtime reading of a thousand insurgents or (at the other) John Ball's distant memory of an evening's conversation?"[2] Besides naming the title character, the broadside alluded to Dowel and Dobet as well as the figure Robert the Robber (B.5.462). Steven Justice suggests that the chastising of "Hobbe the Robbere" relates to some concerted effort to prevent rampaging theft in London, and indeed the mob's failure to loot the Savoy Palace was noted even by the most hostile chroniclers.[3] Knowledge of the poem perhaps suggested also the code name "John Sheep," derived from the narrator's enigmatic self-description in the poem's second line—"I shoop me into a shroud as I a *sheep* weere."

Rustic-sounding pseudonyms such as John Shepherd and John Carter provide an intriguing analogy for the name Will Langland, as does the name John Trueman, with its possible reference to the code phrase *true men* used for Lollards.[4] Did the poet's use of a pen name inspire the rebels, or, the other way around, did the use of code names in 1381 incline the poet to follow their example? "John Nameless" becomes the epitome of an anonymous agent who participated in the conspiracy without running the full risk of exposure. John Ball was apprehended partly because he was rash enough to describe himself as a priest of York and Colchester. As another lesson learned from 1381, Langland's references to his own personal whereabouts may have been intentionally misleading. He mentioned Malvern in the B-text only after he had moved to London; he mentioned Cornhill in the C-text only after he had perhaps retired back to Worcestershire.

As a monk at St. Albans north of London, Walsingham resided close to the events and was almost certainly a witness to John Ball's execution. But events, after they had run their course, were subject to reformulation in the written record with a particular investment of meaning. As an act of posttraumatic repression, the Benedictine historian limited his interpretation of the letter by not explicating its many obscurities (*litteram ænigmatibus plenam*), such as the allusion to Piers Plowman, partly because such understanding would have suggested that he shared an insurgent's understanding of its meaning. His tactic instead was to bracket the seditious letter between two moments of public execution, just as the English was constrained within a disciplinary Latin context. Written by one hanged traitor and found in the pocket of another, the letter itself was offered as a condemned text, one urging lawless revolt in the allegorical language that *Piers Plowman* had already given widespread currency for mobilizing social discontent over rural poverty. Walsingham's literary containment imposed a sense of closure that the violent events themselves did not.

In his summary of John Ball's sermon at Blackheath, Walsingham preserves what might be construed as an explanation of the letter's enigmatic reference to "Peres" in his role as a plowman:

Wherefore they must be prudent, hastening to act after the manner of a good husbandman, tilling his field, and uprooting the tares that are accustomed to destroy the grain; first killing the great lords of the realm, then slaying the lawyers, justices and jurors, and finally rooting out everyone whom they knew to be harmful to the community in future. So at last they would obtain peace . . .[5]

Just as peace purchased through widespread slaughter gives a sinister meaning to the letter's exhortation "seketh pees," the figural equation of the plowman with the exterminator of the upper ranks of English society had the potential of freighting *Piers Plowman* with the fatal burden of criminality. The reference to uprooting tares linked the rebel cause with the theological campaign to uproot heresy, reversing the standard orthodox/heterodox distinction in order to justify punishing corrupt ecclesiasts such as Archbishop Sudbury, who became one of the most famous casualties in London. Wordplay upon the Latin term for tares (*lollium*) was elsewhere mobilized for linking Lollardy with heresy through the parable in Matthew 13:24–30.[6] John Ball's reversal of the standard interpretation of the Parable of the Tares scarcely concealed his support for religious reforms. At a time of legitimate alarm over conspiracy and mob violence, the process of guilt by association had the potential for permanently coloring the reputation of Langland's poem.

This stigma worsened when clerical historians imposed their consensus that John Ball worked as a grassroots agent for John Wyclif. Written within a year of the 1381 uprising, William of Rymington's *XLV Conclusiones* stated that the Oxford theologian's heretical doctrines directly inspired the insurrection of laymen leading to the violence in London.[7] Always the political moralist, Walsingham interpreted the revolt as divine vengeance for allowing the spread of Wyclif's heresies.[8] Not permitting his opponents free sway to define his role for him, Wyclif in *De Blasphemia* rejected civic violence and confirmed his solidarity with the bureaucratic clergy who had become targets of these rebellious laymen.[9] Yet Wyclif's vernacular criticism of ordained clergy such as Sudbury, who held the Church office of archbishop while also serving as chancellor, may have provided exactly the academic support for the antitax revolt that he was accused of.

The later Carmelite *Fasciculi Zizaniorum* offered this report of John Ball's master plan:

He confessed publicly to them that for two years he had been a disciple of Wyclif and had learned from the latter the heresies which he had taught; from Wyclif had arisen the heresy concerning the sacrament of the altar and Ball had openly preached this and other matters taught by him. Ball also declared that there was a certain company of the sect and doctrines of Wyclif which conspired like a secret fraternity [*confoederationem*] and arranged to travel around the whole of England preaching the beliefs taught by Wyclif.[10]

Although the intentions of Ball's original letter remain unclear outside the condemnatory context framed by Walsingham, the principal religious historians made strategic moves to link Wycliffism with the violence of the 1381 rebellion. The Augustinian canon Henry Knighton agreed there was direct collusion between John Wyclif and the rebel leader: "He had John Ball as his precursor, as Christ had John the Baptist, who prepared the way for him in people's minds."[11] Knighton quotes another letter attributed to "Jack Carter" which includes a second unmistakable reference to Langland's title character: "Lat Peres þe Plowman my broþer duelle at home and dyȝt us corne" The sentence reads like a concise summary of *Piers* B.6–7 with its rejection of physical pilgrimage and its substitution of productive farm labor.[12]

These monastic chronicles were not closely coordinated with each other and were not produced in widely read copies, but their initiatives participated in a general campaign to foster realignment of the hierarchies of Church and state. Soon the anti-Lollard campaign was joined by Benedictine preachers such as Thomas Brunton, Uthred of Boldon, and Adam Easton.[13] Traditional solidarities had become dangerously blurred by the Duke of Lancaster's sponsorship of Wyclif and the sympathies of the Lollard knights at Richard II's own court.[14] When two Czech scholars came to England in 1407 searching for copies of Wyclif's theological writings, for example, they visited households connected with the Lollard knight Sir Thomas Latimer.[15] The monastic responses attempted to drive a wedge between John Wyclif and the constituency of his most powerful patron, John of Gaunt, who in 1376 had prompted the Oxford theologian to preach disendowment from church to church in London.

Dobson has observed that "no later English revolutionary movement could ever be quite so inarticulate as that of 1381."[16] This was enforced silence, of course, imposed by the stronger voices within English society. Institutional texts won out, characterizing the rebels as beasts and destructive madmen, while monastic writers portrayed the peasant rabble as enemies of literacy itself.[17] "The accusations of the chroniclers notwithstanding," Paul Strohm has written, "no event occurs unless the actors possess some structured understanding of what they are doing, some way of proceeding in the confidence that their actions are intelligible to themselves and their fellows."[18]

Key to clerical triumph was the outcome of the contest over kingship. The rebels' watchword *Wyth Kynge Richarde and wyth the trew communes* was reported by a Benedictine chronicler in York[19]—echoing Langland's audacious claim "Might of þe communes made hym to regne" (B.Prol.113)—and it introduced a notion of popular sovereignty that would have disenfranchised the titled nobility, the landed gentry and knights, the ecclesiastical authorities, and even the royal justices and bureaucrats in Westminster, in short, all of the vested powers of late fourteenth-century England. Framed in these terms and dramatized by the burning of John of Gaunt's palace, the summary execution of the archbishop of Canterbury, and the grotesque confrontation of Wat Tyler with Richard II at Smithfield, the discursive trajectory of political events was foredoomed to failure. "The rebels wanted what they could not have: sovereignty in a form different from those actually existing."[20] Due largely to the success of the clerical propagandists in imposing their construction upon the English Rising of 1381, the divorce of the Wycliffites from royal and magnate power became the single most important factor in the early failure of this push toward religious reform.[21] The lingering hope of Lollards such as Richard Wyche from Worcester that the knightly class would spearhead the Church's reform came to an end with Oldcastle's failed revolt.[22]

The timing of Lollard activists also provided ammunition to opponents wishing to tie these reformers with the peasant rebels. In 1382 John Aston circulated flysheets around London advertising his unorthodox views on the Eucharist, while Nicholas Hereford and Philip Repingdon nailed their manifestos on the doors of St. Paul's and St. Mary's, London.[23] In the long run, the strategic linkage of Wycliffism with sedition succeeded so completely as a cultural discourse that any manner of social disturbance during the early decades of the fifteenth century, even the Southampton Plot, was almost automatically blamed on Lollard instigation.[24] By criminalizing heresy and adding the new punishment of burning at the stake to the penal code, *De Heretico Comburendo* (1401) was really an antisedition, antidisorder measure enacted when the new Lancastrian regime felt itself most fragile.[25] After the rebellion of the four earls in 1400, for example, Walsingham made this report of one of the traitors: "The Earl of Salisbury, who had been a supporter of Lollards all his life, and a scorner of images, a despiser of the canons, and a scoffer of the sacraments, ended his life without the sacrament of confession."[26]

The Cistercian *Dieulacres Abbey Chronicle* shows the extent to which Langland's poem was implicated in these countermoves by listing "Per Plowman" alongside Jack Straw and John Ball as a principal leader of the 1381 revolt.[27] Textual appropriation became so aggressive that a literary figure was transformed into a historical personage. The fame of the plowman figure, coupled with the anonymity of the author, made this confusion almost inevitable. As one minor witness to the extent that Langland's literary figure had become animated in the reading public's imagination, the scribe of the A-text manuscript Harley 3954 addressed this plea to his readers: "Preyit for pers þe plowmans soule."[28]

Seized in 1381 and pressed into service as a partisan agent, *Piers Plowman* came to figure in the following decades as a prime instance of a text produced and appropriated within the history of more far-reaching productions and social uses.[29] But at least three factors complicate the poem's ideological coherence for literary historians. First, it remains difficult to resist the temptation of seeing *Piers* as part of a political master-narrative with the Puritan teleology that characterizes Christopher Hill's "From Lollards to Levellers."[30] The ex-Carmelite John Bale's history of Wycliffite persecution constructs just such a pattern from his revisionist reading of the *Fasciculi Zizaniorum.*[31] He was therefore poised to fabricate a role for Langland in this retrospective account:

> This, however, appears quite clear that [Langland] was one among the first disciples of John Wyclif, and that, in fervor of spirit, under attractive colors and allegories, he published a pious work in English, which he called *The Vision of Piers Plowman* . . . In this erudite work, on account of various and happy similitudes, he prophetically foresaw many things, which we have seen come to pass in our own days.[32]

Following his lead, Crowley used the preface of his edition of *Piers Plowman* to construct a Catholic Dark Age against which Langland inveighed during the reign of Edward III:

> In whose tyme it pleased God to open the eyes of many to se hys truth, geuing them boldenes of herte to open their mouthes and crye out agaynste the workes of darckenes, as did John Wicklyfe, who also in those dayes translated the holye Byble into the Englische tonge, and this writer who in reportynge certayne visions and dreames, that he fayned hymselfe to haue dreamed, doeth moste christianlye enstructe the weake, and sharplye rebuke the obstynate blynde.[33]

James Simpson's *Reform and Cultural Revolution* revives this retrospective narrative, based on the book catalogues of the literary humanist Leland and the religious reformer Bale, with their first-ever history of an identifiable tradition of English letters covering the now-standard period roughly 1350–1550. Yet Langland's prophetic reforms had been appropriated by a centralizing Tudor regime strangely at odds with the poet's original vision: "*Piers Plowman* both foresaw and forestalled the Reformation, by offering a reformation of its own in which grace is distributed in a wholly decentralized way."[34] No historical moment is repeatable, of course, and fourteenth-century prophecy, once fulfilled, needed to be immediately redefined in the 1550s as non-prophecy.

The second temptation for the literary historian involves some strict polarization of texts into Lollard and anti-Lollard camps, with *Piers Plowman* situated solidly on the heretical side of some unbridgeable division. Again Simpson's *Reform and Cultural Revolution* offers the much-needed corrective that reform had already emerged as the defining feature of a medieval political culture significantly more liberal and free-ranging in its intellectual, theological, and artistic ambitions because unconstrained by the absolutist impulses of Tudor supremacy: "The fundamental condition of that reformism is a sufficiently wide and complex dispersal of jurisdictional power as to disallow any cultural monopoly."[35] Nearly every medieval writer, even John Lydgate, wrote as a reformer.

Long a student of the religious crosscurrents of this period, Anne Hudson emphasizes the challenge of placing individuals as well as texts on the spectrum of religious opinion running from Archbishop Arundel to William Swinderby. "In the mid-point," she notes, "radical orthodoxy and conservative Lollardy might look very much alike."[36] Hudson has refined these views more recently: "Simple binarism is not adequate: there is a vast range of material that shows some sympathy with viewpoints that are characteristic of Lollardy but are not peculiar to that sect, of knowledge of Wycliffite positions without full agreement with them, of allusions (whether mocking or not) to Lollard phraseology and idiom."[37] With their later commitments to provocation and confrontation, Lollards were often unified more by hostility to established practices than by their own coherent program of reforms. Different people thought differently.

Rejecting various unifying principles for a discursive formation, Foucault identified *dispersion* itself as a principle of coherence that nicely describes early Wycliffism, which was therefore perceived as an even greater threat precisely because it refused to materialize as a codified creed.[38] In a heterogeneous culture crisscrossed by so many social and doctrinal fissures, the pejorative label "Lollard" was applied by opponents who projected a monolithic movement as a clearer target.[39] Modern scholarship has often re-enacted this practice. Writings dubbed Wycliffite in modern manuscript descriptions, for example, were not necessarily perceived as heterodox in the fourteenth and early fifteenth centuries.[40] We can detect the free and unproblematic circulation of texts eventually assembled in codices that now seem wildly eclectic, such as the Advocates 19.3.1 compilation described as a "library *in parvo*."[41] In Huntington HM 744, for example, a fascicle containing a Lollard *Commentary on the Ten Commandments* and an extract from the Lollard *Seven Works of Bodily Mercy* became bound with an autograph transcription of poems by the anti-Lollard poet Thomas Hoccleve.[42]

A third temptation for more recent literary historians comes in the form of the subversion-containment model most powerfully articulated by Stephen Greenblatt.[43] This holistic account suggests that cultural orthodoxies maintain themselves not simply by producing and exorcizing their subversive opposites, but also by domesticating and recuperating the dissident elements which thereby lose their antagonistic force.[44] Tracing the evidence of incorporation and containment, my own history of *Piers* takes shape as a series of separate episodes, moments of contestation, accommodation, absorption, and re-emergence, in which social texts operated in a number of different ways under shifting conditions of disciplinary action. Originally written as an irate satire against economic and ecclesiastical corruption, Langland's poem became subject to radical appropriation in John Ball's letters. But it was also available for orthodox domestication in monastic manuscripts such as the Vernon copy of the A-text and Cambridge CUL Dd.1.17 of the B-text with their huge gatherings of historical and orthodox religious texts.[45] Sometimes *Piers* entered a manuscript like Society of Antiquaries 687 (c. 1425) in the company of writings characterized as Wycliffite, and it encouraged the creation of texts such as *Pierce the Ploughman's Crede* far more extreme in their attacks upon corrupt religious practices.[46] Sometimes Langland's text was subjected to crude censorship as in Huntington HM 143 where the name "Piers Plowman" has been systematically erased throughout.[47] And sometimes the poem resisted all manner of factional appropriation to remain safely in a gray area, such as the pristine and apparently untouched Huntington HM 137.[48]

The historical force of *Piers Plowman* sometimes can be felt in texts quite remote from Langland's actual work. Lollard advocacy of plain prayer almost automatically summoned the example of the plowman: "a symple pater nos-ter of a plouʒman þat is in charite is betre þan a þousand massis of coueitouse prelatis & veyn religious."[49] Even the early sixteenth-century *A Lytell Geste howe the Plowman lerned his Pater Noster,* which reversed polarities to make the priest into the figure of upright religion and the plowman into a money-grubbing ignoramus, needs to be understood in terms of a traditional priest-plowman confrontation traceable ultimately to Langland's Pardon Scene. Middleton concludes that the poem's relation to the Lollard movement was cultural rather than textual, and Hudson judges that "*Piers Plowman* in the two and a half centuries after its composition was more honored in the name than in the reading."[50] But every acknowledgment of the text's cultural presence becomes an interpretive act, and all such attempts at rendering the poem meaningful historically become instances of literary police-actions.[51]

The degree to which Langland's poem became implicated in these upheavals of the 1380s should come as no surprise. His widening national audience had reached beyond the original readership of London's scribes, civil servants, and underemployed clergy to merge with the 1381 uprising's demographic of artisans and tradesmen as well as some gentry and clerics in minor orders. This was much the same audience that later Lollard writing attracted, and Emily Steiner's work has shown how these dissident reformists contested the documentary culture of the institutional Church, with its indulgences and letters of fraternity, through their appeal to the Charter of Christ authorizing a purer spiritual community unmediated by ecclesiastical authority.[52]

Hardly the dumb beasts described by monastic chroniclers, participants in the English Rising were already staging their assaults upon official texts in an organized and highly selective manner. Government documents such as tax rolls, charters, and estate archives formed one of the universal targets of rebel violence. Walsingham clearly understood the goal of the peasants: "All court rolls and old muniments should be burnt so that once the memory of ancient customs had been wiped out, their lords would be completely unable to vindicate their rights over them."[53] These rural artisans and agricultural laborers, most likely directed by their clerical leadership, understood that the political culture in which they suffered harsh taxation, limited wages, and restricted movements depended upon written documents such as these. "Each appointment, commission, promulgation, translation, provision, summons, condemnation, and definition executed by documentary writing operates under institutional conditions, and each *enacts* something, gets something done."[54] In order to alter the oppressive circumstances in which they lived, first they needed to seize these records.[55] The St. Albans insurgents seemed to know precisely what they were looking for, even in the details of its physical manufacture: "They demanded a certain ancient charter confirming the liberties of the villeins, with capital letters, one of gold and the other of azure."[56]

Once the rebels reached London, their targets included the men who produced and interpreted texts on behalf of the powerful elite. The *Anonimalle Chronicle* says that "all lawyers, all the men of the Chancery and the Exchequer, and everyone who could write a writ" became candidates for execution.[57] These targeted civil servants would have included Chaucer and most of his literary circle, including Gower who wrote so vehemently against the rebels later in his *Vox Clamantis,*[58] as well as the text-writing professionals presumed as Langland's first readership. When he reports that the rebels forced teachers in grammar schools to swear they would never again offer instruction in religious matters, Walsingham provides grounds for particular fear among all literate clergymen and not only government bureaucrats.[59] Read as public gesture, even the destruction of John of Gaunt's wardrobe, with whatever books it included, constituted an assault upon the economies of textual production over which Church and secular government tried maintaining a strict monopoly.[60]

Leaders of the uprising knew how to marshal their own textual resources. Walsingham and the author of the *Anonimalle Chronicle* reported that the men of Essex spread word of their uprising through letters dispersed from village to village in Kent, Suffolk, and Norfolk.[61] Knighton alleged these communications moved through a network of friends and relatives that would anticipate the system through which Lollard writings were also disseminated. During the Oldcastle rebellion, for example, there were accusations that bills inciting the murder of Henry V and his brothers were circulated through this sort of network.[62] Because she traveled so widely, even Margery Kempe was accused of carrying letters about the countryside on behalf of Oldcastle.[63] John Ball's letters with their references to Piers Plowman constitute primary witnesses to the insurgent literacy investigated so brilliantly by Justice: "Writing itself—both the activity and the product—was at issue in these letters: their composition and copying, recompositon and recopying were so many *acts of assertive literacy.*"[64]

The events of 1381 marked the beginning of a sporadic contest over the production, dissemination, and interpretation of many different kinds of texts which would characterize the ongoing struggle between reformist dissent and established clerical-courtly interests. Earlier generations of scholars suspected that quite orthodox works such as *Prick of Conscience,* Richard

Rolle's *Psalter Commentary,* Thoresby's *Lay Folks' Catechism,* and *Dives et Pauper* were rewritten and altered by Lollard sympathizers.[65] *The Pore Caitif* and even *Ancrene Riwle* appeared sometimes to have been subjected to interpolations that looked suspicious in this contentious context.[66] Such practices were established as spectral if not actual events when Henry Knighton's *Chronicle* charged Wycliffites with erasing passages from orthodox books and rewriting them in places with the teachings of their reformist theology.[67]

Clandestine translation, home-based education in reading and scriptural interpretation, and the secret exchange of vernacular books became essential ingredients in this Lollard subculture. In response, the seizure of books and the examination of their contents became routine threats for the condemnation of heretics by episcopal courts.[68] As Margaret Aston puts it, "Simply to be a reader of English or to own a religious text written in English became in certain circumstances and among certain sorts of people potentially incriminating."[69] The lengths to which overreaction could extend is illustrated by the fact that owning the *Canterbury Tales* served as evidence in the 1464 proceedings against John Baron of Amersham.[70] I use the word *overreaction* tentatively because Chaucer's story collection, subjected to close reading and prosecutorial hermeneutics, could indeed be judged full of suspect views and dangerous opinions.

This first phase of religious dissent in England anticipated the bibliophobia of Reformation print culture.[71] As early as 1384, Cambridge officials examined a copy of the vernacular poem *Speculum Vitae* for errors before it was given formal approval: "If any defects had been found in it, it would have been burnt before the university."[72] The burning of books contributed to the spectacle of repression, becoming the preferred deterrent in an English society apparently reluctant to send men and women to the stake. "Books are one of the most public and persistent means of proclaiming and disseminating heresy," Anne Hudson has observed. "Therefore written materials become the object of official destruction as well as, or even in preference to, the individual heretic."[73] The 1410 bonfire of Wyclif's writings at Carfax in Oxford and the ceremonial burning of Lollard books in London following Perkins's revolt of 1431 testify how the infrequency of these violent occasions served to increase the exemplary impact. Suppression did not always operate so publically, however; two-thirds of the corpus of Wyclif's theological writings, known complete by Thomas Netter in the 1420s, no longer survive in manuscripts in England.[74] When Bishop Pecock was condemned for heresy because he had argued theology in the vernacular, his books were burned. As late as 1521 the Lollard physician John Phip declared that he would rather burn his books than have his books burn him.[75]

As an adjunct to attacks upon outlaw texts, sponsorship of orthodox writers such as Thomas Hoccleve and John Lydgate figured importantly in the Lancastrian counteroffensive. In his poem *To Sir John Oldcastle,* written while the rebel was still at large after 1415, Hoccleve blasted the traitor for his careless regard for right beliefs: "O Oldcastel, allas, what eilid thee / To slippe in to the snare of heresie?" Since Oldcastle's errors included reading the wrong books, Hoccleve prescribed a syllabus appropriate for lay reading and categorized the works befitting a knight's social class:

> Rede the storie of Lancelot de lake,
> Or Vegece of the aart of Chiualrie,
> The Seege of Troie / or Thebes / thee applie
> To thyng þat may to th'ordre of knyght longe![76]

Arthurian romances such as the prose *Lancelot* had established themselves as a staple for chivalric audiences. Sir Simon Burley's library included ten such romances when it was catalogued in 1388, and a French *Romance de Launcelot* was listed among the eighty-four volumes in the Duke of Gloucester's personal collection inventoried at the time of his death in 1397.[77] Commenting on these two book lists, John Scattergood has concluded that "these documents do not represent something casual but a distinctive aristocratic and knightly taste in literature."[78]

Hoccleve also recommended the fourth-century military strategist Vegetius, whose treatise *De Re Militari* provided practical advice on battlefield tactics while offering theoretical justifications for war itself. Thomas of Woodstock owned a volume catalogued as "Vagesse de Chivalrie," and Robert Parker later adapted the work as *Knyghthode and Bataile* for dedication to Henry VI.[79] John Trevisa's patron Lord Berkeley commissioned a translation dated 1408 in the colophon of Bodleian MS Digby 233, which also preserves the unique copy of Trevisa's *The Governance of Kings and Princes.*[80] The manuscript's opening picture shows the aging clergyman presenting his book to a young, clean-shaven prince on a throne, and this idealized image matches the public figure that Prince Henry projected when he established his power on the council prior to 1412.[81] Vegetius provided the source for the last section of Trevisa's principal translation of *De Regimine Principum,* and so Hoccleve could look to this precedence when deciding to write his own *Regiment of Princes* around 1411.[82]

The subject of Troy, also prescribed by Hoccleve, had become standard in collections such as Woodstock's library with its *Ector de Troie, Bataille de Troie,* and *Sege de Troie.* Though no concrete evidence connects the two immediate heirs of the Chaucerian tradition, Lydgate seems to comply with Hoccleve's prospectus for an English syllabus for non-Lollard chivalric readers. During 1412–20 he was laboring at his *Troy Book* apparently at the request of Henry V. This work was actually given Hoccleve's recommended title "Siege of Troy" in some manuscripts. Lydgate's *Siege of Thebes* followed in 1420–22.

The English-language "high art" invented by Chaucer and developed by his successors Hoccleve and Lydgate meant a new kind of literary culture filtering down from the upper ranks of society. This process can be charted in the production of *Canterbury Tales* manuscripts from the first half to the second half of the fifteenth century. Produced for aristocrats, expensively decorated manuscripts such as Petworth, Lichfield, Bodleian 686, Devonshire, and Rawlinson Poet. 223 came at the beginning of the century. These were followed by plainer, cheaper copies such as the Chicago and Glasgow manuscripts meant for lower-ranked readers later in the century.[83] Editors have slighted many of the gorgeous early manuscripts because they lack value for establishing the text of the *Canterbury Tales,* but almost any one of them is superior in material quality to the very best copies of *Piers Plowman.* As the most famous illustrated manuscript of Langland's poem, Bodleian MS Douce 104 (1427) shows intelligence and ingenuity in its seventy-two drawings, as well as some affluence in the gilt decoration of opening initials,[84] but the results fall far short of the ornamental elegance of Chaucer manuscripts such as Harley 7334, Corpus Christi 198, and Lansdowne 851.[85] Doyle's general principle for gauging manuscript survival rates is also worth recalling: "The longer a copy of a text is in use, the lower its chances of survival."[86] These costly manuscripts of the *Canterbury Tales* may have been largely unread and unopened, functioning as elegant trophy books, while the tattered remains of *Piers Plowman* manuscripts such as BL Add. 35287, which is worn, battered, corrected, and scribbled over with massive amounts of later commentary, suggest an avid readership over many decades.[87]

Piers Plowman Before 1381, *Piers Plowman* After 1381

Though a controversial presence throughout the fifteenth and sixteenth centuries, *Piers Plowman* cannot be considered an innocent bystander when first pressed into service by John Ball in 1381. The image of the author in the poem joins with its theological contents and scholastic methods to suggest that Langland belonged to the sizable group of unbeneficed clerks, including Ball himself, who formed the dissident fringe of fourteenth-century English society.[88] These members of the "clerical proletariat" shared a common discourse of homiletic invective against Church corruption and governmental failures, no doubt partly because administrative organizations had failed to provide these individuals with adequate livelihoods.[89]

The poorly shod Will wears a russet habit as he wanders about the countryside as a crazed malcontent showing no respect for his superiors (B.8.1). Such a figure was readily identified with early Wycliffite eccentrics who also wore russet—*vestibus de russeto*—such as William Swinderby and William Smith.[90] Official writings routinely warned against Wycliffite preachers presenting themselves under robes of great sanctity—*sub magnae sanctitatis velamine*—in a phraseology recalling the narrator's initial description of himself "in abite as an hermite vnholy of werkes" (B.Prol.3).[91] If Langland resided in London during the late 1370s, as Skeat inferred, he may have actually heard Wyclif preaching in English when John of Gaunt prompted him to go from church to church throughout the city.[92] More importantly perhaps, he would have heard the various vernacular renditions in the other sermons, schedules, and broadsides so steadily reported by hostile sources.

That Gaunt sponsored Wyclif in 1377 *and* was a target of rebel violence in 1381 complicates the monastic version yoking religious dissent and social protest during these years. Langland's particular relations to Wyclif in matters of private religion, Church wealth, and royal power nonetheless shared enough common ground to explain why *Piers Plowman* might have been viewed as an allied text.[93] Langland's hammering criticism of the religious orders, his suspicion of Church imagery, his emphasis on clerical poverty, and his apocalyptic vision of the Antichrist's army would surely have struck a responsive chord with Wycliffites as well as many conservative laymen and reform-minded clergymen.[94] Langland attacked only the abuses of confession, pilgrimage, and the veneration of saints, however, not their legitimacy as penitential practices, and he never came close to Wyclif's more radical positions on the sacraments, especially the Eucharist.[95] But modern scholars are probably much more alert to the subtleties of the poem's precise meanings. A late fourteenth-century readership would have noticed "hot button" topics in a book already known among dissident clerics by the time the Blackfriars Council condemned Wyclif's errors in 1382. A reference to "Pers" denoting Piers Plowman as a well-known critic of the friars crops up in the macaronic poem *Heu! Quanta Desolatio Angliae Praestatur*—"With an O

and an I, fuerunt pyed freres / Quomodo mutati sunt rogo, dicat Pers"—
which was composed in response to the Blackfriars Council perhaps by the
later renegade mendicant Peter Patershull. The allusion indicates the public
reputation of Langland's title character as an opponent to Wyclif's opponents.[96]

The notorious obscurity of Langland's poem, his eagerness to tackle controversial issues without finally offering clear orthodox resolutions, and his
reliance upon a sort of knotty vernacular disputation—a method that would
become the hallmark of Wycliffite polemic—further rendered *Piers* a text
wide open to both attack and appropriation. Stating that "God cannot be expressed by any philosophical terms," the eighth item in Arundel's *Constitutions* would forbid anyone to "allege or propose any conclusions or proposi-
tions in catholic faith" even though "they defend the same with ever such
curious terms and words." Further difficulties were created for *Piers* by the
medieval text's lack of quotation marks, which might otherwise indicate
where the different allegorical characters voiced extreme opinions, not the
poet expressing his own.[97] *Piers Plowman* remains notoriously difficult to punc-
tuate even in the most recent editions, for example, where Emperor Trajan
stops speaking and the narrator takes over in B.11. Though Langland embraced a nonexclusive concept of the true Church much at odds with evolving Lollard doctrine, David Lawton's famous conclusion would have proved
almost as damning at the time—"the issue is really that Lollards had Langlandian sympathies"[98]—when widespread reformist piety came to be equated
narrowly with Wycliffite heresy during the 1390s.

In the wake of the English Rising and the Blackfriars Council, Langland
rewrote his poem in the form now known as the C-text. The sporadic nature
of the changes and the unaltered form of the final two passus suggest that
these revisions were not completed. Nevill Coghill supported Skeat's original
surmise of 1393 as a plausible end date for the C version, and recent discussion of the C-text's response to the labor statutes issued by the Cambridge
Parliament of 1388 confirms some end date in the early 1390s.[99] Possible draft
versions or "rolling revisions" intermediate between the B-text and the
C-text during the later 1380s hint at the extended length of this rewriting's
time span.[100]

George Russell was ideally qualified as coeditor of the Athlone *C Version*
to detect political prudence underlying a variety of these textual adjustments.
"This poem was circulating at a time when ecclesiastical and political critics
were sensitive to what might appear subversive," he has written. "A maladroit
formulation of a doctrine might easily cause trouble."[101] Careful line-by-line

revision occupied the poet mostly in the Prologue and Passus 1 while longer additions, transpositions, and excisions are concentrated in the center of the poem. The poet's efforts tended to focus upon provocative topics already causing problems for his first audiences. Passages that attracted his attention are often the same that continue to interest modern readers: the Belling of the Cat Fable, the *mede-mercede* distinction, "autobiographical" passages, the characterization of the Seven Sins, the first appearance of Piers, the theology of poverty, the salvation of unbaptized heathens, and the Tree of Charity.[102]

Hudson has examined *Piers* in context of vernacular Wycliffism with particular attention to the concessions made in the C-version to issues that did not seem so dangerous in the late 1370s.[103] These revisions have often disappointed modern readers. For someone such as George Kane who insists upon aesthetic improvement as the principal impulse behind authorial revision,[104] many changes appear miscalculated and therefore inauthentic—the results of scribal interference—unless topical controversies are factored into Langland's motives for making changes. Let me cite one small example. The dreamer Will says his prayers outdoors in the B-text (5.1–8), but in the corresponding passage in the C-text (5.105–8), Langland altered the passage so that Will goes "to þe kirk" to say his Paternoster. Wyclif's *Opus Evangelicum* had characterized churches as latter-day inventions irrelevant to the spiritual life, and his more radical followers recommended that people pray "in þe eire under heven," which was just as sanctified for people's devotions.[105] Doing his revisions during the late 1380s or early 1390s, the poet felt some need to avoid the claim—newly tagged as Wycliffite—that men would be better off saying their prayers outdoors in an open field. So he avoided controversy by having Will proceed to the church to pray.

A more noteworthy instance of strategic revision is the C-text's deletion of the tearing of the Pardon, an episode which in the B-text was pivotal to the progress of the poem's central arguments concerning salvation (B.7.107–48; cf. C.9.282–98).[106] The dispensing of pardons had been seized by the incipient Wycliffite movement for its attack upon ecclesiastical greed.[107] This hostility had been clearly identified as a major tenet by the time Roger Dymmok launched his counterassault in *The Twelve Conclusions of the Lollards*.[108] The rewriting of the Pardon Scene to omit the actual tearing of the document, highlighted in some B-text manuscripts such as Laud Misc. 581 where "Indulgentia Petri" is inserted in the margin (fol. 31b), distanced the C-text from an issue much more dangerous in the early 1390s than it had been in the late 1370s.

Yet no amount of retouching could rid *Piers Plowman* of all doctrinal issues transformed into liabilities by the unfolding of national events. Langland could cut only so much without revising his poem out of existence. How could the poet have eliminated so many large sections such as the pilgrimage in the Half Acre, which accords with the Lollard view that meritorious pilgrimage involved an inward spiritual reorientation instead of a physical journey to some saint's shrine? "It is leueful and medeful to go on pilgrimage to heuenwarde," William Thorpe proclaimed, "doing werkes of penance, werkis of riȝtfulnes and werkis of mercy, and to suche pilgrimage alle men ben boundoun after þer power wile þei lyuen here."[109] Inquiring into an individual's beliefs concerning pilgrimage became one standard means for determining a suspect's heretical views.

Attempts at clarifying issues in the C-revision could have led the poet deeper into controversy. The autobiographical addition (C.5.1–108) offers the outstanding instance of topical rewriting.[110] While the passage underscores the narrator's laziness in ways steadily informed by traditional writings on *acedia* or sloth, Middleton's investigations have shown the extent to which the poet's self-condemnation drew upon the precise language of the 1388 Statutes of Labourers, language that came freighted with its own social provocations.[111] On one point, however, the poet insists upon a scrupulous distinction. As someone dressed in russet robes, he himself was merely "yclothed as a lollare"—he merely *looked* like a Lollard according to his nostalgic pre-Wycliffite definition from the pre-1380s.[112] To the contrary, he claims that he aroused the hostility of "lollares of Londone and lewede ermytes" by targeting these groups for censure in his earlier writings. While the B version damned fraudulent "heremytes on an heep" who trooped to Walsingham with their mistresses (B.Prol.53–57), Langland cagily misrepresents the degree to which this prior satire had targeted *lollares*.

The term *lollare* itself remained novel and lexically unstable during the 1380s. Langland had used it only once in the B-text in conjunction with un-Christlike hermits—"For he nys noȝt in lolleris ne in londleperis heremytes" (B.15.213)—and he continued using it as an omnibus category for fraudulent beggars and maverick friars. The earliest recorded use in reference to a religious sect is commonly understood to have occurred in 1382 when the Cistercian monk Henry Crumpe, who had sat on the Blackfriars Council, was disciplined for accusing Oxford Wycliffites of being heretical *Lollardi*. But Andrew Cole's re-examination of the evidence suggests that the account of Crumpe appeared exclusively in *Fasciculi Zizaniorum* and dates to the period 1393–99 as a retroactive application of the term.[113] Official proclamations and ecclesiastical records did not begin using the word *Lollardi* to mean followers of Wyclif until the end of the 1380s, when the oft-cited 1387 mandate by Bishop Henry Wakefield of Worcester against "Lollardorum confoederati" functioned as a catch-all for preachers of unsound doctrines, including radical friars.[114] Langland used the term *lollare* a grand total of thirteen times in the C-text, with some urgency in the C.5 *apologia* in order to affirm some older non-Wycliffite sense.[115] "Langland goes to the letter of anti-Wycliffite *lollare* discourse and restricts its sense to antifraternal terms," Cole has concluded. "To him the bad 'lollare' heretic is a friar who shuns work—not a Wycliffite."[116]

Sometime by 1390, John Mirk's *Festial* was written partly to compete with the Lollard homily cycles.[117] Specifically, Lollard criticism of church images elicited Mirk's orthodox response in his Corpus Christi sermon: "And þerfor roodes and oþyr ymages ben necessary in holy chirch, whateuer þes Lollardes sayn." Never mentioning other heresies such as the attack on the Eucharist, Mirk expresses only these particular anxieties, an indication that the most notorious Wycliffite tenets were not fully developed or disseminated during the 1380s. Since the Bodleian manuscript used as the base text for the old EETS edition had substituted *Lombards* for *Lollards*—a very peculiar variant—modern readers have not appreciated the full extent of Mirk's objections: "now þese *Lollardis* pursue men of Holi Chirche and ben about in alle þat þei mai to vndon hem."[118] Writing in Shropshire at almost exactly the same time that Langland was working on his C-text, John Mirk kept the meaning of the word *Lollard* sufficiently open-ended to include troublesome mendicants as well as lay heretics.[119] Yet he focused on the one reform that would prove least popular with lay worshipers—the destruction of church images—and would serve also to distinguish Wycliffites from troublesome friars.[120]

Various Latin texts show increased wordplay upon the term *lollium* ("tares") exploiting the image's traditional association with heresy through commentaries on the parable in Matthew 13:24–30. In the Endlink to the Man of Law's Tale, Chaucer aimed this barb at the "Lollere" Parson: "He wolde sowen som difficultye / Or springen cokkel in our clene corn" (*CT*, II, 1182–83). While drawing upon the implications of this parable in his agricultural allegory, Langland's prior strategy called for invoking a different range of meanings—loller, idler, or vagabond—in reference to wayward clerics and extra-regular beggars. He sought to blur distinctions in an effort to disparage all objectionable "gyrovague" misconduct.[121] The 1387 prohibition of the *Lollardi* preachers John Aston and Nicholas Hereford came from the bishop of Worcester,[122] and Langland's references to the Malvern Hills as well as his personal dialect placed him in the same diocese.[123] If the author of the C-text retreated from the high visibility of London, he found himself in another hotbed of Lollard activities back in Worcestershire.

Written as a replacement for the tearing of the Pardon, the longer passage in C.9.98–296 suggests the poet was increasingly aware of the semantic contest when he composed an extended discussion of "lunatyk lollares." These men neither worked nor begged, but sometimes they uttered prophetic messages as God's minstrels.[124] This group differs from those "lollares, lache-draweres, lewede ermites" who performed no honest labor but "lyueth lyke a lollare—Goddes lawe hym dampneth!" The benefits of Piers's Pardon are withheld from these "lollares þat lyuen in sleuthe." It is difficult to gauge what effect Langland intended when he wrestled with this troublesome terminology. He even sought to stabilize the definition by claiming a venerable English usage (C.9.213–16):

> Kyndeliche, by Crist, ben suche ycald "lollares,"
> As by þe Engelisch of our eldres, of olde mennes techynge.
> He þat lolleth is lame, or his leg out of ioynte,
> Or ymaymed in som membre, for to meschief hit souneth.

That is, he asserts some longstanding status for the English word *lollare* predating the Wycliffite controversies. By broadening the scope of the word's meaning, Langland's C-text tries neutralizing the religious stigma by folding the word *lollare* into the poem's relentless condemnation of lazy vagrants. The revised text creates a separate space for "lunatyk lollares" (C.9.107) representing an idealized poverty of true Christian discipleship, as well as a deep identification with the humanity of Christ, entirely separate from the degenerate practice of the mendicant orders.[125]

The textual campaigns by ecclesiastical writers won the contest over lexical control by stipulating *Lollare* as a Wycliffite by the early 1390s.[126] As a result, Langland's own wrestling with the word *lollare* in his C-text provoked more problems than it dispelled. Numerous annotations in the manuscripts testify to the attention drawn to this word. The late fourteenth-century BL Add. 35157 has a note beside C.5.30–31—"lowlars regarded not fridaies fast"—reflecting a standard complaint not against lazy beggars but against Wycliffites.[127] Other additions to the C-text also attracted the attention the poet might have wished to avoid, such as Conscience's condemnations of idolatry and miracles, as well as one topic of unusual concern in the later Reformation period: the cost of wax for devotional candles (C.Prol.96–100).[128] Passages of these sorts suggest that Langland never managed to resolve the tension in *Piers Plowman* between the impulse to criticize corrupt practices and his determination to maintain orthodox theology during this early period of escalating Wycliffite activism and official alarm over "Lollard" threats.

The Public Life of *Piers Plowman*

The C-text *apologia* depicts the poet living in Cornhill, but the dialect of the earliest C-text manuscripts suggests that he was really residing in the West Country at the end of his career. Much else in the poem may have been calculated to mislead the reader about the identity of the writer. No comfortable retirement to a country cottage, Langland's relocation to the Worcester area would be better understood as a retreat to a friendlier provincial setting where his final revisions could proceed without undue risk to the author.[129] Such prudence may have been well invested. The last phase of the poet's career extended over a period when the significance of the Blackfriars Council was coming into sharper focus, and Wycliffism—now elided with "Lollardy"—was being linked with the English Rising in the unambiguous ways represented by religious chroniclers. This was the first period in a cycle of increasing antagonism between those possessing Wycliffite sympathies and those fiercely defending the twin establishments of royal government and ecclesiastical authority. When Walsingham reported that Sir Lewis Clifford renounced his Lollardy and informed against his friends in 1402, the episode signaled a clear shift by an entire social class at the public level.[130]

The second period of antagonism falls in the early fifteenth century when full awareness of the incompatibility of these opposing forces moved to the episcopal courts. This was nonetheless the period when many *Piers Plowman* manuscripts were produced. The enactment of *De Heretico Comburendo* introduced burning as the penalty for relapsed heretics in 1401—with its first victim, the London chaplain William Sawtry—and the terms of violation were spelled out by Arundel's *Constitutions* framed in Oxford in 1407 and issued at St. Paul's in 1409.[131] As a work newly enrolled in the *Piers Plowman* tradition, *Lanterne of Liȝt* testifies to the vehemence of Lollard reaction to "thise newe Constituciouns by whos strengthe Anticrist enterdith chirchis."[132] During Langland's lifetime, however, there is little reason to believe that the first-generation Lollards were pursued with much vigor in remoter part of the realm, and those who held dissenting views lived quietly in the countryside without much fear of trouble. But these circumstances soon changed, culminating with the 1410 burning of the first layman, John Badby, a Worcestershire artisan. One wonders about the extent to which Badby's native Worcestershire dialect—Langland's language preserved even in manuscripts copied in London—had itself become marked as a suspicious Lollard dialect during this period.[133] One of the rebels hanged and not pardoned for taking part in Oldcastle's rising was Sir Roger Acton of Sutton, Worcestershire.

John Badby was an unapologetic heretic who denounced the orthodox doctrine of the Eucharist and denied the exclusive power of priests to perform this sacrament. After failing to convince the obdurate layman to return to the true faith, Bishop Peverell of Worcester referred the case to leaders of the English Church assembled at St. Paul's. A highly theatrical show trial was staged before Archbishop Arundel and other ecclesiasts, including Henry Beaufort and Henry Chichele, along with seven other bishops and prominent members of the laity led by the Duke of York, the recently rehabilitated author of *The Master of Game*.[134] While most dissenters were quick to repent, the stubborn Worcestershire craftsman gave the convocation a special opportunity for generating propaganda. Better than a recantation, his exemplary execution would dramatize the consequences of obstinately holding Lollard beliefs.[135] A royal warrant was issued immediately upon his conviction, and Badby was burned at the stake at Smithfield before a large London audience that included high-ranking churchmen like Richard Courtenay and noblemen like the Prince of Wales. *De Haeretico Comburendo* specified that such burnings should occur in a conspicuous place so that the punishment would strike fear into the hearts of spectators. The dramatic display of ecclesiastical and royal power played out Foucault's "spectacle of the scaffold" as marshaled specifically for what Paul Strohm has described as "the theater of orthodoxy."[136]

Following this 1410 show trial, public executions were used remarkably seldom for stifling religious dissent when compared, for example, with the ferocious persecutions of Cathars. Hundreds of people were burned at the stake in Languedoc, and thousands of others died during a process of inquisition and crusade that lasted over a century.[137] By comparison with inquisitions on the Continent, English heresy trials were surprisingly boring.[138] One explanation for restraint was the lack of involvement by powerful noblemen in the heresy. In England, aristocratic support for Wycliffism waned quickly after 1381 when the Duke of Lancaster began distancing himself. Though deeply pious and committed to the principle of authority, Richard II took little interest in any national witch hunt and shied away from brutal forms of execution. The phrase in the epitaph on Richard II's tomb commissioned for

Westminster Abbey in 1395—"he hammered heretics and scattered their friends"—may have exaggerated his determination *or* may even have been added by Henry V when King Richard was re-entombed in this sepulcher in 1414.[139] Sympathizers included the Lollard knights at his own court, and although King Richard took a personal role in correcting Sir Richard Stury, these free-thinking, reform-minded courtiers enjoyed favor till the end of the monarch's reign and were called to account only under Henry IV.[140]

The fact that Lollardy was a widespread national problem, not a regional one, also helps to account for the lack of massive persecutions.[141] Inquisitors, backed by knights, could not target a single area like Languedoc. Ecclesiastical officials did launch some local campaigns such as the trials in Norwich during the period 1428–31, but no single city or shire offered itself as a site of local infection to be cauterized or cut out entirely.[142] A broad-based national challenge elicited a prolonged national response in the forms of periodic investigations, commissions whenever there seemed a pressing need, and the threat of examining books as part of a textual counterattack.

"If links between heresy and literacy are assessed in terms not of the literate heretics, but of the literate reactors to heresy, further shifts in perspective may occur."[143] As part of this literary response, the first decades of the fifteenth century witnessed the energetic production of the Lancastrian texts that bolstered the linguistic, religious, and political cause of national unity. Some publications showed explicit intentions, as when Archbishop Arundel gave official approval to Nicolas Love's *Mirror of the Life of Christ* and mandated that the book should be distributed to edify the faithful and confute Lollards: "ad fidelium edificationem et hereticorum sive Lollardorum confutationem."[144] Orthodoxy was appropriating the weaponry of the heretics. Dangerous English books encouraged the writing and dissemination of safe English books such as *The Chastising of God's Children,* which attempted, however anxiously, to negotiate an orthodox alliance between the Vulgate and the vernacular.[145] Sheila Lindenbaum detects an array of normalizing discourses to which Lydgate would contribute as a crucial but by no means solitary figure: "Poems like 'Mesure is Tresour' are erected on a scaffolding of underground religious texts—the English translations of the Bible forbidden in the London convocation of 1408, or Lollard tracts like the *Lantern,* burned with its owner John Claydon in 1415."[146]

Exactly contemporary with these events, the first copies of the *Canterbury Tales* in Ellesmere, Harley 7334, and Corpus Christi 198 were manufactured most likely under the direction of individuals with strong commitments to the Lancastrian court, including the poet's son. The Alington family has an early association with the Ellesmere manuscript, for example, and we

know that William Alington worked closely with Thomas Chaucer in asserting Beaufort influence on the council.[147] The first Lancastrians were masterful at the social alchemy that transformed clan allegiances and other power
relations.[148] Although Chaucer himself was never forced to undergo a public
recantation as did his long-time associate Sir Lewis Clifford, Chaucer's works
and his reputation underwent a comparable form of rehabilitation in order
to serve more loyally the orthodoxies of the new regime.

After the 1414 conspiracy that spurred Hoccleve to prescribe a vernacular syllabus notably excluding Langland's poetry, English society entered the
long third period when Lollardy lost social respectability in aristocratic circles so that accusations of Lollardy targeted individuals of the trade and gentry classes.[149] Enforcement of Archbishop Arundel's *Constitutions* at Oxford
and Cambridge also succeeded in depriving Wycliffism of most academic respectability.[150] In 1429 Bishop Richard Fleming founded Oxford's Lincoln
College specifically as a seminary for anti-Lollard preachers. The inferior material quality of later *Piers* manuscripts suggests exclusion from any serious
university readership in circumstances parallel to the exclusion of Wycliffite
texts.[151] By the middle of the fifteenth century, Reginald Pecock conceived
of Wycliffism as a "lay partie" so unsupported by educated clerics that only
layfolk were called "lollardis."[152] During these increasingly repressive years,
Bishop Pecock's own use of the vernacular for combating Lollards contributed to his conviction on charges of heresy.[153]

In terms of these altered political circumstances, Anne Hudson's esti-
mation of the shifting political character of *Piers Plowman* deserves quoting
in full:

> Had Archbishop Arundel read the poem around 1396, he would surely
> have regarded it as dangerous—dangerous because its thrust is so bla-
> tantly hostile to the institutional church, because it advocated disend-
> owment, and because it implied that the individual Christian should
> think and judge for himself on matters concerning his own salvation.
> Had Archbishop Arundel scrutinized the poem again after promul-
> gating the 1409 *Constitutions,* he would surely have had to adjudge
> the poem heretical—it offended against the third, in that criticism of
> the clergy was being paraded before a mixed audience, and against the
> fourth and fifth, in that the sacrament of confession is discussed again
> outside any academic context. One must, I think, conclude that acci-
> dent alone is responsible for the absence of mention of *Piers Plowman*
> from episcopal enquiries into Lollardy.[154]

She further reflects upon this vernacular text's drift from widespread clerical and lay opinion—opinion shared during the 1370s by Oxford theologians and knights of the royal chamber—to an entirely different status within a newly defined religious culture: "The poem was written within the last period when any dispassionate discussion of its issues could have been allowed; its latest version verged dangerously close to the time when loyalties had to be declared—when issues formerly neutral became litmus tests."[155] Doyle's conclusion that the surviving manuscripts represent only a small portion of those that once existed fits the hypothesis that many copies vanished as victims of confiscation and destruction, even destruction by owners wishing to avoid punitive measures.[156] The production and ownership of copies of *Piers* during these decades when possessing far less inflammatory texts could serve as evidence on charges of heresy—and indeed possessing any book in English could be dangerous for someone already under suspicion[157]—figure as features of a larger cultural contest in which the surviving manuscripts, as well as those reckoned to be lost, reflect the destructive energies of those intellectual and spiritual struggles.

In earlier scholarly generations, nearly all work with *Piers* manuscripts was directed toward editorial ends, originally as Early English Text Society editions in service to larger national enterprises such as the *Oxford English Dictionary*.[158] These documents were conceived principally as a massive challenge to editors from Walter Skeat to Carl Schmidt who sought to retrieve Langland's work from scribal carelessness and idiosyncratic rewriting.[159] Recent scholarly initiatives encourage a wider interrogation of *Piers* manuscripts based on the proposition that medieval meaning becomes more legible in terms of medieval usage. The study of the Douce *Piers Plowman* by Kathryn Kerby-Fulton and Denise L. Despres offers a highly instructive guide for exploring and evaluating this manuscript testimony.[160] The whole project of investigating the documents from the fourteenth through the sixteenth centuries has been reconceived as a complex exercise in cultural semantics. The fact that enough manuscripts survive for *Piers Plowman*—59, including fragments and extracts[161]—to make it the third-ranking Middle English poem after *Prick of Conscience* (over 115) and the *Canterbury Tales* (82, including fragments and extracts) can no longer be construed solely as a function of aesthetic tastes detached from other cultural factors.[162] We must also reckon with the absence of evidence for Langland's poem compared with the ownership networks for the *Canterbury Tales* supplied by John M. Manly and Edith Rickert in the first volume of their monumental 1940 edition. The contrast becomes even more impressive for early copies of Gower's *Confessio Amantis*:

There is a significant early group associated with members of the Lancastrian royal family. Huntington Stafford has a coat of arms indicating that it was made for Henry, Earl of Derby, some time between 1393 and 1399, perhaps as a presentation copy; Oxford Christ Church 148 has a coat of arms associating it with Thomas, Duke of Clarence (d. 1421), Henry's second son; Bodley 294 has the autograph motto and *ex libris* inscription (after 1414) of Humphrey, Duke of Gloucester, Henry's fourth son; and there are inscriptions in Cambridge Pembroke 307 connecting it directly with Jaquette de Luxembourg, who married John, Duke of Bedford, Henry's third son, in 1433.[163]

Doyle's impression that *Piers Plowman* was not a leading article of commerce in London after the early years of the fifteenth century suggests more than simply a shift in literary tastes. This census of manuscripts indicates instead a completely altered status of this vernacular poem between the once elegant Ilchester manuscript c. 1400 and the down-market HM 114 c. 1430.[164] Partly to explain this shift, Nicholas Watson describes Arundel's *Constitutions* as "one of the most draconian pieces of censorship in English history" which caught in its wide anti-Lollard net many items of fourteenth-century vernacular theology, including Langland's audacious poem.[165]

Like the elusive identity of the poet, the notorious anonymity of the manuscripts that discouraged Doyle from pursuing a doctoral dissertation on the medieval circulation of *Piers* no longer constitutes a historical fluke or random happenstance.[166] The cautiousness of early scribes and owners needs to be distinguished from the anonymity of most other alliterative poems surviving in single copies, such as *William of Palerne* and the fragmentary *Wit and Will*.[167] In general, the evasive character of *Piers* manuscripts resembles the discretion of most Lollard manuscripts described by Hudson throughout her book *The Premature Reformation*. "Just as Lollard owners rarely wrote their names in their books," she says elsewhere, "so the producers of the books took good care to conceal their activities."[168] The hostile political environment in which these Lollard books were produced necessitated great circumspection for the sake of individuals as well as the larger clandestine community. Even quite orthodox owners took extraordinary care to avoid ecclesiastical authorities.[169] Discovery of Oldcastle's heretical books in a limner's shop in Paternoster Row led to his exposure as a Lollard in 1413,[170] and several named scriveners and parchmeners were implicated in the conspiracy as evidence of their personal commitment to Lollard book production.[171] Though we cannot always trust the accuracy of such reports, we cannot fail to register their ideological meaning: bad men owned bad books.

Since manuscripts routinely served as evidence for prosecution, we should not be surprised that these books did not contain the names of their authors and seldom included any marks of ownership until the sixteenth century.[172] In contrast with the 294 anonymous Wycliffite sermons in over thirty manuscripts, only one brief homily in a single surviving copy actually names its author. He was William Taylor, a Worcestershire man and the Lollard principal of St. Edmund Hall, Oxford, from 1405 to 1406. Taylor's imprudence in attaching his name to a Lollard text is borne out by the fact he was tried before Chichele as an obdurate and relapsed heretic and burned at the stake in 1423.[173]

Like these Lollard manuscripts, copies of *Piers Plowman* are also typically blank. They offer few headings or colophons, and they contain very few names that could have been interpreted as those of medieval owners.[174] BL Harley 6041 from around 1425 bears the arms of the Hoo family of Bedfordshire,[175] and University of London Library V.17 contains the escutcheon of Sir William Clopton, a landowner in Worcestershire. Other evidence of high-status ownership surfaces only later with Bodleian MS Digby 145 copied personally by Sir Adrian Fortescue in 1532. Other inscriptions are difficult to assess as evidence, difficult to date, and often difficult even to read. The large vertical dry-point scrawl *betoun brigge* in the upper right-hand margin of the Huntington HM 128 (fol. 149a) looks more like graffiti than a proper signature of ownership.[176] The name *Johannes Staptun* has been inserted in the National Library of Wales 733B.[177] Two pages after *Piers Plowman* in HM 143, an early sixteenth-century hand scribbled the name of a monk, *Dan Jhon redbery*. Dated to the second quarter of the fifteenth century, Cambridge CUL Ll.4.14 has what might be the signature *A nasshe* (fol. 159b) at the end of a "booke of phisonomye" in the same hand as that of the copyist of *Piers*. With dialect evidence suggesting Oxfordshire copying, Cambridge CUL Ff.5.35 preserves after the explicit what may be the ownership inscription of *Thomas Jakes* (or *Jakeson*), in all likelihood the man admitted to Lincoln's Inn in 1465.[178] Almost impossible to read even under ultraviolet, the name *William Rogger* appears twice in Oriel College MS 79 (fol. 88b), not in the manner of a book-gift but rather like the jotting of a deed-formula.[179]

Scribes named themselves in fewer than a half-dozen instances. At the end of the fourteenth century, when such openness remained relatively safe, the last page of BL MS Add. 35157 included the name *Preston* written and boxed in red as evidence of professional work carefully preserving the language of southwest Worcestershire.[180] Also from the late fourteenth century, Huntington HM 137 is similarly forthright at its conclusion: "Explicit peeres plouheman scriptum p*er* Thom Dankastre" (fol. 89b). No biography readily attaches itself to this professional scribe, however, and expert opinions differ even whether his name reads Thomas Dankastre or Thomas Lankastre.[181] From the first quarter of the fifteenth century, Oriel College MS 79 contains the notation "Nomen scriptoris Iohannes Mallyng" (fol. 88b)—with the scribal tag *Plenus Amoris,* or "full of love"—but this claim of execution, now almost invisible because of cleaning, belongs only to the two Latin verses on the same page and not the previous text of *Piers Plowman* written in a different hand.

Dating probably from the second quarter of the fifteenth century, Bodleian MS Rawlinson Poet. 137 is signed in red after the explicit by a scribe calling himself *Tilot:* "Nome*n* scriptoris . tilot," with the recurring motto "plenus amoris." BL MS Harley 3954's conflation of B+A texts preserves what appears to be the name *Herun:* "Explicit tract*atus* de perys plowman q*uaþ* her*un*."[182] Later owned and signed by John Shirley (d. 1456), Gonville and Caius College MS 669/646 contains a short extract from the C-text (16.182–201a) along with a collection of Richard Rolle texts signed by its apparent copyist, John Cok, a brother of St. Bartholomew's Hospital, London, in 1421.[183] Cok selected a noncontroversial passage from *Piers* on free will which he rendered even more orthodox-looking by placing it under the heading "nota bene de libero arbitrio secundum augustinum & ysidorum." The transition from Preston's openness in the late fourteenth century to Cok's discretion in the fifteenth century parallels the overall shift in tolerance for vernacular religious writings in Lancastrian England.

Little work has been done to trace the careers of individual English copyists aside from the exemplary 1978 study by Doyle and Parkes, followed more recently by the ambitious project of Linne Mooney.[184] Even less progress has been made at establishing biographies for these medieval bookmen.[185] Paleographers often have inherited the prejudice of editors in regarding scribes as intellectual nonentities. But one copyist has attracted close scholarly scrutiny. In their study of the unique Z-text of *Piers Plowman* in Bodley MS 851, A. G. Rigg and Charlotte Brewer focused upon the monk John Wells, who elaborately inscribed his name earlier in the book between pictures of a lion and St. Christopher—"Iste liber constat Fratri Iohanni de WELLIS Monacho Rameseye" (fol. 6b).[186] John Wells was probably the same scholar of Gloucester College, Oxford, who distinguished himself as an outspoken opponent of Wyclif at the Blackfriars Council of 1382 and won mention along with Henry Crumpe in the macaronic poem *Heu! Quanta Desolatio Angliae Praestatur.*[187] He was eulogized as the "hammer of the heretics" by the

chronicler who recorded his death in 1388. Even if the two names refer to
the same man, however, Doyle and Hanna share doubts that the handwriting
of the ownership inscription is also the handwriting of the Z-text scribe.[188]
Though perhaps copied by 1388, the booklet containing this version of *Piers*
(fols. 124a–39b) did not originally belong to the volume now containing the
signature of John Wells. Hanna provides a plausible account for the compilation assembled in its current form, at or near the Benedictine abbey of
Ramsey in Huntingdonshire northwest of Cambridge, as well as an attempt
at historicizing the dissemination of the A-text as a coterie version brought
into later circulation in areas such as the East Midlands by the prior success
of B and C versions.[189]

BL Harley MS 875 has been described as a typical early fifteenth-century
manuscript of Langland's poem, "not conspicuously the type of book written by a clerk for himself, so much as one procured from copyists with some
experience of literary styles of script and presentation, but not in the higher
grades."[190] If Doyle is correct that a scribal signature denotes an amateur or
part-time copyist more often than a commercial textwriter, the five or six
signed *Piers* copies listed above provide a significant index of these men's
personal *interests* so that we would indeed like to know more about them.
Where did they work, in Paternoster Row or at some remove from these professional establishments? What were their institutional affiliations, if any?
Were these textwriters otherwise employed in some government office such
as Chancery? To what literate communities were their book-making efforts
directed? Though other categories of information are often lacking, this last
question can sometimes be approached by considering the other works included in the same bound manuscript, the annotations added to the margins
by the original copyist and later readers, and the degree to which the scribes
edited or rewrote Langland's poem in the process of transcription.

One example of a book homemade by a clergyman for private use is the
late fourteenth-century Cambridge CUL Dd.3.13, whose old-fashioned copyist could have been an exact contemporary of the poet. Oxford Bodleian MS
Laud Misc. 656 also looks like a self-copy with manufacture that is plain, un-
ornamented, and almost ugly.[191] But copying for one's own personal use does
not mean unprofessional work. Elsewhere I have suggested that the good-
quality HM 143, with handwriting that resembles Pinkhurst's, was actually
commissioned by the corrector who supplied a running commentary in the
margins for his own personal use as part of the original copying process.[192]
In Corpus Christi MS 201 from around 1400, the primary scribe operated as
his own rubricator, emphasizing a large number of words as a running commentary on topical interests connected with Chancery clerks.[193]

Langland's poem sometimes found its way into the libraries of monasteries such as St. Augustine's, Canterbury (BL Harley 6041), and the possession of individual monks such as the fifteenth-century Don John Redbery (Huntington HM 143).[194] The massive ledger-books Cambridge CUL Dd.1.17 and Bodleian MS English Poet a.1. (Vernon), both dated around 1400, suggest by their size and double-column format that they were designed for use in religious foundations.[195] Many of the Vernon's English poems are also included in the miscellany compiled during the 1380s or 1390s by John Northwood, a Cistercian monk from the Worcester area.[196] The A-text of *Piers Plowman* is relegated to Vernon's Part IV along with works by Richard Rolle and Walter Hilton as well as pious pieces such as *The Abbey of the Holy Ghost, Ancrene Riwle,* and *Joseph of Arimathea.* This religious context reflects "the industry on the part of orthodoxy in manufacturing didactic treatises, and such industry is borne out in dozens of other vernacular manuscripts of the time."[197] If the A-text was possibly abridged late in his career by a poet hoping to sanitize its contents of theological controversy, A's appearance in Vernon would attest to the success of those ambitions.

The preliminary investigations carried out by Burrow arrived at the conclusion that *Piers* reached two audiences: "the old audience of clerks and the new one of prosperous literate laymen."[198] Middleton adjusted this view somewhat to conclude, "The clerical and lay readers of the poem formed a single audience, not two kinds, an audience interested, by virtue of social location and experience, in the foundations of Christian authority, and right relations as well as faith within the Christian community."[199] Kerby-Fulton widens this range of early readers to include a diverse group of "disenfranchised or underemployed clerks, progressive or satirically inclined clergy, legal scribes, civil servants, and unknown knightly or 'gentel' readers" as well as possibly monastic and aristocratic patrons.[200] Though these assessments are accurate as far as they go, we should remember that surviving evidence does not constitute a statistically sound sampling. Extant manuscripts may represent not a complete profile of original owners and readers but instead a skewed census of the individuals and groups, such as monks, who might have *safely* identified themselves as owners of such books. In their generally orthodox contents, the surviving copies testify to an "above ground" public that could risk the social visibility involved in copying *Piers Plowman,* collecting it in compilations with other vernacular works, and allowing it to circulate as a loan to friends and later as a bequest to heirs.

Known for his bequest of "unum librum vocatum Pers Plewman" in his 1396 will—the earliest on record—the prosperous clerical administrator and prelate Walter Brugge fits comfortably into this visible demography with his other substantial Bibles, missals, and works on canon law, as well as William of Pagula's *Oculus Sacerdotis,* a pastoral manual condemning priestly corruption.[201] Remarking upon the class-based asymmetry of judicial processes, Foucault pointed out that highly placed individuals like Brugge as well as powerful institutions like the religious community that owned the Vernon manuscript operated "in the shade," protected from the full disciplinary force of the laws that they themselves enacted and enforced.[202] The aftermath of the 1381 revolt offers ample testimony to these inequalities. Whereas John Ball, William Grindcobbe, and other lower-class rebels were executed with gruesome bodily violence, gentry participants such as Sir Roger Bacon and Sir William Coggan were granted clemency. As Dobson observed, "The poor found it more difficult than the rich to escape the inequitable workings of a corrupt and partial system of justice."[203]

As with rebels, so with readers. Following innovative Bohemian practices, Queen Anne was reported to have studied the Scriptures in the vernacular. An English tract on biblical translation attributed to John Purvey recalls how Archbishop Arundel himself praised Queen Anne at her 1394 funeral as a reader of scriptural translations after first securing his episcopal approval: "sche hadde on Engliche al the foure gospeleris with the docturis vpon hem."[204] But this famous passage appears only in an English version and not in the Latin source, Richard Ullerston's *Determination on Translation* of 1401, so that the report of Queen Anne's reading habits may have been added by a Lollard redactor in order to fabricate a royal precedent and an episcopal endorsement for the Wycliffite *Glossed Gospels.*[205] Real or fabricated, her reputation as a reader of vernacular Scriptures lent support to John Wyclif for defending English biblical translations: "For it is permitted for the noble queen of England, the sister of the emperor, to have the Gospels written in three languages, that is, in Bohemian and in German and in Latin, and it would smack of Lucifer's pride to call her a heretic!" Wyclif then appealed to patriotic pride: "And since the Germans wish in this matter reasonably to defend their own tongue, so ought the English according to this same argument to defend theirs."[206] This line of defense was joined with an appeal to ancient native practices in the Prologue to the Wycliffite Bible:

> Bede translatide þe Bible and expounide myche in Saxon, þat was Englissh eiþer comoun langage of þis lond in his tyme. And not oneli Bede but also king Alured, þat foundide Oxenford, translatide in hise laste daies þe bigynnyng of þe Sauter into Saxon, and wolde more if he hadde lyued lengere. Also Frensche men, Beemers [Bohemians] and

Britons [Welsh] han þe Bible and oþere bokis of deuocioun and of ex-
posicioun translatid in her modir langauge. Why shulden not English
men haue þe same in here modir langage?[207]

The instance of Alfred the Great as a biblical translator as well as the legendary founder of Oxford University provided another important royal precedent.

Biblical translations predated the emergence of the Lollard movement
as a major textual industry in London,[208] and later not all Wycliffite Bibles
were owned by Wycliffites. Ownership evidence indicates that other late-
medieval grandees besides Queen Anne had exempted themselves from ecclesiastical prohibitions. When inventoried at the time of his death in 1397,
the Duke of Gloucester's library contained only three English books, all of
them biblical translations.[209] Before 1412 Henry IV's son Thomas of Lancaster owned an illuminated copy of the "Early Version" of the Wycliffite
Scriptures bearing his name and motto.[210] At the time of his death, Henry IV
himself had a Bible "in Engelyssh" in the hands of the London stationer
Thomas Marleburgh, a friend of Hoccleve.[211] Henry V himself possessed an
English translation of the Bible, which he left in his will to his son. Henry VI
later donated to the London Carthusian house exactly such a large, beautifully decorated Bible with its Wycliffite Prologue.[212] Arundel's *Constitutions*
stated "that no man hereafter by his own authority translate any text of the
Scripture into English or any other tongue by way of a book libel or treaties,
and that no man read any such book, libel or treatise now lately set forth in
the time of John Wyclif." Yet none of these noblemen played by the rules because none apparently bothered to obtain permission to read these English
translations. Clearly the parameters of vernacular practices were more fractured and porous than the current view of Lancastrian containment and suppression can account for.[213]

Nor do ecclesiastical records before 1413 provide evidence that members of the gentry were often subject to investigation. The sheer number of
Wycliffite biblical translations, over 230 manuscripts including fragments,[214]
indicates the degree to which official controls were disregarded. Hence Lollard book production operated in a manner neither marginal nor opposi-
tional, instead playing a major role in the creation of an English-language
literary culture nonetheless fraught with inconsistencies and divergent motives.[215] The author of the *Longleat Sermons* actually assured his upper-class audience that there was nothing to fear from the bishops: "ʒet non of hem hath
defendit ʒou for connyn þe gospel in Englych . . . non prelat may lettin ʒou

ne dishesin ȝou for connynge ne for kepinge of þe gospel."[216] The full force
of repressive legislation, when mobilized, was borne by artisans such as John
Badby and women below the gentry rank such as Margery Baxter.[217]

John Burrow's pioneering work on Langland's audience focused attention upon the early owners Walter de Brugge, Thomas Stotevyle, Thomas
Roos, and John Wyndhill, extrapolating from this evidence to form conjec-
tures about the social and cultural meaning of Langland's poem during the
century after its composition.[218] One early London owner was perhaps more
typical of the first readership: William Palmere, rector of St. Alphage, Crip-
plegate, from 1397 till his death in 1400.[219] This is probably the same William
Palmere who had the living of Catthorpe, Leicestershire, before his move to
London in 1397. The local presence of Lollards Philip Repingdon, William
Swinderby, and the cell in St. John's Chapel where sympathizers kept a school
(*gignasium*) had made Leicestershire a notorious center for heresy well before
Archbishop Courtenay's visitation in 1389.[220] As a former resident of that region, Palmere looks suspicious because he left a will very different from those
surviving for twelve other London rectors. He described himself simply as a
clerk, he omitted any mention of the Virgin Mary for seeking his soul's re-
pose, and he specified burial in the churchyard rather than the chancel of his
church. Palmere's simple testament recalls the "Lollard will" in *Piers Plowman*,[221] and indeed the only book listed by title in his will was Langland's
poem—"librum meum vocatum peres plowman."

It is also noteworthy that the person named to receive Palmere's book
was a woman, Agnes Eggesfeld. Although *Piers* offers much that might have
attracted women readers, notably the poem's challenges to male authority
and its investment of theological authority in female figures such as Lady
Holy Church, Dame Scripture, and Dame Study,[222] research into wills extant
for the years 1393–1406 indicates that only five other women received books
as bequests, and all other cases involved the primers and psalters that one
might expect for pious female readers.[223] Only Agnes Eggesfeld came into
possession of a text that treated, in the English language, the thorny theological issues that earned such women the hostile label of "great reasoners
in scripture."[224] In his poem condemning Oldcastle's heresy, Hoccleve inveighed against women who argued over Holy Scripture since they lacked
the mental capabilities for anything more than spinning and gossiping.[225]
When laywomen such as Margery Kempe dared to discuss spiritual matters,
however orthodox, they exposed themselves to the risk of being accused
as Lollards.[226] If women were allowed to study and discuss theology, the
next step led to the radical Lollard proposition that women should be per-

mitted to perform priestly duties such as serving the altar, just as the author of *Friar Daw's Reply* viciously accuses: "your sect susteynes wommen to seie massis."[227]

Context as Criticism

Despite its considerable length, *Piers Plowman* was frequently included in larger manuscript anthologies of the kind that offer interpretive contexts suggesting how Langland's poem might have been appreciated and understood. A text bound with other texts was already subjected to some hermeneutic process. Hanna observes that Middle English works were most frequently transmitted within manuscript compilations that "directed reading experiences in ways the modern library edition must ignore."[228] Middleton has given careful consideration to the difficult, elusive, even contradictory principles detected in several of these anthologies. She concludes that they fall into the two general categories of religious instruction and historical narration.[229] A survey reveals that the most frequent companion in five collections, all of them datable to the first half of the fifteenth century, was *Mandeville's Travels*.[230] Richard Rolle's *Form of Living* follows the B-text in the Trinity MS B.15.17 and precedes an extract from the C-text in Gonville and Caius College MS 669/646.[231] A further head count tells us that the stanzaic *Pistill of Susan* accompanies *Piers* three times, the couplet romance *Ypotis* twice, all or part of Chaucer's *Troilus* twice, *The Prick of Conscience* twice, and *The Siege of Jerusalem* twice.[232]

This last work has a profile of composition and manuscript production that may parallel the reception of *Piers*. Mapped by dialect to West Yorkshire and perhaps written at the monastery of Bolton around 1380, *The Siege of Jerusalem* was being copied in London by the period 1410–25. The work's most recent editors have suggested two routes of transmission to the metropolis, one through the copyist Richard Frampton and the administrative channels of the Duchy of Lancaster, the other through Bolton Abbey's patrons, who included Sir Thomas Clifford, a chamber knight under Richard II by 1382.[233]

When assessing codicological evidence, Middleton prudently warns that all inferences from numbers are risky "since the chances that affect manuscript survival have no regard for statistical propriety."[234] This caveat must be joined again with the cautionary reminder that few substantial collections beyond Vernon and CUL Dd.1.17 represent a single scribe's thoroughgoing execution resulting in the bound artifact as it now stands. Separate fascicles may originally have belonged to other volumes, now lost. Leaves or whole gatherings of current collections may have been destroyed by age, accident, or design. Many collections bring together works produced by different scribes working at different times and in different dialects, even different languages. One generalization is worth considering, however. Whereas Chaucer's poems most commonly survive in manuscripts such as Oxford MS Bodley 638 along with English works by John Lydgate, Benedict Burgh, Thomas Hoccleve, Sir John Clanvowe, Sir Richard Roos, Robert Henryson, and Charles of Orleans, *Piers Plowman* is more likely to have been compiled with Latin works in manuscripts such as Oxford MS Bodley 851.[235] During the formation of a Lancastrian syllabus when Chaucer found his audience among respectable courtly and upper-class book owners interested in love and moral conduct, Langland's poem found instead a serious-minded readership of clerics and layfolk with theological interests.

Larger manuscript compilations suggest contests over the ideological standing of *Piers Plowman* into the fifteenth century. The physical production of booklets permitted such texts to be assembled sometimes in an anthology with discernable common themes, sometimes in a large codex for mere convenience of marketing, and sometimes as a melange self-consciously heterogenous and resistant to reductive description, much like the *Canterbury Tales* "compiled by Geffrey Chaucer." Hanna points to HM 128 as a good example of a *Piers* B-text originally meant to accompany the *Prick of Conscience* but then extended with additional quires to include *Siege of Jerusalem* and the even more distantly relevant *How the Good Wife Taught Her Daughter*. Several manuscripts of Langland's poem were similarly planned as complete books only to be joined with supplemental works that shifted the poem's meaning within its newly enlarged context.[236]

One clear attempt at domesticating and naturalizing Langland's poem can be seen in BL Cotton Vespasian B xvi.[237] Here the C-text of *Piers* from about 1400, already editorialized so that the phrase "lollares of Londone" has become "*loreles* of londene," was combined with nine diverse items by nine different scribes, most of them later than the *Piers* copy. Langland's work is preceded in this collection by a fragment of the *South English Legendary,* a poem on the death of the Duke of Suffolk (husband to Alice Chaucer), and a 152-line poem written about 1415 and described by Rossell Hope Robbins as "the sole Middle English poem dealing exclusively with the Lollards."[238] Playing throughout upon the name of Oldcastle, this poem's phraseology and even its use of alliteration—a metrical mode no longer ideologically neutral in the fifteenth century—attempts to negotiate new meaning for Langlandian idiom:

> Euery shepe þat shuld be fed in felde,
> & kepte fro wolfes in her folde,
> Hem nedeth neþer spere ne shulde,
> Ne in no castel to be withholde.
> for þer þe pasture is ful colde,
> in somer seson when hit is drie;
> & namly when þe soyle is solde,
> for lewde lust of lollardie.[239]

Even the phrase "in somer seson" can no longer stand as a mere alliterative formula after the prominence bestowed in the opening line of *Piers Plowman* in all three canonic versions. The Cotton compilation ends with a Latin account of the Holy Blood of Hailes and the indulgences associated with the shrine. Wycliffites had attacked this particular relic—"the blode of Hayles is but the blode of a dog!"—while conservatives responded with a legend describing how the miraculous blood angrily boiled over when a Lollard priest tried saying Mass there.[240]

Far less overt in its anti-Lollard condemnations, Bodleian MS Digby 102 (c. 1400–1425) brings together its imperfect copy of *Piers* C commencing in the middle of Passus 2, written continuously as prose with red-ink virgules separating the alliterative lines, together with a considerable body of pious and topical poetry written in a single hand during the reign of Henry V.[241] Many of these shorter pieces concern subjects that had become central to the period's doctrinal conflicts. Without actually naming an opponent, they acknowledge some antagonistic shadow-presence by asserting orthodox positions on issues such as tithing, transubstantiation, auricular confession, capital punishment, and the legitimacy of religious orders, each of them topics challenged by Lollards. Elsewhere in the Digby 102 poems, heresy is redefined as nothing short of atheism.[242] As clear evidence that Langland's work was read as polemic, *Piers* has been supplied with a total of 480 annotations, more than any other manuscript, one set of sidenotes dated to the copying process, a second set added during the early Tudor period, possibly before the manuscript was acquired by the Oxford scholar Sir Thomas Allen (1540–1632).[243] One fifteenth-century sidenote beside C.9.107—"The whiche aren lynatyk lollares and lepares aboute"—reads simply *lollard* as indication of a reductive interpretation of the poem's controversial contents (fol. 31b). The collection's running commentary epitomizes Middleton's view that during the first two centuries of its public life, *Piers* gradually lost its coherence as narrated action and was instead read as an ideational program framed by various *ordinationes*.[244]

Richard Maidstone's metrical paraphrase of the Seven Penitential Psalms follows Digby 102's assemblage of religious and political poems. Though more famous for his account of Richard II's 1392 entry into London, this Carmelite had participated in anti-Lollard agitation at Oxford and condemned John Aswardby's views on the mendicants as belonging to the *secta lollardum*.[245] John Bale reported that Maidstone wrote two nonextant treatises savaging the heretics, *Contra Wiclevistas* and *Contra Lolhardos*.[246] The manuscript's overall social philosophy, however, reflects populist themes strangely at odds with the authoritarianism of the Lancastrian regime. Although legal *ordinaunce* is recommended for preventing civil war, the formulations of social remedies sometimes retain a distinctly Langlandian resonance: "Thouȝ Holy Chirche shulde fawtes mende / Summe put hem of for Mede."[247] After a patriotic call for arms against France, Poem XIII enters a lengthy advisory section urging the king's reliance upon Parliament, the maintenance of law and justice, and the banishment of corruption from the court. Amid these contradictory signals, Middleton registers the collection's murky political engagements. "The poems lack what one might call the characteristic Lollard public voice and lexicon," she observes, "while sharing some of the broadly ethical and devotional concerns of men of affairs, lay and ecclesiastical, at the coming of the Lancastrians, and are more accurately described as non-Lollard than anti-Lollard."[248]

The date of the Digby 102 poems and their topical engagements are comparable to Bodleian MS Douce 95's unique copy of *The Crowned King*. Addressed to Henry V about 1415, this 144-line poem employs a dream-vision framework and clerical narrator appealing directly to the monarch. Some lines offer clear echoes of *Piers*, such as its own vision of the Fair Field Full of Folk:

> Me thought that y houed an high on a hill,
> And loked down on a dale deppest of othre.
> Ther y sawe in my sight a selcouthe peple—
> The multitude was so moche it myght not be noumbred.[249]

The poem's advice-giving is so unremarkable and meekly expressed, mostly concerned with the cost of war and the burdens of heavy taxation, that it was clearly intended to give no real offense.[250] But the fact that the nameless author imagined his poem actually reaching its intended royal audience serves as evidence how closely the Langlandian tradition lingered near the centers of Lancastrian power.

BL Harley MS 3954 from the first half of the fifteenth century offers a unique instance in which the B-text (through 5.127) is continued with the A-text (5.105 through the end of Passus 11). The scribe Herun conflated and editorialized his text throughout for an audience with an antimendicant bias, a concern for the penitential process, but less ease and comfort with Latin. Herun's *Piers* was accompanied by a series of nine pious works such as "The Merit of Hearing Mass," "The Seven Sacraments," and "Lament of the Blessed Virgin" appropriate for an East Anglian religious house.[251] This collection is headed by a copy of *Mandeville's Travels* with the same red-letter sidenotes as the Langland text but with an ambitious cycle of ninety-nine illustrations, sometimes two pictures per page. Though valued today as a fabulous travelogue, *Mandeville*'s pilgrimage itinerary and account of sacred relics had become something of a monastic text. The narrator, Sir John Mandeville, actually claimed to have been educated at St. Albans. Within this great Benedictine foundation, Thomas Walsingham was influenced by the *Travels,* and a copy was bound together with his histories before 1400. The library of St. Albans originally owned BL MS Egerton 1982, the only complete English version closest to the French original.[252] Kathleen Scott has compared the style of Harley 3954's *Mandeville* illustrations with BL Harley 2278's copy of Lydgate's *Lives of Saints Edmund and Fremund* commissioned by William Curteys, abbot of Bury St. Edmunds, for presentation to Henry VI about 1434 and probably produced in the Bury monastery.[253] This link further suggests copies of Langland's A-text were produced and circulated within a group of religious houses in a small area of South Norfolk and North Suffolk.

The subjects pictured by Harley 3954's illustrations underscore the fact that *Mandeville's Travels* mapped the world according to the shrines and relics of a pilgrimage narrative. Later in the text when the narrative moves beyond the Christian world to the Orient, the illuminations feature the sorts of marvels encountered there by European adventurers.[254] All of the work's accounts of spectacles and pictures of *mirabilia,* it should be noted, stand as a challenge to Lollard prejudices. While these early puritans were notorious for criticizing the wasteful practice of pilgrimage, they also objected to the sorts of sensational wonders central to *Mandeville's Travels.*[255] Even Langland, conservative in most respects, had endorsed the utility of "wondres" as God's summons to the faithful (B.15.482).

In addition to the B-text of *Piers* perhaps produced separately as a freestanding booklet, Newnham College MS 4 now includes a second substantial work as a postproduction addition, *The Lay Folks Mass Book.* Written by the same scribe or second copyist with an almost identical hand,[256] this religious

work figures in the tradition of English-language books such as Thoresby's
Catechism and Mirk's *Instructions* designed to bridge the gap between the Latin
liturgy and the vernacular understanding of the English laity.[257] Such books
encouraged wider comprehension of the sacraments, providing the sorts of
knowledge that permitted lay discussions of theology and eventually debate
over the priest's sacramental powers. The theological wrangling that stimu-
lated much of the *disputatio* within Langland's poem had entered the age's
popular discourses through books such as these, even though Langland de-
plored lay discussions that strayed from orthodox doctrine (B.10.103–10).
Although the *Mass Book* did not include even an English translation of the
Paternoster, it remained vulnerable to the sorts of appropriation that befell
Thoresby's *Catechism*.[258] Owning the *Mass Book* would become dangerous in
the wake of Arundel's *Constitutions*—when the Newnham College manuscript was actually copied in London—since the fifth constitution specifically banned any public or private disputes concerning sacramental doctrines.[259]

Every medieval reading of *Susannah* included contextualizing gestures
because the work never occurs outside a manuscript collection.[260] Since only
five copies survive, it is noteworthy that the stanzaic *Susannah* or *Pistill of
Susan* accompanies Langland's poem three times in these collections.[261] In
the Pierpont Morgan Library M 818, from the middle fifteenth century, the
two poems are joined with a copy of Richard Rolle's *Form of Perfect Living*.[262]
In Huntington HM 114 from the second quarter of the fifteenth century, *Susannah* and *Piers Plowman* are bound together with Chaucer's *Troilus*, *Mandeville's Travels*, and an extract from *The Three Kings of Cologne*. HM 114 places the
stanzaic poem in the central booklet that includes the Oriental matter of *Mandeville* and the *Three Kings*, all three texts sharing a common reference to
"Babylone" and the origins of "bawme." But this collection's third and final
booklet contains the *Epistola Sathanae ad Cleros*, a Lollard work that Hudson
included in her collection *English Wycliffite Writings*.[263]

The story of Susannah was made prominent in the earliest two versions
of the Wycliffite Bible as an addendum to the Book of Daniel—"Here
bigynneth a pistle of holy Sussanne"[264]—and HM 114 actually gave it the title
Susanna and Danyell. The biblical story was reworked to emphasize the heroic
stance of the title character who maintained her fortitude in the face of un-
just prosecution, much like St. Cecilia in Chaucer's Second Nun's Tale. Its account of trial and condemnation anticipates the first-person narratives that
Lollards such as Richard Wyche and William Thorpe developed into an innovative literary genre.[265] On the other hand, *Susannah* was included along

with the A-text of *Piers* in the Vernon manuscript produced for a religious institution presumably heresy-free.[266] The work appears in Vernon's Part III along with the romances *Robert of Sicily* and *The King of Tars* as well as *Prick of Conscience*. Like *Piers,* the *Prick* fell in a "gray area" as a text sometimes subject to appropriation as reformist complaint, but sometimes copied by scribes who also produced courtly manuscripts such as Lydgate's *Siege of Thebes*.[267] Yet the inclusion of *Susannah* in the related Simeon manuscript suggests some connection with the manorial circle of Lollard knights during the fourteenth century.[268] Certainly the story typified the biblicism of Lollard self-defense as episcopal investigations became more aggressive during the opening decades of the fifteenth century.

Lacking any indication of scribe or early ownership, Society of Antiquaries MS no. 687 with its copy of the A-text of *Piers* (c. 1425) perhaps comes closest to a Lollard compilation.[269] The codex's other substantial vernacular poem, *The Prick of Conscience,* represents one of four extant copies of an augmented version dubbed the "Lollard subgroup."[270] Since manuscripts of *Prick* and *Piers* shared a common profile of ownership and circulation,[271] the *Prick* had been drawn into the same contests of appropriation and ideological struggles that Langland's poem experienced. The Lollard library of Richard Colins included the *Prick* along with *Wycklyffes Wycket* around 1421, and the title appears in the list with "Wycliffes dampnable workys" used to convict Richard Hunne of heresy in 1514. Yet the southern version was examined by Winchester diocese authorities in 1473 and returned without further action to its owner, Richard Reder of Petersfield.[272] Hope Emily Allen suggested that the widespread attribution of the *Prick* to Richard Rolle, accepted even by Lydgate, was initiated by Lollard scribes in order to shield their adapted text from orthodox attacks.[273]

Anne Hudson has suggested "deliberate concealment rather than inadvertent confusion" as the motive for interspersing orthodox and nonorthodox texts.[274] Society of Antiquaries MS 687 embodies this brand of ambiguity, since this heterogeneous collection also contains a manual on confession, a treatise on the deadly sins by the anti-Lollard Carmelite Richard Lavenham, and instructions to the clergy based on authority of "our holy fader þe pope of Rome." The problem of inconsistencies in orthodox collections, no less than in Lollard books, complicates doctrinal allegiances in a number of these manuscripts. St. John's College MS G.25 contains the heretical treatises *Vae Octuplex* and *Of Mynystris in þe Chirche* in addition to portions of the English Wycliffite sermon cycle, but it also contains a translation of the orthodox *Elucidarium,* a commentary on Apocalypse, and a devout treatise on the Eucharist.[275] Bodleian Laud Misc. 286 typifies the difficulty experienced in keeping texts entirely orthodox. Its scribe lamented that Rolle's *Psalter Commentary* had been mingled with heresy by "yuel men of lollardy," but then he proceeded to copy the interpolated version with its Lollard views throughout.[276]

The Society of Antiquaries volume assembles vernacular works on suspect or condemned subjects, such as an English prose translation of the Paternoster and Creed, as well as a treatise "in lingua materna" on the Ten Commandments. Though these titles appear quite commonplace, devotional texts were sometimes proscribed on the basis of language alone. Hudson explains the prosecutorial trend: "By the time of Bishop Alnwick's investigations in 1429, knowledge even of the elements of religion, of the Creed, the Paternoster or the Ave in English constituted accepted evidence of heresy."[277] Possession of English versions of the Paternoster and Creed figured in the prosecution of Thomas and Avice Moon in 1428.[278] Commentaries on the Ten Commandments had become especially troublesome because Lollards used the prohibition against worshiping graven images as part of their assault on church statues and paintings of saints.[279] When John Claydon stood convicted as a relapsed heretic before Archbishop Chichele in 1415, his condemnation relied upon evidence that he owned an English translation of the Ten Commandments as part of the *Lanterne of Liȝt*.[280] Within this manuscript context, the ideological affinity of *Piers Plowman* was justly registered by the sixteenth-century reader who inserted this note in the Society of Antiquaries 687: "The author Robert Langland a chiefe disciple of John Wickliffs" (p. 470).

The late fourteenth-century Bodleian Laud Misc. 656 offers a comparable example of a collection both heterogeneous and heterodox.[281] Its C-text of *Piers,* without title or colophon, is followed by an English exposition on "Abraham bileued in God" which defended using the vernacular Creed in defiance of ecclesiastical statutes. This is followed by an English treatise on the Ten Commandments emphasizing "god forbedeþ man for to worschipe any manere of ymagrie made with mannes hondes" (fol. 118a). A separate copy of this treatise was executed in Cambridge Trinity MS B.14.54 by Stephen Doddesham, a monk of Sheen of presumably orthodox credentials, but a third copy survives in Westminster MS 3 connected directly with four other manuscripts containing Wycliffite writings: tracts, scriptural translations, sermon cycles, and commentaries on the Creed, the Paternoster, and the Ave. Hanna concludes with the conjecture that we "might place the composition of the codex in that central East Midland Lollard manuscript factory of which Anne Hudson keeps providing hints."[282]

Standing at the head of Laud Misc. 656 is the earliest of nine surviving copies of the *Siege of Jerusalem* used by all modern editors as the base text.[283] The work's affinities with Langland's poem in other manuscripts remain complicated. The *Siege* comes immediately after *Piers* in Huntington HM 128 in the same booklet, though in a different hand; the HM 114 copyist of *Piers* also copied the *Siege* but did so separately in the Lambeth MS 491.[284] Why this work should have been placed at the beginning of the Laud collection can only be guessed. Was it meant to mask the later, more controversial contents of the manuscript? Did it serve to dramatize the plight of a people targeted for violent reprisals because of their religious beliefs? Were the Jews in the poem intended to suggest a targeted religious minority such as the English Lollards? Originally composed during the 1370s or 1380s, not long after the notorious 1365 attack upon Alexandria in which Chaucer's Knight participated along with other English mercenaries, the *Siege of Jerusalem* aligns itself with a variety of texts designed to bolster the crusader spirit among the English aristocracy at a time when Philippe de Mézières had founded the Military Order of the Passion to restore Christian control over the Holy Land.[285] Recapturing Jerusalem had become the pious fantasy of nearly every late medieval king, and the *Siege* does nothing less than provide a foundational moment for this sort of Christian imperialism under the pretext of avenging Christ's death.[286] Always mindful of the prophecy that he would die in Jerusalem, Henry IV contributed to the construction of the English Tower in the Hospitalers' castle at Bodrum protecting travel to the Holy Land.[287] On his deathbed, Henry V declared his own ambition to rebuild the walls of Jerusalem.[288]

The most recent editors suggest that the text's "meaning" shifted in its various manuscript contexts. *Siege of Jerusalem* in BL Add. 31042 did indeed provoke specific interest in crusading poetry in the company of the Charlemagne poems *Siege of Milan* and *Roland and Otuel*. In Richard Frampton's copy, CUL Mm. 5.14, *The Siege of Jerusalem* becomes another chapter of Roman conquest out of classical history in the tradition of its sources such as Josephus's *Bellum Iudaicum*. In at least four other manuscript compilations, the work can be read as a quasi-biblical narrative continuing the New Testament's account of the conflicts between Jews and Romans.[289] As it was copied during the generation after its original composition, the *Siege of Jerusalem* becomes witness to the pervasive siege mentality fostered to regulate English society during the early fifteenth century. The massacre of the Jews could be read as divine retribution upon the unfaithful as well as the sacred mandate for Christian knighthood to follow the military example of Rome.[290] For an anti-Wycliffite audience, *Siege of Jerusalem* glorifies the enterprise of warfare for the destruction of the nation's enemies, by inference the Lollard community who espoused pacifist opinions in their *Twelve Conclusions*.[291] Also, this alliterative work from the period before 1390 cunningly anticipates the dynamic in which the orthodox majority actually needed some dissenting minority in order to consolidate and direct its scattered energies.[292] Read from this point of view, the work constitutes a thoroughly chilling justification for the deadly violence necessary to defend against the threat of heresy and, therefore, an even odder work to stand as a companion piece with *Piers Plowman*.

Langlandian Writers and Lollard Causes

An impressive number of Chaucerian works by talented successors such as Thomas Hoccleve and John Lydgate, as well as by famous historical figures such as Charles of Orleans and James I of Scotland, survive in a large number of manuscripts, many of them rich and beautiful. By contrast, only a handful of anonymous Langlandian works have come down from the late fourteenth and early fifteenth centuries, none of them particularly engaging as poetry and none of them produced by writers who took effective measures for attaching their names to their works. The "poet almost anonymous" Langland produced a tradition even more thoroughly anonymous. The namelessness of these writers has created special problems for an author-based approach to literary study, and the polemical contents of these texts have failed to attract modern audiences conditioned by Chaucer's kind of literature, which is alive with colorful characters, strong on narrative events, and fully committed to the timeless themes of love and loss. These Langlandian works nonetheless merit attention as the chance survivors of what was probably a much more extensive minority tradition, actually starting in the fourteenth century prior to the Chaucerian tradition, but later forced to share the precarious fortunes of the Lollard demimonde. Like these Wycliffite texts, many of these Langlandian works surfaced only later in the sixteenth century when they became useful for Protestant propaganda.

Not only was *Piers Plowman* the earliest English poem with a national readership during the 1380s, but Langlandian imitations of the 1390s predate Chaucerian works as the earliest influence upon a subsequent generation of vernacular writers.[293] Bruce Holsinger has proposed that the alliterative "The Choristers' Lament" dates from soon after the release of the B-text in the early 1380s and represents perhaps the earliest accretion to the literary afterlife of *Piers*. Its critique of musical extravagance also accords with Lollard attacks upon the elaborate polyphony of liturgical music.[294] If rejected as an authorial version of *Piers,* the Z-text in Bodley MS 851 becomes a stunning instance of "social authorship" in which a nameless scribe, working creatively by 1388, rewrote the poem with passages embodying such a Langland-like quality that many modern scholars have been persuaded of its authenticity, including the editor Carl Schmidt in his parallel-text edition.[295] If not from Langland's pen, the Z-text represents one of the most impressive early contributions to the anonymous *Piers Plowman* tradition as well as an extreme paradigm for the sort of scribal rewriting widespread in surviving copies.[296]

Pierce the Ploughman's Crede* has its earliest possible date determined by its reference to Walter Brut's heresy trial before Bishop Trefnant of Hereford in 1393.[297] "The dependence on Langland is extreme," George Kane notes concerning this antimendicant satire.[298] The Lollard poet drew explicitly upon the section of *Piers Plowman* in which Will encounters the Two Friars (B.8.1–61), and his text makes a bold reference to Wyclif's own campaign against the mendicants:

> Wytnesse on Wycliff, that warned hem with trewthe;
> For he in goodnesse of gost graythliche hem warned
> To wayven her wikednesse and werkes of synne.
> Whou sone this sori men seweden his soule,
> And overal lollede him with heretykes werkes![299]

The poem translated Langland's complex social landscape into the simplistic world of antifraternal tirade appealing to an audience beyond the Lollard community.[300] But if the friars had failed in their mission to provide pastoral instruction to the laity, Lollards afforded an alternative source of Christian education fostered by two victims of persecution named in this primer-like poem, Walter Brut and John Wyclif.[301] Brut's self-description as "laycus agricola cristianus" neatly aligned his identity with Piers Plowman, another farmer adept at quoting Latin to score theological points.[302]

Skeat suspected that the same author wrote the heavy-handed Lollard debate between the Griffin and the Pelican, printed in the sixteenth century as the Chaucerian *Plowman's Tale,* because the text contained a clear back-reference to *Pierce the Ploughman's Crede*—"Of freres I have told before / In a making of a Crede."[303] Skeat also found enough common phrases to suspect this second text was composed relatively soon afterwards, perhaps around 1395.[304] The prose *Jack Upland* also dates from the last decade of the fourteenth century.[305] *Richard the Redeless* followed around 1400.[306] These texts stand as solid evidence of a distinctly Langlandian tradition developing by the 1390s, during the final years of Chaucer's lifetime and more than a decade before the earliest Chaucerian writers Scogan, Hoccleve, and Lydgate.

As the sole Langlandian work extant in more than one copy, *Pierce the Ploughman's Crede* survives complete in only two sixteenth-century manuscripts as well as a black-letter edition. A single-sheet fragment of the *Crede* c. 1460–70 was also included in BL Harley 78, a collection made by the Elizabethan antiquarian John Stow.[307] The superior text in Cambridge Trinity College MS R.3.15 is considered a careful transcription of a copy dating from the fourteenth or early fifteenth century.[308] BL Royal 18.B.xvii uses the *Crede* curiously as an introduction to the C-text of *Piers Plowman* copied in the same scribal hand.[309] This manuscript was produced not much prior to the first printed edition of the *Crede* by Reyner Wolfe in 1553.[310] Publication of Wolfe's London book probably responded to the success of Crowley's edition of Langland's poem.

When Owen Rogers reprinted Crowley's edition in 1561, he combined the *Crede* in the same volume with *Piers Plowman*. Eight sidenotes in this edition serve as guideposts to the printer's chief interests: "Minorites or gray freres," "Minorites," "The augustine freres," "The ploughman," "Caym," "Wicleffe," "Walter Brute," and "The Crede." Thus Rogers bolstered Crowley's characterization of Langland as a Wycliffite sympathizer and nemesis of corrupt friars. The *Crede* remains the most explicitly Lollard contribution to the *Piers Plowman* tradition.[311] Since Whitaker's edition also printed both these works, the 1813 editor confronted the question of Langland's Wycliffism which nearly all subsequent scholars have felt obliged to address.

Somewhere in the survey of Langlandian writers must come large notice of the scribes who creatively copied their exemplars, conflated two or three authorial versions, padded the text with their own lines and passages, and engaged in collaborative writing in imitation of a poem they knew well and cared deeply about. "His scribes, much to the annoyance of modern editors, regarded his text as a living organism, which, owing to the fluidity of manuscript transmission, lay hostage to anyone's zeal for communal authorship."[312] I have already acknowledged the Z-text poet as one of the earliest and most impressive of these co-writers. The HM 114 Scribe adroitly combined his B-text with extra passages that he identified from the A and C versions, while the copyist of the Duke of Westminster's manuscript padded his A-text with passages from B and C. In seven instances copies of the unfinished A-text were shrewdly supplemented with continuation in the C version, while BL Harley 3954 offers a unique instance in which the B-text was abandoned midway through Passus 5 to be continued with the A version to the end of Passus 11. Textual scholars have been so impressed by Scribe D's Prologue for his C-text in the Ilchester manuscript that the status of these lines as authorial or scribal remains the subject of debate.[313]

In his continuation of Passus 12 of the A-text, John But shows himself one of the most knowledgeable and enterprising imitators of *Piers Plowman,* familiar with the work in its A version and perhaps its B and C versions, too. John But seemed intent upon defending his author against Imaginatyf's rebuke for wasting his time on vernacular poetry—"And þow medlest þee wiþ makynges and myʒtest go seye þe sauter" (B.12.16)—as well as the sort of hostile reader-responses recorded in the C-text *apologia* as Langland attempted countering the political fallout of 1381–82.[314] This avid continuator may have had direct contact with the poet's London coterie, with perhaps personal knowledge of Langland himself, but he was careful only to confirm the poet's first name as Will. His own name afforded camouflage verging on anonymity, since the name "John But" was as plentiful as "William Langland" was scarce.[315]

Richard the Redeless survives in only one copy, Cambridge CUL Ll.4.14, executed late in the first half of the fifteenth century probably in London. Skeat was so impressed by the text's echoes as well as the overall competence of its poetic execution that he attributed the work to Langland when including it in his 1886 two-volume edition.[316] In the Cambridge manuscript, *Richard the Redeless* is preceded by a B-text of *Piers Plowman* copied in the same Chancery hand with eight marginal notes drawing attention to the poet's remarks on friars.[317] Yoked with this more topical work written amid the high political drama of Richard II's deposition, Langland's poem underwent a contextual transformation into a polemical tract rendered even more baldly satirical with the addition of these sidenotes. Kerby-Fulton and Justice argue on the basis of precise legal and parliamentary language that the author as well as the copyist of *Richard the Redeless* was a Chancery professional.[318] In addition to these two Langlandian texts, the same scribe copied three prose treatises on arithmetic, astronomy, and physiognomy, making the CUL Ll.4.14 manuscript into a sort of schoolbook on scientific subjects and further emphasizing the intellectual character of *Piers*.[319]

The truncated text of *Richard the Redeless* was later combined by Mabel Day and Robert Steele with the incomplete *Mum and the Sothsegger* from BL Add. 41666, a manuscript dating from the third quarter of the fifteenth century but discovered only in 1928.[320] The two partial texts are now recognized as separate poems composed probably by the same Bristol writer at different times, the first concerning the troubles of Richard II in 1399, and the second, best understood as a sequel, concerning the disappointments of Henry IV's reign about 1403–6.[321] Elsewhere I have suggested that the author of these two works might have been the "Iohan But" who made his first foray into Langlandian poetry in Passus 12 of the A-text. There was a John But recorded as comptroller of customs at Bristol in 1399, the same place and date associated with the composition of *Richard the Redeless*.[322] Whereas Langland mentioned only one contemporary figure by name, the London mayor John Chichester,[323] John But inaugurated the post-Langlandian practice of making precise topical references when naming historical figures such as King Richard himself (A.12.113–15):

> First to rekne Richard, kyng of þis rewme,
> And alle lordes þat louyn him lely in herte,
> God saue hem sound by se and by land.

Also making precise name references, the author of *Richard the Redeless* described the breakdown of feudal allegiance between Richard II and his lords, who then transferred their loyalty to Henry IV:

> So sore were the sawis of bothe two sidis:
> Of Richard that regned so riche and so noble,
> That wyle he werrid be west on the wilde Yrisshe,
> Henrri was entrid on the est half,
> Whom all the londe loued in lengthe and in brede.[324]

If not penned by the same author, the John But Passus, *Richard the Redeless,* and *Mum and the Sothsegger* share the unmistakable Langlandian idiom mobilized by later successors for urging correction in governmental, judiciary, and religious practices, all based upon a strictly political reading of *Piers Plowman* that almost entirely neglected Will's urgent spiritual quest.[325]

Mum avoids doctrinal issues, especially those touching sacramental controversies, as part of an overall reticence on theological topics after the passing of *De Haeretico Comburendo* in 1401.[326] Strongly echoing *Piers* and even modeling the figure of Mum after Lady Mede, the anonymous poet also adopted Langland's meandering rhetoric as part of his own protective strategy: "This self-conscious narrative ineptitude is part of the narrator's ploy to disengage himself from responsibility for discussing political matters."[327] Yet Wycliffite sympathies surface in *Mum*'s mockery of the anti-Lollard friars hanged ("lolled") at Tyburn in 1402 for spreading rumors that Richard II was still alive.[328] Objections to Arundel's restrictions on preaching without a license, satire on the dubious value of academic learning, and a sustained antifraternal diatribe conform with Lollard polemics without posing a direct challenge to the secular authority vested in King Henry.

Also composed at the end of the fourteenth century, the prose *Jack Upland* begins where the B-text of *Piers Plowman* had left off with its vision of the Antichrist's attack upon the Christian community. Langland's allegorical Friar Flatterer has been literalized as "flateringe freris of al the fyve ordris."[329] The title character, Jack Upland, poses a series of almost seventy questions intended as a wide-ranging indictment of the mendicants. Apparently the author was a Lollard with fairly narrow concerns in his battering criticism of the friars. He offers no story and not even the sketchiest attempt at a narrative frame, and "Jack Upland" materializes only as a voice for articulating complaints. The nameless writer does not openly expose other allegiances except in his brief references to trademark Wycliffite topics such as the theology of the Eucharist and the persecution of unlicensed preachers.[330]

Though the date of *Jack Upland* has been much debated, Hudson makes a convincing case for the period 1389–96 on evidence of a series of Latin responses by William Woodford, the Franciscan apologist who devoted considerable energy to defending his religious order against Wycliffites.[331] Though influenced by the Wycliffite sermon *Vae Octuplex* dated prior to 1411, this vernacular work itself survives only in two later manuscripts. BL MS Harley 6041 dates from around 1425 and is written in the same central Midland dialect as so many other Lollard texts. Cambridge CUL Ff.6.2 from the early sixteenth century was perhaps a reliable transcription of a lost medieval exemplar close to the original.[332] *Jack Upland* was printed in John Gough's black-letter edition around 1536, of which only two copies are extant, one at the Huntington Library and the other at Caius College, Cambridge. Gough's title page actually attributed the work to Chaucer: "Jack vp Lande Compyled by the famous Geoffrey Chaucer." Yet the work offers no characteristic Chaucerian charms: "Incoherent in argument, drab and repetitive in style, it has not even the honest vigor that can often redeem the polemics of the unliterary."[333] John Bale's *Index* and John Foxe's *Actes and Monuments* ascribed authorship to Chaucer and thereby contributed to the poet's sixteenth-century reputation as a Wycliffite sympathizer.[334] Speght placed the work last in his 1602 edition of *The Works* along with "Chaucers wordes vnto his owne Scriuener" filling out the second column on the final page.[335]

Jack Upland had ended with a challenge for a rebuttal—"ʒeue Iacke an answere!"—which was first taken up by Woodford's *Responsiones ad Questiones*

LXV. The vernacular work itself had been translated into Latin so that its polemics could be carried forward in the upper levels of clerical culture. The contest then returned to the vernacular, provoking the English *Friar Daw's Reply* by a writer identified boldly as John Walsingham in the unique manuscript's colophon. If Lollards could not publish their names, anti-Lollards could. Bodleian MS Digby 41 dates from around 1420, though internal reference to the hanging of friars moves the text's composition closer to 1404.[336] *Jack Upland* had been antimendicant rather than pro-Lollard, never mentioning Wyclif or his supporters by name. But the spokesman Friar Daw Topias intensifies the tone of the debate by shrilly attacking his opponents as Lollards—"And so lyven this Lollardis in her fals fablis" (24)—and casting Wyclif as a heresiarch on a par with Mani and Arius:

> For he is callid an heretike that rasith oure bileve.
> And he is called an heretike that heresies sowith,
> As Arrians, Wyclyfanes, Sabellyanes, and other.[337]

Whereas Jack Upland had been careful not to self-identify as a Wycliffite, Friar Daw does not hesitate to hurl accusations: "Wermode, Iak, moost verreli was Wiclif your maistir!" (150). As if going back to the conclusion of *Piers Plowman,* John Walsingham works hard to counter any identification of the friars with the Antichrist. In style and rhetoric, the work continues in the Langlandian tradition of weaving biblical quotations into the fabric of its alliterative verse. Though probably written by a Dominican, *Friar Daw's Reply* represents such a scattershot defense that the work actually contributes to antimendicant propaganda by repeating standard complaints in the process of rebutting them.[338]

The unique copy of *Upland's Rejoinder* survives in the same manuscript, Digby 41. Its quasi-alliterative lines have been written out continuously as prose, in tiny handwriting, squeezed mostly into the lower and upper margins surrounding the central text. As a running response to *Friar Daw's Reply,* its precarious survival gives graphic representation of the degree to which Lollard discourses became marginalized quite literally in this manuscript. The text was begun by one writer for 393 lines—probably a holograph by the author himself—and it was continued with three interpolated passages by a second writer. Because one interpolation is very close to the general sense of *Piers* B.10.258–65, these inserted passages were apparently prompted when a second Lollard read *Friar Daw's Reply* and recalled the passage from Langland's poem.[339] This account confirms the currency of *Piers Plowman* during the middle decades of the fifteenth century and the recognition by later readers that Langland's work constituted a major source text in these polemical exchanges with the friars.

In *Upland's Rejoinder,* Jack Upland returns as an antimendicant spokesman whose verbal assault includes accusations of child theft speciously defended by the friars as recruitment:

> Bot thus to stele a childe is a gretter theft
> Than to stele an oxe, for the theft is more.
> Dawe, for thou saist ye robbe hym fro the worlde,
> Ye maken hym more worldly than ever his fadir—
> Yee, thowgh he were a plowman lyvyng trwe lyf,
> Ye robbe hym fro the trwe reule and maken hym apostata
> A begger and a sodomit, for such thai ben many.[340]

Sodomy had always been a source of intense moral anxiety among the single-sex religious orders, and the Langlandian plowman living the Lollard "trwe lyf" became a vulnerable target. Early in their institutional history, the mendicants themselves had energetically mobilized this anxiety in order to incite middle-class supporters to persecute homosexuals in Europe's growing urban centers.[341] In the later medieval period, however, this activist homophobia returned to haunt the mendicants themselves.[342] Wyclif had accused the friars of sodomy in works such as *De Antichristo,* and the *Twelve Conclusions* criticized clerical celibacy and the allied misogynist bias as the causes of homosexuality: "þe lawe of continence annexyd to presthod, þat in preiudys of wimmen was first ordeynid, inducith sodomie in al holy chirche."[343]

Here the Lollard writer of *Upland's Rejoinder* has preempted the commonplace linkage of sodomy and heresy by hurling this accusation back upon the friars themselves.[344] As a former Augustinian friar who embraced the Wycliffite cause, Peter Pateshull created a great commotion in London in 1387 when, backed by a hundred Lollard supporters, he preached a sermon accusing his former religious brothers of sodomy and later nailed his accusations to the door of St. Paul's.[345] A few years later, in 1394, the London transvestite prostitute John Rykener, under arrest in front of the mayor and aldermen in Guildhall, confirmed these suspicions in what Dinshaw describes as "a nightmare of the Lollard imagination" by confessing that his sexual clientele routinely included Franciscans and Carmelites.[346]

A great gap of time separates the 1390s composition of *Pierce the Ploughman's Crede* and *Jack Upland* from their sixteenth-century copies and printings.

There were a few reformist voices crying in the wilderness, literally in the case of the blind poet John Audelay confined to an abbey near Shrewsbury. Audelay's references to *Mede þe maydyn* draw attention to another early fifteenth-century reader of Langland in the West Midlands.[347] Though he had served as chaplain to Lord Lestrange, who searched for Lollards in Shropshire during 1414, Audelay in his retirement around 1426 composed his boldly Langlandian *Marcol and Solomon* with numerous citations from *Piers*. Audelay's fool-figure criticizes ecclesiastical wealth and clerical corruption in explicitly Lollard vocabulary, while the poet admits that such criticisms courted accusation of heresy and burning at the stake.[348]

Therefore it is easy to understand why, except for rarities such as James Yonge's version of the *Secreta Secretorum* (1422) and the middle fifteenth-century *De Veritate et Consciencia* identified as a continuation of the search for Truth in *Piers Plowman*,[349] the Langlandian tradition was overawed and over-shadowed by the prodigious productions of the Chaucerian tradition. This general profile of textual survival suggests that the minority literary tradition shared the same shadow-existence as the minority religious tradition. Anne Hudson's historical view no longer conceives of Lollardy as a reformist project that declined substantially after the 1430s, going almost extinct in the second half of the fifteenth century, only to arise from its cold ashes as Lutheranism during the reigns of Henry VIII and Edward VI.[350] Steven Justice puts it this way: "English Lollardy never died and never joined the mainstream: the mainstream joined it."[351]

Lollardy successfully went underground, then, surviving as a secretive sect during the decades when the greater political threat to the nation came from what McFarlane memorably described as "the broken sequence of battles, murders, executions, and armed clashes between neighbors which we have chosen to miscall the Wars of the Roses."[352] Thomas Bourgchier held office long enough as archbishop of Canterbury during the period 1454–86 to establish his reputation as a persecutor of Lollards, for example, but his long involvement with Lancastrian and Yorkist politics diverted his energies from much active prosecution of heretics.[353] Christopher Hill speaks directly to the special problems in studying the continuities of dissenting beliefs and practices: "A successful underground leaves no traces."[354] Andrew Hope's work has supplied some missing chapters from the Yorkist period and observed that fine-quality Wycliffite Bibles, when they reappeared in the sixteenth century, tended to resurface in the same gentry families.[355] The mapping of actual manuscript production, however, tends to confirm Hudson's larger historical account. The statistical profile for the production of Lollard texts parallels the tracking of *Piers* manuscripts with a drop in actual production after middle fifteenth century, then a resurgence in the early sixteenth century—including the aristocratic production of Sir Adrian and Lady Anne Fortescue—in a process of reinstating Langland's work that culminated in Crowley's edition.[356]

Like manuscripts of the minority religious culture, copies of *Piers Plowman* would have been subjected to the active campaigns of the book-burners as well as the precautions of owners who sometimes destroyed volumes that they feared could prove incriminating. Almost as fatal were the efforts by owners to hide their books in walls, under floorboards, and in holes in the ground.[357] In his *Autobiography,* Benjamin Franklin included an illustrative episode from his own family history:

> They had an English Bible, and to conceal it and place it in safety, it was fastened open with tapes under and within the cover of a joint stool. When my great-grandfather wished to read it to his family, he placed the joint stool on his knees and then turned over the leaves under the tapes. One of the children stood at the door to give notice if he saw the apparitor coming, who was an officer of the spiritual court. In that case the stool was turned down again upon its feet, when the Bible remained concealed under it as before.[358]

One wonders if efforts at concealment led to the fate of the *Piers* C-text fragment (c. 1400) found under old floorboards in a Suffolk vicarage by John Holloway of Queens' College, Cambridge. The place of discovery suggests a clerical owner in the fifteenth or early sixteenth century.[359] The general page-format and ornamental economy of this vellum bifolium resembles important early copies such as Huntington HM 143. Though its dialect is Worcestershire close to Langland's own, it also approximates the language of Scribe D who copied the Ilchester manuscript of *Piers* in London. Taken together, the text's Worcesterisms, the manuscript's London manufacture, and its later Suffolk ownership tell much about the early mobility of Langland's poem.

Complete Langlandian texts that surfaced during the Reformation as handwritten copies and black-letter editions probably constitute only a small portion of the renegade writings produced as part of this minority culture throughout the fifteenth century. Three cases may be signal. The late fourteenth-century *Jack Upland* was still available to be printed by John Gough about 1536. The work entitled *The Praier and complaynte of the ploweman vnto Christe* claims to be a venerable text written "not longe after the yere of oure Lorde A thousande and thre hundred."[360] More likely composed between 1400 and 1440, *The Praier and complaynte* survives in no version earlier than the 1531 Antwerp edition printed by Martin de Keyser.[361] As a third instance, the antimendicant *Plowman's Tale,* partly composed around 1400, was copied in an early sixteenth-century manuscript, now University of Texas Austin MS 8,[362] and was then printed about 1536 "cum priuilegio" by Thomas Godfray. The Huntington Library now owns the only known copy of this black-letter *Plowman's Tale*.[363] Though the first leaf of this sole-surviving copy is missing, a brief snippet of dialogue between the Host and the Plowman indicates that the work had already been supplied with a prologue and adapted for inclusion in Chaucer's collection:

> "Say on," quod our Host, "I the beseche."
> "Syr I am redy at our byddyng.
> I pray you that no man me reproche
> Whyle that I am my tale tellyng."

Thus endeth the prologue / and here foloweth the fyrst parte of this present worke.

Francis Thynne reported that including the *Plowman's Tale* in his father's 1542 edition, with its complete 52-line prologue intact, caused controversy at the highest levels of the royal court.[364] When finally inserted in this second edition of the *Canterbury Tales,* the Lollard poem won sudden prominence and earned a long-lived posterity, indeed fashioning Chaucer's character as a Wycliffite writer for John Foxe, John Dryden, and a host of later literary historians.[365]

It is worth pausing to consider how all our notions of literary traditions, reconstituted as they are from surviving documents, favor those institutions most successful at manufacturing documents with a superior chance for survival. The potency of Robertsonian exegetics, for example, relied entirely upon the sturdiness of the vellum preserving the patristic and later clerical commentaries used by these historicist critics at Princeton, Cornell, and elsewhere to reconstruct interpretive contexts for medieval writings. Texts on the losing side in a social contest, certainly poetry linked with heretical conspiracies within the national community, ran a far greater risk of vanishing entirely. Some works such as *Richard the Redeless* survive as fragments in single copies. Most works such as *Piers Plowman* itself appear without indication of authorship. Even when these texts survive and surface, they invariably lack a contextual documentation as full and informative as Chaucer's *Canterbury Tales.*

When we have the author's name, we have the basis for reconstructing biography, patronage, social relations, and original audience, as well as a sense of human selfhood and lived existence. In 1925 Caroline Spurgeon's *Five Hundred Years of Chaucerian Criticism and Allusion* required three volumes to contain all the materials unearthed before the beginning of the twentieth century. A companion volume entitled *Five Hundred Years of Langlandian Criticism and Allusion* could have fitted into a very slender pamphlet.[366] The first book-length study, Jusserand's *"Piers Plowman": A Contribution to the History of English Mysticism* (1894), was chiefly concerned with illustrating the interests of the commons in Parliament during the later fourteenth century and therefore encouraged the scholarly practice of treating the poem as an archive for historical information, not quite literature.[367]

If *Pierce the Ploughman's Crede* and *Upland's Rejoinder* are indicative of an almost lost literature, the Chaucer tradition underwent progressive redefinition usefully understood in terms of its antagonistic relations with this fifteenth-century Langland tradition. Comparison of the two manuscript archives further testifies to Langland's historical priority. While as many as twenty manuscripts of *Piers Plowman* can be dated paleographically to the fourteenth century,[368] not one copy of Chaucer's works, with the possible exception of Adam Pinkhurst's copy-jobs, can be confidently dated prior to the poet's death in 1400 when he left the *Canterbury Tales* unpublished as well as unfinished.[369] The manufacture of high-quality copies of the *Tales* as well as *Troilus* began during the first two decades of the fifteenth century as part of a campaign mounted under the auspices of Thomas Chaucer and various Lancastrian supporters of Prince Henry, the future Henry V.[370] Their efforts figured in a wide-ranging textual project launched partly in opposition to Lollard book-production along with the continuing cultural presence of *Piers Plowman*.

If Greenblatt is correct that institutional authority seeks to maintain itself by identifying a hostile adversary—even inventing one, as churchmen exaggerated Lollardy's threat to justify surveillance and persecution[371]—these early fifteenth-century Chaucer manuscripts are not free-standing artifacts innocent of outside political influences. While Greenblatt has been criticized for manufacturing the Dark Otherness on behalf of his dominant Tudor-Stuart state,[372] the subversive claims upon Langland's poem can be witnessed from 1381 onward, predating all external evidence of Lancastrian promotion of Chaucer as their official National Poet. Established on the basis of manuscript transmissions and poetic imitations, a virtual antagonistic relationship emerges between the two literary traditions. The minority

Langland tradition lent itself to dissident efforts at contesting prevailing beliefs and practices, while the official Chaucer tradition was strategically constructed by key members of the Lancastrian regime, prompted by ecclesiasts such as Archbishop Arundel and aided by the religious orders such as the Benedictines, to contain these subversive gestures and to persist in these efforts as the very condition of exercising power, even when the armed threat was effectively neutralized by the defeat of Sir John Oldcastle.[373]

Formation of an official Lancastrian canon of the authors Chaucer, Gower, and Lydgate can be newly conceived within this historical field defined by the campaigns against heretical books *and* the sponsorship of orthodox courtly writers. Within this energetic Lancastrian environment, the anonymous Langlandian tradition became more narrowly understood as a medium of minority complaint and antifraternal invective. The escalating fierceness of this debate can be illustrated by comparing *Jack Upland* first with the tempered scholastic tone of William Woodford's Latin *Responsiones* before 1396, then with the English-language hysterics of *Friar Daw's Reply* not later than 1404:

> But sith that wickide worme—Wiclyf be his name—
> Began to sowe the seed of cisme in the erthe,
> Sorowe and shendship hath awaked wyde,
> In lordship and prelacie hath growe þe lasse grace.[374]

For Lollards and their sympathizers, these Langlandian writings served as textual support, truly preaching to the converted, typical of most Wycliffite discourses written during the first half of the fifteenth century. But for Lancastrian adherents in the laity and clergy, these texts incited division throughout the realm—"cisme in þe erþe," as Friar Daw complained—and therefore figured in an ongoing threat to the twin orthodoxies of "lordship and prelacie," the state and the Church.

CHAPTER FIVE

Political Corrections

The Canterbury Tales

MOST LITERARY STUDIES EXAMINE WHAT AN AUTHOR WROTE. THIS chapter examines what Geoffrey Chaucer did not write. I pay special attention to the General Prologue's pilgrims who were slighted or omitted entirely in the later frame-narrative, notably the Plowman, as evidence of the poet's increasingly cautious engagements with the unmentioned and unmentionable presence of *Piers Plowman*. There is hardly a controversial topic in Langland's work that cannot be located somewhere in the *Canterbury Tales,* including overt references to Lollard heresy in the Man of Law's Endlink, but Chaucer clearly tried through various evasions, even self-censorship, to render his own work exempt from the turbulent reception that *Piers Plowman* had attracted and retained.

Though Chaucer left his *Canterbury Tales* in a state far from finished, modern critics have embraced the idea of a work "unfinished but complete."[1] The assumption of completion was necessary to enable discussions of its organic unity and its fulfillment of an authorial design. Yet the fact remains that the work falls drastically short of the 120 tales projected in the General Prologue (*CT,* I, 790–95). Chaucer wrote only twenty-four installments, including the Cook's Tale as a fragment perhaps intended for cancellation[2] and three other narratives interrupted by other pilgrims: the Monk's Tale, Chaucer's Tale of Sir Thopas, and the Squire's Tale. Of the thirty pilgrims introduced in the General Prologue, seven of them are never given any tales at all: the Plowman, the Knight's Yeoman, and the Five Guildsmen. "What the evidence of the manuscripts demands that we recognize," Pearsall has concluded, "is that the *Canterbury Tales* are unfinished—never released or even prepared for publication, and with the stages of revision and recomposition manifest in the surviving manuscripts."[3]

Since Chaucer introduced the Canon's Yeoman as a taleteller not numbered among the original pilgrims gathered at the Tabard Inn, constraints of time and the grim exigencies of mortality cannot fully explain his failure to assign tales to the seven "orphan" pilgrims—or explain the truncation of the Cook's Tale—or even explain the failure of the pilgrims to reach their destination at the shrine of St. Thomas in Canterbury Cathedral. The insertion of the Canon's Yeoman's Tale renders these absences as matters of willful neglect subject to interpretation as authorial intentions. The disruption caused by the unexpected entry of a new taleteller draws attention to Chaucer's decision to omit other pilgrims, rendering them silent, allowing them to slip into partial invisibility, but thereby making their narrative voices available for later appropriation or continued neglect.

This chapter suggests that these omissions are explicable as responses to a variety of pressures felt by the author within the immediate social environment in which he worked—London in the 1390s. More than any of his previous writings, the *Tales* stayed alert to the most controversial issues in the time frame of their composition *and* in later moments of revision, rearrangement, and recomposition. During the decade of 1389–99 when Chaucer worked upon the *Tales,* he engaged in various acts of self-censorship, or more precisely *partial* self-censorship. He canceled portions of his text including perhaps five provocative passages from the Wife of Bath's Prologue,[4] but he allowed these materials such as the Man of Law's Endlink to remain available somewhere in his working papers. He suspended writing on some pieces such as the Cook's Tale, but he allowed this fragment to survive as a challenge to future speculation. He abandoned seven pilgrims in the General Prologue as potential taletellers, but he did not replace them, instead sending them forth as agents provocateurs to instigate later literary responses. And he failed to complete the pilgrimage and bring his company to their destination at the shrine of St. Thomas Becket, but he never changed the General Prologue's announced intentions for the frame-narrative. Although the *Canterbury Tales* with its satires upon corrupt religious practices and the venial clergy might not have signed the poet's death warrant,[5] especially if this project was a closet undertaking, Chaucer was a political survivor clearly intent upon passing these survival skills along to his literary works.

The activities of Chaucer's earliest scribes and successors constitute an important archive of testimony for gauging these reader responses.[6] They provide a diachronic commentary upon the political challenges to which the textual assemblage was subjected when it began to circulate, assume a public life, and become worldly during the first decades after the author's death. Chaucer had left the social logic of the text rigorously undetermined amid the fragments transmitted to his literary executors and the first generations of copyists. The *Canterbury Tales* stands as a supreme example of a literary work given a whole host of semantic inflections within local circumstances of human relations, shifting systems of material production, and networks of cultural agency deployed and redeployed over the next century.[7] The reactions of the early fifteenth-century scribes and continuators, whether they sustained Chaucer's omissions or mended these gaps with supplementary materials, can be explored as attempts at rendering these versions of the *Canterbury Tales* more "politically correct."

In addition to the author's own changes of intention, the fifteenth-century compilers who undertook the business of arranging and copying the unconnected fragments of the *Canterbury Tales* provide a variety of interpretations in their reactions to Chaucer's omissions. We see these texts through sedimented layers of previous interpretations and through the reading habits and categories developed by interpretive traditions.[8] The Knight's Yeoman and the Five Guildsmen were allowed to remain voiceless and slip further into obscurity.[9] The Cook's Tale was supplemented with a variety of spurious conclusions. While twenty-five manuscripts replaced the unfinished tale with the astonishingly un-Chaucerian *Tale of Gamelyn,* the writer of the Oxford MS Bodley 686 staged an even more daring intervention into the tale of Perkyn Revelour by composing a Langlandian survey of London's underworld complete with alliterative language and type-figures reminiscent of Kitte and Calote:

> With Magot and with Mylsent, whan that he mette,
> The bagge with the powder anon was unknette.
> His purs was inperfit, he couthe not welle kepe:
> "Yet let us be mery, while oure sire is aslepe!"
> With pyes and with pykrels, with wynes most swete,
> With loche and with lamprey the childe myght not ete,
> The tapster, the taverner, the koke was nedy,
> Wolde clepe on Perkyn, for his purs was so redy.[10]

This is a signal moment when the very contours of Chaucerian versification are fundamentally altered by a writer succumbing to the powerful influence of Langland's kind of poetry.

Over the course of the next century and a half, other writers and scribal editors would demonstrate their own responses to the Langlandian shadow-presence. The Plowman was provided with two apocryphal tales responsive to the continuing influence of *Piers Plowman*. And there were two attempts at bringing the pilgrims to Canterbury and then setting them back on the road again toward London, Lydgate's Prologue to *The Siege of Thebes* and the anonymous *Canterbury Interlude and Tale of Beryn,* as indicators that the one-way design of the pilgrimage narrative was found somehow unsettling and unacceptable.

Chaucer's own principles of exclusion responded to the immediate field of competing social energies during the period when he worked on the *Canterbury Tales*. The act of writing meant grounding his poem in the world, and Chaucer's own rewritings, whether they took the form of revising, copying, replacing, deleting, or generally anticipating posthumous publication— perhaps by prearrangement with his longtime scribe Adam Pinkhurst— meant grounding the poem in a political landscape that was rapidly shifting. Topics that seemed open to mockery in 1390 became too sensitive as the decade proceeded and the political scene grew increasingly unstable. Intolerance of the Wycliffites escalated during the crisis of 1395 when the *Twelve Conclusions of the Lollards* were posted on the door of Parliament and St. Paul's as some kind of a publicity stunt, more to attack the clergy than arouse the knights and gentry to actual reform, and the king himself returned from Ireland partly due to alarm over the possibility of a second English Rising.[11]

Ideological pressures further contributed to shaping the principles of inclusion and augmentation guiding Chaucer's earliest scribal editors. Political anxieties led to the rushed enactment of *De Heretico Comburendo* in 1401, and the insecurities of the Lancastrian regime persisted even after the stunning royal victory at Agincourt in 1415.[12] Clearly the textual environment of the early decades of the fifteenth century had drastically changed from what it had been about 1390. Specifically, readers became far less tolerant of the social satire that motivated Chaucer's finest work, and they became much more suspicious, even overtly hostile, toward precisely those topics that inspired his most ingenious lampoons.

If current critical practices have rendered interpretation of an author's intentions highly problematic, the prospect of investigating Chaucer's intentions for *not* writing may seem altogether quixotic. Because the unsaid and the barely said can constitute evidence, these absences deserve fuller notice than has been granted for several scholarly generations. The founders of modern Chaucerian studies such as Skeat, Root, Manly, Baugh, and Brown readily speculated about the poet's creative processes, and they were quick to detect evidence of his uncertainties, first shots, makeshift changes, and flagging inspiration.[13] By contrast, New Criticism asked readers to operate on the assumption that a text produced by a literary genius was perfectly executed for the purposes of intensive analysis. Such a text was immune to suspicion of any faltering inspiration on the writer's part, as well as any openness to outside influences, even the biographical and the political. This assumption concerning the stability of the text, even a work-in-progress such as the *Canterbury Tales,* has proved more durable than the New Critical methodology that required it.[14]

These ruptures in the *Tales* contribute to the text's self-declaration within the literary system deployed according to the author's own rules. The General Prologue promised tales from all thirty pilgrims, but Chaucer did not deliver on this promise. Accordingly, my own formulation of *Chaucer the author* ventriloquizes a set of intentions concerning omissions and deletions in the intervening fragments. Key to my interpretation of these strategic silences is the text's duplicity when stubbornly resisting its own narrative assumptions and expectations. Any one of my guesses might be countered with equally convincing accounts, including the longstanding confidence that these gaps would have been mended if only Chaucer had lived long enough to do so. My narrow focus upon specific social pressures to account for these silences proceeds with self-consciousness over the limitations of any historicist explanation. These discussions remain steadily mindful of what Paul Strohm has described as "a considerable receptivity to multiple reference, undecideability, and, especially, the constant instability of relations between what frames and what is framed."[15]

Yet these suppressions are far more consciously intended, I believe, than the repressions that Strohm has located in the textual unconscious. Again, the surprise entry of the Canon's Yeoman with stories about alchemy indicates an authorial decision to omit taletellers originally introduced in the General Prologue and to leave dangling the Cook's Tale, the one narrative that shows no signs of being halted by the Host or other pilgrim. Disregard for the pilgrimage-narrative itself can be interpreted as a signal omission. My overall argument remains suggestive, I hope, in exposing a larger field of the poet's social anxieties and in crediting these anxieties with various evasions during later stages of composing the *Canterbury Tales*. Though Chaucer made the gesture to renounce any objectionable writings in his Retractions, he made no effort to expunge all incriminating evidence from the textual property left to be assembled after his death. He asks people to forgive the shortcomings of his writings, not to burn his papers.

Awareness of social wrangling formed the very ground of Chaucer's creativity and afforded the tensions making possible the dangerous "jokes" that so steadily energize the textual center of his *Tales*. Though we lack the drafts and revisions from Chaucer's workroom, the documentary afterlife of his literary productions has provided ample evidence for his ongoing negotiation between the wildly controversial and the politically correct.

The Cook

The Cook is the one pilgrim clearly identified as a London resident. The General Prologue introduces him as an expert on "Londoun ale" (*CT,* I, 382), and later he is described precisely as "the Cook of Londoun" (*CT,* I, 4325). His Tale makes specific references to Cheapside and Newgate. Because named Roger of Ware after a town in Hertfordshire (*CT,* I, 4336), he was apparently one of those immigrants from the country so typical of the period.[16] He came to London and entered a profession that granted him a civic identity largely superseding his provincial origins.[17]

The unfinished state of the Cook's Tale resulted from the unsettling contents of his tale, not from the unsavory character of the pilgrim. Howard suggested some form of censorship: "Possibly Chaucer or someone else suppressed it, ripped it out of an early copy leaving only what was on the same folio with the ending of the Reeve's Tale."[18] As the first scribe to attempt organizing the fragments of Chaucer's *Tales* in Hengwrt, Adam Pinkhurst left space to add the missing portion of the fabliau, hoping that the stray pages would turn up amid the confusion of the author's working papers. But when no additional sections were delivered, the professional textwriter simply made a note in the margin: "Of this Cokes tale maked Chaucer na moore."[19]

Later copyists continued to struggle with this awkward gap.[20] The incomplete state of the Cook's Tale created a textual rupture between the brilliant series of "quytings" in Fragment I and the isolated sturdiness of the Man of Law's Tale in Fragment II. In ten manuscripts, the problem was remedied by simply dropping the Cook's Tale in order to avoid the appearance of a break. The conscientious scribe of Bodleian Rawlinson Poet. 141 (c. 1425–50) patched together this six-line conclusion with its grim finality:

And had a wyf that hined for a contynaune
A shoppe and swyued for hur sustenaunce
And thus with horedom and bryberye
Togeder thei used till thei honged hye.
For who so evel byeth shal make a sory sale;
And thus I make an ende of my tale.[21]

The landmark manuscripts Corpus Christi 198 and Harley 7334, followed by twenty-three later collections, remedied the problem by adding the 902-line *Tale of Gamelyn* as a continuation. This rustic romance was sometimes connected to the end of the authentic Cook's Tale by a brief bridge passage such as the couplet in BL Royal 18.C.ii: "But here-of I will passe as now / And of yong Gamelyne I wil telle yow."

First printed by John Urry in his Chaucer edition of 1721 and then again as a spurious piece by Skeat in 1884, *Gamelyn* has been largely ignored except for Neil Daniel in his fine doctoral dissertation of 1967.[22] Written in old alexandrine couplets, the romance is thought to have been composed at some time around the middle of the fourteenth century, though no source has been discovered. Even more to the point, no copy of *Gamelyn* survives outside the *Canterbury Tales*. Since the tale occupies the same placement in all but one of the twenty-five manuscripts, Chaucer himself most likely fixed its position at the beginning of the tradition of transmission.[23] And since textual analysis strongly suggests that all copies derive from a single archetype not among the surviving copies, the exemplar was quite possibly discovered among the poet's working papers and made to stand at the head of the tradition for the *Canterbury Tales* as a whole. The rhyme words indicate a text originally composed in northern dialect, but rewritten by a Londoner with some Kentish forms,[24] so the archetype for all later copies may have been one hand-copied by Chaucer himself.

At least two questions have never been given adequate attention. How did this unique copy of *Gamelyn* establish its regular inclusion following the Cook's Tale? And how did *Gamelyn* find such ready acceptance by the early organizers of Corpus Christi 198 and Harley 7334? I have long been inclined to Skeat's suggestion that the unique copy of *Gamelyn* was inserted into the working papers of the *Canterbury Tales* by Chaucer himself in the position immediately following the Cook's fragment.[25] After deciding to discontinue the story of Perkyn Revelour, the poet began to consider a replacement by doing what he always did when planning new work. He searched out a source text. Perhaps in the middle 1390s, Chaucer obtained a copy of *Gamelyn* and decided to use it for a replacement tale. He inserted this quire in his working papers immediately following the Cook's Tale, between Fragments I and II, but he never returned to compose a new tale based on this source. Why not? Perhaps time ran out and Chaucer died before the new tale could be written. Perhaps the rustic Englishness of the romance finally proved uncongenial to a poet who preferred Continental sources. Or perhaps a narrative of an outlaw hiding in the greenwood proved just as problematic as the tale of a criminal apprentice.

An increased threat of outlaws figured in the growing discontent throughout England in the 1390s. The kingdom seemed beset by a crime wave, real or exaggerated, and Richard II was criticized for his inability to remedy the situation. When Jean Froissart returned to England for a visit in 1395, for example, he was shocked how the criminal menace had drastically increased since his prior residency during the 1360s. According to the *Chronicles,* honest men no longer felt safe and no longer expected justice when wronged.[26] While traveling as Clerk of the King's Works in 1390, Chaucer himself was robbed on three separate occasions.[27]

With an uncurbed outbreak of crime later in the decade and a breakdown in the effectiveness of the judicial system, *Gamelyn*'s sympathetic view of outlawry might have proved a miscalculation. Its disrespect for the rule of law would account for Chaucer's neglect of the work as a replacement for the unfinished Cook's Tale. Civil peace under Henry IV and Henry V improved, probably because the outlaws were absorbed back into the army when the wars with France were renewed,[28] and *Gamelyn* could then find a more comfortable placement in the *Canterbury* collection. Since Gamelyn's struggles concerned the right of a son to claim his inheritance, the story also resonated with a Lancastrian public whose kings justified possession of the throne by claiming that Henry IV, as the new Duke of Lancaster in 1399, had been denied his own rights of inheritance by Richard II.[29]

In a unique attempt at remedying the awkwardness of an incomplete narrative, Oxford Bodley 686 (c. 1420–40) padded out the Cook's Tale with thirty-three supplemental lines and a new twelve-line conclusion.[30] Critics have long suspected that Chaucer abandoned the story of Perkyn Revelour because its sexual contents were too indecent, and this continuation confirms some early squeamishness over Chaucer's original. The last authentic line describes how Perkyn's companion had a wife who kept "a shoppe, and swyved for hir sustenance" (*CT,* I, 4422)—that is, she used her shop as a front for prostitution. Bodley 686 altered this ending to read: "A wife he hadde that helde her contenaunce / A schoppe, and *ever sche pleyed* for *his* sustenaunce" (85–86). Like her criminal husband, the prostitute threatened civic controls by practicing the flesh trade in a covert, unregulated manner.[31] More than sexual issues, pervasive anxiety over social threats may have prompted Chaucer to abandon this tale, specifically the threat of unruly apprentices in late fourteenth-century London.

Employed by the Five Guildsmen who belonged to various nonvictualing crafts, the Cook offers a tale about a master "of a craft of vitailliers" (*CT,* I, 4366) who becomes the butt of his rambunctious apprentice. While the long-standing antagonism between victualers and nonvictualers would have appealed to the prejudices of the Cook's employers, the misconduct of Perkyn Revelour threatened the apprenticeship system upon which *all* guilds depended. Though they provided a source of cheap labor, apprentices also constituted the next generation of masters guaranteeing the future success of the craft itself.[32] A guild's patriarchal structure was benevolent as well as disciplinary. Chaucer's grandfather Robert assumed the family name apparently out of filial esteem for his own master, the London mercer John le Chaucer.[33]

Sylvia Thrupp described a system fully responsive to the dynamics of patriarchal rewards and obligations as part of a larger civic role: "The merchant controlled his staff of apprentices and servants by the help of some of the overtones that were to be found in the ideas of lordship and paternity. A man's authority over his apprentices was always semipaternal in nature."[34] An apprentice was forbidden from gambling, visiting taverns, and consorting with women.[35] Contemptuous of authority, Perkyn ran the gamut of misconduct prohibited in the standard contracts of indenture. He was so expert at dice that no other apprentice in London was more skillful (*CT,* I, 4384–86), he preferred to spend his time in taverns rather than in the shop (*CT,* I, 4376), and he chased after women of low repute (*CT,* I, 4372–73).

One of the worst offenses that an apprentice could commit was stealing from his master. Not the victim of subtle pilfering, Perkyn's Master frequently found himself cleaned out completely (*CT,* I, 4390). The Master's long-suffering patience and final leniency are extraordinary. In historical instances involving embezzlement in fourteenth-century London, the guilty apprentice was stripped, beaten bloody in the guild's hall, and then further humiliated with expulsion from the craft.[36] In the Cook's account, the Master endured this in-house robbery for many years before deciding to punish the apprentice by giving him "acquitance" from his contract of service.[37] Perkyn greeted this expulsion more like a welcome release from unwanted restraints. He cast his lot with a companion of his own kind and with the companion's prostitute wife. There the narrative breaks off.

The Cook's Tale halts so prematurely that few scholars have hazarded guessing how Chaucer might have proceeded. Earl Lyon's contribution to

Sources and Analogues of Chaucer's Canterbury Tales worked hard to find plausible analogues.[38] One tale from Robert Greene's *The Blacke Bookes Messenger* suggests how the Master could be drawn back into the story as a continuing character. Since the Master had initiated the plot by sacking Perkyn, the narrative logic required the discharged apprentice to seek his revenge. Like the two preceding fabliaux of the Miller and the Reeve, patriarchal authority would be subverted and the older man would be tricked, cheated, and humiliated.[39]

Whatever its details, such a story would have been told at the expense of a guild master and would have become a provocation to the Cook's employers, the Five Guildsmen. The sense of professional solidarity that motivated the Reeve would have required a firm response from the offended craft members, and Fragment I would have shifted into the arena of London guild controversies. As David Wallace has noted, the great anxiety in the Cook's Tale is generated by Perkyn's efforts to gather a *meynee* or company of similar scoundrels (*CT*, I, 4381).[40] Radically departing from Chaucer's style of language and storytelling, the anonymous versifier of Bodley 686 expanded this statement with lines owing their vehemence as well as alliteration and personification to Langland's complaints over urban corruption (19–23):

> With Rech-never and Recheles this lessoun he lerys
> With Waste and with Wranglere, his owne pley-ferys,
> With Lyght-honde and with Likorouse-mowth, with Unschamfast;
> With Drynke-more and with Drawe-abak, her thryst is y-past,
> With Malaperte and with Mysseavysed—*such meyny they hight.*

The formation of a *meyny* or gang would have touched a deep nerve for any London readership as the threat of secret confederacies continued fueling fear in the wake of the English Rising of 1381. A mayoral proclamation of 1383 criminalized these secret associations.[41] The lurking insecurity finally emerged in the petitions to the Cambridge Parliament of 1388 that targeted every form of civic association, including craft guilds. The early 1390s became a time of maneuvering when crafts as well as parish guilds dissociated themselves from fringe *covens.*[42]

The conclusion of the padded-out Bodley 686 imposes its own severe judgments on Perkyn and his companion (85–98):

> A wife he hadde that helde her contenaunce
> A schoppe, and ever sche pleyed for his sustenaunce.

What thorowe hymselfe and his felawe that sought,
Unto a myschefe bothe they were broght.
The tone y-dampned to presoun perpetually,
The tother to deth for he couthe not of clergye.

While the one gang member is jailed, the other is executed because he had neglected to learn to read and could not claim benefit of clergy.[43] Their namelessness becomes a marker of their outcast status as condemned men. The concluding apostrophe to "yonge men" reasserts the benefits of faithful adherence to guild rules as the surest road to prosperity:

And therfore, yonge men, lerne while ye may
That with mony dyvers thoghtes beth prycked al the day.
Remembre you what myschefe cometh of mysgovernaunce.
Thus mowe ye lerne worschep and come to substaunce.
Thenke how grace and governaunce hath broght hem a boune,
Many pore mannys sonn, chefe state of the towne.
Ever rewle the after the beste man of name,
And God may grace the to come to the same.
HERE ENDETH THE COKES TALE[44]

From good reputation comes financial advancement, and from submission to authority comes the reward of professional success. Even a poor man's son can achieve the highest reward of guild participation by attaining "chefe state of the towne," a success attained by the legendary Dick Whittington. The strikingly Langlandian style of these alliterative lines, with their personifications of Reckless, Waste, Light-Hand and so forth, gives further indication of the rhetorical resources that Chaucer had resisted. *Piers Plowman* had already claimed London's corrupt underworld as its privileged subject matter, and the fate of Langland's poem, permanently embroiled in these civic controversies, warned Chaucer away from a literary terrain off-limits to a poet aiming higher for his posterity.

The Plowman

The Plowman and his brother the Parson are usually recognized as the two pilgrims who come closest to representing the ideals of their estates.[45] In addition to his strict regard for the traditional duties of a parish priest, the Parson has a puritanical streak evidenced by his revulsion at the Host's swearing (*CT,* II, 1163–90).[46] Harry Bailey responds by accusing the Parson of being a Lollard (*CT,* II, 1172–77):

> Oure Host answerde, "O Jankin, be ye there?
> I smelle a Lollere in the wynd," quod he.
> "Now! goode men," quod our Hoste, "herkeneth me;
> Abydeth, for Goddes digne passioun,
> For we schal han a predicacioun;
> This Lollere heer wil prechen us somwhat."

The accusation sounds like a humorous jab rather than a savage attack, even though Knighton had listed objection to swearing oaths as a standard Lollard view by 1388.[47] The Parson's presence among the pilgrims traveling to the shrine of St. Thomas at Canterbury and his orthodox treatise on penance have long been taken as proof-positive that he could not have been a radical religious dissenter. In addition to their objections to auricular confession, true Lollards fiercely criticized the abuses of pilgrimage and specifically the wasteful offerings to Becket's relics.[48] More likely Chaucer's Parson belonged to a sizable population of conservative clerics with austere sensibilities and strong commitments to lay instruction.[49] Yet as the term *lollare* evolved during the 1380s, the Parson's pastoral conduct as a priest who "Cristes gospel trewely wolde preche" but "first he folwed it hymselve" (*CT,* I, 481, 528) perfectly matched the emergent Lollard model described in *Epistola Sathanae ad Cleros*: "ony man will teache þe gospell to oþer men and lyue þeraftur hymself."[50]

Strohm has proposed that the climate of opinion concerning Lollardy remained a "fractured field" throughout the 1380s and 1390s, ending with a jolt only in 1401 with the burning of the heretic William Sawtry.[51] There is evidence to suggest that the jolt came earlier for those closest to the royal court. Prompted by the *Twelve Conclusions,* Roger Dymmok's *Liber contra XII errores et hereses Lollardorum* addressed itself directly to Richard II, and one of these heretical conclusions concerned pilgrimage and the veneration of images: "Pilgrimage, preyeris and offringis made to blynde rodys and to deue ymages of tre and of ston ben ner of kin to ydolatrie."[52] When William Thorpe was questioned before Archbishop Arundel on a variety of religious topics, the savvy Lollard knew exactly how to make a distinction between true and false pilgrims:

I clepe hem trewe pilgrymes trauelynge toward þe blis of heuene whiche, in þe staat, degree or ordre þat God clepiþ hem to, bisien hem feiþfulli for to occupie alle her wittis, bodili and goostli, to knowe treweli and to kepe feiþfulli þe heestis of God, hatynge euere and fleynge alle þe seuene dedli synnes and euery braunche of hem.[53]

Though the Parson's Tale as a treatise on the sacrament of penance seems entirely orthodox[54]—and his contempt for alliterative "rum ram ruf" sets him at odd with Langlandian language—the Parson's Prologue comes perilously close to echoing these Lollard views by dismissing the physical journey of pilgrimage (*CT*, X, 48–51):

> And Jhesu, for his grace, wit me sende
> To shewe yow the wey, in this viage,
> Of thilke parfit glorious pilgrymage
> That highte Jerusalem celestial.

Langland himself had substituted plowing the Half Acre for pilgrimage, and John Ball did much the same, more sinisterly, in his 1381 broadside. So after 1395 the Host's name-calling of "Lollere," prompted by the Parson's puritanism and devotion to preaching, had ceased to be a laughing matter. The Shipman's ensuing reference to sowing "cokkel in our clene corn" also became a standard image for sowing heresy (*CT*, II, 1183).[55] Chaucer caught the decade's political drift and apparently decided to cancel the Man of Law's Endlink. The passage is missing in Hengwrt and Ellesmere as well as in forty-seven later copies of the *Tales*.[56] But obviously the poet left this passage somewhere in his drafts or working papers because it was picked up in Corpus Christi 198 and Harley 7334.

While this passage chiding the Parson as a Lollard was subjected to self-censorship, the Plowman endured a different kind of backlash. His earnest livelihood, combining honest labor and Christian charity, set an ideal example for opposing the money-grubbing farm workers who abandoned their manorial duties to seek cash payments as migrant wage-laborers.[57] Chaucer's contemporaries rarely offered such a positive image of peasant laborers. John Gower's *Mirour de l'Omme* (c. 1374–78) complained about lazy day-workers who exploited the manpower shortage to demand triple wages.[58] Written in the wake of the English Rising when the rebels had demanded the right freely to negotiate wage-labor contracts,[59] Gower's *Vox Clamantis* lashed out even more savagely against day-laborers, castigating them as sluggish, scarce, uncontrollable, and grasping.[60]

The Cambridge Parliament of 1388 led to a renewal of statutes seeking to control the work force, its movements, and its wages, so much so that nearly two-thirds of the statutes spoke directly to labor issues. Thomas Wimbledon's 1388 sermon *Redde Racionem* addressed the proper operation of society's three estates, including farm laborers.[61] Elsewhere I have argued that even *Pearl,* a poem that seems so innocent of political wrangling, incorporated the Parable of the Laborers for the dual purposes of emphasizing the subservience of agricultural workers and affirming the rewards of faithful Christian works.[62]

The spiritual aspect of the Plowman's activities recalls the great literary embodiment of Christian labor in fourteenth-century England. Nevill Coghill long ago pointed out that even the phrases in Chaucer's description of the Plowman echoed those of *Piers Plowman.* The line "He wolde thresshe, and therto dyke and delve" (*CT,* I, 536) recalls the lines "I dyked and I dolue, I do þat he hoteþ; / Som tyme I sowe and som tyme I þresshe" (*Piers* B.5.545–46).[63] Gower also echoes this phrase in a passage condemning Lollard clerics by contrasting them with right-believing laborers:

> Of Scisme, causeth forto bringe
> This newe Secte of Lollardie,
> And also many an heresie
> Among the clerkes in hemselve.
> It were betre *dike and delve*
> And stonde upon the ryhte feith,
> Than knowe al that the bible seith
> And erre as some clerkes do.[64]

Piers Plowman had relentlessly attacked agricultural "wastours" and "lollares" while praising those workers, particularly the poem's title character, who remained faithful to their masters.[65] Even at the very end of his career, Langland's satirical self-portrait in the C-text (5.1–104) relied almost point for point upon the Statute of Laborers enacted by the Cambridge Parliament of 1388.[66]

Andrew Cole's work has brought greater clarity to these issues, but our understanding of the exact relationship between Langland's poem and the early history of Lollardy remains frustrated by a lack of fuller documentation for the early phase of the reform movement.[67] But as the alarm over radical change was felt more urgently after 1381–82, texts such as *Piers Plowman* became tainted with guilt by association. Appropriation of the name "Peres

Ploughman" as a code word in John Ball's letters had already cast a shadow over Langland's poem, especially after Ball was placed on record confessing to be a disciple of John Wyclif, whose errors were condemned at the Blackfriars Council.[68] "Had Archbishop Arundel read the poem around 1396, he would surely have regarded it as dangerous," Hudson has remarked, "dangerous because its thrust is so blatantly hostile to the institutional church, because it advocated disendowment, and because it implied that the individual Christian should think and judge for himself on matters concerning his own salvation."[69] These perils of controversial contents and public notoriety had attached themselves to the plowman figure by the time that Chaucer wrote the General Prologue, and he countered the ideological challenge by transforming Langland's awesome title character into a nameless pilgrim, blandly positive, silent in his initial presentation, and invisible thereafter in the frame-narrative.

The Plowman shares the Parson's innocence as a non-Lollard by reason of his presence on a pilgrimage as well as his eagerness to pay tithes (*CT,* I, 539–40), an obligation that had become another recurrent source of complaint from Lollards.[70] Yet despite these finer distinctions, religious strife had become sufficiently heated by the later 1390s to account for Chaucer's decision to deprive the Plowman of a tale *and* to exclude him from any subsequent appearance in the roadside drama. The pilgrim remains exactly as Lee Patterson describes him: "the psychologically opaque and socially quiescent Plowman, whose portrait assiduously effaces the very real economic struggles of Chaucer's contemporary world, struggles that were in other texts expressed precisely by means of the figure of the plowman."[71]

The ideological energies released by Langland's poem continued to flow in and around Chaucer's Plowman, however, with the result that two very different apocryphal tales were attached to this pilgrim.[72] The Lollard *Complaint of the Ploughman* may have been written around the year 1400 but appeared as the Chaucerian *Plowman's Tale* only when printed in Thomas Godfray's black-letter edition about 1532–36. This spurious tale was then incorporated into William Thynne's second edition of the *Works* in 1542, where it displaced the Retraction to follow the Parson's Tale and cap the collection as a whole.[73] This piece of Reformation propaganda was clearly designed to advance claims for Chaucer as an early literary champion of Wycliffism. Based on his reading of the *Plowman's Tale,* John Foxe concluded that Chaucer "seemeth to be a right Wicklevian, or else there was never any."[74] The mere presence of the Plowman in the General Prologue represented a lingering challenge to some later readers, an opportunity to others.

One fifteenth-century editor of the *Canterbury Tales* responded by giving this mute pilgrim a tale unimpeachable in its orthodox pieties. The complete text of this *Ploughman's Tale* exists only in Christ Church Oxford MS 152 (c. 1450–70), written on pages left blank after the unfinished Squire's Tale and just before the Second Nun's Tale.[75] Apparently the primary scribe had hoped that the missing Part III of the Squire's Oriental romance would turn up. But when time passed and no conclusion was found, Thomas Hoccleve's *Miracle of the Virgin* was provided with a linking prologue and inserted in the sequence of tales. Hoccleve's eighteen-stanza poem, entitled *Item de Beata Virgine* in the autograph Huntington HM 744, had been originally written for Thomas Marleburgh, the London stationer and warden of the guild of Limners and Textwriters in 1423.[76] Since Hoccleve and Marleburgh represent the bookmen directly involved in the production of high-quality manuscripts of Chaucer's works during the early fifteenth century[77]—and Hoccleve's *Regiment* made a point of advertising Chaucer's devout orthodoxy—his own *Miracle of the Virgin* served admirably for supplementing the *Tales* where the voice of unimpeachable orthodoxy was needed.[78]

What makes *The Ploughman's Tale* anti-Lollard? As a writer, Hoccleve showed himself a steady opponent of Lollardy throughout his writings, most famously in his attack on Sir John Oldcastle.[79] This particular narrative praises the devotion of a monk, whereas Lollards expressed opposition to the private religion of monks as well as canons, friars, and even courtly clerics.[80] The tale recounts a miracle of the Virgin, whereas the Lollards criticized the cult of saints and voiced skepticism concerning any miracle as the basis for Christian belief.[81] The tale's praise of virginity, both Mary's and the young monk's, ran counter to Lollard claims that Christ did not privilege the virgin life but instead gave his blessing to the married life, even for clergymen.[82] The exemplum dramatizes how the monk earned promotion to abbot for saying his Paternoster in Latin, whereas Lollards asserted that prayers ought to be recited in English and addressed directly to God, without the sort of mediation performed here by the Virgin Mary.[83] In sum, the anonymous interpolation of *The Ploughman's Tale* foreclosed the possibility of inserting some other narrative related to the Plowman's worldly estate, certainly no narrative further associating him with the notorious title character of Langland's poem. Instead, the anonymous editor of the Christ Church manuscript saddled the Plowman with a pious religious tale incorporating traditional practices and orthodox values, enforcing a clear distinction between Chaucer's Plowman and Langland's.

As one minor instance of "political correction," I want to draw attention to a brief two-stanza poem attributed to Chaucer in John Shirley's collection

BL Add. 16165 and given the modern title *The Plowman's Song*. The first stanza reads as follows:

> Of alle þe crafftes oute blessed be þe ploughe,
> So mury it is to holde to byhinde:
> For whanne þe share is shoven inn depe ynoghe,
> And þe onlere kerveþe in his kuynde
> Þe tydee soyle þat doþe þe lande vnbynde,
> Ageyns þe hil "Tpruk in, tpruk out" I calle,
> For of my ploughe þe best stott is balle.[84]

Langland had developed the figure of plowing toward sublime spiritual meanings, but this versifier has converted the imagery into a thinly veiled euphemism for sexual intercourse—"whanne þe share is shoven inn depe ynoghe"—and his obscene language has been described as nothing more than "elevated bathroom graffiti."[85] Of course Chaucer in his Miller's Tale was perfectly capable of using the *kultour* or plow-blade as a phallic implement meant for Alison's backside but hitting Nicholas's *toute* instead. Furnivall suspected the ballade might be Chaucer's when he published it in 1871. Hammond accepted it as authentic while Brusendorff rejected it. Robinson's *Poetical Works of Chaucer* authoritatively excluded it from the canon on the basis of "tone and subject" and even banished it from the limbo of "Doubtful Poems."[86] But Shirley's readiness to accept this poem among Chaucer's shorter works provides one more instance in which Langland's distinctive subject matter was challenged during the fifteenth century. Though remote from the orthodox piety of the Christ Church *Ploughman's Tale* and the reformist zeal of the sixteenth-century *Plowman's Tale,* this smutty doggerel enacts one of the central functions of the Chaucerian tradition by confronting, countering, and devaluing the powerful symbolism of the plowman figure that elsewhere had the potential to radicalize the Langlandian tradition.

Pilgrimage Narrative: *Canterbury Interlude*

Because public texts open themselves to a multitude of material processes, brilliant performances of the literary imagination such as Chaucer's, even when not deliberately poised for appropriation, become subject to effacement as well as revision through the operations of outside agency.[87] During the first three decades of the fifteenth century, efforts at disseminating Chaucer's fragmentary *Canterbury Tales* aimed at producing books as quality objects for high-status ownership. Yet practical concern for marketability cannot be isolated as the sole motivation for giving his work a more finished look. The incoherence of the Chaucer's frame-narrative invited the imposition of a variety of interpretations, most notably two major efforts at supplementation around 1420: Lydgate's Prologue to *The Siege of Thebes* and the *Canterbury Interlude and Tale of Beryn* in the Northumberland manuscript. In each of these continuations, the pilgrims are shown completing their visit to Canterbury Cathedral before setting off again toward London, continuing their tale-telling during the homeward phase of the journey.

These later efforts to write what Chaucer had left unwritten become legible as interventions of an interpretive nature. Both continuations can be read in terms of strategies of containment designed to impose ideological views on specific topics that had generated intense controversy in the opening decades of the fifteenth century. By situating these two poetic projects in their precise historical environments, I want to investigate how these cultural energies steadily informed their narrative and thematic contents. Each continuation attempts to determine the meaning of the *Canterbury Tales* as the foundational classic of a newly formed vernacular tradition, as well as the political identity of Chaucer as the author whose work had been singled out for this national enterprise.

Chaucer's authentic frame-narrative had proceeded fitfully after the audacious, richly informative beginning in the General Prologue. There was the expansiveness of the Wife of Bath's Prologue, but there were also the minimalist gestures for the Squire and Prioress, and no prologues at all for the Physician and Shipman. What completely disappears in the prologue + tale format is something that hardly existed in the first place, namely, the story of the pilgrimage itself. Readers seldom appreciate how unexpectedly the Canterbury pilgrimage is announced after the famous opening lines and how obliquely the destination at the shrine of St. Thomas Becket is described: "to Caunterbury they wende, / The hooly blisful martir for to seke" (*CT,* I, 16–17). The saint's name is not mentioned here and occurs only three times in the entire work, only in casual oaths.[88] The relics of Becket's shrine are almost exclusively encrypted in the poet's most wicked lampoons.[89] Even more significantly, the pilgrims never arrive at their destination in Canterbury, getting no closer than the outskirts of a village mentioned in the vaguest terms as the "thropes ende" in the Parson's Prologue (X, 12).

For the generation of Chaucer's readers schooled in New Criticism, the incompleteness of the pilgrimage narrative presented an urgent challenge for reconstituting the author's final intentions in order to formulate a sense of the work's organic wholeness. E. Talbot Donaldson suggested the simplest solution: "The pilgrimage seems no longer to have Canterbury as its destination but rather, I suspect, the Celestial City of which the Parson speaks."[90] Ralph Baldwin's *The Unity of the Canterbury Tales* (1955) exerted tremendous influence with its thesis that the Parson's metaphorical concept of pilgrimage imposed a retroactive structure upon the entire collection.[91] The poet intended—and could *only* have intended—a one-way journey from Southwark to Canterbury. This view breathed new life into the consensus of the nineteenth-century Chaucer Society that Ellesmere's ordering of the fragments could be conveniently repaired by the Bradshaw Shift aligning the geographical references for a one-way journey to Canterbury.[92] D. W. Robertson's *Preface to Chaucer* (1962) imposed this pre-emptive construction upon the entire collection: "Any pilgrimage during the Middle Ages, whether it was made on the knees in a labyrinth set in a cathedral floor, or, more strenuously, to the Holy Land, was ideally a figure for the pilgrimage of the Christian soul through the world's wilderness toward the celestial Jerusalem."[93] Donald Howard elaborated this view in the most impressive volume of Chaucer criticism published in the 1970s,[94] and V. A. Kolve's *Chaucer and the Imagery of Narrative* reformulated the notion for the 1980s when he proposed a parabolic movement away from a literal journey toward a spiritual highway at the poem's close.[95] For the 1990s, Lee Patterson deconstructs the literality of pilgrimage as a unidirectional pattern without challenging the Ellesmere order so strongly implying this sense of linear purpose.[96]

The Parson's concept of pilgrimage as a spiritual redirection to the celestial Jerusalem relied upon theological authorities such as St. Augustine, and its literary currency derived from vernacular texts such as Guillaume de Deguileville's *Le Pèlerinage de la vie humaine*.[97] But less critical attention has been paid to the heated controversies surrounding the actual practice of pilgrimage during the late fourteenth and early fifteenth centuries, especially pilgrimages to the shrine of St. Thomas at Canterbury.[98] Far from universally accepted, the practices were condemned as a waste of money as well as the occasion for drunkenness and lechery, and these condemnations became fiercely voiced by the lay and clerical dissidents increasingly identified as Lollards. Although John Wyclif concerned himself less with pilgrimage than with the veneration of images, even defending the saintly status of Becket, his followers soon harshened their rhetoric and made St. Thomas their principal target for popular abuses in England.[99]

The boundary between orthodoxy and heresy remained ambiguous during the last two decades of the fourteenth century when much common

ground persisted between acceptable and condemned forms of devotion.[100]
Rejection of the physical pilgrimage in favor of a metaphorical concept had
already found literary expression in *Piers Plowman,* which predates the emergence of more radical forms of Wycliffism, but it became a standard topic in
the catalogue of Lollard beliefs precisely during the period when Chaucer
was writing his *Tales* in the 1390s. Likely composed at the end of the fourteenth century, *Sixteen Points on Which the Bishops Accuse Lollards* surveyed the
questions routinely asked of suspected heretics. The following response
would have amounted to self-incrimination:

> Also we graunten þat it is leueful and medeful to go on pilgrimage to
> heuenwarde, doing werkes of penance, werkis of riȝtfulnes and werkis
> of mercy, and to suche pilgrimage alle men ben boundoun after þer
> power wile þei lyuen here.[101]

The *Twelve Conclusions of the Lollards* rejected pilgrimage more pointedly as the
occasion for idolatry, concluding with a swipe at Becket's status as an authentic martyr.[102] Since Dymmok addressed his response *Liber contra XII errores et
hereses Lollardorum* directly to Richard II, ideological work at the highest
official levels was clearly undertaken during the mid-1390s.

The campaign for branding reformists as heretics meant isolating and
condemning many widely held attitudes, including these complaints against
pilgrimage abuses. Though Dymmok's reply deals mostly with venerating
saints and making offerings to sacred images, he cites various scriptural examples that support pilgrimage by drawing upon the same practical benefit
singled out by Chaucer: healing the sick.[103] There is one important difference.
Whereas Dymmok claims that pilgrims received miraculous cures by visiting
the relics of a saint, Chaucer's pilgrims traveled to Canterbury to render
thanks for recoveries already effected at home by prior intercession of the
martyr: "That hem hath holpen whan that they were seeke" (I, 18). Lydgate's
Prologue to *Thebes* also avoided controversy by stating that he visited the
Canterbury shrine to give thanks for health already restored: "The holy seynt
pleynly to visite / Aftere sikness, my vow to aquyte."[104]

Archbishop Arundel alleged that William Thorpe had been preaching
his Lollard heresies for more than twenty years prior to his 1407 examination, that is, during the same period when Chaucer was working on his
Tales.[105] Because Thorpe's extended comments on the misconduct of contemporary pilgrims have often been cited as commentary on Chaucer's fictional pilgrims, his remarks are worth quoting at length:

Also, sire, I knowe wel þat whanne dyuerse men and wymmen wolen
goen þus aftir her owne willis and fyndingis out on pilgrimageyngis,
þei wolen ordeyne biforehonde to haue wiþ hem boþe men and wymmen þat kunnen wel synge rowtinge songis, and also summe of þese
pilgrimes wolen haue wiþ hem beggepipis so þat in eche toun þat þei
comen þoruȝ, what wiþ noyse of her syngynge, and wiþ þe soun of
her pipinge, and wiþ þe gingelynge of her Cantirbirie bellis, and wiþ
þe berkynge out of dogges aftir hem, þese maken more noyse þan if
þe king came þere awey wiþ his clarioneris and manye oþer mynys-
trals. And if þese men and wymmen ben a moneþe oute in her pilgrymage, manye of hem an half ȝeere aftir schulen be greete iangelers,
tale tellers and lyeris.[106]

Here we find complaints against the Miller's bagpiping, the singing of the
Summoner and the Pardoner, the jingling bells on the Monk's bridle, and
particularly the reputation of pilgrims as great tellers of made-up tales. What
cannot be omitted from critical evaluation is the fact that these complaints,
which Chaucer assimilated from some broad stratum of popular disapproval,
became linked in the 1390s with the repertory of Lollard invectives by religious writers such as Roger Dymmok.

Concerning Chaucer's sympathies amid these religious controversies,
sixteenth-century readers were prejudiced by the Lollard tract adapted as *The
Plowman's Tale* in Thynne's 1542 edition of the *Canterbury Tales* and retained by
John Stow in his edition of 1561.[107] Together with the puritanical sentiments
of the Parson, this attribution meant that Reformation readers associated
Chaucer with the teachings of Wyclif and the proto-Protestant doctrines of
his followers.[108] Members of the nineteenth-century Chaucer Society found
this view congenial to their notion of a right-thinking poet ahead of his
times as a proponent of religious reform.[109] But when searching the decades
immediately after the poet's death for evidence of the earliest reader-
responses, one is struck by the degree to which his writings were *not* implicated in investigations of Lollardy. The most famous episode is probably
the least typical, when a copy of the *Canterbury Tales* was produced for prose-
cuting a case of heresy against John Baron in 1464.[110]

In his *Regiment of Princes,* Hoccleve set the example by rendering Chaucer as a staunchly orthodox writer. These strategies of containment become
particularly telling when Hoccleve's scribal colleagues attempted mending
and completing the pilgrimage narrative. The longest and most dramatically
rich continuation of Chaucer's *Tales* remains the 732-line *Canterbury Interlude*

otherwise known as the Prologue to *The Tale of Beryn*. The text is commonly thought to belong to the period around 1420, although it survives uniquely in Northumberland MS 455 dated c. 1450–70.[111] Like Lydgate's Prologue to the *Siege of Thebes,* the *Canterbury Interlude* serves as evidence that the generations of readers following Chaucer's death did not instinctively view the *Tales* as "unfinished but complete," nor did they assume that the pilgrimage narrative necessarily generated a one-way design.

The escalating controversy over pilgrimages constitutes an important component in the textual environment when considering whether the Parson speaks only for himself as he allegorized the pilgrimage as a one-way journey toward the Celestial Jerusalem. Charles Owen long upheld the views of Root and Manly that the poet intended some tales for the homeward journey.[112] The fact that no early manuscript of the *Tales* correctly arranged the fragments in an order aligning the geographical references to create a one-way trip suggests that no medieval readers actually enforced the formalist determinism proposed by Baldwin. My own article "Alternative Ideas of the *Canterbury Tales*" (1985) used Lydgate's *Thebes* and the Northumberland's *Canterbury Interlude* as evidence to argue that these two fifteenth-century responses endorsed the poet's original announcement of a round-trip for the collection as a whole. My own prior investigation neglected to consider how this narrative realism might have served specific ideological ends.

The ninth item in Arundel's *Constitutions* of 1409 defended pilgrimage and the veneration of relics in considerable detail: "It shall be commonly taught and preached that the cross and image of the crucifix and other images of saints, in honor of them whom they represent, are to be worshiped with procession, bowing of knees, offering of frankincense, kissing, oblations, lighting of candles, and pilgrimages."[113] Like Lydgate's Prologue to the *Siege of Thebes,* the *Canterbury Interlude* brings Chaucer's pilgrims to their destination in the cathedral, allowing them the completion of the sacred rite *and* the continuation of their profane lives. The anonymous poet negotiates the delicate operation of reviving some of Chaucer's satirical themes while neutralizing the more contentious features. The pilgrims arrive in Canterbury, they visit the cathedral, they venerate the shrine of St. Thomas, and they make their donations to his relics.[114] The fifteenth-century continuator invested such expert knowledge in describing these local practices that Peter Brown has proposed that the *Beryn* Poet may have been one of the Benedictine monks actually charged with custody of the shrine.[115] Whoever actually executed this missing link in the larger narrative, he scrupulously maintained the literality of the pilgrimage without allowing it to rocket upward into some spiritual metaphor.

As a highly individual attempt at editorial reorganization, the Northumberland manuscript itself resisted the concept of a one-way journey by arranging the fragments to provide tales for the homeward trip. After the turnaround episode of the *Interlude* itself, there come the Merchant's *Tale of Beryn* (his second tale), the concluding episode of the Summoner's Tale, Chaucer's Melibee (his second tale), the Monk's Tale, the Nun's Priest's Tale, the Manciple's Tale, and the Parson's Tale.[116] Because the manuscript has lost leaves at the end, we cannot know whether the anonymous writer also provided a conclusion that would have brought the pilgrims back to the Tabard Inn for the announcement of the Host's verdict followed by a lively banquet. I think not. The writer probably concentrated his modest talents upon the real ideological business of the continuation, and this project meant fulfilling the intention for the pilgrims to visit Canterbury's shrine of St. Thomas. The poet's enterprise has therefore done more than reshape the roadside drama.[117] The Northumberland manuscript reinstated the round-trip pattern of pilgrimage, which was actually practiced by orthodox but fallible Christians in fifteenth-century England, as the dominant narrative structure in order to block the metaphor of a one-way spiritual journey increasingly associated with Lollards.

Finally, the continuator's concern for the literal enactment of pilgrimage accounts for the stylistic register of the *Canterbury Interlude* where the tone and contents are "distinctly uncourtly."[118] By contrast, Lydgate directed his *Thebes* Prologue to a noble audience, and the high-quality Arundel 119 manuscript boasts the arms of the Duke of Suffolk as indication that the work found this aristocratic audience even if the original patron, Henry V, had died before the work was completed. The nondeluxe Northumberland manuscript, like so many copies from the later fifteenth century, reflects the *Canterbury Interlude*'s lower social aim.[119] If I am correct in my sense that this continuation partly engages in an ideological enterprise, the writer felt no need to pursue this work at the level of courtly address. Although Wycliffism had found some sympathizers in the household of Richard II, the reform movement rapidly lost its social cachet during the first decade of the fifteenth century, and the heresy was largely extinct as an aristocratic phenomenon after Oldcastle's rebellion. Supported by gentry patronage in some scattered communities, Lollards were concentrated in the large middle stratum of English society, the stratum occupied by the unfortunate John Baron whose copy of the *Canterbury Tales* served as evidence of heresy in 1464.[120] Deeply invested in mercantile financial values,[121] the *Beryn* Poet directed his continuation to this bourgeois sector of Chaucer's widening national audience as a defense of the Canterbury pilgrimage as a legitimate religious practice.

The Pardoner

The *Canterbury Interlude* provides more action than the whole of Chaucer's own frame-narrative. So engaging are the voices and personalities in the original *Tales* that we seldom notice how few events actually occur within this dramatic frame. The Knight draws the first lot, the Pardoner and the Host kiss, the drunken Cook falls off his horse, and the unnamed narrator calculates the time of day by measuring his shadow. The *Interlude*'s scenes in which the Knight and Squire inspect the city's fortification while the Wife of Bath rests in the inn's herb garden with the Prioress, for example, are crosscut with episodes of the Pardoner's fabliau misadventure with the tapster Kit.[122] As a tactic for distracting attention from the actual veneration of Becket's relics, this bustling activity becomes a cunning substitution for moral complexity and class-bound strife.

Glending Olson has detected a strain of social conservatism in the *Canterbury Interlude* that "mutes or at least dampens some of the most ebullient and anti-authoritarian Canterbury voices."[123] Since the pilgrims as a group have been largely silenced as agents of challenge, contest, and confrontation, the Pardoner becomes the principal figure for rewriting Chaucer's most disturbing and subversive personalities. The *Beryn* Poet has recast the Pardoner so that he entirely lacks the qualities that attracted so much attention in the original *Tales*. He no longer has a high-pitched voice or a prissy concern for fashion. He is no longer beardless with long blond hair. In short, he no longer arouses suspicion as a eunuch or homosexual.[124] If the Pardoner is effeminate, he is effeminate in the strictly medieval sense of a man who seeks the company of women.[125] Whereas Lydgate confuses the figures of the Pardoner and the Summoner in his Prologue to the *Siege of Thebes*,[126] the *Beryn* Poet actually switches their personalities, transforming the Pardoner into a lecherous woman-chaser like the Summoner notorious for consorting with low-life "younge girles" such as Kit the Tapster (*CT*, I, 663–65). This newly imagined Pardoner is invested with the greedy cunning and wide-ranging sexuality that had been central to Chaucer's characterization of the Summoner.[127] All queerness disappears in the process. The moral imperatives of Lancastrian poetics created space for a rapacious sexual predator, however much a failure, but not a sexual deviant.

This normalizing process extends from the sexual to the religious as the *Canterbury Interlude* erases another whole area of deviance. Nothing is said about the Pardoner's professional chicanery as a purveyor of pardons, and there is no mention of the sham religious artifacts that had provoked the edgy distinction between authentic relics and pig bones.[128] This fifteenth-century Pardoner has also been denied any psychological depth. The logic of fabliau debasement reduces him to a sleazy scoundrel tricked, robbed, beaten, humiliated, and allowed to slink away as a comic butt. He is trivialized as a cliché of the low-humor genre.[129] In the process, he entirely ceases to operate as a weapon of satire against Canterbury relics.

The *Canterbury Interlude* pursues a middle course by describing how the pilgrims reach their destination at the shrine of St. Thomas while allowing that some individuals misbehaved before and after. The Friar sneaks a peek at the Nun under her veil, the Miller stupidly guesses at the images in the stained-glass windows, and the Summoner squabbles over a cache of Canterbury souvenirs shoplifted by the Miller and Pardoner.[130] This brief scene (175–92) actually dramatizes a "divorce" between the Pardoner and the Summoner as a couple. They no longer form the partnership originally described by Chaucer—"With hym ther rood a gentil Pardoner / Of Rouncivale, his freend and his compeer" (*CT,* I, 669–70)—and they do not travel side by side as they were positioned during the Wife of Bath's Prologue. The imperative of heterosexuality required a parting of the ways emphasized here by the squabble over the stolen souvenirs.

Despite the commotion stirring around the fringes, hardly a hint of criticism impinges upon the act of devotion central to the pilgrimage ritual (163–70):

> Then passed they forth boystly, goglyng with hir hedes,
> Kneled adown tofore the shryne, and hertlich hir bedes
> They preyd to Seynt Thomas, in such wise as they couth.
> And sith the holy relikes ech man with his mowth
> Kissed, as a goodly monke the names told and taught.
> And sith to other places of holynes they raughte
> And were in hir devocioun tyl service were al doon,
> And sith they drowgh to dynerward, as it drew to noon.

Segregated in its own profane space, the Pardoner's unhappy encounter with Kit remains entirely separate from the solemnity of devotion at the shrine. The conniving female's double-dealings nonetheless confirm William Thorpe's caustic remarks on the seedy side of the pilgrimage trade: "Siche madde peple wasten blamfulli Goddis goodis in her veyne pilgrymageyng, spend-ynge þese goodis vpon vicious hosteleris and vpon tapsters, whiche ben ofte vnclene wymmen of her bodies."[131] The continuator does not blink at these abuses. Quite the contrary, he rejoices in the retribution visited upon a con man whose misconduct so grossly compromised the sacred journey.

What the *Beryn* Poet leaves entirely intact is the validity of the pilgrimage itself, in theory and in practice, as a pious ritual that Chaucer had slighted in the General Prologue and omitted altogether at the end. Linda Georgianna has nicely gauged this ambivalence in the *Tales* overall: "Chaucer is drawn to the practice precisely because it provides Christians *both* an opportunity to heed a profound spiritual call to renewal and redemption *and* a way to defer and displace the full recognition of the need for mercy for as long as possible."[132] The split plot of the *Canterbury Interlude* dramatizes this finely registered sense of doubleness. The pilgrims as a group successfully complete their spiritual rendezvous with Becket's relics, while the Pardoner fails miserably in his sexual rendezvous with the scheming tapster Kit.

CHAPTER SIX

The House of Chaucer & Son

The Business of Lancastrian Canon-Formation

GEOFFREY CHAUCER WAS NEARING SIXTY IN DECEMBER 1399 WHEN he took a lease on a house in the garden of the Lady Chapel of Westminster Abbey. The term of the lease, set at fifty-three years, proved excessively optimistic since Chaucer died during the first year of occupancy.[1] These facts are often rehearsed. The scant evidence has been colorfully embroidered by the novelistic imagination of John Gardner and used as evidence for a murder mystery by Terry Jones, while the historian Gervase Rosser explains Chaucer's relocation more practically in terms of the osmotic movements of other courtiers between the Palace of Westminster and the convent enclave of Westminster Abbey.[2] Far less attention has been paid to the Warden's Accounts indicating that a lease on this same residence was maintained by Thomas Chaucer, the poet's only known son, from 1411 until his own death in 1434.

Abbey records are imprecise as well as incomplete for the period 1400–1411. For the years immediately following Chaucer's death, a lease agreement for a tenement survives for "Master Pol," probably the Frenchman Paul de la Mounte who had served as Richard II's chief clerk and physician. Next comes William Horscroft, the chief skinner who had supplied King Richard with an enormous quantity of furs, cloaks, and hoods. But their rents were higher than the 53s. 4d. paid quarterly by the poet and his immediate predecessor, John Edrich. Since Abbey records refer to these houses in the plural (*de domibus in gardino capelle Beate Marie*), the subsequent tenants probably occupied residences different from the one leased to Chaucer.[3] As Ricardian loyalists, however, Horscroft and Master Paul belonged to the same group of men who may have needed safe houses during the early years of Henry IV's regime and moreover, as neighbors or sublets, may also have been entrusted as custodians for whatever Geoffrey Chaucer left behind in his last earthly residence.

The more likely scenario has Thomas Chaucer inheriting this leasehold and maintaining it for the rest of his own life rather than returning to this residence over a decade after his father's decease. Since Geoffrey's lease terminated upon his death without obligation on the part of his heir to continue for the allotted fifty-three years—and indeed the lease contained a clause permitting re-entry immediately after the lessee's death—we are left with a question that is quite modest on the face of things but far-reaching in its implications. Why did Thomas Chaucer, wealthy country squire and busy man of national and international affairs, make this effort to continue leasing the house where his father had died at Westminster Abbey?

Since he could have sold the lease immediately after his father's death, Thomas Chaucer's long-term involvement with this residence becomes all the more puzzling in light of the extensive inventory of his other properties recorded in the Postmortem Inquisitions during the year after his death, November 1434 to May 1435.[4] Retained for life by John of Gaunt in 1389, the younger Chaucer became extremely active in court politics and performed considerable service to the first three Lancastrian kings. His principal residence at Ewelme in Oxfordshire was convenient to Henry VI's favorite palace at Windsor.[5] He was knight of the shire for Oxfordshire in eleven Westminster parliaments from 1400 to 1431, and he was speaker of the Commons in three of them.[6] But the fifteenth-century Parliament did not convene regularly, it did not meet always in Westminster, and no session lasted long enough to justify a permanent Westminster address except perhaps the unexpected 171-day session in 1406.[7]

Thomas Chaucer served as chief butler of England for over thirty years after his initial appointment in 1402 with only two interruptions, most likely punitive suspensions as a result of his participation in Prince Henry's faction.[8] The position of butler required purveying wine for the king's mobile household as well as castles, ships, and armies. The butler also collected duties on wine imported through Southampton, Bristol, Lynn, and the eight other main ports.[9] Since these dealings required Thomas's presence in the port of London, a residence in the City made better sense. It is therefore not surprising the posthumous Inquisitions recorded a residence in Goldynglane at a rent twice that paid on the Westminster tenement. This grander household better suited the man who served as a member of Henry VI's council for the years 1424–27.[10] So why did Thomas Chaucer maintain a Westminster house that he otherwise did not need for discharging his official duties? And for that matter, why did Chaucer's son have the property basically for free, since records indicate the 66s. 8d. was paid partly by the sacrist, partly by the wardens of the lands of Queen Anne and Richard II?[11]

Reasons for Geoffrey Chaucer's move to the abbey precincts in the first place have engaged the speculation of his biographers.[12] With his tenement wedged between Westminster Palace and Westminster Abbey, he would have been close to the court, and during his waning weeks of life, he would have been enwrapped in the sacred atmosphere of the ancient monastery. His later burial in the Abbey reflected this dual status as a resident of the monastic precincts *and* a longtime royal servant honored with a burial near the royal mausoleum of Plantagenet kings.[13] Actually mentioned in his lease agreement, the Abbey's immunities protected him from arrest, although the poet himself lived apart from the unsavory sanctuary-seekers along the street appropriately named Thieving Lane.[14] Political currents were uncertain in the weeks following Henry IV's seizure of the throne, and the deposed Richard II soon died under mysterious circumstances. Though no guarantee, residence in the monastic compound meant greater security for Chaucer, his household, and his personal belongings.

Though often characterized as a spiritual retreat, Westminster Abbey actually remained a hotbed of pro-Ricardian intrigue during the months following the monarch's arrest. The monastery had received enormous patronage from Richard II and retained strong loyalties. Abbot William Colchester marshaled opposition to the new regime by taking into custody the earls of Huntingdon, Kent, Rutland, and Salisbury as well as hosting the demoted bishop of Carlisle, Thomas Merks, and the deposed archbishop of Canterbury, Roger Walden. By December 17 of 1399, these stalwarts were conspiring rebellion at the abbot's house. The coup plotters were joined by "John Paule," probably the Master Paul de la Mounte later recorded as a tenement-holder in the same document recording Chaucer's lease. Perhaps intentionally set in motion by Henry IV and Archbishop Arundel to flush out traitors, the Epiphany Uprising of January 1400 failed spectacularly. A whole host of opponents were eliminated or neutralized, while events were set in motion for Richard II's death.[15] Though Chaucer may have been physically close to the conspiracy—if not in Calais early in 1400 as his *Life-Records* suggest[16]— he was not accustomed to risking his life in an uncertain cause.

Caution had been the hallmark of Chaucer's entire career. It is evident in his adroit withdrawal from public life during 1386–89, and it can be read in his decision to relocate to the sanctuary of Westminster Abbey in 1399. Caution can also be discerned in his steady guardedness toward his life's work as a writer. The courtly poems *Book of the Duchess* and *Parliament of Fowls* apparently had limited circulation since these two dream-visions are not well attested, appearing in humbler manuscripts such as Fairfax 16, Tanner 346, Bodley 638, and CUL MS Ff.1.6 for which the exemplars became available surprisingly late, perhaps as an afterthought from Thomas Chaucer or even the poet's granddaughter Alice, Duchess of Suffolk (d. 1475).[17] These anthologies, even a late collection such as Bodleian MS Digby 181 from the last quarter of the fifteenth century, rarely attached Chaucer's name to these courtly works. Even the familiar lyrics to friends were more likely than the dream-visions to be attributed to Chaucer in Fairfax 16: the *ABC* "Par Chaucer" (fol. 191a), "Lenvoy de Chaucer a Scogan" (fol. 192b), "The Complaynt of Chaucer to his Purse" (fol. 193a), and "Lenvoy de Chaucer a Bukton" (fol. 193b).[18] Attribution of the dream-visions rests mostly in the self-generated catalogues in the Retraction and the Prologue to the *Legend of Good Women,* which was another dream-vision known narrowly within a royal circle that included courtiers such as Edward, Second Duke of York, who refers to the work in his *Master of Game.* Most scholars who have studied the manuscripts of the *Canterbury Tales* agree that this work, too, was never published during Chaucer's lifetime, certainly not as a whole, probably not even in part.[19] Hengwrt is the only manuscript of the *Tales* that might arguably be dated to his lifetime, probably as a fair copy for the author's own use.

So Chaucer had this great hoard of literary manuscripts with him at the end of his life for the occasional revision and retouching, as well as for security's sake. This literary treasure trove would have included his authorial exemplars for the dream poems, the fair copies for *Troilus* and *Boece* produced by Adam Pinkhurst, the draft versions of works such as the *Equatorie of the Planetis,* and the fair copies as well as working drafts of the *Canterbury Tales.* All of these literary manuscripts as well as his extensive personal library— described as "sixty bokes olde and newe" in the Prologue of the *Legend of Good Women* (G.273)—would most likely have remained in his home at Westminster conveniently near his original coterie of civil servants such as Thomas Hoccleve. Perhaps more important in terms of posterity, local scribes and professional textwriters such as Adam Pinkhurst already had some firsthand knowledge of the poet's projects and would later play an instrumental role in preparing the *Canterbury Tales* for official publication.[20]

Although the poet's will does not survive, ownership of these manuscripts would have passed to his heir.[21] Thomas Chaucer naturally filled the
role of literary executor for his father's writings, particularly the unpublished
and largely unknown *Canterbury Tales.* This is the real reason, I would suggest,
that Thomas maintained the lease on the Westminster house. The residence
was not for him but for his father's books. It became a manuscript archive
where Geoffrey Chaucer's literary remains were safely stored inside the monastic precincts, sorted out by experienced copyists such as the poet's long-
time scribe Pinkhurst, and read by approved parties such as John Lydgate. If
Pinkhurst had experience at arranging the *Tales* in Hengwrt under Chaucer's
personal supervision prior to his death, as Linne Mooney has suggested, he
still required access and financial support from Thomas Chaucer in order to
complete Ellesmere as well as the other later copy represented by the Cambridge CUL Kk.1.3/20 fragment.[22]

Here at the Westminster tenement at some later date, the exemplars
were further compared and assembled for copying by other local textwriters
such as Scribe D in order to produce Corpus Christi 198 and Harley 7334.[23]
Perhaps this long-range project figured in Geoffrey's own strategic plans,
shared with his son, when he undertook a lease for the extraordinary dura-
tion of fifty-three years. Perhaps this project of national importance also explains why the rent was paid out of revenues from the lands of Queen Anne
and Richard II? Speculation that Chaucer left England during the political
crisis of 1399–1400 for safe haven in the Low Countries—supported by the
mysterious evidence that Chaucer was in Calais during the first half of
1400[24]—would mean that the Westminster tenement served primarily as a
book depository rather than sanctuary for the poet himself.

John Fisher has remarked quite rightly that Thomas Chaucer had both
motive and opportunity for commissioning professional scribes to sift
through his father's literary papers in order to produce an elegant presentation copy of *Troilus and Criseyde* for Prince Henry and the most orderly text
possible of *The Canterbury Tales,* first Hengwrt and finally Ellesmere.[25] Commercial profit was not a likely motive, however, since Thomas had married
the wealthy heiress Maud Burghersh in 1395 and was already well on his way
to becoming one of the richest men in England. These early bespoke manuscripts cost somebody a considerable sum but fattened the purses only of
the textwriters, limners, and bookbinders who produced them.[26] In short,
posthumous publication did not directly bolster family fortunes in the manner enjoyed by the heirs of Ernest Hemingway and J. R. R. Tolkien.

In this regard, Thomas Chaucer's marble tomb in the church at Ewelme becomes instructive. Described as one of the most extensive collections of medieval coats of arms found on any tomb in England, the elaborate table-top design actually omitted the heraldic shield of Geoffrey Chaucer himself. Thomas evidently preferred the socially prestigious connections through his mother, Roet, and his wife, Burghersh.[27] The arms that are included strongly indicate the congruence of Thomas Chaucer's family consciousness and his social ambitions. Here we find John of Gaunt and his third wife, Katherine Roet, the sister of Thomas's mother, Philippa. Next follow Gaunt's and Katherine's son Henry Beaufort, Cardinal Bishop of Winchester; their youngest son, Thomas Beaufort, Duke of Exeter; and Ralph Neville, Earl of Westmoreland and husband of Joan Beaufort.[28] Also proudly displayed are Thomas Montagu, Earl of Salisbury and second husband of Alice Chaucer, Thomas Chaucer's only child; William de la Pole, Duke of Suffolk and Alice Chaucer's third husband—and so on. The design of Thomas Chaucer's tomb advertised an elaborate family tree connecting the important noble houses of England in the early fifteenth century, including Mowbray, Stafford, Beauchamp, Courtenay, Despenser, and Percy, but slighting his own father, who did not derive from this same aristocratic elite.[29] Since details of the genealogical design date from the year of Maud Chaucer's death in 1438, two years after her husband's, and tomb might partly reflect the wishes of Thomas, partly the sense of family prestige carried forward by Alice Chaucer. She expanded this grand genealogical program of coats of arms on her own nearby tomb, dating from the early 1470s, where the inscription actually inflated her own title as "Princess Alice": ORATE PRO ANIMA SERENISSIMAE PRINCIPESSAE ALICIAE DUCISSAE SUFFOLCHIA. In addition to her relatively insignificant first husband, Sir John Phelip, her grandfather the poet remains missing from this ostentatious lineup of heraldic dignitaries.[30]

Within this far-reaching social network, Thomas Chaucer undertook disseminating his father's literary works. His motivation was not primarily artistic patronage or even filial devotion, but more a desire to contribute an important cultural strand—which was also a clan strand—to the vital network of English associations supporting the Lancastrian monarch. Since the younger Chaucer joined with his cousins Thomas and Henry Beaufort to become the real architects of Prince Henry's emergence in 1412 more than a year before Henry IV's death, it can be no coincidence that the only early Chaucer manuscript with definite indication of ownership is the Campsall *Troilus and Criseyde* bearing the arms of Henry as Prince of Wales.[31] Doyle thinks that the Corpus Christi manuscript of *Troilus* with its famous frontispiece that shows the poet reading to a youthful king was also intended for Henry V.[32] Crudely described, the project of promoting Geoffrey Chaucer as literary royalty—"of makyng souereyne," in Lydgate's phrase—paralleled the campaign for bolstering Prince Henry's campaign for legitimacy as England's next king from around 1410. Chaucer's foundational position was readily equated with John of Gaunt's position from the fourteenth century as the two father figures in poetry and politics. Thomas Chaucer had clear motivations for promoting these twin legacies as furtherance of his own ambitions.

This speculation concerning the poet's Westminster Abbey tenement as the original "Center for Chaucer Studies" remains admittedly as imaginative as John Gardner's description of the elderly Chaucer spying on young lovers in the abbey garden. My scenario nonetheless accounts for much that passes as common scholarly lore as well as a good deal of textual evidence not previously brought together into a single coherent account. Thomas Chaucer emerges as the agent instrumental in preserving his father's literary materials, facilitating production of copies for friends and political allies of the future Henry V, and affording his patronage to later writers, primarily John Lydgate, for developing the well-defined Chaucerian poetics—really *Lancastrian poetics*—committed to social stability and religious orthodoxy.[33] By establishing an official succession of named poets as a counterpart to the orderly succession of monarchs, Thomas Chaucer emerges as a true entrepreneur in the business of canon-formation, which was a project as politically freighted then as now.[34]

The older poet John Gower's efforts at self-promotion included rededicating his *Confessio Amantis* to Henry Bolingbroke, writing the viciously anti-Ricardian *Tripartite Chronicle* after the king's fall, and dedicating his *Cinkante Balades* to Henry IV after the French poet Christine de Pizan turned down an invitation to join the Lancastrian court. And yet the triumvirate of canonic authors to emerge from these historical negotiations firmly established Chaucer's priority in a succession that became standard: Chaucer first, and then Gower and Lydgate. To secure his own position in this literary genealogy, Lydgate repeatedly claimed Chaucer's status as the founder:

> *ffyrste* in any age / That amendede our language . . .
> glorye / Of wel seying *first* in our language . . .
> the noble rethor Poete of breteine / that made *firste* to distille
>   and reyne . . .[35]

Hoccleve may have anticipated this whole notion of patriarchal succession, but he failed to place himself solidly in this official canon partly because he belonged to the original nonaristocratic readership of bureaucrats *and* because he tried too hard to assert his claims as son and heir. Sibling rivalry can be read in the competing claims of Thomas Hoccleve and Thomas Chaucer, and the hapless Privy Seal poet with his "strategy for poetic usurpation" lost out to the more powerful Lancastrian captain.[36]

In this nascent canon of English authors materializing during the first decades of the fifteenth century, Thomas Chaucer took measures to install Geoffrey Chaucer as the patriarch of English letters, a father very much created by his own son. The older Chaucer had made signal advances in inventing the category of English literature, but the younger Chaucer extended this project by fostering the concept of canon-formation *and* constructing literary tradition in terms of the genealogy of legitimate descent. Not universally honored as a poet during his lifetime—never once mentioned as a poet in six hundred pages of *Life-Records*—Chaucer soon came to occupy the role later imposed upon Shakespeare as the official National Poet defining the substance of aristocratic culture, standardizing a single literary dialect, and shaping England's social consciousness for generations to come.

Thomas Hocccleve: The Insider Locked Out

Thomas Hoccleve worked the hardest to install Geoffrey Chaucer as the father of English poetry and to claim his own position as direct lineal heir. The notion of a patrilineal inheritance was already formulated within a generation of the poet's death when Hoccleve sought to place himself in this family tree of immediate literary descendants in his famous commendation from *The Regiment of Princes*:

> O maistir deere and fadir reverent,
> My maistir Chaucer, flour of eloquence,
> Mirour of fructuous entendement,
> O universel fadir in science![37]

These stanzas mourning Chaucer dramatized Hoccleve's claims as a beneficiary according to the social logic that the one who grieves is the one with the right to inherit.[38]

Yet despite his enterprise at establishing right of descent, Hoccleve failed to secure this legacy. After the early success of his *Regiment,* he gradually ceded his position to an altogether unlikely rival poet, the monk John Lydgate from Bury St. Edmunds, whose religious vocation and provincial location in East Anglia otherwise seemed to disqualify him as a complete outsider. Apparently Hoccleve did not even realize that Lydgate was writing at the same time during the first quarter of the fifteenth century.[39] The trinity of writers was eventually formulated as Chaucer, Gower, and Lydgate. So why was Hoccleve, the total insider, eventually locked out of the House of Chaucer & Son and excluded from the literary tradition that he himself did so much to secure?

Although we normally associate Hoccleve with the fifteenth century, he was born around 1367 (probably the same year as Thomas Chaucer) and began work as a clerk in the office of the Privy Seal in 1387. This was a propitious time to have arrived in London, but also an ominous time. Chaucer had just completed *Troilus* and was embarking on the *Canterbury Tales,* and Hoccleve began moving in the circles of the literate civil servants who participated as members of Chaucer's first audience.[40] But it was also the time when the Appellants began their attack upon Richard II, and disaster befell some of the king's closest supporters, including the writer and political opportunist Thomas Usk, who moved in many of these same professional circles.[41] Chaucer himself found it prudent to retrench during 1386–89. But the young Hoccleve maintained his position safely throughout the 1390s, and he was quick to transfer his loyalties to the Lancastrian rulers after the deposition of King Richard. Henry IV granted annuities of £10 to each of the four clerks at the Privy Seal in 1399, and Hoccleve's annuity was increased to twenty marks in 1409.[42] Though he himself made some decisions that were detrimental to his career, such as his marriage, he had ample opportunity to prosper along with other Privy Seal clerks under the new regime.

When Hoccleve names himself in the *Regiment,* the Old Man immediately associates him with the pre-eminent writer of the previous generation—"Thow were aqweyntid with Chaucer, pardee" (1867). Claims of personal and artistic affiliation should not be hastily dismissed.[43] The fatherly Chaucer can easily be imagined reading juvenile drafts just as Hoccleve implies: "And fadir Chaucer fayn wolde han me taght / But I was dul and lerned lyte or naght."[44] Perhaps among his earliest efforts, Hoccleve's Marian poems may owe a direct debt.[45] Chaucer's own devotional *ABC to the Virgin* and the Second Nun's Prologue became the subject of his praise in the *Regiment*

(4983–91).[46] It has even been suggested that Hoccleve was one of the privileged literary men chosen to help sort out Chaucer's papers after his death, editing and preparing exemplars for the unfinished *Canterbury Tales*.[47] Although he collaborated on the Trinity *Confessio Amantis* with the professional textwriter Adam Pinkhurst who copied Hengwrt and Ellesmere, Hoccleve himself shows surprisingly little direct knowledge of Chaucer's poetry.[48] Even though he was ideally situated in London and Westminster and he had all the right connections in the literate culture of the metropolis, Hoccleve was familiar with Chaucer the man, his literary reputation, and even some ringing phrases, but he shows no detailed mastery of the works themselves. Knowing the man but not the works, he is the opposite of the Man of Law, who read the works but did not recognize the man himself.

Hoccleve's exclusion from the pantheon of early English poets is hard to explain in terms of his assiduous efforts at inclusion. His contribution to constructing a literary genealogy clearly paralleled the formulation of a legitimate royal descent for the Lancastrians. The *Regiment*'s references to the Lancastrian forebears John of Gaunt (512), Edward III (2556), and Henry of Grosmont, the first duke of Lancaster (2646), complement the evocation of his own Chaucerian literary ancestry.[49] Hoccleve rigorously followed the Lancastrian line in hammering away at the Lollards in poems such as *To Sir John Oldcastle*, which contributed to the portrayal of the heretic Oldcastle as a grotesque parody of a discredited father figure.[50] Taking some risks by writing in English about theological matters after Arundel's *Constitutions* in 1409, Hoccleve in other poems such as "To Henry V and the Knights of the Garter" and the account of the burning of the heretic John Badby in the *Regiment* (281–329) worked at banishing any suspicions that Henry himself had been lenient to Lollards.[51] The final appeal of the *Regiment* for the kings of England and France to make war on "mescreantz" and "foos of Cryst" sounds like a call for persecuting heretics rather than liberating the Holy Land.

Book production by clerical writers such as Hoccleve figured as an unmistakable maneuver in the Lancastrian offensive against its religious opponents. To this end, Hoccleve did important service by recruiting Chaucer posthumously to the cause of orthodoxy. The BL Harley 4866 manuscript of his *Regiment* includes a famous portrait of Chaucer closely resembling the picture in the Ellesmere manuscript c. 1400–1410.[52] This decorative image accompanies Hoccleve's stanzas praising Chaucer's devout service to the Virgin. The picture is followed immediately by a defense of images against unnamed opponents:

Yit sum men holde oppinioun and seye
That noon ymages shoulde ymakid be.
They erren foule and goon out of the weye.[53]

These antagonists are not mentioned by name, but "sum men" are certainly understood as Lollards. Chaucer had long-term associations with the Lollard knights Sir Richard Stury and Sir Lewis Clifford, and some of his writings such as the Wife of Bath's Prologue could be read as containing a wide range of Lollard views.[54] In addition to denying that Prince Henry had been soft on heretics, Hoccleve needed to deny Chaucer's reformist sympathies and redefine his cultural identity in ways wholly orthodox and deeply pious.

Apparently to supplement his livelihood, Hoccleve joined with other professionals to copy and disseminate the works of Lancastrian poets such as John Gower.[55] By working jointly on a transcription of the *Confessio Amantis* with the two scribes who also produced the landmark manuscripts of the *Canterbury Tales*—Hengwrt, Ellesmere, Harley 7334, and Corpus Christi 198—Hoccleve took a hands-on role in manufacturing literary works by the authors whose standing at the head of the English tradition he labored so diligently to promote in the *Regiment*. As further evidence of the creation of a prestige readership for these vernacular works, Hoccleve made tactical efforts to address his own poems to grandees such as Edward, Duke of York, John, Duke of Bedford, Humphrey, Duke of Gloucester, Joan FitzAlan, Countess of Hereford, and of course Henry V himself. In addition to presentation copies of the *Regiment*, he sent a collection of ballades to the Duke of Gloucester and a "little pamfilet" of poems to the Duke of York.[56] As the recipient of his holograph *Series*, Joan Neville, Countess of Westmoreland, typified Hoccleve's ambitions for forming relationships with great and influential persons. Joan Beaufort was the second wife of Ralph Neville, Earl of Westmoreland, mother-in-law to Mowbray, the Earl Marshal, sister-in-law to Thomas Neville, Lord Furnival, and aunt to both Duke Humphrey and Henry V—as well as niece of Geoffrey Chaucer, through Gaunt's liaison with the poet's sister-in-law Katherine, and mother of the Earl of Salisbury who married Chaucer's granddaughter, Alice.[57]

We have unique evidence for Hoccleve's copying out his own *Series* in Durham University MS Cosin V.iii.9 under circumstances that amounted to authorial publication. The two Huntington holographs HM 744 and HM 111 indicate a sense of "collected works" as an enterprise of signal importance in the formation of a distinct English literary tradition.[58] Charles Blyth thinks that the two best extant manuscripts of the *Regiment*, BL Harley 4866 and BL

Arundel 38, were executed under Hoccleve's direct supervision so that they constitute authorized editions of the work. The third manuscript, BL Royal 17.D.xviii, derived perhaps from a copy written in Hoccleve's own hand.[59]

Ironically, Hoccleve's increased authority over his texts and his industry at distributing them failed to secure his own status as a canonic author.[60] Whereas Chaucer exercised less rigorous control over textual transmission, the fragmentary nature of his works did not weaken his position as an author. To the contrary, the open-endedness and inchoate structure of his big, all-inclusive *Canterbury Tales* actually rendered him a stronger cultural presence. The obvious incompleteness of his oeuvre invited imitators and other entrepreneurial talents to compose their own textual supplements in works such as *The Kingis Quair, The Siege of Thebes, The Fall of Princes, The Testament of Cresseid,* and *The Canterbury Interlude and Tale of Beryn.* As Ethan Knapp has rightly observed in his fine study of Hoccleve's bureaucratic identity, the Privy Seal poet differed from Chaucer and Lydgate because he had no progeny.[61]

Hoccleve's failure to insert himself permanently in the English canon is all the more puzzling since he made so many of the right moves. Chaucer's death in 1400 left a "poet vacuum" at the new and insecure Lancastrian court. Hoccleve's earliest datable poem, *The Letter of Cupid* (c. 1402), aligned itself with the courtly tastes of the moment, rendering into English the *Epistre au Dieu d'Amours* by Christine de Pizan.[62] English connections with the celebrated French poet had begun late in the reign of Richard II. Christine's son Jean came to England around 1398 to join the household of the Earl of Salisbury, where his companions included Thomas Montagu, second husband of Alice Chaucer. Chaucer's granddaughter would own her own copy of Christine's *Cité des dames.* Henry IV acquired the manuscripts of works that Christine had given to Salisbury, and the new Lancastrian monarch tried unsuccessfully to lure her to England to join her son, who was kept almost as a hostage to apply pressure upon the French writer.[63] Since Christine succeeded in arranging the return of her son without accepting the English king's invitation, Hoccleve spotted an opening and quickly attempted to fill it. But he may have miscalculated.[64] When Henry V began an aggressive nationalist campaign that eventually renewed hostilities with France, the robust Englishness of Chaucer's *Canterbury Tales* better suited the new national culture. As further miscalculation, Hoccleve's pacificist conclusion to the *Regiment,* in which he appealed to the English and French rulers to seek "pees and reste," conflicted with Henry V's militarist policies that led to his victory at Agincourt and the long-term English occupation of French territories.[65]

The clear and immediate success of his *Regiment,* with forty-four extant manuscripts, six of them deluxe, deepens the mystery of Hoccleve's failure. Marcia Marzec provides a concise summary of the outstanding quality of these manuscripts as well as the impressive line-up of recipients:

> There must have been at least five such patronic copies: the copy presumably presented to Prince Henry in 1412 (no longer extant); those copies presented to Edward, Duke of York, and John, Duke of Bedford, as is indicated by surviving dedicatory verses; the British Library MS. Arundel 38, bearing the arms of the FitzAlans, Earls of Arundel; and the British Library MS. Harley 4866, almost exactly like MS. Arundel 38 in bibliographical format. Moreover, there were other members of the royal circle who were patrons of other Hoccleve works and who would have been likely recipients of the *Regiment,* viz., Humphrey, Duke of Gloucester, Joan Beaufort, Countess of Westmoreland, Robert Chichele, and Joan FitzAlan, Countess of Hereford, possibly the recipient of the MS. Arundel 38.[66]

Despite all of its early prestige, however, the *Regiment* did not permanently secure its place as a literary masterpiece.[67] Though the poet engaged in self-naming inside the text—"Hoccleve, fadir myn, men clepen me"—most manuscripts of the *Regiment* do not identify the author in an incipit or colophon.[68] Since all of the manuscripts are fifteenth-century copies and nearly all represent the scribal dialect of the Southeast Midlands, the text's transmission appears limited in time and place. John Shirley's middle fifteenth-century copy in Huntington EL 26.A.13 shows some quality workmanship, with fine red and blue initials as well as the conscientious inclusion of Latin glosses, but later copies such as HM 135 are plain transcriptions on coarser paper without ornament or textual apparatus.[69]

Regiment of Princes is composed in Chaucerian verse-form, but otherwise the work lacks the Chaucerian characteristics that became most dearly prized by posterity. Specifically, Hoccleve does not excel at storytelling, almost as if he had internalized the puritanical suspicion of "fablis" and "veyne stories" expressed by the Lollard sermon *Vae Octuplex* dated 1411, exactly when he was writing his *Regiment.*[70] He is not a narrative poet except in a few scattered pieces, such as his verse renderings "Jereslaus's Wife" and "Jonathas" from the *Gesta Romanorum.* Even his lyrics are unlike Chaucer's, either more personal in their direct address to well-placed recipients or more conventional in their indebtedness to French models.[71] Yet it was exactly Chaucer's retreat into fiction that served as a strategy for avoiding direct confrontation with the topical controversies of public life which rendered his works so enduring, embodying the contradictory qualities of looking so lively *and* safe.[72] Though the *Regiment* is studded with instructional *exempla,* Hoccleve did not compose the sorts of extended narratives that Chaucer wrote so brilliantly, and though he enjoined Oldcastle to read chivalric romances and heroic epics, he himself eschewed writing the "jeestis of batailles and fals cronyclis" condemned by Lollard tracts.[73] Imaginative storytelling would become the dominant literary mode, but it was not Hoccleve's.

Though he survived Henry V by four years, Hoccleve did not live long enough to establish himself firmly in the later Lancastrian era. He died just when Lydgate was reaching the apogee of his career with a large number of commissions such as his seven Mummings. Duke Humphrey of Gloucester took an active interest in literary patronage during the years 1430–41, mostly at the end of this period, when Lydgate was able to take best advantage of these opportunities. Dedicated to Gloucester, the large-scale *The Fall of Princes* survives in several costly, illustrated manuscripts.[74] With additional patronage from the Earl of Warwick and the Duke of Bedford—whose personal interest in books is indicated by his desire to acquire the French royal library—the Monk of Bury came to enjoy the role as "Laureate Lydgate" until his own death in 1449.[75] Size matters, too, and in terms of securing canonic status through quantity of production, Hoccleve's output looks slim compared to Lydgate's massive outpouring of poetic works totaling almost 140,000 lines.

When considered in its precise historical context, Hoccleve's advice-giving belonged to a very specific period in Lancastrian history, and therefore his *Regiment* established the logic of its own short-lived popularity. The work was produced during the years 1410–12 when the ailing Henry IV continued to consolidate power after the deposition of Richard II while also facing challenges to his authority from his own son Prince Henry. It was an open secret that the heir was already finding means to erode his father's prerogative.[76] Since Prince Henry stands as a constant figural presence throughout the *Regiment* while the reigning monarch, Henry IV, is notably absent— alluded to only indirectly as "the kyng which that is now" (816)—Hoccleve's convoluted treatments of sovereignty and paternity assume a subversive quality within the larger strategy of localizing authority. Knapp writes with great insight about the risks that the poet pursued: "In writing propaganda for the prince, Hoccleve was not just writing for Lancastrian interests. He was also stepping into a potentially dangerous feud within the Lancastrian house itself, a feud between father and son, at a moment at which notions of

paternity, inheritance, and counsel could not be used simply and inno-
cently."[77] The rapid decline of the poem's literary fortunes can partly be interpreted in light of its narrow political ambitions within this limited time
frame. A later fifteenth-century manuscript continued to advertise this connection in its title: *Liber qui Hocclyf compositus a Rege Henrico Quinto*.[78] Tied to a
particular historical moment, the *Regiment* bore a political stigma that was
also a family stain, one that Henry V worked hard to purge as soon as he ascended the throne in 1413.

Hoccleve's failure as an author may also relate directly to his undistin-
guished record as a government careerist. Though openly money-grubbing,
he did not skillfully exploit the lucrative opportunities open to him in the
governmental economy of the English capital.[79] In a society where advanta-
geous connections meant everything, Hoccleve pictures himself a perpetual
loner, wandering the streets and haunting the taverns, settling for all the
wrong company.[80] The Privy Seal also proved an unfortunate choice of government offices, because it offered the least opportunity for upward mobility
in royal administration. What is more, Hoccleve's marriage came at exactly
the wrong time, when Henry V ascended the house the throne and began insisting
upon more rigorous enforcement of traditional rules excluding married
clerks from government service.

"As a professional bureaucrat," Malcolm Richardson concludes, "Hoccleve was exactly what he tells us he was, a bungler, misfit, and perpetual
also-ran."[81] His disappointments must have been increased by the successes
of office peers such as Robert Frye, who became clerk of the council and a
prosperous, well-connected businessman, and the university graduate and
pluralist John Prophete, who served as secretary to Henry IV and then became keeper of the Privy Seal.[82] The almost perfect correspondence between
Hoccleve's middling career and his poetry's account of these shortcomings
further undercut his claims for any literary posterity. The description of his
chaotic lifestyle in *La Male Regle* stigmatized Hoccleve in conventional but
deeply unflattering terms as someone with dubious authority to advise a
prince in the *Regiment*. Parodying the conventions of penitential confession
did not exempt the poet from the implications of his own disorderly conduct.[83] How could a clerk so ill-regulated in his personal life presume to dic-
tate the regimen for a prince?

Specifically, Hoccleve's mental health posed a serious problem. In addition to confessing his inadequacies in love, finance, and poetic skill, he used
confessional disclosures to talk about himself with such raw frankness that
even modern readers have felt distinctly uncomfortable. Going beyond

Chaucer's self-deprecatory portraiture, Hoccleve's autobiographical writings become unnerving in their honesty, especially when depicting periods of insanity. His openness more closely resembles the Pardoner's or the Wife of Bath's, with all of the moral judgment and opprobrium that such naked honesty entailed. A severe medical crisis in 1414 was particularly unfortunate in its timing.[84] The threshold of Henry V's new reign was not a propitious moment for Hoccleve to acquire a reputation for personal instability when political stability was so much at stake.[85] Instead of explaining away this episode, Hoccleve revisited it in his *Complaint* and *Dialogue with a Friend.*[86] Although his later autobiographical works may have been intended to facilitate his social rehabilitation, these proclamations may have had the opposite effect of fostering a public image that was deeply repugnant. Though fascinating to modern readers, his declarations of insanity provide one more explanation why Hoccleve was quickly excluded from a literary genealogy that he himself had done so much to create.

Though his last name suggests Bedfordshire origins, the documentary evidence as well as the poetic testimony confirms Hoccleve as a fully naturalized Londoner. Literary historians have long valued Hoccleve specifically because his poetry provides such a realistic look at contemporary urban life. "The world of London and Westminster is more vividly present in his writings than in those of his fellow-citizen Chaucer."[87] These modern appreciations expose what may actually have been a fatal flaw in the poet's choice of subject matter. David Wallace has suggested that one of Chaucer's secrets for literary longevity lay precisely in his decision to render London as the "absent city" in his writings. By avoiding London as a setting for his work, most famously in his decision to situate the General Prologue across the river in Southwark, Chaucer evaded any messy encounter with the civic controversies that both energized and threatened the world in which he operated in his professional life.[88] Chaucer even avoided the controversy surrounding London's cathedral, since Lollards began attacking pilgrimage to the famous rood at the north door of St. Paul's in 1389.[89] London as a setting, as well as a problem for literary exploration, had become instead the signature subject of *Piers Plowman,* as Skeat long ago observed: "One great merit of the poem consists in its exhibition of *London* life and *London* opinions."[90] This was not a literary association that worked to Hoccleve's advantage.

Despite its Chaucerian versification and its outright support of the religious and political status quo, Hoccleve's *Regiment* represents an uneasy hybrid of authorial autobiography and Mirror of Princes which resembles poetry of the Langlandian tradition. Pearsall's brief summary underscores the work's similarity to *Piers Plowman*: "a loosely sprawling medley of auto-biography, complaint, social satire and moral reflection stamped with the mark of an individual and arresting poetic personality."[91] Spearing has also detected the Langlandian quality in Hoccleve's persistent use of small-scale personification.[92] For example, Langland's allegorical representation of Favel seems to have encouraged Hoccleve to make repeated use of this particular personification in similar moral contexts: "Favel is weddid to plesant deceit / And in that wedlok treewe is his conceit."[93] Sarah Tolmie has registered an open-ended conflation of moral allegory and urban realism which brings Hoccleve even closer to the practices in *Piers*.[94] Patterson compares the poet-protagonist of the *Male Regle* specifically to Langland's London waferer Haw-kyn,[95] while Knapp detects Hoccleve's circumspect "tones of *clergie*" that show affinity with his older London contemporary.[96]

Hoccleve's early education took place during the 1380s perhaps at the Inns of Chancery among the scribes and civil servants where *Piers Plowman* very likely found its earliest and most politically astute readership.[97] Lang-land's representation of himself as an idle waster—"Y am to wayke to worche with sykel or with sythe / And to long, lef me, lowe to stoupe" (C.5.23–24)—seems to have influenced Hoccleve's self-portrayal as a layabout who could not engage in physical labor, with plow or harrow, but who vigorously de-fends the legitimacy of writing as an alternative occupation:

> With plow can I nat medlen ne with harwe,
> Ne woot nat what lond good is for what corn,
> And for to lade a cart or fille a barwe,
> To which I nevere usid was toforn;
> My bak unbuxum hath swich thyng forsworn,
> At instaunce of wrytynge, his werreyour,
> That stowpynge hath him spilt with labour.[98]

Overall, too, the *Regiment*'s long introductory section with its first-person de-scription of the cleric's sad and insecure livelihood verges dangerously close to Langland's literary turf. Hoccleve's poem becomes a larger, earlier version of *The Crowned King* (c. 1415) in which Langland's dream-vision, his lunatic petitioner, and even verbal echoes from *Piers* combine in an advisory poem directed to the same recipient, now Henry V, as he embarked on his French campaigns. My early book *Crisis of Will in "Piers Plowman"* detected a resem-blance between Langland's and Hoccleve's self-representations as witless wanderers, as well as their attitudes toward the dangerous stresses of the

writing profession, but I had not suspected then, as I do now, that Hoccleve might have been encouraged in these attitudes by actually reading *Piers
Plowman*.[99]

Barron and Pearsall have confirmed Skeat's view that Langland, despite
his Worcestershire dialect and claims of Malvern origins, was a thoroughly
London poet: "Insofar as Langland's poem is rooted in time and place, it is
rooted in the streets of London in the 1370s."[100] Recent work also confirms
Skeat's sense of an end point for the writing of *Piers* in the early years of the
1390s. Since Hoccleve began work at the Privy Seal in 1387, there is a strong
likelihood that Langland was still alive and *Piers Plowman* avidly read in London when the younger would-be poet arrived upon the literary scene.[101]
Langland's writings remained a strong textual presence in the metropolis
during Hoccleve's formative years. Three closely related B-text manuscripts
seem to have descended in a stemma from a West Midland scribe working
earlier in London.[102] Doyle and Parkes have identified the London copyist
Scribe D who produced the Ilchester manuscript of *Piers Plowman* C-text
around 1400.[103] The London textwriter Adam Pinkhurst has now been identified as the copyist of the B-text in Trinity B.15.17.[104] His handwriting has
been judged similar to the professional hands in at least three other manuscripts of *Piers Plowman*: Huntington HM 143, BL Add. 35287, and the Holloway Fragment.[105] Used as the copy-text for the Russell-Kane *C Version,*
HM 143's Worcestershire language nonetheless shows evidence of dialect interference indicative of London copying, and Simon Horobin makes the argument that C-manuscripts mapped by dialect to the Worcester area were
actually copied in London by scribes who carefully preserved the poet's regional language.[106]

This census has important implications for suggesting London as the
principal center for producing copies of Langland's poem in the B and C versions. Since Hoccleve worked in association with Pinkhurst and Scribe D on
the Trinity R.3.2 manuscript of *Confessio Amantis* around 1408, he was professionally situated in this same textual community with direct hands-on knowledge of Langland's poem. Finally, the Duke of Westminster's manuscript of
Piers A, creatively conflated with passages from B and C, was written in an elegant secretarial hand of the kind employed in the Privy Seal at the beginning
of the fifteenth century, and Doyle has hazarded a guess that it was commissioned and executed in that milieu.[107] In sum, Langland's poem was a well-
known work in exactly the same professional environment in which Hoccleve
operated when he wrote his *Regiment*.

As a political advice-giver in the early fifteenth century, Hoccleve placed himself awkwardly in this same *Piers Plowman* tradition and may have drawn directly from Langland's poem, with debts to specific passages such as the C-text *apologia*.[108] He criticized the extravagant wardrobes of courtiers in the same manner as the Langlandian *Mum and the Sothsegger* and almost resembles Lollards when echoing their puritanical complaint against luxury crafts.[109] The highly topical *Mum* was written shortly after 1409 and surveyed the first decade of Henry IV's reign leading up to Arundel's *Constitutions*. Written just before the *Regiment,* this Langlandian poem embodied a realistic fear of retribution altogether missing in Hoccleve's performance. Since Richard II's refusal to accept advice had been listed as one of the Articles of Deposition, the new Lancastrian kings had incurred an obligation to *seem* welcoming of wise counsel.[110] Hoccleve's enterprise was perhaps a put-up job encouraged by Prince Henry's followers in order to publicize his wisdom as a promoter of good governance on the council. Writing the *Regiment* may have been encouraged by Henry himself in order to bolster his image as a prince willing to heed advice, playing the English Alexander to Hoccleve's quirky, pedantic Aristotle.[111]

By participating in an episode of royal gamesmanship between Prince Henry and Henry IV, Hoccleve ran the risk of engaging in topical controversies without Langland's tactic for sheltering beneath the obscurities of allegory—for example, the Belling of the Cat Fable (B.Prol.146–208) as reference to John of Gaunt's meddling in civic politics[112]—and without attaching his poem to the sorts of durable social issues that gained a permanent foothold for *Piers Plowman*. While Langland's poem persevered during the fifteenth century as a sort of cult classic among religious dissenters to emerge as an official Reformation book when printed in 1550, Hoccleve's standing quickly eroded. William Caxton chose not to print his *Regiment of Princes*.[113] Renaissance readers took little notice. There was no complete printed text until Thomas Wright's edition for the Roxburghe Club in 1860.[114]

Following more closely the example of his master Chaucer, John Lydgate managed to avoid topical controversies even in his anti-Lollard poem *A Defence of Holy Church,* probably written around the time of Henry V's accession in 1413.[115] In addition to his success as a court poet, Lydgate managed to insert himself into the robust vernacular culture of the City with poems such as *Dance of Death,* commissioned by the common clerk John Carpenter, and *Mesure Is Tresour,* where he became bolder in his attack upon Lollards as a threat to civic stability.[116] In the long run, the Monk of Bury succeeded in filling the "poet vacuum" as the author of explicitly Chaucerian works such as his *Troy Book*—which made an appeal to Londoners such as Carpenter, whose own *Liber Albus* imagined the capital as a New Troy[117]—as well as his *Siege of Thebes* and *Fall of Princes* with their seemingly timeless, universal lessons for princely governance.

John Lydgate: The Outsider Let In

As Chaucer's heir with access to the unpublished works, particularly the *Canterbury Tales,* Thomas Chaucer played a key role in the formation of an official literary tradition that was Chaucerian in style and subject matter, Lancastrian in its social affiliations. With no clear connection to Hoccleve, the younger Chaucer's role as a literary benefactor found its chief fulfillment in the career of John Lydgate, a monk of the great Benedictine abbey of Bury St. Edmunds. Lydgate may have made initial contact with the Thomas Chaucer circle at Ewelme while he was studying in the early 1400s at Gloucester College, Oxford, but he never seemed to enjoy any personal acquaintance with the great poet himself. "Their paths would not have crossed," Pearsall has remarked.[118] While it is entirely likely that Hoccleve knew Geoffrey Chaucer personally and professionally, Lydgate built a more successful literary career upon his connections with Thomas Chaucer.

It is noteworthy that Lydgate's short poem *On the Departing of Thomas Chaucer* makes no mention of his poetic father figure, the addressee's natural father, but instead refers to Thomas as "my maystre Chaucyer" and praises him for his generosity and his brilliant household.[119] Dating from 1414 when Thomas Chaucer went to France to discuss Henry V's marriage or from 1417 when he negotiated a final settlement of the war, the poem testifies to the younger Chaucer's key role in Lancastrian foreign policy. On the domestic front, Thomas is praised as a social magnet attracting gentlemen such as Sir William Moleyns (d. 1429). Here we begin to glimpse the wealthy and well-connected household in addition to the larger circle of "gentilmen dwelling envyroun" (57) to which the ambitious monastic writer was eager to dedicate his talents.

Lydgate's earliest Chaucerian productions were probably inspired by the courtly dream-visions that apparently had limited circulation. *The Complaint of the Black Knight* was based upon *The Book of the Duchess,* and *The Temple of Glass* upon *The House of Fame.*[120] Since Chaucer's own dream-poems survive mostly in the same anthologies with these imitations—notably Fairfax 16 and Bodley 638—Lydgate seems to have benefited from the sort of privileged early access to Chaucer's literary papers that was possible only through family permission. The history of his later productions testifies to some continuing affinity with the poet's descendants. Lydgate wrote *My Lady Dere* for Maud Chaucer, the poet's daughter-in-law. He composed *Virtues of the Mass* for the poet's only known grandchild, the thrice-married Alice Chaucer (c. 1404–75).[121] Her second husband, Thomas Montagu, Earl of Salisbury and John of Bedford's deputy in France, commissioned a translation of the vast *Pilgrimage of the Life of Man* in 1426, two years before his death at the siege of Orléans. The work was later donated in a less expensive paper volume by Alice to the Ewelme Almshouse: "Item, a boke of English, in paper, of þe pilgrymage, translated by dom. John Lydgate out of frensh."[122] Officially thanked for her donation of volumes to Oxford's Divinity School in 1454, Alice Chaucer distinguished herself as a woman with well-documented interests in literary as well as liturgical books.[123]

Alice Chaucer and her third husband, William de la Pole, maintained an ongoing relationship with Lydgate after they were admitted to the fraternity of Bury St. Edmunds. The Duke of Suffolk owned the best surviving manuscript of the *Siege of Thebes* (BL Arundel 119) executed by a scribe whose handwriting has also been identified in copies of Gower's *Confessio Amantis* and John Walton's verse translation of *The Consolation of Philosophy*.[124] It has been suggested that this prestige manuscript of Lydgate's *Thebes* was actually commissioned by Alice for her husband, William.[125] Though the evidence for attribution is slight, Suffolk himself has been identified as the author of the "Fairfax sequence" of verses wittily mocking Lydgate for defaming women and speaking ill of love, perhaps really chiding the poet for defecting from the Chaucer-Beaufort faction.[126] Indeed, Lydgate had begun receiving commissions from the head of the opposing court party, Duke Humphrey of Gloucester, the great bibliophile whose collection grew to an estimated five hundred volumes.[127] For this patron, Lydgate produced his only prose work, *Serpent of Division* (1422), and later the massive *Fall of Princes* (1431–38) as well as shorter poems such as "On Gloucester's Approaching Marriage" and "Letter to Gloucester."[128] But there does not appear to have been a permanent breach, since Suffolk sponsored Lydgate's petition in 1441 for resolving problems with his official annuity of ten marks.[129]

Lydgate's steady contact with the Chaucer family ran parallel to his growing knowledge of Geoffrey Chaucer's poetry. He spent much time in London, probably at the abbot's townhouse of Buries Markes in St. Mary Axe. John Shirley reported that one of Lydgate's poems was written "by night as he lay in his bedde at London."[130] Not isolated in East Anglia, the Bury monk had opportunity to become one of the early readers granted access to the Chaucer archives housed at the Westminster tenement, as well as those copies already circulating in the metropolis. This would account for his acquaintance with the full corpus of Chaucer's works later catalogued in the *Fall of Princes,*[131] but also his frequent confusion and mistakes over contents indicative of someone unable to consult personal copies and lacking easy access to someone else's.

While the Bury St. Edmunds catalogues list French-language romances, Chaucer's *Canterbury Tales* was not the sort of book likely to enter a monastic library.[132] Still, a large proportion of a monastic library's holdings came by way of donations, and with no way for the monks to exert control over gift-giving, these collections often resembled what David Knowles described as "a heap."[133] Cambridge CUL Gg.4.27 was copied around 1420 in the Cambridgeshire dialect by a scribe working perhaps in Cambridge or Ely. As Chaucer's first real "collected work" that included *Troilus, Canterbury Tales, Legend of Good Women, Parliament of Fowls,* and several lyrics such as *Truth* and *Scogan,* Cambridge Gg represents exactly the sort of manuscript that we would like to imagine Lydgate reading and even commissioning for his own personal use.[134] In one small but telling example of limited access, the Bury monk announces that he will include Chaucer's *ABC,* an excerpt originally translated from Deguileville, in his own complete translation of the *Pèlerinage de la vie humaine*:

> Therefore, as I am bounde off dette,
> In thys book I wyl hym sette,
> And ympen thys Oryson
> Affter hys translacion . . .
> That men may knowe and pleynly se
> Off Our Lady the .A. B. C.[135]

Yet the lyric was not actually included in any of the early manuscripts where spaces were left for the missing lines. Lydgate knew that Chaucer had written this poem but did not have a copy at hand to insert into his own *Pilgrimage of the Life of Man.*[136]

Seldom heavy handed when pursuing his mission as a Lancastrian apologist, Lydgate avoided the risk of topicality by following his monastic instincts and projecting political themes backward into history. Catching the innovative terminology of Chaucer's poem *To His Purse* on the accession of Henry IV—"by lyne and free eleccion / Been verray kyng" (23–24)—

Lydgate's *Siege of Thebes* (1197–1205) provided a classical precedent when Adrastus became king of Argos "of fre eleccioun."[137] While still Prince of Wales during the early 1400s, Henry V had taken an interest in Lydgate's progress as a student at Oxford.[138] Pearsall summarizes the many motives behind this royal patronage: "Henry had his attention drawn to Lydgate's facility as a versifier, recognized his promise as a future Lancastrian propagandist, and perhaps saw too the possibilities for a kind of high-style religious poetry in English that would embody his own austerely orthodox piety, fulfil his desire to promote the English language as an engine of nationhood, and preempt the claims of the Lollards on the vernacular as a language of religion."[139] Later, too, the agency of Chaucerian writing and the construction of English authorship figured as one more component in Henry V's larger campaign of territorial expansion abroad.[140]

When the first stage of foreign aggression was crowned with victory at Agincourt in 1415, the strategy of the military expedition was replaced by a campaign of territorial settlement and colonization in Normandy.[141] Froissart's *Chronicles* recorded the prior episodes of English expansion into the European mainland, and Edward III initiated an early experiment in colonial displacement when he announced his intention to repeople Calais with Englishmen.[142] This plan continued after the Treaty of Brétigny in 1360 when the port city and its surrounding territories became a border community like Wales as an extended part of the British Isles, and in 1379 during the papal schism the city's ecclesiastical assignment was transferred to the diocese of Canterbury. The welfare of these later Normandy colonists would become a major consideration during all Anglo-French negotiations following the Treaty of Troyes in 1420—a date associated, not coincidentally, with the production of the most conspicuous Chaucerian continuation, John Lydgate's *Siege of Thebes*.[143] Describing the unpredictable consequences of wars that ravaged kingdoms and toppled great men, Lydgate's *Thebes* actually alluded to the language of the Treaty of Troyes, which was circulated in an English translation as a singular instance of the Crown's use of the vernacular for mass communication purposes.[144] Again, the network of personal and poetic connections is unusually tight. Thomas Chaucer had partly negotiated this treaty, and he was re-elected speaker of the Commons charged with its ratification in May 1421.[145]

The reconquest of Normandy became a theme of considerable importance in Lancastrian historiography. Even sacred prophecies were rewritten: the English king anointed with the holy oil of St. Thomas Becket would recover the lost territories of Normandy and Aquitaine.[146] Walsingham produced his *Ypodigma Neustriae* (*The Paradigm of Normandy*) between 1419 and 1422 in order to provide a new frame for national history, now bracketed between Rollo's first conquest of Normandy in 911 and Henry V's reassertion of sovereignty over the territory in 1420, an account "which draws on and compresses his other writings into a structure, not of conquests of England, but of English conquests modeled on the Conquest itself."[147] Thus the works of these two monastic writers, Walsingham from St. Albans and Lydgate from Bury St. Edmunds, testify to an expanded role for the Benedictines in buttressing Lancastrian claims. Though Henry V made plans for founding three religious houses for the Carthusians, Bridgettines, and Celestines,[148] ongoing support was expected from the venerable Benedictines, whose credibility as historians was therefore much at stake.

The Monk: Prologue to the *Siege of Thebes*

Lydgate's *Troy Book* had been undertaken for Prince Henry in 1412 in order to bring the great story of chivalric adventure into English—"And y-writen as wel in oure langage / As in latyn and in frensche it is"—and to help to consolidate English national identity along with Prince Henry's legitimacy as heir to royal power.[149] Begun about the same time that Hoccleve's *Regiment* was being completed, the Trojan-theme epic also contributed to the rehabilitation of Chaucer's reputation in the wake of Arundel's *Constitutions* of 1409. Taking a somewhat different view, Lydgate's *Siege of Thebes* was completed after the Treaty of Troyes in May 1420 and probably around the time of Henry V's death in August 1422.[150] The idealized representation of Tydeus as an exemplar of knightly virtues reads like a compliment to the English king, but Lydgate's failure to address the poem to Henry V suggests that he lost his royal patron just before publishing the work.[151]

The relationship between the *Siege* and the king who served as Lydgate's patron has been brilliantly explored by Patterson, and it is my view that the Prologue was also composed with Henry V and his immediate circle as its primary audience.[152] The poet engages in a defense of his religious lifestyle at exactly the moment when the king focused official criticism upon the Benedictine order. His Prologue represents a personal self-justification that can be extended to an entire institutional culture as part of the centuries-old practice of monastic *apologia:* "It may not be so surprising that Black Monks were the first to compose such apologias. New monks and new masters had still to make their way, and they did so in good part by attacking what had gone wrong in the recent past. Black Monks were compelled thus to defend either the appropriateness or the quality of their work as scribes, teachers, administrators and theologians."[153] By restaging the pilgrimage of the *Canterbury Tales* and fitting it to the genre of monastic self-defense, Lydgate appeals to the Chaucerian tradition to emphasize that the business of canon-formation, like the business of writing history, was an enterprise in which religious writers made indispensable contributions.

As a sequel to the *Canterbury Tales,* Lydgate's *Thebes* draws attention to the radical incompleteness of the pilgrimage narrative in the very act of supplementing it. His Prologue extends the frame by imagining that Chaucer's pilgrims had actually arrived at Canterbury, where the Host invites the monastic poet to join their company. Compared with the *Canterbury Interlude,* his continuation comes off as a disappointment. The visit to the shrine has already been accomplished, and the original pilgrims are never described as actual presences, only as a jumbled group of characters vaguely remembered and sometimes misremembered. After a section praising the original author as a national treasure for all of Britain—"Floure of poetes thorghout al Breteyne" (40)—Lydgate displaces not only Chaucer but all other pilgrims as well, installing himself as the exclusive focus of the Prologue in his confrontation with the talkative Host.[154] Seen in the long-standing tradition of Benedictine defensiveness, the Prologue becomes a justification, placed in the mouth of this secular authority figure, of what could easily be construed as the monk's irregular conduct.

It has long been recognized that Lydgate's self-portrait draws upon the topics and even the precise phrases used to describe Chaucer's Monk in the *Canterbury Tales.*[155] This fifteenth-century rewriting of the monastic figure functions largely to refute the accusations of corruption and excess that informed Chaucer's caricature. But Lydgate's performance does more than "correct" Chaucer's original. Recent microscopic investigation of the Ellesmere miniatures reveals some repainting of the Monk's portrait (fol. 169a), with sober black pigment covering over the original golden pin and love-knot around his neck (*CT,* I, 195–97).[156] This retouching accords with the more wide-ranging project of rendering Chaucer, his pilgrims, and his works themselves more respectable for fifteenth-century readers. It is hardly coincidental that Ellesmere's touched-up image of the Monk comes to resemble the portrait of the pious Monk Lydgate in the famous illustration from the BL Royal 18 D.ii manuscript of the *Siege of Thebes.*[157]

What has seldom been factored into these critical assessments is the urgent topicality of Lydgate's response to these complaints against monks. In

March of 1421, at precisely the time the *Thebes* was being written, the king took a sudden interest in the laxity of Benedictine foundations in England. Henry V's sense of Christian kingship obliged him to rehabilitate older institutions rather than simply found new ones.[158] To this end, he sent a letter to the abbot of Bury St. Edmunds asking him to convene a General Chapter in Westminster at the beginning of May. The king's representatives formulated his complaints in thirteen articles, and monastic committees answered these charges in two separate responses, one coauthored by William Courtney, the future abbot of Bury St. Edmunds.[159] Then Henry V departed for France in June 1421. By the time the Benedictine commission had completed its final report in July 1423, their royal critic had died and the government of his infant heir, Henry VI, had more pressing business than improving standards of monastic conduct.

Lydgate's *Thebes* Prologue was composed amid the heat of these controversies. His tactics were different from those of the Benedictine committees, which tended to defend modern practices by citing revision of canonist authorities and deferring to the authority of the abbots to regulate behavior within their separate houses. Lydgate gave every appearance of siding with the king's sentiments, offering his own self-figuration as an upright example adhering to the ancient ideals and practices of St. Benedict's *Rule*. Any apparent irregularities in his livelihood became defensible in terms of exemptions carefully spelled out in this authoritative text. These were the same appeals to original standards that Henry V extolled concerning the pristine religion of the monks (*de pristina religione monachorum*) when he personally attended the Westminster convocation in May 1421.[160]

Chaucer had cannily anticipated these criticisms when his Monk rejected ancient standards of conduct: "This ilke Monk leet olde thynges pace / And heeld after the newe world the space" (*CT,* I, 175–76). Because the *Tales* quickly became a staple of Lancastrian literary culture, it is conceivable that Chaucer's caricature of the Monk contributed to Henry V's concern for laxity among the Benedictines. Article 11 of the king's criticisms targeted exactly these same abuses, for example, condemning monks who left their cloister to seek amusements such as outdoor sports that were the favorites of Chaucer's Monk: "Of prikyng and of huntyng for the hare / Was al his lust, for no cost wolde he spare" (*CT,* I, 191–92).[161]

Espousing the venerable traditions of monastic austerity, Lydgate counters these charges by depicting himself as a pious pilgrim traveling to Canterbury with the utmost humility (70–76):

That me byfil to entren into toun,
The holy seynt pleynly to visite
Aftere siknesse, my vowes to aquyte,
In a cope of blak and not of grene,
On a palfrey slender, long and lene,
With rusty brydel mad nat for the sale,
My man toforn with a voide male.

Barbara Harvey observes that well-off monks routinely made pilgrimages to sites such as Canterbury, and for a monk struggling with ill health, as Lydgate describes himself, there was no questions of the "therapeutic value of the holiday."[162]

Whereas Article 5 repeated Chaucer's charge that Benedictines had begun wearing elaborate habits made from expensive dyed cloth (*CT,* I, 193–97),[163] Lydgate describes himself wearing the standard black habit. His "thred-bare hood" (90) was actually inferior to what the *Rule* directed monks to wear when journeying outside the cloister: "Those who are sent on a journey . . . let their cowls and tunics be somewhat better than what they usually wear."[164] Lydgate's skinny horse contrasts with the stable of fine thoroughbreds provided for Chaucer's Monk (*CT,* I, 168). Article 2 criticized decorations on monastic horses, especially gilt bosses and elaborate bridles such as the Monk's jingling gear (*CT,* I, 169–71).[165] These complaints are answered by Lydgate's description of his rusty bridle and later by the Host's observation that the monk's "bridel have neither boos ne belle" (85).

Living like gentry, fifteenth-century Benedictines, who numbered sixty to eighty at Bury St. Edmunds, belonged to a wealthy foundation that enjoyed an annual income around £2000 and employed a staff of around two hundred servants. The sumptuous liveries of these servants figured in Article 2's complaints.[166] Yet Lydgate describes himself traveling with only a single manservant, who wears no livery and carries in his lap an empty purse. Though easily taken as a plea for more generous patronage, the reference to an empty purse also replies to Article 4's restrictions on monks having any personal money.[167] When the Host observes that "to ben a monk, sclender is youre koyse!" (102), the poet refutes another popular prejudice, expressed in Article 7, that monks ignored their obligation for fasting by overindulging in all manner of luxury foods, such as the Monk's roasted swan (*CT,* I, 206). Consequently real-life monks were "surely on average rather obese."[168] By contrast, the Host's recommendation that Lydgate should dine on pudding and haggis, followed by an omelette or a pancake, lay well within the approved menu of minced meats and dairy products. The *Rule* permitted meat to sick monks even during seasons of fasting.[169]

Lydgate's Prologue continues this line of response, shifting responsibility for any irregularities to the Host's directions. Since he has been sick, Lydgate is told to neglect his Divine Office by not rising at midnight and to improve his rest by sleeping with a pillow and wrapping his head in turbanlike scarves (109–21). These comforts violated the *Rule*'s guidelines for proper monastic bedclothes according to Henry V's Article 13.[170] Moreover, Article 9 forbade monks from owning personal books such as the collection of a hundred tragedies that Chaucer's Monk keeps in his cell (*CT,* VII, 1971–72). Because a good monk had only scriptural writings borrowed from the library by giving a document of indenture to the prior,[171] Lydgate is described as reading piously from a portable breviary (162). Here he follows the *Rule*'s requirement that monks should not neglect their service while on a journey.

When instructed by the Host to tell a merry tale, Lydgate offers his 4540-line epic chronicling the disastrous careers of a series of Theban rulers, from Edipus to Creon.[172] Its conclusion dovetails with the beginning of the Knight's Tale, closing the circle of the *Canterbury Tales* by ending where the taletelling had begun, with the war between Athens and Thebes.[173] Chaucer's original Monk's Tale had been interrupted by the Knight, who wanted to hear about no more tragic reversals that had befallen kings. These included Peter Lusignan, King of Cyprus—"That Alisandre wan by heigh maistrie" (*CT,* VII, 2391–98)—whom the Knight had served in the first campaign described in his portrait in the General Prologue: "At Alisuandre he was whan it was wonne" (I, 51). Chaucer's Monk has drummed away relentlessly at the reality of violence, defeat, death, and dispossession which a warrior needed to repress as precondition for a military career:

> But what the Monk has to say in his strangely mechanical way is quite dreadful. And this does not simply prove his insensitivity to dreadfulness. He emphasizes that it is the business of tragedy to "bewail." He raises the stakes of tragedy, catastrophizes it further; tragedy is not just about an "overturning" or an unhappy end, but about falling to an end utterly without resources . . . Tragedy invokes the limit beyond which action, technology, enhancements of sentience are relevant.[174]

Addressing his own cautionary history to Henry V after his military victory in France, the Monk of Bury returns to this dreadful, forbidden subject by offering a prequel to the Knight's Tale with its own version of chivalric triumph undercut by tragedy. Lydgate renews the clerical claim that aristocratic ambitions were always inevitably subject to the downturn of Fortune's wheel, here offering a chilling riposte to the Knight as the embodiment of these chivalric values and self-deluding aspirations.[175] Later in the fifteenth century when dynastic conflict seemed destined for civil war, Lydgate wrote *The Fall of Princes* in which he trumped Chaucer's Monk with the sheer number of changeful histories of great men, whose downfalls lacked even the predictability of a single or simple meaning.[176]

Lydgate's *Troy Book* had already dramatized the suicidal dynamic of conquest and territorial expansion.[177] If Chaucer's Monk had stripped his tragedies down to the bare bones of arbitrary and inanimate laws devoid of consolation, Lydgate inflated the dimensions of his storytelling and gave greater scope to his characters, using this distention of time to intensify the pathos of inevitable outcomes and provoke forethought for his readers: "Beware!" Despite his modern reputation as a Lancastrian apologist, Lydgate took pains in his two ostensibly heroic *romans anciens* to prepare England's military rulers for the catastrophic fiasco that France became, while later works, particularly the *Fall of Princes,* assailed their imperialist ambitions and domestic infighting.[178] This tragic viewpoint remained the default discourse for monastic historians such as Walsingham who automatically configured the English Rising, for example, as a tragedy for Richard II and his nobility.[179] Because *The Siege of Thebes* figures in Lydgate's continuing counsel to royalty, specifically warning Bedford and Gloucester against fraternal strife after the death of Henry V, the Prologue works ingeniously at reclaiming his credibility as a monk in order to validate this advisory role.[180] By representing himself as an upright example, Lydgate averted the mistake that Hoccleve made when describing himself publicly as unstable and unsound.

This persistent exculpation of personal conduct invites further speculation about Lydgate's circumstances for poetic occupation, which may also have fallen within the purview of King Henry's 1421 criticisms. Article 10 stated that no monk should have a private room or cell separate from the communal dormitory. Yet monastic officials such as the cellarer and sexton—that is, administrative offices of the kind that Harry Bailey assumes the Monk fills (*CT,* VII, 1935–38)—did invariably occupy private apartments, as did other monks clearly less distinguished, inside and outside the cloister, than John Lydgate.[181] His vast output of verse would have been impossible if the writer had participated fully in the monastery's communal worship. The religious lifestyle included repeated interruptions for long liturgical services, day and night, shoulder to shoulder with the lowly novices mentioned so disparagingly by Harry Bailey (*CT,* VII, 1939).

Henry V's Article 10 made one important exception to this prohibition against private quarters, as well as allowing dispensation from dietary restrictions and the regular round of liturgical services. The *Rule* itself made this same exception for monks who were infirm, whether by illness or old age or both.[182] Here I suggest Lydgate exploited a major loophole, seizing upon Chaucer's original rationale for the Canterbury pilgrimage to give thanks to the saint who helped people "whan that they were seeke" (*CT,* I, 18).[183] Lydgate too claims that he traveled to Canterbury "aftere siknesse" to fulfill a vow to the saint. What is more, the monastic poet goes out of his way to disclose his advancing age in the same line where he gives his name: "I answerde my name was Lydgate / Monk of Bery, nygh fyfty yere of age" (92–93).[184] The Host becomes almost obsessed with Lydgate's status as an aging invalid and uses the monk's lingering ill health as pretext for relaxing religious strictures following his overnight stay in Canterbury. Focusing his concern on the intestinal ailment "collis passioun," the Host observes that Lydgate looks so sickly that he should eat heartily and season his meal with medicinal spices such as fennel, anise, cumin, and coriander.[185] He must also bundle up warmly for bed and refrain from rising at midnight (113–20). The Host even stresses the therapeutic value of their merry companionship: "A company, parde, shal do you good!" (125).[186]

Lydgate needed to proceed cautiously. Branded by Benedictine regulations with the Latin verb *lordicare,* a malingering monk could fall under the same suspicion of *lurdici et loselli*—in the vernacular "lollers and losels"— well established in the age's lexicon for those who feigned illness or infirmity to enjoy an idle life.[187] So the poet uses the Host as the voice of secular authority to ventriloquize permission for irregular actions already taken, exemptions already exploited, and dispensations already transformed by Lydgate into a lifestyle of mobility, personal comfort, and social-climbing ambition. This erasure of criticism becomes part of what Patterson describes as "overcoming division, correcting waywardness and suppressing dissent" in the sense that the Host's allowances coincide exactly with Lydgate's chosen lifestyle.[188] Their social solidarity offers contemporary correction to the recurrent tragedy of political divisiveness dramatized throughout *The Siege of Thebes.* Any potential friction between Henry V and Lydgate has been translated into a jocular exchange between the robust innkeeper and the weedy monk. The Host's bantering tone conceals the poet's anxiety over any threat to the long-standing, mutually beneficial alliance between Crown and cloister in 1421.

In her study of the wealthy community of Westminster Abbey, Barbara Harvey observes that chambers in the monastery's infirmary became highly desirable, because their occupants were automatically relieved of the obligation to participate in the monastic routine *and* because these quarters were comfortable and quiet. Since the infirmary was closed off from the foot traffic that was almost constant elsewhere, it became the place favored by those absorbed in their studies.[189] One of the official responses to the king's articles stressed this same point, maintaining that private chambers were necessary for the careful concentration required by students, advanced scholars, and administrative officials.[190] But Lydgate eschews such arguments by falling back on the allowance made by the king's own articles for the elderly and infirm. By appealing to ancient practices, he justified exactly the exemptions that he needed to perform his work as a writer and advice-giver to royalty: personal privacy, healthy diet, undisturbed sleep, and plenty of peace and quiet. Speculation stops just short of proposing a forerunner to Marcel Proust sequestered in his cork-lined bedroom and complaining of ill health, real or fancied, while producing a vast amount of writing in these sheltered accommodations.

Finally, Lydgate's decision to represent himself as a pilgrim to the shrine of St. Thomas has additional significance in light of the saint's controversial status during this period. The poet shows devotion to the same saint singled out for veneration by his royal patron's father. Henry IV had shown special devotion to Becket including his choice of a burial place. Perhaps uncomfortable with the prospect of being surrounded by the monuments of the Plantagenets whom he had supplanted—including the still-empty tomb of Richard II, whose specter haunted him psychologically and politically[191]— he followed the example of his uncle the Black Prince by preferring entombment at Canterbury Cathedral instead of Westminster Abbey. The 1410 burial of his half-brother John Beaufort, Earl of Somerset, indicates that Canterbury was already functioning as a mausoleum for the Lancastrian dynasty. Henry IV's connection with the cathedral grew stronger after he was anointed with the holy oil discovered there and believed to have been the Virgin's gift to St. Thomas Becket.

In short, Henry V's father had wagered heavily upon the sanctity of St. Thomas of Canterbury. "The claim to have received unction with the oil of St. Thomas put the Lancastrian succession under the patronage of Canterbury's and England's premier saint in the most public and unambiguous manner."[192] Royal endorsement on such a grand ceremonial scale prepared for Henry V himself to grant devotion publicly to the cult of St. Thomas. In the arena of international competition, too, the saint's Englishness rivaled the Frenchness of St. Denis and St. Clovis.[193] Lydgate's literary enactment of the Canterbury pilgrimage with his grateful homage to the saint's restorative powers—and his forthright confidence in the rite's legitimacy proclaimed boldly "I ha therof no shame!" (95)—implied recognition of the political status of the martyr while offering tacit rebuttal to Becket's most vocal critics. Though Lydgate praised Gloucester as a foe of Lollards in the *Fall of Princes,* the poet himself was usually much more reticent about religious controversy.[194] Here his maneuver has the added advantage of positioning Chaucer, as the original author of the Canterbury pilgrimage, more solidly on the orthodox side of a religious division that became more perilous during the two decades after his death.

Within the achieved text of the *Canterbury Tales,* Chaucer had included a whole array of gaps, interruptions, ruptures, ellipses, and discursive fragments which in turn invited a variety of responses from later readers. Attempts by Lydgate and the anonymous author of the *Canterbury Interlude* to supply those missing parts constitute a second category of evidence, offering a second occasion for interpretation. "What is methodologically interesting," Patterson has noted, "is precisely the amount of interpretation that is required to recover the act of interpretation itself."[195] Chaucer's poetry drew its fiercest wit and its most disturbing human truths from the social tensions that energized English life during the 1390s. His textual engagements persisted after his death, among those producing manuscripts of this work, to aggravate those tensions *or* provoke responses calculated to dampen those energies. Some social antagonisms simply passed from the scene. Others, such as the criticism of monks and the debate over pilgrimage, assumed greater urgency and involved the full technology of institutional self-protection.

The real subversiveness of Chaucer's literary provocations can be detected in his ability to lure later continuators into a sort of ambush, forcing them to refocus attention on precisely these controversies in their efforts to adjust, qualify, and correct. Lydgate entered into the controversies surrounding the laxity of the Benedictines, and he managed in the *Thebes* Prologue and other writings such as *The Serpent of Division,* completed soon afterward, to remove any doubt of his loyalty and usefulness.[196] In February 1423, as evidence of Lydgate's success, the King's Council granted him a portion of some rents and, later that year, appointed him prior of a small Benedictine house in Essex that he would hold until 1430. Residing at Hatfield where the daily regime was more relaxed, Lydgate could pursue the literary projects that became considerable as commissions rolled in. In 1439 he finally received an annual grant of ten marks from the royal exchequer, though a hitch developed for exactly the reason that he had previously addressed—the prohibition against monks receiving cash payments.[197] By 1440, as explicit recognition of his status as a professional poet, Lydgate received direct payment of £3.6s.8d. for writing *St. Albon and St. Amphibalus* for Abbot Whethamstead of St. Albans. This entry in the abbot's register constitutes the first English record of a payment specifically for literary services.[198] Official payment from a Benedictine abbot clearly indicates that the *Rule*'s prohibition had ceased to pose the same practical concern that worried Lydgate around 1421. Chaucer had created the cultural category of the English author, and now Lydgate proceeded to establish the terms of a writer's professional contracts and earnings.

CHAPTER SEVEN

Piers Plowman, Print, and Protestantism

WHEN WILLIAM CAXTON (C. 1420–92) RETURNED TO ENGLAND AND re-established his publishing business in 1476, he set up shop in Westminster in order to appeal specifically to members of the royal court and civil service with money and long-established interests in vernacular reading. Appealing to this clientele of better-off citizens, churchmen, and visitors from the shires, the printer ensured his capital venture by providing courtly and pious subject matter while avoiding home-grown controversies. His prologue to the *History of Troy* stated that he was born in Kent and spoke the "brode and rude Englissh" of his provincial origins. Kent and especially the Weald had become a notorious center for Lollardy in the late fifteenth century perhaps through a network of artisans involved in the local cloth industry,[1] and therefore Caxton, a mercer by profession, may have worked especially hard to distance himself from guilt by association during his publishing career. Any hint of heresy would have jeopardized his bottom line.

Serving as publisher blurbs, Caxton's prologues and epilogues reflected what he took to be the acceptable standards of literary connoisseurship during the Yorkist and early Tudor periods. His translations also mirrored the preferences of aristocratic readers by excluding old-fashioned "rude" native writings out of touch with metropolitan stylishness.[2] From the beginning, the new print technology contributed powerfully to the narrowing of linguistic and metrical possibilities for English literature.[3] Much of Chaucer's canon was represented in Caxton's printing of *The House of Fame, Boece, Anelida and Arcite, Parliament of Fowls, Troilus and Criseyde,* and two separate editions of the *Canterbury Tales.* He printed John Gower's courtly *Confessio Amantis,* appealing to readers who might want "dyuers hystoryes and fables towchynge euery matere,"[4] but he regarded John Lydgate narrowly as a monk-poet best represented by didactic and religious works such as *The Court of Sapience* and *Life of Our Lady.* While these three named poets had already established themselves as the favorites of scribal workshops geared to commercial production prior to the printing press,[5] Caxton's acceptance of Chaucer, Gower, and Lydgate as the originators of English poetry proved decisive in establishing the canonic authors of the poetic tradition and indeed promulgating the whole idea of vernacular authorship.

Caxton's printing of a prose version of the *Pilgrimage of the Soul* instead of Lydgate's verse translation of Deguileville's *Pèlerinage de la vie humaine* reflects his general preference for prose works. His neglect of the English Bible is therefore remarkable. Its omission probably reflects the continuing cloud of suspicion after Archbishop Arundel's *Constitutions* banned vernacular renderings of sacred Scripture. Instead, he printed Nicholas Love's *Speculum Vitae Christi* as one of the officially sanctioned English-language religious works; Arundel himself had actually mandated its distribution in order to confute Lollards. This concern for avoiding religious controversy, together with his rejection of outdated poetical language, would account for his other glaring omission—William Langland's *Piers Plowman.*[6]

In his preface to the second edition of the *Canterbury Tales* in 1484, Caxton carefully qualified his notion of Chaucer's role as a national poet by placing strict limits on proper writers and preferred genres. He publicized the wholesome variety of stories—"whyche ben of noblesse, wysedom, gentyl-esse, myrthe, and also of veray holynesse and vertue"—to assure buyers that they would get good value for their investment. He shrewdly sensed the marketability of his wares when excluding other writings from the national canon on the basis of style: "in thys royame was had rude speche & incongrue / as yet it appiereth by olde bookes / whyche at thys day ought not to haue place."[7] What was this rude language? Which were the old books? In comparison with the Winchester manuscript, his 1485 adaptation of Malory's *Le Morte Darthur* reveals how Caxton removed objectionable features of non-London diction and particularly alliteration.[8] Though defended on aesthetic grounds, his rejection of the non-Chaucerian tradition epitomized by *Piers Plowman* can be interpreted as Caxton's commitment of his new technology

to the religious orthodoxy as well as the social values of his named patrons
William FitzAlan, Earl of Arundel, John de Vere, Earl of Oxford, Margaret,
Duchess of Somerset and mother of Henry VII, and the Woodvilles—Anthony,
Earl Rivers, Elizabeth, wife of Edward IV, and her daughter Elizabeth,
wedded to Henry VII in 1486.[9] Clearly there was a close connection
between Caxton's decision to locate his press in Westminster and his choice
of books for printing. Records show that for the week Parliament was sitting
in 1477, Caxton rented a nearby shop to exhibit his wares directly to this target
audience.[10] At a time when the economy of medieval Westminster was
based primarily upon the entrapment of consumers, Caxton's printing projects
succeeded by retailing certain books in the metropolitan marketplace
while excluding others.[11]

Denied wider distribution during the earliest period of the print revolution,
Piers Plowman continued to be read by friends and foes alike. James
Simpson's view that ongoing censorship caused a withering of the Langland
tradition and a failure to exert any real influence on later literature is skewed
by a sense of "literature" and "influence" essentially Chaucerian.[12] As Fiona
Somerset's recent work makes clear, the Langlandian mode far transcended
alliterative style and recurring plowman figures to infiltrate a wide range of
dissenting Latin as well as vernacular discourses, palpable in nearly every
form of reformist writing, eventually contributing to the redefinition of
Chaucer's own literary identity in Tudor England.[13]

In the first half of the sixteenth century, the manuscript evidence indicates
that *Piers* remained the hand-copied object of various political constructions
such as BL Royal 18.B.xvii and Cambridge CUL Gg.4.31. The
latter's sidenotes and extensive table of contents emphasized prophecies
concerning the king, bishops, and religious orders.[14] With occasional marginalia
by the main scribe around 1400, BL Cotton Vespasian B.xvi was later
supplied with at least three series of sixteenth-century annotations.[15] Written
in the second quarter of the fifteenth century, Cambridge CUL Ll.4.14 includes
a glossary that was added over a hundred years later, perhaps by Robert
Crowley himself as an early stage in his editorial project.[16]

Textual activities in 1532 provide ample testimony to the continuing public
life of *Piers Plowman*. In this year, Sir Adrian Fortescue copied out in his
own hand, signed, and dated the intact manuscript Bodleian MS Digby 145
with an A-text followed by a C continuation (fols. 2a–130a).[17] Langland's
poem is then followed by a transcription of *The Dyfference betwene Dominium
Regale et Dominium Politicum & Regale* (fols. 133a–159a). Sir Adrian's great-uncle
Sir John Fortescue (c. 1395–c. 1477), chief justice of the King's Bench, had
written this essay on the differences between French absolute monarchy and

English constitutional monarchy, a distinction much at issue during the reign of Henry VIII.[18] These two apparently disparate works have as their common denominator an Aristotelian conviction in the rule of reason by which the king is answerable to the body politic from which he derives his sovereignty. Each urges reform by a return to earlier, better practices. A few notes and marginal markings were even added to *Piers* by Sir Adrian's young wife, Anne, with two actual signatures, as evidence of an intelligent, fully engaged female reader.[19]

As a copyist, Sir Adrian was remarkable in his conservative handling of the text. Although he may have had access to two exemplars, he did not otherwise attempt to intervene, censor, or modernize the language.[20] Following prior practices that he may have discovered in his copy-texts, he provided a full series of annotations, also dated 1532, serving as a guide to topics, and he employed the occasional *nota bene* to draw attention to particular lines. These sidenotes refer to the long-familiar controversies over hermits, beggars, pilgrims, idolatry, penance, confession, laborers, marriage, and the priesthood. There are at least twenty-seven remarks on friars. In his thorough study of this manuscript, Thorlac Turville-Petre suggests that the C-text further highlighted issues of the 1530s such as clerical negligence and false relics as well as the authority of the bishops, royal servants, and the king himself.[21]

Sir Adrian's mother was the great-aunt of Anne Boleyn, and he enjoyed favor at court when copying these texts, receiving grants of land previously in the possession of Cardinal Wolsey. Yet the younger Fortescue witnessed with alarm the turn of royal power against the Crown's traditional ally, the Church. His notations revived a pre-1381 view of *Piers Plowman* as a poem of sweeping social vision, whose moral insights might be applied to the current political scene to repair rather than discard existing religious institutions. Also in 1532, Sir Adrian was admitted as a lay associate of the Knights of the Order of St. John of Malta, and a year after the Langland transcription, he joined the confraternity of the Black Friars in Oxford. Both moves represented rebuffs to radical reformers. He nonetheless bought a copy of *The Plowman's Tale* during the year after it was published by Thomas Godfray. The same year saw passage of the Submission of the Clergy moving decisively toward Henry VIII's goal of becoming supreme head of the English Church.

Turville-Petre's conclusion seems balanced: "If Fortescue's attitudes can be simply characterized, perhaps the right description for them is Henrician; if he was orthodox, then he was orthodox in the same way as the king himself, sharing his ferocious anticlericalism and apparently supporting his absolutist tendencies."[22] Whatever the precise reasons for Sir Adrian's fall from royal favor and execution without trial in 1539, later Catholics promoted him as one of their martyrs. His work on behalf of Langland's poem can be construed as a last-ditch effort at moderation mounted against the forces of a stronger Reformation movement. When his manuscript came into the collection of Kenelm Digby, a passionate convert to Catholicism, it was safeguarded from further tampering as if accorded the status of a holy object, the relic of a martyr.[23]

Also dated 1532, the Catholic prose debate-piece *The Banckett of Iohan the Reve vnto Pers Ploughman* survives only in BL Harley 207.[24] Here the Protestant serving man Jack Jolie quotes Martin Luther and other reformers on the Eucharist. Uncharacteristically, the latter-day Pers functions as a defender of the orthodox Catholic position. He gives voice to a rural conservatism reflecting the fact that country parishes, far from London, usually clung most ardently to the older conventions of religious devotion. He grows extremely angry, as originally Piers Plowman did in the Pardon Scene, and vents his hostility by calling his opponent a "fals heritike." Pers remains the enemy of newfangled ideas throughout the symposium, defending the doctrine of the true presence by citing "catholicke writers" such as Augustine, Ambrose, Jerome, Tertullian, and Gregory. He attacks the Protestant position with the tactic, previously used amid Lollard debates, of appealing to original traditions stretching back "XV hundred ʒeares and more."

Another work contemporary with Fortescue's *Piers* transcription, *The Praier and Complaynte of the Ploweman* reasserts the reformist Protestant version of the plowman figure.[25] This pamphlet was printed in Antwerp probably in 1531 and reprinted in London the next year by Thomas Godfray, the same printer who produced *The Plowman's Tale*. John Bale and John Foxe attributed the publication to William Tyndale,[26] and Sir Thomas More condemned the "Ploughmans Prayour" in his *Confutation of Tyndale's Answer* in 1532. Its self-conscious connection with the Wycliffite tradition is further suggested by borrowings from *The Examinacion of Master William Thorpe* printed in 1530. There are further textual relations with the Lollard *Lanterne of Lyʒt* also printed in the early 1530s.[27]

Never actually called Piers, the plowman in *The Praier and Complaynte* assumes the role of the principal Protestant spokesman. Although the prose style owes no clear debt to Langlandian idiom and the author shows no direct knowledge of *Piers Plowman,* the work's archaic vocabulary required the first printer to include a one-page glossary of hard words, suggesting it was partly an authentic Lollard text and not completely a sixteenth-century forgery.[28] The preface refutes conservatives who argued that the reformed religion offered "new lerninge" by showing that these doctrines actually had long-standing authority. The work claims its own venerable status as a document written "not longe after the yere of oure Lorde a thousande and three hundred / in his awne olde english." While the Ploweman chiefly quotes the Old Testament for its foundational wisdom, the text's own old-fashioned language served a similar purpose by bestowing authority on doctrines that otherwise seemed like innovations. Crowley would claim much the same privilege for reform theology by appealing to the fourteenth-century example of John Wyclif.

A great deal of revision and interpolation sharpened polemical points in the *Praier and Complaynte.* Long-standing Wycliffite positions surfaced in the rejection of auricular confession, attacks on the mendicants, a shift in the doctrine of the Eucharist, defensiveness over charges of heresy, anger at the greed of the priesthood, attacks on religious imagery—"blynde mawmetes of stokes and of stones"—and denial of the pope's legitimacy as successor to St. Peter. In the manner firmly established when Jerome Barlowe and William Roye published their *Proper dyaloge betwene a Gentillman and an Husbandman* in 1530—a work that assimilates a Wycliffite tract described as "an olde treatyse made about the tyme of kinge Rychard the seconde"[29]—the Ploweman practices honest prayer uncorrupted by a desire for financial reward and stands as a representative of the impoverished laborers neglected by the priesthood. Indeed, the *Praier and Complaynte* preserves one of the clearest articulations of the extreme Lollard belief that property should be owned communally.[30]

The literary as well as political climate changed radically during the reign of Edward VI (1547–53).[31] The young king's uncle Edward Seymour led a faction of Protestant aristocrats to relax Crown censorship. This move triggered an explosion of radical publications, some new and some old, such as the 1553 printing of late fourteenth-century *Pierce the Ploughman's Crede.*[32] One new work was *Pyers Plowmans exhortation vnto the lordes, knightes and burgoysses of the Parlyamenthouse,* dedicated to King Edward. This prose text was printed in London about 1550 by Anthony Scoloker and possibly composed by the *Piers* editor Crowley.[33] Suddenly the Langlandian tradition had become both official and orthodox, ideologically aligned with the royalist cause and the new state religion.

Addressing the economic consequences of the Reformation, Pyers Plowman expresses heart-felt sympathy for the poor with an egalitarian tone harkening back to the Blackheath sermon of John Ball. "It is not agreable with the gospel," says Pyers, "that a fewe parsons shall lyue in so great aboundaunce of wealth and suffer so many their christen brothers to lyue in extreme pouertie." The address to the Parliament also distantly echoes the *Twelve Conclusions of the Lollards.* Yet here we find a new humanist plowman who appeals

to natural law in confronting the social ills that resulted from the dissolution
of the abbeys, when so many monks, friars, hermits, and chantry priests have
been dumped upon the labor market. He also laments the impact of so many
formerly celibate priests and nuns now freely procreating and creating a baby
boom. Pyers voices chagrin at the amount of spare time created by the abo-
lition of pilgrimages, holidays, and image making, and he offers a solution
consonant with the views of Langland's original plowman: "all must be put
to labour." The interplay of royal governance, labor capital, and a moneyed
economy on a national level—"that this litell realme is like to florish and
excell in wealth and prosperite all the realms in the world"—offers a prag-
matic formulation of many of the social themes originally sounded in *Piers
Plowman*.

Hugh Latimer's *Sermon on the Plowers,* delivered in 1548 and published
later in the same year, attests to the continuing currency of the plowman figure as a powerful trope for urging ecclesiastical reform.[34] Printed possibly in
1550, the small black-letter book *I playne Piers which can not flatter* departs from
the narrow concern with eucharistic controversies to address a great many
distinctly Langlandian social concerns. The greed of the old priesthood
brought suffering upon the poor, even though poverty is recommended as a
virtue; the violent persecution of popish agents is offensive, even though
such disciplinary powers are endorsed as the king's rights. Belying the title's
claim of a plain-speaking Piers, these contradictions reflected the confusion
and disillusion late in Henry VIII's reign when enthusiasm for religious
change collided with the monarch's own religious conservatism. This Protestant Piers called for allowing layfolk to read the Bible in the vernacular instead of secular works by poets such as John Gower: "You allowe they say
Legenda Aurea, Roben Hoode, Beuys and Gower and al bagage besyd, but
Gods word ye may not abyde."[35]

Despite its allusions to Thomas More, William Tyndale and other figures
of the 1530s and 1540s, *I playne Piers* also incorporates material from the
fifteenth-century Lollard poem elsewhere provided with a Chaucerian prologue and printed as the *Plowman's Tale.* Although written in prose, the piece
breaks into poetical doggerel at three points with discernible meter and
rhyme scheme.[36] The slim volume concludes with the little poem *God Speed
the Plow,* eerily recalling the broadsides of 1381:

> God saue the kynge and speede the ploughe.
> And sende the prelates care ynoughe.
> Ynoughe, ynoughe, ynoughe.[37]

The text possibly incorporated portions of other Lollard works that survive nowhere else and therefore remain unidentifiable.

Mostly concerned with the doctrine of the Eucharist, the prose *A Godly dyalogue and dysputacyon betwene Pyers plowman and a popysh preest* was printed twice in 1550 by W. Copland and therefore participated in the reformist zeal evident in Crowley's edition of *Piers Plowman.* This fiercely Protestant Pyers stands in sharp contrast to another plowman figure in *A Lytell Geste How the Plowman Lerned his Pater Noster,* a 208-line couplet composition published as early as 1510 by Wynkyn de Worde. Here a greedy farmer was tricked by his parson into memorizing the Latin prayer by attaching each separate word to a donation.[38] By contrast, the twelve-page *Godly dyalogue* resuscitates Langland's hero as an inspired theologian opposing four ignorant priests gathered for a neighborhood dinner. The sole subject of the debate is another sort of meal, the sacrament of the altar. Moved by the Holy Spirit, Pyers immediately demonstrates his theological erudition. When accused of heresy, he responds with a barrage of quotations from Augustine supporting the doctrine of Christ's symbolic presence in the bread and wine, sometimes quoting the original Latin in order to overwhelm and humiliate the ill-educated clergymen. As a gesture of desperation, one priest's remarks served as a reminder that Arundel's *Constitutions* were still in effect until 1529: "Forsoth, it were a straunge matter to reason uppon before the laye people." The other priests rebuke laymen "busy in readynge of Englysh," a complaint also standard throughout fifteenth-century campaigns against Lollards and persistent in prosecutions during the 1520s.[39]

Robert Crowley's 1550 edition of *Piers* with its engraved title page—and its bold proclamation "cum priuilegio"—marks the poem's official recuperation for Protestant England. Finally confirmed as a named author, Langland achieved his position as Father of English Literary Dissent when his brand of religious reform was channeled back into the mainstream and became temporarily the new orthodoxy.[40] Crowley's text went through three quarto editions during its first year, with each of the two reprints embodying changes based on collations with new manuscripts.[41] These additional print runs suggest that the initial publication met with even greater success than Crowley had anticipated, sparking a real vogue in Langland-inspired texts that included *I playne Piers, A Godly dyalogue,* and *Pyers Plowmans exhortation.*[42]

Boldly advertising the name of John Wyclif, previously condemned as England's great heresiarch, Crowley's preface followed John Bale's *Image of Bothe Churches* by looking back to the reign of Edward III as a time when God inspired certain pious men with the gift of reforming vision expressed in the vernacular:

to open their mouthes and crye oute agaynste the workes of darck-
enes, as did John Wicklefe, who also in those dayes translated the
holye Bible into the Englishe tonge, and this writer who in reportynge
certaine visions and dreames, that he fayned himselfe to haue
dreamed.

Bale had originally conjectured that Wyclif wrote *Petrus Agricola,* then retreated to the position that its author was one of Wyclif's leading disciples.[43]
Yet despite the fact that fifteenth-century *Piers Plowman* manuscripts such as
Oxford MS Bodley 814 contain sixteenth-century marginalia emphasizing
the poem's prophetic contents,[44] Crowley remained suspicious of the poem's
prophetic strains and rejected these features as spurious accretions: "And
that whiche foloweth and geueth it the face of a prophecye is lyke to be a
thinge added of some other man than the fyrste autour." He cast Langland
as a visionary precursor of the Reformation instead of an apocalyptic writer
predicting pessimistically the end of time. This is the moral note upon which
Crowley ended his preface: "Loke not vpon this boke therfore to talke of
wonders paste or to come, but to amende thyne owne misse."[45] A sidenote
for Passus 3 in the second printing extended this sense of caution: "Thys is
no prophecye, but a truth gathered of the scriptures." In sum, Crowley's
preface and especially the "Principall Poyntes" prefixed as a plot summary
encouraged the hortatory themes in contemporary reformist works such as
I playne Piers and *Pyers Plowmans exhortation.*

The teleology of Reformation historiography extended to the construction of literary history. John Bale had surveyed the entire range of English
literary works from the previous two centuries even as the monastic libraries
that safeguarded them were being dispersed and destroyed. Finally printed in
1557–59, his *Catalogus* offered some fourteen hundred bio-bibliographic en-
tries to create a "unified field theory" of Protestant textual production.[46]
John Wyclif, "Robert" Langland, Richard Maidstone, John Gower, Geoffrey
Chaucer, William Thorpe, John Lydgate, and Reginald Pecock are grouped
together in one large corporate enterprise. Bale made Thomas Hoccleve into
a closet Lollard and John Trevisa into a translator of the Wycliffite Bible as
signal efforts at bolstering this account of a literary run-up to the Tudor reform movement.[47]

Protestant makeovers had already begun among the printers. Around
1536, John Gough had printed "cum priuilegio Regali" the Lollard diatribe
Jack Upland in a small black-letter volume bearing the title "Jack vp Lande /
Compyled by the / famous Geoffrey / Chaucer."[48] Around 1540, John Le-

land included this remark in his list of Chaucer's works: "But the Tale of Piers Plowman [*fabula Petri Aratoris*], which by the common consent of the learned is attributed to Chaucer as its true author, has been suppressed in each edition, because it vigorously inveighed against the bad morals of priests."[49] Dedicated to Henry VIII and later reported to have been produced under direct supervision by the king, William Thynne's 1542 edition of the *Canterbury Tales* used its Lollard *Plowman's Tale* to complete the collection immediately after the Parson's Tale.

Continuing this revisionist project, John Foxe renewed attribution of *Jack Upland* to Chaucer in the 1570 edition of *Actes and Monumentes,* and Speght's second edition of 1602 formally admitted the work into the Chaucer canon.[50] Lifted from Speght's edition, the work was separately printed in 1606 when it was supplied with more than five hundred sidenotes described as "a gold mine of information on Puritan attitudes on medieval poetry and religion."[51] A stanza asserting the authority of secular rulers against the pope was quoted by John Milton in his 1641 tract *On the Reformation of Church Government.*[52] The work remained a staple in Chaucer's oeuvre until removed by Skeat in his *Works of Geoffrey Chaucer* in the last decade of the nineteenth century.[53]

By attributing to Chaucer these two hand-me-down Lollard texts *The Plowman's Tale* and *Jack Upland,* Speght's editions did much to fix the poet's Wycliffite identity for future readers. John Dryden's Preface to the *Fables* in 1700 lent his authority for transmitting this prevailing view to modern readers: "As for the Religion of our Poet, he seems to have some little Byas towards the Opinions of Wickliff, after John of Ghant his Patron; somewhat of which appears in the Tale of *Piers Plowman.*"[54] To a large extent, this version of Chaucer as a relentless critic of religious corruption—an aspect of his literary preoccupations almost entirely lacking in the fifteenth-century appreciations of his works—continues to influence today's critical and classroom discussions. As an integral component in this long-term project, Crowley's edition completed the process by which *Piers Plowman* was elevated from its demimonde existence and drawn into the cultural mainstream by a religious as well as political movement. Working to ally the *Canterbury Tales* with *Piers Plowman* from the 1530s until 1550s, Protestant bookmen realized a convergence of the separate, antagonistic literary traditions of Langland and Chaucer which had reached back as far as the 1380s. The persistence of this revisionist literary history is evident, for example, in Dryden's willingness to associate the title *Piers Plowman* so easily with the authorship of Geoffrey Chaucer.

But the triumph of *Piers* in 1550 was short-lived just as the printing of other Langlandian texts, like other Lollard printed books, remained entirely incidental. "They had little theological usefulness," as Justice has concluded. "They were valued above all for their mere survival, as living proof that reform was no novelty, but a proud English tradition."[55] Chaucer would win the official competition all over again. Starting in 1360, my own survey ends almost two centuries later around the time when Nicholas Brigham moved the poet's remains from around the corner to Westminster Abbey's transept and erected the current above-ground altar tomb in 1556.[56] Chaucer's place of honor in the abbey church likely reflected his service to the king, not his service to literature. Imitating the French example of Charles V at St. Denis, Richard II promoted Westminster Abbey as the burial place for distinguished courtiers of nonroyal birth such as the chamber knights Sir James Berners and Sir John Salisbury, and eventually favorite servants such as Sir Bernard Brocas and Sir John Golafre.[57] Chaucer's original interment in St. Benedict's Chapel represented a belated instance of this Ricardian practice of honoring valued royal retainers. It is also likely that the poet himself specified this burial site in his will, now lost, as a privilege granted to residents of the abbey, really an adjunct to his efforts at ensuring a literary posterity after his death. Newly memorialized in Brigham's sepulcher, Chaucer became the first resident of Poets' Corner as the future mausoleum of England's literary royalty. "The story is clear," says Pearsall, "how a poet became a national monument."[58]

Although the *Canterbury Tales* just narrowly won royal approval, according to Francis Thynne's account, Chaucer's works continued to be printed later in the sixteenth century by Stow (1561) and Speght (1598), in the seventeenth century by reprints of Speght (1602, 1687), and in the eighteenth century by Urry (1721) and quite spectacularly by Tyrwhitt (1775).[59] After Owen Rogers's hasty reprint of Crowley's edition in 1561, however, Langland's name would largely vanish from literary history. *Piers Plowman* would not again be printed until the C-text was produced in 1813 by Thomas Whitaker. Working during a period of alarm over radicalism during the Regency period, this country vicar initiated efforts at denying Langland's religious nonconformity: "That he believed and taught almost all the fundamental doctrines of Christianity has no tendency to prove him a Wickliffite or Lollard."[60]

Whitaker's conclusions denied the unsettling theological elements that had actually created an audience for *Piers* during the first two centuries of its public life, as well as the book's potent but largely subliminal afterlife among Puritan readers of the sixteenth and seventeenth centuries.[61] The Langland-

ian tradition remained essentially the tradition of minority dissent marginalized in those same social fringes where A. G. Dickens located the residual
beliefs of Wycliffism.[62] R. W. Chambers agreed that "the spiritual successors of *Piers Plowman* are to be found among the Puritans and the rebels with
Foxe and Bunyan and Whitfield and Blake."[63] When the Puritans migrated
to New England, the Langland tradition arrived with this exile community
of dissenters. Though in many ways self-evident, the Langlandian migration
across the Atlantic can actually be documented. Aboard the *Arbella* in
transit to America in 1630, Thomas Dudley carried with him a copy of *Piers
Plowman*[64]—and Dudley's daughter would establish herself as the first great
American poet, Anne Bradstreet (1612–72). With this secure line of transmission, Langland deserves credit as the unacknowledged progenitor of an
American literary tradition that remains essentially a mosaic of minority lit-
eratures marked by spiritual restlessness, an obsession with social reform,
and the urgent need for self-definition so long established in the prior English tradition by *Piers Plowman*.[65]

Notes

CHAPTER ONE

Introduction

1. A. C. Spearing, *Medieval to Renaissance in English Poetry* (Cambridge: Cambridge University Press, 1985), 92; Seth Lerer, *Chaucer and His Readers: Imagining the Author in Late-Medieval England* (Princeton: Princeton University Press, 1993), 23; and Stephanie Trigg, *Congenial Souls: Reading Chaucer from Medieval to Modern* (Minneapolis: University of Minnesota Press, 2002), xix, who takes her title from Dryden: "I found I had a Soul congenial to his." See also Carolyn Collette, "Afterlife," *A Companion to Chaucer*, ed. Peter Brown (Oxford: Blackwell, 2000), 8–22.

2. *Chaucer: The Critical Heritage*, vol. 1, *1385–1837*, ed. Derek Brewer (London: Routledge & Kegan Paul, 1978), 164. Dryden began this preface with a forceful statement of literary genealogy: "for we have our lineal descents and clans as well as other families."

3. Thomas Hoccleve, *The Regiment of Princes*, ed. Charles R. Blyth (Kalamazoo: Medieval Institute Publications, 1999), 185 (lines 4982–83). See Ethan Knapp, "Eulogies and Usurpations: Hoccleve and Chaucer Revisited," *SAC* 21 (1999): 247–73, and Tim William Machan, "Textual Authority and the Works of Hoccleve, Lydgate and Henryson," *Viator* 23 (1992): 281–99.

4. *The Idea of the Vernacular: An Anthology of Middle English Literary Theory, 1280–1520*, ed. Jocelyn Wogan-Browne, Nicholas Watson, Andrew Taylor, and Ruth Evans (University Park: Pennsylvania State University Press, 1999), esp. Nicholas Watson's "The Politics of Middle English Writing," 331–52, which provides the best recent discussion of the diverse developments of vernacular writing during this period.

5. A. I. Doyle, "A Survey of the Origins and Circulation of Theological Writings in English in the 14th, 15th, and Early 16th Centuries with Special Consideration of the Part of the Clergy Therein," 2 vols. (Ph.D. diss., Cambridge University, 1953).

6. Michel Foucault, "Nietzsche, Genealogy, History" (1971), *The Foucault Reader,* ed. Paul Rabinow (New York: Pantheon Books, 1984), 76–100, and Jacques Derrida, *Of Grammatology,* trans. Gayatri Chakravorty Spivak (Baltimore: Johns Hopkins University Press, 1976), 4: "The idea of writing—therefore also of the science of writing—is meaningful for us only in terms of an origin."

7. Christopher Cannon, "The Myth of Origin and the Making of Chaucer's English," *Speculum* 71 (1996): 646–75 at 675; these reflections are expanded in his book *The Making of Chaucer's English* (Cambridge: Cambridge University Press, 1998).

8. James Simpson, "Contemporary English Writers," *Companion to Chaucer,* ed. Peter Brown, 114–32 at 118–21. Books such as J. A. Burrow, *Ricardian Poetry: Chaucer, Gower, Langland and the "Gawain" Poet* (London: Routledge & Kegan Paul, 1971), and David Aers, *Chaucer, Langland, and the Creative Imagination* (London: Routledge & Kegan Paul, 1980), assume a common historical frame for the two poets without precisely describing their chronological and geographical relationship within this shared cultural context.

9. Helen Cooper, "Langland's and Chaucer's Prologues," *YLS* 1 (1987): 71–81, continues the work of Nevill Coghill, "Two Notes on *Piers Plowman*: I. The Abbot of Abingdon and the Date of the C-Text; II. Chaucer's Debt to Langland," *MÆ* 4 (1935): 83–94, and J. A. W. Bennett, "Chaucer's Contemporary," *"Piers Plowman": Critical Approaches,* ed. S. S. Hussey (London: Methuen, 1969), 310–24 at 320. See also Jill Mann, *Chaucer and Medieval Estate Satire* (Cambridge: Cambridge University Press, 1973), 208–12, and A. V. C. Schmidt, ed., *The Vision of Piers Plowman: A Critical Edition of the B-Text* (London: J. M. Dent; New York: E. P. Dutton, 1978), xvi.

10. Frank Grady, "Chaucer Reading Langland: *The House of Fame,*" *SAC* 18 (1996): 3–23.

11. Harold Bloom, *The Anxiety of Influence: A Theory of Poetry* (Oxford and New York: Oxford University Press, 1973), 11, and Spearing, *Medieval to Renaissance,* "The Chaucerian Tradition," 59–120.

12. George Kane, "Langland and Chaucer: An Obligatory Conjunction" and "Chaucer and Langland II," *Chaucer and Langland: Historical and Textual Approaches* (Berkeley and Los Angeles: University of California Press, 1989), 123–33 and 134–49, and Lee Patterson, *Chaucer and the Subject of History* (Madison: University of Wisconsin Press, 1991), 393–97. Michael Olmert, "Troilus in *Piers Plowman*: A Contemporary View of Chaucer's *Troilus and Criseyde,*" *Chaucer Newsletter* 2 (1980): 13–14, points out the verb *troyledest* (deceived) in C.20.319 as perhaps inspired by some understanding of Troilus as a well-known victim of deception. A revised version of Anne Middleton's 1991 MLA paper "Commentary on an Unacknowledged Text: Chaucer's Debt to Langland" will appear in the final section of her forthcoming book on Langland.

13. Ralph Hanna, *London Literature, 1300–1380* (Cambridge: Cambridge University Press, 2005), 253–57: "Chaucer 'does Langland' and not the reverse" (253).

14. Bloom, *Anxiety of Influence,* 5.

15. R. Allen Shoaf, ed., *Thomas Usk: The Testament of Love* (Kalamazoo: Medieval Institute Publications, 1998), 14–17, detects even more pervasive borrowing from

Troilus than recorded by Walter W. Skeat, ed., *The Testament of Love* in *Chaucerian and Other Pieces: Being a Supplement to the Complete Works of Geoffrey Chaucer* (London: Oxford University Press, 1897), xviii–xxxi, 1–145, 451–84, while finding less evidence of Langland's C-text. Shoaf cites my "Dating *Piers Plowman*: Testing the Testimony of Usk's *Testament*," *YLS* 13 (1999): 65–100, discounting Skeat's claims of C-text quotations in Usk's text.

16. Anne Middleton, "The Audience and Public of *Piers Plowman*," *Middle English Alliterative Poetry and Its Literary Background,* ed. David Lawton (Cambridge: D. S. Brewer, 1982), 101–23 and notes 147–54 at 106, takes notice that *Troilus* twice became a traveling companion with *Piers* in the manuscripts Huntington HM 114 (full texts) and HM 143 with only two leaves of *Troilus* (1:71–140, 421–90) written in a different fifteenth-century hand.

17. Martha Woodmansee and Peter Jaszi, eds., *The Construction of Authorship: Textual Appropriation in Law and Literature* (Durham, NC: Duke University Press, 1994), situate this category of the author only later in the eighteenth century.

18. Anne Middleton, "William Langland's 'Kynde Name': Authorial Signature and Social Identity in Late Fourteenth-Century England," *Literary Practice and Social Change in Britain 1380–1530,* ed. Lee Patterson (Berkeley and Los Angeles: University of California Press, 1990), 15–82 at 15.

19. Though Langland's Latin citations are integral to the method and meaning of his poem, he is casual about his knowledge of the French language: "Frenche men and fre men affaiteth thus hire children: / *Bele vertue est suffraunce, mal dire est petite vengeance*" (B.11.384–85), but he equates a lack of French with sinful neglect when Covetousness admits, "I lerned never rede on boke / And I kan no Frenssh" (B.5.234–35). Unless otherwise noted, my citations come from William Langland, *Piers Plowman: A Parallel-Text Edition of the A, B, C and Z Versions.* vol. 1: *Text,* ed. A. V. C. Schmidt (London and New York: Longman, 1995).

20. Robert Langland, *Visio Willi de Petro Plouhman, Item Visiones ejusdem de Dowel, Dobet, et Dobest,* ed. Thomas Dunham Whitaker (London: John Murray, 1813), xxxvi.

21. A. I. Doyle, "Remarks on Surviving Manuscripts of *Piers Plowman*," *Medieval English Religious and Ethical Literature: Essays in Honour of G. H. Russell,* ed. Gregory Kratzmann and James Simpson (Cambridge: D. S. Brewer, 1986), 35–48 at 36.

22. Kathleen L. Scott, "An Hours and Psalter by Two Ellesmere Illuminators," *The Ellesmere Chaucer: Essays in Interpretation,* ed. Martin Stevens and Daniel Woodward (San Marino: Huntington Library, 1997), 87–119, and Ralph Hanna III, *Pursuing History: Middle English Manuscripts and Their Texts* (Stanford: Stanford University Press, 1996), "The Hengwrt Manuscript and the Canon of *The Canterbury Tales*," 140–55, have made the most convincing case for dating Hengwrt before 1400. Following Estelle Stubbs, "Observations," *The Hengwrt Chaucer Digital Facsimile* CD-ROM (Leicester: Scholarly Digital Editions, 2000), Simon Horobin, *The Language of the Chaucer Tradition* (Cambridge: D. S. Brewer, 2003), 139, and Linne R. Mooney, "Chaucer's Scribe," *Speculum* 81 (2006): 97–138 at 119–20, speculate that Adam Pinkhurst worked under the poet's direct supervision to produce Hengwrt and perhaps also Ellesmere.

23. Mooney, "Chaucer's Scribe," gives details of Adam Pinkhurst's identification first presented in "New Evidence on the Hengwrt/Ellesmere Scribe and the City" at the fourteenth biennial congress of the New Chaucer Society in Glasgow (17 July 2004); I am grateful to Professor Mooney for sharing the prepublication version of this important article.

24. Beverly Boyd, "The Infamous B-text of the *Canterbury Tales*," *Manuscripta* 34 (1990): 233–38 at 235, attempts to explain the disorder of the Helmingham MS (Princeton Firestone Library MS 100).

25. Aage Brusendorff, *The Chaucer Tradition* (Oxford: Clarendon, 1925). See also Lerer, *Chaucer and His Readers,* and Helen Cooper and Sally Mapstone, eds., *The Long Fifteenth Century: Essays for Douglas Gray* (Oxford: Clarendon, 1997).

26. See especially Ralph Hanna III, "(The) Editing (of) the Ellesmere Text," *Ellesmere Chaucer,* ed. Stevens and Woodward, 225–43.

27. Michel Foucault, *The Order of Things: An Archaeology of the Human Sciences* (New York: Vintage Books, 1973), 147.

28. Raymond Williams, *Keywords: A Vocabulary of Culture and Society* (Oxford: Oxford University Press, 1976), 268–69.

29. F. D. Matthew, ed., *The English Works of Wyclif Hitherto Unprinted,* EETS o.s. 74, 1880, 2nd rev. ed., 1902, 392.

30. Andrew Jotischky, *The Carmelites and Antiquity: Mendicants and Their Pasts in the Middle Ages* (Oxford: Oxford University Press, 2002).

31. John Lydgate, *Troy Book* ed. Henry Bergen, EETS e.s. 97, 103, 106, 126, 1906–35, 311 (2.5831–34).

32. T. S. Eliot, *Selected Essays: New Edition* (New York: Harcourt, Brace & World, 1950), 3–11 at 5.

33. Brusendorff, *The Chaucer Tradition,* 13.

34. Northrop Frye, *Anatomy of Criticism* (Princeton: Princeton University Press, 1957), 18. See more recently Wendell V. Harris, "Canonicity," *PMLA* 106 (1991): 110–21.

35. Cannon, "The Myth of Origin and the Making of Chaucer's English," 670.

36. Donald R. Howard, *Chaucer: His Life, His Works, His World* (New York: Fawcett Columbine, 1987), "Reading Boccaccio," 260–82, and "Boccaccio and the Birth of Fiction," 283–303.

37. Terry Jones, *Chaucer's Knight: The Portrait of a Medieval Mercenary* (Baton Rouge: Louisiana State University Press, 1980); see also his follow-up study "The Image of Chaucer's Knight," *Speaking Images: Essays in Honor of V. A. Kolve,* ed. R. F. Yeager and Charlotte C. Morse (Asheville: Pegasus Press, 2001), 205–36.

38. *The Riverside Chaucer,* 3rd ed., gen. ed. Larry D. Benson (Boston: Houghton Mifflin, 1987), 65 (*CT,* I, 3012–15). This edition is cited throughout.

39. *The Riverside Chaucer,* 650–51.

40. Eric Hobsbawm, "Introduction: Inventing Traditions," *The Invention of Tradition,* ed. Eric Hobsbawm and Terrence Ranger (Cambridge: Cambridge University Press, 1983), 1–14 at 1.

41. Jaroslav Pelikan, *The Vindication of Tradition* (New Haven and London: Yale University Press, 1984), 6.

42. Williams, *Keywords,* 269.

43. George Kane, "Langland and Chaucer: An Obligatory Conjunction" (1980) and "Langland and Chaucer II" (1980), *Chaucer and Langland,* 123–33 and 134–49 at 149. Kane points to shared backgrounds in Latin rhetoric and French dream-visions; he compares Langland's C.5 *apologia* to Chaucer's Retraction and notes that both poets failed to conclude their final large-scale undertakings, with the *Canterbury Tales* incomplete and the C-revision of *Piers* unfinished. Mary Clemente Davlin, O.P., "Chaucer and Langland as Religious Writers," *William Langland's "Piers Plowman": A Book of Essays,* ed. Kathleen M. Hewett-Smith (New York and London: Routledge, 2001), 119–41, finds another area of overlap with marked differences.

44. Spearing, *Medieval to Renaissance in English Poetry,* typifies prior histories by offering a literary survey without including a single chapter or even a substantial discussion devoted to Langland's *Piers Plowman.*

45. Middleton, "The Audience and Public of *Piers Plowman,*" Anne Hudson, "Epilogue: The Legacy of *Piers Plowman,*" *A Companion to "Piers Plowman,"* ed. John A. Alford (Berkeley and Los Angeles: University of California Press, 1988), 251–66; Barbara A. Johnson, *Reading "Piers Plowman" and "The Pilgrim's Progress": Reception and the Protestant Reader* (Carbondale: Southern Illinois University Press, 1992), esp. 63–98; and Helen Barr, *Signes and Sothe: Language in the "Piers Plowman" Tradition* (Cambridge: D. S. Brewer, 1994).

46. David R. Carlson, *Chaucer's Jobs* (New York: Palgrave Macmillan, 2004), 1–31, and Jeremy Catto, "Religious Change under Henry V," *Henry V: The Practice of Kingship,* ed. G. L. Harriss (1985; rpt. Dover, NH: Alan Sutton, 1993), 97–115.

47. James Simpson, *Reform and Cultural Revolution, 1350–1547* (Oxford: Oxford University Press, 2002), 1–6.

48. Simon Horobin, "'In London and Opelond': The Dialect and Circulation of the C Version of *Piers Plowman,*" *MÆ* 74 (2005): 248–69, argues that many C manuscripts such as HM 143, previously mapped by dialect to the Worcester area, were actually produced in London.

49. Ralph Hanna, "Alliterative Poetry," *Cambridge History of Medieval English Literature,* ed. David Wallace (Cambridge: Cambridge University Press, 1999), 488–512 at 511.

50. Gerald Harriss, *Shaping the Nation: England, 1360–1461* (Oxford: Clarendon, 2005), also establishes this year as his starting point.

51. Anne Hudson, ed., *Selections from English Wycliffite Writings* (Cambridge: Cambridge University Press, 1978), *Twelve Conclusions of the Lollards,* 24–29 at 24, illustrates the vocabulary of *reformaciun* central to the Lollard project.

52. Andrew Galloway, "Authority," *Companion to Chaucer,* ed. Peter Brown, 23–39. For later periods, see John Guilllory, *Poetic Authority: Spenser, Milton, and Literary History* (New York: Columbia University Press, 1983).

53. For an earlier phase in this development, see Barnaby Keeney, "Military Service and the Development of Nationalism in England, 1272–1327," *Speculum* 22 (1947): 534–49.

54. Edward W. Said, *Beginnings: Intention and Method* (New York: Basic Books, 1975), 3.

55. See Allen J. Frantzen, *Desire for Origins: New Language, Old English, and Teaching the Tradition* (New Brunswick and London: Rutgers University Press, 1990), esp. 22–26.

56. Erich Auerbach, *Mimesis: The Representation of Reality in Western Literature,* trans. Willard R. Trask (Princeton: Princeton University Press, 1953), 548–49.

57. Derek Pearsall, ed., *Piers Plowman: An Edition of the C-text* (Berkeley and Los Angeles: University of California Press, 1978), 10, notes that the C-reviser worked "outward from certain cores of dissatisfaction" rather than executing a thorough rewriting of the B-text from start to finish.

58. For norms of self-explanatory introductions, see A. J. Minnis, "The Influence of Academic Prologues on the Prologues and Literary Attitudes of Late Medieval English Writers," *MS* 43 (1981): 342–83. My book *The Crisis of Will in "Piers Plowman"* (Washington, DC: Catholic University of America Press, 1986), "The Question of Will in His Waking Life," 129–64, addressed the baffling quality of the poem's nonvisionary sections. Hanna, *London Literature,* 258, believes that Langland accepted the presumptions of the antiromance prologue established earlier in his century (see his 149–52).

59. For the question of Langland's hermits, see Bowers, *The Crisis of Will in "Piers Plowman,"* 97–128; Edward Jones, "Langland and Hermits," *YLS* 11 (1997): 67–86; and Ralph Hanna III, "Will's Work," *Written Work: Langland, Labor, and Authorship,* ed. Steven Justice and Kathryn Kerby-Fulton (Philadelphia: University of Pennsylvania Press, 1997), 23–66.

60. Anne Middleton, "Langland's Lives: Reflections on Late-Medieval Religious and Literary Vocabulary," *The Idea of Medieval Literature: New Essays on Chaucer and Medieval Culture in Honor of Donald R. Howard,* ed. James M. Dean and Christian K. Zacher (Newark: University of Delaware Press, 1992), 227–42.

61. D. Vance Smith, *The Book of Incipit: Beginnings in the Fourteenth Century* (Minneapolis: University of Minnesota Press, 2001), esp. 113–39.

62. Anne Middleton, "Acts of Vagrancy: The C Version 'Autobiography' and the Statute of 1388," *Written Work,* ed. Justice and Kerby-Fulton, 208–317 at 275.

63. Mary J. Carruthers, "Time, Apocalypse, and the Plot of *Piers Plowman,*" *Acts of Interpretation: The Text in Its Contexts 700–1600: Essays on Medieval and Renaissance Literature in Honor of E. Talbot Donaldson,* ed. Mary J. Carruthers and Elizabeth D. Kirk (Norman, OK: Pilgrim Books, 1982), 175–88 at 176. See also William Elford Rogers, *Interpretation in "Piers Plowman"* (Washington, DC: Catholic University of America Press, 2002), 24–30.

64. Anne Middleton, "Narration and the Invention of Experience: Episodic Form in *Piers Plowman,*" *The Wisdom of Poetry: Essays in Early English Literature in Honor of Morton W. Bloomfield,* ed. Larry D. Benson and Siegfried Wenzel (Kalamazoo: Medieval Institute Publications, 1982), 91–122 and notes 280–83 at 119.

65. Derek Pearsall, "Langland and Lollardy: From B to C," *YLS* 17 (2003): 7–23 at 23.

66. J. A. Burrow, "The Action of Langland's Second Vision," *Essays in Criticism* 15 (1965): 247–68.

67. Thorlac Turville-Petre, "The Prologue of *Wynner and Wastoure*," *LSE* n.s. 18 (1987): 19–29 at 20–21; Hanna, *Pursuing History,* 232; and Helen Barr, "Constructing Social Realities," *Socioliterary Practice in Late Medieval England* (Oxford: Oxford University Press, 2001), 10–39. David A. Lawton, "The Unity of Middle English Alliterative Poetry," *Speculum* 58 (1983): 72–94, finds so many crosscurrents of affiliation that the direction of influence between texts is difficult to chart.

68. Hanna, *London Literature,* 256.

69. The editors A. G. Rigg and Charlotte Brewer in William Langland, *Piers Plowman: The Z Version* (Toronto: Pontifical Institute of Mediaeval Studies, no. 59, 1983), argue for the authorial status of this version. George Kane, "The 'Z Version' of *Piers Plowman*," *Speculum* 60 (1985): 910–30, and Hanna, *Pursuing History,* "MS. Bodley 851 and the Dissemination of *Piers Plowman*," 195–202, disagree. A. V. C. Schmidt, "The Authenticity of the Z-text of *Piers Plowman*: A Metrical Examination," *MÆ* 53 (1984): 295–300, and Hoyt N. Duggan, "The Authenticity of the Z-text of *Piers Plowman*: Further Notes on Metrical Evidence," *MÆ* 56 (1987): 25–45, identify alliterative practices unique to the three canonic versions of *Piers* as well as the Z-text.

70. Jill Mann, "The Power of the Alphabet: A Reassessment of the Relation between the A and the B Versions of *Piers Plowman*," *YLS* 8 (1994): 21–50, and John M. Bowers, "*Piers Plowman*'s William Langland: Editing the Text, Writing the Author's Life," *YLS* 9 (1995): 65–102 at 82–87.

71. Thomas Netter, *Fasciculi Zizaniorum,* ed. Walter Waddington Shirley (London: Rolls Series, 1858), 493–97, lists these condemned theological conclusions. See James Simpson, "The Constraints of Satire in *Piers Plowman* and *Mum and the Sothsegger*," *Langland, the Mystics and the Medieval English Religious Tradition: Essays in Honour of S. S. Hussey,* ed. Helen Phillips (Cambridge: D. S. Brewer, 1990), 11–30; Anne Hudson, *The Premature Reformation: Wycliffite Texts and Lollard History* (Oxford: Clarendon, 1988), 398–408; Anne Hudson, "*Piers Plowman* and the Peasants' Revolt: A Problem Revisited," *YLS* 8 (1994): 85–106; and Kathryn Kerby-Fulton, "Langland and the Bibliographic Ego," *Written Work,* ed. Justice and Kerby-Fulton, 67–143 at 75–76. Andrew Galloway, "Latin England," *Imagining a Medieval English Nation,* ed. Kathy Lavezzo (Minneapolis: University of Minnesota Press, 2004), 41–95 at 73–86, discusses Walsingham's evolving responses to national events into the fifteenth century.

72. See two studies by George H. Russell: "Poet as Reviser: The Metamorphosis of the Confession of the Seven Deadly Sins in *Piers Plowman*," *Acts of Interpretation,* ed. Carruthers and Kirk, 53–65, and "The Imperative of Revision in the C Version of *Piers Plowman*," *Medieval English Studies Presented to George Kane,* ed. Edward Donald Kennedy, Ronald Waldron, and Joseph S. Wittig (Cambridge: D. S. Brewer, 1988), 233–42.

73. Geoffrey of Vinsauf, *Poetria Nova,* trans. Margaret F. Nims (Toronto: Pontifical Institute of Mediaeval Studies, 1967), 16–17 (lines 43–45); Vinsauf is also cited in the Nun's Priest's Tale (*CT,* VII, 3347–51). Judith M. Davidoff, *Beginning Well: Framing Fictions in Late Middle English Poetry* (London and Toronto: Associated University Presses, 1988), 101–34, places Chaucer's introductions in context of other medieval practices.

74. Caroline M. Barron, "William Langland: A London Poet," *Chaucer's England: Literature in Historical Context,* ed. Barbara Hanawalt (Minneapolis: University of Minnesota Press, 1992), 91–109; Derek Pearsall, "Langland's London," *Written Work,* ed. Justice and Kerby-Fulton, 185–207; and John M. Bowers, *The Politics of "Pearl": Court Poetry in the Age of Richard II* (Cambridge: D. S. Brewer, 2001), 12–16.

75. For a survey of the critical tradition, see William A. Quinn, "Chaucer's Problematic *Priere: An ABC* as Artifact and Critical Issue," *SAC* 23 (2001): 109–41. Terry Jones with Robert Yeager, Terry Dolan, Alan Fletcher, and Juliette Dor, *Who Murdered Chaucer? A Medieval Mystery* (New York: St. Martin's, 2004), 337–43, argue that Chaucer wrote the *ABC* very late in his career as a "theological make-over."

76. John P. H. Clark, "Trinovantum—The Evolution of a Legend," *JMH* 7 (1981): 135–51, details specifically the myth of London's Trojan origins. See also Sylvia Federico, *New Troy: Fantasies of Empire in the Late Middle Ages* (Minneapolis: University of Minnesota Press, 2003), esp. "Late-Fourteenth-Century London as the New Troy," 1–28.

77. Like history, cartography could also be organized alphabetically; see Kathleen Biddick, "The ABC of Ptolemy: Mapping the World with the Alphabet," *Texts and Territory: Geographical Imagination in the European Middle Ages,* ed. Sylvia Tomasch and Sealy Gilles (Philadelphia: University of Pennsylvania Press, 1998), 268–93.

78. The selections assembled in *The Idea of the Vernacular,* ed. Wogan-Browne et al., show other early writers explicit about their concerns for literary tradition, the status of the author, and the instability of the English language in ways that qualify Chaucer's self-conscious sense of singularity.

79. Ian Robinson, *Chaucer and the English Tradition* (Cambridge: Cambridge University Press, 1972); Elizabeth D. Kirk, "Chaucer and His English Contemporaries," *Geoffrey Chaucer: A Collection of Original Articles* (New York: McGraw-Hill, 1975), 111–27; and W. A. Davenport, *Chaucer and His English Contemporaries: Prologue and Tale in "The Canterbury Tales"* (New York: St. Martin's Press, 1998), suggest the degree to which Chaucer neglected and ignored other Middle English writings.

80. Homer's reputation must have been strong during Chaucer's lifetime, since Richard II's tomb includes this inscription: ANIMO PRUDENS UT HOMERUS — "prudent in spirit like Homer." Michael J. Bennett, "The Court of Richard II and the Promotion of Literature," *Chaucer's England,* ed. Hanawalt, 3–20 at 16, speculates on the significance of this panegyric, while Jones et al., *Who Murdered Chaucer?* 92–95, suggest that the inscription was added not at Richard II's command in 1395 but under Henry V's direction in 1413.

81. *Chaucer Life-Records,* ed. Martin M. Crow and Clair C. Olson (Oxford: Clarendon, 1966), produces no wills for John Chaucer or Geoffrey Chaucer, but the historical archive shows a pattern of property transmitted from single son to single son, with an overall increase in family prosperity and status.

82. P. M. Kean, *Chaucer and the Making of English Poetry,* 2 vols. (London and Boston: Routledge & Kegan Paul, 1972), "Chaucer and the English Tradition," 1:1–30, describes the manner in which Chaucer *made* English poetry.

83. Osbern Bokenham, *Legendys of Hooly Wummen,* ed. Mary S. Serjeantson, EETS o.s. 206, 1938, 3 (lines 83–96).

84. For a redating of the *House of Fame* to the later 1380s after the completion of *Troilus* and at the end of the poet's residence of Aldgate 1374–86, see E. K. Rand, "Chaucer in Error," *Speculum* 1 (1926): 222–25 at 224–25, and Helen Cooper, "Welcome to the House of Fame: 600 Years Dead: Chaucer's Deserved Reputation as 'the Father of English Poetry,'" *TLS* 5091 (27 October 2000): 3–4. See also Cooper, "The Four Last Things in Dante and Chaucer: Ugolino in the House of Rumour," *NML* 3 (1999): 39–66, and "Chaucerian Representation," *New Readings of Chaucer's Poetry,* ed. Robert G. Benson and Susan J. Ridyard, intro. Derek Brewer (Cambridge: D. S. Brewer, 2003), 7–29.

85. John M. Bowers, "Chaucer after Smithfield: From Postcolonial Writer to Imperialist Author," *The Postcolonial Middle Ages,* ed. Jeffrey Cohen (New York: St. Martin's Press, 2000), 53–66.

86. William Provost, "Chaucer's Endings," *New Readings of Chaucer's Poetry,* ed. Benson and Ridyard, 91–105, makes the point that earlier poems have clearer endings than the later works.

87. See Rosemarie McGerr, *Chaucer's Open Books: Resistance to Closure in Medieval Discourse* (Gainesville: University Press of Florida, 1998).

88. The entirety of *Midsummer Night's Dream* grows out of a single line—"And of the feste that was at hir weddynge" (*CT,* I, 883)—in which Chaucer advertised what had been omitted from the Knight's Tale. For a fine account of these literary transactions, see E. Talbot Donaldson, *The Swan at the Well: Shakespeare Reading Chaucer* (New Haven: Yale University Press, 1985).

89. Derek Pearsall, "Lydgate as Innovator," *MLQ* 53 (1992): 5–22 at 6.

90. Lynn Staley, "Personal Identity," *Companion to Chaucer,* ed. Brown, 360–77, and for a general history from classical times, Charles Taylor, *Sources of the Self: The Making of Modern Identity* (Cambridge: Harvard University Press, 1989).

91. Ernest Renan, "What Is a Nation?" (1882), trans. Martin Thom, *Nation and Narration,* ed. Homi K. Bhabha (London and New York: Routledge, 1991), 8–22 at 11. See also Homi K. Bhabha, "DissemiNation: Time, Narrative, and the Margins of the Modern Nation," *Nation and Narration,* 291–322 at 310: "It is this forgetting—a minus in the origin—that constitutes the *beginning* of the nation's narration."

92. Smith, *The Book of Incipit,* 118–19.

93. Bede, *Ecclesiastical History of the English People,* ed. Bertram Colgrave and R. A. B. Mynors (Oxford: Clarendon, 1969), 414–21 (IV, 24).

94. Christopher Cannon, "Monastic Productions," *Cambridge History of Medieval English Literature,* ed. Wallace, 316–48.

95. Hanna, "Alliterative Poetry," *Cambridge History of Medieval English Literature,* ed. Wallace, 488–512 at 493.

96. R. M. Wilson, *The Lost Literature of Medieval England,* 2nd ed. (London: Methuen, 1970), 1–23, begins with this sobering reminder: "How much of the heroic poetry of the Germanic peoples has been lost will never be known." See also

C. E. Wright, "The Dispersal of the Monastic Libraries and the Beginnings of Anglo-Saxon Studies," *Transactions of the Cambridge Bibliographical Society* 1 (1949–53): 208–37.

97. For a concise survey of the thirteenth and early fourteenth centuries, see Derek Pearsall, *Old English and Middle English Poetry* (London: Routledge & Kegan Paul, 1977), esp. 119–49, and Thomas Hahn, "Early Middle English," *Cambridge History of Medieval English Literature,* ed. Wallace, 61–91. Hanna, *London Literature,* "Reading Romance in London," 104–47, places provincial-looking works such as *Havelock* and *King Horn* in context of London's Auchinleck manuscript.

98. B. D. H. Miller, "The Early History of Bodleian MS Digby 86," *Annuale Medievale* 4 (1963): 23–56; but see Siegfried Wenzel, *Preachers, Poets, and the Early English Lyric* (Princeton: Princeton University Press, 1986). For recent work on Harley 2253 from the 1330s–40s, see Susanna Fein, ed., *Studies in the Harley Manuscript: The Scribes, Contents and Social Contexts of British Library MS Harley 2253* (Kalamazoo: Medieval Institute Publications, 2000).

99. Thorlac Turville-Petre, *England the Nation: Language, Literature, and National Identity, 1290–1340* (Oxford: Clarendon, 1996); Christopher Cannon, *The Grounds of English Literature* (Oxford: Oxford University Press, 2004); and Hanna, *London Literature,* "English Vernacular Culture in London before 1380: The Evidence," 1–43.

100. Katherine O'Brien O'Keeffe and Linda Georgianna have undertaken volume 1, *To 1350: The Literary Cultures of Early England,* while Simpson takes up the story in volume 2, *1350–1547: Reform and Cultural Revolution.*

101. Laura Hibbard Loomis, "Chaucer and the Breton Lays of the Auchinleck MS," *SP* 38 (1941): 14–33; Loomis, "The Auchinleck Manuscript and a Possible London Bookshop of 1330–1340," *PMLA* 57 (1942): 595–627; *The Auchinleck Manuscript: National Library of Scotland, Advocates' MS 19.2.1,* intro. Derek Pearsall and I. C. Cunningham (London: Scolar Press, 1977); and Timothy A. Shonk, "A Study of the Auchinleck Manuscript: Bookmen and Bookmaking in the Early Fourteenth Century," *Speculum* 60 (1985): 71–91.

102. Kathryn Kerby-Fulton and Steven Justice, "Langlandian Reading Circles and the Civil Service in London and Dublin, 1380–1427," *NML* 1 (1997): 59–83, suggest that Langland as well as both Chaucer and Gower had a coterie of metropolitan readers with legal and parliamentary interests possibly concentrated in Chancery. For other aspects of the London literary scene, see Bennett, "The Court of Richard II and the Promotion of Literature." Chaucer's knowledge of *Sir Gawain* is suggested by a passage from the Squire's Tale (*CT,* V, 89–104).

103. Andrew Galloway, "Making History Legal: *Piers Plowman* and the Rebels of Fourteenth-Century England," *William Langland's "Piers Plowman,"* ed. Hewett-Smith, 7–39 at 25–28, explicates this passage by reference to Earl Randolf II of Chester as a symbolic liberator anticipating the political hopes of 1381.

104. Hanna, "Alliterative Poetry," argues for a continuous survival rather than a spontaneous revival. Christine Chism, *Alliterative Revivals* (Philadelphia: University of Pennsylvania Press, 2002), 14–15, might overreach in her claim that Anglo-Saxon language was "probably indecipherable to fourteenth-century readers." Hoyt N. Duggan, "Evidential Basis for Old English Metrics," *SP* 85 (1988): 145–63, and

"Stress Assignment in Middle English Alliterative Poetry," *JEGP* 89 (1990): 309–29, nonetheless confirms the essential differences in early and later metrical practices concluded by J. P. Oakden, *Alliterative Poetry in Middle English,* 2 vols. (Manchester: Manchester University Press, 1930–35).

105. Kerby-Fulton, "Langland and the Bibliographic Ego," 105.

106. George Kane, "Outstanding Problems of Middle English Scholarship" (1977), *Chaucer and Langland,* 228–41 at 238, raised this question: "What is the significance of Langland's choice of the alliterative long line, presuming him to have wanted a national audience?" His essay "Music 'Neither Unpleasant nor Monotonous'" (1981), *Chaucer and Langland,* 77–89, starts answering this important question.

107. S. S. Hussey, "Langland's Reading of Alliterative Poetry," *MLR* 60 (1965): 163–70, and Thorlac Turville-Petre, *The Alliterative Revival* (Cambridge: D. S. Brewer, 1977), 31–32. See also John Scattergood, *The Lost Tradition: Essays on Middle English Alliterative Poetry* (Dublin: Four Courts Press, 2000).

108. Bowers, *The Crisis of Will in "Piers Plowman,"* 191–218.

109. John A. Alford, "The Role of the Quotations in *Piers Plowman,*" *Speculum* 52 (1977): 80–99, and Judson Boyce Allen, "Langland's Reading and Writing: *Detractor* and the Pardon Scene," *Speculum* 59 (1984): 342–62.

110. Morton W. Bloomfield, *"Piers Plowman" as a Fourteenth-Century Apocalypse* (New Brunswick: Rutgers University Press, 1962), 32.

111. Hanna, "On the Versions of *Piers Plowman,*" *Pursuing History,* 202–43 at 229–43, frames an account of the anguished process of composition and revision even within the A version.

112. Emily Steiner, "Langland's Documents," *YLS* 14 (2000): 95–115; see the expanded version of this discussion in her book *Documentary Culture and the Making of Medieval English Literature* (Cambridge: Cambridge University Press, 2003), 93–115. Middleton, "Audience and Public," 110, noted that *Piers* was included in manuscripts with other works framed as charters, wills, and letters, such as *The Charter of the Abbey of the Holy Ghost,* "the written instruments by which possessions and offices were transferred and diplomatic relations sustained."

113. Kerby-Fulton and Justice, "Langlandian Reading Circle," 63–64, build usefully upon the prior investigations of Rudolf Kirk, "References to the Law in *Piers Plowman,*" *PMLA* 48 (1933): 322–28, and John A. Alford, *Piers Plowman: A Glossary of Legal Diction* (Cambridge: D. S. Brewer, 1988).

114. Elizabeth Salter, "Langland and the Contexts of *Piers Plowman,*" *E&S* n.s. 32 (1979): 19–25.

115. George Shuffelton, *"Piers Plowman* and the Case of the Missing Book," *YLS* 18 (2004): 55–72: "In all of his wanderings and in all of his encounters, Will never sees a book" (56). For contrasting attitudes, see Jesse M. Gellrich, *The Idea of the Book in the Middle Ages* (Ithaca: Cornell University Press, 1985), and A. V. C. Schmidt, "Langland's Visions and Revisions," *YLS* 14 (2000): 5–27, esp. 12–13.

116. Nicholas Watson, *Richard Rolle and the Invention of Authority* (Cambridge: Cambridge University Press, 1991), "Epilogue: Rolle as a Late Medieval *Auctor,*" 257–70. Simpson, *Reform,* 23 n. 24, notes that Rolle is the first English-language writer

acknowledged by John Bale's *Catalogus.* Mooney, "Chaucer's Scribe," 113, suggests that Adam Pinkhurst copied Rolle's *Form of Living* around the same time that he copied the Trinity B.15.17 manuscript of *Piers.*

117. Aers, *Chaucer, Langland and the Creative Imagination,* "Langland, Apocalypse and the *Saeculum,*" esp. 70–79, and Larry Scanlon, "King, Commons, and Kind Wit: Langland's National Vision and the Rising of 1381," *Imagining a Medieval English Nation,* ed. Lavezzo, 191–233 at 196–97.

118. George Kane, *Piers Plowman: The Evidence for Authorship* (London: Athlone Press, 1965), 26–28.

119. Middleton, "William Langland's 'Kynde Name': Authorial Signature and Social Identity in Late Fourteenth-Century England," 25 and 42; later scribes often noted these passages without being able to unravel the enigma of authorial identity. For James le Palmer, see Lucy Freeman Sandler, "*Omne Bonum: Compilatio* and *Ordinatio* in an English Illustrated Encyclopedia of the Fourteenth Century," *Medieval Book Production: Assessing the Evidence,* ed. Linda L. Brownrigg (Los Altos Hills, CA: Anderson-Lovelace, 1990), 183–200 at 189, and Kerby-Fulton, "Langland and the Bibliographical Ego," 113.

120. The five manuscripts are HM 143, University of London MS S.L. V. 88 (Ilchester), Bodleian MS Digby 102, BM MS Add. 35157, and Bodleian MS Douce 104.

121. Charlotte Brewer, "Authorial vs. Scribal Writing in *Piers Plowman,*" *Medieval Literature: Texts and Interpretation,* ed. Tim William Machan (Binghamton: Medieval & Renaissance Texts & Studies, 1991), 59–89; Hanna, *Pursuing History,* 201–43; and Andrew Galloway, "Uncharacterizable Entities: The Poetics of Middle English Scribal Culture and the Definitive *Piers Plowman,*" *SB* 52 (1999): 59–87, address the challenge of editing a literary text so much open to a process of scribal rewriting not always distinguishable from authorial revision.

122. Hanna, *Pursuing History,* 236–37.

123. A. S. G. Edwards, "The Early Reception of Chaucer and Langland," *Florilegium* 15 (1998): 1–23 at 4. On Charleton's collection, see K. B. McFarlane, "The Education of the Nobility in Later Medieval England," *The Nobility of Later Medieval England* (Oxford: Clarendon, 1973), 228–47 at 237–38.

124. Since Langland's name was unavailable and could not be acknowledged by later writers, modern scholars have experienced even greater challenges in tracing this subsequent lineage. As with his exaggeration of C-text quotations in Thomas Usk's *Testament of Love,* Walter W. Skeat was too quick to claim the influence of *Piers* upon other works; see Joseph M. P. Donatelli, ed., *Death and Liffe* (Cambridge, MA: Medieval Academy of America, Speculum Anniversary Monographs, 1989), 30–32.

125. E. Talbot Donaldson, "MSS R and F in the B-Tradition of *Piers Plowman,*" *Transactions of the Connecticut Academy of Arts and Sciences* 39 (1955): 177–212 at 211: "merely historical accidents, haphazard milestones in the history of a poem that was begun but never finished, photographs that caught a static image of a living organism at a given but not necessarily significant moment of time." While rejecting the

authorial status of the Z-text, Hanna, *Pursuing History,* 203–43, allows for a process of "rolling revision" that produced intermediate texts such as the RF version. Lawrence Warner, "The Ur-B *Piers Plowman* and the Earliest Production of C and B," *YLS* 16 (2002): 3–39, suggests degrees of authorial variation not posited since Skeat.

126. *Letters from Petrarch,* ed. and trans. Morris Bishop (Bloomington and London: Indiana University Press, 1966), "Epistle to Posterity" (1351), 5–12.

127. On literary warnings against the perils of seeking fame, see B. G. Koonce, *Chaucer and the Tradition of Fame: Symbolism in "The House of Fame"* (Princeton: Princeton University Press, 1966), 32–45.

128. Justice, "Lollardy," *Cambridge History of Medieval English Literature,* ed. Wallace, 662–89 at 672; he furthermore reads the dream-vision as a cultural debate between the courtly nightingale and the Lollard cuckoo (671). For more on Clanvowe, see Siegrid Düll, Anthony Luttrell, and Maurice Keen, "Faithful unto Death: The Tomb Slab of Sir William Neville and Sir John Clanvowe, Constantinople, 1391," *The Antiquaries Journal* 71 (1991): 174–90; Lee Patterson, "Court Politics and the Invention of Literature: The Case of Sir John Clanvowe," *Culture and History, 1350–1600,* ed. David Aers (Detroit: Wayne State University Press, 1992), 7–41; and John M. Bowers, "Three Readings of *The Knight's Tale*: Sir John Clanvowe, Geoffrey Chaucer, and James I of Scotland," *JMEMS* 34 (2004): 279–307 at 279–87.

129. See my book *The Politics of "Pearl,"* esp. 187–95. It is noteworthy that the Cheshire knight Sir John Stanley of Hooton (d. 1469) commissioned the Chaucerian collection Bodleian MS Fairfax 16, since the Stanleys were likely patrons for the *Pearl* Poet during the reign of Richard II. See John Norton-Smith, intro., *Bodleian Library, MS Fairfax 16* (London: Scolar Press, 1979), xiii–xiv; Edward Wilson, "*Sir Gawain and the Green Knight* and the Stanley Family of Stanley, Storeton, and Hooton," *RES* n.s. 30 (1979): 308–16; and Theresa Tinkle, "The Imagined Chaucerian Community of Bodleian MS Fairfax 16," *Chaucer and the Challenges of Medievalism: Studies in Honor of H. A. Kelly,* ed. Donka Minkova and Theresa Tinkle (Frankfurt am Main: Peter Lang, 2003), 157–74.

130. Julia Boffey and John J. Thompson, "Anthologies and Miscellanies: Production and Choice of Texts," *Book Production and Publishing in Britain, 1374–1475,* ed. Jeremy Griffiths and Derek Pearsall (Cambridge: Cambridge University Press, 1989), 279–315 at 280.

131. John Gower, *The English Works,* ed. G. C. Macaulay, 2 vols., EETS e.s. 81 and 82, 1900–1901, 2:466 (lines 2941*–2957*).

132. M. B. Parkes and Richard Beadle, eds., *Poetical Works: A Facsimile of Cambridge University Library MS GG.4.27,* 3 vols. (Cambridge: D. S. Brewer, 1980–81), and Michael Seymour, *A Catalogue of Chaucer Manuscripts,* vol. I: *Works before the "Canterbury Tales"* (Aldershot: Scolar Press, 1995), 68–70. See also A. S. G. Edwards, "Fifteenth-Century Middle English Verse Author Collections," *The English Medieval Book: Studies in Memory of Jeremy Griffiths,* ed. A. S. G. Edwards, Vincent Gillespie, and Ralph Hanna (London: The British Library, 2000), 101–12.

133. Paul Strohm, *England's Empty Throne: Usurpation and the Language of Legitima-tion, 1399–1422* (New Haven: Yale University Press, 1998), "Reburying Richard: Cere-mony and Symbolic Relegitimation," 101–27.

134. Sylvia Wright, "The Author Portraits in the Bedford Psalter-Hours: Gower, Chaucer and Hoccleve," *British Library Journal* 18 (1992): 190–201, suggests a portrait gallery of the most politically fashionable poets, with of course Langland noticeably missing.

135. Eamon Duffy, *The Stripping of the Altars: Traditional Religion in England, c. 1400–c. 1580* (New Haven and London: Yale University Press, 1992), esp. 338–76.

136. K. B. McFarlane, *Lancastrian Kings and Lollard Knights* (Oxford: Clarendon, 1972), 210–20.

137. E. A. Greening Lamborn, "The Arms on the Chaucer Tomb at Ewelme," *Oxoniensia* 5 (1940): 78–93.

138. John A. A. Goodall, *God's House at Ewelme* (Aldershot: Ashgate, 2001), 7–35.

139. John Hines, Nathalie Cohen, and Simon Roffey, "*Iohannes Gower, Armiger, Poeta*: Records and Memorials of His Life and Death," *A Companion to Gower,* ed. Siân Echard (Cambridge: D. S. Brewer, 2004), 23–41 at 36–41.

140. *Speculum* 64 (1989): 130–34 at 133.

141. Stephen Greenblatt, "Towards a Poetics of Culture," *The New Historicism,* ed. H. Aram Veeser (New York and London: Routledge, 1989), 1–14, offers elegant reflections upon these critical practices. See also his essay "What Is the History of Literature?" *Critical Inquiry* 23 (1997): 460–81.

142. On HM 114, see G. H. Russell and Venetia Nathan, "A *Piers Plowman* Manu-script at the Huntington Library," *HLQ* 26 (1963): 119–30.

143. Thomas Tyrwhitt, ed., *The Canterbury Tales of Chaucer,* 5 vols. (London: T. Payne, 1775–78). On the signal achievement of this edition, see B. A. Windeatt, "Thomas Tyrwhitt (1730–1786)," *Editing Chaucer: The Great Tradition,* ed. Paul G. Rug-giers (Norman, OK: Pilgrim Books, 1984), 117–43. Recent books help to place Tyr-whitt's enterprise in historical context: Jonathan Brody Kramnick, *Making the English Canon: Print-Capitalism and the Cultural Past, 1700–1770* (Cambridge: Cambridge Univer-sity Press, 1999); Trevor Ross, *The Making of the English Literary Canon: From the Middle Ages to the Late Eighteenth Century* (Montreal: McGill-Queen's University Press, 1998); and David Matthews, *The Making of Middle English, 1765–1910* (Minneapolis: University of Minnesota Press, 1999).

144. Frank Kermode, *Pleasure and Change: The Aesthetics of Canon,* ed. Robert Alter (Oxford: Oxford University Press, 2004). Dr. Johnson's criterion of judgment, echoing the Horatian platitude from *Ars Poetica* (343–44), endorsed the standard al-ready set forth by Harry Bailey in the General Prologue: "Tales of best sentence and moost solaas" (*CT,* I, 798).

145. Resistance to accepting the authenticity of the Z-text perhaps derives partly from reluctance to having a fourth version to factor into critical discussions. By switching from a B to an A exemplar, the copyist of BL Harley 3954 offers one instance in which a medieval scribe made an effort to shorten *Piers.*

146. Steven Justice, *Writing and Rebellion: England in 1381* (Berkeley and Los Angeles: University of California Press, 1994), "Insurgent Literacy," 13–66, provides one of the best current interpretations of these texts.

147. Walsingham's account is translated by A. R. Myers, ed., *English Historical Documents, 1327–1485* (New York: Oxford University Press, 1969), 140–42. For Wyclif's actual Oxford disciples such as Hereford and Repingdon, see Jeremy I. Catto, "Fellows and Helpers: The Religious Identity of the Followers of Wyclif," *The Medieval Church: Universities, Heresy, and the Religious Life,* ed. Peter Biller and Barrie Dobson (Woodbridge: Boydell, 1999), 141–61. On the careers of Walsingham and Knighton, see Antonia Gransden, *Historical Writing in England c. 1307 to the Early Sixteenth Century* (Ithaca: Cornell University Press, 1982), 118–56, 159–60, and 166–71, and Louisa DeSaussure Duls, *Richard II in the Early Chronicles* (Paris and The Hague: Mouton, 1975), 205–14. Geoffrey Martin, "Knighton's Lollards," *Lollardy and the Gentry in the Later Middle Ages,* ed. Margaret Aston and Colin Richmond (New York: St. Martin's Press, 1997), 28–40, observes how the historian telescoped all the disruptive events of the early 1380s.

148. Justice, *Writing and Rebellion,* "Wyclif in the Rising," 67–101 at 90. Harriss, *Shaping the Nation,* "Wyclif and Wycliffism," 376–95, places the Oxford theologian's career in a larger national context.

149. *The Chronicle of Adam Usk, 1377–1421,* ed. and trans. C. Given-Wilson (Oxford: Clarendon, 1997), 6–7.

150. Helen Barr, "Wycliffite Representations of the Third Estate," *Lollards and Their Influence in Late Medieval England,* ed. Fiona Somerset, Jill C. Havens, and Derrick G. Pitard (Woodbridge: Boydell, 2003), 197–216, examines unanimous obedience to secular authority *and* sympathetic idealization of the rural poor represented by the plowman figure.

151. Justice, "Lollardy," *Cambridge History of Medieval English Literature,* ed. Wallace, 673.

152. Terry Jones et al., *Who Murdered Chaucer?* "Henry Meets Arundel," 123–28, and "Chaucer's Enemies Gain Power," 146–64, make Archbishop Arundel the brains as well as the prime mover in the Lancastrian revolution. R. G. Davies, "Thomas Arundel as Archbishop of Canterbury, 1396–1414," *Journal of Ecclesiastical History* 14 (1973): 9–21, takes a more clement view of the prelate's career, and Margaret Aston, *Thomas Arundel: A Study of Church Life in the Reign of Richard II* (Oxford: Clarendon, 1967), "Arundel and Heresy, 1382–97," 320–35, shows that his defense of orthodoxy was no sudden obsession after 1399.

153. Anne Hudson, "Wycliffism in Oxford," *Wyclif in His Times,* ed. Anthony Kenny (Oxford: Clarendon, 1986), 67–84 at 76.

154. Paul Strohm, "Hoccleve, Lydgate and the Lancastrian Court," *Cambridge History of Medieval English Literature,* ed. Wallace, 640–61 at 645–47.

155. Jones et al., *Who Murdered Chaucer?* 161–64 ("War on Heresy").

156. Catto, "Religious Change under Henry V," 101. John A. F. Thomson, *The Later Lollards, 1414–1520* (Oxford: Oxford University Press, 1965), "Lollardy after the Oldcastle Rising," 5–19.

157. Anne Hudson, "Trial and Error: Wyclif's Works in Cambridge, Trinity College MS B.16.2," *New Science out of Old Books: Studies in Manuscripts and Early Printed Books in Honour of A. I. Doyle,* ed. Richard Beadle and A. J. Piper (Aldershot: Scolar Press, 1995), 53–80.

158. Anne Hudson and Pamela Gradon, eds., *English Wycliffite Sermons,* vol. 1 (Oxford: Clarendon, 1983), 189–207. Hanna, *Pursuing History,* "Two Lollard Codices and Lollard Book Production," 48–59 at 58–59, proposes that the use of fascicular exemplars in other Lollard collections resembles the process of copying student texts at Oxford; for more on university-based book production, see Malcolm B. Parkes, "The Provision of Books," *History of the University of Oxford, Vol. 2: Late Medieval Oxford,* ed. J. I. Catto and Ralph Evans (Oxford: Clarendon, 1992), 407–83.

159. Jill C. Havens, "'As Englishe Is Comoun Langage to Oure Puple': The Lollards and Their Imagined 'English' Community," *Imagining a Medieval English Nation,* ed. Lavezzo, 96–128.

160. John H. Fisher, "*Piers Plowman* and the Chancery Tradition," *Medieval English Studies Presented to George Kane,* ed. Donald et al., 267–78. See also Kerby-Fulton and Justice, "Langlandian Reading Circles," 66–67, and Kathleen E. Kennedy, "Retaining a Court of Chancery in *Piers Plowman,*" *YLS* 17 (2003): 175–89.

161. Doyle, "Manuscripts of *Piers Plowman,*" 44, and Ralph Hanna III, *William Langland* (Brookfield, VT: Variorum, 1993), 34. Newnham College MS 4 has an unidentified badge indicating another armigerous owner. Turville-Petre, *The Alliterative Revival,* 46, suggests knights, gentry, and franklins among Langland's immediate audience.

162. A. I. Doyle and M. B. Parkes, "The Production of Copies of the *Canterbury Tales* and the *Confessio Amantis* in the Early Fifteenth Century," *Medieval Scribes, Manuscripts and Libraries: Essays Presented to N. R. Ker,* ed. M. B. Parkes and A. G. Watson (London: Scolar Press, 1978), 163–210, "Appendix C: Evidence of Original Owners," 208–9. Derek Pearsall, "The Manuscripts and Illustrations of Gower's Works," *Companion to Gower,* ed. Echard, 73–97 at 81 and 94–95, on Scribe D's work as a copyist of the *Confessio Amantis.* Kate Harris, "Patrons, Buyers and Owners," *Book Production,* ed. Griffiths and Pearsall, 168–69, reminds us that only a small fraction of manuscripts preserve any evidence of original ownership.

163. Of the eight manuscripts of *Confessio Amantis* produced by this copyist, Kathryn Kerby-Fulton and Steven Justice, "Scribe D and the Marketing of Ricardian Literature," *The Medieval Professional Reader at Work,* ed. Kathryn Kerby-Fulton and Maidie Hilmo (Victoria: University of Victoria English Literary Studies, 2001), 217–33, concentrate upon Princeton University Library Taylor MS 5 as a signal instance of Gower's early pre-eminence. See also M. B. Parkes, "Patterns of Scribal Activity and Revisions of the Text in Early Copies of Works by John Gower," *New Science out of Old Books,* ed. Beadle and Piper, 81–104.

164. Simon Horobin and Linne R. Mooney, "A *Piers Plowman* Manuscript by the Hengwrt/Ellesmere Scribe and Its Implications for London Standard English," *SAC* 26 (2004): 65–112. J. S. P. Tatlock, "The *Canterbury Tales* in 1400," *PMLA* 50 (1935): 100–139 at 128, first noted that Hengwrt and Ellesmere were copied by the same scribe.

165. Estelle Stubbs, "A New Manuscript by the Hengwrt/Ellesmere Scribe? Aberystwyth, National Library of Wales, MS. Peniarth 393D," *Journal of the Early Book Society* 5 (2002): 161–68 at 114–29.

166. John M. Bowers, "Two Professional Readers of Chaucer and Langland: Scribe D and the HM 114 Scribe," *SAC* 26 (2004): 113–46.

167. Kerby-Fulton and Justice, "Scribe D and the Marketing of Ricardian Literature," 222–26, had already suggested such specialties: Scribe D for Gower's *Confessio* and Scribe Δ for Trevisa's *Polychronicon*. The Edmund-Fremund Scribe specialized in Lydgate with ten manuscripts to his credit in the middle decades of the fifteenth century; see Kathleen L. Scott, "Lydgate's Lives of Saints Edmund and Fremund: A Newly-Located Manuscript in Arundel Castle," *Viator* 13 (1982): 335–66.

168. Alcuin Blamires, "Crisis and Dissent," *Companion to Chaucer,* ed. Peter Brown, 133–48.

169. Myrta Ethel McGinnis, *"Piers the Plowman* in England, 1362–1625" (Ph.D. diss., Yale University, 1932), demonstrates the abundance of evidence for a Langlandian tradition but also the difficulty of rendering it coherent.

170. Laurence de Looze, "Signing Off in the Middle Ages: Medieval Textuality and Strategies of Authorial Self-Naming," *Vox Intexta: Orality and Textuality in the Middle Ages,* ed. A. N. Doan and Carol Braun Pasternak (Madison: University of Wisconsin Press, 1991), 162–78 at 165.

171. Derek Pearsall, "The Idea of Englishness in the Fifteenth Century," *Nation, Court and Culture: New Essays on Fifteenth-Century English Poetry,* ed. Helen Cooney (Dublin: Four Courts Press, 2001), 15–27 at 25, raises considerable doubt about the extent of this project beyond the years 1410–20. John H. Fisher, "Chancery and the Emergence of Standard Written English in the Fifteenth Century," *Speculum* 52 (1977): 870–99, and Malcolm Richardson, "Henry V, the English Chancery, and Chancery English," *Speculum* 55 (1980): 726–50, suggest something far-reaching like royal sponsorship of a standard vernacular.

172. Lucy Freeman Sandler, "Lancastrian Heraldry in the Bohun Manuscripts," *The Lancastrian Court,* ed. Jenny Stratford, *Harlaxton Medieval Studies,* n.s. 13 (2003): 221–32, and Sandler, "Political Imagery in the Bohun Manuscripts," *Decorations and Illustration in Medieval English Manuscripts, English Manuscript Studies* 10 (2002): 114–53.

173. For the affluence of Richard II, see Bowers, *The Politics of "Pearl,"* 77–132. Poverty was the hallmark of Henry IV's reign; K. B. McFarlane, "England: The Lancastrian Kings, 1399–1461," *The Cambridge Medieval History* (Cambridge: Cambridge University Press, 1936), 8:362–417 at 376, suggests that the Lollard Endowment petition of 1410 appealed to this royal poverty by proposing to remedy the country's financial difficulties by confiscating Church estates.

174. Jones et al., *Who Murdered Chaucer?* 228–31 ("The Missing Royal Library"), continues my speculation in *The Politics of "Pearl"* that Richard II's book collection, along with those volumes inherited from the previous two monarchs, may have been scattered as part of the eradication of his court culture after 1399.

175. Edith Rickert, "King Richard II's Books," *The Library* 4th ser., 13 (1933): 144–47; Richard Firth Green, "King Richard II's Books Revisited," *The Library* 5th

ser., 31 (1976): 235–39; A. I. Doyle, "English Books in and out of Court from Edward III to Henry VII," *English Court Culture in the Later Middle Ages,* ed. V. J. Scattergood and J. W. Sherborne (New York: St. Martin's, 1983), 163–81; V. J. Scattergood, "Literary Culture at the Court of Richard II," *English Court Culture in the Later Middle Ages,* 29–43; Jeanne E. Krochalis, "The Books and Reading of Henry V and His Circle," *ChauR* 23 (1988): 50–77 at 57–60; and Bowers, *Politics of "Pearl,"* 77–132.

176. See two contributions to Lotte Hellinga and J. B. Trapp, eds., *Cambridge History of the Book in Britain,* vol. 3, *1400–1557* (Cambridge: Cambridge University Press, 1999): Jenny Stratford, "The Early Royal Collections and the Royal Library to 1461," 255–66, and Janet Backhouse, "The Royal Library from Edward IV and Henry VII," 267–73 at 260–61.

177. Lucy Freeman Sandler, *The Lichtenthal Psalter and the Manuscript Patronage of the Bohun Family* (London and Turnhout: Harvey Miller Publishers, 2004), 11–28 and 145–51.

178. *A Facsimile of Corpus Christi College Cambridge MS 61,* intro. M. B. Parkes and Elizabeth Salter (Cambridge: D. S. Brewer, 1978). See also Patrick Strong and Felicity Strong, "The Last Will and Codicils of Henry V," *EHR* 96 (1981): 79–102 at 99–100, and Stratford, "The Early Royal Collections," 266.

179. C. Paul Christianson, "A Community of Book Artisans in Chaucer's London," *Viator* 20 (1989): 207–18, and J. J. G. Alexander, "Foreign Illuminators and Illuminated Manuscripts," *The Cambridge History of the Book in Britain,* vol. 3: ed. Hellinga and Trapp, 47–64.

180. K. B. McFarlane, "Henry V, Bishop Beaufort and the Red Hat, 1417–1421" (1945), rpt. *England in the Fifteenth Century,* intro. G. L. Harriss (London: Hambledon, 1981), 79–113 at 102, and Derek Pearsall, "The Literary Milieu of Charles of Orléans and the Duke of Suffolk, and the Authorship of the Fairfax Sequence," *Charles d'Orléans in England (1415–1440),* ed. Mary-Jo Arn (Cambridge: D. S. Brewer, 2000), 145–56 at 149.

181. Now Pierpont Morgan Library M 817; see B. A. Windeatt, ed., *Troilus and Criseyde* (London and New York: Longman, 1984), 68–69.

182. Kerby-Fulton and Justice, "Scribe D and the Marketing of Ricardian Literature," 226. On the standardized ways of writing civic documents, see Sheila Lindenbaum, "London Texts and Literate Practices," *Cambridge History of Medieval English Literature,* ed. Wallace, 284–309. The high quality of these decorated books can be better appreciated in Richard K. Emmerson, "Reading Gower in a Manuscript Culture: Latin and English in Illustrated Manuscripts of the *Confessio Amantis," SAC* 21 (1999): 143–86.

183. Derek Brewer, "Chaucer's Anti-Ricardian Poetry," *The Living Middle Ages: A Festschrift for Karl Heinz Göller,* ed. Uwe Böker, Manfred Markus, and Rainer Schöwerling (Stuttgart: Belser, 1989), 115–28.

184. Doyle, "English Books in and out of Court," 171–72. For more on this textwriter's activities, see M. L. Samuels, "The Scribe of the Hengwrt and Ellesmere Manuscripts of the *Canterbury Tales," SAC* 5 (1983): 49–65, and A. I. Doyle, "The Copyist of the Ellesmere *Canterbury Tales," Ellesmere Chaucer,* ed. Stevens and Woodward, 49–67.

185. Tyrwhitt, ed., *The Canterbury Tales of Chaucer,* 4:188–89.

186. J. S. Roskell, *The Commons and Their Speakers in English Parliaments, 1376–1523* (Manchester: Manchester University Press, 1965), 159–61 and 172–74.

187. McFarlane, "Henry V, Bishop Beaufort and the Red Hat, 1417–1421," 89–91.

188. Carol M. Meale, "Patrons, Buyers and Owners: Book Production and Social Status," *Book Production,* ed. Griffiths and Pearsall, 201–38 at 218.

189. David Carlson, *Chaucer's Jobs,* 1.

190. Derek Pearsall, "Thomas Speght (ca. 1550–?)," *Editing Chaucer,* ed. Ruggiers, 71–92.

191. Geoffrey Chaucer, *The Works (1532) with Supplementary Material from the Editions of 1542, 1561, 1598 and 1602,* facsimile ed., D. S. Brewer (London: Scolar Press, 1978). Since Thomas Chaucer's tomb actually omitted his father Geoffrey, Speght's frontispiece corrected the deficiency by placing Payne Roet at the top as if he were the common ancestor, through his two daughters, of both the Lancastrians and the Chaucers.

192. This later process is the subject of Michael Dobson, *The Making of the National Poet: Shakespeare, Adaptation and Authorship, 1660–1769* (Oxford: Clarendon, 1992).

193. Christopher Cannon, *The Making of Chaucer's English,* esp. 179–220, and David Burnley, "Language," *Companion to Chaucer,* ed. Brown, 235–50, adjust this longstanding view.

194. Edwin Ford Piper, "The Royal Boar and the Ellesmere Chaucer," *PQ* 5 (1926): 330–40; C. W. Dutschke, *Guide to Medieval and Renaissance Manuscripts in the Huntington Library,* 2 vols. (San Marino: Huntington Library, 1989), 1:41–50; and Ralph Hanna III and A. S. G. Edwards, "Rotheley, the De Vere Circle, and the Ellesmere Chaucer," *Reading from the Margins: Textual Studies, Chaucer, and Medieval Culture,* ed. Seth Lerer (San Marino: Huntington Library, 1996), 11–35. See also Kate Harris, "Patrons, Buyers and Owners: The Evidence for Ownership and the Role of Book Owners in Book Production and the Book Trade," *Book Production and Publishing in Britain, 1375–1475,* ed. Griffiths and Pearsall, 163–99.

195. Clifford Geertz, "Thick Description: Toward an Interpretive Theory of Culture," *The Interpretation of Cultures* (New York: Basic Books, 1973), 3–30 at 10.

196. B. A. Windeatt, "The Scribes as Chaucer's Early Critics," *SAC* 1 (1979): 119–41, and Derek Pearsall, "Texts, Textual Criticism, and Fifteenth Century Manuscript Production," *Fifteenth-Century Studies: Recent Essays,* ed. Robert F. Yeager (Hamden, CT: Archon Books, 1984), 121–36, encouraged this reassessment of scribal activities.

197. Kathryn Kerby-Fulton, "Professional Readers of Langland at Home and Abroad: New Directions in the Political and Bureaucratic Codicology of *Piers Plowman,*" *New Directions in Later Medieval Manuscript Studies,* ed. Derek Pearsall (Woodbridge: Boydell, for York Medieval Press, 2000), 103–29 at 103.

198. Malcolm Richardson, "The Earliest Known Owners of *Canterbury Tales* MSS and Chaucer's Secondary Audience," *ChauR* 25 (1990): 17–32. See also *The Text*

of the Canterbury Tales, ed. John M. Manly and Edith Rickert, 8 vols. (Chicago: University of Chicago Press, 1940), 1:606–7.

199. Eleanor Prescott Hammond, "Poet and Patron in the *Fall of Princes*: Lydgate and Humphrey of Gloucester," *Anglia* 38 (1914): 121–36, and Peter J. Lucas, "The Growth and Development of English Literary Patronage in the Later Middle Ages and Early Renaissance," *The Library* 6th ser., 4 (1982): 219–48 at 225–27. Harriss, *Shaping the Nation,* "The Court as a Religious and Cultural Centre," 31–40, reminds us that goldsmiths were more likely than writers to receive royal commissions.

200. Robert Crowley, ed., *The Vision of Pierce Plowman* (1550), intro. to facsimile ed. by J. A. W. Bennett (London: David Paradine Developments, 1976).

201. N. F. Blake, "William Caxton: His Choice of Texts," *Anglia* 83 (1965): 289–307, and "Caxton and Chaucer," *LSE* n.s. 1 (1967): 19–36. See also David R. Carlson, "Chaucer, Humanism, and Printing: Conditions of Authorship in Fifteenth-Century England," *University of Toronto Quarterly* 64 (1995): 274–88.

202. Beverly Boyd, "William Caxton (1422?–1491)," *Editing Chaucer,* ed. Ruggiers, 13–34.

203. Lerer, *Chaucer and His Readers,* "At Chaucer's Tomb: Laureation and Paternity in Caxton's Criticism," 147–75.

204. Wendy Scase, "'Strange and Wonderful Bills': Bill-Casting and Political Discourse in Late Medieval England," *NML* 2 (1998): 225–47, breaks new ground in our understanding of these ephemeral writings. Wilson, *Lost Literature of the Medieval England,* "Political and Satirical Poetry," 187–208, begins with works in the *Piers Plowman* tradition.

205. Sharon L. Jansen, "British Library MS Sloane 2578 and Popular Unrest in England, 1554–1556," *Manuscripta* 29 (1985): 30–41, and "Politics, Protest, and a New *Piers Plowman* Fragment: The Voice of the Past in Tudor England," *RES* n.s. 40 (1989): 93–99.

206. *The workes of Geffray Chaucer newly printed, with dyuers workes whych were neuer in print before,* ed. William Thynne, 1542. Francis Thynne, *Animadversions upon Thynne's First Edition of Chaucers Workes,* rev. ed. F. J. Furnivall (London: Chaucer Society, ser. 2, no. 13, 1876), 10, recollected the problematic inclusion of the Plowman's Tale "with muche ado permitted to passe with the reste."

207. Tim William Machan, "Thomas Berthelette and Gower's *Confessio,*" *SAC* 18 (1996): 143–66, discusses Gower's neglect after Caxton. Simpson, *Reform,* 40–41, documents an energetic printing of Lydgate during the 1530s through the 1550s, then a sudden closing down of the monastic poet's prospects.

208. James E. Blodgett, "William Thynne (d. 1546)," *Editing Chaucer,* ed. Ruggiers, 35–52. Seth Lerer, *Courtly Letters in the Age of Henry VIII: Literary Culture and the Arts of Deceit* (Cambridge: Cambridge University Press, 1997), is chiefly concerned with Tudor publication of Chaucer's *Troilus*. See also Pamela Neville-Sington, "Press, Politics and Religion," *Cambridge History of the Book in Britain,* vol. 3, ed. Hellinga and Trapp, 576–607.

209. Peter Brown, "Higden's Britain," *Medieval Europeans: Studies in Ethnic Identity and National Perspectives in Medieval Europe,* ed. Alfred P. Smyth (New York: St. Mar-

tin's Press, 1998), 103–18, and Kathy Lavezzo, "Introduction," *Imagining a Medieval English Nation,* vii–xxxiv. See also Alice Miskimin, *The Renaissance Chaucer* (New Haven: Yale University Press, 1975), and John Watkins, "'Wrastling for This World': Wyatt and the Tudor Canonization of Chaucer," *Refiguring Chaucer in the Renaissance,* ed. Theresa M. Krier (Gainesville: University Press of Florida, 1998), 21–39 at 28.

210. Thynne, *Adimadversions,* 9–10.

211. Furnivall, 77–98, prints the "Pilgrim's Tale" from the incomplete blackletter edition *Courte of Venus* in Bodleian Douce frag. g.3, fols. 31b–45b (STC 24650). See Joseph A. Dane, "Bibliographical History versus Bibliographical Evidence: *The Plowman's Tale* and Early Chaucer Editions," *BJRL* 78 (1996): 50–64. The text cannot have been accepted as authentic since it names Chaucer as an outside authority (lines 93 and 740). For a careful consideration of dating, see *The Court of Venus,* ed. Russell A. Fraser (Durham, NC: Duke University Press, 1955), 11–14 and 82–110.

212. John Bale, *Index Britanniae Scriptorum,* ed. Reginald Lane Poole and Mary Bateson (Oxford: Clarendon, 1902), 389. See Ritchie D. Kendall, *The Drama of Dissent: The Radical Poetics of Nonconformity, 1380–1590* (Chapel Hill: University of North Carolina Press, 1986), "John Bale: The Cloistered Imagination," 90–131, and generally Peter Happé, *John Bale* (New York: Twayne Publishers, 1996).

213. Alan J. Fletcher, "Chaucer the Heretic," *SAC* 25 (2003): 53–121, returns to a view commonplace in the second half of the nineteenth century but completely out of fashion during the second half of the twentieth century.

214. Catherine Gallagher and Stephen Greenblatt, *Practicing New Historicism* (Chicago and London: University of Chicago Press, 2000), 16–17.

215. Thynne, *Animadversions,* 10.

216. Langland still attracted some imitators such as the author of *The Conference between Simon Certain and Pierce Plowman* and some noteworthy readers such as Edmund Spenser; see Hudson, "Legacy of *Piers Plowman,*" 261–62, and Johnson, *Reading "Piers Plowman" and "The Pilgrim's Progress,"* "Renaissance Readings of *Piers Plowman,*" 128–59.

217. Ros King, *The Works of Richard Edwards: Politics, Poetry and Performance in Sixteenth-Century England* (Manchester: Manchester University Press, 2001), 63–87.

218. Helen Cooper, "Jacobean Chaucer: *The Two Noble Kinsmen* and Other Chaucerian Plays," *Refiguring Chaucer in the Renaissance,* ed. Krier, 189–209.

219. Clare R. Kinney, "Thomas Speght's Renaissance Chaucer and the *Solaas* of *Sentence* in *Troilus and Criseyde,*" *Refiguring Chaucer in the Renaissance,* ed. Krier, 66–84.

220. Edwards, "The Early Reception of Chaucer and Langland," 21n.72, draws attention to New Haven, Beinecke MS Osborn a.18, fols. 1a–12b, which preserves a text suggesting Catholic sympathies later in the sixteenth century: "Peers plowghman hys answer to the doctours / interogatoryes & scryves of the lawe in stede / of an Apology for the late martyrs of noble memory." As a reversal of fortunes, while the official print medium worked to advance the cause of Protestant authorities, Catholics relied heavily upon handwritten books to preserve their stories and identities during the period 1580–1688, much like the Lollard underground during the preceding two centuries; see Arthur F. Marotti, *Religious Ideology and Cultural Fantasy: Catholic*

and Anti-Catholic Discourses in Early Modern England (Notre Dame, IN: University of Notre Dame Press, 2005).

221. *The Mirror for Magistrates,* ed. Lily B. Campbell (Cambridge: Cambridge University Press, 1938), 95 (lines 92–93). See also Judith H. Anderson, "Langland, William," *Spenser Encyclopedia,* ed. A. C. Hamilton (Toronto: University of Toronto Press, 1990), 425–26, and Leslie-Anne Crowley, *The Quest for Holiness: Spenser's Debt to Langland* (Milan: Arcipelago Edizioni, Letterature in Lingua Inglese, no. 5, 1992).

222. Jean-François Lyotard, *The Postmodern Condition: A Report on Knowledge,* trans. Geoff Bennington and Brian Massumi (Minneapolis: University of Minnesota Press, 1984), 37.

223. Hayden White, *The Content of the Form: Narrative Discourse and Historical Representation* (Baltimore and London: Johns Hopkins University Press, 1987), ix.

224. Joel Fineman, "The History of the Anecdote: Fiction and Fiction," *The New Historicism,* ed. Veeser, 49–76.

225. Auerbach's *Mimesis,* 552, for "emphasis on the random occurrence." Gallagher and Greenblatt, *Practicing New Historicism,* 20–48 at 35 (Greenblatt) and 49–74 (Gallagher), acknowledge Auerbach's contribution; see also the valuable collection *Literary History and the Challenge of Philology: The Legacy of Erich Auerbach,* ed. Seth Lerer (Stanford: Stanford University Press, 1996).

226. Strohm, *England's Empty Throne,* "Reconsidering the 'Oldcastle Rebellion,'" 65–86.

227. Carolyn Dinshaw, *Getting Medieval: Sexualities and Communities, Pre- and Postmodern* (Durham, NC: Duke University Press, 1999), esp. 12–34, refines our understanding of these minority communities in terms of collective self-fashioning; see also Jacob Torfing, *New Theories of Discourse: Laclau, Mouffe and Žižek* (Oxford: Blackwell, 1999), "Social Antagonism," 120–31.

228. Elizabeth Fowler, "Misogyny and Economic Person in Skelton, Langland, and Chaucer," *Spenser Studies* 10 (1992): 245–73.

229. Trevor Ross, "Dissolution and the Making of the English Literary Canon: The Catalogues of Leland and Bale," *Renaissance and Reformation,* n.s. 15 (1991): 57–80; Simpson, *Reform,* "The Melancholy of John Leland and the Beginnings of English Literary History," 7–33; and James P. Carley, "'Cum excuterem puluerem et blattas': John Bale, John Leland, and the *Chronicon Tinemutensis coenobii," Text and Controversy from Wyclif to Bale: Essays in Honour of Anne Hudson,* ed. Helen Barr and Ann M. Hutchison (Turnhout, Belgium: Brepols, 2005), 163–87.

230. Ernesto Laclau and Chantal Mouffe, *Hegemony and Socialist Strategy,* trans. Winston Moore and Paul Cammack (London: Verso, 1985), "Antagonism and Objectivity," 122–27, and Slavoj Žižek, *The Sublime Object of Ideology* (London and New York: Verso, 1989), "How Did Marx Invent the Symptom?" 11–53.

231. Slavoj Žižek, "Beyond Discourse Analysis," *New Reflections on the Revolution of Our Time,* ed. Ernesto Laclau (London: Verso, 1990), 249–60.

232. Pearsall, "The Idea of Englishness," 26–27.

233. E. H. Gombrich, *The Story of Art,* 16th rev. ed. (New York: Phaedon, 1995), 15.

234. Bernhard ten Brink, *History of English Literature:* vol. 1: *Early English Literature to Wyclif,* trans. Horace Milton Kennedy, and vol. 2: *Wyclif, Chaucer, Earliest Drama, Renaissance,* trans. William Clarke Robinson (London: George Bell & Sons, 1893).

235. Nicholas Watson, "Desire for the Past," *SAC* 21 (1999): 59–97 at 91.

236. Stanley Fish, "Commentary: The Young and the Restless," *The New Historicism,* ed. Veeser, 303–16 at 303.

CHAPTER TWO   **Beginnings**

1. The same start-up date of 1360 is selected by Gerald Harriss for his volume of the New Oxford History of England, *Shaping the Nation.* Simpson, *Reform,* 2, decided to begin his survey at roughly 1350 with the death of Richard Rolle and to end about 1547 with the death of Henry VIII.

2. Michael Hanly, "France," *Companion to Chaucer,* ed. Brown, 149–66.

3. William Langland, *The Vision of William concerning Piers the Plowman in Three Parallel Texts together with Richard the Redeless,* ed. Walter W. Skeat, 2 vols. (Oxford: Oxford University Press, 1886), 2:48–49, identified the allusion to the Treaty of Brétigny. His conclusion was confirmed by J. A. W. Bennett, "The Date of the A-Text of *Piers Plowman,*" *PMLA* 58 (1943): 566–72. The evidence for dating all three versions is reviewed by Hanna, *William Langland,* 11–17.

4. Gransden, *Historical Writing in England c. 1307 to the Early Sixteenth Century,* 111–13.

5. *Anonimalle Chronicle, 1333–1381,* ed. V. H. Galbraith (Manchester: Manchester University Press, 1927), 49, trans. John Barnie, *War in Medieval English Society: Social Values in the Hundred Years War, 1337–99* (Ithaca: Cornell University Press, 1974), 13–14.

6. Sir Thomas Gray, *Scalacronica: The Reigns of Edward I, Edward II, and Edward III,* ed. and trans. Sir Herbert Maxwell (Glasgow: James Maclehose & Sons, 1907), 165.

7. McFarlane, *Nobility of Later Medieval England,* 33.

8. Barnie, *War in Medieval English Society,* 33, and Christopher Allmand, *The Hundred Years War: England and France at War c. 1300–c. 1450* (Cambridge: Cambridge University Press, 1988), 47.

9. May McKisack, *The Fourteenth Century, 1307–1399* (Oxford: Clarendon, 1959), 254.

10. John L. Selzer, "Topical Allegory in *Piers Plowman*: Lady Mede's B-Text Debate with Conscience," *PQ* 59 (1980): 257–67.

11. K. B. McFarlane, "War, the Economy and Social Change: England and the Hundred Years War" (1962), rpt. *England in the Fifteenth Century,* 139–49.

12. Myers, ed., *English Historical Documents,* 103–8 at 105.

13. Charles Tilly, *Coercion, Capital and European States, AD 990–1990* (Oxford: Blackwell, 1990), "War Drives State Formation and Transformation," 20–88.

14. Quoted by Michael Powicke, "The English Aristocracy and the War," *The Hundred Years War,* ed. Kenneth Fowler (London: Macmillan, 1971), 122–34 at 130.

15. Edouard Perroy, *The Hundred Years War,* trans. David C. Douglas (Bloomington: Indiana University Press, 1959), 132–42, and Jonathan Sumption, *The Hundred Years War,* vol. 2: *Trial by Fire* (Philadelphia: University of Pennsylvania Press, 1999), "Edward III's Last Campaign," 405–54, summarize the entire military operation and its aftermath.

16. Allmand, *Hundred Years War,* 37–38.

17. Denise N. Baker, "Mede and the Economics of Chivalry in *Piers Plowman,*" *Inscribing the Hundred Years' War in French and English Cultures,* ed. Denise N. Baker (Albany: State University of New York Press, 2000), 55–72 at 63–64.

18. *The Brut, or The Chronicles of England,* ed. Friedrich W. D. Brie, EETS o.s. 131 and 136, 1906 and 1908, 311.

19. *The Chronicle of Jean de Venette,* ed. Richard A. Newhall, trans. Jean Birdsall (New York: Columbia University Press, 1953), 103.

20. Baker, "Mede and the Economics of Chivalry," 66, translates *Chroniques de J. Froissart,* ed. Siméon Luce (Paris: Libraire de la Société de l'Histoire de France, 1876), 6:4–5.

21. Baker, "Mede and the Economics of Chivalry," 67.

22. Richard W. Kaeuper, *War, Justice, and Public Order: England and France in the Later Middle Ages* (Oxford: Clarendon, 1988), esp. 170–83.

23. M. M. Postan, "The Costs of the Hundred Years' War," *P&P* 27 (1964): 34–53.

24. C. C. Bayley, "The Campaign of 1375 and the Good Parliament," *EHR* 55 (1940): 370–83.

25. R. B. Dobson, ed., *The Peasants' Revolt of 1381,* 2nd ed. (London: Macmillan, 1983), 103–22, collects documents relating to these three poll taxes.

26. Patricia DeMarco, "An Arthur for the Ricardian Age: Crown, Nobility, and the Alliterative *Morte Arthure,*" *Speculum* 80 (2005): 464–93, discusses the conflicting interests of the king and the warrior class.

27. Anna P. Baldwin, "The Historical Context," *Companion to "Piers Plowman,"* ed. Alford, 67–86 at 76–77. Baldwin continues her discussion of these antiwar elements resembling Wycliffite positions in "Patient Politics in *Piers Plowman,*" *YLS* 15 (2001): 99–108.

28. Langland, *Piers Plowman: An Edition of the C-text,* ed. Pearsall, 75.

29. Hudson, *Premature Reformation,* 367–68. See John Wyclif, *Tractatus de Ecclesia,* ed. Iohann Loserth (London: Wyclif Society, 1886), 427.

30. For Walsingham's account of the crusade, see *English Historical Documents,* ed. Myers, 145–47. Margaret Aston, "The Impeachment of Bishop Despenser," *Bulletin of the Institute of Historical Research* 38 (1965): 127–48; A. K. McHardy, "Liturgy and Propaganda in the Diocese of Lincoln during the Hundred Years War," *SCH* 18 (1982): 215–27 at 222–25; and Hudson, *Premature Reformation,* 368. C. T. Allmand, "The War and the Non-combatant," *The Hundred Years War,* ed. Fowler, 163–83 at

176, places these Wycliffite criticisms in context of larger clerical discontent with warfare.

31. A. K. McHardy, "Bishop Buckingham and the Lollards of Lincoln Diocese," *SCH* 9 (1972): 131–45, prints Coryngham's views from the bishop's register.

32. Hudson, ed., *English Wycliffite Writings,* 28.

33. This explanation was promulgated by monastic historians such as Thomas Walsingham, *Historia Anglicana,* ed. Henry Thomas Riley, 2 vols. (London, Rolls Series, 1863–64), 2:215–17. J. J. N. Palmer, *England, France and Christendom, 1377–99* (London: Routledge & Kegan Paul, 1972), 166–68, thinks Richard rushed back to England because of a sudden deterioration in peace negotiations with the French.

34. Roger Dymmok, *Liber contra XII Errores et Hereses Lollardorum,* ed. H. S. Cronin (London: Wyclif Society, 1922), 238–40 and 243; Kathleen L. Scott, *Dated and Datable English Manuscript Borders, c. 1395–1499* (London: British Library for the Bibliographical Society, 2002), 17 and 22–25, for the presentation manuscript Cambridge, Trinity Hall MS 17. The English version of the *Conclusions* has been separately edited by Hudson, ed., *English Wycliffite Writings,* 24–29 with commentary 150–55; see also Hudson, *Premature Reformation,* 49–50. Another Latin version of the *Conclusions* is preserved in *Fasciculi Zizaniorum,* 360–69. See also Fiona Somerset, *Clerical Discourse and Lay Audience in Late Medieval England* (Cambridge: Cambridge University Press, 1998), "Answering the *Twelve Conclusions*: Dymmok's Halfhearted Gestures toward Publication," 103–34.

35. Justice, "Lollardy," *Cambridge History of Medieval English Literature,* ed. Wallace, 684, on the movement as a catchall for many sorts of dissenting opinion.

36. *Fasciculi Zizaniorum,* 431–32. See Hudson, *Premature Reformation,* 37, and generally Steven Justice, "Inquisition, Speech and Writing: A Case from Late-Medieval Norwich," *Representations* 48 (1994): 1–29.

37. Hudson, *Premature Reformation,* 496–97.

38. Wilbur Gaffney, "The Allegory of the Christ-Knight in *Piers Plowman,*" *PMLA* 46 (1931): 155–68; Rosemary Woolf, "The Theme of Christ the Lover-Knight in Medieval English Literature," *RES* 13 (1962): 1–16; and Lawrence Warner, "Jesus the Jouster: The Christ-Knight and Medieval Theories of the Atonement in *Piers Plowman* and the 'Round Table' Sermons," *YLS* 10 (1996): 129–43.

39. Bowers, *Politics of "Pearl,"* 89–93.

40. F. R. H. Du Boulay, *The England of "Piers Plowman": William Langland and His Vision of the Fourteenth Century* (Cambridge: D. S. Brewer, 1991).

41. *Chaucer Life-Records,* 23–28: "Galfrido Chaucer capto per inimicos in partibus Francie in subsidium redempcionis sue de consimili dono regis die et anno supradictis xvi li."

42. *Chaucer Life-Records,* 370. Derek Brewer, *Chaucer and His World,* 2nd ed. (Cambridge: D. S. Brewer, 1992), 56–61, offers an imaginative fleshing-out of these events.

43. *Knighton's Chronicle, 1337–1396,* ed. and trans. G. H. Martin (Oxford: Clarendon, 1995), 176–77.

44. Chandos Herald, *The Life and Campaigns of the Black Prince,* ed. and trans. Richard Barber (New York: St. Martin's, 1986), 104. See Desmond Seward, *The Hundred Years War* (New York: Atheneum, 1978), 97–101.

45. Barnie, *War in Medieval English Society,* 28–29. See also John Keegan, *The Face of War* (Harmondsworth: Penguin, 1978), 70–72.

46. Gray, *Scalacronica,* 158–59.

47. John Palmer, "The War Aims of the Protagonists and Negotiations for Peace," *The Hundred Years War,* ed. Fowler, 59–63.

48. Derek Pearsall, *The Life of Geoffrey Chaucer* (Oxford: Blackwell, 1992), 55–73.

49. Howard, *Chaucer: His Life, His Works, His World,* 71–73. See also James I. Wimsatt, *Chaucer and His French Contemporaries* (Toronto: University of Toronto Press, 1991), 78–84, and Anne Walters Robertson, *Guillaume de Machaut and Reims* (Cambridge: Cambridge University Press, 2002).

50. Froissart, *Chronicles,* trans. Geoffrey Brereton (Harmondsworth: Penguin, 1978), 69.

51. Anthony Tuck, "Why Men Fought in the 100 Years War," *History Today* 33 (April 1983): 35–40 at 38. C. T. Allmand, *Society at War: The Experience of England and France during the Hundred Years War* (Edinburgh: Oliver & Boyd, 1973), 83–85, gathers contemporary statements on the treatment of prisoners.

52. H. J. Hewitt, *The Organization of War under Edward III, 1338–62* (New York: Barnes & Noble, 1966), 93–139; Allmand, "The War and the Non-combatant," *The Hundred Years War,* ed. Fowler, 163–83; and Nicholas Wright, *Knights and Peasants: The Hundred Years' War in the French Countryside* (Woodbridge: Boydell Press, 1998).

53. *Knighton's Chronicle,* 176–77.

54. Evidence of the poet's pacifism is assessed by V. J. Scattergood, "Chaucer and the French War: *Sir Thopas* and *Melibee,*" *Court and Poet,* ed. Glyn S. Burgess et al. (Liverpool: Cairns, 1981), 287–96, and R. F. Yeager, "*Pax Poetica*: On the Pacifism of Chaucer and Gower," *SAC* 9 (1987): 97–121.

55. *The Chronicle of Jean de Venette,* 92, and generally 87–107, describing the terrible misery of French civilians during 1359–60.

56. Kenneth Fowler, "Introduction: War and Change in Late Medieval France and England," *The Hundred Years War,* ed. Fowler, 1–27 at 22.

57. Richard Cazelles, "The Jacquerie," *The English Rising of 1381,* ed. R. H. Hilton and T. H. Aston (Cambridge: Cambridge University Press, 1984), 74–83.

58. Sir Thomas Gray's *Scalacronica,* 158–59, on the scarcity of victuals during the winter of 1359–60.

59. *Knighton's Chronicle,* 178–79.

60. Burrow, *Ricardian Poetry,* 93–102, detects a persistently unheroic attitude even in the Knight's Tale. Pearsall, *Life of Geoffrey Chaucer,* 40–46, admits that warfare did not provide Chaucer with his favorite subject. See also Elizabeth Porter, "Chaucer's Knight, the Alliterative *Morte Arthure,* and Medieval Laws of War: A Reconsideration," *Nottingham Medieval Studies* 27 (1983): 56–78, and Simon Meecham-Jones, "The Invisible Siege—The Depiction of Warfare in the Poetry of Chaucer," *Writing War: Medieval Literary Responses to Warfare,* ed. Corinne Saunders, Françoise Le Saux, and Neil Thomas (Cambridge: D. S. Brewer, 2004), 147–67.

61. On the provinciality of French spoken in England, see Albert C. Baugh, *A History of the English Language,* 2nd ed. (New York: Appleton-Century-Crofts, 1957), 167–68, and two articles by W. Rothwell: "Stratford atte Bowe and Paris," *MLR* 80 (1985): 39–54, and "Chaucer and Stratford atte Bowe," *BJRL* 74 (1992): 3–28.

62. George Neilson, *Caudatus Anglicus: A Mediaeval Slander* (Edinburgh: George P. Johnson, 1896), esp. 15–18, and Peter Rickard, *"Anglois coué* and *l'Anglois qui couve,"* *French Studies* 7 (1953): 48–55.

63. Wimsatt, *Chaucer and His French Contemporaries,* 239–40. Paul Meyvaert, "'Rainaldus est malus scriptor Francigenus'—Voicing National Antipathy in the Middle Ages," *Speculum* 66 (1991): 743–63, notes that the terms of ethnic derision were always subject to particular historical circumstances, here the ongoing hostilities between England and France.

64. David Wallace, *Premodern Places: Calais to Surinam, Chaucer to Aphra Behn* (Oxford: Blackwell, 2004), "At Calais Gate," 22–90 at 48–61.

65. Fowler, "Introduction," *Hundred Years War,* ed. Fowler, 22.

66. Pearsall, *Life of Geoffrey Chaucer,* "Writing a Life of Chaucer," 1–8, and Janette Dillon, "Life Histories," *Companion to Chaucer,* ed. Peter Brown, 251–65, review the challenges of extracting a biography from the *Chaucer Life-Records.*

67. Anthony Goodman, *John of Gaunt* (Harlow: Longman, 1992), 46–49.

68. *Chaucer Life-Records,* 31–32.

69. For a fuller account, see Bowers, "Chaucer after Retters: The Wartime Origins of English Literature," *Inscribing the Hundred Years' War,* ed. Baker, 91–125.

CHAPTER THREE   **Naming Names**

1. "What Is an Author?" (1969), *The Foucault Reader,* 101–20 at 105–7.

2. Dutschke, *Guide to Medieval and Renaissance Manuscripts in the Huntington Library,* 1:35–39 and 185–90. On the mingling of Chaucer's poems with works by imitators, see John J. Thompson, "Thomas Hoccleve and Manuscript Culture," *Nation, Court and Culture,* ed. Cooney, 81–94 at 87–88.

3. Henry Noble MacCracken, "More Odd Texts of Chaucer's *Troilus,*" *MLN* 25 (1910): 126–27. On Shirley's contribution to the canonicity of the shorter poems, see Lerer, *Chaucer and His Readers,* 117–46.

4. Kathleen Forni, *The Chaucerian Apocrypha: A Counterfeit Canon* (Gainesville: University Press of Florida, 2001), examines how authentic and spurious texts moved from manuscripts to Tudor folio editions. Even Tyrwhitt, ed., *The Canterbury Tales,* 1: xxiv–xxxvi, "An Abstract of the Historical Passages of the Life of Chaucer," accepted the biographical evidence of *Testament of Love.*

5. See generally A. S. G. Edwards, "Walter Skeat (1835–1912)," *Editing Chaucer,* ed. Ruggiers, 171–89.

6. Bokenham, *Legendys of Hooly Wummen,* ed. Serjeantson, 6 (lines 199–200) and 289.

7. Middleton, "William Langland's 'Kynde Name': Authorial Signature and Social Identity in Late Fourteenth-Century England," 15.

8. Kerby-Fulton, "Langland and the Bibliographic Ego," 113–14.

9. Kane, *Evidence for Authorship*, 26–51.

10. Translated as "William made the book *who* is called Piers Plowman," the Latin wording equivocates whether Piers is a book or a person. For an earlier investigation, see E. St. John Brooks, "The *Piers Plowman* Manuscripts in Trinity College, Dublin," *The Library* 5th ser., 6 (1951): 141–53.

11. George H. Russell, "'As They Read It': Some Notes on Early Responses to the C-Version of *Piers Plowman*," *LSE* n.s. 20 (1989): 173–89 at 186–87.

12. Ralph Hanna, "Emendations to a 1993 'Vita de Ne'erdowel,'" *YLS* 14 (2000): 185–98 at 186, summarizes Lister Matheson's views favoring *Langland* as a pen name.

13. Kane, *Evidence for Authorship*, 29. Oscar Cargill, "The Langland Myth," *PMLA* 50 (1935): 36–56 at 41–42, allowed for a conspiracy since the poet took real risks by attacking the mendicants and championing the Good Parliament of 1376. Cargill, 46–56, did important research unearthing references to men named William Rokayle during the fourteenth century. Anne Middleton, *"Piers Plowman,"* in *A Manual of the Writings in Middle English, 1050–1500*, gen. ed. Albert E. Hartung, vol. 7 (New Haven: Connecticut Academy of Arts and Sciences, 1986), 2224–27 and 2429–31, reviews the history of the authorship controversy.

14. A. I. Doyle, "The Manuscripts," *Middle English Alliterative Poetry and Its Literary Background,* ed. Lawton, 88–100 and notes 142–47, at 90. The question of the sequence of canonic versions has been reopened by Mann, "The Power of the Alphabet: A Reassessment of the Relation between the A and the B Versions of *Piers Plowman,"* and Bowers, *"Piers Plowman'*s William Langland: Editing the Text, Writing the Author's Life," 82–87. Hanna, *Pursuing History,* 195–201, suggests another scenario in which A copies were exported by members of Langland's London coterie to their provincial houses and hence to local religious houses under the patronage of these coterie members.

15. Steven Justice, "Introduction: Authorial Work and Literary Ideology," *Written Work,* ed. Justice and Kerby-Fulton, 1–12 at 8, concerning B.15.504–69. For self-censoring revision in the C-text, see Andrew Galloway, "The Rhetoric of Riddling in Late-Medieval England: The 'Oxford' Riddles, the *Secretum Philosophorum,* and the Riddles in *Piers Plowman,"* *Speculum* 70 (1995): 68–105.

16. Michael Wilks, *"Thesaurus Ecclesiae* (Presidential Address)," *The Church and Wealth,* ed. W. J. Sheils and Diana Wood (Oxford: Blackwell, 1987), xv–xlv.

17. George Kane, "The Text," *Companion to "Piers Plowman,"* 175–200 at 190. Charlotte Brewer, *Editing "Piers Plowman": The Evolution of the Text* (Cambridge: Cambridge University Press, 1996), "The Athlone B-Text," 380–408, places this project in context of the full history of *Piers* editing; this study has informed the discussions that follow more steadily than the footnotes have been able to acknowledge.

18. G. H. Russell, "The Evolution of a Poem: Some Reflections on the Textual Tradition of *Piers Plowman,"* *Arts* 2 (1962): 33–46 at 39–40.

19. Hanna, *Pursuing History,* 240. By contrast, the Fairfax and Huntington Stafford manuscripts of *Confessio Amantis* were copied from exemplars prepared most

likely under John Gower's direct supervision as models for the standard format of early fifteenth-century copies; see Pearsall, "Manuscripts and Illustrations," *Companion to Gower,* ed. Echard, 80.

20. Russell, "As They Read It," 175–76; see also Wendy Scase, "Two *Piers Plowman* C-Text Interpolations: Evidence for a Second Textual Tradition," *N&Q* n.s. 34 (1987): 456–63, and Kerby-Fulton, "Langland and the Bibliographic Ego," 100–102.

21. Kerby-Fulton and Justice, "Langlandian Reading Circles," 72–73, suggest that both But and Langland were pen names: "a 'butt' is, like a 'longland,' a feature of a ploughman's lexis: a 'longland' is a long strip of ploughland, and a 'butt,' by contrast, is a short strip at the end of a row." Rawlinson Poet. 38 (fol. 101a) ends with what appears to be the ownership signature of "William Butte." On this testimony, see Lawrence Warner, "John But and Other Works That Will Wrought (*Piers Plowman* A XII 101–02)," *N&Q* n.s. 52 (2005): 13–18.

22. Skeat, ed., *Piers the Plowman,* 2:xxvii–xxxii at xxxi. Walter W. Skeat emerges the real hero of Brewer, *Editing "Piers Plowman,"* 91–178.

23. Bowers, *Crisis of Will in "Piers Plowman,"* esp. 41–60.

24. Middleton, "William Langland's 'Kynde Name,'" esp. 42–52.

25. Brewer, *Editing "Piers Plowman,"* 32–33, notes Tyrwhitt's contribution to Langland scholarship, including the change of first names from Robert to William, in his edition of Chaucer's *Canterbury Tales.*

26. Andrew Cole's two studies "William Langland and the Invention of Lollardy," *Lollards and Their Influence,* ed. Somerset, Havens, and Pitard, 37–58, and "William Langland's Lollardy," *YLS* 17 (2003): 25–54, bring much-needed clarity to the original meaning and emerging redefinition of *lollare* during the poet's career.

27. John M. Bowers, "Piers Plowman and the Police: Notes toward a History of the Wycliffite Langland," *YLS* 6 (1992): 1–50 at 2–10.

28. McKisack, *The Fourteenth Century,* 514.

29. The necessity for secrecy is central to the concerns of the Langlandian *Richard the Redeless* around 1400: "For yit it is secrette and so it shall lenger / Tyll wyser wittis han waytid it ouere / That it be lore laweffull and lusty to here" (1:61–63); Helen Barr, ed., *The Piers Plowman Tradition* (London: J. M. Dent, 1993), 103.

30. Simpson, "The Constraints of Satire in *Piers Plowman* and *Mum and the Sothsegger.*"

31. *Knighton's Chronicle,* 520–23. See also Richard H. Helmholz, ed., *Select Cases on Defamation to 1600* (London: Selden Society, 1985).

32. *Mum and the Sothsegger* (lines 165–70), ed. Barr, *The Piers Plowman Tradition,* 143.

33. Middleton, "Acts of Vagrancy: The C Version 'Autobiography' and the Statute of 1388," *Written Work,* ed. Justice and Kerby-Fulton, 208–317, assesses Langland's responses to the Cambridge Parliament. Wendy Scase, "'First to Reckon Richard': John But's *Piers Plowman,*" *YLS* 11 (1997): 49–66, points to A.12.113 as an instance of royal rhetoric that Richard II assumed only after 1388. See also Edwin D. Craun, *Lies, Slander, and Obscenity in Medieval English Literature* (Cambridge: Cambridge

University Press, 1997), "Reforming Deviant Social Practices: *Turpiloquium/Scurrilitas* in the B Version of *Piers Plowman,*" 157–86.

34. Michaela Paasche Grudin, *Chaucer and the Politics of Discourse* (Columbia: University of South Carolina Press, 1996), "Speech and the Commonwealth," 1–26 at 23–24.

35. Jones et al., *Who Murdered Chaucer?* 144: "He actually made legal history as the first victim of treason by the spoken word."

36. M. L. Samuels, "Langland's Dialect," *MÆ* 54 (1985): 232–47 at 240, and "Dialect and Grammar," *A Companion to "Piers Plowman,"* ed. Alford, 201–21. But see Horobin, "The Dialect and Circulation of the C Version of *Piers Plowman.*"

37. *Piers Plowman: The C Version,* ed. George Russell and George Kane (London: Athlone Press; Berkeley: University of California Press, 1997), 5–6 and 102.

38. Pearsall, "Langland's London," 198–99.

39. Middleton, "William Langland's 'Kynde Name,'" 20, and Hanna, "Emendations to a 1993 'Vita de Ne'erdowel,'" 186–87, 190.

40. Christopher Allmand, *Henry V* (Berkeley: University of California Press, 1992), "Lollardy and Sedition," 280–305 at 288; see also Thomson, *Later Lollards,* "Bristol and the West Country," 20–52. The first layman burned as a heretic in 1410 was John Badby, a Worcestershire artisan; Peter McNiven, *Heresy and Politics in the Reign of Henry IV: The Burning of John Badby* (Woodbridge: Boydell, 1987), 199–219.

41. Jeremy J. Smith's analysis of language in *Lollard Sermons,* ed. Gloria Cigman, EETS o.s. 294, 1989, notes that both scribes of BL Add. 41321 display distinctive Worcestershire dialect features (xl–xli). Alan J. Fletcher, "The Essential (Ephemeral) William Langland: Textual Revision as Ethical Process in *Piers Plowman,*" *YLS* 15 (2001): 61–84 at 82–84, connects these Lollard sermons with an expanded Langland tradition.

42. Hudson, *Premature Reformation,* 3. Cole, "William Langland and the Invention of Lollardy," 43–45, notes that the prevailing first usage by Henry Crumpe in 1382 was a "back-formation" created by the Carmelite compiler of *Fasciculi Zizaniorum.* The Apocalypse commentary *Opus Arduum* around 1389 marked the first recorded occasion when a Wycliffite writer acknowledged the heretical label of "Lolardi"; see Anne Hudson, "A Neglected Wycliffite Text" (1978), *Lollards and Their Books* (London: Hambledon Press, 1985), 43–66.

43. Bowers, "Dating *Piers Plowman*: Testing the Testimony of Usk's *Testament,*" removes the date of Usk's death in 1388 as the *terminus ante quem* for Langland's career. Middleton, "Acts of Vagrancy: The C Version 'Autobiography' and the Statute of 1388," assesses Langland's responses following the Cambridge Parliament of 1388.

44. Wendy Scase, *"Piers Plowman" and the New Anticlericalism* (Cambridge: Cambridge University Press, 1989), "From the Gyrovague to the Loller," 125–37. Joseph S. Wittig, "'Culture Wars' and the Persona in *Piers Plowman,*" *YLS* 15 (2001): 167–95 at 195, provides a census of the word *lollare*'s occurrences, only once in B but thirteen times in C.

45. For the most rigorous assessment of the Ilchester Prologue, see Hanna, *Pursuing History,* "On the Versions of *Piers Plowman,*" 204–14; his view that Ilchester

and HM 114 preserve an earlier archetype suggests that the controversial *lollare* material predates the manuscript's production c. 1400. Ilchester (fol. 3b) preserves Langland's insistence that the term *loller* is not newfangled but instead a word with a venerable native tradition: "kyndely by holy crist ben suche cleped lollers / by heryng of oure eldres of olde mennes techin[ge]" (cf. C.9.214–15).

46. Cole, "Langland and the Invention of Lollardy," 57.

47. Middleton, "Audience and Public," 105–6, on the conjunction of these two works.

48. For some recent assessments of "Mandeville" as traveler and author, see M. C. Seymour, *Sir John Mandeville* (Aldershot: Variorum Authors of the Middle Ages, vol. 1, no. 1, 1994), 1–40; Iain Macleod Higgins, *Writing East: The "Travels" of Sir John Mandeville* (Philadelphia: University of Pennsylvania Press, 1997); and Rosemary Tzanaki, *Mandeville's Medieval Audiences: A Study on the Reception of the "Book" of Sir John Mandeville (1371–1550)* (Aldershot, England, and Burlington, VT: Ashgate Publishing, 2003).

49. Lawrence Warner, "Langland and the Problem of *William of Palerne*," *Viator* 37 (2006): 397–415, renews the suggestion that the "William" commissioned to translate this poem for Humphrey de Bohun was in fact William Langland. If so, Langland's career began in the near-anonymous obscurity in which it remained.

50. Allan H. Bright, *New Light on "Piers Plowman"* (London: Oxford University Press, 1928), 75.

51. Skeat, ed., *Piers the Plowman,* 2:xxix.

52. Kane, *Evidence for Authorship,* 29 and 35–37.

53. John M. Bowers, "Langland's *Piers Plowman* in HM 143: Copy, Commentary, Censorship," *YLS* 19 (2005): 137–68.

54. Anne Ferry, "*Anonymity*: The Literary History of a Word," *NLH* 33 (2002): 193–214, stands as the first article in a number of *New Literary History* (33/2) devoted to the issue of anonymous literature.

55. Bale, *Index Britanniae Scriptorum,* ed. Poole and Bateson, 383.

56. Crowley, ed., *The Vision of Pierce Plowman* (1550); see also John N. King, *English Reformation Literature: The Tudor Origins of the Protestant Tradition* (Princeton: Princeton University Press, 1982), 326; J. W. Martin, "The Publishing Career of Robert Crowley," *Publishing History* 14 (1983): 85–98; and Johnson, *Reading "Piers Plowman" and "The Pilgrim's Progress,"* 99–127.

57. Skeat, ed., *Piers the Plowman,* 2:xxxii.

58. E. A. Quain, "The Medieval *Accessus ad Auctores*," *Traditio* 3 (1945): 228–42; A. J. Minnis, *Medieval Theory of Authorship,* 2nd ed. (Philadelphia: University of Pennsylvania Press, 1988), 9–39; and A. J. Minnis and A. B. Scott, with David Wallace, ed., *Medieval Literary Theory and Criticism c. 1100–c. 1375,* rev. ed. (Oxford: Clarendon, 1991), 12–36.

59. Kane, *Evidence for Authorship,* 3.

60. Lee Patterson, "The Logic of Textual Criticism and the Way of Genius: The Kane-Donaldson *Piers Plowman* in Historical Perspective" (1985), *Negotiating the Past: The Historical Understanding of Medieval Literature* (Madison: University of Wisconsin Press, 1987), 77–113 at 101.

61. Hanna, *William Langland,* 17–24, has made the most recent effort at sorting out the documentary testimony while also formulating what he terms "Langland's Represented Life," that is, the biography so strongly implied by the three versions of the poem. Prior efforts include Howard Meroney, "The Life and Death of Longe Will," *ELH* 17 (1950): 1–35. J. A. Burrow, *Langland's Fictions* (Oxford: Clarendon, 1993), 82–108, reminds us how hard it is to resist the leap in logical inference when the first-person narrator insists upon describing himself as the writer.

62. Brewer, *Editing "Piers Plowman,"* "Crowley," 7–19, provides a comprehensive assessment of Langland's first print editor.

63. *Piers Plowman: The B Version,* ed. George Kane and E. Talbot Donaldson (London: Athlone, Press, 1975), 6–7.

64. William R. Crawford, "Robert Crowley's Editions of *Piers Plowman*: A Bibliographical and Textual Study" (Ph.D. diss., Yale University, 1957), and J. R. Thorne and Marie-Claire Uhart, "Robert Crowley's *Piers Plowman,*" *MÆ* 55 (1986): 248–54. The Sion College manuscript is now in the private collection of Toshiyuki Takamiya; see C. David Benson and Lynne S. Blanchfield, *The Manuscripts of "Piers Plowman": The B-Version* (Cambridge: D. S. Brewer, 1997), 112–15.

65. Simpson, *Reform,* 22, identifies this conservative tendency in the recovery projects of Leland and Bale.

66. John N. King, "Freedom of the Press, Protestant Propaganda, and Protector Somerset," *HLQ* 40 (1976): 1–9; Christopher Haigh, *English Reformations: Religion, Politics, and Society under the Tudors* (Oxford: Clarendon, 1993), 168–83; and Jennifer Loach, *Edward VI,* ed. George Bernard and Penry Williams (New Haven and London: Yale University Press, 1999), 39–57.

67. For two recent examples, see Steve Hindle, *The State and Social Change in Early Modern England c. 1550–1640* (New York: St. Martin's, 2000), and Michael J. Braddick, *State Formation in Early Modern England c. 1550–1700* (Cambridge: Cambridge University Press, 2000).

68. Duffy, *Stripping of the Altars,* 448–77. For the Protestant editor's polemical writings, most of them also published in 1550, see *The Select Works of Robert Crowley,* ed. J. M. Cowper, EETS e.s. 15, 1872.

69. Cf. Roland Barthes, "The Death of the Author," *Image—Music—Text,* trans. Stephen Heath (New York: Noonday Press, 1977), 142–48 at 142–43.

70. *Westminster Chronicle, 1381–1394,* ed. and trans. L. C. Hector and Barbara F. Harvey (Oxford: Clarendon, 1982), 436–39. See also John M. Theilmann, "Political Canonization and Political Symbolism in Medieval England," *Journal of British Studies* 29 (1990): 241–66 at 253–64, and Chris Given-Wilson, "Richard II, Edward II, and the Lancastrian Inheritance," *EHR* 109 (1994): 553–71. A generation later, *The Book of Margery Kempe* was produced in a failed attempt to secure sainthood for the Lynn housewife; see Gail McMurray Gibson, *The Theater of Devotion: East Anglian Drama and Society in the Late Middle Ages* (Chicago: University of Chicago Press, 1989), "St. Margery: *The Book of Margery Kempe,*" 47–65.

71. See King, *English Reformation Literature,* 330–31. The lines praising the monastic life are found only in two early B manuscripts representing a separate line of

transmission—Oxford Corpus Christi College 201 and BL Lansdowne 398/Bodleian Rawlinson poet. 38—so it is uncertain whether this passage was known to Crowley; see Thorne and Uhart, "Robert Crowley's *Piers Plowman,*" 252.

72. See Brewer, *Editing "Piers Plowman,"* "Whitaker and Price," 37–49.

73. Robert Langland, *Visio Willi de Petro Plouhman,* ed. Whitaker, v–vi.

74. Whitaker, ed., iv. The editor intensified this obscurity by printing the text in blackletter font with medieval orthography; see Sarah A. Kelen, *"Piers Plouhman* and the 'Formidable Array of Blackletter' in the Early Nineteenth Century," *Illuminating Letters: Typography and Literary Interpretation,* ed. Paul C. Gutjahr and Megan L. Benton (Amherst: University of Massachusetts Press, 2001), 47–67.

75. For a similar view, see David A. Lawton, "The Idea of Alliterative Poetry: Alliterative Meter and *Piers Plowman,*" *Suche Werkis to Werche: Essays on "Piers Plowman" in Honor of David C. Fowler,* ed. Míceál F. Vaughan (East Lansing: Colleagues Press, 1993), 147–68 at 166–68.

76. Annabel M. Patterson, *Censorship and Interpretation: The Conditions of Writing and Reading in Early Modern England* (Madison: University of Wisconsin Press, 1984), 14–15, cites Quintillian's *Institutio Oratoria* (IX.ii.67).

77. Whitaker, ed., iv.

78. Ibid., v.

79. Ibid., xxxix–xl.

80. Brewer, *Editing "Piers Plowman,"* "Wright," 50–62. On his contribution to Chaucer scholarship, see Thomas W. Ross, "Thomas Wright (1810–1877)," *Editing Chaucer,* ed. Ruggiers, 145–56.

81. Thomas Wright, ed., *Three Chapters of Letters Relating to the Suppression of the Monasteries* (Camden Society o.s. 26, 1843), and *Political Poems and Songs Relating to English History Composed during the Period from the Accession of Edward III to that of Richard III,* 2 vols. (London: Rolls Series, 1859–61).

82. Thomas Wright, ed., *The Vision and Creed of Piers Ploughman,* 2 vols., 2nd ed. (London: Reeves and Turner, 1887), 1:v.

83. Wright, ed., *Piers Ploughman,* 1:viii.

84. Benson and Blanchfield, *Manuscripts of "Piers Plowman": The B-Version,* 56–59. On Thomas Wright's "best-text" approach to *Piers,* see Eric Dahl, *"Diuerse Copies Haue It Diuerselye:* An Unorthodox Survey of *Piers Plowman* Textual Scholarship from Crowley to Skeat," *Suche Werkis to Werche,* ed. Vaughan, 53–80 at 68–69.

85. Wright, ed., *Piers Ploughman,* 1:xxiii.

86. Ibid., 1:xxii–xxiii.

87. Bright, *New Light on "Piers Plowman,"* 41–42 , proposed that the poet was the Great Malvern monk Willelmus de Colewell, ordained in 1348 by John de Trillek, bishop of Hereford. Morton W. Bloomfield, "Was William Langland a Benedictine Monk?" *MLQ* 4 (1943): 57–61, extended this speculation. Elizabeth M. Orsten, "'Heaven on Earth': Langland's Vision of Life within the Cloister," *American Benedictine Review* 21 (1970): 526–34, finds no internal textual evidence to support this view, although Kathryn Kerby-Fulton, *"Piers Plowman," Cambridge History of Medieval*

English Literature, ed. Wallace, 513–38 at 530–33, discusses the pervasive influence of monastic literature as well as early monastic ownership of *Piers* manuscripts.

88. Wright, ed., *Piers Ploughman,* 1:ix note.

89. Skeat, ed., *Piers the Plowman,* 2:xxxii–xxxviii.

90. Ibid., 2:xxxviii.

91. Ibid., 2:xxii–xxiii.

92. Quoted by Brewer, *Editing "Piers Plowman,"* 234.

93. Kerby-Fulton and Justice, "Langlandian Reading Circles," 61 n., cite Skeat's letter in support of their own speculation about the poet's professional coterie; see also Kerby-Fulton, "Langland and the Bibliographic Ego," 84, on further speculation that Langland worked as a legal scribe.

94. Walter W. Skeat, ed., *The Vision of Piers Plowman, II: Text B,* EETS o.s. 38, 1869, ix. See also Marie-Claire Uhart, "The Early Reception of *Piers Plowman*" (Ph.D. diss., University of Leicester, 1986), 306–7.

95. Skeat, ed., *Piers the Plowman,* 2:xxxvi.

96. John M. Manly, "The Lost Leaf of *Piers the Plowman,*" *MP* 3 (1906): 359–66. On the ramifications of their scholarly feud, see Brewer, *Editing "Piers Plowman,"* "Manly versus Chambers and Grattan," 181–208.

97. John M. Manly, *"Piers Plowman and Its Sequence," The Cambridge History of English Literature,* vol. 2: *The End of the Middle Ages* (Cambridge: Cambridge University Press, 1908), 1–42 at 28 and 31.

98. Brewer, *Editing "Piers Plowman,"* "Chamber versus Knott," 237–55, and "Knott and Fowler, Donaldson, Mitchell, and Russell," 329–40.

99. Thomas A. Knott, "An Essay toward the Critical Text of the A-Version of *Piers the Plowman,*" *MP* 12 (1915): 389–421 at 410–15.

100. *Piers the Plowman: A Critical Edition of the A-Version,* ed. Thomas A. Knott and David C. Fowler (Baltimore: Johns Hopkins University Press, 1952), 8–15.

101. Brewer, *Editing "Piers Plowman,"* 219–309. As instances of this debate, see R. W. Chambers, "The Authorship of *Piers Plowman,*" *MLR* 5 (1910): 1–32; Mabel Day, "The Revisions of *Piers Plowman,*" *MLR* 23 (1928): 1–27; and R. W. Chambers and J. H. G. Grattan, "The Text of *Piers Plowman,*" *MLR* 26 (1931): 1–51.

102. Patterson, "The Logic of Textual Criticism and the Way of Genius: The Kane-Donaldson *Piers Plowman* in Historical Perspective," *Negotiating the Past,* 77–113.

103. Tim William Machan, "Late Middle English Texts and the Higher and Lower Criticisms," *Medieval Literature,* ed. Machan, 3–15, and Derek Pearsall, "Theory and Practice in Middle English Editing," *Text* 7 (1994): 107–26 at 118–24, summarize important reactions to the Kane-Donaldson *B Version.*

104. See Patterson, "The Logic of Textual Criticism and the Way of Genius"; Tim William Machan, "Middle English Text Production and Modern Textual Criticism," *Crux and Controversy in Middle English Textual Criticism,* ed. A. J. Minnis and Charlotte Brewer (Woodbridge and Rochester: Boydell & Brewer, 1992), 1–18; and Brewer, *Editing "Piers Plowman,"* "The Athlone Press Edition," 343–408, for assessments of this monumental editorial project.

105. Foucault, "What Is an Author?" 119.

106. Katherine O'Brien O'Keeffe, "Texts and Works: Some Historical Questions on the Editing of Old English Verse," *New Historical Literary Study,* ed. Jeffrey N. Cox and Larry J. Reynolds (Princeton: Princeton University Press, 1993), 54–68 at 63.

107. E. Talbot Donaldson, *The C-Text and Its Poet* (New Haven: Yale Studies in English, no. 113, 1949).

108. Gallagher and Greenblatt, *Practicing New Historicism,* 11–12.

109. Kane, *Evidence for Authorship,* 4.

110. George Kane, *Middle English Literature: A Critical Study of the Romance, the Religious Lyrics, "Piers Plowman"* (London: Methuen, 1951), 250–51.

111. Kane, "The Autobiographical Fallacy in Chaucer and Langland Studies" (1965), *Chaucer and Langland,* 1–14 at 1.

112. Kane, "Langland and Chaucer II" (1980), *Chaucer and Langland,* 147.

113. Kane, *Chaucer and Langland,* 159.

114. Kane and Donaldson, eds., *The B Version,* 84.

115. Ibid., 13 n. 9. See Horobin and Mooney, "A *Piers Plowman* Manuscript by the Hengwrt/Ellesmere Scribe," and Mooney, "Chaucer's Scribe."

116. Kane and Donaldson, eds., *The B Version,* 215 n. 181 and 214.

117. Ibid., 215 n. 184, 220, and 215 n. 181. On the varieties of the metropolitan vernacular, see Jeremy J. Smith, "John Gower and London English," *Companion to Gower,* ed. Echard, 61–72.

118. Brewer, *Editing "Piers Plowman,"* "The Athlone Aftermath: Schmidt, Pearsall, Rigg-Brewer, et al.," 409–33.

119. Raymond Williams, *Marxism and Literature* (Oxford: Oxford University Press, 1977), "Authors," 192–98 at 196. Since Jerome McGann was the most influential proponent for "social textual criticism" derived in large measure from Williams, it is not surprising that Pearsall's "Editing Medieval Texts: Some Developments and Some Problems," reasserting his views on the social embeddedness of *Piers,* appeared in McGann's collection *Textual Criticism and Literary Interpretation* (Chicago: University of Chicago Press, 1985), 92–106.

120. Pearsall, ed., *Piers Plowman: An Edition of the C-text,* 16, with comments on self-censorship, 39–40. See also Derek Pearsall, "Authorial Revision in Some Late-Medieval English Texts," *Crux and Controversy,* ed. Minnis and Brewer, 39–48.

121. Schmidt, ed., *The Vision of Piers Plowman: A Critical Edition of the B-Text,* xiii.

122. Hanna, *William Langland,* 2–6.

123. See Lister M. Matheson's review of Hanna's *William Langland, YLS* 8 (1994): 192–94 at 193.

124. Michael Calabrese, *"[Piers] the [Plowman]:* The Corrections, Interventions, and Erasures of Huntington MS Hm 143 (X)," *YLS* 19 (2005): 169–99, exposes a variety of alterations that bring the text closer to reformist views.

125. Kane and Donaldson, ed., *The B Version,* 122 n. 47.

126. Ralph Hanna III, "Sir Thomas Berkeley and His Patronage," *Speculum* 64 (1989): 878–916; "Producing Manuscripts and Editions," *Crux and Controversy,* ed.

Minnis and Brewer, 109–30; and in modified form *Pursuing History,* "On the Versions of *Piers Plowman,*" 225–29. See also Ronald Waldron, "John Trevisa and the Use of English," *PBA* 74 (1988): 171–202, and Somerset, *Clerical Discourse and Lay Audience,* "John Trevisa, Sir Thomas Berkeley, and Their Project of 'Englysch Translacion,'" 62–100.

127. Hoyt N. Duggan, "The Electronic *Piers Plowman* B: A New Diplomatic-Critical Edition," *Æstel* 1 (1993): 55–75, offers early suggestions of the scope of his own hypertext project. For the first fruits, see *The "Piers Plowman" Electronic Archive: Corpus Christi College, Oxford MS 201,* ed. Robert Adams with M. Gail Duggan and Catherine A. Farley (Ann Arbor: University of Michigan Press, 2000). For the future of CD-ROM and Internet publications, see Martha W. Driver, "Medieval Manuscripts and Electronic Media: Observations on Future Possibilities," *New Directions in Later Medieval Manuscript Studies,* ed. Pearsall, 53–64.

128. Foucault, "What Is an Author?" 113.

129. Hanna, *Pursuing History,* 242, concludes with a somewhat different account: "I imagine a poet who wrote only one full text (what is customarily called B, my B stage 2), who allowed an earlier fragment of the poem to escape to the public (A), and who may have returned to the poem [in C] only to counter what he took to be its misuse (and perhaps its misuse in limited areas) by others."

130. R. W. Chambers, *Man's Unconquerable Mind* (London: Jonathan Cape, 1939), 15. For the chapters on *Piers Plowman,* see 88–131 and 132–71.

131. Ibid., 168–69 and 164.

132. Ibid., 68–69. For the heroic strain in the Hobbit's saga, see T. A. Shippey, *J. R. R. Tolkien: Author of the Century* (Boston: Houghton Mifflin, 2001), esp. 147–55.

133. Olive Sayce, "Chaucer's 'Retractions': The Conclusion of the *Canterbury Tales* and Its Place in Literary Tradition," *MÆ* 40 (1971): 230–48.

134. Hines, Cohen, and Roffey, "*Iohannes Gower, Armiger, Poeta*: Records and Memorials of His Life and Death," *Companion to Gower,* ed. Echard, 25. Ralph Strode, who moved from Merton College to become a common serjeant for the city of London in 1373, corresponded with his former Oxford colleague Wyclif and thus serves as a direct personal and intellectual link between Wyclif and Chaucer; see J. A. W. Bennett, *Chaucer at Oxford and Cambridge* (Oxford: Clarendon, 1974), "Men of Merton," 58–85. Maureen Jurkowski, "Lawyers and Lollardy in the Early Fifteenth Century," *Lollardy and the Gentry,* ed. Aston and Richmond, 155–82 at 155–57, provides useful background on this professional group in late medieval England.

135. Kerby-Fulton and Justice, "Langlandian Reading Circles." Justice, *Writing and Rebellion,* 218, believes that these lines contain "winks and nudges and nods" bespeaking the jocular intimacy of a coterie.

136. Brewer, ed., *Chaucer: The Critical Heritage,* 1:40–41.

137. John Gower, *Mirour de l'Omme,* trans. William Burton Wilson, rev. Nancy Wilson Van Baak (East Lansing: Colleagues Press, 1992), 76 (lines 5245–56).

138. Usk, *The Testament of Love,* ed. Shoaf, 266–67. Caroline M. Barron, "New Light on Thomas Usk," *Chaucer Newsletter* 26/2 (Fall 2004): 1, finds Usk working as a scribe for the Grocers, just as Pinkhurst worked for the Mercers, with the suggestion

that both men worked as freelance copyists. Elsewhere I have suggested that Usk knew *Troilus* so thoroughly because he had copied it as a scribe; see "Testing the Testimony of Usk's *Testament*," 91–92.

139. *The Works of Sir John Clanvowe*, ed. V. J. Scattergood (Cambridge: D. S. Brewer, 1975), 35, quotes lines from the Knight's Tale (*CT*, I, 1785–1825) that represent an important original supplement to Boccaccio's *Teseida*. On Clanvowe as a particular kind of Squire-like reader, see Lerer, *Chaucer and His Readers*, 57–84.

140. Gower, *The English Works*, 2:466 (lines 2941*–42*).

141. John H. Fisher, *John Gower: Moral Philosopher and Friend of Chaucer* (London: Methuen, 1965), 27–32 and 117–21, reviews the issues of the Lancastrian revision. See also Peter Nicholson, "Gower's Revisions in the *Confessio Amantis*," ChauR 19 (1984): 123–43, and Nicholson, "The Dedications of Gower's *Confessio Amantis*," Mediaevalia 10 (1984): 159–80. Pearsall, "Manuscripts and Illustrations," *Companion to Gower*, ed. Echard, 93, suggests physical erasure of praise for Richard II and Chaucer in the Fairfax manuscript.

142. Carolyn Dinshaw, "Rivalry, Rape and Manhood: Gower and Chaucer," *Chaucer and Gower: Difference, Mutuality, Exchange*, ed. Robert F. Yeager (Victoria, BC: University of Victoria English Literary Studies, no. 51, 1991), 130–52, revisits the "quarrel" between the two poets.

143. *Chaucer Life-Records*, 54 and 60.

144. David Wallace, "Italy," *Companion to Chaucer*, ed. Brown, 218–34.

145. Howard, *Chaucer*, 121. Pearsall, *Life of Geoffrey Chaucer*, 53–54, is more skeptical but admits "it is pleasing to picture him there, in the company of Froissart and the venerable Petrarch."

146. David Wallace, *Chaucerian Polity: Absolutist Lineages and Associational Forms in England and Italy* (Stanford: Stanford University Press, 1997), "'Whan She Translated Was': Humanism, Tyranny, and the Petrarchan Academy," 261–98 at 262.

147. Philippe de Mézières, *Letter to King Richard II: A Plea Made in 1395 for Peace between England and France*, ed. and trans. G. W. Coopland (Liverpool: Liverpool University Press, 1975), 42.

148. Claire Sponsler, "The Captivity of Henry Chrystede: Froissart's *Chroniques*, Ireland, and Fourteenth-Century Nationalism," *Imagining a Medieval English Nation*, ed. Lavezzo, 304–39, reflects upon Froissart's own sense of a "mongrel identity," moving from nation to nation while belonging to none of them.

149. Dobson, ed., *Peasants' Revolt of 1381*, 160 and 364.

150. *Knighton's Chronicle*, 214–15.

151. *The Westminster Chronicle*, 4–5.

152. Howard, *Chaucer*, 88.

153. Duffy, *Stripping of the Altars*, 338–76.

154. Koonce, *Chaucer and the Tradition of Fame*, "Dante in Inglissh," 73–88.

155. Kane, *Chaucer and Langland*, 24–25, has no doubt that Chaucer was a reader of *Piers Plowman*.

156. Grady's "Chaucer Reading Langland" makes even better sense now that *The House of Fame* can be dated to the later 1380s, when its author had had more time to assimilate the full impact of the B-text.

157. Barr, "The Regal Image of Richard II and the *Prologue to the Legend of Good Women*," *Socioliterary Practice in Late Medieval England,* 80–105, discusses the poet's confrontation with Richard II over charges of heresy. See also Helen Phillips, "Register, Politics, and the *Legend of Good Women*," *ChauR* 37 (2002): 101–28, on the revision of the G Prologue to reflect the poet's heightened anxiety over "dangerous talk."

158. H. G. Richardson, "Heresy and the Lay Power under Richard II," *EHR* 51 (1936): 1–28 at 11.

159. Kellie Robertson, "Laboring in the God of Love's Garden: Chaucer's Prologue to *The Legend of Good Women*," *SAC* 24 (2002): 115–47, reads this inquisition into proper forms of labor in light of the 1388 Statute of Labourers, much as Middleton has read Langland's C.5 self-indictment in her "Acts of Vagrancy."

160. Myers, ed., *English Historical Documents,* 177–78, translates Walsingham's *Historia Anglicana,* 2:230, for the year 1399.

161. *Riverside Chaucer,* 328.

162. J. A. F. Thomson, "Knightly Piety and the Margins of Lollardy," *Lollardy and the Gentry,* ed. Aston and Richmond, 95–111. For Alice Chaucer's double-decker tomb, see Pearsall, *Life of Geoffrey Chaucer,* 282–83.

163. Jones et al., *Who Murdered Chaucer?* 319–29, suggests the heretic's recantation as a new art form to which Chaucer's Retraction gestures.

164. Froissart, *Chronicles,* 469. James R. Hulbert, *Chaucer's Official Life* (1912; rpt. New York: Phaeton Press, 1970), long ago showed that Chaucer as a royal esquire was rewarded no more generously than his colleagues who were not poets.

165. Jones et al., *Who Murdered Chaucer?* 296–314, make the intriguing suggestion that the poet might have absconded to the Low Countries, his wife Philippa's homeland, to ride out the storm of 1399–1400 as perhaps he had done during the prior crisis of 1388–89.

166. Edmund Burke, *Reflections on the Revolution in France,* ed. Conor Cruise O'Brien (New York: Penguin, 1982), 194–95.

167. Larry D. Benson, "The Occasion of *The Parliament of Fowls*," *The Wisdom of Poetry,* ed. Benson and Wenzel, 123–44.

168. For the poet-patron model provided by Machaut and Froissart, see Sylvia Huot, *From Song to Book* (Ithaca and London: Cornell University Press, 1987), 211–327.

169. V. J. Scattergood, "The Shorter Poems," *Oxford Guides to Chaucer: The Shorter Poems,* ed. A. J. Minnis with V. J. Scattergood and J. J. Smith (Oxford: Clarendon, 1995), 455–512 at 510–12.

170. Brewer, ed., *Chaucer: The Critical Heritage,* 1:40–41. See also Michael Hanly, "Courtiers and Poets: An International Network of Literary Exchange," *Viator* 28 (1997): 305–32.

171. Paul Strohm, *Social Chaucer* (Cambridge, MA: Harvard University Press, 1989), 28–29, 39–40, 42–46. For a concise survey of these named contacts, see Pearsall, *Life of Geoffrey Chaucer,* "The 'Chaucer Circle,'" 181–85.

172. George Lyman Kittredge, "Chaucer and Some of His Friends," *MP* 1 (1903): 1–18. Kittredge, "Lewis Chaucer or Lewis Clifford?" *MP* 14 (1917): 513–18,

suggested that the death of Clifford's son in 1391 prompted Chaucer to "drop his pen in the middle of a sentence when the *Astrolabe* was still far from completion" (130).

173. Edith Rickert, "Thou Vache," *MP* 11 (1913–14): 209–25; Alfred David, "The Truth about 'Vache,'" *ChauR* 11 (1977): 334–37; and Strohm, *Social Chaucer,* 39–46.

174. Anne Middleton, "Chaucer's 'New Men' and the Good of Poetry," *Literature and Society,* ed. Edward Said (Baltimore: Johns Hopkins University Press, 1980), 15–56.

175. Richard Maidstone, *Concordia: The Reconciliation of Richard II with London,* ed. David R. Carlson, trans. A. G. Rigg (Kalamazoo: Medieval Institute Publications, 2003), 56: "Iste velud Troylus vel ut Absolon ipse docorus" (line 112).

176. *Riverside Chaucer,* 650.

177. *Riverside Chaucer,* 649; see Scattergood, "The Shorter Poems," *Oxford Guides to Chaucer: The Shorter Poems,* ed. Minnis et al., 466–68.

178. *The Chaucer Variorum,* vol. 5: *The Minor Poems, Part 1,* ed. George B. Pace and Alfred David (Norman: University of Oklahoma Press, 1982), 140.

179. G. L. Kittredge, "Henry Scogan," *Harvard Studies and Notes* 1 (1892): 109–17; Strohm, *Social Chaucer,* 72–75; and Andrew James Johnston, *Clerks and Courtiers: Chaucer, Late Middle English Literature and the State Formation Process* (Heidelberg: C. Winter, 2001), 227–50.

180. Alfred David, "Chaucer's Good Counsel to Scogan," *ChauR* 3 (1968–69): 265–74; R. T. Lenaghan, "Chaucer's *Envoy to Scogan*: The Uses of Literary Conventions," *ChauR* 10 (1975–76): 46–61; Lenaghan, "Chaucer's Circle of Gentlemen and Clerks," *ChauR* 18 (1983): 155–60; and Robert Epstein, "Chaucer's Scogan and Scogan's Chaucer," *SP* 96 (1999): 1–21.

181. Walter W. Skeat, ed., *Chaucerian and Other Pieces, Being a Supplement to the Complete Works of Geoffrey Chaucer,* vol. 7 (London: Oxford University Press, 1897), 237–44 at 237 (lines 3–4).

182. "Here foloweth next a Moral Balade, to my lord the Prince, to my lord of Clarence, to my lord of Bedford, and to my lord of Gloucestre, by Henry Scogan; at a souper of feorthe merchande in the Vyntre in London, at the hous of Lowys Johan." Skeat, ed., *Chaucerian and Other Pieces,* xlii–xliii and 237, works out the issues of the guild supper as the poem's original occasion. Pearsall, *Life of Geoffrey Chaucer,* 21–22, credits Shirley's testimony for the sort of grand social occasion when Chaucer's poetry—and later Scogan's and Lydgate's—might have been presented.

183. *Hoccleve's Works: The Minor Poems,* ed. Frederick J. Furnivall and I. Gollancz, rev. Jerome Mitchell and A. I. Doyle, EETS e.s. 61 and 73, 1892 and 1925, rev. 1970, 64–66. See J. A. Burrow, *Thomas Hoccleve* (Aldershot and Brookfield: Variorum, Authors of the Middle Ages, no. 4, 1994), 28–29: "This poem, with its glimpse of a 'clubbable London clerk of literary leanings,' stands as a reminder of how little we know of the poet's social and private life."

184. Immediately after his mother's death in 1381, the poet had quitclaimed his father's house in St. Martin's parish to another London vintner, Henry Herbury; see

Chaucer Life-Records, 1. Alfred Allan Kern, *The Ancestry of Chaucer* (Baltimore: Lord Baltimore Press, 1906), 100, surveys John Chaucer's London holdings.

185. Roskell, *The Commons and Their Speakers,* 90, and Antony D. Carr, "Sir Lewis John—A Medieval London Welshman," *Bulletin of the Board of Celtic Studies* 22 (1968): 260–70.

186. Alfred David, "The Ownership and Use of the Ellesmere Manuscript," *Ellesmere Chaucer,* ed. Stevens and Woodward, 307–26. His second wife was the daughter of John Montagu, Earl of Salisbury, and Alice Chaucer's second husband was Thomas Montagu, Earl of Salisbury—so the family connections remained tight.

187. May Newman Hallmundsson, "Chaucer's Circle: Henry Scogan and His Friends," *M&H,* n.s. 10 (1981): 129–39 at 134, uncovers a connection between Thomas Chaucer and Scogan's son, Robert.

188. Paul Strohm, "Chaucer's Fifteenth-Century Audience and the Narrowing of the 'Chaucer Tradition,'" *SAC* 4 (1982): 3–32 at 11–12.

189. For a preview of these implications, see John M. Bowers, "The House of Chaucer & Son: The Business of Lancastrian Canon-Formation," *Medieval Perspectives* 6 (1991): 135–43.

190. Patterson, *Chaucer and the Subject of History,* 17, as part of a fuller contrast between Scogan's Chaucer and Dryden's Chaucer (16–22).

191. Miri Rubin, "Small Groups, Identity and Solidarity in the Late Middle Ages," *Enterprise and Individuals in Fifteenth-Century England,* ed. Jennifer Kermode (Wolfeboro Falls, NH: Sutton, 1991), 132–50.

192. Norman Davis, Douglas Gray, Patricia Ingham, and Anne Wallace-Hadrill, eds., *A Chaucer Glossary* (Oxford: Clarendon, 1979), 30.

193. George Unwin, *The Gilds and Companies of London,* 4th ed. (London: Frank Cass, 1963), 127–54; Sylvia L. Thrupp, *The Merchant Class of Medieval London* (Ann Arbor: University of Michigan Press, 1948), 66–80; Ruth Bird, *The Turbulent London of Richard II* (London: Longmans, Green and Co., 1949), 44–101; McKisack, *The Fourteenth Century,* 370–80; Antony Black, *Guilds and Civil Society in European Political Thought from the Twelfth Century to the Present* (Ithaca: Cornell University Press, 1984), 66–75; and Pamela Nightingale, "Capitalists, Crafts and Constitutional Change in Late Fourteenth-Century London," *P&P* 124 (1989): 3–35.

194. J. A. Tuck, "The Cambridge Parliament, 1388," *EHR* 84 (1969): 225–43. See also Caroline M. Barron, "The Parish Fraternities of Medieval London," *The Church in Pre-Reformation Society,* ed. Caroline M. Barron and Christopher Harper-Bill (Woodbridge: Boydell, 1985), 13–37.

195. R. W. Chambers and Marjorie Daunt, eds., *A Book of London English, 1384–1425* (Oxford: Clarendon, 1931), 44. On the importance of these new charters, see W. Carew Hazlitt, *The Livery Companies of the City of London* (1892; rpt. New York and London: Benjamin Blom, 1969), 170, 235, 252–53; T. F. Reddaway, *The Early History of the Goldsmiths' Company 1327–1509* (London: Edward Arnold, 1975), 70–71; and Caroline M. Barron, "The London Middle English Guild Certificates of 1388–89," *Nottingham Medieval Studies* 39 (1995): 108–18.

196. *Riverside Chaucer,* 656 (line 29).

197. Thomas Hoccleve, *Complaint and Dialogue,* ed. J. A. Burrow, EETS o.s. 313, 1999, 67–68 (lines 694–97).

198. John Lydgate, *The Minor Poems: Religious Poems and Secular Poems,* 2 vols., ed. Henry Noble MacCracken, EETS e.s. 107, 1911, and o.s. 192, 1934, 2:679 (lines 168–71). Once attributed to Lydgate, *The Chaunces of the Dyse* criticizes the dubious reading habits of dice throwers: "Ye han by rote the wifes lyfe of Bathe"; see Caroline F. E. Spurgeon, ed., *Five Hundred Years of Chaucerian Criticism and Allusion, 1357–1900,* 3 vols. (1925; rpt. New York: Russell & Russell, 1960), 1:44–45. James D. Johnson, "Identifying Chaucer Allusions, 1953–1980: An Annotated Bibliography," *ChauR* 19 (1984): 62–86, supplements Spurgeon's foundational study.

199. Brusendorff, *Chaucer Tradition,* 254–55.

200. Strohm, "Chaucer's Audience," 19. See also Johannes Petrus Maria Jansen, *The "Suffolk" Poems: An Edition of the Love Lyrics in Fairfax 16 Attributed to William de la Pole* (Groningen: Universiteitsdrukkerij, 1989), esp. 13–30 and 52–72; Julia Boffey, "Charles of Orleans Reading Chaucer's Dream Visions," *Mediaevalitas: Reading the Middle Ages,* ed. Piero Boitani and Anna Torti (Cambridge: D. S. Brewer, 1996), 43–62; A. E. B. Coldiron, *Canon, Period, and the Poetry of Charles of Orleans* (Ann Arbor: University of Michigan Press, 2000); and two chapters in Arn, ed., *Charles d'Orléans in England*: Mary-Jo Arn, "Two Manuscripts, One Mind: Charles d'Orléans and the Production of Manuscripts in Two Languages," 61–78, and A. E. B. Coldiron, "Translation, Canons, and Cultural Capital: Manuscripts and Reception of Charles d'Orléans's English Poetry," 183–214.

201. James I of Scotland, *The Kingis Quair,* ed. John Norton-Smith (Oxford: Clarendon Press, 1971), 1 (lines 13–16). For this aspect of Chaucer's contribution to vernacular culture, see Roger Ellis, "Translation," *Companion to Chaucer,* ed. Brown, 443–58.

202. John Walton, *Boethius: De Consolatione Philosophiae,* ed. Mark Science, EETS o.s. 170, 1927, 2 (stanza 5); twenty-four manuscripts survive. The early copy of *Boece* in Peniarth 393D, perhaps made by Pinkhurst with Chaucer's own corrections, suggests how an Osney canon might have gained his familiarity with this prose work before 1410. Frederick J. Furnivall, ed., *The Fifty Earliest English Wills,* EETS o.s. 78, 1882, 136, cites the 1420 will of John Brinchele with mention of an English version of Boethius in addition to "librum meum vocatum Talys of Caunterbury."

203. Fols. 100a–111b. See Dutschke, *Guide to Medieval and Renaissance Manuscripts in the Huntington Library,* 1:197–203, and Kate Harris, "Unnoticed Extracts from Chaucer and Hoccleve: Huntington MS HM 144, Trinity College, Oxford MS D 29 and *The Canterbury Tales,*" *SAC* 20 (1998): 167–99. The 1998 congress of the New Chaucer Society meeting in Paris included a distinguished panel reassessing this tale's importance; see "Colloquium on *The Monk's Tale,*" *SAC* 22 (2000): 381–440.

204. On the success of this substantial work, see Alexandra Gillespie, "Framing Lydgate's *Fall of Princes*: The Evidence of Book History," *Mediaevalia* 20 (2001): 153–78.

205. Jones et al., *Who Murdered Chaucer?* 260–66.

206. Ibid., 265.

207. M. C. Seymour, *A Catalogue of Chaucer Manuscripts,* vol. 2: *"The Canterbury Tales"* (Aldershot: Scolar Press, 1997), 31. Jones et al., *Who Murdered Chaucer?* 240–43 and 274–75, suggest that work on Hengwrt ceased with Chaucer's death, with some unbound leaves gnawed by rats, and then completed only with the rehabilitation of the poet's reputation under Prince Henry around 1410.

208. Geoffrey Chaucer, *The Canterbury Tales: A Facsimile and Transcription of the Hengwrt Manuscript,* ed. Paul G. Ruggiers, intro. Donald C. Baker, and A. I. Doyle and M. B. Parkes (Norman: University of Oklahoma Press, 1979), xliii–xliv.

209. Huntington EL 26.C.9 (fol. 153b). For various assessments of the Chaucer portraits, see M. H. Spielmann, *The Portraits of Geoffrey Chaucer* (London: Chaucer Society, ser. 2, no. 31, 1900); Brusendorff, *Chaucer Tradition,* 13–27; Michael Seymour, "Manuscript Portraits of Chaucer and Hoccleve," *Burlington Magazine* 124 (1982): 618–23; Jeanne Krochalis, "Hoccleve's Chaucer Portrait," *ChauR* 21 (1986): 234–45; David R. Carlson, "Thomas Hoccleve and the Chaucer Portrait," *HLQ* 54 (1991): 283–300; Leger Brosnahan, "The Pendant in the Chaucer Portraits," *ChauR* 26 (1992): 424–31; Pearsall, *The Life of Geoffrey Chaucer,* 285–305; A. S. G. Edwards, "The Chaucer Portraits in the Harley and Rosenbach Manuscripts," *English Manuscript Studies, 1100–1700,* vol. 4, ed. Peter Beal and Jeremy Griffiths (London: British Library, 1993), 268–71; and Alan T. Gaylord, "Portrait of a Poet," *Ellesmere Chaucer,* ed. Stevens and Woodward, 121–42.

210. Hoccleve, *Regiment of Princes,* ed. Blyth, 186 (lines 4992–5008).

211. Johnston, *Clerks and Courtiers,* "Chaucer's Visual Image and the Identity of the Poet," 251–61.

212. Anne Hudson, "A Lollard Sermon Cycle and Its Implications," *MÆ* 40 (1971): 142–56.

213. Justice, "Lollardy," *Cambridge History of Medieval English Literature,* ed. Wallace, 670–73 ("Lollardy at Court").

214. McFarlane, *Lancastrian Kings and Lollard Knights;* Jeremy I. Catto, "Sir William Beauchamp between Chivalry and Lollardy," *The Ideals and Practice of Medieval Knighthood,* ed. Christopher Harper-Bill and Ruth Harvey (Woodbridge: Boydell, 1990), 39–48; and Martin, "Knighton's Lollards," *Lollardy and the Gentry,* ed. Aston and Richmond, 31.

215. Andrew Cole, "Chaucer's English Lesson," *Speculum* 77 (2002): 1128–67; see also Ralph Hanna III, "The Difficulty of Ricardian Prose Translation: The Case of the Lollards," *MLQ* 51 (1990): 319–40, and Kantik Ghosh, *The Wycliffite Heresy: Authority and the Interpretation of Texts* (Cambridge: Cambridge University Press, 2002), "Vernacular Translations of the Bible and 'Authority,'" 86–111.

216. *Works of Sir John Clanvowe,* ed. Scattergood, 57. Anne Hudson, "Langland and Lollardy?" *YLS* 17 (2003): 93–105 at 99, points out that this reference occurs in only one of the two surviving manuscripts, Oxford University College 97, made after Clanvowe's death in 1391 and is therefore a flimsy foundation for building an argument on his understanding of this term during the 1380s.

217. Hudson, *Premature Reformation,* 390–94, considers Wycliffite elements in Chaucer's writings. For a more specific examination, see Michael Wilks, "Chaucer

and the Mystical Marriage in Medieval Political Thought," *BJRL* 44 (1962): 489–530, and Alcuin Blamires, "The Wife of Bath and Lollardy," *MÆ* 58 (1989): 224–42.

218. Matti Peikola, "'Whom Clepist Þou Trewe Pilgrimes?': Lollard Discourse on Pilgrimages in *The Testimony of William Thorpe*," *Essayes and Explorations: A "Freund-schrift" for Liisa Dahl,* ed. Marita Gustafsson (Turku, Finland: University of Turku, Anglicana Turkuensia, 15, 1996), 73–84. See also John M. Bowers, "Controversy and Criticism: Lydgate's *Thebes* and the Prologue to *Beryn*," *Chaucer Yearbook* 5 (1998): 91–115 at 105–7, and Somerset, *Clerical Discourse and Lay Audience,* "Vernacular Argumentation in *The Testimony of William Thorpe*," 179–215.

219. *Regiment,* ed. Blyth, 96 (1970–73).

220. James H. McGregor, "The Iconography of Chaucer in Hoccleve's *Regiment Principum* and in the *Troilus* Frontispiece," *ChauR* 11 (1976–77): 338–50.

221. Accusations of heresy function here much as later charges of atheism. See Stephen Greenblatt, "Invisible Bullets" (1981), rpt. *Shakespearean Negotiations* (Berkeley and Los Angeles: University of California Press, 1988), 21–65 at 22.

222. McFarlane, *Lancastrian Kings,* 95–96. On Henry IV's ability to gain parliamentary backing, see A. L. Brown, "The Reign of Henry IV," *Fifteenth Century England, 1399–1509: Studies in Politics and Society,* ed. S. B. Chrimes, C. D. Ross, and R. A. Griffiths, 2nd ed. (Stroud: Sutton, 1995), 1–28 at 24, and Douglas Biggs, "The Reign of Henry IV: The Revolution of 1399 and the Establishment of the Lancastrian Regime," *Fourteenth Century England,* ed. Nigel Saul (Woodbridge: Boydell, 2000), 195–210 at 209.

223. Hudson, *English Wycliffite Writings,* 135–37 and 203–7. The gist of the Disendowment Bill had already been articulated by earlier Lollards such as John Purvey according to *Fasciculi Zizaniorum,* 393–95. Such a bill may have existed in 1406 and even as early as 1395, and it was still circulating in 1431 when its posting coincided with a minor Lollard revolt; see R. W. Hoyle, "The Origins of the Dissolution of the Monasteries," *Historical Journal* 38 (1995): 275–305, and Justice, "Lollardy," *Cambridge History of Medieval English Literature,* ed. Wallace, 674.

224. Derek Pearsall, "Hoccleve's *Regement of Princes*: The Poetics of Royal Self-Representation," *Speculum* 69 (1994): 386–410 at 397–408, and Pearsall, *John Lydgate (1371–1449): A Bio-bibliography* (Victoria: University of Victoria English Literary Studies, no. 71, 1997), 18–19.

225. Estelle Stubbs, "Clare Priory, the London Austin Friars and Manuscripts of Chaucer's *Canterbury Tales,*" *Middle English Poetry,* ed. Minnis, 17–26, suggests how even friars were willing to overlook Chaucer's antifraternal views.

226. Hudson, *Premature Reformation,* "The Context of Vernacular Wycliffism," 390–445 and particularly 390–94, describes the dangerous textual environment in which the *Canterbury Tales* might have been enmeshed if the poet and his son Thomas Chaucer had not been so usefully connected with the Lancastrians.

227. Hobsbawm, "Inventing Tradition," 10.

228. John M. Bowers, ed., *The Canterbury Tales: Fifteenth-Century Continuations and Additions,* 2nd rev. ed. (Kalamazoo: Medieval Institute Publications, 1999), 60–79; the work survives only later in the Northumberland manuscript c. 1450–70.

229. John M. Bowers, "*The Tale of Beryn* and *The Siege of Thebes*: Alternative Ideas of the *Canterbury Tales*," *SAC* 7 (1985): 23–50 at 27–38; this article has been reprinted in *Writing after Chaucer: Essential Readings in Chaucer and the Fifteenth Century,* ed. Daniel Pinti (New York: Garland, 1998), 201–26.

230. On the early and later phases of this controversial cult, see two recent studies in *Pilgrimage: The English Experience from Becket to Bunyan,* ed. Colin Morris and Peter Roberts (Cambridge: Cambridge University Press, 2002): Richard Gameson, "The Early Imagery of Thomas Becket," 46–89, and Peter Roberts, "Politics, Drama and the Cult of Thomas Becket in the Sixteenth Century," 199–237.

231. Bowers, ed., *The Canterbury Tales: Fifteenth-Century Continuations and Additions,* 13–17. Chaucer does not include any self-portrait in the General Prologue; the Man of Law does not seem to know the poet is present (*CT,* II, 46–89); and the Host does not know his identity when he asks Chaucer the pilgrim to tell a tale (VII, 694–704). See Lee Patterson, "'What Man Artow?': Authorial Self-Definition in *The Tale of Sir Thopas* and *The Tale of Melibee*," *SAC* 11 (1989): 117–75.

232. John Lydgate, *The Siege of Thebes,* ed. Robert R. Edwards (Kalamazoo: Medieval Institute Publications, 2001), 5.

233. John J. Thompson, "After Chaucer: Resituating Middle English Poetry in the Late Medieval and Early Modern Period," *New Directions in Later Medieval Manuscript Studies,* ed. Pearsall, 183–99 at 185.

234. Lydgate, *Siege of Thebes,* ed. Edwards, 145 (line 4501).

235. Ibid., 145 (lines 4520–24).

236. Spurgeon, ed., *Five Hundred Years of Chaucerian Criticism and Allusion,* 1:14. For the corrected date, see Pearsall, *John Lydgate* (1997), 50.

237. Lydgate, *Siege of Thebes,* ed. Edwards, 111 (line 3200).

238. Edward, Second Duke of York, *The Master of Game,* ed. William A. Baillie-Grohman and F. N. Baillie-Grohman, intro. Theodore Roosevelt (London: Ballantyne, Hanson & Co., 1904), 3–4, provides the original and a modern translation of BL Cotton Vespasian B.xii; the modernized version of this edition has been reprinted as Edward of Norwich, *The Master of Game* (Philadelphia: University of Pennsylvania Press, 2005). Portions are included in Spurgeon, ed., *Five Hundred Years of Chaucerian Criticism and Allusion,* 1:18; Edith Rickert, ed., *Chaucer's World* (New York: Columbia University Press, 1948), 218–25; and Douglas Gray, ed., *The Oxford Book of Late Medieval Verse and Prose* (Oxford: Clarendon, 1985), 145–48. Nicholas Orme, "Medieval Hunting: Fact and Fancy," *Chaucer's England,* ed. Hanawalt, 133–53 at 138–39, places this work in context of other hunting treatises.

239. Bowers, "Three Readings of *The Knight's Tale*: Sir John Clanvowe, Geoffrey Chaucer, and James I of Scotland," 291–97. For other members of this "captive audience," see Martin Michael Crow, "John of Angoulême and His Chaucer Manuscript," *Speculum* 17 (1942): 86–99; Paul Strohm, "Jean of Angoulême: A Fifteenth-Century Reader of Chaucer," *NM* 72 (1971): 69–76; Diane R. Marks, "Poems from Prison: James I of Scotland and Charles d'Orléans," *Fifteenth-Century Studies* 15 (1989): 245–58; A. C. Spearing, "Prison, Writing, Absence: Representing the Subject in the English Poems of Charles d'Orléans," *MLQ* 53 (1992): 83–99; Joanna Summers, *Late-*

Medieval Prison Writing and the Politics of Autobiography (Oxford: Clarendon, 2004), 60–107; and Linne R. Mooney and Mary-Jo Arn, eds., *"The Kingis Quair" and Other Prison Poems* (Kalamazoo: Medieval Institute Publications, 2005). For the circumstances of royal prisoners, see Christopher Harding, Bill Hines, Richard Ireland, and Philip Rawlings, *Imprisonment in England and Wales* (London: Croom Helm, 1985).

240. John Lydgate, *The Minor Poems: Secular Poems,* 2:417 (lines 236–37).

241. John Lydgate, *Poems,* ed. John Norton-Smith (Oxford: Clarendon, 1966), 70 (line 110).

242. Lydgate, *Minor Poems: Secular Poems,* 2:542 (lines 76–77). On the unfinished status of the Squire's Tale, see David Seaman, "'The Wordes of the Frankeleyn to the Squier': An Interruption?" *ELN* 24 (1986): 12–18.

243. Brewer, ed., *The Critical Heritage,* 1:46.

244. Ibid., 48–49; my italics.

245. Lydgate, *Minor Poems: Secular Poems,* 2:828 (lines 188–91).

246. John Lydgate, *Fall of Princes,* ed. Henry Bergen, EETS e.s 121–24, 1924–27, part I, 7–8 (book I, lines 246–50). The review of Chaucer's works continues 8–10 (lines 281–357).

247. Dante was not entirely unknown in England, since Bishop Robert Hallum of Salisbury and Bishop Nicholas Bubwith of Bath and Wells cosponsored a translation of the *Divine Comedy* into Latin by Giovanni Bertoldi de Serravalle in 1416; John Leland reported seeing a copy in the Wells Cathedral library and the commentary in Duke Humphrey's library at Oxford. See R. A. Shoaf, "'Noon Englissh Digne': Dante in Late Medieval England," *Dante Now: Current Trends in Dante Studies,* ed. Theodore J. Cachey, Jr. (Notre Dame, IN: University of Notre Dame Press, 1995), 189–203, and David Wallace, "Dante in Somerset: Ghosts, Historiography, Periodization," *NML* 3 (1999): 9–38.

248. Patterson, *Chaucer and the Subject of History,* "'Thirled with the Poynt of Remembraunce': The Theban Writing of *Anelida and Arcite,*" 47–83.

249. Andrew Taylor, "Anne of Bohemia and the Making of Chaucer," *SAC* 19 (1997): 95–119.

250. Lydgate, *Fall of Princes,* part I, 10 (lines 346–50).

251. Ibid., part I, 49 (lines 1783–85).

252. Ibid., part III, 436 (lines 3858–64).

253. For the text, see *Riverside Chaucer,* 656.

254. Pearsall, "The *Troilus* Frontispiece and Chaucer's Audience," *YES* 7 (1977): 68–74. For more on this artist, see two pieces in *Prestige, Authority and Power in Late Medieval Manuscripts and Texts,* ed. Felicity Riddy (Woodbridge: Boydell & Brewer for York Medieval Press, 2000): Kathleen L. Scott, "Limner-Power: A Book Artist in England c. 1420," 55–75, and Kate Harris, "The Patronage and Dating of Longleat House MS 24, a Prestige Copy of the *Pupilla Oculi* Illuminated by the Master of the *Troilus* Frontispiece," 35–54.

255. Paul Strohm, *Hochon's Arrow: The Social Imagination of Fourteenth-Century Texts* (Princeton: Princeton University Press, 1992), "Saving the Appearances: Chaucer's

'Purse' and the Fabrication of the Lancastrian Claim," 75–94, explores the political implications of the late lyric.

256. Alixe Bovey, *The Chaworth Roll: A Fourteenth-Century Genealogy of the Kings of England* (London: Sam Fogg Gallery, 2005).

257. Lydgate, *Minor Poems: Secular Poems,* 613–22. The poet was not alone in invoking this propagandistic genealogy; see J. W. McKenna, "Henry VI of England and the Dual Monarchy: Aspects of Royal Political Propaganda, 1422–1432," *Journal of the Warburg and Courtauld Institutes* 28 (1965): 145–62.

258. Seymour, *A Catalogue of Chaucer Manuscripts,* vol. 1: *Works before the "Canterbury Tales,"* 85–87.

259. Lydgate, *Siege of Thebes,* ed. Edwards, 120 (lines 3538–43).

260. Hope Emily Allen, *The Authorship of "The Prick of Conscience"* (Boston and New York: Radcliffe College Monographs, no. 15, 1910), showed the work was not Rolle's. Pearsall, *Old English and Middle English Poetry,* 139, thinks the work was assigned to Rolle in order "to cleanse it from heretical taint after it had been interpolated in some versions with Lollard material."

261. Lydgate, *Fall of Princes,* part III, 1015–16 (book IX, lines 3410–14).

262. Ibid., part III, 1016 (book IX, lines 3422–27).

263. Cannon, "Monastic Productions," *Cambridge History of English Medieval Literature,* ed. Wallace, 343.

264. Lydgate, *Fall of Princes,* part III, 1016 (book IX, lines 3431–35).

265. A. S. G. Edwards, "The Influence of Lydgate's *Fall of Princes* c. 1440–1559: A Survey," *Medieval Studies* 39 (1977): 424–39, and Alexandra Gillespie, "The Lydgate Canon in Print from 1476 to 1534," *Journal of the Early Book Society* 4 (2000): 59–93, trace this work's long afterlife.

266. Doyle, "English Books in and out of Court," 174. John M. Bowers, "*Mankind* and the Political Interests of Bury St. Edmunds," *Æstel* 2 (1994): 77–103, suggests regional knowledge of Lydgate and his distinctive aureate diction.

267. Oxford, Bodleian MS Laud misc. 233, fol. 125b; see Pearsall, *John Lydgate* (1997), 67, item 30.

CHAPTER FOUR   *Piers Plowman* and the Impulse to Antagonism

1. Dobson, ed., *The Peasants' Revolt of 1381,* 380–81, translates Walsingham's *Historia,* 2:33–34. See also Anne Middleton, "Introduction: The Critical Heritage," *Companion to "Piers Plowman,"* ed. Alford, 1–25 at 4–6; Richard Firth Green, "John Ball's Letters: Literary History and Historical Literature," *Chaucer's England,* ed. Hanawalt, 176–200; and Justice, *Writing and Rebellion,* 13–66.

2. Justice, *Writing and Rebellion,* "*Piers Plowman* in the Rising," 102–39 at 119.

3. Justice, *Writing and Rebellion,* 90–93.

4. Anne Hudson, "A Lollard Sect Vocabulary?" (1981), *Lollards and Their Books,* 165–80 at 166–67, and Peggy Knapp, *Chaucer and the Social Contest* (New York and London: Routledge, 1990), "Coming to Terms with Wyclif," 63–76.

5. Dobson, ed., *The Peasants' Revolt,* 375, translates Walsingham 2:32–33.

6. Lorraine Kochanske Stock, "Parable, Allegory, History, and *Piers Plowman,*" *YLS* 5 (1991): 143–64 at 155–60.

7. Oxford Bodley MS 158, fol. 202a. Rymington's concern for civic disorder underscores the new importance of London as the national capital—"capital civitas regni"—and therefore the seat of royal administration and governance.

8. Gransden, *Historical Writing in England,* 130; for the value and vested interests in these chronicles, see Geoffrey Martin, "Wyclif, Lollards, and Historians, 1384–1984," *Lollards and Their Influence,* ed. Somerset, Havens, and Pitard, 237–50.

9. Margaret Aston, "Lollardy and Sedition 1381–1431" (1960), rpt. *Lollards and Reformers: Images and Literacy in Late Medieval Religion* (London: Hambledon Press, 1984), 3–4, and Anne Hudson, "*Hermofodrita or Ambidexter*: Wycliffite Views on Clerks in Secular Office," *Lollardy and the Gentry,* ed. Aston and Richmond, 41–51.

10. Dobson, ed., *The Peasants' Revolt,* 378, translates from *Fasciculi Zizaniorum,* 273–74.

11. *Knighton's Chronicle,* 242–43.

12. *Knighton's Chronicle,* 222–23, with other accounts of Ball's misconduct, 210–11. Justice, *Writing and Rebellion,* 122–24.

13. David Knowles, *The Religious Orders in England,* 3 vols. (Cambridge: Cambridge University Press, 1948–59), 2:48–60.

14. McFarlane, *Lancastrian Kings and Lollard Knights,* 148–76, and Justice, "Lollardy," *Cambridge History of Medieval English Literature,* ed. Wallace, 670–73 ("Lollardy at Court"). Margaret Aston, "Lollardy and Literacy" (1977), rpt. *Lollards and Reformers,* 193–217 at 206, on the "elevated alarmism" motivating these chronicle accounts. Even after 1381–82 Gaunt continued to shield Wyclif and protect followers such as Repingdon and Hereford; see Joseph H. Dahmus, *The Prosecution of John Wyclif* (New Haven: Yale University Press, 1952), 113–14 and 135.

15. Anne Hudson, "Lollard Book Production," *Book Production,* ed. Griffiths and Pearsall, 125–42 at 129.

16. Dobson, ed., *The Peasants' Revolt,* 338 and 380. See also John Taylor, *English Historical Literature in the Fourteenth Century* (Oxford: Clarendon, 1987), 318–24, and Andrew Prescott, "Writing about Rebellion: Using the Records of the Peasants' Revolt of 1381," *History Workshop Journal* 45 (1998): 1–27.

17. Susan Crane, "The Writing Lesson of 1381," *Chaucer's England,* ed. Hanawalt, 201–21 at 202.

18. Strohm, *Hochon's Arrow,* "'A Revelle!': Chronicle Evidence and the Rebel Voice," 33–56 at 51; see Derek Pearsall, "Interpretative Models for the Peasants' Revolt," *Hermeneutics and Medieval Culture,* ed. Patrick J. Gallacher and Helen Damico (Albany: State University of New York Press, 1989), 63–70.

19. *Anonimalle Chronicle,* ed. Galbraith, 139.

20. Scanlon, "King, Commons, and Kind Wit," 218–19.

21. Michael Wilks, "'Reformatio Regni': Wyclif and Hus as Leaders of Religious Protest Movements," *SCH* 9 (1972): 109–30 at 127–30; see also Harriet Merete Hansen, "The Peasants' Revolt of 1381 and the Chronicles," *JMH* 6 (1980): 393–415.

22. Christina von Nolcken, "Richard Wyche, a Certain Knight, and the Beginning of the End," *Lollardy and the Gentry,* ed. Aston and Richmond, 127–54; see also F. D. Matthew, "Trial of Richard Wyche," *EHR* 5 (1890): 530–44.

23. *Fasciculi Zizaniorum,* 318–25, 329–31; see also *Knighton's Chronicle,* ed. Martin, 276–83.

24. T. B. Pugh, *Henry V and the Southampton Plot of 1415* (Southampton: Southampton University Press, 1988), 19 and 126–27.

25. A. K. McHardy, "*De Heretico Comburendo,* 1401," *Lollardy and the Gentry,* ed. Aston and Richmond, 112–26, provides new insights into this drastic legislation.

26. Myers, ed., *English Historical Documents,* 188. See also David Crook, "Central England and the Revolt of the Earls, January 1400," *Historical Research* 64 (1991): 403–10, and A. Rogers, "The Political Crisis of 1401," *Nottingham Mediaeval Studies* 12 (1968): 85–96.

27. M. V. Clarke and V. H. Galbraith, eds., *Chronicle of Dieulacres Abbey, 1381–1403, BJRL* 14 (1930): 164–81 at 164–65: "Iohannis B., Iak Strawe, Per Plowman et ceteri." See Hudson, *Premature Reformation,* 399–400, and Baldwin, "The Historical Context," 72–73.

28. *Piers Plowman: The A Version,* ed. George Kane (London: Athlone Press, 1960), 48.

29. Louis A. Montrose, "Professing the Renaissance: The Poetics and Politics of Culture," *The New Historicism,* ed. Veeser, 15–36, describes a similar sort of textual space in which so many cultural codes converge that ideological coherence becomes permanently disrupted.

30. Christopher Hill, "From Lollards to Levellers" (1978), rpt. *The Collected Essays,* 3 vols. (Amherst: University of Massachusetts Press, 1986), 2:89–116.

31. Margaret Aston, "Lollardy and the Reformation: Survival or Revival?" (1964), rpt. *Lollards and Reformers,* 219–42 at 234–40.

32. Bale's *Catalogus* is translated by Simpson, *Reform,* 27.

33. Crowley, ed., *The Vision of Pierce Plowman* (1550), facsimile edition by J. A. W. Bennett. Christopher Hill's observation, "From Lollards to Levellers," 96, that Crowley came from an old Lollard area in Gloucestershire fits the picture almost too precisely. See also John N. King, "Robert Crowley's Editions of *Piers Plowman*: A Tudor Apocalypse," *MP* 73 (1976): 342–52.

34. Simpson, *Reform,* 328–29.

35. Simpson, *Reform,* 62, remarks upon Lydgate as a critic of his own aristocratic patrons.

36. Hudson, *Premature Reformation,* 429.

37. Anne Hudson, "Preface," *Lollards and Their Influence,* ed. Somerset, Havens, and Pitard, 1–8 at 8. See also Justice, "Lollardy," *Cambridge History of Medieval English Literature,* ed. Wallace, 683–84 ("The Problem of Definition") and 684–85 ("Doctrinal Diversity in Lollardy"), and Jill C. Havens, "Shading the Grey Area: Determining Heresy in Middle English Texts," *Text and Controversy from Wyclif to Bale,* ed. Barr and Hutchison, 337–52.

38. Michel Foucault, *The Archaeology of Knowledge,* trans. A. M. Sheridan Smith (New York: Pantheon Books, 1972), 31–39.

39. Andrew E. Larsen, "Are All Lollards Lollards?" *Lollards and Their Influence,* ed. Somerset, Havens, and Pitard, 59–72, argues for many brands of unorthodox beliefs: "The corollary to the myth that there was no heresy in England before 1377 is that all heresy occurring in England after 1377 must be associated with Wyclif and Lollardy" (63). See also Gloria Cigman, "*Luceat Lux Vestra*: The Lollard Preacher as Truth and Light," *RES* n.s. 40 (1989): 479–96.

40. Hanna, *Pursuing History,* "Two Lollard Codices," 57–58, points to works that appear in both Lollard and non-Lollard compilations.

41. Phillipa Hardman, "A Medieval 'Library *in Parvo,*'" *MÆ* 47 (1978): 262–73.

42. Dutschke, *Guide to Medieval and Renaissance Manuscripts in the Huntington Library,* 1:248–50. For the two religious works, see A. L. Kellogg and E. W. Talbert, "The Wycliffite *Pater Noster* and *Ten Commandments* with Special Reference to English MSS 85 and 90 in the John Rylands Library," *BJRL* 42 (1959–60): 345–77, and *Select English Works of John Wyclif,* ed. Thomas Arnold, 3 vols. (Oxford: Clarendon, 1869–71), 3:168–69.

43. Greenblatt, *Shakespearean Negotiations,* 21–65.

44. Jean E. Howard, "The New Historicism in Renaissance Studies," *Renaissance Historicism,* ed. Arthur F. Kinney and Dan S. Collins (Amherst: University of Massachusetts Press, 1987), 3–33 at 29–30.

45. Middleton, "Audience and Public," 105–6, reviews the contents of these two enormous collections. Hanna, *Pursuing History,* 231, thinks that Vernon "was surely a communal lectern book, perhaps for a community of women." See Kathleen L. Scott, *A Survey of Manuscripts Illuminated in the British Isles,* gen. ed. J. J. G. Alexander, vol. 6: *Later Gothic Manuscripts, 1390–1490,* 2 vols. (London: Harvey Miller, 1996), 2:19–24 for Vernon, and Benson and Blanchfield, *Manuscripts of "Piers Plowman,"* 32–38, for CUL Dd. Bruce W. Holsinger, "Langland's Musical Reader: Liturgy, Law, and the Constraints of Performance," *SAC* 21 (1999): 99–141 at 130–32, remarks how the early Langlandian spinoff "The Choisters' Lament" is preserved in the Benedictine manuscript BL Arundel 292.

46. *Pierce the Ploughmans Crede (and God Spede the Plough),* ed. Walter W. Skeat, EETS o.s. 30, 1867, has been newly edited by James M. Dean, *Six Ecclesiastical Satires* (Kalamazoo: Medieval Institute Publications, 1991), 1–49, and Barr, ed., *The Piers Plowman Tradition,* 9–14, 61–97, 213–46.

47. G. H. Russell, "Some Early Responses to the C-Version of *Piers Plowman,*" *Viator* 15 (1984): 275–303 at 276–78, and my article "Langland's *Piers Plowman* in HM 143: Copy, Commentary, Censorship."

48. Uhart, "The Early Reception of *Piers Plowman,*" 324–25, for the running subject-guide in HM 137.

49. Matthew, ed., *The English Works of Wyclif,* 274.

50. Middleton, "The Audience and Public of *Piers Plowman,*" 107, and Hudson, "The Legacy of *Piers Plowman,*" 263.

51. Frank Lentricchia, *Ariel and the Police: Michel Foucault, William James, Wallace Stevens* (Madison: University of Wisconsin Press, 1988), 25–26.

52. Steiner, *Documentary Culture,* "Lollard Community and the *Charters of Christ,*" 193–228, situates Langland's contribution to this reformist assault upon the claims of intercessory power invested in Church documents.

53. Dobson, ed., *Peasants' Revolt,* 133–34, translates Walsingham 1:455.

54. Justice, *Writing and Rebellion,* 116.

55. Rodney Hilton, *Bond Men Made Free: Medieval Peasant Movements and the English Rising of 1381* (1973; rpt. London and New York: Routledge, 1988), 176–85; David Aers, "*Vox Populi* and the Literature of 1381," *Cambridge History of Medieval English Literature,* ed. Wallace, 432–53 at 438–39; and Simpson, *Reform,* 343–46.

56. Quoted and translated from Walsingham's *Gesta* by Justice, *Writing and Rebellion,* 256–57.

57. Dobson, ed., *Peasants' Revolt,* 160. Walsingham, *Historia,* 1:445, shows how Kentish insurgents anticipated the plans of Cade's rebels in Shakespeare's *2 Henry VI* (4.2.77): "The first thing we do, let's kill all the lawyers."

58. Andrew Galloway, "Gower in His Most Learned Role and the Peasants' Revolt of 1381," *Mediaevalia* 16 (1993 for 1990): 329–47.

59. Walsingham, *Historia,* 2:9.

60. Nick Ronan, "1381: Writing in Revolt—Signs of Confederacy in the Chronicle Accounts of the English Rising," *Forum for Modern Language Studies* 25 (1989): 304–14.

61. Walsingham 1:453, and *Anonimalle Chronicle,* 135.

62. Dobson, ed., *Peasants' Revolt,* 125–26, 132, 136. See also Aston, "Lollardy and Sedition," 25–26.

63. *The Book of Margery Kempe,* ed. Sanford Brown Meech and Hope Emily Allen, EETS o.s. 212, 1940, 132.

64. Justice, *Writing and Rebellion,* "Insurgent Literacy," 13–66 at 24.

65. Aston, "Lollardy and Literacy," *Lollards and Reformers,* 208–12; Hudson, *Premature Reformation,* 27–28, 259–64, 247–59, and generally "The Context of Vernacular Wycliffism," 390–445. *Lay Folks' Catechism: Archbishop Thoresby's Instruction for the People,* ed. T. F. Simmons and H. E. Nolloth, EETS o.s. 118, 1901, xx–xxvii, discusses the principal additions (82–85) in Lambeth MS 408 of a work dating from 1357. See Curt F. Bühler, "A Lollard Tract: On Translating the Bible into English," *MÆ* 7 (1938): 167–83; Anne Hudson, "A New Look at the Lay Folks' Catechism," *Viator* 16 (1985): 243–58; R. N. Swanson, "The Origins of *The Lay Folks' Catechism,*" *MÆ* 60 (1991): 92–100; Susan Powell, "The Transmission and Circulation of *The Lay Folks' Catechism,*" *Late-Medieval Religious Texts and Their Transmission,* ed. Minnis, 67–84; and Emily Steiner, "Lollardy and the Legal Document," *Lollards and Their Influence,* ed. Somerset, Havens, and Pitard, 155–74.

66. On the "Lollard" features of *Pore Caitif,* see Doyle, "A Survey of the Origins and Circulation of Theological Writings in English," 1:48–56, and Sr. Mary Teresa Brady, "Lollard Interpolations and Omissions in Manuscripts of *The Pore Caitif,*" *Cella in Seculum: Religious and Secular Life and Devotion in Late Medieval England,* ed. Mi-

chael G. Sargent (Cambridge: D. S. Brewer, 1989), 183–203. See *Ancrene Riwle: Edited from Magdalene College, Cambridge MS. Pepys 2498,* ed. A. Zettersten, EETS o.s. 274, 1976, xxii, and Eric Colledge, "*The Recluse*: A Lollard Interpolated Version of the *Ancren Riwle*," *RES* 15 (1939): 1–15 and 129–45, at 13–14 for a list of the "Lollard" interpolations. Doyle, "Survey of Origins," 1:231–32, pronounced this manuscript "heavily interpolated with radical Lollard opinions."

67. *Knighton's Chronicle,* 252–53: Wyclif and his followers "had erased ancient books of the solid faith of the church and in many places imposed the literal doctrine of their new opinions." Cited by Justice, "Lollardy," *Cambridge History of Medieval English Literature,* ed. Wallace, 682. Though Knighton includes this account under the year 1382, such alarmist claims might represent back-formations fictionalized during the mid-1390s.

68. Hudson, *Premature Reformation,* 157–68.

69. Aston, "Lollardy and Literacy," *Lollards and Reformers,* 207.

70. Margaret Deanesly, *The Lollard Bible and Other Medieval Biblical Versions* (Cambridge: Cambridge University Press, 1920), 363, and Anne Hudson, "Lollardy: The English Heresy?" (1982), *Lollards and Their Books,* 141–63 at 142.

71. Brian Cummings, "Iconoclasm and Bibliophobia in the English Reformation, 1521–1558," *Images, Idolatry, and Iconoclasm in Late Medieval England,* ed. Jeremy Dimmick, James Simpson, and Nicolette Zeeman (Oxford: Oxford University Press, 2002), 185–206.

72. Hope Emily Allen, "The *Speculum Vitae*: Addendum," *PMLA* 25 (1917): 133–62 at 147–48.

73. Anne Hudson, "*Laicus Litteratus*: The Paradox of Lollardy," *Heresy and Literacy, 1000–1530,* ed. Peter Biller and Anne Hudson (Cambridge: Cambridge University Press, 1994), 222–36 at 233.

74. Williel R. Thomson, *The Latin Writings of John Wyclif: An Annotated Catalog* (Toronto: Pontifical Institute of Medieval Studies, Subsidia Mediaevalia, no. 14, 1983).

75. Hudson, "*Laicus Litteratus*," 233.

76. *Hoccleve's Works: The Minor Poems,* 9 and 14 (lines 25–26 and 195–98). On the subject of Oldcastle's books, see Ruth Nissé, "'Oure Fadres Olde and Modres': Gender, Heresy, and Hoccleve's Literary Politics," *SAC* 21 (1999): 275–99 at 294–98, and Barr, *Socioliterary Practice in Late Medieval England,* 26–39.

77. Maude Violet Clarke, *Fourteenth Century Studies,* ed. L. S. Sutherland and M. McKisack (Oxford: Clarendon, 1937), "Forfeitures and Treason," 120–21, lists other works in Burley's collection. See also Viscount Dillon and W. H. St. John Hope, "Inventory of the Goods and Chattels Belonging to Thomas, Duke of Gloucester, and Seized in His Castle at Pleshy, Co. Essex, 21 Richard II (1397), with Their Values, as Shown in the Escheator's Accounts," *Archaeological Journal* 54 (1897): 275–308, esp. 281–82 and 300–303.

78. V. J. Scattergood, "Two Medieval Book Lists," *The Library* 5th ser., 23 (1968): 236–39.

79. Allmand, *The Hundred Years War,* 157–58. Pearsall, *Old English and Middle English Poetry,* 239–40, and Hanna, "Sir Thomas Berkeley and His Patronage," 891–92, discuss English renderings of the treatise. Charles R. Shrader, "A Handlist of Extant Manuscripts Containing the *De Re Militari* of Flavius Vegetius Renatus," *Scriptorium* 33 (1979): 280–305, attests to the wide circulation of this work.

80. *"The Governance of Kings and Princes": John Trevisa's Middle English Translation of the "De Regimine Principum" of Aegidius Romanus,* ed. David C. Fowler, Charles F. Briggs, and Paul G. Remley (New York and London: Garland, 1997), xi–xii for dating MS Digby 233, and 2 for a plate of the presentation portrait (fol. 1a). Charles F. Briggs, *Giles of Rome's "De Regimine Principum": Reading and Writing Politics at Court and University, c. 1275–c. 1525* (Cambridge: Cambridge University Press, 1999), 84–90, offers a history of composition and transmission.

81. Doyle, "English Books in and out of Court," 173.

82. Richard Firth Green, *Poets and Princepleasers: Literature and the English Court in the Late Middle Ages* (Toronto: University of Toronto Press, 1980), 144–45, and Harriss, *Shaping the Nation,* "The Literary Model of Governance," 6–13.

83. Seymour, ed., *Catalogue of Chaucer Manuscripts: "The Canterbury Tales,"* provides descriptions for Huntington Library MS El.26.C.9 at one end of the scale (230–35) and University of Chicago Library MS 564 at the other end (74–76) . Not all later copies were unimpressive; Bodleian MS Arch. Selden B.14 c. 1460 was expensive to produce and remains beautiful to admire.

84. Russell, "Some Early Responses to the C-Version," 278–81; Kathleen L. Scott, "The Illustrations of *Piers Plowman* in Bodleian Library MS Douce 104," *YLS* 4 (1990): 1–86; Derek Pearsall, "Manuscript Illustration of Late Middle English Literary Texts, with Special Reference to the Illustration of *Piers Plowman* in Bodleian Library MS Douce 104," *Suche Werkis to Werche,* ed. Vaughan, 191–210; and *Piers Plowman: A Facsimile of Bodleian Library, Oxford, MS Douce 104,* intro. Derek Pearsall, catalogue of illustrations by Kathleen Scott (Cambridge: D. S. Brewer, 1992). For the annotations accompanying these pictures, see Uhart, "The Early Reception of *Piers Plowman,*" 363–73.

85. *Text of the Canterbury Tales,* ed. Manly and Rickert, 1:plates II–IV, gives some sense of the richness of these lesser-known Chaucer manuscripts. Scott, "The Ellesmere Illuminators," *Ellesmere Chaucer,* ed. Stevens and Woodward, 104, believes that the same master limner influenced or supervised Harley 7334 and Lansdowne 851.

86. Doyle, "The Manuscripts," *Middle English Alliterative Poetry,* ed. Lawton, 88.

87. Uhart, "The Early Reception of *Piers Plowman,*" 353–62. Thorlac Turville-Petre, "Putting It Right: The Corrections of Huntington Library MS Hm 128 and BL Additional MS 35287," *YLS* 16 (2002): 41–65, examines one category of readerly engagement.

88. Bowers, *The Crisis of Will in "Piers Plowman,"* 165–89, on the poet's image in the poem.

89. For the "clerical proletariat," see Alison K. McHardy, "Careers and Disappointments in the Late-Medieval Church: Some English Evidence," *SCH* 26 (1989): 111–30, and R. N. Swanson, *Church and Society in Late Medieval England* (Oxford: Blackwell, 1989), 40–50.

90. Hudson, *Premature Reformation,* 74–76 and 146–47, on the russet color of Lollard clothing. See also Walsingham, *Historia,* 1:324.

91. Aston, "Lollardy and Sedition," 6.

92. Goodman, *John of Gaunt,* 60–61.

93. Pamela Gradon, "Langland and the Ideology of Dissent," *PBA* 66 (1980): 179–205; David Lawton, "Lollardy and the 'Piers Plowman' Tradition," *MLR* 76 (1981): 780–93; Anne Hudson, "The Legacy of *Piers Plowman,*" 251–66; and Christina Von Nolcken, "*Piers Plowman,* the Wycliffites, and *Pierce the Plowman's Creed,*" *YLS* 2 (1988): 71–102. See Matthew, *The English Works of Wyclif,* 108–13 and 254–62, for some issues of common interest.

94. On the early history of these controversial topics, see Margaret Aston, "Caim's Castles: Poverty, Politics and Disendowment," *Faith and Fire: Popular and Unpopular Religion, 1350–1600* (London: Hambledon, 1993), 95–131.

95. David Aers, "The Sacrament of the Altar in *Piers Plowman* and the Late Medieval Church," *Images, Idolatry, and Iconoclasm,* ed. Dimmick, Simpson, and Zeeman, 63–80; see Anthony Kenny, *Wyclif* (Oxford: Oxford University Press, 1985), 80–90, and Pearsall, "Langland and Lollardy: From B to C," 13.

96. Wright, ed., *Political Poems and Songs,* 1:253–63 at 262 (lines 263–64). Anne Hudson, "Peter Pateshull: One-Time Friar and Poet?" *Interstices: Studies in Late Middle English and Anglo-Latin Texts in Honor of A. G. Rigg,* ed. Richard Firth Green and Linne R. Mooney (Toronto: University of Toronto Press, 2004), 167–83, proposes an author for the piece. Wendy Scase, "'Heu! Quanta Desolatio Angliae Praestatur': A Wycliffite Libel and the Naming of Heretics, Oxford 1382," *Lollards and Their Influence,* ed. Somerset, Havens, and Pitard, 19–36 at 33, explicates "Pers" as a critic of the Carmelites. See also A. G. Rigg, *A History of Anglo-Latin Literature 1066–1422* (Cambridge: Cambridge University Press, 1992), 281–82; Ralph Hanna III, "With an O (Yorks) or an I (Salop)? The Middle English Lyrics of British Library Additional 45896," *SB* 48 (1995): 290–97, on the genre; and Kathryn Kerby-Fulton, "Prophecy and Suspicion: Closet Radicalism, Reformist Politics, and the Vogue for Hildegardiana in Ricardian England," *Speculum* 75 (2000): 318–41 at 336.

97. Joel Fredell, "The Lowly Paraf: Transmitting Manuscript Design in *The Canterbury Tales,*" *SAC* 22 (2000): 213–80 at 226–27, notices that careful markings and divisions, as the equivalent of modern punctuation, appear only in high-end *Piers* manuscripts like Cambridge Dd.1.17.

98. Lawton, "Lollardy and the 'Piers Plowman' Tradition," 793; see more recently Barr, "'Blessed are the horny hands of toil': Wycliffite Representations of the Third Estate," *Socioliterary Practice,* 128–57. Simpson, *Reform,* 370–74, explains why he thinks Lollards did *not* have Langlandian sympathies.

99. *Piers the Plowman,* ed. Skeat, 2:xxxv, and Coghill, "Two Notes on *Piers Plowman.*" Cargill, "The Langland Myth," also focused on the date 1393/94. See more recently Anne Middleton, "Acts of Vagrancy: The C Version 'Autobiography' and the Statute of 1388."

100. Donaldson, "MSS R and F in the B-Tradition of *Piers Plowman*"; Scase, "Two *Piers Plowman* C-Text Interpolations: Evidence for a Second Textual Tradition"; Hanna, *Pursuing History,* "On the Versions of *Piers Plowman,*" 215–29 and

238–39; Sean Taylor, "The Lost Revision of *Piers Plowman* B," *YLS* 11 (1997): 97–134; and Warner, "The Ur-B *Piers Plowman* and the Earliest Production of C and B." See Hanna, *Pursuing History*, "Authorial Versions, Rolling Revision, Scribal Error? Or, The Truth about *Truth*," 159–73, for the process of "rolling revision."

101. George H. Russell, "Some Aspects of the Process of Revision in *Piers Plowman*," *"Piers Plowman": Critical Approaches*, ed. Hussey, 27–49 at 39.

102. Russell, "As They Read It," 175.

103. Hudson, *Premature Reformation*, 398–408. See also David A. Lawton, "English Poetry and English Society," *The Radical Reader*, ed. Stephen Knight and Michael Wilding (Sydney: Wild & Woolley, 1977), 145–68 at 149–52.

104. See Kane, "John M. Manly (1865–1940) and Edith Rickert (1871–1938)," *Chaucer and Langland*, 178–205 at 202–3.

105. Hudson, *Premature Reformation*, 322–23. See also Bowers, *The Crisis of Will*, 139–43, and Vincent Gillespie, "'Thy Will Be Done': *Piers Plowman* and the *Pater Noster*," *Late-Medieval Religious Texts and Their Transmission: Essays in Honour of A. I. Doyle*, ed. A. J. Minnis (Cambridge: D. S. Brewer, 1994), 95–119.

106. This episode represents a crux that elicited important critical studies from Nevill Coghill, "The Pardon of Piers Plowman," *PBA* 30 (1944): 303–57; Rosemary Woolf, "The Tearing of the Pardon," *"Piers Plowman": Critical Approaches*, ed. Hussey, 50–75; and Mary Carruthers, "*Piers Plowman*: The Tearing of the Pardon," *PQ* 49 (1970): 8–18.

107. Hudson, *Premature Reformation*, 299–301.

108. Hudson, ed., *English Wycliffite Writings*, 27–28 and 150–54.

109. Ibid., 23. See also Hudson, *Premature Reformation*, 307–9. Burrow, "The Action of Langland's Second Vision," discusses Langland's abandonment of pilgrimage as a geographical journey in the Half Acre.

110. *Written Work*, ed. Justice and Kerby-Fulton.

111. Middleton, "Acts of Vagrancy," esp. 216–46; see also Bowers, *Crisis of Will*, 165–89. Hanna, *William Langland*, 31–32, lays out evidence supporting his view that the C-text autobiography responded specifically to the language of the 1388 Statute of Labourers.

112. Lawrence M. Clopper, "Franciscans, Lollards, and Reform," *Lollards and Their Influence*, ed. Somerset, Havens, and Pitard, 177–96, suggests that many of these *lollare* references were actually invoked by reform-minded Franciscan dissidents.

113. Cole, "William Langland and the Invention of Lollardy," *Lollards and Their Influence*, ed. Somerset, Havens, and Pitard, 40–43, describes as a back-formation the testimony of the *Fasciculi Zizaniorum*, 311–12: "suspenditur Henricus Crumpe, magister in theologia, . . . quia vocavit haereticos 'Lollardos.'"

114. Cole, "The Invention of Lollardy," 43–50.

115. Wittig, "'Culture Wars' and the Persona in *Piers Plowman*," 195, provides a census of the word *lollare*'s occurrences, once in B and thirteen times in C. Middleton, "Acts of Vagrancy," 276–77 and 280–87, reads C.5 as the final part of the revision and the poet's last effort at subordinating this volatile term.

116. Cole, "Invention of Lollardy," 53.

117. A. I. Doyle, "Publications by Members of the Religious Orders," *Book Production,* ed. Griffiths and Pearsall, 109–23 at 115; see also Susan Powell, ed., *The Advent and Nativity Sermons from a Fifteenth-Century Revision of John Mirk's "Festial"* (Heidelberg: Middle English Texts, no. 13, 1981), esp. 18–32.

118. Quoted from the Oxford Bodleian MS Rawlinson A. 381 by Alan J. Fletcher, "John Mirk and the Lollards," *MÆ* 56 (1987): 217–24 at 218. See also Fletcher, "Unnoticed Sermons from John Mirk's *Festial,*" *Speculum* 55 (1980): 514–22.

119. Susan Powell, "A New Dating of John Mirk's *Festial,*" *N&Q* n.s. 29 (1982): 487–89, suggests the period 1350–90 so that Mirk may have been the earliest extant writer to use the term *Lollard.*

120. W. R. Jones, "Lollards and Images: The Defense of Religious Art in Later Medieval England," *Journal of the History of Ideas* 34 (1973): 27–50.

121. Scase, *"Piers Plowman" and the New Anticlericalism,* "'Kyndeliche, by Christ, ben suche ycald *lollares*': The New Satire under Siege," 149–60.

122. Hudson, *Premature Reformation,* 3.

123. Samuels, "Langland's Dialect," 240.

124. Derek Pearsall, "'Lunatyk Lollares' in *Piers Plowman,*" *Religion in the Poetry and Drama of the Late Middle Ages in England,* ed. Piero Boitani and Anna Torti (Cambridge: D. S. Brewer, 1990), 163–78 at 170, avoids the issue with a parenthetical remark: "The question of Langland's association with Lollardy is a vexed one."

125. David Aers, "The Humanity of Christ: Representations in Wycliffite Texts and *Piers Plowman,*" *The Powers of the Holy,* ed. David Aers and Lynn Staley (University Park: Pennsylvania State University Press, 1996), 43–76, and Cole, "William Langland's Lollardy."

126. Hudson, *Premature Reformation,* 4, decided not to differentiate between *Wycliffite* and *Lollard* for the later period when the terms were fused, but she made a more careful distinction in "Wyclif and the English Language," *Wyclif in His Times,* ed. Kenny, 85–103 at 85–86.

127. Hudson, *Premature Reformation,* 147–48, discusses Lollard objections to fasts. Carl James Grindley, "Reading *Piers Plowman* C-text Annotations: Notes toward the Classification of Printed and Written Marginalia in Texts from the British Isles 1300–1641," *Medieval Professional Reader at Work,* ed. Kerby-Fulton and Hilmo, 73–141, includes Add. 35157 among his star witnesses. See also Russell, "Some Early Responses to the C-Version," 281–83, and Uhart, "The Early Reception of *Piers Plowman,*" 374–93.

128. See Duffy, *Stripping of the Altars,* "Coins, Candles, and Contracts," 183–86.

129. S. S. Hussey, "Langland the Outsider," *Middle English Poetry: Texts and Traditions: Essays in Honour of Derek Pearsall,* ed. A. J. Minnis (Woodbridge: York Medieval Press, with Boydell Press, 2001), 129–37.

130. McFarlane, *Lancastrian Kings and Lollard Knights,* 212.

131. Paul Strohm, *Theory and the Premodern Text* (Minneapolis: University of Minnesota Press, 2000), "Walking Fire," 20–32, on the imaginative preparations for Sawtry's burning. Arundel's *Constitutions* can be read in John Foxe's *Acts and Monuments* (1563), ed. George Townsend (1843–49; rpt. New York: AMS Press, 1965), 3:242–48.

132. *Lanterne of Li3t Edited from MS Harl. 2324,* ed. Lilian M. Swinburn, EETS o.s. 151, 1917, 17; see Fiona Somerset, "Expanding the Langlandian Canon: Radical Latin and the Stylistics of Reform," *YLS* 17 (2003): 73–92.

133. Tim William Machan, *English in the Middle Ages* (Oxford: Oxford University Press, 2003), argues that without a "standard" version of the vernacular, a "dialect" became a figure of social tension identified through regional variety.

134. Meale, "Patrons, Buyers and Owners: Book Production and Social Status," 223 n. 13, suggests that Henry V's 1421 order for twelve hunting books, perhaps as gifts, would have included Edward of York's translation of *Livre de la Chasse.*

135. McNiven, *Heresy and Politics in the Reign of Henry IV: The Burning of John Badby,* 199–219 at 203. See also E. F. Jacob, *The Fifteenth Century, 1399–1485* (Oxford: Clarendon, 1961), 95–96.

136. Michael Foucault, *Discipline and Punish: The Birth of the Prison,* trans. Alan Sheridan (New York: Vintage Books, 1979), 32–69, and Strohm, *England's Empty Throne,* "Heretic Burning: The Lollard as Menace and Victim," 32–62 at 53–57.

137. Recent examinations include Malcolm Barber, *The Cathars: Dualist Heretics in Languedoc in the High Middle Ages* (New York: Longman, 2000); Stephen O'Shea, *The Perfect Heresy: The Revolutionary Life and Death of the Cathars* (New York: Walker & Co., 2000); and René Weis, *The Yellow Cross: The Story of the Last Cathars, 1290–1329* (New York: Knopf, 2001).

138. John H. Arnold, "Lollard Trials and Inquisitorial Discourse," *Fourteenth-Century England II,* ed. Chris Given-Wilson (Woodbridge: Boydell, 2002), 81–94 at 93; he nonetheless notes a "haunting familiarity" between the Languedoc and Norwich heresy trials.

139. Jones et al., *Who Murdered Chaucer?* "Richard's Extraordinary Epitaph," 92–95, raises questions about dating, whether 1395 at the time of the tomb's commission or 1414 at the time of Richard's reburial by Henry V. See also "Chaucer's Last Bloody Year," 137–45, on the violent methods of Henry IV as opposed to the relative restraint of Richard II.

140. *Annales Ricardi Secundi et Henrici Quarti,* ed. Henry Thomas Riley (London: Rolls Series, 1866), 183. J. A. Tuck, "Carthusian Monks and Lollard Knights: Religious Attitude at the Court of Richard II," *Studies in the Age of Chaucer, Proceedings, No. 1, 1984: Reconstructing Chaucer,* ed. Paul Strohm and Thomas J. Heffernan (Knoxville: New Chaucer Society, 1985), 149–61 at 153 for the king's epitaph.

141. Harriss, *Shaping the Nation,* "The Persecution of Lollardy," 395–402, wonders whether most examinations of suspects were merely *pro forma* responses.

142. Norman P. Tanner, ed., *Heresy Trials in the Diocese of Norwich, 1428–31* (London: Camden, 4th ser., vol. 20, 1977). See also Ruth Nissé, "Grace under Pressure: Conduct and Representation in the Norwich Heresy Trials," *Medieval Conduct,* ed. Kathleen Ashley and Robert L. A. Clark (Minneapolis: University of Minnesota Press, 2001), 207–25.

143. R. N. Swanson, "Literacy, Heresy, History and Orthodoxy: Perspectives and Permutations for the Later Middle Ages," *Heresy and Literacy,* ed. Biller and Hudson, 279–93 at 279.

144. Nicholas Love, *Mirror of the Blessed Life of Jesus Christ,* ed. Michael G. Sargent (New York: Garland Medieval Texts, no. 18, 1992), xlv. See also A. I. Doyle, "Reflections on Some Manuscripts of Nicholas Love's *Myrrour of the Blessed Lyf of Jesu Christ,*" *LSE* n.s. 14 (1983): 82–93; Vincent Gillespie, "Vernacular Books of Religion," *Book Production,* ed. Griffiths and Pearsall, 317–44 at 323–24; and Kantik Ghosh, "Manuscripts of Nicholas Love's *The Mirror of the Blessed Life of Jesus Christ* and Wycliffite Notions of 'Authority,'" *Prestige, Authority and Power,* ed. Riddy, 17–54.

145. Annie Sutherland, "*The Chastising of God's Children*: A Neglected Text," *Text and Controversy from Wyclif to Bale,* ed. Barr and Hutchison, 353–73.

146. Lindenbaum, "London Texts and Literary Practice," 298, and Justice, "Lollardy," *Cambridge History of Medieval English Literature,* ed. Wallace, 677–78.

147. Manly and Rickert, eds., *The Canterbury Tales,* 1:152–55, and G. L. Harriss, *Cardinal Beaufort: A Study of Lancastrian Ascendancy and Decline* (Oxford: Clarendon, 1988), 120.

148. Strohm, *Theory and the Premodern Text,* "Henry IV as Social Alchemist," 42–45.

149. Maureen Jurkowski, "Lancastrian Royal Service, Lollardy and Forgery: The Career of Thomas Tykhill," *Crown, Government, and People in the Fifteenth Century,* ed. Rowena E. Archer (New York: St. Martin's, 1995), 33–52, and "Lollardy in Oxfordshire and Northamptonshire: The Two Thomas Compworths," *Lollards and Their Influence,* ed. Somerset, Havens, and Pitard, 73–95. See McFarlane, *John Wycliffe,* 160–85, and Aston, *Lollards and Reformers,* 24–38, on the ramifications of the abortive Oldcastle rebellion.

150. Gordon Leff, *Heresy in the Later Middle Ages,* 2 vols. (Manchester: Manchester University Press, 1967), 2:559–605, and Hudson, "Wycliffism in Oxford."

151. Middleton, "Audience and Public," 109.

152. Hudson, *Premature Reformation,* 55–58.

153. *Reginald Pecock's Book of Faith,* ed. J. L. Morison (Glasgow: J. Maclehose & Sons, 1909), 114. See Charles W. Brockwell, Jr., *Bishop Reginald Pecock and the Lancastrian Church: Securing the Foundations of Cultural Authority* (Lewiston, NY: Edwin Mellen Press, 1985); Wendy Scase, *Reginald Pecock* (Aldershot: Variorum Authors of the Middle Ages, vol. 3, no. 8, 1996); Johnston, *Clerks and Courtiers,* "Reginald Pecock and the Tragedy of Clerkly Ambition," 359–74; Mishtooni Bose, "Reginald Pecock's Vernacular Voice," *Lollards and Their Influence,* ed. Somerset, Havens, and Pitard, 217–36; and Kantik Ghosh, "Bishop Reginald Pecock and the Idea of 'Lollardy,'" *Text and Controversy from Wyclif to Bale,* ed. Barr and Hutchison, 252–65.

154. Hudson, *Premature Reformation,* 408.

155. Ibid.

156. Doyle, "Manuscripts of *Piers Plowman,*" 36.

157. Anne Hudson, "The Examination of Lollards" (1973), *Lollards and Their Books,* 125–40, and "Preface," *Lollards and Their Influence,* ed. Somerset, Havens, and Pitard, 3.

158. Brewer, *Editing "Piers Plowman,"* "The Early English Text Society and Its Editorial Context," 65–90; Frederick J. Furnivall wrote bluntly about these nationalist

objectives: "The study of the national literature has a moral effect as well. *It is the true ground and foundation of patriotism . . .*" (73).

159. A. V. C. Schmidt, *"Ars* or *Scientia*? Reflections on Editing *Piers Plowman,"* *YLS* 18 (2004): 31–54, provides the most current status report.

160. Kathryn Kerby-Fulton and Denise L. Despres, *Iconography and the Professional Reader: The Politics of Book Production in the Douce "Piers Plowman"* (Minneapolis: University of Minnesota Press, 1999).

161. Hanna, "Emendations to a 1993 'Vita de Ne'erdowel,'" 194, includes a new fragment of Prologue 1–4 found by Thorlac Turville-Petre at the Public Record Office.

162. For English-language prose works, there are over 230 copies of the Wycliffite Bible and at least 169 manuscripts of the *Brut*; see Lister M. Matheson, "The Middle English Prose *Brut*: A Location List of the Manuscripts and Early Printed Editions," *Analytical and Enumerative Bibliography* 3 (1979): 254–66.

163. Pearsall, "Manuscripts and Illustrations," *Companion to Gower,* ed. Echard, 95.

164. Doyle, "Manuscripts of *Piers Plowman,"* 47–48; see also Bowers, "Two Professional Readers of Chaucer and Langland: Scribe D and the HM 114 Scribe."

165. Nicholas Watson, "Censorship and Cultural Change in Late-Medieval England: Vernacular Theology, the Oxford Translation Debate, and Arundel's Constitutions of 1409," *Speculum* 70 (1995): 822–64 at 825–26, and Simpson, *Reform,* 333–43.

166. A. I. Doyle, "Recent Directions in Medieval Manuscript Study," *New Directions in Later Medieval Manuscript Studies,* ed. Pearsall, 1–14: "I started in English literature by trying to discover who were the earliest readers and hearers of the late fourteenth-century alliterative poem of *Piers Plowman . . .* when I decided that I could not find enough direct and indirect evidence about that work" (1).

167. Doyle, "The Manuscripts," 90 and 88. See, for example, Thorlac Turville-Petre, "The Author of *The Destruction of Troy,"* *MÆ* 57 (1988): 264–69.

168. Hudson, "Lollard Book Production," 129.

169. Wendy Scase, "Reginald Pecock, John Carpenter and John Colop's 'Common-Profit' Books: Aspects of Book Ownership and Circulation in Fifteenth-Century London," *MÆ* 61 (1992): 261–74 at 268–70.

170. Graham Pollard, "The Company of Stationers before 1557," *The Library* 4th ser., 18 (1937): 1–38 at 14, and Hudson, *Premature Reformation,* 206. Strohm, *England's Empty Throne,* 65–86, casts much doubt on the reliability of these accounts of Oldcastle.

171. Maureen Jurkowski, "Lollard Book Producers in London in 1414," *Text and Controversy from Wyclif to Bale,* ed. Barr and Hutchison, 201–26.

172. Harris, "Patrons, Buyers and Owners," 169. For example, the early sixteenth-century Kentish monk William Holyngborne added his name to Harley 6041 (fol. 96b); see *The A Version,* ed. Kane, 7. Walter W. Skeat, ed., *The Vision of William Concerning Piers Plowman: The B Text,* EETS o.s. 38, 1869, vii–viii, indicates a memorandum on the last leaf of Laud Misc. 581 (fol. 93a): "Raffe Coppynges. Mem. þat I

haue lent to Nicholas brigham the pers ploughman wech I borowed of Mr Le of Addyngton." Nicholas Brigham (d. 1558) was the Marian loyalist and antiquarian who built Westminster Abbey's marble altar-tomb in which Chaucer's bones were placed about 1556. Bale's *Index,* 383 and 479, indicates Brigham knew *Mum and the Sothsegger* in addition to possessing two copies of *Piers Plowman.*

173. Anne Hudson, ed., *Two Wycliffite Texts: The Sermon of William Taylor 1406, The Testimony of William Thorpe 1407,* EETS o.s. 301, 1993, "Introduction: The Sermon of William Taylor," xi–xxvi. It should be noted that almost all non-Wycliffite sermon collections before 1415 were also anonymous, with the well-known exception of John Mirk's *Festial.* See Martyn F. Wakelin, "The Manuscripts of John Mirk's *Festial,*" *LSE* n.s. 1 (1967): 93–118.

174. See Uhart, "The Early Reception of *Piers Plowman.*"

175. Matthew Giancarlo, *"Piers Plowman,* Parliament, and the Public Voice," *YLS* 17 (2003): 135–74 at 141, identifies Sir William Hoo as the son of Sir Thomas Hoo, who experienced a prophetic dream eerily like Will's while attending a session of Parliament; see Anthony Goodman, "Sir Thomas Hoo and the Parliament of 1376," *Bulletin of the Institute of Historical Research* 41 (1968): 139–49.

176. The text begins without title (fol. 113a) and ends in black-ink lettering not much larger than the main hand, "Explicit visio petri ploughman" (fol. 205a). HM 128 is described in *The B Version,* ed. Kane, 9–10; Benson and Blanchfield, *Manuscripts of "Piers Plowman": The B-Version,* 106–11; and *The "Piers Plowman" Electronic Archive: San Marino, Huntington Library, HM 128,* ed. Michael Calabrese, with Hoyt N. Duggan and Thorlac Turville-Petre (forthcoming).

177. Doyle, "Manuscripts of *Piers Plowman,*" 46 n. 43.

178. Russell and Kane, eds., *The C Version,* 5.

179. Personal correspondence from A. I. Doyle (20 August 1990). See also Kane and Donaldson, eds., *The B Version,* 12, and Benson and Blanchfield, *Manuscripts of "Piers Plowman": The B-Version,* 87.

180. Doyle, "Manuscripts of *Piers Plowman,*" 43 n. 30.

181. Dutschke, *Guide to Medieval and Renaissance Manuscripts in the Huntington Library,* 1:183–84. See Russell, "As They Read It," 188 n. 8, and Hanna, *William Langland,* 41: "Copied by Thomas Dankastre (Lancastre?)."

182. Uhart, "The Early Reception of *Piers Plowman,*" 279–80.

183. Cok's extract agrees textually with CUL Ff.5.35 containing a complete C-text. See Doyle, "Survey of Origins," "John Shirley, John Cok, and St. Bartholomew's Close," 2:200–202; Doyle, "Manuscripts of *Piers Plowman,*" 45; and Russell and Kane, eds., *The C Version,* 2–3.

184. A. I. Doyle and M. B. Parkes, "The Production of Copies of the *Canterbury Tales* and the *Confessio Amantis* in the Early Fifteenth Century," *Medieval Scribes, Manuscripts and Libraries: Essays Presented to N. R. Ker,* ed. Parkes and Watson, 163–210. Linne R. Mooney, "Professional Scribes? Identifying English Scribes Who Had a Hand in More Than One Manuscript," *New Directions in Later Medieval Manuscript Studies,* ed. Pearsall, 131–41, proposes seeking a fuller record of productions by individual scribes.

185. In addition to the two studies already cited, C. Paul Christianson has pursued this investigation in *Memorials of the Book Trade in Medieval London* (Cambridge: D. S. Brewer, 1987), and "Evidence for the Study of London's Late Medieval Manuscripts-Book Trade," *Book Production,* ed. Griffiths and Pearsall, 87–108.

186. *Piers Plowman: The Z Version,* ed. Rigg and Brewer, 3–5. See also Brewer and Rigg, eds., *Piers Plowman: A Facsimile of the Z-Text,* 25.

187. Scase, "A Wycliffite Libel and the Naming of Heretics," 25.

188. Doyle, "Manuscripts of *Piers Plowman,*" 37, and Ralph Hanna III, "Studies in the Manuscripts of *Piers Plowman,*" *YLS* 7 (1993): 1–25 at 21.

189. Hanna, *Pursuing History,* "MS. Bodley 851 and the Dissemination of *Piers Plowman,*" 195–202.

190. Doyle, "Manuscripts of *Piers Plowman,*" 38 and 48.

191. Ibid., 42–43, and Uhart, "The Early Reception of *Piers Plowman,*" 315–16.

192. Bowers, "Langland's *Piers Plowman* in HM 143: Copy, Commentary, Censorship." Uhart, "The Early Reception of *Piers Plowman,*" 332–39, provided a transcription of these sidenotes improved by Grindley, "Reading *Piers Plowman* C-Text Annotations: Notes toward the Classification of Printed and Written Marginalia in Texts from the British Isles 1300–1641," 127–35.

193. Kerby-Fulton, "Professional Readers of Langland," 109–11, suggests that the handwriting also connects the manuscript with Chancery clerks. See also Benson and Blanchfield, *Manuscripts of "Piers Plowman": The B-Version,* 208–26. A. I. Doyle, "Ushaw College, Durham, MS 50: Fragments of the *Prick of Conscience,* by the Same Scribe as Oxford, Corpus Christi College, MS 201, of the B Text of *Piers Plowman,*" *English Medieval Book,* ed. Edwards, Gillespie, and Hanna, 43–49.

194. Russell, "As They Read It," 182–83, and Carl Grindley, "A New Fragment of *Piers Plowman* C Text?" *YLS* 11 (1997): 135–40. Hanna, *William Langland,* 34–35, shows a surprising number of Langland manuscripts associated with monasteries.

195. A. I. Doyle, "The Shaping of the Vernon and Simeon Manuscripts," *Chaucer and Middle English Studies in Honor of Rossell Hope Robbins,* ed. Beryl Rowland (London: Allen & Unwin, 1974), 328–41 at 331, and Middleton, "The Audience and Public," 105–6.

196. Andrew Galloway, "*Piers Plowman* and the Schools," *YLS* 6 (1992): 89–107 at 101, references Nita Scudder Baugh, "A Worcestershire Miscellany Compiled by John Northwood, c. 1400, Edited from British Museum MS. Add. 37,787" (Philadelphia: Bryn Mawr College dissertation, 1956).

197. Thomas J. Heffernan, "Orthodoxies' *Redux*: The *Northern Homily Cycle* in the Vernon Manuscript and Its Textual Affiliations," *Studies in the Vernon Manuscript,* ed. Derek Pearsall (Cambridge: D. S. Brewer, 1990), 75–87 at 79. See the back paste-in pages of *The Vernon Manuscript: A Facsimile of Bodleian Library, Oxford, MS English Poet.a.1,* intro. A. I. Doyle (Cambridge: D. S. Brewer, 1987), for "Summary Contents-List of Vernon."

198. John A. Burrow, "The Audience of *Piers Plowman,*" *Anglia* 75 (1957): 373–84 at 378.

199. Middleton, "The Audience and Public of *Piers Plowman,*" 104.

200. Kerby-Fulton, "Langland and the Bibliographic Ego," 122.

201. Rees Davies, "The Life, Travels, and Library of an Early Reader of *Piers Plowman,*" *YLS* 13 (1999): 49–64; see Leonard E. Boyle, "The *Oculus Sacerdotis* and Some Other Works of William of Pagula," *TRHS* 5th ser., 5 (1955): 81–110. Jurkowski, "Lawyers and Lollardy in the Early Fifteenth Century," thinks that legal professionals shared the Lollards' hostility toward the Caesarian clergy out of a sense of professional rivalry.

202. Foucault, *Discipline and Punish,* 276. Vincent Gillespie, "The Mole in the Vineyard: Wyclif at Syon in the Fifteenth Century," *Text and Controversy from Wyclif to Bale,* ed. Barr and Hutchison, 131–62, shows how unorthodox texts could infiltrate a pious institutional collection.

203. Dobson, ed., *The Peasants' Revolt,* 303.

204. Deanesly, *Lollard Bible,* 445, 278–79, and 437–38. See also Susan Groag Bell, "Medieval Women Book Owners: Arbiters of Lay Piety and Ambassadors of Culture," *Women and Power in the Middle Ages,* ed. Mary Erler and Maryanne Kowaleski (Athens, GA, and London: University of Georgia Press, 1988), 149–87 at 177.

205. Hudson, "The Debate on Bible Translation, Oxford 1401" (1975), *Lollards and Their Books,* 67–84 at 71, and *Premature Reformation,* 248. For a broad survey of practices, see David Lawton, "Englishing the Bible, 1066–1549," *Cambridge History of Medieval English Literature,* ed. Wallace, 545–82, and Fiona Somerset, "Professionalizing Translation at the Turn of the Fifteenth Century: Ullerston's *Determinacio,* Arundel's *Constitutiones,*" *The Vulgar Tongue: Medieval and Postmedieval Vernacularity,* ed. Fiona Somerset and Nicolas Watson (University Park: Pennsylvania State University Press, 2003), 145–57.

206. John Wyclif, *De Triplici Vinculo Amoris,* in *Polemical Works in Latin,* ed. Rudolf Buddensieg, 2 vols. (London: Wyclif Society, 1883), 168; my translation. See Deanesly, *Lollard Bible,* 248, and Hudson, "Lollardy: The English Heresy?" *Lollards and Their Books,* 154. For women's use of the vernacular, see František Šmahel, "Literacy and Heresy in Hussite Bohemia," *Heresy and Literacy,* ed. Biller and Hudson, 237–54; Alfred Thomas, *Anne's Bohemia: Czech Literature and Society, 1310–1420* (Minneapolis: University of Minnesota Press, 1998), esp. 33–49; and Taylor, "Anne of Bohemia and the Making of Chaucer."

207. Hudson, ed., *English Wycliffite Writings,* 67–72 at 71.

208. Ralph Hanna, "English Biblical Texts before Lollardy and Their Fate," *Lollards and Their Influence,* ed. Somerset, Havens, and Pitard, 141–53.

209. Dillon and St. John Hope, "Inventory of the Goods and Chattels Belonging to Thomas, Duke of Gloucester," esp. 281 and 300–302: "un bible en Engleys," "un livre Dengleis de les evangelies," and "un novel livre de les Evangelies gloseȝ en Engleis." The illustrated Bible survives as BL Egerton MS 617–18.

210. Wolfenbüttel, Herzog-August Bibliothek MS Guelf.Aug.A.2.

211. Meale, "Patrons, Buyers and Owners," 203.

212. Oxford Bodley MS 277 is marked on its modern binding "Bible Wickcliffe." See Doyle, "English Books in and out of Court," 168–69, and Krochalis, "The Books and Reading of Henry V and His Circle," 51 and 69.

213. Hanna, *London Literature,* 311–12, provides other evidence that includes Gaunt's sponsorship of Wyclif, Thomas of Woodstock's ownership of four Lollard books, Henry IV's strenuous anticlericalism, and the Lollard knight Sir John Cheyne's membership in the council until 1410.

214. Conrad Lindberg, "The Manuscripts and Versions of the Wycliffite Bible: A Preliminary Survey," *Studia Neophilologica* 42 (1970): 333–47.

215. Hanna, "English Biblical Texts before Lollardy and Their Fate," 151–53.

216. Watson, "Censorship and Cultural Change," 856–57, and Hudson, *Premature Reformation,* 420.

217. Malcolm Lambert, *Medieval Heresy: Popular Movements from Bogomil to Hus* (New York: Holmes & Meier, 1977), 257–59; Hudson, *Premature Reformation,* 129–33; Shannon McSheffrey, *Gender and Heresy: Women and Men in Lollard Communities, 1420–1530* (Philadelphia: University of Pennsylvania Press, 1995), "Prominent Women in Lollardy," 109–24; and Steiner, *Documentary Culture,* "Lollard Rhetoric and the Written Word: Margery Baxter and William Thorpe," 229–39.

218. Manly and Rickert, eds., *Canterbury Tales,* 1:610, record that around 1460 the Suffolk man Thomas Stotevyle bequeathed six literary books that included both "Petrus Plowman" and the "Narraciones Cantuarienses" or *Canterbury Tales.* For a full listing, see Hanna, *William Langland,* 34–36. Jonathan Hughes, *Pastors and Visionaries: Religion and Secular Life in Late Medieval Yorkshire* (Woodbridge: Boydell & Brewer, 1988), 205, finds another reference to *Piers* in the will of John Kendale, vicar choral of York Minster in 1409.

219. Robert A. Wood, "A Fourteenth-Century London Owner of *Piers Plowman,*" *MÆ* 53 (1984): 83–90.

220. James Crompton, "Leicestershire Lollards," *Transactions of the Leicestershire Archaeological and Historical Society* 44 (1968/69): 11–44 at 11–14; Martin, "Knighton's Lollards," *Lollardy and the Gentry,* ed. Aston and Richmond, 28–40; and Justice, "Lollardy," *Cambridge History of Medieval English Literature,* ed. Wallace, 668–69.

221. Wood, "Fourteenth-Century London Owner," 84; see McFarlane, *Lancastrian Kings and Lollard Knights,* 207–20. This view has been adjusted by Thomson, "Knightly Piety and the Margins of Lollardy," 106: "Requests for a humble burial can be found in wills of individuals whose orthodoxy cannot be questioned."

222. Kathryn Kerby-Fulton, "The Women Readers in Langland's Earliest Audience: Some Codicological Evidence," *Learning and Literacy in Medieval England and Abroad,* ed. Sarah Rees Jones (Turnhout: Brepols, 2003), 121–34, draws attention to evidence of women readers or women owners for six *Piers* manuscripts, though only Lady Anne Fortescue in 1532 showed herself an engaged reader in Digby 145. Nicolette Zeeman, "'Studying' in the Middle Ages—and in *Piers Plowman,*" *NML* 3 (1999): 185–212 at 200–212, explores a discipline open to women because free of the classroom, while Ralph Hanna III, "School and Scorn: Gender in *Piers Plowman,*" *NML* 3 (1999): 213–27, looks at ways that medieval schooling maimed the masculinity of figures such as Will the Dreamer.

223. Wood, "Fourteenth-Century London Owner," 88. Bell, "Medieval Women Book Owners," 160, believes that devotional literature was viewed as less offensive

by Church officials because of its private nature; see Aston, "Devotional Literacy," *Lollards and Reformers,* 122–25. More evidence of female book-owning practices is provided by Mary C. Erler, "Exchange of Books between Nuns and Laywomen: Three Surviving Examples," *New Science out of Old Books,* ed. Beadle and Piper, 361–73.

224. Aston, "Lollard Women Priests?" *Lollards and Reformers,* 49–70, and Claire Cross, "'Great Reasoners in Scripture': The Activities of Women Lollards, 1380–1530," *Medieval Women,* ed. Derek Baker (Oxford: Blackwell, 1978), 359–80.

225. Hoccleve, *Minor Poems,* 13 (lines 145–49).

226. *The Book of Margery Kempe,* 28, tells how she was threatened: "þow xalt be brent, fals lollare!" See Steiner, *Documentary Culture,* 240–46.

227. Dean, ed., *Six Ecclesiastical Satires,* 175 (line 869). Alastair Minnis, "'Respondet Waltherus Bryth . . .': Walter Brut in Debate on Women Priests," *Text and Controversy from Wyclif to Bale,* ed. Barr and Hutchison, 229–49, reviews one argument from the 1390s.

228. Hanna, *Pursuing History,* "Introduction," 1–17 at 9.

229. Middleton, "Audience and Public," 104.

230. University of London Library V.17's copy of *Piers Plowman* was originally accompanied by a copy of *Mandeville's Travels,* now a separate manuscript; see Doyle, "Manuscripts of *Piers Plowman,*" 44.

231. Benson and Blanchfield, *Manuscripts of "Piers Plowman": The B-Version,* 57, and Russell and Kane, eds., *The C Version,* 2.

232. Doyle, "Ushaw College, Durham, MS 50 Fragments of the *Prick of Conscience,*" has discovered a further instance of the same scribe copying *Piers,* though in a different manuscript. The significance of extracts from *Troilus* has been discussed by Julia Boffey, "Proverbial Chaucer and the Chaucer Canon," *Reading from the Margins,* ed. Lerer, 37–47.

233. Hanna and Lawton, eds., *Siege of Jerusalem,* lxviii–lxix.

234. Middleton, "Audience and Public," 105.

235. MS Bodley 851 includes predominantly satirical works such as Walter Map's *De Nugis Curialium, Apocalypsis Goliae,* and *Bridlington's Prophecy;* see Russell and Kane, eds., *The C Version,* 17. For a minor exception, see Thorlac Turville-Petre, "Poems by Chaucer in John Harpur's Psalter," *SAC* 21 (1999): 301–13.

236. Hanna, *Pursuing History,* "Booklets in Medieval Manuscripts," 21–34 at 24–25.

237. Russell and Kane, eds., *The C Version,* 8–9.

238. Rossell Hope Robbins, "Dissent in Middle English Literature: The Spirit of (Thirteen) Seventy-Six," *M&H* n.s. 9 (1979), 25–51 at 36. The ballad on the death of William de la Pole, Duke of Suffolk, is edited from this manuscript by Rossell Hope Robbins, ed., *Historical Poems of the XIVth and XVth Centuries* (New York: Columbia University Press, 1959), 187–89. Latin attacks on Lollards are printed by Wright, ed., *Political Poems and Songs,* 1:231–49 and 2:128.

239. Robbins, ed., *Historical Poems,* 154 (lines 49–56).

240. Hudson, *Premature Reformation*, 304, and J. C. T. Oates, "Richard Pynson and the Holy Blood of Hayles," *The Library* 5th ser., 13 (1958): 269–77.

241. Russell and Kane, eds., *The C Version*, 16.

242. J. Kail, ed., *Twenty-Six Political and Other Poems from Oxford MSS Digby 102 and Douce 322*, EETS o.s. 124, 1904, 29 (lines 76–80).

243. Tanya Schaap, "From Professional to Private Readership: A Discussion and Transcription of the Fifteenth- and Sixteenth-Century Marginalia in *Piers Plowman* C-Text, Oxford, Bodleian Library, MS Digby 102," *The Medieval Reader: Reception and Cultural History in the Late Medieval Manuscript*, ed. Kathryn Kerby-Fulton and Maidie Hilmo (New York: AMS Press, 2001), 81–116.

244. Middleton, "Audience and Public," 150.

245. Hudson, *Premature Reformation*, 95–97.

246. Mabel Day, ed., *The Wheatley Manuscript*, EETS o.s. 155, 1921, 19–59, and Valerie Edden, *Richard Maidstone's Penitential Psalms* (Heidelberg: Winter Middle English Texts, no. 22, 1990). See also Valerie Edden, "Richard Maidstone's *Penitential Psalms*," *Leeds Studies in English* n.s. 17 (1986): 77–94.

247. Kail, ed., *Twenty-Six Political and Other Poems*, 19 (lines 137–38).

248. Middleton, "Audience and Public," 108. See Janet Coleman, *Medieval Readers and Writers, 1350–1400* (New York: Columbia University Press, 1981), 98–111, on the twenty-four political poems.

249. Barr, ed., *The Piers Plowman Tradition*, 30–35, 205–10, 368–75 at 206 (lines 31–34).

250. Hudson, "The Legacy of *Piers Plowman*," 254.

251. Simon Horobin, "Harley 3954 and the Audience of *Piers Plowman*," *Medieval Texts in Context*, ed. Graham D. Caie and Denis Renevey (New York and London: Routledge, forthcoming), suggests East Anglian manufacture of A manuscripts including Bodley 851 (Z) and Society of Antiquaries 687 for local religious houses. See also Kane, ed., *The A Version*, 7–8, and Benson and Blanchfield, *Manuscripts of "Piers Plowman": The B-Version*, 72–75.

252. M. C. Seymour, "The Origin of the Egerton Version of *Mandeville's Travels*," *MÆ* 30 (1961): 159–69; Hanna, "Mandeville"; and Gransden, *Historical Writing in England*, 127.

253. Scott, *Later Gothic Manuscripts, 1390–1490*, 2:207–11 and 2:225–29 at 2:210.

254. Scott Lightsey, "Chaucer's Secular Marvels and the Medieval Economy of Wonder," *SAC* 23 (2001): 289–316, identifies a movement away from Mandeville's supernatural marvels to instances of mechanical trickery.

255. Hudson, *Premature Reformation*, 301–4.

256. Hanna, *Pursuing History*, "Booklets in Medieval Manuscripts," 24. Kane and Donaldson, eds., *The B Version*, 14; Hanna, *William Langland*, 39; and Benson and Blanchfield, *Manuscripts of "Piers Plowman": The B-Version*, 50–54.

257. *The Lay Folks Mass Book*, ed. Thomas Frederick Simmons, EETS o.s. 71, 1879.

258. Doyle, "Survey of the Origins," 30–35, judges the interpolations found in Lambeth 408 and York Cathedral XVI L 12 as Lollard features, while BL Add. 24202

is a "strongly Lollard volume." See also Moira Fitzgibbons, "Disruptive Simplicity: Gaytryge's Translation of Archbishop Thoresby's *Injunctions*," *The Vernacular Spirit: Essays on Medieval Religious Literature,* ed. Renate Blumenfeld-Kosinski, Duncan Robertson, and Nancy Bradley Warren (New York: Palgrave, 2002), 39–58.

259. Aston, "Lollardy and Literacy," 216, and Hudson, "A New Look at the *Lay Folks' Catechism.*"

260. Hanna, *Pursuing History,* "Producing Manuscripts and Editions," 63–82 at 76.

261. *Susannah: Alliterative Poem of the Fourteenth Century,* ed. Alice Miskimin (New Haven: Yale University Press, 1969), 22–24.

262. Kane, ed., *The A Version,* 8.

263. Hudson, ed., *English Wycliffite Writings,* 89–93 and 182–85; *Premature Reformation,* 335; and Cole, "William Langland's Lollardy," 35–37. See also Ralph Hanna III, "The Scribe of Huntington HM 114," *SB* 42 (1989): 120–33, and Bowers, "Two Professional Readers of Chaucer and Langland: Scribe D and the HM 114 Scribe," 129–45.

264. *The Holy Bible Made from the Latin Vulgate by John Wycliffe and His Followers,* ed. Josiah Forshall and Sir Frederic Madden, 4 vols. (Oxford: Oxford University Press, 1850), 3:662–67.

265. Justice, "Lollardy," 682–83, and Hudson, ed., *Two Wycliffite Texts,* "The Genre of Thorpe's Text," liii–lix. Lynn Staley Johnson, "Chaucer's Tale of the Second Nun and the Strategies of Dissent," *SP* 89 (1992): 314–33, considers St. Cecilia's courtroom defense as another anticipation of this Lollard genre.

266. Derek Pearsall, "Introduction," *Studies in the Vernon Manuscript,* x. For the placement of *Susannah,* see the rear paste-down "Summary Contents-List" in *Vernon Manuscript: A Facsimile,* intro. Doyle, which supersedes Mary S. Serjeantson, "The Index of the Vernon Manuscript," *MLR* 32 (1937): 222–61.

267. A. I. Doyle, "Stephen Dodesham of Witham and Sheen," *Of the Making of Books: Medieval Manuscripts, Their Scribes and Readers: Essays Presented to M. B. Parkes,* ed. P. R. Robinson and Rivkah Zim (Aldershot: Scolar Press, 1977), 94–115.

268. David Lyle Jeffrey, "Victimization and Legal Abuse: The Wycliffite Retelling of the Story of Susannah," *Retelling Tales: Essays in Honor of Russell Peck,* ed. Thomas Hahn and Alan Lupack (Cambridge: D. S. Brewer, 1997), 161–78 at 162–64.

269. Kane, ed., *The A Version,* 11–12. Derek Pearsall, "The 'Ilchester' Manuscript of *Piers Plowman,*" *NM* 82 (1981): 181–93 at 192, thinks Scribe D "may have had Lollard inclinations," while Merja Black, "A Scribal Translation of *Piers Plowman,*" *MÆ* 67 (1998): 257–90 at 269, suggests that changes in BL Harley 2376 also reflect Lollard attitudes locally in Herefordshire.

270. Robert E. Lewis and Angus McIntosh, *A Descriptive Guide to the Manuscripts of the "Prick of Conscience"* (Oxford: Medium Ævum Monographs, n.s. 12, 1982), 84–85.

271. Doyle, "Manuscripts of *Piers Plowman,*" 47, adds the *Speculum Vitae* and *South English Legendary* to this common profile. R. J. Lyall, "Materials: The Paper

Revolution," *Book Production,* ed. Griffiths and Pearsall, 11–29 at 14, concludes that the paper copies of *Prick* were most commonly owned by parish priests, members of religious orders, and pious layfolk.

272. Hudson, *Premature Reformation,* 464, 485, 205n.

273. Hope Emily Allen, ed., *English Writings of Richard Rolle, Hermit of Hampole* (Oxford: Clarendon, 1931), 393.

274. Hudson, "Preface," *Lollards and Their Influence,* ed. Somerset, Havens, and Pitard, 3.

275. Hudson, *Premature Reformation,* 426.

276. Hudson, "Lollard Book Production," 135.

277. Hudson, *Premature Reformation,* 31, and Kellogg and Talbert, "The Wycliffite *Pater Noster* and *Ten Commandments.*" See also Matthew, ed., *English Wycliffite Writings,* 197–202.

278. Cross, "Great Reasoners in Scripture," 363.

279. Hudson, *Premature Reformation,* 167.

280. *Lanterne of Liȝt,* viii–ix and 81–127; Claydon's own servant David Berde swore he had heard the book read aloud and recalled it contained the English exposition on the Commandments. See Aston, *Lollards and Reformers,* 149, and Hudson, "Lollard Book Production," 125–26.

281. Russell and Kane, eds., *The C Version,* 4.

282. Ralph Hanna III, "The Origins and Production of Westminster School MS. 3," *SB* 41 (1988): 197–218, esp. 206–12.

283. *Siege of Jerusalem Edited from MS Laud Misc. 656,* ed. E. Kölbing and Mabel Day, EETS o.s. 188, 1932, and *The Siege of Jerusalem,* ed. Ralph Hanna and David Lawton, EETS o.s. 320, 2003. See also J. R. Hulbert, "The Text of *The Siege of Jerusalem,*" *SP* 28 (1931): 602–12; Doyle, "The Manuscripts," *Middle English Alliterative Poetry,* ed. Lawton, 93–94; and Hanna, *Pursuing History,* "On Stemmatics," 83–93.

284. In addition to *Siege of Jerusalem,* Lambeth Palace MS 491 contains the prose *Brut,* unique English prose *Three Kings of Cologne,* alliterative *Awntyrs off Arthure,* verse *Book of Hunting,* and *Prick of Conscience.* For other descriptions of Lambeth 491 and HM 128, see Hanna and Lawton, eds., xx–xxiv.

285. Mary Hamel, "*The Siege of Jerusalem* as a Crusading Poem," *Journeys toward God: Pilgrimage and Crusade,* ed. Barbara N. Sargent-Baur (Kalamazoo: Medieval Institute Publications, 1992), 177–94, and Bonnie Millar, "*The Siege of Jerusalem*" in Its Physical, Literary and Historical Contexts (Dublin: Four Courts Press, 2000). Philippe de Mézières, *Letter to King Richard II: A Plea Made in 1395 for Peace between England and France,* ed. and trans. G. W. Coopland (Liverpool: Liverpool University Press, 1975), continued his appeal for a crusade; see Bowers, *The Politics of "Pearl,"* 34–35, 89–90, and figs. 4–5.

286. Chism, *Alliterative Revivals,* "Profiting from Precursors in *The Siege of Jerusalem,*" 155–88.

287. Richard Kyngeston, *Expeditions to Prussia and the Holy Land Made by Henry Earl of Derby (afterwards King Henry IV) in the Years 1390–1 and 1392–3,* ed. Lucy Toulmin Smith (London: Camden Society, n.s. 52, 1894), chronicles Henry's travels in the eastern Mediterranean. Anthony Tuck, "Henry IV and Chivalry," *Henry IV: The Estab-*

lishment of the Regime, 1399–1406, ed. Gwilym Dodd and Douglas Biggs (Woodbridge: Boydell & Brewer for York Medieval Press, 2003), 55–71, suggest that this "grand tour" gave an opportunity for Henry to establish the international network that supported diplomatically his later usurpation.

288. Allmand, *Henry V,* 174.

289. Hanna and Lawton, eds., *Siege of Jerusalem,* xxvii.

290. Malcolm Hebron, *The Medieval Siege: Theme and Image in Middle English Romance* (Oxford: Clarendon, 1997), "The Siege of Jerusalem," 112–35.

291. Ralph Hanna III, "Contextualizing *The Siege of Jerusalem,*" *YLS* 6 (1992): 109–21 at 119–20: "After 1402, Lollard sectarians who did violence to God's body similar to that attributed to the Jews . . . became 'fair game.'"

292. This forms part of the complex analysis of Chism's chapter in *Alliterative Revivals.*

293. I exclude Thomas Usk from the ranks of Chaucerian imitators because the prose *Testament of Love* never really departs from the predominant influence of Boethius. Though Sir John Clanvowe quotes a single line from the Knight's Tale when it was still the free-standing "Love of Palamon and Arcite," his *Boke of Cupide* remains closer to the French tradition of Deschamps and may actually have influenced Chaucer's own *LGW* Prologue. I also exclude John Gower, who was the senior poet and may have influenced Chaucer more than the other way around. Yeager, ed., *Chaucer and Gower,* includes several essays that draw attention to this direction of indebtedness: Chauncey Wood, "Chaucer's Most 'Gowerian' Tale," 75–84; Peter Nicholson, "Chaucer Borrows from Gower: The Sources of the *Man of Law's Tale,*" 85–99; and Peter G. Beidler, "Transformations in Gower's *Tale of Florent* and Chaucer's *Wife of Bath's Tale,*" 100–114.

294. Holsinger, "Langland's Musical Reader," 101 on date and 132–34 on Lollard features.

295. Schmidt, ed., viii: "The inclusion of the Z-text implies my acceptance of its Langlandian authorship as overwhelmingly likely." James Simpson, "The Power of Impropriety: Authorial Naming in *Piers Plowman,*" *William Langland's "Piers Plowman,"* ed. Hewett-Smith, 145–65, on the nameless writer's invitation to communal authorship.

296. Calabrese, "Corrections, Interventions, and Erasures in Huntington MS Hm 143 (X)," demonstrates how Hand 2's corrections have the effect of rewriting even in the manuscript that has served as the copy-text for all three modern editions of C.

297. For a specific examination of this famous heretic, see David Aers, "Walter Brut's Theology of the Sacrament of the Altar," *Lollards and Their Influence,* ed. Somerset, Havens, and Pitard, 115–26.

298. George Kane, "Some Fourteenth-Century 'Political' Poems," *Medieval English Religious and Ethical Literature,* ed. Kratzmann and Simpson, 82–91 at 89–90.

299. Dean, ed., *Six Ecclesiastical Satires,* 24 (lines 528–32). David Lampe, "The Satiric Strategy of *Peres the Ploughmans Crede,*" *The Alliterative Tradition in the Fourteenth Century,* ed. Bernard S. Levy and Paul E. Szarmach (Kent, OH: Kent State University Press, 1981), 69–80; Penn R. Szittya, *The Antifraternal Tradition in Medieval Literature*

(Princeton: Princeton University Press, 1986), 199–230; and Barr, *Signes and Sothe: The Language in the "Piers Plowman" Tradition,* esp. 83–94.

300. Matti Peikola, "'And after all, myn Aue-Marie almost to the ende': *Pierce the Ploughman's Crede* and Lollard Expositions of the Ave Maria," *ES* 81 (2000): 273–92, explicates features of the poem readily recognized as problems by Wycliffite readers.

301. John Scattergood, "*Pierce the Ploughman's Crede*: Lollardy and Texts," *Lollardy and the Gentry,* ed. Aston and Richmond, 77–94.

302. Dean, ed., *Six Ecclesiastical Satires,* 28 (lines 657–63); see also Hudson, "*Laicus Litteratus,*" 222–23.

303. Skeat, ed., *Chaucerian and Other Pieces,* xxxi–xxxv, and Von Nolcken, "*Piers Plowman,* the Wycliffites, and *Pierce the Plowman's Creed,*" 90–94.

304. Walter W. Skeat, *The Chaucer Canon* (Oxford: Clarendon, 1900), 99–100. See also Andrew Wawn, "The Genesis of *The Plowman's Tale,*" *YES* 2 (1972): 21–40.

305. Hudson, *Premature Reformation,* 97; and Somerset, *Clerical Discourse and Lay Audience,* "The *Upland Series* and the Invention of Invective, 1350–1410," 135–78, and "Appendix: The Dating of the *Upland* Series," 216–20.

306. Barr, ed., *The Piers Plowman Tradition,* 14–22, detects a reference to the Cirencester uprising that suggests the poem was written some months after the accession of Henry IV in 1400 (16 and 261).

307. Doyle, "An Unrecognized Piece of *Piers the Ploughman's Creed* and Other Work by Its Scribe." For the career of this antiquarian, see *John Stow (1525–1605) and the Making of the English Past,* ed. Ian Gadd and Alexandra Gillespie (London: British Library, 2004).

308. Dean, ed., *Six Ecclesiastical Satires,* 1. See also Doyle, "The Manuscripts," 98, and Barr, ed., *The Piers Plowman Tradition,* 8–14.

309. Russell and Kane, eds., *The C Version,* 12.

310. Doyle, "The Manuscripts," 98. Wolfe found the language difficult enough to require a brief glossary on the last leaf. The front plate of this 1553 edition of the *Crede* illustrates the double suicide of Pyramus and Thisbe, clearly makeshift and purely ornamental.

311. Kendall, *Drama of Dissent,* 73–80, and Hudson, "Legacy of *Piers Plowman,*" 255–56.

312. Kerby-Fulton and Justice, "Langlandian Reading Circles," 70–73, include John But in their conspectus of scribal enthusiasts.

313. Hanna, *Pursuing History,* 195–214, has summarized the state of the problem with the Z-text and the Ilchester Prologue.

314. Kerby-Fulton, "Langland and the Bibliographic Ego," 70, announces this exploration of the *apologia* "written in a particular historical context in response to the pressures, political, ecclesiastical and authorial, created, among other things, by the misappropriation of his poem by rebels in 1381."

315. Kerby-Fulton and Justice, "Langlandian Reading Circles," 72–73.

316. Skeat, ed., *Piers the Plowman,* 2:lxxxiv–lxxxv.

317. Kane and Donaldson, eds., *The B Version,* 4, and Benson and Blanchfield, *Manuscripts of "Piers Plowman": The B-Version,* 44–48 and 137–43.

318. Kerby-Fulton and Justice, "Langlandian Reading Circles," 76–80.

319. Galloway, "*Piers Plowman* and the Schools," 100–104, compares these scientific contents to the Oxford notebook of the Cistercian monk Richard Dove; see David Bell, "A Cistercian at Oxford: Richard Dove of Buckfast and London BL Sloane 513," *Studia Monastica* 31 (1989): 69–87. For the treatises on arithmetic and physiognomy, see Robert Steele, ed., *The Earliest Arithmetics in English,* EETS e.s. 118, 1922, v; Jeanne Krochalis and Edward Peters, eds. and trans., *The World of Piers Plowman* (Philadelphia: University of Pennsylvania Press, 1975), 218–28; and generally Linda Ehrsam Voights, "Scientific and Medical Books," *Book Production,* ed. Griffiths and Pearsall, 345–402.

320. *Mum and the Sothsegger,* ed. Mabel Day and Robert Steele, EETS o.s. 199, 1936; see now Barr, ed., *The Piers Plowman Tradition,* 14–22, 101–33, 247–91.

321. Don Embree, "*Richard the Redeless* and *Mum and the Sothsegger*: A Case of Mistaken Identity," *N&Q* 220 (1975): 4–12, and Helen Barr, "The Relationship of *Richard the Redeless* and *Mum and the Sothsegger*: Some New Evidence," *YLS* 4 (1990): 105–33. See also Barr, *Socioliterary Practice in Late Medieval England,* 63–79.

322. Bowers, "*Piers Plowman*'s William Langland," 87–89. Simon Horobin, "The Dialect and Authorship of *Richard the Redeless* and *Mum and the Sothsegger,*" *YLS* 18 (2004): 133–52, confirms the Bristol dialect for both poems.

323. Also probably a punning reference to the Dominican William Jordan (*Piers* B.13.270 and 13.84); see Hanna, *William Langland,* 13. For details on the goldsmith Chichester's career, see T. F. Reddaway, *Early History of the Goldsmiths' Company,* 289–92.

324. Barr, ed., *The Piers Plowman Tradition,* 101 (lines 8–12).

325. Arthur B. Ferguson, "The Problem of Counsel in *Mum and the Sothsegger,*" *Studies in the Renaissance* 2 (1955): 67–83; Alcuin G. Blamires, "*Mum and the Sothsegger* and Langlandian Idiom," *NM* 76 (1975): 583–604; Andrew N. Wawn, "Truth-telling and the Tradition of *Mum and the Sothsegger,*" *YES* 13 (1983): 270–87; and Barr, *Socioliterary Practice in Late Medieval England,* 158–87.

326. Barr, ed., *The Piers Plowman Tradition,* 22–30, 137–202, 291–368.

327. Ibid., 27.

328. *Mum and the Sothsegger* (lines 416–20), ed. Barr, *The Piers Plowman Tradition,* 152. See also Peter McNiven, "Rebellion, Sedition, and the Legend of Richard II's Survival," *BJRL* 76 (1994): 93–117, and Philip Morgan, "Henry IV and the Shadow of Richard II," *Crown, Government, and People,* ed. Archer, 1–31.

329. Dean, ed., *Six Ecclesiastical Satires,* 122 (line 68).

330. P. L. Heyworth, ed., *Jack Upland, Friar Daw's Reply, and Upland's Rejoinder* (Oxford: Oxford University Press, 1968), 65 (lines 244–50), 65 (lines 251–56), and 71 (lines 390–93).

331. Hudson, *Premature Reformation,* 97 and 146, discusses Woodford's *Responsiones ad Questiones LXV* in Oxford Bodley MS 703.

332. Hudson, "'No Newe Thyng': The Printing of Medieval Texts in the Early Reformation Period" (1983), *Lollards and Their Books,* 227–48 at 239–40.

333. P. L. Heyworth, "The Earliest Black-Letter Editions of *Jack Upland,*" *HLQ* 30 (1967): 307–14.

334. John A. F. Thomson, "John Foxe and Some Sources for Lollard History: Notes for a Critical Appraisal," *Studies in Church History* 2 (1965): 251–57.

335. Chaucer, *The Works (1532) with Supplementary Material from the Editions of 1542, 1561, 1598 and 1602,* facsimile ed., Brewer, fols. 348a–50b.

336. Somerset, *Clerical Discourse and Lay Audience,* "The Dating of the *Upland* Series," 216–20.

337. Dean, ed., *Six Ecclesiastical Satires,* 169 (lines 660–62), and also 154 (line 157).

338. Ibid., 145–47. Fiona Somerset, "Here, There, and Everywhere? Wycliffite Conceptions of the Eucharist and Chaucer's 'Other' Lollard Joke," *Lollards and Their Influence,* ed. Somerset, Havens, and Pitard, 127–38, argues that the *Upland Series,* rather than confused in thought, was highly nuanced in understanding the eucharistic debates. Lawrence M. Clopper, "Langland's Persona: An Anatomy of the Mendicant Orders," *Written Work,* ed. Justice and Kerby-Fulton, 144–84, argues that the antifraternalism employed by writers such as Langland typified the reformist polemics generated within the fraternal orders themselves.

339. P. L. Heyworth, "*Jack Upland's Rejoinder,* a Lollard Interpolator, and *Piers Plowman* B.X.249f," *MÆ* 36 (1967): 242–48.

340. Dean, ed., *Six Ecclesiastical Satires,* 211–12 (lines 257–63). Francis Lee Utley, "How Judicare Came in the Creed," *MS* 8 (1946): 303–9, explores some of the schoolboy language in *Friar Daw's Reply.*

341. Michael Goodich, *The Unmentionable Vice: Homosexuality in the Later Medieval Period* (Santa Barbara, CA, and Oxford: ABC-Clio, 1979), 86; David F. Greenberg, *The Construction of Homosexuality* (Chicago: University of Chicago Press, 1988), 272, 280–86, and 296–98; and Jeffrey Richards, *Sex, Dissidence and Damnation: Minority Groups in the Middle Ages* (London and New York: Routledge, 1991), 145.

342. Carolly Erickson, "The Fourteenth-Century Franciscans and Their Critics," *Franciscan Studies* 35 (1975): 107–35 at 112–13 and 116–18, and Penn R. Szittya, "The Antifraternal Tradition in Middle English Literature," *Speculum* 52 (1977): 287–313 at 300.

343. Hudson, ed., *English Wycliffite Writings,* 25. For the longstanding linkage of heresy and sodomy, see John Boswell, *Christianity, Social Tolerance, and Homosexuality* (Chicago and London: University of Chicago Press, 1980), 283–86.

344. The discourses of heresy and sexual irregularity become a major preoccupation for Dinshaw, *Getting Medieval,* esp. "It Takes One to Know One: Lollards, Sodomites, and Their Accusers," 55–99.

345. Walsingham, *Historia,* 2:158: "Dicit insuper eos sodomitas existere." For his earlier career, see Hudson, "Peter Pateshull: One-Time Friar and Poet?" *Interstices,* ed. Green and Mooney.

346. Ruth Mazo Karras and David Lorenzo Boyd, "'Ut cum mulier': A Male Transvestite Prostitute in Fourteenth-Century London," *Premodern Sexualities,* ed. Louise Fradenburg and Carla Freccero (New York and London: Routledge, 1996), 101–16 at 103, with transcript 111–12. Dinshaw, *Getting Medieval,* "Good Vibrations: John/Eleanor, Dame Alys, the Pardoner, and Foucault," 100–142 at 101.

347. *The Poems of John Audelay,* ed. Ella Keats Whiting, EETS o.s. 184, 1931, xvii for poems 7 (705) and 12 (11).

348. Simpson, *Reform,* 378–80, explicates the Lollard themes and Langlandian ingredients of the poem that he entitles *Marcol and Solomon;* he elaborates this discussion in "Saving Satire after Arundel's *Constitutions*: John Audelay's 'Marcol and Solomon,'" *Text and Controversy,* ed. Barr and Hutchison, 387–404. On the poet's background, see Michael Bennett, "John Audelay: Some New Evidence on His Life and Work," *ChauR* 16 (1982): 344–55.

349. Kerby-Fulton and Justice, "Langlandian Reading Circles," 81–82, and George Kane, "The Middle English Verse in Wellcome 1493," *London Mediaeval Studies* 2 (1951): 54–58 and 61–65.

350. Hudson, *Premature Reformation,* 60–62 and 494–507; Thomson, *Later Lollards,* traces the movement's largely invisible history in the second half of the fifteenth century. See also the cautionary remarks of Christine Carpenter, "The Religion of the Gentry of Fifteenth-Century England," *England in the Fifteenth Century: Proceedings of the 1986 Harlaxton Symposium,* ed. Daniel Williams (Woodbridge: Boydell Press, 1987), 53–74.

351. Justice, "Lollardy," *Cambridge History of Medieval English Literature,* ed. Wallace, 662; see also the recent concise history of Richard Rex, *The Lollards* (New York: Palgrave, 2002).

352. K. B. McFarlane, "The Wars of the Roses" (1964), rpt. *England in the Fifteenth Century,* 231–61 at 231 and 259.

353. Hudson, *Premature Reformation,* 448. F. Donald Logan, "Archbishop Thomas Bourgchier Revisited," *Church in Pre-Reformation Society,* ed. Barron and Harper-Bill, 170–88 at 175–76, finds only a brief period in the late 1450s when the archbishop took a stern interest in Wycliffite Bibles and especially the writings of Reginald Pecock.

354. Hill, "From Lollards to Levellers," 2:90.

355. Andrew Hope, "Lollardy: The Stone the Builders Rejected?" *Protestantism and the National Church in Sixteenth-Century England,* ed. Peter Lake and Maria Dowling (London: Croom Helm, 1987), 1–35, and "The Lady and the Bailiff: Lollardy among the Gentry in Yorkist and Early Tudor England," *Lollardy and the Gentry,* ed. Aston and Richmond, 250–77.

356. Hudson, *Premature Reformation,* 18, and Doyle, "Manuscripts of *Piers Plowman,*" 36.

357. Aston, *Lollards and Reformers,* 202–3.

358. Benjamin Franklin, *The Autobiography* (New York: Barnes & Noble, 1995), 6.

359. Russell and Kane, eds., *The C Version,* 6: "It was found at the Old Vicarage, Wickhambrook, Suffolk, under original or at least 16th century floorboards . . . in the oldest part of the house, c. 1500." See Hanna, "Studies in the Manuscripts of *Piers Plowman,*" 1–14.

360. Douglas H. Parker, ed., *The Praier and Complaynte of the Ploweman vnto Christe* (Toronto: University of Toronto Press, 1997), 107. The work was previously printed

by John Foxe in his *Acts and Monuments,* ed. Townsend, 2:728–47, and in the *Harleian Miscellany,* 8 vols. (London, 1744–46), 6:84–106.

361. Anthea Hume, "English Protestant Books Printed Abroad, 1525–1535," *The Complete Works of St. Thomas More,* ed. Louis L. Martz et al. (New Haven: Yale University Press, 1963–), 8:1065–91 at 1078–79. See also Donald Dean Smeeton, *Lollard Themes in the Reformation Theology of William Tyndale* (Kirkville, MO: Sixteenth Century Journal Publishers, 1986).

362. Annie S. Irvine, "A Manuscript Copy of *The Plowman's Tale,*" *University of Texas Studies in English* 12 (1932): 27–56.

363. *The Plowman's Tale: The c. 1532 and 1606 Editions of a Spurious Canterbury Tale,* ed. Mary Rhinelander McCarl (New York and London: Garland, 1997). Andrew N. Wawn, "Chaucer, *The Plowman's Tale* and Reformation Propaganda: The Testimonies of Thomas Godfray and *I Playne Piers,*" *BJRL* 56 (1973): 174–92, determined that lines 1–52 and 205–28 were sixteenth-century accretions added to an early fifteenth-century text in order to insert the figure of the plowman. See also Forni, *The Chaucerian Apocrypha,* 88–105.

364. Thynne, *Animadversions,* 10; for the text, see Chaucer, *The Works (1532) with Supplementary Material from the Editions of 1542, 1561, 1598 and 1602,* facsimile ed., Brewer, fols. cxix–cxxvi. Robert Costomiris, "The Yoke of Canon: Chaucerian Aspects of *The Plowman's Tale,*" *PQ* 71 (1992): 185–98, discusses how the work was fitted into the *Canterbury Tales.*

365. Helen C. White, *Social Criticism in Popular Literature of the Sixteenth Century* (New York: Macmillan, 1944), 35–40, and Thomas J. Heffernan, "Aspects of the Chaucerian Apocrypha: Animadversions on William Thynne's Edition of the *Plowman's Tale,*" *Chaucer Traditions: Studies in Honour of Derek Brewer,* ed. Ruth Morse and Barry Windeatt (Cambridge: Cambridge University Press, 1990), 155–67.

366. Skeat, ed., *Piers the Plowman,* 2:xxxviii–lvii, includes the bulk of the commentary available before 1886.

367. J. J. Jusserand, *"Piers Plowman": A Contribution to the History of English Mysticism,* trans. M. E. R. (London: T. Fisher Unwin, 1894); see Middleton, "The Critical Heritage," 3–4.

368. Doyle, "Manuscripts of *Piers Plowman,*" 36.

369. Stubbs, "A New Manuscript by the Hengwrt/Ellesmere Scribe?" and Mooney, "Chaucer's Scribe," 98–105, date Pinkhurst's *Boece* and Hengwrt manuscripts during Chaucer's lifetime. The prior view that no copies survived from the poet's lifetime was proposed by Tatlock, "The *Canterbury Tales* in 1400," 104–6, and John H. Fisher, "Animadversions on the Text of Chaucer, 1988," *Speculum* 63 (1988): 779–93.

370. John H. Fisher, *The Importance of Chaucer* (Carbondale and Edwardsville: Southern Illinois University Press, 1992), 1–35.

371. Greenblatt, *Shakespearean Negotiations,* 21–65, and Justice, "Lollardy," *Cambridge History of Medieval English Literature,* ed. Wallace, 668–69.

372. Howard, "The New Historicism in Renaissance Studies," 29, and Montrose, "Professing the Renaissance," 21–22.

373. Strohm, *Theory and the Premodern Text,* "Shakespeare's Oldcastle: Another Ill-Framed Knight," 132–48. See also J. R. Lander, *Conflict and Stability in Fifteenth-Century England* (London: Hutchinson, 1969), 48–90 and 115–40.

374. Dean, ed., *Six Ecclesiastical Satires,* 152 (lines 71–74). Somerset, *Clerical Discourse and Lay Audience,* 216–20, dates *Friar Daw's Reply* to the period 1388–99 with perhaps a revision after 1404.

CHAPTER FIVE   **Political Corrections**

1. Donald R. Howard, *The Idea of the Canterbury Tales* (Berkeley and Los Angeles: University of California Press, 1976), 1.

2. V. A. Kolve, *Chaucer and the Imagery of Narrative: The First Five Canterbury Tales* (Stanford: Stanford University Press, 1984), 275–85.

3. Pearsall, "Theory and Practice in Middle English Editing," 113; see also Tim William Machan, "Texts," *Companion to Chaucer,* ed. Brown, 428–42.

4. Missing from the best manuscripts, these five passages from the Wife of Bath's Prologue (*CT,* III, 44a–f, 575–84, 605–12, 619–26, 717–20) can be viewed as late additions or last-minute excisions.

5. For a different reading of the evidence, see Jones et al., *Who Murdered Chaucer?* 183–227 ("The *Canterbury Tales* as Death-Warrant").

6. Bowers, "*The Tale of Beryn* and *The Siege of Thebes:* Alternative Ideas of the *Canterbury Tales,*" and Bowers, ed., *The Canterbury Tales: Fifteenth-Century Continuations and Additions,* esp. 1–4.

7. Gabrielle M. Spiegel, "History, Historicism, and the Social Logic of the Text in the Middle Ages," *Speculum* 65 (1990): 59–86 at 77.

8. Fredric Jameson, *The Political Unconscious: Narrative as a Socially Symbolic Act* (Ithaca: Cornell University Press, 1981), 9.

9. John M. Bowers, "Chaucer's *Canterbury Tales*—Politically Corrected," *Rewriting Chaucer: Culture, Authority, and the Idea of the Authentic Text, 1400–1602,* ed. Thomas A. Prendergast and Barbara Kline (Columbus: Ohio State University Press, 1999), 13–44, accounts for the omissions of the Knight's Yeoman (16–19) and the Five Guildsmen (24–27).

10. Bowers, ed., *The Canterbury Tales: Fifteenth-Century Continuations and Additions,* 36 (lines 31–38). See Daniel J. Pinti, "Governing the Cook's Tale in Bodley 686," *ChauR* 30 (1996): 379–88, and David Lorenzo Boyd, "Social Texts: Bodley 686 and the Politics of the Cook's Tale," *Reading from the Margins,* ed. Lerer, 81–97.

11. Wendy Scase, "The Audience and Framers of the *Twelve Conclusions of the Lollards,*" *Text and Controversy from Wyclif to Bale,* ed. Barr and Hutchison, 283–301.

12. The regime became stable only from the victory at Agincourt until the young king's death in 1422. Henry V's strategies for shoring up the Lancastrian regime have formed the subject of a number of studies: P. S. Lewis, "War Propaganda and Historiography in Fifteenth-Century France and England," *TRHS* 5th ser., 15 (1965): 1–21; C. T. Allmand, *Lancastrian Normandy 1415–1450: The History of a Medieval*

Occupation (Oxford: Clarendon, 1983); Harriss, ed., *Henry V: The Practice of Kingship*; Edward Powell, *Kingship, Law, and Society: Criminal Justice in the Reign of Henry V* (Oxford: Oxford University Press, 1989); John H. Fisher, "A Language Policy for Lancastrian England," *PMLA* 107 (1992): 1168–80; and Allmand, *Henry V,* 306–32.

13. See for example Walter W. Skeat, *The Evolution of the "Canterbury Tales"* (London: Chaucer Society, 2nd ser., no. 38, 1907); Robert K. Root, "The Manciple's Prologue," *MLN* 44 (1929): 493–96; John M. Manly, "Tales of the Homeward Journey," *SP* 28 (1931): 613–17; Albert C. Baugh, "The Original Teller of the Merchant's Tale," *MP* 35 (1937): 15–26; and Carleton Brown, "Author's Revisions in the *Canterbury Tales*," *PMLA* 57 (1942): 29–50.

14. These issues are assessed by Patterson, *Negotiating the Past,* 3–39.

15. Paul Strohm, "Chaucer's Lollard Joke: History and the Textual Unconscious," *SAC* 17 (1995): 23–42 at 42.

16. Edith Rickert, "Chaucer's 'Hodge of Ware,'" *TLS* (20 October 1932): 761, and Earl D. Lyon, "Roger de Ware, Cook," *MLN* 52 (1937): 491–94.

17. Steven A. Epstein, *Wage, Labor and Guilds in Medieval Europe* (Chapel Hill: University of North Carolina Press, 1991), 197–202.

18. Howard, *Idea of the Canterbury Tales,* 244. See also E. G. Stanley, "Of This Cokes Tale Maked Chaucer Na Moore," *Poetica* 5 (1976): 36–59; M. C. Seymour, "Of This Cokes Tale," *ChauR* 24 (1990): 259–62; and Richard Beadle, "'I wol nat telle it yit': John Selden and a Lost Version of the *Cook's Tale,*" *Chaucer and Shakespeare: Essays in Honour of Shinsuke Ando,* ed. Toshiyuki Takamiya and Richard Beadle (Cambridge: D. S. Brewer, 1992), 55–66.

19. *A Facsimile and Transcription of the Hengwrt Manuscript,* ed. Ruggiers, intro. Baker, Doyle, and Parkes, 224–25. Doyle and Parkes, "The Production of Copies," xxvii, note that the copyist did not fill the space with an explicit as elsewhere in the manuscript; this suggests that Pinkhurst or his director had not given up hope of receiving additional materials. Some scholars speculate that the poet completed the tale but pages went missing from his working papers; see M. C. Seymour, "Hypothesis, Hyperbole, and the Hengwrt Manuscript of the *Canterbury Tales,*" *ES* 68 (1987): 214–19.

20. Kolve, *Chaucer and the Imagery of Narrative,* "Crossing the Hengwrt/Ellesmere Gap," 257–96, and Stephen Partridge, "Minding the Gap: Interpreting the Manuscript Evidence of the Cook's Tale and the Squire's Tale," *English Medieval Book,* ed. Edwards, Gillespie, and Hanna, 51–85.

21. Fol. 29a; see Bowers, ed., *Continuations and Additions,* 33–34.

22. Neil Daniel, ed., *"The Tale of Gamelyn:* A New Edition" (Ph.D. diss., Indiana University, 1967), 1–2, on the editorial tradition.

23. The exception is one eccentric late collection, Rawlinson Poet. 149 (c. 1450–75), which places *Gamelyn* after the Merchant's Tale and before the Wife of Bath's Tale.

24. Daniel, ed., 28–29, with assessment of textual transmission, 34–38.

25. W. W. Skeat, ed., *The Tale of Gamelyn* (Oxford: Clarendon Press, 1884), xvi, and Tatlock, "The *Canterbury Tales* in 1400," 112. Brusendorff, *The Chaucer Tradition,*

72–73, thought that Chaucer placed *Gamelyn* in his working papers with the intention of assigning it to the Yeoman, not the Cook.

26. Froissart, *Chronicles,* 441.

27. Pearsall, *The Life of Geoffrey Chaucer,* 213.

28. Edward Powell, "The Restoration of Law and Order," *Henry V: Practice of Kingship,* ed. Harriss, 53–74.

29. For the revocation of rights of inheritance, see Myers, ed., *English Historical Documents,* 178–79. This justification is critiqued by Michael Bennett, "Henry Bolingbroke and the Revolution of 1399," *Henry IV,* ed. Dodd and Biggs, 9–33. Stephen Knight, *Robin Hood: A Complete Study of the English Outlaw* (Oxford: Blackwell, 1994), 41, notes that *Gamelyn*'s account of a disinherited gentleman of the knightly class distinguishes it among other stories of heroic outlaws. See also John Scattergood, "*The Tale of Gamelyn*: The Noble Robber as Provincial Hero," *Reading the Past: Essays on Medieval and Renaissance Literature* (Dublin: Four Courts Press, 1996), 80–113.

30. Fols. 54b–55b; see Bowers, ed., *Continuations and Additions,* 33–39, and Seymour, *Catalogue of Chaucer Manuscripts: "The Canterbury Tales,"* 168–71. Chaucer's *Tales* heads this collection with a gorgeously decorated front page including a fine pictorial initial; it is followed by works of Lydgate.

31. Ruth Mazo Karras, "The Regulation of Brothels in Later Medieval England," *Signs* 14 (1989): 399–433.

32. Hazlitt, *The Livery Companies,* 75–76.

33. Lister M. Matheson, "Chaucer's Ancestry: Historical and Philological Reassessments," *ChauR* 25 (1991): 171–89 at 179–81.

34. Thrupp, *The Merchant Class of Medieval London,* 16–17.

35. Ibid., 169.

36. For accounts of these ceremonial floggings, see Thrupp, *The Merchant Class of Medieval London,* 169, and Reddaway, *The Early History of the Goldsmiths' Company,* 83–84 and 147.

37. Reginald Call, "'Whan He His Papir Sought' (Chaucer's *Cook's Tale,* A 4404)," *MLQ* 4 (1943): 167–76.

38. Earl D. Lyon, "The Cook's Tale," *Sources and Analogues of Chaucer's Canterbury Tales,* ed. W. F. Bryan and Germaine Dempster (London: Routledge & Kegan Paul, 1941), 148–54 at 151. John Scattergood, "The Cook's Tale," *Sources and Analogues of the Canterbury Tales,* vol. 1, ed. Robert M. Correale and Mary Hamel (Cambridge: D. S. Brewer, 2002), 75–86, decides that instead of searching for narrative sources, scholars should consult contemporary documents on London life.

39. V. J. Scattergood, "Perkyn Revelour and the *Cook's Tale,*" *ChauR* 19 (1984): 14–23 at 21, suggests that the completed tale would have involved trickery of some older victim.

40. Wallace, *Chaucerian Polity,* "Chaucer's Cook and the Limits of Associational Ideology," 167–76. See also Michael Hanrahan, "London," *Companion to Chaucer,* ed. Brown, 266–80.

41. *Memorials of London and London Life in the XIIIth, XIVth and XVth Centuries, A.D. 1276–1419,* ed. Henry Thomas Riley (London: Longmans, Green, and Co., 1868),

480. Specific fears in the aftermath of 1381 have been detected by Paul Strohm, "'Lad with Revel to Newegate': Chaucerian Narrative and Historical Metanarrative," *Theory and the Premodern Text,* 51–64; see also Andrew Prescott, "London in the Peasants' Revolt: A Portrait Gallery," *London Journal* 7 (1981): 125–43 at 131–33.

42. Barbara A. Hanawalt and Ben R. McRee, "The Guilds of *Homo Prudens* in Late-Medieval England," *Continuity and Change* 7 (1992): 163–79.

43. Peter Heath, *The English Parish Clergy on the Eve of the Reformation* (London: Routledge & Kegan Paul, 1969), 119–33.

44. Bowers, ed., *The Canterbury Tales: Fifteenth-Century Continuations and Additions,* 37.

45. D. W. Robertson, Jr., "Chaucer and the 'Commune Profit': The Manor," *Mediaevalia* 6 (1980): 239–59; D. Higgs, "The Old Order and the 'Newe World' in the General Prologue to the *Canterbury Tales,*" *HLQ* 45 (1982): 155–73; Larry Scanlon, *Narrative, Authority, and Power: The Medieval Exemplum and the Chaucerian Tradition* (Cambridge: Cambridge University Press, 1994), "Chaucer's Parson," 3–26; and Paul Hardwick, "The Poet as Ploughman," *ChauR* 33 (1998): 146–56. For a somewhat dissenting view, see Robert N. Swanson, "Chaucer's Parson and Other Priests," *SAC* 13 (1991): 41–80.

46. Rosemary Woolf, *The English Religious Lyric in the Middle Ages* (Oxford: Clarendon, 1968), "Complaints Against Swearing," 395–400.

47. "Quod non licet aliquo modo jurare"; see Hudson, *Premature Reformation,* 371–74, on swearing oaths.

48. Hudson, *Premature Reformation,* 294–301 on confession, 301–9 on pilgrimage, and 390–94 on Chaucer's Parson himself. Lawrence Warner, "Becket and the Hopping Bishops," *YLS* 17 (2003): 107–34, finds that Langland's rejection of commercial pilgrimage does not sully St. Thomas.

49. Douglas J. Wurtele, "The Anti-Lollardry of Chaucer's Parson," *Mediaevalia* 11 (1989 for 1985): 151–68, and Katherine Little, "Chaucer's Parson and the Specter of Wycliffism," *SAC* 23 (2001): 225–53, negotiate the contradiction in the Parson's identity between the General Prologue and the Parson's Tale.

50. Hudson, ed., *English Wycliffite Writings,* 92 (lines 136–48). Cole, "William Langland's Lollardy," 35–37, clarifies use of the word *Lollers* in the *Epistola.*

51. Strohm, "Chaucer's Lollard Joke: History and the Textual Unconscious," 29–32.

52. Hudson, ed., *English Wycliffite Writings,* 27 (lines 94–95).

53. Hudson, ed., *Two Wycliffite Texts,* 61–62. On the strategies of minority evasiveness, see Rita Copeland, "William Thorpe and His Lollard Community: Intellectual Labor and the Representation of Dissent," *Bodies and Disciplines,* ed. Barbara A. Hanawalt and David Wallace (Minneapolis: University of Minnesota Press, 1996), 199–221, and Somerset, *Clerical Discourse,* "Vernacular Argumentation in *The Testimony of William Thorpe,*" 179–215.

54. Derrick G. Pitard, "Sowing Difficulty: *The Parson's Tale,* Vernacular Commentary, and the Nature of Chaucerian Dissent," *SAC* 26 (2004): 299–330, challenges this view on the basis of the text's vernacularity.

55. Disagreement in the manuscripts whether this speaker is the Shipman, Squire, or Summoner attests to the draft nature of whatever was found in Chaucer's working papers.

56. See Hanna's textual note in *Riverside Chaucer,* 1126.

57. Gardiner Stillwell, "Chaucer's Plowman and the Contemporary English Peasant," *ELH* 6 (1939): 285–90; Joseph Horrell, "Chaucer's Symbolic Plowman," *Speculum* 14 (1939): 82–92; and Daniel F. Pigg, "With Hym Ther Was a Plowman, Was His Brother," *Chaucer's Pilgrims: An Historical Guide to the Pilgrims in "The Canterbury Tales,"* ed. Laura C. Lambdin and Robert T. Lambdin (Westport and London: Greenwood Press, 1996), 263–70.

58. Gower, *Mirour de l'Omme* (lines 26,425–84), trans. Wilson, 347.

59. J. L. Bolton, *The Medieval English Economy, 1150–1500* (Totowa, NJ: Rowman & Littlefield, 1980), "Crisis and Change in the Agrarian Economy," 207–45 at 215. *The English Rising of 1381,* ed. Hilton and Aston, offers two studies especially pertinent here: Christopher Dyer, "The Social and Economic Background to the Rural Revolt of 1381," 9–42, and J. A. Tuck, "Nobles, Commons and the Great Revolt of 1381," 194–212.

60. *The Major Latin Works of John Gower* (5.9–10), trans. Eric W. Stockton (Seattle: University of Washington Press, 1962), 208–10.

61. Nancy H. Owen, "Thomas Wimbledon's Sermon: 'Redde racionem villicacionis tue,'" *MS* 28 (1966): 176–97 at 178. The homiletic literature of the late fourteenth century is unanimous in its condemnation of lazy laborers; G. R. Owst, *Literature and Pulpit in Medieval England* (1933; rpt. Oxford: Blackwell, 1966), 362–67 and 553–74. See also Bertha H. Putnam, "Maximum Wage-Laws for Priests after the Black Death, 1348–1381," *American Historical Review* 21 (1915): 12–32, and A. K. McHardy, "Ecclesiastics and Economics: Poor Priests, Prosperous Laymen, and Proud Prelates in the Reign of Richard II," *The Church and Wealth,* ed. Sheils and Wood, 129–37.

62. Bowers, *The Politics of "Pearl,"* 41–49.

63. Coghill, "Two Notes on *Piers Plowman*: I. The Abbot of Abingdon and the Date of the C-text; II. Chaucer's Debt to Langland," 89–94.

64. Gower, *English Works,* 1:14 (lines 348–55).

65. James Simpson, "Spirituality and Economics in Passus 1–7 of the B-text," *YLS* 1 (1987): 83–103 at 99. Other studies of Langland's conservative response to economic changes include John M. Bowers, "*Piers Plowman* and the Unwillingness to Work," *Mediaevalia* 9 (1987 for 1983): 239–49; Bowers, *The Crisis of Will in "Piers Plowman,"* esp. 97–128; Baldwin, "The Historical Context," 70–71; Aers, "*Piers Plowman*: Poverty, Work, and Community," Helen Jewell, "*Piers Plowman*—A Poem of Crisis: An Analysis of Political Instability in Langland's England," *Politics and Crisis in Fourteenth-Century England,* ed. John Taylor and Wendy Childs (Wolfeboro Falls, NH: Alan Sutton, 1990), 59–80, esp. 61–64; and Clopper, "Need Men and Women Labor? Langland's Wanderer and the Labor Ordinances."

66. Hanna, *William Langland,* 16–17 and 31–32, and Middleton, "Acts of Vagrancy."

67. *Yearbook of Langland Studies* devoted volume 17 (2003) to "Langland and Lollardy."

68. Bowers, "Piers Plowman and the Police," 2–10.

69. Hudson, *Premature Reformation,* 408.

70. Ibid., 152–53 and 342–44.

71. Patterson, *Chaucer and the Subject of History,* 31.

72. Helen Cooper, *Oxford Guides to Chaucer: The Canterbury Tales* (Oxford: Clarendon, 1989), 415–18.

73. Dean, ed., *Six Ecclesiastical Satires,* 51–114. Thynne, *Animadversions,* 68–69, noted the problem of placing this tale last. See also Wawn, "Chaucer, *The Plowman's Tale* and Reformation Propaganda: The Testimonies of Thomas Godfray and *I Playne Piers,*" and Heffernan, "Aspects of the Chaucerian Apocrypha: Animadversions on William Thynne's Edition of the *Plowman's Tale,*" 155–67.

74. John Foxe's *Actes and Monumentes* (1570), ed. Josiah Pratt and John Stoughton, 8 vols. (London: Religious Tract Society, 1877), 4:249–50.

75. Bowers, ed., *Continuations and Additions,* 23–32.

76. Huntington HM 744, fol. 36a: "Ce feust *faite* a l'instance de T. Marleburgh." A scribal copy survives in Trinity College, Cambridge, MS R.3.21; see Beverly Boyd, ed., *The Middle English Miracles of the Virgin* (San Marino, CA: Huntington Library, 1964), 50–55 and 119–22.

77. Christianson, "A Community of Book Artisans in Chaucer's London," 217–18. Christianson, *A Directory of London Stationers and Book Artisans, 1300–1500* (New York: Bibliographical Society of America, 1990), 131–32, traces Thomas Marleburgh's professional activities and associations.

78. Hanna, *Pursuing History,* 312 n. 25, agrees with Manly and Rickert that Christ Church's textual conservatism reflects access to something like the exemplar available to Hengwrt.

79. Hoccleve's fierce anti-Lollard stance forms the subject of three important studies: David Lawton, "Dullness in the Fifteenth Century," *ELH* 54 (1987): 761–99; Larry Scanlon, "The King's Two Voices: Narrative and Power in Hoccleve's *Regement of Princes,*" *Literary Practice and Social Change,* ed. Patterson, 216–47; and Pearsall, "Hoccleve's *Regement of Princes*: The Poetics of Royal Self-Representation."

80. Hudson, *Premature Reformation,* 347–51.

81. Ibid., 302–4.

82. Ibid., 357–58.

83. Ibid., 310–13.

84. The full text of the poem is printed by Julia Boffey and A. S. G. Edwards, "'Chaucer's Chronicle,' John Shirley, and the Canon of Chaucer's Shorter Poems," *SAC* 20 (1998): 201–18 at 217–18.

85. Forni, *Chaucerian Apocrypha,* 149–50.

86. *The Poetic Works of Chaucer,* ed. F. N. Robinson (Boston: Houghton Mifflin, 1933), 981, allowed that the language was not "positively incompatible with the theory that Chaucer was the author"; see Brusendorff, *Chaucer Tradition,* 279, with facsimile of the stanzas from BL Add. 16165, fol. 244v.

87. Strohm, *Hochon's Arrow,* 7.

88. *CT,* I, 3291, 3425, 3461. Even the specificity of these oaths is far from certain; see Ed Malone, "Doubting Thomas and John the Carpenter's Oaths in the *Miller's Tale,*" *ELN* 29 (1991): 15–17.

89. Daniel Knapp, "The Relyk of a Seint: A Gloss on Chaucer's Pilgrimage," *ELH* 39 (1972): 1–26; Melvin Storm, "The Pardoner's Invitation: Quaestor's Bag or Becket's Shrine," *PMLA* 97 (1982): 810–18; John V. Fleming, "Chaucer and Erasmus on the Pilgrimage to Canterbury: An Iconographical Speculation," *The Popular Literature of Medieval England,* ed. Thomas J. Heffernan (Knoxville: Tennessee Studies in Literature, vol. 28, 1985), 148–66; and Julia Bolton Holloway, *The Pilgrim and the Book: A Study of Dante, Langland and Chaucer* (New York and Frankfurt: Peter Lang, 1987), 93–135.

90. E. Talbot Donaldson, "Chaucer the Pilgrim" (1954), rpt. *Speaking of Chaucer* (London: Athlone, 1970), 1–12 at 10.

91. Ralph Baldwin, *The Unity of the Canterbury Tales* (Copenhagen: Rosenkilde and Bagger, 1955), 92.

92. For a review of these issues of tale order, see Bowers, "*The Tale of Beryn* and *The Siege of Thebes*: Alternative Ideas of the *Canterbury Tales,*" 23–27.

93. D. W. Robertson, Jr., *A Preface to Chaucer* (Princeton: Princeton University Press, 1962), 373.

94. Howard, *The Idea of the Canterbury Tales,* 30 and later 159–73. See also Donald R. Howard, *Writers and Pilgrims: Medieval Pilgrimage Narratives and Their Posterity* (Berkeley and Los Angeles: University of California Press, 1980), 77–103.

95. Kolve, *Chaucer and the Imagery of Narrative,* 231.

96. Patterson, *Chaucer and the Subject of History,* 20, and his acceptance of Ellesmere's authority, 41–46. See also Helen Cooper, "The Order of Tales in the Ellesmere Manuscript," *Ellesmere Chaucer,* ed. Stevens and Woodward, 245–61.

97. Susan K. Hagen, *Allegorical Remembrance: A Study of "The Pilgrimage of the Life of Man" as a Medieval Treatise on Seeing and Remembering* (Athens: University of Georgia Press, 1990).

98. Long neglected, too, has been the literality of the Canterbury pilgrimage that fascinated Victorian scholars such as Frederick J. Furnivall, *Temporary Preface to the Six-Text Edition of Chaucer's "Canterbury Tales"* (London: Chaucer Society, 2nd series 3, 1868), with two appendices, one on Queen Isabella's pilgrimage of 1358, the second on King Jean II of France's pilgrimage of 1360. Henry Littlehales, *Some Notes on the Road from London to Canterbury in the Middle Ages* (London: Chaucer Society, ser. 2, no. 30, 1898), offered a series of maps. For a more recent bibliography, see Linda Kay Davidson and Maryjane Dunn-Wood, *Pilgrimage in the Middle Ages: A Research Guide* (New York and London: Garland, 1993), 176–78. It is seldom noted that the "Pilgrim's Way" led to Canterbury from Winchester, not from the London starting point of Chaucer's band; see Julia Mary Cartwright Ady, *The Pilgrims' Way from Winchester to Canterbury* (1893; rpt. New York: AMS Press, 1974).

99. J. F. Davis, "Lollards, Reformers and St. Thomas of Canterbury," *University of Birmingham Historical Journal* 9 (1963): 1–15; Jonathan Sumption, *Pilgrimage: An*

Notes to Pages 176–178

Image of Mediaeval Religion (Totowa: Rowman and Littlefield, 1975), 272–73; Aston, "Lollards and Images," *Lollards and Reformers,* 132–43; and Hudson, *Premature Reformation,* 301–9.

100. J. A. F. Thomson, "Orthodox Religion and the Origins of Lollardy," *History* 74 (1989): 39–55.

101. Hudson, ed., *English Wycliffite Writings,* 23, with comments on the manuscript and dating of the text, 145.

102. Ibid., 27. Phyllis B. Roberts, "The Unmaking of a Saint: The Suppression of the Cult of St. Thomas of Canterbury," *Hagiographica* 7 (2000): 35–46, describes the final assault upon the cult whose history has been recounted by Anne Duggan, *Thomas Becket* (Oxford: Oxford University Press, 2004).

103. Dymmok, *Liber Contra XII Errores et Hereses Lollardorum,* ed. Cronin, 192 (viii, 7).

104. Bowers, ed., *Fifteenth-Century Continuations and Additions,* 14–15 (lines 71–72).

105. Hudson, ed., *Two Wycliffite Texts,* xlv–liii, considers the dating of the actual interrogation as opposed to the dating of the manuscript.

106. Ibid., 64. Rickert, *Chaucer's World,* 264–65, quotes Thorpe's complaints as a gloss on Chaucer's pilgrims.

107. Anne Hudson, "John Stow (1525?–1605)," *Editing Chaucer,* ed. Ruggiers, 53–70 at 59.

108. See David Lyle Jeffrey, "Chaucer and Wyclif: Biblical Hermeneutic and Literary Theory in XIVth Century," *Chaucer and Scriptural Tradition,* ed. David Lyle Jeffrey (Ottawa: University of Ottawa Press, 1984), 109–40, and Linda Georgianna, "The Protestant Chaucer," *Chaucer's Religious Tales,* ed. C. David Benson and Elizabeth Robertson (Woodbridge, Suffolk, and Wolfeboro, NH: D. S. Brewer, 1990), 55–69.

109. Hugo Simon, "Chaucer a Wicliffite: An Essay on Chaucer's Parson and Parson's Tale," *Essays on Chaucer* (London: Chaucer Society, 2nd ser., no. 16, 1876), 227–92. Andrew N. Wawn, "Chaucer, Wyclif and the Court of Apollo," *ELN* 10 (1972): 15–20, reviews the durable tradition that Chaucer had some personal connection with Wyclif.

110. Hudson, "Lollardy: The English Heresy?" *Lollards and Their Books,* 142, and Aston, "Lollardy and Literacy," *Lollards and Reformers,* 208.

111. Bowers, ed., *Fifteenth-Century Continuations and Additions,* 60–79, and Seymour, *Catalogue of Chaucer Manuscripts: "The Canterbury Tales,"* 34–39.

112. Charles A. Owen, Jr., "The Alternative Reading of *The Canterbury Tales:* Chaucer's Text and the Early Manuscripts," *PMLA* 97 (1982): 237–50. Earlier proponents of the round-trip theory included Manly, "Tales of the Homeward Journey."

113. *The Constitutions of Thomas Arundel,* quoted from Lynn Staley, ed., *The Book of Margery Kempe* (New York: Norton, 2001), 187–96 at 193.

114. Stephen Medcalf, "Motives for Pilgrimage: *The Tale of Beryn,*" *England in the Fourteenth Century: Proceedings of the 1991 Harlaxton Symposium,* ed. Nicholas Rogers (Stamford, CT: Paul Watkins, 1993), 97–108, proposes that these pilgrims are more genuinely spiritual than usually understood.

115. Peter Brown, "Journey's End: The Prologue to *The Tale of Beryn*," *Chaucer and Fifteenth-Century Poetry*, ed. Boffey and Cowen, 143–74. For a different view of authorship, see Richard Firth Green, "Legal Satire in *The Tale of Beryn*," *SAC* 11 (1989): 43–62.

116. Bowers, "Alternative Ideas of *The Canterbury Tales*," 33–38, and Seymour, *Catalogue of Chaucer Manuscripts: "The Canterbury Tales,"* 34–39, describe the idiosyncratic organization of Northumberland.

117. See Robert M. Lumiansky, *Of Sundry Folk: The Dramatic Principle in the "Canterbury Tales"* (Austin: University of Texas Press, 1955); Charles A. Owen, Jr., *Pilgrimage and Storytelling in the "Canterbury Tales"* (Norman: University of Oklahoma Press, 1977); and Frederick B. Jonassen, "The Inn, the Cathedral, and the Pilgrimage of the *Canterbury Tales*," *Rebels and Rivals: The Contestive Spirit in the "Canterbury Tales,"* ed. Susanna Freer Fein, David Raybin, and Peter C. Braeger (Kalamazoo: Medieval Institute Publications, 1991), 1–35.

118. Jean E. Jost, "From Southwark's Tabard Inn to Canterbury's Cheker-of-the-Hope: The Un-Chaucerian *Tale of Beryn*," *FCS* 21 (1994): 133–48 at 133–34.

119. Doyle, "English Books in and out of Court," 178–79.

120. The essays collected in *Lollardy and the Gentry in the Later Middle Ages*, ed. Aston and Richmond, have begun rewriting the history of gentry participation and patronage in the underground Lollard movement during the fifteenth and into the sixteenth century.

121. Jenny Adams, "Exchequers and Balances: Anxieties of Exchange in *The Tale of Beryn*," *SAC* 26 (2004): 267–97.

122. See Bowers, "Alternative Ideas of *The Canterbury Tales*," 27–30, and Karen A. Winstead, "The *Beryn*-Writer as a Reader of Chaucer," *ChauR* 22 (1988): 225–33.

123. Glending Olson, "The Misreadings of the *Beryn* Prologue," *Mediaevalia* 18 (1993): 201–19 at 204.

124. Alastair Minnis, "Chaucer and the Queering Eunuch," *NML* 6 (2003): 107–28.

125. Henry Ansgar Kelly, "The Pardoner's Voice: Disjunctive Narrative and Modes of Effemination," *Speaking Images*, ed. Yeager and Morse, 411–44.

126. Bowers, ed., *Fifteenth-Century Continuations and Additions*, 13–14 (lines 32–36).

127. John M. Bowers, "Queering the Summoner: Same-Sex Union in Chaucer's *Canterbury Tales*," *Speaking Images*, ed. Yeager and Morse, 301–24.

128. Alfred L. Kellogg and Louis A. Haselmayer, "Chaucer's Satire of the Pardoner," *PMLA* 66 (1951): 251–77; Siegfried Wenzel, "Chaucer's Pardoner and His Relics," *SAC* 11 (1989): 37–41; William Komowski, "'Coillons,' Relics, Skepticism and Faith on Chaucer's Road to Canterbury: An Observation on the Pardoner's and the Host's Confrontation," *ELN* 28 (1991): 1–8; and Alastair Minnis, "Reclaiming the Pardoners," *JMEMS* 33 (2003): 311–34.

129. Frederick B. Jonassen, "Cathedral, Inn, and Pardoner in the Prologue to the *Tale of Beryn*," *FCS* 18 (1991): 109–32.

130. David Wallace, "Pilgrim Signs and the Ellesmere Chaucer," *Chaucer Newsletter* 11.2 (1989): 1–3.

131. Hudson, ed., *Two Wycliffite Texts,* 64.

132. Linda Georgianna, "Love So Dearly Bought: The Terms of Redemption in *The Canterbury Tales,*" *SAC* 12 (1990): 85–116 at 98. See also David Lawton, "Chaucer's Two Ways: The Pilgrimage Frame of *The Canterbury Tales,*" *SAC* 9 (1987): 3–40.

CHAPTER SIX   **The House of Chaucer & Son**

1. *Chaucer Life-Records,* 535–40. The document's abbreviation can actually be read as 43 or 53 years.

2. Gervase Rosser, *Medieval Westminster, 1200–1540* (Oxford: Clarendon, 1989), 160–61. For more speculative accounts, see John Gardner, *The Life and Times of Chaucer* (New York: Knopf, 1977), 309–14, and Terry Jones et al., *Who Murdered Chaucer?* 5–7 and 276–95 ("Chaucer's Final Days").

3. *Chaucer Life-Records,* 539 n.3.

4. Martin B. Ruud, *Thomas Chaucer* (Minneapolis: University of Minnesota Studies in Language and Literature, no. 9, 1926), 109–15. The *Life Records* published by the Chaucer Society are open to many interpretations; see Albert C. Baugh, "Kirk's Life Records of Thomas Chaucer," *PMLA* 47 (1932): 461–515, and "Thomas Chaucer, One Man or Two?" *PMLA* 47 (1933): 328–39. Russell Krauss, "Chaucerian Problems Especially the Petherton Forestership and the Question of Thomas Chaucer," *Three Chaucer Studies,* ed. Carleton Brown (New York: Oxford University Press, 1932), esp. 131–69 ("The Paternity of Thomas Chaucer"), encouraged the bizarre speculation Thomas might have been John of Gaunt's illegitimate son. For refutation, see H. Ansgar Kelly, "Shades of Incest and Cuckoldry: Pandarus and John of Gaunt," *SAC* 13 (1991): 121–40.

5. G. L. Harriss, "The Court of the Lancastrian Kings," *The Lancastrian Court: Proceedings of the 2001 Harlaxton Symposium,* ed. Jenny Stratford (Donington: Shaun Tyas, 2003), 1–18.

6. Ruud, *Thomas Chaucer,* 33; he was an MP in a total of fourteen parliaments, serving a remarkable five times as speaker. Roskell, *The Commons and Their Speakers,* 336, notes that Thomas Chaucer was one of only two speakers elected in three consecutive parliaments during the medieval period. See J. S. Roskell, Linda Clark, and Carole Rawcliffe, *The History of Parliament: The House of Commons 1386–1421,* vol. 2: *Members A–D* (Stroud: Alan Sutton, 1992), 524–32. Thomas Chaucer's close association with the Lancastrian mainstays is discussed by McFarlane, "Henry V, Bishop Beaufort and the Red Hat, 1417–1421," *England in the Fifteenth Century,* 79–113. A. L. Brown, *The Governance of Late Medieval England, 1272–1461* (Stanford: Stanford University Press, 1989), "The Evolution of Parliamentary Procedure," 207–15, indicates that by the end of the fourteenth century, the speaker was charged with not only organizing the business of the Commons but also speaking on their behalf, requiring a rhetorical skill that seems to have run in the Chaucer family.

7. The session dragged on because illness prevented the king from presiding while he recuperated, not in Westminster but in London at the palace of Bishop

Langley; see A. J. Pollard, "The Lancastrian Constitutional Experiment Revisited: Henry IV, Sir John Tiptoft and the Parliament of 1406," *Parliamentary History* 14 (1995): 103–19, and Douglas Biggs, "The Politics of Health: Henry IV and the Long Parliament of 1406," *Henry IV,* ed. Dodd and Biggs, 185–202.

8. Roskell, *Commons and Their Speakers,* 72 and 101–2. Henry IV actually voiced irritation with Thomas Chaucer's *novelleries* when he was elected speaker of the Commons in 1411.

9. Ruud, *Thomas Chaucer,* 38–56.

10. Ibid., 115.

11. *Chaucer Life-Records,* 538.

12. See Howard, *Chaucer,* 482–86.

13. Pearsall, "Chaucer's Tomb," and Bowers, *Politics of "Pearl,"* 125–26. His burial here seems neither obscure nor suspicious as suggested by Jones et al., *Who Murdered Chaucer?* 305–7 and 314–17.

14. Marjorie B. Honeybourne, "The Sanctuary Boundaries and Environs of Westminster Abbey and the College of St. Martin-Le-Grand," *Transactions of the British Archaeological Association* n.s. 38 (1932): 316–33, and N. H. MacMichael, "Sanctuary at Westminster," *Westminster Abbey Occasional Papers* 27 (1971): 9–14.

15. "Even if Henry and Arundel hadn't organized it themselves, the outcome couldn't have been more satisfactory": Jones et al., *Who Murdered Chaucer?* 156–59 at 159; see also 289–91: "The sanctuary itself was a stronghold of Ricardian opposition to the new regime, and Chaucer may have composed the *Complaint to his Purse* around the time the plotters met at the Abbot's house to discuss bringing Richard back" (178).

16. *Chaucer Life-Records,* ed. Crow and Olson, 532–33. Chaucer's earliest Renaissance biographers recounted how Chaucer fled to the Continent when things became dangerous in England, a possibility revived by Jones et al., *Who Murdered Chaucer?* 310–11.

17. Doyle, "English Books in and out of Court," 178.

18. For an important critical assessment, see Julia Boffey, *Manuscripts of English Courtly Love Lyrics in the Later Middle Ages* (Cambridge: D. S. Brewer, 1985).

19. Tatlock, "The *Canterbury Tales* in 1400," 104–7; Fisher, "Animadversions on the Text of Chaucer, 1988"; and A. S. G. Edwards and Derek Pearsall, "The Manuscripts of the Major English Poetic Texts," *Book Production,* ed. Griffiths and Pearsall, 257–78.

20. N. F. Blake, "Geoffrey Chaucer and the Manuscripts of *The Canterbury Tales,*" *Journal of the Early Book Society* 1 (1997): 96–122, speculates on the state of the poet's literary papers prior to his death. Kerby-Fulton, "Langland and the Bibliographic Ego," esp. 110–22, makes the case for an overlap between the first readers and first copyists of the London poets Langland and Chaucer. Ethan Knapp, *Bureaucratic Muse: Thomas Hoccleve and the Literature of Late Medieval England* (University Park: Pennsylvania State University Press, 2001), esp. "Bureaucratic Identity," 17–43, traces ways that the audience-responses of these governmental bookmen helped shape Chaucer's identity as an author.

21. If Chaucer had a son Lewis and a daughter Elizabeth, they had become such shadow-figures in the documents that they do not represent likely heirs; see *Chaucer Life-Records,* 544–46.

22. Manly and Rickert, eds., *The Canterbury Tales,* 1:159, concluded that Thomas Chaucer must have been responsible for commissioning Ellesmere at Westminster. Stubbs, "The Treatment of the Cook's Tale in Hg," *Hengwrt Facsimile*; Jones et al., *Who Murdered Chaucer?* 240–43; and Mooney, "Chaucer's Scribe," 105, suspect that Pinkhurst wrote "Of this Cokes tale maked Chaucer na moore" because the poet had actually died while his copyist was working on Fragment I of the *Tales.*

23. Fisher, "Animadversions," 788–89. No hard evidence confirms that Chaucer supervised any early manuscript even if work began on Ellesmere before 1400; see Blake, "Geoffrey Chaucer and the Manuscripts of *The Canterbury Tales.*"

24. *Chaucer Life-Records,* 532–33; see Jones et al., *Who Murdered Chaucer?* 296–314.

25. Fisher, "Animadversions," 789.

26. For an excellent description of the physical process of book making, see Christopher De Hamel, *Scribes and Illuminators* (Toronto: University of Toronto Press, 1992).

27. Greening Lamborn, "The Arms on the Chaucer Tomb at Ewelme," 78. See Russell Krauss's "An Examination of the Heraldic Decorations on Thomas Chaucer's Tomb," *Three Chaucerian Studies,* 31–56; Pearsall, *Life of Geoffrey Chaucer,* 279–80; and Mary-Jo Arn, "Thomas Chaucer and William Paston Take Care of Business: HLS Deeds 349," *SAC* 24 (2002): 237–67 at 250–64 ("Chaucer's Seal").

28. Richard II had legitimated the Beaufort offspring in 1397 after Gaunt wedded Katherine as his third wife; see Myers, ed., *English Historical Documents,* 169. Jeannette Lucraft, "Missing from History," *History Today* 52/5 (2002): 11–17, concludes that Katherine Swynford possessed a high standard of education as well as considerable piety, which she passed along to her children.

29. For context of this tomb within the family church, see Goodall, *God's House at Ewelme.* Anne McGee Morganstern, *Gothic Tombs of Kinship in France, the Low Countries, and England* (University Park: Pennsylvania State University Press, 2000), explores the genealogical programs in a wide variety of aristocratic tombs.

30. Goodall, *God's House at Ewelme,* 169–99.

31. G. L. Harriss, "Henry Beaufort, 'Cardinal of England,'" *England in the Fifteenth Century,* ed. Williams, 111–27.

32. Doyle, "English Books in and out of Court," 175, thinks the monarch's unexpected death in 1422 might explain the abandonment of the manuscript's later illustrations; see also Edwards and Pearsall, "Manuscripts of the Major English Poetic Texts," *Book Production,* ed. Griffiths and Pearsall, 266–67.

33. Mine provides an account very different from the story of deliberate manuscript destruction offered by Jones et al., *Who Murdered Chaucer?* 228–45 ("What Happened to Chaucer's Works?"), although we agree that not much manuscript production occurred during the first years of the fifteenth century, immediately after the poet died and while Henry IV and Arundel staged their harshest crackdowns: "The revival of Chaucer's reputation seems to have owed nothing to Henry IV but everything to his son, the Prince of Wales" (235).

34. Jones et al., *Who Murdered Chaucer?* 291–95, also provide a different account for the tenement's leasing by Thomas Chaucer, who perhaps wanted a safe house of his own after 1410 when Prince Henry's faction experienced a series of setbacks and the speaker of the Commons had incurred the displeasure of both Henry IV and Archbishop Arundel.

35. These praises are gathered for convenient review in Lois A. Ebin's *Illuminator, Makar, Vates: Visions of Poetry in the Fifteenth Century* (Lincoln: University of Nebraska Press, 1988), 4.

36. Knapp, *Bureaucratic Muse: Thomas Hoccleve and the Literature of Late Medieval England,* 109, notes that Hoccleve's support for Prince Henry could become a challenge to Chaucer's prerogative, read here as a challenge to Thomas Chaucer's prior right of inheritance.

37. Hoccleve, *The Regiment of Princes,* ed. Blyth, 96 (lines 1961–64).

38. Ibid., 96 (lines 1975–81). See Charles Blyth, "Thomas Hoccleve's Other Master," *Mediaevalia* 16 (1993): 349–59, on the poet's indebtedness to Gower.

39. Pearsall, *Old English and Middle English Poetry,* 236–38, remarks on the nonintersecting careers of Hoccleve and Lydgate.

40. Thomas Frederick Tout, "Literature and Learning in the English Civil Service in the Fourteenth Century," *Speculum* 4 (1929): 365–89, and Strohm, *Social Chaucer,* "Audience," 47–83.

41. Strohm, "Politics and Poetics: Usk and Chaucer in the 1380s," *Literary Practice and Social Change in Britain, 1380–1530,* ed. Patterson, 83–112.

42. Burrow, *Thomas Hoccleve,* 1–17.

43. Jerome Mitchell, "Hoccleve's Supposed Friendship with Chaucer," *ELN* 4 (1966): 9–12, and J. A. Burrow, "Autobiographical Poetry in the Middle Ages: The Case of Thomas Hoccleve," *PBA* 68 (1982): 389–412. For a very useful survey of the criticism, see Jerome Mitchell, "Hoccleve Studies, 1965–1981," *Fifteenth-Century Studies,* ed. Yeager, 49–63.

44. *Regiment,* ed. Blyth, 100 (lines 2078–79). Burrow, *Thomas Hoccleve,* 10–11, draws upon the work of Judith A. Jefferson, "The Hoccleve Holographs and Hoccleve's Metrical Practice," *Manuscripts and Texts: Editorial Problems in Later Middle English Literature,* ed. Derek Pearsall (Cambridge: D. S. Brewer, 1987), 95–109.

45. *Hoccleve's Works: The Minor Poems,* "The Compleynte of the Virgin before the Cross," 1–8, the two pieces entitled "Ad Beatam Virginem," 43–47 and 52–56, and "Balade to the Virgin and Christ," 67–72.

46. Beverly Boyd, "Our Lady According to Geoffrey Chaucer: Translation and Collage," *Florilegium* 9 (1990 for 1987): 147–54, explains how the poet's Marian pieces, as layered adaptations, have completely orthodox contents.

47. Pearsall, *The Life of Geoffrey Chaucer,* 289.

48. Derek Pearsall, "The English Chaucerians," *Chaucer and Chaucerians,* ed. D. S. Brewer (University: University of Alabama Press, 1966), 201–39, and Albrecht Classen, "Hoccleve's Independence from Chaucer: A Study of Poetic Emancipation," *FCS* 16 (1990): 59–81. Doyle and Parkes, "The Production of Copies of the *Canterbury Tales* and the *Confessio Amantis,*" identified the stints copied by Hoccleve and the Ellesmere Scribe.

49. Scanlon, *Narrative, Authority, and Power,* 313–14, and Simpson, *Reform,* 204–14.

50. Strohm, *England's Empty Throne,* "Reconsidering the 'Oldcastle Rebellion,'" 65–86, and Ruth Nissé, "'Oure Fadres Olde and Modres': Gender, Heresy, and Hoccleve's Literary Politics."

51. Lawton, "Dullness and the Fifteenth Century," 764; Burrow, *Thomas Hoccleve,* 22; and Pearsall, "Hoccleve's *Regiment of Princes*: The Poetics of Royal Self-Representation," 401–8. On the risks of Hoccleve's project, see Watson, "Censorship and Cultural Change in Late-Medieval England," 848–49.

52. Scott, "An Hours and Psalter by Two Ellesmere Illuminators," *Ellesmere Chaucer,* ed. Stevens and Woodward, 106, suggests the earlier period 1400–1405.

53. *Regiment,* ed. Blyth, 186 (lines 5006–8).

54. Hudson, *Premature Reformation,* 390–94, considers Wycliffite elements in Chaucer's writings.

55. Doyle and Parkes, "The Production of Copies of the *Canterbury Tales* and *Confessio Amantis,*" 182–85 and 199–203. See also J. J. Smith, "The Trinity Gower D-Scribe and His Work on Two Early *Canterbury Tales* Manuscripts," *The English of Chaucer and His Contemporaries,* ed. J. J. Smith (Aberdeen: Aberdeen University Press 1988), 51–69.

56. *Hoccleve's Works: The Minor Poems,* 49 (line 1).

57. Burrow, *Thomas Hoccleve,* 28. See also John Burrow, "Hoccleve's *Series*: Experience and Books," *Fifteenth-Century Studies,* ed. Yeager, 261–73; J. A. Burrow, ed., *Thomas Hoccleve's Complaint and Dialogue,* EETS o.s. 313, 1999, "The Making of the 'Series': Humphrey, Duke of Gloucester," lv–lvii; and especially John J. Thompson, "A Poet's Contacts with the Great and the Good: Further Consideration of Thomas Hoccleve's Texts and Manuscripts," *Prestige, Authority and Power,* ed. Riddy, 77–101.

58. John M. Bowers, "Hoccleve's Huntington Holographs: The First 'Collected Poems' in English," *Fifteenth-Century Studies* 15 (1989): 27–51, suggests that the two Huntington autograph manuscripts HM 744 and HM 111 were originally a single no-frills book containing the poet's shorter works. For French antecedents, see Huot, *From Song to Book,* "The Vernacular Poet as Compiler: The Rise of the Single-Authored Codex in the Fourteenth Century," 211–41.

59. Blyth, ed., *Regiment,* 16–17.

60. For a close study of the poet's work as his own copyist, see John M. Bowers, "Hoccleve's Two Copies of *Lerne to Dye*: Implications for Textual Critics," *PBSA* 83 (1989): 437–72, and Burrow, ed., *Complaint and Dialogue,* 111–18.

61. Knapp, *Bureaucratic Muse: Thomas Hoccleve and the Literature of Late Medieval England,* 11; Hoccleve's civil service instincts for care and completion may have contributed strongly to his sense of literary texts but actually worked to his disadvantage, as an aspiring author, because a mere functionary's professional status lacked the prestige that even a monastic poet such as Lydgate might claim.

62. Hoccleve's clerical attitudes colored his views of women and may have contributed to his failure to attract women readers as an important segment of the emerging vernacular public. See Anna Torti, "Hoccleve's Attitude toward Women,"

A Wyf Ther Was: Essays in Honour of Paule Mertens-Fonck, ed. Juliette Dor (Liège: Université de Liège, 1992), 264–74; Karen A. Winstead, "'I Am Al Other to Yow Than Yee Weene': Hoccleve, Women and the *Series,*" *PQ* 72 (1993): 143–55; and Catherine Batt, "Hoccleve and . . . Feminism? Negotiating Meaning in the *Regement of Princes,*" *Essays on Thomas Hoccleve,* ed. Catherine Batt (Brepols, Belgium: Westfield Publications in Medieval Studies, no. 10, 1996), 55–84.

63. J. C. Laidlaw, "Christine de Pizan, the Earl of Salisbury and Henry IV," *French Studies* 36 (1982): 129–43, exposes the complications of these textual and political negotiations. See also Sandra Hindman, "The Composition of the Manuscript of Christine de Pizan's Collected Works in the British Library: A Reassessment," *British Library Journal* 9 (1983): 93–123, and Roger Ellis, "Chaucer, Christine de Pizan and Hoccleve: *The Letter of Cupid,*" *Essays on Thomas Hoccleve,* ed. Batt, 29–54.

64. John Burrow, "Hoccleve and the Middle French Poets," *The Long Fifteenth Century,* ed. Cooper and Mapstone, 35–49, writes specifically of Hoccleve's metrical precision compared with Chaucer's: "He may be regarded as more Gallic than his master—perhaps too Gallic, indeed, for native readers" (39). With his French-language *Cinkante Balades* dated to this period, Gower may have made his own bid to fill the "poet vacuum" after Christine demurred.

65. Richard Ager Newhall, *The English Conquest of Normandy, 1416–1424* (New Haven: Yale University Press, 1924), and Allmand, *Lancastrian Normandy 1415–1450: The History of a Medieval Occupation.*

66. Marcia Smith Marzec, "The Latin Marginalia of the *Regiment of Princes* as an Aid to Stemmatic Analysis," *Text* 3 (1987): 269–84 at 270–71. See also M. C. Seymour, "Manuscripts of Hoccleve's *Regiment of Princes,*" *Edinburgh Bibliographical Society Transactions* 4/7 (1974): 253–97 at 255–56; Kate Harris, "The Patron of British Library MS. Arundel 38," *N&Q* n.s. 31 (1984): 462–63; and Douglas J. McMillan, "The Single Most Popular of Thomas Hoccleve's Poems: *The Regement of Princes,*" *NM* 89 (1988): 63–71. On the literary activities of John, Duke of Bedford, see M. J. Barber, "The Books and Patronage of Learning of a Fifteenth-Century Prince," *Book Collector* 12 (1963): 308–15, and Jenny Stratford, *The Bedford Inventories: The Worldly Goods of John, Duke of Bedford, Regent of France (1389–1435)* (London: Society of Antiquaries, 1993), "Manuscripts," 91–96. Sandler, *Lichtenthal Psalter,* 26–27, traces Joan FitzAlan's patronage of translations and book production within the Bohun family back to the 1380s when volumes were produced for her daughter Mary and son-in-law Henry Bolingbroke.

67. Thompson, "Thomas Hoccleve and Manuscript Culture," 94, concludes that the poet's publishing ambitions were even more far-reaching: "He was personally responsible for compiling together both the *Regement* and the *Series* as part of an original exercise in authorial self-promotion."

68. *Regiment,* ed. Blyth, 93 (line 1864). The editor remarks upon the anonymity of his copy-text Arundel 38 "with neither title nor incipit nor rubric" (201). See also Scott, *Dated and Datable English Manuscript Borders,* 42–43.

69. Dutschke, *Guide to Medieval and Renaissance Manuscripts in the Huntington Library,* 1:35–39 and 180–81.

70. Hudson, ed., *English Wycliffite Writings,* 75.

71. J. A. Burrow, "Hoccleve and Chaucer," *Chaucer Traditions,* ed. Morse and Windeatt, 54–61 at 56.

72. L. O. Aranye Fradenburg, *Sacrifice Your Love: Psychoanalysis, Historicism, Chaucer* (Minneapolis: University of Minnesota Press, 2002), describes the reversal of this contradictory pair of qualities already embodied in the Monk's Tale: "What interests me is the question of how it is possible that the Monk could be both terrorizing and stupefyingly boring" (146).

73. Arnold, ed., *Select English Works of John Wyclif,* 3:196.

74. Lydgate, *Fall of Princes,* 1:2 (I, line 403), makes early reference to Gloucester's role in suppressing the Lollard rising of 1431: "That in this land no Lollard dar abide." Meale, "Patrons, Buyers and Owners," 209, mentions these exceptionally elaborate manuscripts, such as BL Harley 1776 with 157 miniatures; see also A. S. G. Edwards, "The Huntington *Fall of Princes* (HM 268) and Sloane 2452," *Manuscripta* 16 (1972): 37–40.

75. Derek Pearsall, *John Lydgate* (Charlottesville: University Press of Virginia, 1970), 160–91, and Pearsall, *John Lydgate (1371–1449): A Bio-bibliography,* "Lancastrian Propagandist and Laureate Poet to Crown and Commons, 1426–32," 28–32. For Bedford's impulses as a book collector, see Jenny Stratford, "The Manuscripts of John, Duke of Bedford: Library and Chapel," *England in the Fifteenth Century,* ed. Williams, 329–50.

76. McFarlane, *Lancastrian Kings and Lollard Knights,* "Father and Son," 102–13; Peter McNiven, "Prince Henry and the Political Crisis of 1412," *History* 65 (1980): 1–16; and Allmand, *Henry V,* 39–58. Anthony Tuck, "Henry IV and Europe: A Dynasty's Search for Recognition," *The McFarlane Legacy,* ed. R. H. Britnell and A. J. Pollard (New York: St. Martin's, 1995), 107–25, investigates another aspect of this campaign for legitimacy.

77. Knapp, *Bureaucratic Muse: Thomas Hoccleve and the Literature of Late Medieval England,* "Fathers and Sons, 1410–12," 124–27 at 126.

78. Dutschke, *Guide to Medieval and Renaissance Manuscripts in the Huntington Library,* 1:180, restores the cropped heading for HM 135, which is dated from the third quarter of the fifteenth century. The defective text is written on paper without decoration after the three rubricated initials on fol. 1a. At the beginning of the royal section, where elegant pictures are placed in Arundel 38 and Harley 4866, there is only a black-ink title "Hic trattat de principum regimine" (fol. 34b).

79. The great increase in these opportunities has been discussed by T. F. Tout, "The Beginnings of a Modern Capital: London and Westminster in the Fourteenth Century," *PBA* 10 (1923): 487–511.

80. James Simpson, "Nobody's Man: Thomas Hoccleve's *Regement of Princes,*" *London and Europe in the Later Middle Ages,* ed. Julia Boffey and Pamela King (London: Westfield Publications in Medieval Studies, no. 9, 1995), 149–80, suggests some strategic advantages to Hoccleve's posture as a patronless poet.

81. Malcolm Richardson, "Hoccleve in His Social Context," *ChauR* 20 (1986): 313–22 at 321; see also A. Compton Reeves, "The World of Thomas Hoccleve,"

FCS 2 (1979): 187–201. J. A. Burrow, "Hoccleve and the 'Court,'" *Nation, Court and Culture,* ed. Cooney, 70–80 at 73, qualifies this view of a professional failure.

82. A. L. Brown, "The Privy Seal Clerks in the Early Fifteenth Century," *The Study of Medieval Records: Essays in Honour of Kathleen Major,* ed. D. A. Bullough and R. L. Storey (Oxford: Clarendon, 1971), 260–81, compares the careers of these three men.

83. Eva M. Thornley, "The ME Penitential Lyric and Hoccleve's Autobiographical Poetry," *NM* 68 (1967): 295–321.

84. Lee Patterson, "'What Is Me?': Self and Society in the Poetry of Thomas Hoccleve," *SAC* 23 (2001): 437–70, reads Hoccleve's whole career as a tragicomedy of missteps, tactless gestures, and bad timing.

85. Burrow, *Thomas Hoccleve,* 22. For closer discussion of his mental illness, see Penelope Doob, *Nebuchadnezzar's Children: Conventions of Madness in Middle English Literature* (New Haven: Yale University Press, 1974), 210–30, and Burrow, ed., *Complaint and Dialogue,* "Hoccleve's 'Wylde Infirmitee,'" lx–lxii.

86. James Simpson, "Madness and Texts: Hoccleve's *Series,*" *Chaucer and Fifteenth-Century Poetry,* ed. Julia Boffey and Janet Cowen (London: King's College London Medieval Studies, no. 5, 1991), 15–29. See also D. C. Greetham, "Self-Referential Artifacts: Hoccleve's Persona as a Literary Device," *MP* 86 (1989): 242–51; Antony J. Hasler, "Hoccleve's Unregimented Body," *Paragraph* 13 (1990): 164–83; Ethan Knapp, "Bureaucratic Identity and the Construction of the Self in Hoccleve's *Formulary* and *La Male Regle,*" *Speculum* 74 (1999): 357–76; and Matthew Boyd Goldie, "Psychosomatic Illness and Identity in London, 1416–1421: Hoccleve's *Complaint* and *Dialogue with a Friend,*" *Exemplaria* 11 (1999): 23–52.

87. Burrow, *Thomas Hoccleve,* 7. See also H. S. Bennett, *Chaucer and the Fifteenth Century* (Oxford: Clarendon, 1947), esp. 146–47.

88. Wallace, *Chaucerian Polity,* "Absent City," 156–81.

89. Margaret Aston, "Lollards and the Cross," *Lollards and Their Influence,* ed. Somerset, Havens, and Pitard, 99–113 at 101.

90. Skeat, ed., *Piers Plowman,* 2:3: "To remember the *London* origin of, at any rate, the larger portion of the poem, is the true key to the right understanding of it."

91. Pearsall, "The English Chaucerians," 223.

92. Spearing, *Medieval to Renaissance in English Poetry,* 110–20 at 119.

93. *Regiment,* ed. Blyth, 129 (lines 3051–52). This personification returns so strongly through the work that the editor capitalizes the name Favel but not, for example, Plesant Deceit.

94. Sarah Tolmie, "The *Prive Scilence* of Thomas Hoccleve," *SAC* 22 (2000): 281–309 at 285.

95. Patterson, "Who Is Me?" 469.

96. Knapp, *Bureaucratic Muse: Thomas Hoccleve and the Literature of Late Medieval England,* 71.

97. Kerby-Fulton, "Langland and the Bibliographic Ego," 110–17. Burrow, *Thomas Hoccleve,* 2 n. 5, traces speculation that the poet studied at an Inn of Chancery.

98. *Regiment,* ed. Blyth, 67 (lines 981–87) and continuing, 68–69. On poetry as a lazy man's occupation, see Bowers, *The Crisis of Will in "Piers Plowman,"* "The Poet as Worker," 191–218, and Middleton, "Acts of Vagrancy."

99. Bowers, *Crisis of Will in "Piers Plowman,"* 150–51 and 208–9.

100. Barron, "William Langland: A London Poet," 91–109 at 93, and Pearsall, "Langland's London," 185–207. Lawrence M. Clopper, "The Engaged Spectator: Langland and Chaucer on Civic Spectacle and the *Theatrum," SAC* 22 (2000): 115–39, assesses Langland's responses to two London events, the Pageant of the Lady of the Sun in 1366 and Richard II's coronation procession in 1377.

101. See Kerby-Fulton and Justice, "Langlandian Reading Circles," 60–61.

102. M. L. Samuels, "Scribes and Manuscript Traditions," *Regionalism in Late Medieval Manuscripts and Texts,* ed. Felicity Riddy (Cambridge: D. S. Brewer, 1991), 1–7 at 3, discusses the London prehistory of BL Add. 10574, Oxford Bodley 814, and BL Cotton Caligula A.xi. See also Bryan P. Davis, "The Rationale for a Copy of a Text: Constructing the Exemplar for BL Additional MS. 10574," *YLS* 11 (1997): 141–55.

103. Doyle and Parkes, "The Production of Copies of the *Canterbury Tales* and the *Confessio Amantis* in the Early Fifteenth Century," 174–82 and 192–98. See also Pearsall, "The 'Ilchester' Manuscript of *Piers Plowman*"; Kerby-Fulton and Justice, "Scribe D and the Marketing of Ricardian Literature," 218–22; and Bowers, "Two Professional Readers of Chaucer and Langland: Scribe D and the HM 114 Scribe," 114–29.

104. Horobin and Mooney, "A *Piers Plowman* Manuscript by the Hengwrt/Ellesmere Scribe and Its Implications for London Standard English," established this identification before Mooney provided a name for this professional textwriter.

105. *Piers Plowman: The B Version,* ed. Kane and Donaldson, 13 n. 91 on the Trinity B.15.17 hand, and 50–51 on textual affiliations. On the hand of BL Add. 35287, see Doyle, "Manuscripts of *Piers Plowman,"* 39–40, and *The B Version,* 11 n. 73. On the Holloway fragment, see Hanna, "Studies in the Manuscripts of *Piers Plowman,"* 4. Ralph Hanna III, "Reconsidering the Auchinleck Manuscript," *New Directions in Later Medieval Manuscript Studies,* ed. Derek Pearsall (Woodbridge: Boydell for York Medieval Press, 2000), 91–102 at 101 n. 33, remarks that the hand of Scribe B resembles Huntington HM 143 and the Holloway Fragment now in the collection of Martin Schøyen of Oslo.

106. Horobin, "Dialect and Circulation of the C Version of *Piers Plowman."*

107. Doyle, "Manuscripts of *Piers Plowman,"* 46. Since the manuscript is dated on paleological grounds to the third quarter of the fifteenth century, the handwriting may represent a throwback in terms of style. Lincoln's Inn MS Hale 150 can be added to the short list of A manuscripts associated with London and specifically the legal profession.

108. Kerby-Fulton, "Langland and the Bibliographic Ego," and Middleton, "Acts of Vagrancy," also detect the influence of Langland's *apologia* upon Hoccleve's anxious self-portrait.

109. Blyth, ed., 206, notes the similarities between the *Regiment* (lines 419–553) and *Mum* (lines 121–81). Bowers, *The Politics of "Pearl,"* 26–28, discusses the attack on

luxury crafts in the 1395 *Twelve Conclusions of the Lollards* and the defense of royal magnificence by Roger Dymmok in *Liber contra XII Errores et Hereses Lollardorum.*

110. Chris Given-Wilson, ed., *Chronicles of the Revolution 1397–1400: The Reign of Richard II* (Manchester and New York: Manchester University Press, 1993), 179. McFarlane, *Lancastrian Kings and Lollard Knights,* 87–89, notes that the Commons immediately in 1399 urged Henry IV to seek the advice of the council before making grants.

111. G. L. Harriss, "Introduction: The Exemplar of Kingship," *Henry V: The Practice of Kingship,* 1–29 at 8–9, and Pearsall, "Hoccleve's *Regiment,*" 389. Simpson, *Reform,* 191–254, stresses the Aristotelian nature of all late medieval political writing.

112. Baldwin, "Historical Context," 78–79.

113. *Caxton's Book of Curtesye,* ed. Frederick J. Furnivall, EETS e.s. 3, 1868, 37 (lines 351–64), nonetheless placed Hoccleve and his *Regiment* on his approved syllabus along with Chaucer, Gower, and Lydgate. This view is adjusted somewhat by Nicholas Perkins, *Hoccleve's "Regiment of Princes": Counsel and Constraint* (Cambridge: D. S. Brewer, 2001), "The Afterlife of the Poem," 151–91.

114. Thomas Occleve, *De Regimine Principum: A Poem Written in the Reign of Henry IV,* ed. Thomas Wright (London: Roxburghe Club, 1860).

115. See Lerer, *Chaucer and His Readers,* esp. 22–56, on Lydgate's success at establishing himself as Chaucer's heir.

116. Lydgate, *Minor Poems,* 779 (line 127).

117. Lindenbaum, "London Texts," 299; see also William Kellaway, "John Carpenter's *Liber Albus,*" *Guildhall Studies in London History* 3 (1978): 67–84.

118. Pearsall, *John Lydgate* (1997), 14. See also Pearsall, *John Lydgate* (1970), 160–63, and Walter F. Schirmer, *John Lydgate: A Study in the Culture of the XVth Century,* trans. Ann E. Keep (London: Methuen, 1961), 232–35. For Benedictines at Oxford during this period, see Joan Greatrex, "Monk Students from Norwich Cathedral Priory at Oxford and Cambridge, c. 1300 to 1530," *EHR* 106/420 (1991): 555–83.

119. Lydgate, *Minor Poems,* ed. MacCracken, 2:657–59, and Lydgate, *Poems,* ed. Norton-Smith, 4–6 and 119–20 on the question of dating.

120. Sue Bianco, "New Perspectives on Lydgate's Courtly Verse," *Nation, Court and Culture,* ed. Cooney, 95–115, reads these poems as comments on Bolingbroke's early career before and immediately after ascending the throne as Henry IV. Connections with a bygone period of Lancastrian history, one that later apologists, including Lydgate himself, were eager to airbrush away, might explain the relative neglect of these *dits amoureux* in the manuscripts.

121. Oxford, St. John's College MS 56: "Hyc incipit interpretatio misse in lingua materna secundum Iohannen litgate monanchum de Buria ad rogatum domine Countesse de Suthefolchia."

122. *Royal Commission on Historical Manuscripts: Eighth Report and Appendix (Part I)* (London: Eyre and Spottiswoode, 1881), 629; see also Pearsall, *John Lydgate* (1997), 27. This collection also included "a frensh boke of La Cite des Dames," clearly Christine de Pizan's *Cité des dames.* Alice's "frensh boke of temps pastoure" may have been Christine's *Le Dit de la pastoure.*

123. Carol M. Meale, "Reading Women's Culture in Fifteenth-Century England: The Case of Alice Chaucer," *Mediaevalitas: Reading in the Middle Ages,* ed. Piero Boitani and Anna Torti (Cambridge: D. S. Brewer, 1996), 81–101.

124. Jeremy Griffiths, "Thomas Hyngham, Monk of Bury and the Macro Plays Manuscript," *English Manuscript Studies* 5 (1995): 214–19, and Richard Beadle, "Monk Thomas Hyngham's Hand in the Macro Manuscript," *New Science out of Old Books,* ed. Beadle and Piper, 315–41. Edwards and Pearsall, "Manuscripts of the Major English Poetic Texts," *Book Production,* ed. Griffiths and Pearsall, 264, note the imposition of an *ordinatio* on Arundel 119 remarkably similar to the Ellesmere Chaucer. Other vernacular literary activity centered on the monastic community has been discussed by Gail McMurray Gibson, "Bury St. Edmunds, Lydgate, and the N-Town Cycle," *Speculum* 56 (1981): 56–90, and Bowers, "*Mankind* and the Political Interests of Bury St. Edmunds." The monastery's local political, economic, and social engagements are examined by Robert S. Gottfried, *Bury St. Edmunds and the Urban Crisis: 1290–1539* (Princeton: Princeton University Press, 1982).

125. Meale, "Reading Women's Culture in Fifteenth-Century England: The Case of Alice Chaucer," 92–93.

126. On Suffolk's verse reply to Lydgate, see Henry Noble MacCracken, "An English Friend of Charles of Orleans," *PMLA* 26 (1911): 142–80, text at 168–71. Boffey, *Manuscripts of English Courtly Love Lyrics,* 65–67, questions John Shirley's credibility concerning Suffolk's authorship, while Jansen, *The "Suffolk" Poems,* "Date and Authorship," 13–30, concludes, "The tone adopted in the reproof to Lydgate would suggest a noble patron such as Suffolk" (30). Pearsall, "The Literary Milieu of Charles of Orléans and the Duke of Suffolk, and the Authorship of the Fairfax Sequence," 156, laments the scholarly preoccupation with attaching this fine sequence to any named author.

127. Malcolm Parkes, "The Literacy of the Laity" (1973), *Scribes, Scripts and Readers: Studies in the Communication, Presentation and Dissemination of Medieval Texts* (London: Hambledon Press, 1991), 275–97 at 290–91, and Susanne Saygin, *Humphrey, Duke of Gloucester (1390–1447) and the Italian Humanists* (Leiden, Boston, and Cologne: Brill, 2002).

128. For speculation on the political contexts of these poems, see Tony Davenport, "Fifteenth-Century Complaints and Duke Humphrey's Wives," *Nation, Court and Culture,* ed. Cooney, 129–52.

129. Pearsall, *John Lydgate* (1997), 38–39.

130. Ibid., 31.

131. Lydgate, *Fall of Princes,* ed. Bergen, part 1, 8–10 (lines 281–357).

132. Cannon, "Monastic Productions," *Cambridge History of Medieval English Literature,* ed. Wallace, 326. For earlier histories of the collection, see Montague Rhodes James, *On the Abbey of S. Edmund at Bury,* vol. 1: *The Library* (Cambridge: Cambridge Antiquarian Society, no. 28, 1895); Montague Rhodes James, "Bury St. Edmunds Manuscripts," *EHR* 41 (1926): 251–60; and Rodney M. Thomson, "The Library of Bury St. Edmunds Abbey in the Eleventh and Twelfth Centures," *Speculum* 47 (1972): 617–45. Doyle, "Publications by Members of the Religious Orders," *Book Production,* ed. Griffiths and Pearsall, 117–18, thinks that even Lydgate's local scribes were lay

professionals rather than monastic copyists. For recent work on local manuscript production, see Nicholas J. Rogers, "Fitzwilliam Museum MS 3–1979: A Bury St. Edmunds Book of Hours and the Origins of the Bury Style," *England in the Fifteenth Century*, ed. Williams, 229–43.

133. Knowles, *Religious Orders of England*, 332. David N. Bell, "Monastic Libraries, 1400–1557," *Cambridge History of the Book in Britain*, vol. 3, ed. Hellinga and Trapp, 229–54 at 239, notes that a copy of *The Owl and the Nightingale* crops up in the library catalogue for Titchfield c. 1400 (239).

134. Parkes and Beadle, eds., *Poetical Works: A Facsimile of Cambridge University Library MS GG.4.27*, 63, and Seymour, *Catalogue of Chaucer Manuscripts: "The Canterbury Tales,"* 47–51. Later, in 1476, Glasgow Hunterian MS U.1.1 (197) was copied at Norwich by the scrivener Geoffrey Spirleng and his son Thomas. Richard Beadle, "Geoffrey Spirleng (c. 1426–c. 1494): A Scribe of the *Canterbury Tales* in His Time," *Of the Making of Books*, ed. Robinson and Zim, 116–46, traces the career of this copyist.

135. John Lydgate, *The Pilgrimage of the Life of Man*, ed. F. J. Furnivall and K. B. Locock, EETS e.s. 77, 83, 92 (1899, 1901, 1904), lines 19,777–80 and 19,789–90.

136. John J. Thompson, "After Chaucer," 192–99, discusses this "embarrassing gap" (195); see also Thompson, "Chaucer's *An ABC* in and out of Context," *Poetica* 37 (1993): 38–48.

137. Strohm, "Saving the Appearances: Chaucer's 'Purse' and the Fabrication of the Lancastrian Claim," *Hochon's Arrow*, 75–94 at 88–90, points to the importance of the term *eleccion*.

138. Pearsall, *John Lydgate* (1997), 15 and 56–57.

139. Ibid., 17.

140. Harriss, "Introduction: The Exemplar of Kingship," *Henry V: Practice of Kingship*, 1–29.

141. Newhall, *The English Conquest of Normandy*, esp. 143–89.

142. Wallace, *Premodern Places*, 22–90 at 33–44 ("Repeopling Calais"); see R. R. Davies, *The First English Empire: Power and Identities in the British Isles, 1093–1343* (Oxford: Oxford University Press, 2000), 149.

143. Pearsall, *John Lydgate* (1997), 77–79, catalogues the thirty manuscripts and early printings of the *Siege of Thebes*.

144. Bowers, ed., *Fifteenth-Century Continuations and Additions*, esp. 1–12 and 55–57. For Henry V's English version of the Treaty of Troyes, see W. M. Ormrod, "The Use of English: Language, Law, and Political Culture in Fourteenth-Century England," *Speculum* 78 (2003): 750–787 at 786.

145. Roskell, *The Commons and Their Speakers*, 173.

146. Strohm, *Theory and the Premodern Text*, 43–44.

147. Galloway, "Latin England," 75; see also Gransden, *Historical Writing in England*, 126.

148. Allmand, *Henry V*, 272–79; see specifically Neil Beckett, "The Relations between St. Bridget, Henry V, and Syon Abbey," *Studies in St. Birgitta and the Brigittine Order*, ed. James Hogg, 2 vols. (Salzburg: Universität Salzburg, 1993), 2:125–50.

149. Lydgate, *Troy Book,* 4 (Prol. 114–15). See also Nicholas Watson, "Outdoing Chaucer: Lydgate's *Troy Book* and Henryson's *Testament of Cresseid* as Competitive Imitations of *Troilus and Criseyde," Shifts and Transpositions in Medieval Narrative,* ed. Karen Pratt (Cambridge: D. S. Brewer, 1994), 89–108, and Alan S. Ambrisco and Paul Strohm, "Succession and Sovereignty in Lydgate's Prologue to *The Troy Book," ChauR* 30 (1995): 40–57.

150. Bowers, ed., *Fifteenth-Century Continuations and Additions,* 11–22; see Schirmer, *John Lydgate,* 59–65, and Pearsall, *John Lydgate* (1970), 151–59. Johnstone Parr, "Astronomical Dating for Some of Lydgate's Poems," *PMLA* 67 (1952): 251–58, dates the action to April 27, 1421.

151. Lee Patterson, "Making Identities in Fifteenth-Century England: Henry V and John Lydgate," *New Historical Literary Studies,* ed. Cox and Reynolds, 69–107 at 76, believes *Thebes* was completed before Henry V's death. James Simpson, "'Dysemol Daies and Fatal Houres': Lydgate's *Destruction of Thebes* and Chaucer's *Knight's Tale," The Long Fifteenth Century,* ed. Cooper and Mapstone, 15–33 at 15–16, believes that *Thebes* was completed after Henry V's death, when its narrative assumed more pressing significance as Gloucester and Bedford began re-enacting the fraternal strife of Ethyocles and Polymyte; see also Paul M. Clogan, "Lydgate and the *Roman Antique," Florilegium* 11 (1992): 7–22 at 12.

152. John M. Ganim, *Style and Consciousness in Middle English Narrative* (Princeton: Princeton University Press, 1983), "Mannerism and Moralism in Lydgate's *Siege of Thebes,"* 103–22, interprets the monumental style as an attempt to bridge the gap between the cloister and the court. Rosamund S. Allen, *"The Siege of Thebes*: Lydgate's Canterbury Tale," *Chaucer and Fifteenth-Century Poetry,* ed. Boffey and Cowen, 122–42, expands the notion of the courtly audience to include "dowager queens, princesses and royal nannies as well" (129).

153. John H. van Engen, *Rupert of Deutz* (Berkeley and Los Angeles: University of California Press, 1983), 349. Earlier episodes of Benedictine self-defense have been explored by Barbara H. Rosenwein, Thomas Head, and Sharon Farmer, "Monks and Their Enemies: A Comparative Approach," *Speculum* 66 (1991): 764–96. Kerby-Fulton, "Langland and the Bibliographic Ego," 91–97, proposes that this monastic genre informs the *apologias* of both Langland and Hoccleve.

154. Though not included in the text, the name "Chaucer" is placed prominently in the margin beside this passage in the Arundel manuscript. Paul Strohm, "Fourteenth- and Fifteenth-Century Writers as Readers of Chaucer," *Genres, Themes, and Images in English Literature from the Fourteenth to the Fifteenth Century,* ed. Piero Boitani and Anna Torti (Tübingen: Gunter Narr Verlag, 1988), 90–104, notes that all later successors lost the multiplicity of voices that had been one of Chaucer's most engaging achievements.

155. E. Beichner, "Daun Piers, Monk and Business Administrator," *Speculum* 34 (1959): 611–19; Robertson, *A Preface to Chaucer,* 253–56; Kumiko Shikii, "Chaucer's Anti-clericalism as Seen in the Monk," *The Fleur-de-Lis Review* (25 December 1980): 25–54; and John V. Fleming, "Daun Piers and Dom Pier: Waterless Fish and Unholy Hunters," *ChauR* 15 (1981): 287–94.

156. Terry Jones et al., *Who Murdered Chaucer?* 253–55, date the censorship around 1407 in response to Archbishop Arundel, but I prefer around 1421 in response to Henry V.

157. Used on the cover of the *Riverside Chaucer* paperback, this picture is discussed by Trigg, *Congenial Souls,* xiii–xvi.

158. Harriss, "Introduction," *Henry V: Practice of Kingship,* 24–25; see also Patterson, "Henry V and John Lydgate," 93–95.

159. All of the relevant documents are assembled by William Abel Pantin, ed., *Documents Illustrating the Activities of the General and Provincial Chapters of the English Black Monks, 1215–1540,* vol. 2, Camden 3rd ser., no. 47 (London: Camden Society, 1933), 98–134.

160. Walsingham, *Historia,* 2:337–38.

161. Cf. Pantin, ed., 115.

162. Barbara Harvey, *Living and Dying in England, 1100–1540: The Monastic Experience* (Oxford: Clarendon, 1993), 80–82 and 99.

163. John V. Fleming, "Gospel Asceticism: Some Chaucerian Images of Perfection," *Chaucer and Scriptural Tradition,* ed. Jeffrey, 183–95, and Laura F. Hodges, "A Reconsideration of the Monk's Costume," *ChauR* 26 (1991): 133–46, contribute to the scriptural and social contexts for this satire.

164. *St. Benedict's Rule for Monasteries,* trans. Leonard J. Doyle (Collegeville, MN: Liturgical Press, 1948), 76 (55).

165. Pantin, ed., 111.

166. Ibid. See also Harvey, *Living and Dying,* 146–78.

167. Pantin, ed., 111.

168. Harvey, *Living and Dying,* 71. Her study focuses upon Westminster Abbey. Since Chaucer's Monk (*CT,* VII, 1970) offers to tell the life of St. Edward the Confessor, founder of Westminster, this was probably his monastery.

169. *Rule* (36), 55; see also Harvey, *Living and Dying,* 51–56 and 61–62.

170. *Rule* (22), 42–43, and Pantin, ed., 115. Harvey, *Living and Dying,* 131, mentions the wearing of special nightclothes at Westminster.

171. Pantin, ed., 114. This article makes more detailed the prohibition of the *Rule* (33), 51.

172. Daniel T. Kline, "Father Chaucer and the *Siege of Thebes*: Literary Paternity, Aggressive Deference, and the Prologue to Lydgate's Oedipal *Canterbury Tales,*" *ChauR* 34 (1999): 217–35, reads the choice of historical subject back into Lydgate's struggles with the anxiety of influence.

173. A. C. Spearing, "Lydgate's Canterbury Tale: *The Siege of Thebes* and Fifteenth-Century Chaucerianism," *Fifteenth-Century Studies,* ed. Yeager, 333–64; Bowers, "Alternative Ideas of *The Canterbury Tales*"; and Simpson, "Lydgate's *Destruction of Thebes* and Chaucer's *Knight's Tale,*" 21–33.

174. Fradenburg, *Sacrifice Your Love,* "The Ninety-Six Tears of Chaucer's Monk," 113–54 at 137–38.

175. Simpson, *Reform,* "The Tragic," 68–120.

176. Wallace, *Chaucerian Polity,* "All That Fall: Chaucer's Monk and 'Every Myghty Man,'" 299–336.

177. Scott-Morgan Straker, "Rivalry and Reciprocity in Lydgate's *Troy Book," NML* 3 (1999): 119–47.

178. Simpson, *Reform,* "The Energies of John Lydgate," 34–67 at 56, find reformist impulses throughout the monk-poet's courtly works.

179. Walsingham, *Historia,* 2:13: "Scripsimus non sine labore in præcedentibus historiam tragicam."

180. Patterson, "Henry V and John Lydgate," 73–77 and 93–97, and Scanlon, *Narrative, Authority, and Power,* 332–50.

181. Pantin, ed., 114. Harvey, *Living and Dying,* 77, notes that private apartments had become the norm for officials and distinguished brothers. See also J. E. Madden, "Business Monks, Banker Monks, Bankrupt Monks: The English Cistercians in the Thirteenth Century," *Catholic Historical Review* 49 (1963): 341–64.

182. *Rule* (36–37), 54–55.

183. For the health-giving benefits of pilgrimage, see Ronald C. Finucane, *Miracles and Pilgrims: Popular Beliefs in Medieval England* (London: J. M. Dent, 1977), 59–82.

184. John Burrow, *The Ages of Man* (Oxford: Clarendon, 1988), 30–32, shows how Lydgate followed Avicenna's four-ages scheme with old age beginning at forty. Though he lived until 1449, Lydgate in 1420 might have understood himself well into old age.

185. *On the Properties of Things: John Trevisa's Translation of Bartholomaeus Anglicus "De Proprietatibus Rerum,"* gen. ed. M. C. Seymour, 2 vols. (Oxford: Clarendon Press, 1975), 252, described *colica passio* as a potentially fatal intestinal blockage.

186. Lydgate's much-copied *Dietary* began with similar advice: "Who will been holle & kepe hym from sekenesse . . . Lat hym be glad & voide al hevynesse"; *Minor Poems: Secular Poems,* 2:702. See also Charles F. Mullett, "John Lydgate: A Mirror of Medieval Medicine," *Bulletin of the History of Medicine* 22 (1948): 403–15; Glending Olson, *Literature as Recreation in the Middle Ages* (Ithaca and London: Cornell University Press, 1982), 52 and 173–74; and Claire Sponsler, "Eating Lessons: Lydgate's 'Dietary' and Consumer Conduct," *Medieval Conduct,* ed. Ashley and Clark, 1–22, on eating as a marker for social status.

187. Scase, "A Wycliffite Libel and the Naming of Heretics," 23.

188. Patterson, "Henry V and John Lydgate," 72.

189. Harvey, *Living and Dying,* 87–88.

190. Pantin, ed., 120.

191. Paul Strohm, "The Trouble with Richard: The Reburial of Richard II and Lancastrian Symbolic Strategy," *Speculum* 71 (1996): 87–111 at 101–5; this article has been revised as "Reburying Richard: Ceremony and Symbolic Relegitimation," *England's Empty Throne,* 101–27.

192. Christopher Wilson, "The Tomb of Henry IV and the Holy Oil of St. Thomas of Canterbury," *Medieval Architecture and Its Intellectual Context,* ed. Eric Fernie and Paul Crossley (London: Hambledon, 1990), 181–90 at 186. See also Walter Ullmann, "Thomas Becket's Miraculous Oil," *Journal of Theological Studies* 8 (1957):

129–33; T. A. Sandquist, "The Holy Oil of St. Thomas of Canterbury," *Essays in Medieval History Presented to Bertie Wilkinson,* ed. T. A. Sandquist and M. R. Powicke (Toronto: University of Toronto Press, 1969), 330–44; and Joel Burden, "How Do You Bury a Deposed King? The Funeral of Richard II and the Establishment of Lancastrian Royal Authority in 1400," *Henry IV,* ed. Dodd and Biggs, 35–53, esp. 37–39.

193. Allmand, *Henry V,* 415–17. See generally Simon Walker, "Political Saints in Later Medieval England," *McFarlane Legacy,* ed. Britnell and Pollard, 77–106.

194. In *The Legend of St. Austin at Compton (Minor Poems* 1:193, lines 387–88) he warned against those who complained about paying tithes—a clear reference to Lollard objectors—but he simply summoned the standard imagery of enemies sowing cockles amid the good corn.

195. Patterson, "Ambiguity and Interpretation: A Fifteenth-Century Reading of *Troilus and Criseyde*" (1979), rpt. *Negotiating the Past,* 116.

196. Maura B. Nolan, "The Art of History Writing: Lydgate's *Serpent of Division,*" *Speculum* 78 (2003): 99–127, reads this work in context of the national political crisis following Henry V's death.

197. Pearsall, *John Lydgate* (1997), 23–25 and 36–38.

198. Green, *Poets and Princepleasers,* 157, and Pearsall, *John Lydgate* (1997), 35–36 and 59.

CHAPTER SEVEN   *Piers Plowman,* **Print, and Protestantism**

1. Thomson, *Later Lollards,* "Kent and the South-East," 173–91, and John F. Davis, "Lollard Survival and the Textile Industry in the Southeast of England," *SCH* 3 (1966): 191–201; see also Hudson, *Premature Reformation,* 456–66, and Rob Lutton, "Connections between Lollards, Townsfolk and Gentry in Tenterden in the Late Fifteenth and Early Sixteenth Centuries," *Lollardy and the Gentry,* ed. Aston and Richmond, 198–228.

2. N. F. Blake, *Caxton and His World* (London: Deutsch, 1969), 70; Margaret Kekewich, "Edward IV, William Caxton, and Literary Patronage in Yorkist England," *MLR* 66 (1971): 481–87; King, *English Reformation Literature,* 36–37; and Pearsall, "The Idea of Englishness," 26.

3. Lotte Hellinga, *Caxton in Focus: The Beginning of Printing in England* (London: British Library, 1982); N. F. Blake, *William Caxton* (Aldershot: Variorum Press, English Writers of the Late Middle Ages, no. 7, 1996); and Seth Lerer, "William Caxton," *Cambridge History of Medieval English Literature,* ed. Wallace, 720–38.

4. Martha W. Driver, "Printing the *Confessio Amantis*: Caxton's Edition in Context," *Re-Visioning Gower,* ed. R. F. Yeager (Asheville, NC: Pegasus Press, 1998), 269–303, and Siân Echard, "Gower in Print," *Companion to Gower,* ed. Echard, 115–35 at 115–16.

5. Linne R. Mooney and Lister M. Matheson, "The Beryn Scribe and His Texts: Evidence for Multiple-Copy Production of Manuscripts in Fifteenth-Century England," *The Library* ser. 7, 4 (2003): 347–70; Linne R. Mooney, "John Shirley's

Heirs," *YES* 33 (2003): 182–98; and N. F. Blake, "Manuscript to Print," *William Caxton and English Literary Culture* (London: Hambledon, 1991), 275–93.

6. R. Carter Hailey, "'Geuyng Light to the Reader': Robert Crowley's Editions of *Piers Plowman* (1550)," *PBSA* 95 (2001): 483–502, proposes that Caxton felt Langland's archaic diction and outmoded meter, not the controversial contents, disqualified the poem from his early printing project.

7. Brewer, ed., *Chaucer: The Critical Heritage,* 1:76; see also Alexandra Gillespie, "Caxton's Chaucer and Lydgate Quartos: Miscellanies from Manuscript to Print," *Transactions of the Cambridge Bibliographical Society* 12 (2000): 1–25.

8. N. F. Blake, "Late Medieval Prose," *The Middle Ages,* ed. W. F. Bolton (1970; rpt. New York: P. Bedrick, 1987), 369–99 at 397. Printed from the Winchester Manuscript (BL Add. 59,678), Sir Thomas Malory's *Le Morte Darthur,* ed. Stephen H. A. Shepherd (New York: W. W. Norton, 2004), 814–19, includes Caxton's Prologue and Epilogue from his 1485 edition.

9. Blake, *Caxton and His World,* 84–93.

10. Ibid., 79–100 at 83. See also Barbara Belyea, "Caxton's Reading Public," *ELN* 19 (1981): 14–19.

11. Rosser, *Medieval Westminster,* 161, and William Kuskin, "Reading Caxton: Transformations in Capital, Authority, Print, and Persona in the Late Fifteenth Century," *NML* 3 (1999): 149–83. See also Kuskin, ed., *Caxton's Trace: Studies in the History of English Printing* (Notre Dame IN: University of Notre Dame Press, 2006).

12. Simpson, *Reform and Cultural Revolution,* esp. 333–43.

13. Somerset, "Expanding the Langlandian Canon: Radical Latin and the Stylistics of Reform."

14. Uhart, "The Early Reception of *Piers Plowman,*" 300–302 and 326–27, and Benson and Blanchfield, *Manuscripts of "Piers Plowman": The B-Version,* 40–43 and 129–36.

15. Russell and Kane, eds., *The C Version,* 8–9.

16. Uhart, "The Early Reception of *Piers Plowman,*" 394–95, for a transcription. See also Thorne and Uhart, "Robert Crowley's *Piers Plowman,*" 248, and Benson and Blanchfield, *Manuscripts of "Piers Plowman": The B-Version,* 47 and 148–49.

17. See Kane, ed., *The A Version,* 9–10 and 30–31.

18. G. L. Harriss, "Political Society and Growth of Government in Late Medieval England," *P&P* 138 (1993): 28–57, and Simpson, *Reform,* 219–29.

19. Kerby-Fulton, "Women Readers in Langland's Earliest Audience," 126–34, includes reproductions of the two manuscript pages with Anne Fortescue's signatures as well as her pointing-finger manicules.

20. Hanna, *Pursuing History,* 318 n. 44.

21. Thorlac Turville-Petre, "Sir Adrian Fortescue and His Copy of *Piers Plowman,*" *YLS* 14 (2000): 29–48 at 39–40; see Uhart, "The Early Reception of *Piers Plowman,*" 340–52, for a transcript of these sidenotes. Sir Adrian was not the only Tudor courtier to take an interest in *Piers Plowman.* The Blage anthology of sixteenth-century courtly verse, mainly by Wyatt and his circle, includes a poem with an unmistakable Langlandian beginning: "In soumer seson, as soune as the sonne"; see Derek Brewer, "An Unpublished Late Alliterative Poem," *English Philological Studies* 9 (1965):

84–88. James Simpson, "Grace Abounding: Evangelical Centralization and the End of *Piers Plowman*," *YLS* 14 (2000): 49–73, sees Wyatt's *Penitential Psalms* as another entry point for Langland's emergence in Henry VIII's England.

22. Turville-Petre, "Fortescue and His Copy of *Piers Plowman*," 43. Turville-Petre, 44, reports the purchase of *The Plowman's Tale* in Fortescue's account books deposited in the Public Record Office.

23. Richard Rex, "Blessed Adrian Fortescue: A Martyr Without a Cause?" *Analecta Bollandiana* 115 (1997): 307–53.

24. Hudson, "Legacy of *Piers Plowman*," 260.

25. Sarah A. Kelen, "Plowing the Past: 'Piers Protestant' and the Authority of Medieval Literary History," *YLS* 13 (1999): 101–36, provides a smart survey of Langland's plowman figure during this period. See also Hudson, "Legacy of *Piers Plowman*," 257–58.

26. Hudson, *Premature Reformation,* 493.

27. Parker, ed., *The Praier and Complaynte,* 20–24 and 31–32, makes these connections.

28. Hudson, "'No Newe Thyng': The Printing of Medieval Texts in the Early Reformation Period," *Lollards and Their Books,* 230 and 246.

29. Parker, ed., *The Praier and Complaynte,* 20 and 65, describes the composite makeup of this work, which includes a reference to the *Sixteen Points on which the Bishops Accuse Lollards.* Hudson, ed., *English Wycliffite Writings,* 145, comments on the early history of the *Sixteen Points* and its possible composition in the late fourteenth century.

30. Hudson, *Premature Reformation,* 375, and Simpson, *Reform,* 363–70.

31. John N. King, "The Book-Trade under Edward VI and Mary I," *Cambridge History of the Book in Britain,* vol. 3, ed. Hellinga and Trapp, 164–75.

32. King, *English Reformation Literature,* 3–5 and 323–25.

33. Hudson, "Legacy of *Piers Plowman*," 258–59, and King, *English Reformation Literature,* 474.

34. *Selected Sermons of Hugh Latimer,* ed. Allan G. Chester (Charlottesville: University Press of Virginia, 1968), 28–49. See Robert L. Kelly, "Hugh Latimer as Piers Plowman," *Studies in English Literature* 17 (1977): 13–26.

35. Hudson, "Legacy of *Piers Plowman*," 259.

36. Parker, ed., *Praier and Complaynte of the Ploweman,* "The Ploughman Tradition of Complaint," 52–78 at 68. Wawn, "Chaucer, *The Plowman's Tale* and Reformation Propaganda: The Testimonies of Thomas Godfray and *I Playne Piers,*" 184–88.

37. The text is different from the BL Lansdowne 762 edited by James M. Dean, *Medieval English Political Writings* (Kalamazoo: Medieval Institute Publication, 1996), 254–56.

38. Duffy, *Stripping the Altars,* 84–85, discusses briefly *How the Plowman Lerned his Pater Noster.*

39. Hudson, "Lollardy: The English Heresy?" *Lollards and Their Books,* 141–63.

40. Middleton, "The Critical Heritage," 2, and King, *English Reformation Literature,* 319–57.

41. Kane and Donaldson, eds., *The B Version,* 6–7.

42. Hudson, "Legacy of *Piers Plowman*," 258–59.

43. Ibid., 261.

44. Benson and Blanchfield, *Manuscripts of "Piers Plowman": The B-Version,* 190, and Uhart, "The Early Reception of *Piers Plowman*," 90–92.

45. Richard K. Emmerson, "'Or Yernen to Rede Redels?': *Piers Plowman* and Prophecy," *YLS* 7 (1993): 27–76, places Langland in context of medieval prophetic traditions first explored at length by Bloomfield's *"Piers Plowman" as a Fourteenth-Century Apocalypse.*

46. C. E. Wright, "The Dispersal of the Libraries in the Sixteenth Century," *The English Library before 1700: Studies in Its History,* ed. Francis Wormald and C. E. Wright (London: Athlone, 1958), 148–75.

47. Simpson, *Reform,* 23–31.

48. Heyworth, "The Earliest Black-Letter Editions of *Jack Upland*," 313, remarks that "here *Cum priuiligio Regali* is not a perfunctory and permissive formula but constitutes the royal assent to what is essentially an act of policy," preparing for Cromwell's suppression of the religious establishments.

49. Brewer, ed., *Chaucer: The Critical Heritage,* 1:94.

50. Foxe's *Actes and Monumentes* (1570), ed. Pratt and Stoughton, 2:357. See also Pearsall, "Thomas Speght (c. 1550–?)," *Editing Chaucer,* ed. Ruggiers, 88.

51. McCarl, ed., *Plowman's Tale,* 16–17.

52. John Milton, *Of Reformation Touching Church-Discipline in England,* ed. Will Taliaferro Hale (New Haven: Yale Studies in English, no. 54, 1916), 44.

53. Skeat included the text of *The Plowman's Tale* in his supplementary volume *Chaucerian and Other Pieces,* xxxi–xxxv and 147–90. See also Kathleen Forni, "The Chaucer Apocrypha: Did Usk's 'Testament of Love' and the 'Plowman's Tale' Ruin Chaucer's Early Reputation?" *NM* 98 (1997): 261–72. Forni, *The Chaucerian Apocrypha,* 88–105, discusses how these spurious works actually enhanced Chaucer's reputation in sixteenth-century Reformation England.

54. Brewer, ed., *Chaucer: The Critical Heritage,* 1:166.

55. Justice, "Lollardy," *Cambridge History of Medieval English Literature,* ed. Wallace, 688. "By the middle of the sixteenth-century, Piers the Plowman is too old to be anyone's brother," says Kelen, "Plowing the Past: 'Piers Protestant' and the Authority of Medieval Literary History," 105, "and that is exactly why he is useful to those who invoke his authority."

56. Joseph A. Dane, *Who Is Buried in Chaucer's Tomb?* (East Lansing: Michigan State University Press, 1998), 11–32, surveys the history of Chaucer's burial as the introduction to the relationship between treatment of the poet's body and editorial embalming of the body of his work. For some adjustment of these views, see Joseph A. Dane and Alexandra Gillespie, "Back at Chaucer's Tomb—Inscriptions in Two Early Copies of Chaucer's *Workes*," *SB* 52 (1999): 89–96, and Thomas A. Prendergast, *Chaucer's Dead Body: From Corpse to Corpus* (New York and London: Routledge, 2004).

57. Paul Binski, *Westminster Abbey and the Plantagenets: Kingship and the Representation of Power, 1200–1400* (New Haven and London: Yale University Press, 1995), 193–94. See also Nigel Saul, "Richard II and Westminster Abbey," *The Cloister and the*

World: Essays in Medieval History in Honour of Barbara Harvey, ed. John Blair and Brian Golding (Oxford: Clarendon, 1996), 196–218 at 212.

58. Derek Pearsall, "Chaucer's Tomb: The Politics of Reburial," *MÆ* 64 (1995): 51–73 at 67.

59. Chaucer, *The Works (1532) with Supplementary Material from the Editions of 1542, 1561, 1598 and 1602,* facsimile ed., Brewer.

60. Whitaker, ed., *Visio Willi de Petro Plouhman,* xvii–xviii.

61. Alvin Kernan, *The Cankered Muse* (1959; rpt. Hamden, CT: Archon Books, 1976), "The Mask of the Plowman," 40–54.

62. A. G. Dickens, *The English Reformation,* 2nd ed. (London: Batsford, 1989), 49–56 at 53, on the "Lollard Survival" in Tudor England into the 1530s: "All save a few belonged to the common people—weavers, wheelwrights, smiths, carpenters, shoemakers, tailors and other tradesmen, 'of whom,' writes Foxe, 'few or none were learned, being simple labourers and artificers, but as it pleased the Lord to work in them knowledge and understanding by reading a few books, such as they could get in corner.'"

63. Chambers, *Man's Unconquerable Mind,* 89.

64. McCarl, ed., *The Plowman's Tale,* 9, reports discovering this fact while reading seventeenth-century New England probate inventories.

65. See my forthcoming study "William Langland, Father of American Literature."

Works Cited

Primary Sources

Ancrene Riwle: Edited from Magdalene College, Cambridge MS. Pepys 2498. Ed. A. Zettersten. EETS o.s. 274, 1976.

Annales Ricardi Secundi et Henrici Quarti. Ed. Henry Thomas Riley. London: Rolls Series, 1866.

Anonimalle Chronicle, 1333–1381. Ed. V. H. Galbraith. Manchester: Manchester University Press, 1927.

The Auchinleck Manuscript: National Library of Scotland, Advocates' MS 19.2.1. Intro. Derek Pearsall and I. C. Cunningham. London: Scolar Press, 1977.

Audelay, John. *The Poems of John Audelay.* Ed. Ella Keats Whiting. EETS o.s. 184, 1931.

Bale, John. *Index Britanniae Scriptorum.* Ed. Reginald Lane Poole and Mary Bateson. Oxford: Clarendon, 1902.

Barr, Helen, ed. *The Piers Plowman Tradition.* London: J. M. Dent, 1993.

Bartholomaeus Anglicus. *On the Properties of Things: John Trevisa's Translation of Bartholomaeus Anglicus "De Proprietatibus Rerum."* Gen. ed. M. C. Seymour. 2 vols. Oxford: Clarendon Press, 1975.

Bede. *Ecclesiastical History of the English People.* Ed. Bertram Colgrave and R. A. B. Mynors. Oxford: Clarendon, 1969.

Benedict, St. *St. Benedict's Rule for Monasteries.* Trans. Leonard J. Doyle. Collegeville, MN: Liturgical Press, 1948.

Bokenham, Osbern. *Legendys of Hooly Wummen.* Ed. Mary S. Serjeantson. EETS o.s. 206, 1938.

Bowers, John M., ed. *The Canterbury Tales: 15th-Century Continuations and Additions.* 2nd ed. rev. Kalamazoo: Medieval Institute Publications, 1999.

Boyd, Beverly, ed. *The Middle English Miracles of the Virgin.* San Marino, CA: Huntington Library, 1964.

Brewer, Derek, ed. *Chaucer: The Critical Heritage*. Vol. 1: *1385–1837*. London: Routledge & Kegan Paul, 1978.

The Brut, or The Chronicles of England. Ed. Friedrich W. D. Brie. EETS o.s. 136, 1908.

Caxton, William. *Caxton's Book of Curtesye*. Ed. Frederick J. Furnivall. EETS e.s. 3, 1868.

Chambers, R. W., and Marjorie Daunt, eds. *A Book of London English, 1384–1425*. Oxford: Clarendon, 1931.

Chandos Herald. *The Life and Campaigns of the Black Prince*. Ed. and trans. Richard Barber. New York: St. Martin's, 1986.

Chaucer, Geoffrey. *Bodleian Library, MS Fairfax 16*. Intro. John Norton-Smith. London: Scolar Press, 1979.

———. *The Canterbury Tales of Chaucer*. Ed. Thomas Tyrwhitt. 5 vols. London: T. Payne, 1775–78.

———. *The Canterbury Tales: A Facsimile and Transcription of the Hengwrt Manuscript*. Ed. Paul G. Ruggiers. Intro. Donald C. Baker, and A. I. Doyle and M. B. Parkes. Norman: University of Oklahoma Press, 1979.

———. *The Chaucer Variorum*, vol. 5: *The Minor Poems, Part 1*. Ed. George B. Pace and Alfred David. Norman: University of Oklahoma Press, 1982.

———. *The Complete Works of Geoffrey Chaucer*. Ed. Walter W. Skeat. 6 vols. Oxford: Clarendon, 1894.

———. *A Facsimile of Corpus Christi College Cambridge MS 61*. Intro. M. B. Parkes and Elizabeth Salter. Cambridge: D. S. Brewer, 1978.

———. *The Hengwrt Chaucer Digital Facsimile*. Ed. Estelle Stubbs. CD-ROM. Leicester: Scholarly Digital Editions, 2000.

———. *The Poetic Works of Chaucer*. Ed. F. N. Robinson. Boston: Houghton Mifflin, 1933.

———. *Poetical Works: A Facsimile of Cambridge University Library MS GG.4.27*. Commentary by M. B. Parkes and Richard Beadle. 3 vols. Cambridge: D. S. Brewer, 1980–81.

———. *The Riverside Chaucer*. 3rd ed. Gen. ed. Larry D. Benson. Boston: Houghton Mifflin, 1987.

———. *The Text of the Canterbury Tales*. Ed. John M. Manley and Edith Rickert. 8 vols. Chicago: University of Chicago Press, 1940.

———. *Troilus and Criseyde*. Ed. B. A. Windeatt. London: Longman, 1984.

———. *The workes of Geffray Chaucer newly printed, with dyuers workes whych were neuer in print before*. Ed. William Thynne, 1542.

———. *The Works (1532) with Supplementary Material from the Editions of 1542, 1561, 1598 and 1602*. Facsimile edition by D. S. Brewer. London: Scolar Press, 1978.

Chaucer Life-Records. Ed. Martin M. Crow and Clair C. Olson. Oxford: Clarendon, 1966.

Chaucerian and Other Pieces: Being a Supplement to the Complete Works of Geoffrey Chaucer. Ed. Walter W. Skeat. Oxford: Clarendon, 1897.

Clanvowe, Sir John. *The Works of Sir John Clanvowe*. Ed. V. J. Scattergood. Cambridge: D. S. Brewer, 1975.

Court of Venus. Ed. Russell A. Fraser. Durham, NC: Duke University Press, 1955. 82–110.

Crowley, Robert. *The Select Works of Robert Crowley*. Ed. J. M. Cowper. EETS e.s. 15, 1872.

Dean, James M., ed. *Medieval English Political Writings*. Kalamazoo: Medieval Institute Publications, 1996.

———, ed. *Six Ecclesiastical Satires*. Kalamazoo: Medieval Institute Publications, 1991.

Death and Liffe. Ed. Joseph M. P. Donatelli. Cambridge, MA: Medieval Academy of America, Speculum Anniversary Monographs, 1989.

Dymmok, Roger. *Liber Contra XII Errores et Hereses Lollardorum*. Ed. H. S. Cronin. London: Wyclif Society, 1922.

Edward, Second Duke of York. *The Master of Game*. Ed. William A. Baillie-Grohman and F. N. Baillie-Grohman. Intro. Theodore Roosevelt. London: Ballantyne, Hanson & Co., 1904. Modernized version of this edition reprinted as Edward of Norwich. *Master of Game*. Philadelphia: University of Pennsylvania Press, 2005.

Eliot, T. S. *Selected Essays: New Edition*. New York: Harcourt, Brace & World, 1950.

Foxe, John. *Acts and Monuments* (1563). Ed. George Townsend. 1843–49; rpt. New York: AMS Press, 1965.

———. *The Actes and Monuments* (1570). Ed. Josiah Pratt and John Stoughton. 8 vols. London: Religious Tract Society, 1877.

Franklin, Benjamin. *The Autobiography*. New York: Barnes & Noble, 1995.

Froissart, Jean. *Chronicles*. Trans. Geoffrey Brereton. Harmondsworth: Penguin, 1978.

———. *Chroniques de J. Froissart*. Ed. Siméon Luce. Paris: Libraire de la Société de l'Histoire de France, 1876.

Furnivall, Frederick J., ed. *The Fifty Earliest English Wills*. EETS o.s. 78, 1882.

Geoffrey of Vinsauf. *Poetria Nova*. Trans. Margaret F. Nims. Toronto: Pontifical Institute of Mediaeval Studies, 1967.

Godly dyalogue and dysputacyon betwene Pyers plowman and a popysh preest (STC 19903).

Gower, John. *The English Works*. Ed. G. C. Macaulay. 2 vols. EETS e.s. 81 and 82, 1900–1901.

———. *Mirour de l'Omme*. Trans. William Burton Wilson. Rev. by Nancy Wilson Van Baak. East Lansing, MI: Colleagues Press, 1992.

———. *Vox Clamantis. The Major Latin Works*. Trans. Eric W. Stockton. Seattle: University of Washington Press, 1962.

Gray, Douglas, ed. *The Oxford Book of Late Medieval Verse and Prose*. Oxford: Clarendon, 1985.

Gray, Sir Thomas. *Scalacronica: The Reigns of Edward I, Edward II, and Edward III*. Ed. and trans. Sir Herbert Maxwell. Glasgow: James Maclehose & Sons, 1907.

Heyworth, P. L., ed. *Jack Upland, Friar Daw's Reply, and Upland's Rejoinder*. Oxford: Oxford University Press, 1968.

Hoccleve, Thomas. *Complaint and Dialogue*. Ed. J. A. Burrow. EETS o.s. 313, 1999.

————. *De Regimine Principum: A Poem Written in the Reign of Henry IV.* Ed. Thomas Wright. London: Roxburghe Club, 1860.

————. *Hoccleve's Works: The Minor Poems.* Ed. Frederick J. Furnivall and I. Gollancz, rev. Jerome Mitchell and A. I. Doyle. EETS e.s. 61 and 73, 1892 and 1925, rev. 1970.

————. *The Regiment of Princes.* Ed. Charles R. Blyth. Kalamazoo: Medieval Institute Publications, 1999.

Holy Bible Made from the Latin Vulgate by John Wycliffe and His Followers. Ed. Josiah Forshall and Sir Frederic Madden. 4 vols. Oxford: Oxford University Press, 1850.

Hudson, Anne, ed. *Selections from English Wycliffite Writings.* Cambridge: Cambridge University Press, 1978.

————, ed. *Two Wycliffite Texts: The Sermon of William Taylor 1406, The Testimony of William Thorpe 1407.* EETS o.s. 301, 1993.

————, and Pamela Gradon, eds. *English Wycliffite Sermons.* Vol. 1. Oxford: Clarendon, 1983.

I playne Piers which can not flatter (STC 19903a).

Jack Upland (STC 5098).

James I of Scotland. *The Kingis Quair.* Ed. John Norton-Smith. Oxford: Clarendon Press, 1971.

Jansen, Johannes Petrus Maria, ed. *The "Suffolk" Poems: An Edition of the Love Lyrics in Fairfax 16 Attributed to William de la Pole.* Groningen: Universiteitsdrukkerij, 1989.

Jean de Venette. *The Chronicle of Jean de Venette.* Ed. Richard A. Newhall. Trans. Jean Birdsall. New York: Columbia University Press, 1953.

Kail, J., ed. *Twenty-Six Political and Other Poems from Oxford MSS Digby 102 and Douce 322.* EETS o.s. 124, 1904.

Kempe, Margery. *The Book of Margery Kempe.* Ed. Sanford Brown Meech and Hope Emily Allen. EETS o.s. 212, 1940.

————. *The Book of Margery Kempe.* Ed. Lynn Staley. New York: Norton, 2001.

Knighton's Chronicle, 1337–1396. Ed. and trans. G. H. Martin. Oxford: Clarendon, 1995.

Langland, Robert. *Visio Willi de Petro Plouhman, Item Visiones eiusdem de Dowel, Dobet, et Dobest.* Ed. Thomas Dunham Whitaker. London: John Murray, 1813.

————. *The Vision of Pierce Plowman.* Ed. Robert Crowley. London, 1550 (STC 19906), 2nd printing 1550 with notes (STC 19907), 3rd printing 1550 (STC 19907a).

————. *The Vision of Pierce Plowman* (1550). Ed. Robert Crowley. Intro. to facsimile edition by J. A. W. Bennett. London: David Paradine Developments Ltd., 1976.

Langland, William. *Piers Plowman: The A Version.* Ed. George Kane. London: Athlone Press, 1960.

————. *Piers Plowman: The B Version.* Ed. George Kane and E. Talbot Donaldson. London: Athlone Press, 1975.

————. *Piers Plowman: The C Version.* Ed. George Russell and George Kane. London: Athlone Press; Berkeley: University of California Press, 1997.

————. *Piers the Plowman: A Critical Edition of the A-Version.* Ed. Thomas A. Knott and David C. Fowler. Baltimore: Johns Hopkins University Press, 1952.

———. *Piers Plowman: An Edition of the C-text*. Ed. Derek Pearsall. Berkeley and Los Angeles: University of California Press, 1978.

———. *The "Piers Plowman" Electronic Archive: Corpus Christi College, Oxford MS 201*. Ed. Robert Adams with M. Gail Duggan and Catherine A. Farley. Ann Arbor: University of Michigan Press, 2000.

———. *The "Piers Plowman" Electronic Archive: San Marino, Huntington Library, HM 128*. Ed. Michael A. Calabrese with Hoyt N. Duggan and Thorlac Turville-Petre. (Forthcoming.)

———. *Piers Plowman: A Facsimile of Bodleian Library, Oxford, MS Douce 104*. Intro. Derek Pearsall. Catalogue of illustrations, Kathleen Scott. Cambridge: D. S. Brewer, 1992.

———. *Piers Plowman: A Facsimile of the Z-text in Bodleian Library, Oxford, MS Bodley 851*. Ed. Charlotte Brewer and A. G. Rigg. Cambridge: D. S. Brewer, 1994.

———. *Piers Plowman: A Parallel-Text Edition of the A, B, C and Z Versions*. Vol. 1: *Text*. Ed. A. V. C. Schmidt. London and New York: Longman, 1995.

———. *Piers Plowman: The Z Version*. Ed. A. G. Rigg and Charlotte Brewer. Toronto: Pontifical Institute of Mediaeval Studies, no. 59, 1983.

———. *The Vision and Creed of Piers Ploughman*. Ed. Thomas Wright. 2 vols. 2nd ed. London: Reeves and Turner, 1887.

———. *The Vision of Piers Plowman: A Critical Edition of the B-Text*. Ed. A. V. C. Schmidt. London and New York: Dent/Dutton, 1978.

———. *The Vision of Piers Plowman, II: Text B*. Ed. Walter W. Skeat. EETS o.s. 38, 1869.

———. *The Vision of William concerning Piers the Plowman in Three Parallel Texts together with Richard the Redeless*. Ed. Walter W. Skeat. 2 vols. Oxford: Oxford University Press, 1886.

Lanterne of Liȝt Edited from MS Harl. 2324. Ed. Lilian M. Swinburn. EETS o.s. 151, 1917.

Latimer, Hugh. *Selected Sermons of Hugh Latimer*. Ed. Allan G. Chester. Charlottesville: University Press of Virginia, 1968.

Lay Folks' Catechism: Archbishop Thoresby's Instruction for the People. Ed. T. F. Simmons and H. E. Nolloth. EETS o.s. 118, 1901.

The Lay Folks Mass Book. Ed. Thomas Frederick Simmons. EETS o.s. 71, 1879.

Lollard Sermons. Ed. Gloria Cigman. EETS o.s. 294, 1989.

Love, Nicholas. *Mirror of the Blessed Life of Jesus Christ*. Ed. Michael G. Sargent. New York: Garland Medieval Texts, no. 18, 1992.

Lydgate, John. *Fall of Princes*. Ed. Henry Bergen. EETS e.s. 121–24, 1924–27.

———. *The Minor Poems: Religious Poems and Secular Poems*. 2 vols. Ed. Henry Noble MacCracken. EETS e.s. 107, 1911, and o.s. 192, 1934.

———. *The Pilgrimage of the Life of Man*. Ed. F. J. Furnivall and K. B. Locock. EETS e.s. 77, 83, 92, 1899, 1901, 1904.

———. *Poems*. Ed. John Norton-Smith. Oxford: Clarendon, 1966.

———. *The Siege of Thebes*. Ed. Robert R. Edwards. Kalamazoo: Medieval Institute Publications, 2001.

————. *Troy Book*. Ed. Henry Bergen. EETS e.s. 97, 103, 106, 126, 1906–35.

Lytell Geste how the Plowman lerned his Pater Noster (STC 20034).

Maidstone, Richard. *Concordia: The Reconciliation of Richard II with London*. Ed. David R. Carlson. Trans. A. G. Rigg. Kalamazoo: Medieval Institute Publications, 2003.

————. *Penitential Psalms*. Ed. Valerie Edden. Heidelberg: Winter Middle English Texts, no. 22, 1990.

Malory, Sir Thomas. *Le Morte Darthur*. Ed. Stephen H. A. Shepherd. New York: W. W. Norton, 2004.

Matthew, F. D., ed. *The English Works of Wyclif Hitherto Unprinted*. EETS o.s. 74, 1880, 2nd ed. rev. 1902.

Memorials of London and London Life in the XIIIth, XIVth and XVth Centuries, A.D. 1276–1419. Ed. Henry Thomas Riley. London: Longmans, Green, and Co., 1868.

Milton, John. *Of Reformation Touching Church-Discipline in England*. Ed. Will Taliaferro Hale. New Haven: Yale Studies in English, no. 54, 1916.

Mirror for Magistrates. Ed. Lily B. Campbell. Cambridge: Cambridge University Press, 1938.

Mum and the Sothsegger. Ed. Mabel Day and Robert Steele. EETS o.s. 199, 1936.

Myers, A. R., ed. *English Historical Documents, 1327–1485*. New York: Oxford University Press, 1969.

Netter, Thomas. *Fasciculi Zizaniorum*. Ed. Walter Waddington Shirley. London: Rolls Series, 1858.

Owen, Nancy H. "Thomas Wimbledon's Sermon: 'Redde racionem villicacionis tue.'" *MS* 28 (1966): 176–97.

Pantin, William Abel, ed. *Documents Illustrating the Activities of the General and Provincial Chapters of the English Black Monks, 1215–1540*. Vol. 2. London: Camden Society, 3rd ser., no. 47, 1933.

Pecock, Reginald. *Reginald Pecock's Book of Faith*. Ed. J. L. Morison. Glasgow: J. Maclehose & Sons, 1909.

Petrarch. *Letters*. Ed. and trans. Morris Bishop. Bloomington and London: Indiana University Press, 1966.

Philippe de Mézières. *Letter to King Richard II*. Ed. and trans. G. W. Coopland. Liverpool: Liverpool University Press, 1975.

Pierce the Ploughmans Crede (and God Spede the Plough). Ed. Walter W. Skeat. EETS o.s. 30, 1867.

The Pilgrim's Tale. Thynne. *Animadversions*. 77–98.

The Plowman's Tale: The c. 1532 and 1606 Editions of a Spurious Canterbury Tale. Ed. Mary Rhinelander McCarl. New York and London: Garland, 1997.

Powell, Susan, ed. *The Advent and Nativity Sermons from a Fifteenth-Century Revision of John Mirk's "Festial."* Heidelberg: Middle English Texts, no. 13, 1981.

The Praier and Complaynte of the Ploweman vnto Christe. Ed. Douglas H. Parker. Toronto: University of Toronto Press, 1997.

Puttenham, George. *The Arte of English Poesie*. Ed. Gladys Doidge Willcock and Alice Walker. Cambridge: Cambridge University Press, 1936.

Pyers Plowmans exhortation vnto the lordes, knightes and burgoysses of the Parlyamenthouse. (STC 19905).

Robbins, Rossell Hope, ed. *Historical Poems of the XIVth and XVth Centuries*. New York: Columbia University Press, 1959.

Rolle, Richard. *English Writings of Richard Rolle, Hermit of Hampole*. Ed. Hope Emily Allen. Oxford: Clarendon, 1931.

Royal Commission on Historical Manuscripts: Eighth Report and Appendix (Part I). London: Eyre and Spottiswoode, 1881.

Siege of Jerusalem Edited from MS Laud Misc. 656. Ed. E. Kölbing and Mabel Day. EETS o.s. 188, 1932.

The Siege of Jerusalem. Ed. Ralph Hanna and David Lawton. EETS o.s. 320, 2003.

Spurgeon, Caroline F. E., ed. *Five Hundred Years of Chaucerian Criticism and Allusion, 1357–1900*. 3 vols. 1925; rpt. New York: Russell & Russell, 1960.

Susannah: Alliterative Poem of the Fourteenth Century. Ed. Alice Miskimin. New Haven: Yale University Press, 1969.

The Tale of Gamelyn. Ed. W. W. Skeat. Oxford: Clarendon Press, 1884.

"*The Tale of Gamelyn*: A New Edition." Ed. Neil Daniel. Ph.D. diss., Indiana University, 1967.

Thynne, Francis. *Animadversions upon Thynne's First Edition of Chaucers Workes*. Ed. F. J. Furnivall. London: Chaucer Society, ser. 2, no. 13, 1876.

Trevisa, John. "*The Governance of Kings and Princes*": *John Trevisa's Middle English Translation of the "De Regimine Principum" of Aegidius Romanus*. Ed. David C. Fowler, Charles F. Briggs, and Paul G. Remley. New York and London: Garland, 1997.

Usk, Adam. *The Chronicle of Adam Usk, 1377–1421*. Ed. and trans. C. Given-Wilson. Oxford: Clarendon, 1997.

Usk, Thomas. *The Testament of Love*. Ed. R. Allen Shoaf. Kalamazoo: Medieval Institute Publications, 1998.

———. *The Testament of Love. Chaucerian and Other Pieces*. Ed. Skeat. xviii–xxxi, 1–145, 451–84.

The Vernon Manuscript: A Facsimile of Bodleian Library, Oxford, MS English Poet.a.1. Intro. A. I. Doyle. Cambridge: D. S. Brewer, 1987.

Walsingham, Thomas. *Historia Anglicana*. Ed. Henry Thomas Riley. 2 vols. London: Rolls Series, 1863–64.

Walton, John. *Boethius: De Consolatione Philosophiae*. Ed. Mark Science. EETS o.s. 170, 1927.

Westminster Chronicle, 1381–1394. Ed. and trans. L. C. Hector and Barbara F. Harvey. Oxford: Clarendon, 1982.

The Wheatley Manuscript. Ed. Mabel Day. EETS o.s. 155, 1921.

Wright, Thomas, ed. *Political Poems and Songs Relating to English History Composed during the Period from the Accession of Edward III to that of Richard III*. 2 vols. London: Rolls Series, 1859–61.

———, ed. *Three Chapters of Letters Relating to the Suppression of the Monasteries*. Camden Society o.s. 26, 1843.

Wyclif, John. *Polemical Works in Latin*. Ed. Rudolf Buddensieg. 2 vols. London: Wyclif Society, 1883.

———. *Select English Works of John Wyclif*. Ed. Thomas Arnold. 3 vols. Oxford: Clarendon, 1869–71.

Secondary Sources

Adams, Jenny. "Exchequers and Balances: Anxieties of Exchange in *The Tale of Beryn*." *SAC* 26 (2004): 267–97.

Ady, Julia Mary Cartwright. *The Pilgrims' Way from Winchester to Canterbury*. 1893; rpt. New York: AMS Press, 1974.

Aers, David. *Chaucer, Langland, and the Creative Imagination*. London: Routledge & Kegan Paul, 1980.

———. "The Sacrament of the Altar in *Piers Plowman* and the Late Medieval Church." *Images, Idolatry, and Iconoclasm*. Ed. Dimmick, Simpson, and Zeeman. 63–80.

———. "*Vox Populi* and the Literature of 1381." *Cambridge History of Medieval English Literature*. Ed. Wallace. 432–53.

———. "Walter Brut's Theology of the Sacrament of the Altar." *Lollards and Their Influence*. Ed. Somerset, Havens, and Pitard. 115–26.

———, and Lynn Staley. *The Powers of the Holy*. University Park: Pennsylvania State University Press, 1996.

Alexander, J. J. G. "Foreign Illuminators and Illuminated Manuscripts." *Cambridge History of the Book in Britain,* vol. 3. Ed. Hellinga and Trapp. 47–64.

Alford, John A. *Piers Plowman: A Glossary of Legal Diction*. Cambridge: D. S. Brewer, 1988.

———. "The Role of the Quotations in *Piers Plowman*." *Speculum* 52 (1977): 80–99.

———, ed. *A Companion to "Piers Plowman."* Berkeley and Los Angeles: University of California Press, 1988.

Allen, Hope Emily. *The Authorship of "The Prick of Conscience."* Boston and New York: Radcliffe College Monographs, no. 15, 1910.

———. "The *Speculum Vitae*: Addendum." *PMLA* 32 (1917): 133–62.

Allen, Judson Boyce. "Langland's Reading and Writing: *Detractor* and the Pardon Scene." *Speculum* 59 (1984): 342–62.

Allen, Rosamund S. "*The Siege of Thebes*: Lydgate's Canterbury Tale." *Chaucer and Fifteenth-Century Poetry*. Ed. Boffey and Cowen. 122–42.

Allmand, Christopher. *Henry V*. Berkeley and Los Angeles: University of California Press, 1992.

———. *The Hundred Years War: England and France at War c. 1300–c. 1450*. Cambridge: Cambridge University Press, 1988.

———. *Lancastrian Normandy 1415–1450: The History of a Medieval Occupation*. Oxford: Clarendon, 1983.

———. *Society at War: The Experience of England and France during the Hundred Years War*. Edinburgh: Oliver & Boyd, 1973.

Ambrisco, Alan S., and Paul Strohm. "Succession and Sovereignty in Lydgate's Prologue to *The Troy Book*." *ChauR* 30 (1995): 40–57.

Anderson, Judith H. "Langland, William." *Spenser Encyclopedia*. Ed. A. C. Hamilton. Toronto: University of Toronto Press, 1990. 425–26.

Archer, Rowena E., ed. *Crown, Government, and People in the Fifteenth Century*. New York: St. Martin's, 1995.

Arn, Mary-Jo. "Thomas Chaucer and William Paston Take Care of Business: HLS Deeds 349." *SAC* 24 (2002): 237–67.

———. "Two Manuscripts, One Mind: Charles d'Orléans and the Production of Manuscripts in Two Languages." *Charles d'Orléans in England.* Ed. Arn. 61–78.

———, ed. *Charles d'Orléans in England (1415–1440).* Cambridge: D. S. Brewer, 2000.

Arnold, John H. "Lollard Trials and Inquisitorial Discourse." *Fourteenth-Century England II.* Ed. Chris Given-Wilson. Woodbridge: Boydell, 2002. 81–94.

Ashley, Kathleen, and Robert L. A. Clark, eds. *Medieval Conduct.* Minneapolis: University of Minnesota Press, 2001.

Aston, Margaret. *Faith and Fire: Popular and Unpopular Religion, 1350–1600.* London: Hambledon, 1993.

———. "Lollards and the Cross." *Lollards and Their Influence.* Ed. Somerset, Havens, and Pitard. 99–113.

———. *Lollards and Reformers: Images and Literacy in Late Medieval Religion.* London: Hambledon Press, 1984.

———. *Thomas Arundel: A Study of Church Life in the Reign of Richard II.* Oxford: Clarendon, 1967.

———, and Colin Richmond, eds. *Lollardy and the Gentry in the Later Middle Ages.* New York: St. Martin's Press, 1997.

Auerbach, Erich. *Mimesis: The Representation of Reality in Western Literature.* Trans. Willard R. Trask. Princeton: Princeton University Press, 1953.

Backhouse, Janet. "The Royal Library from Edward IV and Henry VII." *Cambridge History of the Book in Britain,* vol. 3. Ed. Hellinga and Trapp. 267–73.

Baker, Denise N., ed. *Inscribing the Hundred Years' War in French and English Cultures.* Albany: State University of New York Press, 2000.

———. "Mede and the Economics of Chivalry in *Piers Plowman.*" *Inscribing the Hundred Years' War.* Ed. Baker. 55–72.

Baldwin, Anna P. "The Historical Context." *Companion to "Piers Plowman."* Ed. Alford. 67–86.

———. "Patient Politics in *Piers Plowman.*" *YLS* 15 (2001): 99–108.

Baldwin, Ralph. *The Unity of the Canterbury Tales.* Copenhagen: Rosenkilde and Bagger, 1955.

Barber, M. J. "The Books and Patronage of Learning of a Fifteenth-Century Prince." *Book Collector* 12 (1963): 308–15.

Barber, Malcolm. *The Cathars: Dualist Heretics in Languedoc in the High Middle Ages.* New York: Longman, 2000.

Barnie, John. *War in Medieval English Society: Social Values in the Hundred Years War, 1337–99.* Ithaca: Cornell University Press, 1974.

Barr, Helen. "The Relationship of *Richard the Redeless* and *Mum and the Sothsegger*: Some New Evidence." *YLS* 4 (1990): 105–33.

———. *Signes and Sothe: Language in the "Piers Plowman" Tradition.* Cambridge: D. S. Brewer, 1994.

———. *Socioliterary Practice in Late Medieval England.* Oxford: Oxford University Press, 2001.

———. "Wycliffite Representations of the Third Estate." *Lollards and Their Influence.* Ed. Somerset, Havens, and Pitard. 197–216.

————, and Ann M. Hutchison, eds. *Text and Controversy from Wyclif to Bale: Essays in Honour of Anne Hudson*. Turnhout, Belgium: Brepols, 2005.

Barron, Caroline M. "The London Middle English Guild Certificates of 1388–89." *Nottingham Medieval Studies* 39 (1995): 108–18.

————. "New Light on Thomas Usk." *Chaucer Newsletter* 26/2 (Fall 2004): 1.

————. "The Parish Fraternities of Medieval London." *Church in Pre-Reformation Society*. Ed. Barron and Harper-Bill. 13–37.

————. "William Langland: A London Poet." *Chaucer's England*. Ed. Hanawalt. 91–109.

————, and Christopher Harper-Bill, eds. *The Church in Pre-Reformation Society*. Woodbridge: Boydell, 1985.

Barthes, Roland. "The Death of the Author." *Image—Music—Text*. Trans. Stephen Heath. New York: Noonday Press, 1977. 142–48.

Batt, Catherine. "Hoccleve and . . . Feminism? Negotiating Meaning in the *Regement of Princes*." *Essays on Thomas Hoccleve*. Ed. Batt. 55–84.

————, ed. *Essays on Thomas Hoccleve*. Brepols, Belgium: Westfield Publications in Medieval Studies, no. 10, 1996.

Baugh, Albert C. *A History of the English Language*. 2nd ed. New York: Appleton-Century-Crofts, 1957.

————. "Kirk's Life Records of Thomas Chaucer." *PMLA* 47 (1932): 461–515.

————. "The Original Teller of the Merchant's Tale." *MP* 35 (1937): 15–26.

————. "Thomas Chaucer, One Man or Two?" *PMLA* 47 (1933): 328–39.

Baugh, Nita Scudder. "A Worcestershire Miscellany Compiled by John Northwood, c. 1400, Edited from British Museum MS. Add. 37,787." Philadelphia: Bryn Mawr College dissertation, 1956.

Bayley, C. C. "The Campaign of 1375 and the Good Parliament." *EHR* 55 (1940): 370–83.

Beadle, Richard. "Geoffrey Spirleng (c. 1426–c. 1494): A Scribe of the *Canterbury Tales* in His Time." *Of the Making of Books*. Ed. Robinson and Zim. 116–46.

————. "'I wol nat telle it yit': John Selden and a Lost Version of the *Cook's Tale*." *Chaucer and Shakespeare: Essays in Honour of Shinsuke Ando*. Ed. Toshiyuki Takamiya and Richard Beadle. Cambridge: D. S. Brewer, 1992. 55–66.

————. "Monk Thomas Hyngham's Hand in the Macro Manuscript." *New Science out of Old Books*. Ed. Beadle and Piper. 315–41.

————, and A. J. Piper, eds. *New Science out of Old Books: Studies in Manuscripts and Early Printed Books in Honour of A. I. Doyle*. Aldershot: Scolar Press, 1995.

Beckett, Neil. "The Relations between St. Bridget, Henry V, and Syon Abbey." *Studies in St. Birgitta and the Brigittine Order*. Ed. James Hogg. 2 vols. Salzburg: Universität Salzburg, 1993. 2:125–50.

Beichner, Paul E. "Daun Piers, Monk and Business Administrator." *Speculum* 34 (1959): 611–19.

Beidler, Peter G. "Transformations in Gower's *Tale of Florent* and Chaucer's *Wife of Bath's Tale*." *Chaucer and Gower*. Ed. Yeager. 100–114.

Bell, David. "A Cistercian at Oxford: Richard Dove of Buckfast and London BL Sloane 513." *Studia Monastica* 31 (1989): 69–87.

————. "Monastic Libraries, 1400–1557." *Cambridge History of the Book in Britain,* vol. 3. Ed. Hellinga and Trapp. 229–54.

Bell, Susan Groag. "Medieval Women Book Owners: Arbiters of Lay Piety and Ambassadors of Culture." *Women and Power in the Middle Ages.* Ed. Mary Erler and Maryanne Kowaleski. Athens and London: University of Georgia Press, 1988. 149–87.

Belyea, Barbara. "Caxton's Reading Public." *ELN* 19 (1981): 14–19.

Bennett, H. S. *Chaucer and the Fifteenth Century.* Oxford: Clarendon, 1947.

Bennett, J. A. W. "Chaucer's Contemporary." *"Piers Plowman": Critical Approaches.* Ed. Hussey. 310–24.

————. "The Date of the A-Text of *Piers Plowman.*" *PMLA* 58 (1943): 566–72.

Bennett, Michael J. "The Court of Richard II and the Promotion of Literature." *Chaucer's England.* Ed. Hanawalt. 3–20.

————. "Henry Bolingbroke and the Revolution of 1399." *Henry IV.* Ed. Dodd and Biggs. 9–33.

————. "John Audelay: Some New Evidence on His Life and Work." *ChauR* 16 (1982): 344–55.

Benson, C. David, and Lynne S. Blanchfield. *The Manuscripts of "Piers Plowman": The B-Version.* Cambridge: D. S. Brewer, 1997.

Benson, Larry D. "The Occasion of *The Parliament of Fowls.*" *Wisdom of Poetry.* Ed. Benson and Wenzel. 123–44.

————, and Siegfried Wenzel, eds. *The Wisdom of Poetry: Essays in Early English Literature in Honor of Morton W. Bloomfield.* Kalamazoo: Medieval Institute Publications, 1982.

Bhabha, Homi K., ed. *Nation and Narration.* London and New York: Routledge, 1991.

Bianco, Sue. "New Perspectives on Lydgate's Courtly Verse." *Nation, Court and Culture.* Ed. Cooney. 95–115.

Biddick, Kathleen. "The ABC of Ptolemy: Mapping the World with the Alphabet." *Texts and Territory: Geographical Imagination in the European Middle Ages.* Ed. Sylvia Tomasch and Sealy Gilles. Philadelphia: University of Pennsylvania Press, 1998. 268–93.

Biggs, Douglas. "The Politics of Health: Henry IV and the Long Parliament of 1406." *Henry IV.* Ed. Dodd and Biggs. 185–202.

————. "The Reign of Henry IV: The Revolution of 1399 and the Establishment of the Lancastrian Regime." *Fourteenth Century England.* Ed. Nigel Saul. Woodbridge: Boydell, 2000. 195–210.

Biller, Peter, and Anne Hudson, eds. *Heresy and Literacy, 1000–1530.* Cambridge: Cambridge University Press, 1994.

Binski, Paul. *Westminster Abbey and the Plantagenets: Kingship and the Representation of Power, 1200–1400.* New Haven and London: Yale University Press, 1995.

Bird, Ruth. *The Turbulent London of Richard II.* London: Longmans, Green and Co., 1949.

Black, Antony. *Guilds and Civil Society in European Political Thought from the Twelfth Century to the Present.* Ithaca: Cornell University Press, 1984.

Black, Merja. "A Scribal Translation of *Piers Plowman*." *MÆ* 67 (1998): 257–90.

Blake, Norman F. "Caxton and Chaucer." *LSE* n.s. 1 (1967): 19–36.

———. *Caxton and His World*. London: Deutsch, 1969.

———. "Geoffrey Chaucer and the Manuscripts of the *Canterbury Tales*." *Journal of the Early Book Society* 1 (1997): 96–122.

———. "Late Medieval Prose." *The Middle Ages*. Ed. W. F. Bolton. 1970; rpt. New York: P. Bedrick, 1987. 369–99.

———. *William Caxton*. Aldershot: Variorum Press, English Writers of the Late Middle Ages, no. 7, 1996.

———. *William Caxton and English Literary Culture*. London: Hambledon, 1991.

———. "William Caxton: His Choice of Texts." *Anglia* 83 (1965): 289–307.

Blamires, Alcuin G. "Crisis and Dissent." *Companion to Chaucer*. Ed. Brown. 133–48.

———. "*Mum and the Sothsegger* and Langlandian Idiom." *NM* 76 (1975): 583–604.

———. "The Wife of Bath and Lollardy." *MÆ* 58 (1989): 224–42.

Blodgett, James E. "William Thynne (d. 1546)." *Editing Chaucer*. Ed. Ruggiers. 35–52.

Bloom, Harold. *The Anxiety of Influence: A Theory of Poetry*. Oxford and New York: Oxford University Press, 1973.

Bloomfield, Morton W. *"Piers Plowman" as a Fourteenth-Century Apocalypse*. New Brunswick: Rutgers University Press, 1962.

———. "Was William Langland a Benedictine Monk?" *MLQ* 4 (1943): 57–61.

Blyth, Charles. "Thomas Hoccleve's Other Master." *Mediaevalia* 16 (1993): 349–59.

Boffey, Julia. "Charles of Orleans Reading Chaucer's Dream Visions." *Mediaevalitas: Reading the Middle Ages*. Ed. Piero Boitani and Anna Torti. Cambridge: D. S. Brewer, 1996. 43–62.

———. *Manuscripts of English Courtly Love Lyrics in the Later Middle Ages*. Cambridge: D. S. Brewer, 1985.

———. "Proverbial Chaucer and the Chaucer Canon." *Reading from the Margins*. Ed. Lerer. 37–47.

———, and A. S. G. Edwards. "'Chaucer's Chronicle,' John Shirley, and the Canon of Chaucer's Shorter Poems." *SAC* 20 (1998): 201–18.

———, and John J. Thompson. "Anthologies and Miscellanies: Production and Choice of Texts." *Book Production*. Ed. Griffiths and Pearsall. 279–315.

———, and Janet Cowen, eds. *Chaucer and Fifteenth-Century Poetry*. London: King's College London Medieval Studies, no. 5, 1991.

Bolton, J. L. *The Medieval English Economy, 1150–1500*. Totowa, NJ: Rowman & Littlefield, 1980.

Bose, Mishtooni. "Reginald Pecock's Vernacular Voice." *Lollards and Their Influence*. Ed. Somerset, Havens, and Pitard. 217–36.

Boswell, John. *Christianity, Social Tolerance, and Homosexuality*. Chicago and London: University of Chicago Press, 1980.

Bovey, Alixe. *The Chaworth Roll: A Fourteenth-Century Genealogy of the Kings of England*. London: Sam Fogg Gallery, 2005.

Bowers, John M. "Chaucer after Retters: The Wartime Origins of English Literature." *Inscribing the Hundred Years' War*. Ed. Baker. 91–125.

————. "Chaucer after Smithfield: From Postcolonial Writer to Imperialist Author." *The Postcolonial Middle Ages*. Ed. Jeffrey Cohen. New York: St. Martin's Press, 2000. 53–66.

————. "Chaucer's *Canterbury Tales*—Politically Corrected." *Rewriting Chaucer: Culture, Authority, and the Idea of the Authentic Text, 1400–1602*. Ed. Thomas A. Prendergast and Barbara Kline. Columbus: Ohio State University Press, 1999. 13–44.

————. "Controversy and Criticism: Lydgate's *Thebes* and the Prologue to *Beryn*." *Chaucer Yearbook* 5 (1998): 91–115.

————. *The Crisis of Will in "Piers Plowman."* Washington, DC: Catholic University of America Press, 1986.

————. "Dating *Piers Plowman*: Testing the Testimony of Usk's *Testament*." *YLS* 13 (1999): 65–100.

————. "Hoccleve's Huntington Holographs: The First 'Collected Poems' in English." *FCS* 15 (1989): 24–51.

————. "Hoccleve's Two Copies of *Lerne to Dye*: Implications for Textual Critics." *PBSA* 83 (1989): 437–72.

————. "The House of Chaucer & Son: The Business of Lancastrian Canon-Formation." *Medieval Perspectives* 6 (1991): 135–43.

————. "Langland's *Piers Plowman* in HM 143: Copy, Commentary, Censorship." *YLS* 19 (2005): 137–68.

————. "*Mankind* and the Political Interests of Bury St. Edmunds." *Æstel* 2 (1994): 77–103.

————. "Piers Plowman and the Police: Notes toward a History of the Wycliffite Langland." *YLS* 6 (1992): 1–50.

————. "*Piers Plowman* and the Unwillingness to Work." *Mediaevalia* 9 (1987 for 1983): 239–49.

————. "*Piers Plowman's* William Langland: Editing the Text, Writing the Author's Life." *YLS* 9 (1995): 65–102.

————. *The Politics of "Pearl": Court Poetry in the Age of Richard II*. Cambridge: D. S. Brewer, 2001.

————. "Queering the Summoner: Same-Sex Union in Chaucer's *Canterbury Tales*." *Speaking Images*. Ed. Yeager and Morse. 301–24.

————. "*The Tale of Beryn* and *The Siege of Thebes*: Alternative Ideas of the *Canterbury Tales*." *SAC* 7 (1985): 23–50. Reprinted in *Writing after Chaucer: Essential Readings in Chaucer and the Fifteenth Century*. Ed. Daniel Pinti. New York: Garland, 1998. 201–26.

————. "Three Readings of *The Knight's Tale*: Sir John Clanvowe, Geoffrey Chaucer, and James I of Scotland." *JMEMS* 34 (2004): 279–307.

————. "Two Professional Readers of Chaucer and Langland: Scribe D and the HM 114 Scribe." *SAC* 26 (2004): 113–46.

Boyd, Beverly. "The Infamous B-text of the *Canterbury Tales*." *Manuscripta* 34 (1990): 233–38.

———. "Our Lady According to Geoffrey Chaucer: Translation and Collage." *Florilegium* 9 (1990 for 1987): 147–54.

———. "William Caxton (1422?-1491)." *Editing Chaucer*. Ed. Ruggiers. 13–34.

Boyd, David Lorenzo. "Social Texts: Bodley 686 and the Politics of the Cook's Tale." *Reading from the Margins*. Ed. Lerer. 81–97.

Boyle, Leonard E. "The *Oculus Sacerdotis* and Some Other Works of William of Pagula." *TRHS* 5th ser., 5 (1955): 81–110.

Braddick, Michael J. *State Formation in Early Modern England c. 1550–1700*. Cambridge: Cambridge University Press, 2000.

Brady, Sr. M. Teresa. "Lollard Interpolations and Omissions in Manuscripts of *The Pore Caitif.*" *Cella in Seculum: Religious and Secular Life and Devotion in Late Medieval England*. Ed. Michael G. Sargent. Cambridge: D. S. Brewer, 1989. 183–203.

Brewer, Charlotte. "Authorial vs. Scribal Writing in *Piers Plowman*." *Medieval Literature*. Ed. Machan. 59–89.

———. *Editing "Piers Plowman": The Evolution of the Text*. Cambridge: Cambridge University Press, 1996.

Brewer, Derek. *Chaucer and His World*. 2nd ed. Cambridge: D. S. Brewer, 1992.

———. "Chaucer's Anti-Ricardian Poetry." *The Living Middle Ages: A Festschrift for Karl Heinz Göller*. Ed. Uwe Böker, Manfred Markus, and Rainer Schöwerling. Stuttgart: Belser, 1989. 115–28.

———. "An Unpublished Late Alliterative Poem." *English Philological Studies* 9 (1965): 84–88.

Briggs, Charles F. *Giles of Rome's "De Regime Principum": Reading and Writing Politics at Court and University, c. 1275–c. 1525*. Cambridge: Cambridge University Press, 1999.

Bright, Allan H. *New Light on "Piers Plowman."* London: Oxford University Press, 1928.

Brink, Bernhard ten. *History of English Literature*. Vol. 1: *Early English Literature to Wyclif*. Trans. Horace Milton Kennedy. Vol. 2: *Wyclif, Chaucer, Earliest Drama, Renaissance*. Trans. William Clarke Robinson. London: George Bell & Sons, 1893.

Britnell, R. H., and A. J. Pollard, eds. *The McFarlane Legacy: Studies in Late Medieval Politics and Society*. New York: St. Martin's, 1995.

Brockwell, Charles W., Jr. *Bishop Reginald Pecock and the Lancastrian Church: Securing the Foundations of Cultural Authority*. Lewiston, NY: Edwin Mellen Press, 1985.

Brooks, E. St. John. "The *Piers Plowman* Manuscripts in Trinity College, Dublin." *The Library* 5th ser., 6 (1951): 141–53.

Brosnahan, Leger. "The Pendant in the Chaucer Portraits." *ChauR* 26 (1992): 424–31.

Brown, A. L. *The Governance of Late Medieval England, 1272–1461*. Stanford: Stanford University Press, 1989.

———. "The Privy Seal Clerks in the Early Fifteenth Century." *The Study of Medieval Records: Essays in Honour of Kathleen Major*. Ed. D. A. Bullough and R. L. Storey. Oxford: Clarendon, 1971. 260–81.

————. "The Reign of Henry IV." *Fifteenth Century England, 1399–1509: Studies in Politics and Society.* Ed. S. B. Chrimes, C. D. Ross, and R. A. Griffiths. 2nd ed. Stroud: Sutton, 1995. 1–28.

Brown, Carleton. "Author's Revisions in the *Canterbury Tales.*" *PMLA* 57 (1942): 29–50.

Brown, Peter. "Higden's Britain." *Medieval Europeans: Studies in Ethnic Identity and National Perspectives in Medieval Europe.* Ed. Alfred P. Smyth. New York: St. Martin's Press, 1998. 103–18.

————. "Journey's End: The Prologue to *The Tale of Beryn.*" *Chaucer and Fifteenth-Century Poetry.* Ed. Boffey and Cowen. 143–74.

————, ed. *A Companion to Chaucer.* Oxford: Blackwell, 2000.

Brusendorff, Aage. *The Chaucer Tradition.* Oxford: Clarendon, 1925.

Bryan, W. F., and Germaine Dempster, eds. *Sources and Analogues of Chaucer's "Canterbury Tales."* London: Routledge & Kegan Paul, 1941.

Bühler, Curt F. "A Lollard Tract: On Translating the Bible into English." *MÆ* 7 (1938): 167–83.

Burden, Joel. "How Do You Bury a Deposed King? The Funeral of Richard II and the Establishment of Lancastrian Royal Authority in 1400." *Henry IV.* Ed. Dodd and Biggs. 35–53.

Burke, Edmund. *Reflections on the Revolution in France.* Ed. Conor Cruise O'Brien. New York: Penguin, 1982.

Burnley, David. "Language." *Companion to Chaucer.* Ed. Brown. 235–50.

Burrow, John A. "The Action of Langland's Second Vision." *EIC* 15 (1965): 247–68.

————. *The Ages of Man.* Oxford: Clarendon, 1988.

————. "The Audience of *Piers Plowman.*" *Anglia* 75 (1957): 373–84.

————. "Autobiographical Poetry in the Middle Ages: The Case of Thomas Hoccleve." *PBA* 68 (1982): 389–412.

————. "Hoccleve and Chaucer." *Chaucer Traditions.* Ed. Morse and Windeatt. 54–61.

————. "Hoccleve and the 'Court.'" *Nation, Court and Culture.* Ed. Cooney. 70–80.

————. "Hoccleve and the Middle French Poets." *The Long Fifteenth Century.* Ed. Cooper and Mapstone. 35–49.

————. "Hoccleve's *Series*: Experience and Books." *Fifteenth-Century Studies.* Ed. Yeager. 261–73.

————. *Langland's Fictions.* Oxford: Clarendon, 1993.

————. *Ricardian Poetry: Chaucer, Gower, Langland and the "Gawain" Poet.* London: Routledge & Kegan Paul, 1971.

————. *Thomas Hoccleve.* Aldershot and Brookfield: Variorum, Authors of the Middle Ages, no. 4, 1994.

Calabrese, Michael. "*[Piers] the [Plowman]*: The Corrections, Interventions, and Erasures in Huntington MS Hm 143 (X)." *YLS* 19 (2005): 169–99.

Call, Reginald. "'Whan He His Papir Sought' (Chaucer's *Cook's Tale,* A 4404)." *MLQ* 4 (1943): 167–76.

Cannon, Christopher. *The Grounds of English Literature*. Oxford: Oxford University Press, 2004.

———. *The Making of Chaucer's English*. Cambridge: Cambridge University Press, 1998.

———. "Monastic Productions." *Cambridge History of Medieval English Literature*. Ed. Wallace. 316–48.

———. "The Myth of Origin and the Making of Chaucer's English." *Speculum* 71 (1996): 646–75.

Cargill, Oscar. "The Langland Myth." *PMLA* 50 (1935): 36–56.

Carley, James P. "'Cum excuterem puluerem et blattas': John Bale, John Leland, and the *Chronicon Tinemutensis coenobii*." *Text and Controversy from Wyclif to Bale*. Ed. Barr and Hutchison. 163–87.

Carlson, David R. *Chaucer's Jobs*. New York: Palgrave Macmillan, 2004.

———. "Thomas Hoccleve and the Chaucer Portrait." *HLQ* 54 (1991): 283–300.

Carpenter, Christine. "The Religion of the Gentry of Fifteenth-Century England." *England in the Fifteenth Century*. Ed. Williams. 53–74.

Carr, Antony D. "Sir Lewis John—A Medieval London Welshman." *Bulletin of the Board of Celtic Studies* 22 (1968): 260–70.

Carruthers, Mary J. "*Piers Plowman*: The Tearing of the Pardon." *PQ* 49 (1970): 8–18.

———. "Time, Apocalypse, and the Plot of *Piers Plowman*." *Acts of Interpretation: The Text in Its Contexts 700–1600. Essays on Medieval and Renaissance Literature in Honor of E. Talbot Donaldson*. Ed. Mary J. Carruthers and Elizabeth D. Kirk. Norman, OK: Pilgrim Books, 1982. 175–88.

Catto, Jeremy. "Fellows and Helpers: The Religious Identity of the Followers of Wyclif." *The Medieval Church: Universities, Heresy, and the Religious Life*. Ed. Peter Biller and Barrie Dobson. Woodbridge: Boydell, 1999. 141–61.

———. "Religious Change under Henry V." *Henry V: The Practice of Kingship*. Ed. Harriss. 75–115.

———. "Sir William Beauchamp between Chivalry and Lollardy." *The Ideals and Practice of Medieval Knighthood*. Ed. Christopher Harper-Bill and Ruth Harvey. Woodbridge: Boydell, 1990. 39–48.

Cazelles, Richard. "The Jacquerie." *The English Rising of 1381*. Ed. Hilton and Aston. 74–83.

Chambers, R. W. "The Authorship of *Piers Plowman*." *MLR* 5 (1910): 1–32.

———. *Man's Unconquerable Mind*. London: Jonathan Cape, 1939.

———, and J. H. G. Grattan. "The Text of *Piers Plowman*." *MLR* 26 (1931): 1–51.

Chism, Christine. *Alliterative Revivals*. Philadelphia: University of Pennsylvania Press, 2002.

Christianson, C. Paul. "A Community of Book Artisans in Chaucer's London." *Viator* 20 (1989): 207–18.

———. *A Directory of London Stationers and Book Artisans, 1300–1500*. New York: Bibliographical Society of America, 1990.

———. "Evidence for the Study of London's Late Medieval Manuscripts-Book Trade." *Book Production*. Ed. Griffiths and Pearsall. 87–108.

————. *Memorials of the Book Trade in Medieval London*. Cambridge: D. S. Brewer, 1987.

Cigman, Gloria. "*Luceat Lux Vestra*: The Lollard Preacher as Truth and Light." *RES* n.s. 40 (1989): 479–96.

Clark, John P. H. "Trinovantum—The Evolution of a Legend." *Journal of Medieval History* 7 (1981): 135–51.

Clarke, Maude Violet. *Fourteenth Century Studies*. Ed. L. S. Sutherland and M. McKisack. Oxford: Clarendon, 1937.

————, and V. H. Galbraith, eds. "*Chronicle of Dieulacres Abbey, 1381–1403.*" *BJRL* 14 (1930): 164–81.

Classen, Albrecht. "Hoccleve's Independence from Chaucer: A Study of Poetic Emancipation." *FCS* 16 (1990): 59–81.

Clogan, Paul M. "Lydgate and the *Roman Antique*." *Florilegium* 11 (1992): 7–22.

Clopper, Lawrence M. "The Engaged Spectator: Langland and Chaucer on Civic Spectacle and the *Theatrum*." *SAC* 22 (2000): 115–39.

————. "Franciscans, Lollards, and Reform." *Lollards and Their Influence*. Ed. Somerset, Havens, and Pitard. 177–96.

————. "Langland's Persona: An Anatomy of the Mendicant Orders." *Written Work*. Ed. Justice and Kerby-Fulton. 144–84.

————. "Need Men and Women Labor? Langland's Wanderer and the Labor Ordinances." *Chaucer's England*. Ed. Hanawalt. 110–29.

Coghill, Nevill. "The Pardon of Piers Plowman." *PBA* 30 (1944): 303–57.

————. "Two Notes on *Piers Plowman*: I. The Abbot of Abingdon and the Date of the C-Text; II. Chaucer's Debt to Langland." *MÆ* 4 (1935): 83–94.

Coldiron, A. E. B. *Canon, Period, and the Poetry of Charles of Orleans*. Ann Arbor: University of Michigan Press, 2000.

————. "Translation, Canons, and Cultural Capital: Manuscripts and Reception of Charles d'Orléans's English Poetry." *Charles d'Orléans in England*. Ed. Arn. 183–214.

Cole, Andrew. "Chaucer's English Lesson." *Speculum* 77 (2002): 1128–67.

————. "William Langland and the Invention of Lollardy." *Lollards and Their Influence*. Ed. Somerset, Havens, and Pitard. 37–58.

————. "William Langland's Lollardy." *YLS* 17 (2003): 25–54.

Coleman, Janet. *Medieval Readers and Writers, 1350–1400*. New York: Columbia University Press, 1981.

Colledge, Eric. "*The Recluse*: A Lollard Interpolated Version of the *Ancren Riwle*." *RES* 15 (1939): 1–15 and 129–45.

Collette, Carolyn. "Afterlife." *Companion to Chaucer*. Ed. Brown. 8–22.

Cooney, Helen, ed. *Nation, Court and Culture: New Essays on Fifteenth-Century English Poetry*. Dublin: Four Courts Press, 2001.

Cooper, Helen. "Chaucerian Representation." *New Readings of Chaucer's Poetry*. Ed. Robert G. Benson and Susan J. Ridyard. Intro. Derek Brewer. Cambridge: D. S. Brewer, 2003. 7–29.

———. "The Four Last Things in Dante and Chaucer: Ugolino in the House of Rumour." *NML* 3 (1999): 39–66.

———. "Jacobean Chaucer: *The Two Noble Kinsmen* and Other Chaucerian Plays." *Refiguring Chaucer in the Renaissance*. Ed. Krier. 189–209.

———. "Langland's and Chaucer's Prologues." *YLS* 1 (1987): 71–81.

———. "The Order of Tales in the Ellesmere Manuscript." *Ellesmere Chaucer*. Ed. Stevens and Woodward. 245–61.

———. *Oxford Guides to Chaucer: The Canterbury Tales*. Oxford: Clarendon, 1989.

———. "Welcome to the House of Fame: 600 Years Dead: Chaucer's Deserved Reputation as 'the Father of English Poetry.'" *TLS* 5091 (27 October 2000): 3–4.

———, and Sally Mapstone, eds. *The Long Fifteenth Century: Essays for Douglas Gray*. Oxford: Clarendon, 1997.

Copeland, Rita. "William Thorpe and His Lollard Community: Intellectual Labor and the Representation of Dissent." *Bodies and Disciplines*. Ed. Barbara A. Hanawalt and David Wallace. Minneapolis: University of Minnesota Press, 1996. 199–221.

Correale, Robert M., and Mary Hamel, eds. *Sources and Analogues of the "Canterbury Tales": Volume I*. Cambridge: D. S. Brewer, 2002.

Costomiris, Robert. "The Yoke of Canon: Chaucerian Aspects of *The Plowman's Tale*." *PQ* 71 (1992): 185–98.

Cox, Jeffrey N., and Larry J. Reynolds, eds. *New Historical Literary Study*. Princeton: Princeton University Press, 1993.

Crane, Susan. "The Writing Lesson of 1381." *Chaucer's England*. Ed. Hanawalt. 201–21.

Craun, Edwin D. *Lies, Slander, and Obscenity in Medieval English Literature*. Cambridge: Cambridge University Press, 1997.

Crawford, William R. "Robert Crowley's Editions of *Piers Plowman*: A Bibliographical and Textual Study." Ph.D. diss., Yale University, 1957.

Crompton, James. "Leicestershire Lollards." *Transactions of the Leicestershire Archaeological and Historical Society* 44 (1968/69): 11–44.

Crook, David. "Central England and the Revolt of the Earls, January 1400." *Historical Research* 64 (1991): 403–10.

Cross, Claire. "'Great Reasoners in Scripture': The Activities of Women Lollards, 1380–1530." *Medieval Women*. Ed. Derek Baker. Oxford: Blackwell, 1978. 359–80.

Crow, Martin Michael. "John of Angoulême and His Chaucer Manuscript." *Speculum* 17 (1942): 86–99.

Crowley, Leslie-Anne. *The Quest for Holiness: Spenser's Debt to Langland*. Milan: Arcipelago Edizioni, Letterature in Lingua Inglese, no. 5, 1992.

Cummings, Brian. "Iconoclasm and Bibliophobia in the English Reformation, 1521–1558." *Images, Idolatry, and Iconoclasm in Late Medieval England*. Ed. Dimmick, Simpson, and Zeeman. 185–206.

Dahl, Eric. "*Diuerse Copies Haue It Diuerselye*: An Unorthodox Survey of *Piers Plowman* Textual Scholarship from Crowley to Skeat." *Suche Werkis to Werche*. Ed. Vaughan. 53–80.

Dahmus, Joseph H. *The Prosecution of John Wyclif.* New Haven: Yale University Press, 1952.

Dane, Joseph A. "Bibliographical History versus Bibliographical Evidence: *The Plowman's Tale* and Early Chaucer Editions." *BJRL* 78 (1996): 50–64.

———. *Who Is Buried in Chaucer's Tomb?* East Lansing: Michigan State University Press, 1998.

———, and Alexandra Gillespie. "Back at Chaucer's Tomb—Inscriptions in Two Early Copies of Chaucer's *Workes*." *SB* 52 (1999): 89–96.

Davenport, W. A. *Chaucer and His English Contemporaries: Prologue and Tale in "The Canterbury Tales."* New York: St. Martin's Press, 1998.

———. "Fifteenth-Century Complaints and Duke Humphrey's Wives." *Nation, Court and Culture.* Ed. Cooney. 129–52.

David, Alfred. "Chaucer's Good Counsel to Scogan." *ChauR* 3 (1968–69): 265–74.

———. "The Ownership and Use of the Ellesmere Manuscript." *Ellesmere Chaucer.* Ed. Stevens and Woodward. 307–26.

———. "The Truth about 'Vache.'" *ChauR* 11 (1977): 334–37.

Davidoff, Judith M. *Beginning Well: Framing Fictions in Late Middle English Poetry.* London and Toronto: Associated University Presses, 1988.

Davidson, Linda Kay, and Maryjane Dunn-Wood. *Pilgrimage in the Middle Ages: A Research Guide.* New York and London: Garland, 1993.

Davies, R. G. "Thomas Arundel as Archbishop of Canterbury, 1396–1414." *Journal of Ecclesiastical History* 14 (1973): 9–21.

Davies, R. R. *The First English Empire: Power and Identities in the British Isles, 1093–1343.* Oxford: Oxford University Press, 2000.

———. "The Life, Travels, and Library of an Early Reader of *Piers Plowman*." *YLS* 13 (1999): 49–64.

Davis, Bryan P. "The Rationale for a Copy of a Text: Constructing the Exemplar for BL Additional MS. 10574." *YLS* 11 (1997): 141–55.

Davis, John F. "Lollard Survival and the Textile Industry in the Southeast of England." *SCH* 3 (1966): 191–201.

———. "Lollards, Reformers and St. Thomas of Canterbury." *University of Birmingham Historical Journal* 9 (1963): 1–15.

Davis, Norman, Douglas Gray, Patricia Ingham, and Anne Wallace-Hadrill, eds. *A Chaucer Glossary.* Oxford: Clarendon, 1979.

Davlin, Mary Clemente, O.P. "Chaucer and Langland as Religious Writers." *William Langland's "Piers Plowman."* Ed. Hewett-Smith. 119–41.

Day, Mabel. "The Revisions of *Piers Plowman*." *MLR* 23 (1928): 1–27.

Deanesly, Margaret. *The Lollard Bible and Other Medieval Biblical Versions.* Cambridge: Cambridge University Press, 1920.

De Hamel, Christopher. *Scribes and Illuminators.* Toronto: University of Toronto Press, 1992.

De Looze, Laurence. "Signing Off in the Middle Ages: Medieval Textuality and Strategies of Authorial Self-Naming." *Vox Intexta: Orality and Textuality in the Middle Ages.* Ed. A. N. Doan and Carol Braun Pasternak. Madison: University of Wisconsin Press, 1991. 162–78.

DeMarco, Patricia. "An Arthur for the Ricardian Age: Crown, Nobility, and the Alliterative *Morte Arthure*." *Speculum* 80 (2005): 464–93.

Derrida, Jacques. *Of Grammatology*. Trans. Gayatri Chakravorty Spivak. Baltimore: Johns Hopkins University Press, 1976.

Dickens, A. G. *The English Reformation*. 2nd ed. London: Batsford, 1989.

Dillon, Janette. "Life Histories." *Companion to Chaucer*. Ed. Brown. 251–65.

Dillon, Viscount, and W. H. St. John Hope. "Inventory of the Goods and Chattels Belonging to Thomas, Duke of Gloucester, and Seized in His Castle at Pleshy, Co. Essex, 21 Richard II (1397), with Their Values, as Shown in the Escheator's Accounts." *Archaeological Journal* 54 (1897): 275–308.

Dimmick, Jeremy, James Simpson, and Nicolette Zeeman, eds. *Images, Idolatry, and Iconoclasm in Late Medieval England*. Oxford: Oxford University Press, 2002.

Dinshaw, Carolyn. *Getting Medieval*. Durham: Duke University Press, 1999.

———. "Rivalry, Rape and Manhood: Gower and Chaucer." *Chaucer and Gower*. Ed. Yeager. 130–52

Dobson, Michael. *The Making of the National Poet: Shakespeare, Adaptation and Authorship, 1660–1769*. Oxford: Clarendon, 1992.

Dobson, R. B., ed. *The Peasants' Revolt of 1381*. 2nd ed. London: Macmillan, 1983.

Dodd, Gwilym, and Douglas Biggs, eds. *Henry IV: The Establishment of the Regime, 1399–1406*. Woodbridge: Boydell & Brewer for York Medieval Press, 2003.

Donaldson, E. Talbot. "MSS R and F in the B-Tradition of *Piers Plowman*." *Transactions of the Connecticut Academy of Arts and Sciences* 39 (1955): 177–212.

———. *"Piers Plowman": The C-Text and Its Poet*. New Haven: Yale Studies in English, no. 113, 1949.

———. *Speaking of Chaucer*. London: Athlone, 1970.

———. *The Swan at the Well: Shakespeare Reading Chaucer*. New Haven: Yale University Press, 1985.

Doob, Penelope. *Nebuchadnezzar's Children: Conventions of Madness in Middle English Literature*. New Haven: Yale University Press, 1974.

Doyle, A. I. "The Copyist of the Ellesmere *Canterbury Tales*." *Ellesmere Chaucer*. Ed. Stevens and Woodward. 49–67.

———. "English Books in and out of Court from Edward III to Henry VII." *English Court Culture in the Later Middle Ages*. Ed. Scattergood and Sherborne. 163–81.

———. "The Manuscripts." *Middle English Alliterative Poetry and Its Literary Background*. Ed. Lawton. 88–100 and notes 142–47.

———. "Publications by Members of the Religious Orders." *Book Production*. Ed. Griffiths and Pearsall. 109–23.

———. "Recent Directions in Medieval Manuscript Study." *New Directions in Later Medieval Manuscript Studies*. Ed. Pearsall. 1–14.

———. "Reflections on Some Manuscripts of Nicholas Love's *Myrrour of the Blessed Lyf of Jesu Christ*." *LSE* n.s. 14 (1983): 82–93.

———. "Remarks on Surviving Manuscripts of *Piers Plowman*." *Medieval English Religious and Ethical Literature: Essays in Honour of G. H. Russell*. Ed. Gregory Kratzmann and James Simpson. Cambridge: D. S. Brewer, 1986. 35–48.

————. "The Shaping of the Vernon and Simeon Manuscripts." *Chaucer and Middle English Studies in Honor of Rossell Hope Robbins*. Ed. Beryl Rowland. London: Allen & Unwin, 1974. 328–41.

————. "Stephen Dodesham of Witham and Sheen." *Of the Making of Books*. Ed. Robinson and Zim. 94–115.

————. "A Survey of the Origins and Circulation of Theological Writings in English in the 14th, 15th, and Early 16th Centuries with Special Consideration of the Part of the Clergy Therein." 2 vols. Ph.D. diss., Cambridge University, 1953.

————. "An Unrecognized Piece of *Piers the Ploughman's Creed* and Other Work by Its Scribe." *Speculum* 34 (1959): 428–36.

————. "Ushaw College, Durham, MS 50: Fragments of the *Prick of Conscience*, by the Same Scribe as Oxford, Corpus Christi College, MS 201 of the B Text of *Piers Plowman*." *English Medieval Book*. Ed. Edwards, Gillespie, and Hanna. 43–49.

————, and M. B. Parkes. "The Production of Copies of the *Canterbury Tales* and the *Confessio Amantis* in the Early Fifteenth Century." *Medieval Scribes, Manuscripts and Libraries: Essays Presented to N. R. Ker*. Ed. M. B. Parkes and A. G. Watson. London: Scolar Press, 1978. 163–210.

Driver, Martha W. "Medieval Manuscripts and Electronic Media: Observations on Future Possibilities." *New Directions in Late Medieval Manuscript Studies*. Ed. Pearsall. 53–64.

————. "Printing the *Confessio Amantis*: Caxton's Edition in Context." *Re-Visioning Gower*. Ed. R. F. Yeager. Asheville, NC: Pegasus Press, 1998. 269–303.

Du Boulay, F. R. H. *The England of "Piers Plowman": William Langland and His Vision of the Fourteenth Century*. Cambridge: D. S. Brewer, 1991.

Duffy, Eamon. *The Stripping of the Altars: Traditional Religion in England, c. 1400–c. 1580*. New Haven and London: Yale University Press, 1992.

Duggan, Anne. *Thomas Becket*. Oxford: Oxford University Press, 2004.

Duggan, Hoyt N. "The Authenticity of the Z-text of *Piers Plowman*: Further Notes on Metrical Evidence." *MÆ* 56 (1987): 25–45.

————. "The Electronic *Piers Plowman* B: A New Diplomatic-Critical Edition." *Æstel* 1 (1993): 55–75.

————. "Evidential Basis for Old English Metrics." *SP* 85 (1988): 145–63.

————. "Stress Assignment in Middle English Alliterative Poetry." *JEGP* 89 (1990): 309–29.

Düll, Siegrid, Anthony Luttrell, and Maurice Keen. "Faithful unto Death: The Tomb Slab of Sir William Neville and Sir John Clanvowe, Constantinople, 1391." *The Antiquaries Journal* 71 (1991): 174–90.

Duls, Louisa DeSaussure. *Richard II in the Early Chronicles*. Paris and The Hague: Mouton, 1975.

Dutschke, C. W. *Guide to Medieval and Renaissance Manuscripts in the Huntington Library*. 2 vols. San Marino: Huntington Library, 1989.

Dyer, Christopher. "The Social and Economic Background to the Rural Revolt of 1381." *The English Rising of 1381*. Ed. Hilton and Aston. 9–42.

Ebin, Lois A. *Illuminator, Makar, Vates: Visions of Poetry in the Fifteenth Century*. Lincoln: University of Nebraska Press, 1988.

Echard, Siân. "Gower in Print." *Companion to Gower*. Ed. Echard. 115–35.

———, ed. *A Companion to Gower*. Cambridge: D. S. Brewer, 2004.

Edden, Valerie. "Richard Maidstone's *Penitential Psalms*." *Leeds Studies in English* n.s. 17 (1986): 77–94.

Edwards, A. S. G. "The Chaucer Portraits in the Harley and Rosenbach Manuscripts." *English Manuscript Studies, 1100–1700*. Ed. Peter Beal and Jeremy Griffiths. Vol. 4. London: British Library, 1993. 268–71.

———. "The Early Reception of Chaucer and Langland." *Florilegium* 15 (1998): 1–23.

———. "Fifteenth-Century Middle English Verse Author Collections." *English Medieval Book*. Ed. Edwards, Gillespie, and Hanna. 101–12.

———. "The Huntington *Fall of Princes* (HM 268) and Sloane 2452." *Manuscripta* 16 (1972): 37–40.

———. "The Influence of Lydgate's *Fall of Princes* c. 1440–1559: A Survey." *Medieval Studies* 39 (1977): 424–39.

———. "Walter Skeat (1835–1912)." *Editing Chaucer*. Ed. Ruggiers. 171–89.

———, and Derek Pearsall. "The Manuscripts of the Major English Poetic Texts." *Book Production*. Ed. Griffiths and Pearsall. 257–78.

———, Vincent Gillespie, and Ralph Hanna, eds. *The English Medieval Book: Studies in Memory of Jeremy Griffiths*. London: British Library, 2000.

Ellis, Roger. "Chaucer, Christine de Pizan and Hoccleve: *The Letter of Cupid*." *Essays on Thomas Hoccleve*. Ed. Batt. 29–54.

———. "Translation." *Companion to Chaucer*. Ed. Brown. 443–58.

Embree, Don. "*Richard the Redeless* and *Mum and the Sothsegger*: A Case of Mistaken Identity." *N&Q* 220 (1975): 4–12.

Emmerson, Richard K. "'Or Yernen to Rede Redels?' *Piers Plowman* and Prophecy." *YLS* 7 (1993): 27–76.

———. "Reading Gower in a Manuscript Culture: Latin and English in Illustrated Manuscripts of the *Confessio Amantis*." *SAC* 21 (1999): 143–86.

Epstein, Robert. "Chaucer's Scogan and Scogan's Chaucer." *SP* 96 (1999): 1–21.

Epstein, Steven A. *Wage, Labor and Guilds in Medieval Europe*. Chapel Hill: University of North Carolina Press, 1991.

Erickson, Carolly. "The Fourteenth-Century Franciscans and Their Critics." *Franciscan Studies* 35 (1975): 107–35.

Erler, Mary C. "Exchange of Books between Nuns and Laywomen: Three Surviving Examples." *New Science out of Old Books*. Ed. Beadle and Piper. 361–73.

Federico, Sylvia. *New Troy: Fantasies of Empire in the Late Middle Ages*. Minneapolis and London: University of Minnesota Press, 2003.

Fein, Susanna, ed. *Studies in the Harley Manuscript: The Scribes, Contents and Social Contexts of British Library MS Harley 2253*. Kalamazoo: Medieval Institute Publications, 2000.

———, David Raybin, and Peter C. Braeger, eds. *Rebels and Rivals: The Contestive Spirit in the "Canterbury Tales."* Kalamazoo: Medieval Institute Publications, 1991.

Ferguson, Arthur B. "The Problem of Counsel in *Mum and the Sothsegger*." *Studies in the Renaissance* 2 (1955): 67–83.

Ferry, Anne. "*Anonymity*: The Literary History of a Word." *NLH* 33 (2002): 193–214.

Fineman, Joel. "The History of the Anecdote: Fiction and Fiction." *The New Historicism*. Ed. Veeser. 49–76.

Finucane, Ronald C. *Miracles and Pilgrims: Popular Beliefs in Medieval England*. London: J. M. Dent, 1977.

Fish, Stanley. "Commentary: The Young and the Restless." *The New Historicism*. Ed. Veeser. 303–16.

Fisher, John H. "Animadversions on the Text of Chaucer, 1988." *Speculum* 63 (1988): 779–93.

———. "Chancery and the Emergence of Standard Written English in the Fifteenth Century." *Speculum* 52 (1977): 870–99.

———. *The Importance of Chaucer*. Carbondale and Edwardsville: Southern Illinois University Press, 1992.

———. *John Gower: Moral Philosopher and Friend of Chaucer*. London: Methuen, 1965.

———. "A Language Policy for Lancastrian England." *PMLA* 107 (1992): 1168–80.

———. "*Piers Plowman* and the Chancery Tradition." *Medieval English Studies Presented to George Kane*. Ed. Kennedy et al. 267–78.

Fitzgibbons, Moira. "Disruptive Simplicity: Gaytryge's Translation of Archbishop Thoresby's *Injunctions*." *The Vernacular Spirit: Essays on Medieval Religious Literature*. Ed. Renate Blumenfeld-Kosinski, Duncan Robertson, and Nancy Bradley Warren. New York: Palgrave, 2002. 39–58.

Fleming, John V. "Chaucer and Erasmus on the Pilgrimage to Canterbury: An Iconographical Speculation." *The Popular Literature of Medieval England*. Ed. Thomas J. Heffernan. Knoxville: Tennessee Studies in Literature, vol. 28, 1985. 148–66.

———. "Daun Piers and Dom Pier: Waterless Fish and Unholy Hunters." *ChauR* 15 (1981): 287–94.

———. "Gospel Asceticism: Some Chaucerian Images of Perfection." *Chaucer and Scriptural Tradition*. Ed. Jeffrey. 183–95.

Fletcher, Alan J. "Chaucer the Heretic." *SAC* 25 (2003): 53–121.

———. "The Essential (Ephemeral) William Langland: Textual Revision as Ethical Process in *Piers Plowman*." *YLS* 15 (2001): 61–84.

———. "John Mirk and the Lollards." *MÆ* 56 (1987): 217–24.

———. "Unnoticed Sermons from John Mirk's *Festial*." *Speculum* 55 (1980): 514–22.

Forni, Kathleen. "The Chaucer Apocrypha: Did Usk's 'Testament of Love' and the 'Plowman's Tale' Ruin Chaucer's Early Reputation?" *NM* 98 (1997): 261–72.

———. *The Chaucerian Apocrypha: A Counterfeit Canon*. Gainesville: University Press of Florida, 2001.

Foucault, Michel. *The Archaeology of Knowledge*. Trans. A. M. Sheridan Smith. New York: Pantheon Books, 1972.

———. *Discipline and Punish: The Birth of the Prison*. Trans. Alan Sheridan. New York: Vintage Books, 1979.

———. *The Foucault Reader*. Ed. Paul Rabinow. New York: Pantheon Books, 1984.

———. *The Order of Things: An Archaeology of the Human Sciences*. New York: Vintage Books, 1973.

Fowler, Elizabeth. "Misogyny and Economic Person in Skelton, Langland, and Chaucer." *Spenser Studies* 10 (1992): 245–73.

Fowler, Kenneth, ed. *The Hundred Years War*. London: Macmillan, 1971.

Fradenburg, L. O. Aranye. *Sacrifice Your Love: Psychoanalysis, Historicism, Chaucer*. Minneapolis: University of Minnesota Press, 2002.

Frantzen, Allen J. *Desire for Origins: New Language, Old English, and Teaching the Tradition*. New Brunswick and London: Rutgers University Press, 1990.

Fredell, Joel. "The Lowly Paraf: Transmitting Manuscript Design in *The Canterbury Tales*." *SAC* 22 (2000): 213–80.

Frye, Northrop. *Anatomy of Criticism*. Princeton: Princeton University Press, 1957.

Furnivall, Frederick J. *Temporary Preface to the Six-Text Edition of Chaucer's "Canterbury Tales."* London: Chaucer Society, 2nd ser. 3, 1868.

Gadd, Ian, and Alexandra Gillespie, eds. *John Stow (1525–1605) and the Making of the English Past*. London: British Library, 2004.

Gaffney, Wilbur. "The Allegory of the Christ-Knight in *Piers Plowman*." *PMLA* 46 (1931): 155–68.

Gallagher, Catherine, and Stephen Greenblatt. *Practicing New Historicism*. Chicago and London: University of Chicago Press, 2000.

Galloway, Andrew. "Authority." *Companion to Chaucer*. Ed. Brown. 23–39.

———. "Gower in His Most Learned Role and the Peasants' Revolt of 1381." *Mediaevalia* 16 (1993 for 1990): 329–47.

———. "Latin England." *Imagining a Medieval English Nation*. Ed. Lavezzo. 41–95.

———. "Making History Legal: *Piers Plowman* and the Rebels of Fourteenth-Century England." *William Langland's "Piers Plowman."* Ed. Hewett-Smith. 7–39.

———. "*Piers Plowman* and the Schools." *YLS* 6 (1992): 89–107.

———. "The Rhetoric of Riddling in Late-Medieval England: The 'Oxford' Riddles, the *Secretum Philosophorum,* and the Riddles in *Piers Plowman*." *Speculum* 70 (1995): 68–105.

———. "Uncharacterizable Entities: The Poetics of Middle English Scribal Culture and the Definitive *Piers Plowman*." *SB* 52 (1999): 59–87.

Ganim, John M. *Style and Consciousness in Middle English Narrative*. Princeton: Princeton University Press, 1983.

Gardner, John. *The Life and Times of Chaucer*. New York: Knopf, 1977.

Gaylord, Alan T. "Portrait of a Poet." *Ellesmere Chaucer*. Ed. Stevens and Woodward. 121–42.

Geertz, Clifford. *The Interpretation of Cultures*. New York: Basic Books, 1973.

Georgianna, Linda. "Love So Dearly Bought: The Terms of Redemption in *The Canterbury Tales*." *SAC* 12 (1990): 85–116.

———. "The Protestant Chaucer." *Chaucer's Religious Tales*. Ed. C. David Benson and Elizabeth Robertson. Cambridge: D. S. Brewer, 1990. 55–69.

Ghosh, Kantik. "Bishop Reginald Pecock and the Idea of 'Lollardy.'" *Text and Controversy from Wyclif to Bale*. Ed. Barr and Hutchison. 252–65.

———. "Manuscripts of Nicholas Love's *The Mirror of the Blessed Life of Jesus Christ* and Wycliffite Notions of 'Authority.'" *Prestige, Authority and Power*. Ed. Riddy. 17–54.

————. *The Wycliffite Heresy: Authority and the Interpretation of Texts.* Cambridge: Cambridge University Press, 2002.

Giancarlo, Matthew. "*Piers Plowman,* Parliament, and the Public Voice." *YLS* 17 (2003): 135–74.

Gibson, Gail McMurray. "Bury St. Edmunds, Lydgate, and the N-Town Cycle." *Speculum* 56 (1981): 56–90.

————. *The Theater of Devotion: East Anglian Drama and Society in the Late Middle Ages.* Chicago: University of Chicago Press, 1989.

Gillespie, Alexandra. "Caxton's Chaucer and Lydgate Quartos: Miscellanies from Manuscript to Print." *Transactions of the Cambridge Bibliographical Society* 12 (2000): 1–25.

————. "Framing Lydgate's *Fall of Princes*: The Evidence of Book History." *Mediaevalia* 20 (2001): 153–78.

————. "The Lydgate Canon in Print from 1476 to 1534." *Journal of the Early Book Society* 4 (2000): 59–93.

Gillespie, Vincent. "The Mole in the Vineyard: Wyclif at Syon in the Fifteenth Century." *Text and Controversy from Wyclif to Bale.* Ed. Barr and Hutchison. 131–62.

————. "'Thy Will Be Done': *Piers Plowman* and the *Pater Noster*." *Late-Medieval Religious Texts and Their Transmission.* Ed. Minnis. 95–119.

————. "Vernacular Books of Religion." *Book Production.* Ed. Griffiths and Pearsall. 317–44.

Given-Wilson, Chris. *Chronicles of the Revolution 1397–1400: The Reign of Richard II.* Manchester and New York: Manchester University Press, 1993.

————. "Richard II, Edward II, and the Lancastrian Inheritance." *EHR* 109 (1994): 553–71.

Goldie, Matthew Boyd. "Psychosomatic Illness and Identity in London, 1416–1421: Hoccleve's *Complaint* and *Dialogue with a Friend*." *Exemplaria* 11 (1999): 23–52.

Gombrich, E. H. *The Story of Art.* 16th ed. rev. New York: Phaedon, 1995.

Goodall, John A. A. *God's House at Ewelme.* Aldershot: Ashgate, 2001.

Goodich, Michael. *The Unmentionable Vice: Homosexuality in the Later Medieval Period.* Santa Barbara and Oxford: ABC-Clio, 1979.

Goodman, Anthony. *John of Gaunt.* Harlow: Longman, 1992.

————. "Sir Thomas Hoo and the Parliament of 1376." *Bulletin of the Institute of Historical Research* 41 (1968): 139–49.

Gottfried, Robert S. *Bury St. Edmunds and the Urban Crisis: 1290–1539.* Princeton: Princeton University Press, 1982.

Gradon, Pamela. "Langland and the Ideology of Dissent." *PBA* 66 (1980): 179–205.

Grady, Frank. "Chaucer Reading Langland: *The House of Fame.*" *SAC* 18 (1996): 3–23.

Gransden, Antonia. *Historical Writing in England c. 1307 to the Early Sixteenth Century.* Ithaca: Cornell University Press, 1982.

Greatrex, Joan. "Monk Students from Norwich Cathedral Priory at Oxford and Cambridge, c. 1300 to 1530." *EHR* 106/420 (1991): 555–83.

Green, Richard Firth. "John Ball's Letters: Literary History and Historical Literature." *Chaucer's England.* Ed. Hanawalt. 176–200.

————. "King Richard II's Books Revisited." *The Library* 5th ser., 31 (1976): 235–39.

————. "Legal Satire in *The Tale of Beryn*." *SAC* 11 (1989): 43–62.

————. *Poets and Princepleasers: Literature and the English Court in the Late Middle Ages.* Toronto: University of Toronto Press, 1980.

Greenberg, David F. *The Construction of Homosexuality.* Chicago: University of Chicago Press, 1988.

Greenblatt, Stephen. *Shakespearean Negotiations: The Circulation of Social Energy in Renaissance England.* Berkeley and Los Angeles: University of California Press, 1988.

————. "Towards a Poetics of Culture." *The New Historicism.* Ed. Vecser. 1–14.

————. "What Is the History of Literature?" *Critical Inquiry* 23 (1997): 460–81.

Greening Lamborn, E. A. "The Arms on the Chaucer Tomb at Ewelme." *Oxoniensia* 5 (1940): 78–93.

Greetham, D. C. "Self-Referential Artifacts: Hoccleve's Persona as a Literary Device." *MP* 86 (1989): 242–51.

Griffiths, Jeremy. "Thomas Hyngham, Monk of Bury and the Macro Plays Manuscript." *English Manuscript Studies* 5 (1995): 214–19.

————, and Derek Pearsall, eds. *Book Production and Publishing in Britain, 1375–1475.* Cambridge: Cambridge University Press, 1989.

Grindley, Carl. "A New Fragment of *Piers Plowman* C Text?" *YLS* 11 (1997): 135–40.

————. "Reading *Piers Plowman* C-text Annotations: Notes toward the Classification of Printed and Written Marginalia in Texts from the British Isles 1300–1641." *Medieval Professional Reader at Work.* Ed. Kerby-Fulton and Hilmo. 73–141.

Grudin, Michaela Paasche. *Chaucer and the Politics of Discourse.* Columbia: University of South Carolina Press, 1996.

Guillory, John. *Poetic Authority: Spenser, Milton, and Literary History.* New York: Columbia University Press, 1983.

Hagen, Susan K. *Allegorical Remembrance: A Study of "The Pilgrimage of the Life of Man" as a Medieval Treatise on Seeing and Remembering.* Athens: University of Georgia Press, 1990.

Hahn, Thomas. "Early Middle English." *Cambridge History of Medieval English Literature.* Ed. Wallace. 61–91.

————, and Alan Lupack, eds. *Retelling Tales: Essays in Honor of Russell Peck.* Cambridge: D. S. Brewer, 1997.

Haigh, Christopher. *English Reformations: Religion, Politics, and Society under the Tudors.* Oxford: Clarendon, 1993.

Hailey, R. Carter. "'Geuyng Light to the Reader': Robert Crowley's Editions of *Piers Plowman* (1550)." *PBSA* 95 (2001): 483–502.

Hallmundsson, May Newman. "Chaucer's Circle: Henry Scogan and His Friends." *M&H* n.s. 10 (1981): 129–39.

Hamel, Mary. "*The Siege of Jerusalem* as a Crusading Poem." *Journeys toward God: Pilgrimage and Crusade.* Ed. Barbara N. Sargent-Baur. Kalamazoo: Medieval Institute Publications, 1992. 177–94.

Hammond, Eleanor Prescott. "Poet and Patron in the *Fall of Princes*: Lydgate and Humphrey of Gloucester." *Anglia* 38 (1914): 121–36.

Hanawalt, Barbara, ed. *Chaucer's England: Literature in Historical Context.* Minneapolis: University of Minnesota Press, 1991.

———, and Ben R. McRee. "The Guilds of *Homo Prudens* in Late-Medieval England." *Continuity and Change* 7 (1992): 163–79.

Hanly, Michael. "Courtiers and Poets: An International Network of Literary Exchange." *Viator* 28 (1997): 305–32.

———. "France." *Companion to Chaucer.* Ed. Brown. 149–66.

Hanna, Ralph, III. "Alliterative Poetry." *Cambridge History of Medieval English Literature.* Ed. Wallace. 488–512.

———. "Contextualizing *The Siege of Jerusalem.*" *YLS* 6 (1992): 109–21.

———. "The Difficulty of Ricardian Prose Translation: The Case of the Lollards. " *MLQ* 51 (1990): 319–40.

———. "(The) Editing (of) the Ellesmere Text." *Ellesmere Chaucer.* Ed. Stevens and Woodward. 225–43.

———. "Emendations to a 1993 'Vita de Ne'erdowel.'" *YLS* 14 (2000): 185–98.

———. "English Biblical Texts before Lollardy and Their Fate." *Lollards and Their Influence.* Ed. Somerset, Havens, and Pitard. 141–51.

———. *London Literature, 1300–1380.* Cambridge: Cambridge University Press, 2005.

———. "The Origins and Production of Westminster School MS. 3." *SB* 41 (1988): 197–218.

———. "Producing Manuscripts and Editions." *Crux and Controversy.* Ed. Minnis and Brewer. 109–30.

———. *Pursuing History: Middle English Manuscripts and Their Texts.* Stanford: Stanford University Press, 1996.

———. "Reconsidering the Auchinleck Manuscript." *New Directions in Later Medieval Manuscript Studies.* Ed. Pearsall. 91–102.

———. "School and Scorn: Gender in *Piers Plowman.*" *NML* 3 (1999): 213–27.

———. "The Scribe of Huntington HM 114." *SB* 42 (1989): 120–33.

———. "Sir Thomas Berkeley and His Patronage." *Speculum* 64 (1989): 878–916.

———. "Studies in the Manuscripts of *Piers Plowman.*" *YLS* 7 (1993): 1–25.

———. *William Langland.* Brookfield, VT: Variorum, 1993.

———. "Will's Work." *Written Work.* Ed. Justice and Kerby-Fulton. 23–66.

———. "With an O (Yorks) or an I (Salop)? The Middle English Lyrics of British Library Additional 45896." *SB* 48 (1995): 290–97.

———, and A. S. G. Edwards. "Rotheley, the De Vere Circle, and the Ellesmere Chaucer." *Reading from the Margins.* Ed. Lerer. 11–35.

Hanrahan, Michael. "London." *Companion to Chaucer.* Ed. Brown. 266–80.

Hansen, Harriet Merete. "The Peasants' Revolt of 1381 and the Chronicles." *JMH* 6 (1980): 393–415.

Happé, Peter. *John Bale.* New York: Twayne Publishers, 1996.

Harding, Christopher, Bill Hines, Richard Ireland, and Philip Rawlings. *Imprisonment in England and Wales.* London: Croom Helm, 1985.

Hardman, Phillipa. "A Medieval 'Library *in Parvo.*'" *MÆ* 47 (1978): 262–73.

Hardwick, Paul. "The Poet as Ploughman." *ChauR* 33 (1998): 146–56.

Harris, Kate. "The Patron of British Library MS. Arundel 38." *N&Q* n.s. 31 (1984): 462–63.

———. "The Patronage and Dating of Longleat House MS 24, a Prestige Copy of the *Pupilla Oculi* Illuminated by the Master of the *Troilus* Frontispiece." *Prestige, Authority and Power.* Ed. Riddy. 35–54.

———. "Patrons, Buyers and Owners: The Evidence for Ownership and the Role of Book Owners in Book Production and the Book Trade." *Book Production.* Ed. Griffiths and Pearsall. 163–99.

———. "Unnoticed Extracts from Chaucer and Hoccleve: Huntington MS HM 144, Trinity College, Oxford MS D 29 and *The Canterbury Tales.*" *SAC* 20 (1998): 167–99.

Harris, Wendell V. "Canonicity." *PMLA* 106 (1991): 110–21.

Harriss, G. L. *Cardinal Beaufort: A Study of Lancastrian Ascendancy and Decline.* Oxford: Clarendon, 1988.

———. "The Court of the Lancastrian Kings." *The Lancastrian Court: Proceedings of the 2001 Harlaxton Symposium.* Ed. Jenny Stratford. Donington: Shaun Tyas, 2003. 1–18.

———. "Henry Beaufort, 'Cardinal of England.'" *England in the Fifteenth Century.* Ed. Williams. 111–27.

———. "Political Society and Growth of Government in Late Medieval England." *P&P* 138 (1993): 28–57.

———. *Shaping the Nation: England, 1360–1461.* Oxford: Clarendon, 2005.

———, ed. *Henry V: The Practice of Kingship.* 1985; rpt. Dover, NH: Alan Sutton, 1993.

Harvey, Barbara. *Living and Dying in England, 1100–1540: The Monastic Experience.* Oxford: Clarendon, 1993.

Hasler, Antony J. "Hoccleve's Unregimented Body." *Paragraph* 13 (1990): 164–83.

Havens, Jill C. "'As Englishe Is Comoun Langage to Oure Puple': The Lollards and Their Imagined 'English' Community." *Imagining a Medieval English Nation.* Ed. Lavezzo. 96–128.

———. "Shading the Grey Area: Determining Heresy in Middle English Texts." *Text and Controversy from Wyclif to Bale.* Ed. Barr and Hutchison. 337–52.

Hazlitt, W. Carew. *The Livery Companies of the City of London.* 1892; rpt. New York and London: Benjamin Blom, 1969.

Heath, Peter. *The English Parish Clergy on the Eve of the Reformation.* London: Routledge & Kegan Paul, 1969.

Hebron, Malcolm. *The Medieval Siege: Theme and Image in Middle English Romance.* Oxford: Clarendon, 1997.

Heffernan, Thomas J. "Aspects of the Chaucerian Apocrypha: Animadversions on William Thynne's Edition of the *Plowman's Tale.*" *Chaucer Traditions.* Ed. Morse and Windeatt. 155–67.

———. "'Orthodoxies' Redux: The *Northern Homily Cycle* in the Vernon Manuscript and Its Textual Affiliations." *Studies in the Vernon Manuscript.* Ed. Pearsall. 75–87.

Hellinga, Lotte. *Caxton in Focus: The Beginning of Printing in England.* London: British Library, 1982.

————, and J. B. Trapp, eds. *Cambridge History of the Book in Britain,* vol. 3: *1400–1557.* Cambridge: Cambridge University Press, 1999.

Helmholz, Richard H., ed. *Select Cases on Defamation to 1600.* London: Selden Society, 1985.

Hewett-Smith, Kathleen M., ed. *William Langland's "Piers Plowman": A Book of Essays.* New York and London: Routledge, 2001.

Heyworth, P. L. "The Earliest Black-Letter Editions of *Jack Upland.*" *HLQ* 30 (1967): 307–14.

————. "*Jack Upland's Rejoinder,* a Lollard Interpolator, and *Piers Plowman* B.X.249f." *MÆ* 36 (1967): 242–48.

Higgins, Iain Macleod. *Writing East: The "Travels" of Sir John Mandeville.* Philadelphia: University of Pennsylvania Press, 1997.

Higgs, Elton D. "The Old Order and the 'Newe World' in the General Prologue to the *Canterbury Tales.*" *HLQ* 45 (1982): 155–73.

Hill, Christopher. "From Lollards to Levellers." 1978; rpt. *The Collected Essays.* 3 vols. Amherst: University of Massachusetts Press, 1986. 2:89–116.

Hilton, Rodney. *Bond Men Made Free: Medieval Peasant Movements and the English Rising of 1381.* 1973; rpt. London and New York: Routledge, 1988.

————, and T. H. Aston, eds. *The English Rising of 1381.* Cambridge: Cambridge University Press, 1984.

Hindle, Steve. *The State and Social Change in Early Modern England c. 1550–1640.* New York: St. Martin's, 2000.

Hindman, Sandra. "The Composition of the Manuscript of Christine de Pizan's Collected Works in the British Library: A Reassessment." *British Library Journal* 9 (1983): 93–123.

Hines, John, Nathalie Cohen, and Simon Roffey. "*Iohannes Gower, Armiger, Poeta*: Records and Memorials of His Life and Death." *Companion to Gower.* Ed. Echard. 23–41.

Hobsbawm, Eric, and Terence Ranger, eds. *The Invention of Tradition.* Cambridge: Cambridge University Press, 1983.

Hodges, Laura F. "A Reconsideration of the Monk's Costume." *ChauR* 26 (1991): 133–46.

Holloway, Julia Bolton. *The Pilgrim and the Book: A Study of Dante, Langland and Chaucer.* New York and Frankfurt: Peter Lang, 1987.

Holsinger, Bruce W. "Langland's Musical Reader: Liturgy, Law, and the Constraints of Performance." *SAC* 21 (1999): 99–141.

Honeybourne, Marjorie B. "The Sanctuary Boundaries and Environs of Westminster Abbey and the College of St. Martin-Le-Grand." *Transactions of the British Archaeological Association* n.s. 38 (1932): 316–33.

Hope, Andrew. "The Lady and the Bailiff: Lollardy Among the Gentry in Yorkist and Early Tudor England." *Lollardy and the Gentry.* Ed. Aston and Richmond. 250–77.

————. "Lollardy: The Stone the Builders Rejected?" *Protestantism and the National Church in Sixteenthh-Century England.* Ed. Peter Lake and Maria Dowling. London: Croom Helm, 1987. 1–35.

Horobin, Simon. "The Dialect and Authorship of *Richard the Redeless* and *Mum and the Sothsegger*." *YLS* 18 (2004): 133–52.

———. "Harley 3954 and the Audience of *Piers Plowman*." *Medieval Texts in Context*. Ed. Graham D. Caie and Denis Renevey. New York and London: Routledge, forthcoming.

———. "'In London and Opelond': Dialect and Circulation of the C Version of *Piers Plowman*." *MÆ* 74 (2005): 248–69.

———. *The Language of the Chaucer Tradition*. Cambridge: D. S. Brewer, 2003.

———, and Linne R. Mooney. "A *Piers Plowman* Manuscript by the Hengwrt/Ellesmere Scribe and Its Implications for London Standard English." *SAC* 26 (2004): 65–112.

Horrell, Joseph. "Chaucer's Symbolic Plowman." *Speculum* 14 (1939): 82–92.

Howard, Donald R. *Chaucer: His Life, His Works, His World*. New York: Fawcett Columbine, 1987.

———. *The Idea of the Canterbury Tales*. Berkeley and Los Angeles: University of California Press, 1976.

———. *Writers and Pilgrims: Medieval Pilgrimage Narratives and Their Posterity*. Berkeley and Los Angeles: University of California Press, 1980.

Howard, Jean E. "The New Historicism in Renaissance Studies." *Renaissance Historicism*. Ed. Arthur F. Kinney and Dan S. Collins. Amherst: University of Massachusetts Press, 1987. 3–33.

Hoyle, R. W. "The Origins of the Dissolution of the Monasteries." *Historical Journal* 38 (1995): 275–305.

Hudson, Anne. "Epilogue: The Legacy of *Piers Plowman*." *Companion to "Piers Plowman*." Ed. Alford. 251–66.

———. "*Hermofodrita or Ambidexter*: Wycliffite Views on Clerks in Secular Office." *Lollardy and the Gentry*. Ed. Aston and Richmond. 41–51.

———. "John Stow (1525?–1605)." *Editing Chaucer*. Ed. Ruggiers. 53–70.

———. "*Laicus Litteratus*: The Paradox of Lollardy." *Heresy and Literacy*. Ed. Biller and Hudson. 222–36.

———. "Langland and Lollardy?" *YLS* 17 (2003): 93–105.

———. "Lollard Book Production." *Book Production*. Ed. Griffiths and Pearsall. 125–42.

———. "A Lollard Sermon Cycle and Its Implications." *MÆ* 40 (1971): 142–56.

———. *Lollards and Their Books*. London: Hambledon Press, 1985.

———. "A New Look at the *Lay Folks' Catechism*." *Viator* 16 (1985): 243–58.

———. "Peter Pateshull: One-Time Friar and Poet?" *Interstices: Studies in Late Middle English and Anglo-Latin Texts in Honor of A. G. Rigg*. Ed. Richard Firth Green and Linne R. Mooney. Toronto: University of Toronto Press, 2004. 167–83.

———. "*Piers Plowman* and the Peasants' Revolt: A Problem Revisited." *YLS* 8 (1994): 85–106.

———. "Preface." *Lollards and Their Influence*. Ed. Somerset, Havens, and Pitard. 1–8.

———. *The Premature Reformation: Wycliffite Texts and Lollard History*. Oxford: Clarendon, 1988.

————. "Trial and Error: Wyclif's Works in Cambridge, Trinity College MS B.16.2." *New Science out of Old Books*. Ed. Beadle and Piper. 53–80.

————. "Wyclif and the English Language." *Wyclif in His Times*. Ed. Kenny. 85–103.

————. "Wycliffism in Oxford." *Wyclif in His Times*. Ed. Kenny. 67–84.

Hughes, Jonathan. *Pastors and Visionaries: Religion and Secular Life in Late Medieval Yorkshire*. Woodbridge: Boydell & Brewer, 1988.

Hulbert, J. R. *Chaucer's Official Life*. 1912; rpt. New York: Phaeton Press, 1970.

————. "The Text of *The Siege of Jerusalem*." *SP* 28 (1931): 602–12.

Hume, Anthea. "English Protestant Books Printed Abroad, 1525–1535." *The Complete Works of St. Thomas More*. Ed. Louis L. Martz et al. New Haven: Yale University Press, 1963– . 8:1065–91.

Huot, Sylvia. *From Song to Book*. Ithaca and London: Cornell University Press, 1987.

Hussey, S. S. "Langland the Outsider." *Middle English Poetry*. Ed. Minnis. 129–37.

————. "Langland's Reading of Alliterative Poetry." *MLR* 60 (1965): 163–70.

————, ed. *"Piers Plowman": Critical Approaches*. London: Methuen, 1969.

Irvine, Annie S. "A Manuscript Copy of *The Plowman's Tale*." *University of Texas Studies in English* 12 (1932): 27–56.

Jacob, E. F. *The Fifteenth Century, 1399–1485*. Oxford: Clarendon, 1961.

James, Montague Rhodes. "Bury St. Edmunds Manuscripts." *EHR* 41 (1926): 251–60.

————. *On the Abbey of S. Edmund at Bury*, vol. 1: *The Library*. Cambridge: Cambridge Antiquarian Society, no. 28, 1895.

Jameson, Fredric. *The Political Unconscious: Narrative as a Socially Symbolic Act*. Ithaca: Cornell University Press, 1981.

Jansen, Sharon L. "British Library MS Sloane 2578 and Popular Unrest in England, 1554–1556." *Manuscripta* 29 (1985): 30–41.

————. "Politics, Protest, and a New *Piers Plowman* Fragment: The Voice of the Past in Tudor England." *RES* n.s. 40 (1989): 93–99.

Jefferson, Judith A. "The Hoccleve Holographs and Hoccleve's Metrical Practice." *Manuscripts and Texts: Editorial Problems in Later Middle English Literature*. Ed. Derek Pearsall. Cambridge: D. S. Brewer, 1987. 95–109.

Jeffrey, David Lyle. "Chaucer and Wyclif: Biblical Hermeneutic and Literary Theory in XIVth Century." *Chaucer and Scriptural Tradition*. Ed. Jeffrey. 109–40.

————. "Victimization and Legal Abuse: The Wycliffite Retelling of the Story of Susannah." *Retelling Tales*. Ed. Hahn and Lupack. 161–78.

————, ed. *Chaucer and Scriptural Tradition*. Ottawa: University of Ottawa Press, 1984.

Jewell, Helen. "*Piers Plowman*—A Poem of Crisis: An Analysis of Political Instability in Langland's England." *Politics and Crisis in Fourteenth-Century England*. Ed. John Taylor and Wendy Childs. Wolfeboro Falls, NH: Alan Sutton, 1990. 59–80.

Johnson, Barbara A. *Reading "Piers Plowman" and "The Pilgrim's Progress": Reception and the Protestant Reader*. Carbondale: Southern Illinois University Press, 1992.

Johnson, James D. "Identifying Chaucer Allusions, 1953–1980: An Annotated Bibliography." *ChauR* 19 (1984): 62–86.

Johnston, Andrew James. *Clerks and Courtiers: Chaucer, Late Middle English Literature and the State Formation Process.* Heidelberg: C. Winter, 2001.

Jonassen, Frederick B. "Cathedral, Inn, and Pardoner in the Prologue to the *Tale of Beryn.*" *FCS* 18 (1991): 109–32.

———. "The Inn, the Cathedral, and the Pilgrimage of the *Canterbury Tales.*" *Rebels and Rivals.* Ed. Fein et al. 1–35.

Jones, Alex I. "MS Harley 7334 and the Construction of *The Canterbury Tales.*" *ELN* 23 (1985): 9–15.

Jones, Edward. "Langland and Hermits." *YLS* 11 (1997): 67–86.

Jones, Terry. *Chaucer's Knight: The Portrait of a Medieval Mercenary.* Baton Rouge: Louisiana State University Press, 1980.

———. "The Image of Chaucer's Knight." *Speaking Images.* Ed. Yeager and Morse. 205–36.

———, with Robert Yeager, Terry Dolan, Alan Fletcher, and Juliette Dor. *Who Murdered Chaucer? A Medieval Mystery.* New York: St. Martin's, 2004.

Jones, W. R. "Lollards and Images: The Defense of Religious Art in Later Medieval England." *Journal of the History of Ideas* 34 (1973): 27–50.

Jost, Jean E. "From Southwark's Tabard Inn to Canterbury's Cheker-of-the-Hope: The Un-Chaucerian *Tale of Beryn.*" *FCS* 21 (1994): 133–48.

Jurkowski, Maureen. "Lancastrian Royal Service, Lollardy and Forgery: The Career of Thomas Tykhill." *Crown, Government, and People.* Ed. Archer. 33–52.

———. "Lawyers and Lollardy in the Early Fifteenth Century." *Lollardy and the Gentry.* Ed. Aston and Richmond. 155–82.

———. "Lollard Book Producers in London in 1414." *Text and Controversy from Wyclif to Bale.* Ed. Barr and Hutchison. 201–26.

———. "Lollardy in Oxfordshire and Northamptonshire: The Two Thomas Compworths." *Lollards and Their Influence.* Ed. Somerset, Havens, and Pitard. 73–95.

Jusserand, J. J. *"Piers Plowman": A Contribution to the History of English Mysticism.* Trans. M. E. R. London: T. Fisher Unwin, 1894.

Justice, Steven. "Inquisition, Speech and Writing: A Case from Late-Medieval Norwich." *Representations* 48 (1994): 1–29.

———. "Introduction: Authorial Work and Literary Ideology." *Written Work.* Ed. Justice and Kerby-Fulton. 1–12.

———. "Lollardy." *Cambridge History of Medieval English Literature.* Ed. Wallace. 662–89.

———. *Writing and Rebellion: England in 1381.* Berkeley and Los Angeles: University of California Press, 1994.

———, and Kathryn Kerby-Fulton, eds. *Written Work: Langland, Labor, and Authorship.* Philadelphia: University of Pennsylvania Press, 1997.

Kamowski, William. "'Coillons,' Relics, Skepticism and Faith on Chaucer's Road to Canterbury: An Observation on the Pardoner's and the Host's Confrontation." *ELN* 28 (1991): 1–8.

Kane, George. *Chaucer and Langland: Historical and Textual Approaches.* Berkeley and Los Angeles: University of California Press, 1989.

———. *Middle English Literature: A Critical Study of the Romance, the Religious Lyrics, "Piers Plowman."* London: Methuen, 1951.

———. *Piers Plowman: The Evidence for Authorship.* London: Athlone Press, 1965.

———. "Some Fourteenth-Century 'Political' Poems." *Medieval English Religious and Ethical Literature.* Ed. Kratzmann and Simpson. 82–91.

———. "The Text." *A Companion to "Piers Plowman."* Ed. Alford. 175–200.

———. "The 'Z Version' of *Piers Plowman*." *Speculum* 60 (1985): 910–30.

Karras, Ruth Mazo. "The Regulation of Brothels in Later Medieval England." *Signs* 14 (1989): 399–433.

———, and David Lorenzo Boyd. "'Ut cum mulier': A Male Transvestite Prostitute in Fourteenth-Century London." *Premodern Sexualities.* Ed. Louise Olga Fradenburg and Carla Freccero. New York and London: Routledge, 1996. 101–16.

Kean, P. M. *Chaucer and the Making of English Poetry.* 2 vols. London: Routledge & Kegan Paul, 1972.

Keegan, John. *The Face of War.* Harmondsworth: Penguin, 1978.

Keeney, Barnaby. "Military Service and the Development of Nationalism in England, 1272–1327." *Speculum* 22 (1947): 534–49.

Kekewich, Margaret. "Edward IV, William Caxton, and Literary Patronage in Yorkist England." *MLR* 66 (1971): 481–87.

Kelen, Sarah A. "*Piers Plouhman* and the 'Formidable Array of Blackletter' in the Early Nineteenth Century." *Illuminating Letters: Typography and Literary Interpretation.* Ed. Paul C. Gutjahr and Megan L. Benton. Amherst: University of Massachusetts Press, 2001. 47–67.

———. "Plowing the Past: 'Piers Protestant' and the Authority of Medieval Literary History." *YLS* 13 (1999): 101–36.

Kellaway, William. "John Carpenter's *Liber Albus*." *Guildhall Studies in London History* 3 (1978): 67–84.

Kellogg, Alfred L., and Louis A. Haselmayer. "Chaucer's Satire of the Pardoner." *PMLA* 66 (1951): 251–77.

Kellogg, Alfred L., and Ernest W. Talbert. "The Wycliffite *Pater Noster* and *Ten Commandments*." *BJRL* 42 (1960): 345–77.

Kelly, Henry Ansgar. "The Pardoner's Voice: Disjunctive Narrative and Modes of Effemination." *Speaking Images.* Ed. Yeager and Morse. 411–44.

———. "Shades of Incest and Cuckoldry: Pandarus and John of Gaunt." *SAC* 13 (1991): 121–40.

Kelly, Robert L. "Hugh Latimer as Piers Plowman." *Studies in English Literature* 17 (1977): 13–26.

Kendall, Ritchie D. *The Drama of Dissent: The Radical Poetics of Nonconformity, 1380–1590.* Chapel Hill: University of North Carolina Press, 1986.

Kennedy, Edward Donald, Ronald Waldron, and Joseph S. Wittig, eds. *Medieval English Studies Presented to George Kane.* Cambridge: D. S. Brewer, 1988.

Kennedy, Kathleen E. "Retaining a Court of Chancery in *Piers Plowman*." *YLS* 17 (2003): 175–89.

Kenny, Anthony. *Wyclif.* Oxford: Oxford University Press, 1985.

————, ed. *Wyclif in His Times*. Oxford: Clarendon, 1986.

Kerby-Fulton, Kathryn. "Langland and the Bibliographic Ego." *Written Work*. Ed. Justice and Kerby-Fulton. 67–143.

————. "Professional Readers of Langland at Home and Abroad: New Directions in the Political and Bureaucratic Codicology of *Piers Plowman*." *New Directions in Later Medieval Manuscript Studies*. Ed. Pearsall. 103–29.

————. "Prophecy and Suspicion: Closet Radicalism, Reformist Politics, and the Vogue for Hildegardiana in Ricardian England." *Speculum* 75 (2000): 318–41.

————. "The Women Readers in Langland's Earliest Audience: Some Codicological Evidence." *Learning and Literacy in Medieval England and Abroad*. Ed. Sarah Rees Jones. Turnhout: Brepols, 2003. 121–34.

————, and Denise L. Despres. *Iconography and the Professional Reader: The Politics of Book Production in the Douce "Piers Plowman."* Minneapolis: University of Minnesota Press, 1999.

————, and Steven Justice. "Langlandian Reading Circles and the Civil Service in London and Dublin, 1380–1427." *NML* 1 (1997): 59–83.

————, and Steven Justice. "Scribe D and the Marketing of Ricardian Literature." *Medieval Professional Reader at Work*. Ed. Kerby-Fulton and Hilmo. 217–33.

————, and Maidie Hilmo, eds. *The Medieval Professional Reader at Work*. Victoria: University of Victoria English Literary Studies, 2001.

Kern, Alfred Allan. *The Ancestry of Chaucer*. Baltimore: Lord Baltimore Press, 1906.

Kernan, Alvin. *The Cankered Muse*. 1959; rpt. Hamden, CT: Archon Books, 1976.

King, John N. "The Book-Trade under Edward VI and Mary I." *Cambridge History of the Book in Britain,* vol. 3. Ed. Hellinga and Trapp. 164–75.

————. *English Reformation Literature: The Tudor Origins of the Protestant Tradition*. Princeton: Princeton University Press, 1982.

————. "Freedom of the Press, Protestant Propaganda, and Protector Somerset." *HLQ* 40 (1976): 1–9.

————. "Robert Crowley's Editions of *Piers Plowman*: A Tudor Apocalypse." *MP* 73 (1976): 342–52.

Kinney, Clare R. "Thomas Speght's Renaissance Chaucer and the *Solaas* of *Sentence* in *Troilus and Criseyde*." *Refiguring Chaucer in the Renaissance*. Ed. Krier. 66–84.

Kirk, Elizabeth D. "Chaucer and His English Contemporaries." *Geoffrey Chaucer: A Collection of Original Articles*. New York: McGraw-Hill, 1975. 111–27.

Kirk, Rudolf. "References to the Law in *Piers Plowman*." *PMLA* 48 (1933): 322–28.

Kittredge, George Lyman. "Chaucer and Some of His Friends." *MP* 1 (1903): 1–18.

————. "Henry Scogan." *Harvard Studies and Notes* 1 (1892): 109–17.

————. "Lewis Chaucer or Lewis Clifford?" *MP* 14 (1917): 513–18.

Kline, Daniel T. "Father Chaucer and the *Siege of Thebes*: Literary Paternity, Aggressive Deference, and the Prologue to Lydgate's Oedipal *Canterbury Tales*." *ChauR* 34 (1999): 217–35.

Knapp, Daniel. "The Relyk of a Seint: A Gloss on Chaucer's Pilgrimage." *ELH* 39 (1972): 1–26.

Knapp, Ethan. "Bureaucratic Identity and the Construction of the Self in Hoccleve's *Formulary* and *La Male Regle*." *Speculum* 74 (1999): 357–76.

————. *Bureaucratic Muse: Thomas Hoccleve and the Literature of Late Medieval England.* University Park: Pennsylvania State University Press, 2001.

————. "Eulogies and Usurpations: Hoccleve and Chaucer Revisited." *SAC* 21 (1999): 247–73.

Knapp, Peggy. *Chaucer and the Social Contest.* New York and London: Routledge, 1990.

Knight, Stephen. *Robin Hood: A Complete Study of the English Outlaw.* Oxford: Blackwell, 1994.

Knott, Thomas A. "An Essay toward the Critical Text of the A-Version of *Piers the Plowman*." *MP* 12 (1915): 389–421.

Knowles, David. *The Religious Orders in England.* 3 vols. Cambridge: Cambridge University Press, 1948–59.

Kolve, V. A. *Chaucer and the Imagery of Narrative: The First Five Canterbury Tales.* Stanford: Stanford University Press, 1984.

Koonce, B. G. *Chaucer and the Tradition of Fame: Symbolism in "The House of Fame."* Princeton: Princeton University Press, 1966.

Kramnick, Jonathan Brody. *Making the English Canon: Print-Capitalism and the Cultural Past, 1700–1770.* Cambridge: Cambridge University Press, 1999.

Kratzmann, Gregory, and James Simpson, eds. *Medieval English Religious and Ethical Literature: Essays in Honour of G. H. Russell.* Cambridge: D. S. Brewer, 1986.

Krauss, Russell. "An Examination of the Heraldic Decorations on Thomas Chaucer's Tomb" and "Chaucerian Problems Especially the Petherton Forestership and the Question of Thomas Chaucer." *Three Chaucer Studies.* Ed. Carleton Brown. New York: Oxford University Press, 1932. 31–56 and 131–69.

Krier, Theresa, ed. *Refiguring Chaucer in the Renaissance.* Gainesville: University Press of Florida, 1998.

Krochalis, Jeanne E. "The Books and Reading of Henry V and His Circle." *ChauR* 23 (1988): 50–77.

————. "Hoccleve's Chaucer Portrait." *ChauR* 21 (1986): 234–45.

————, and Edward Peters, eds. and trans. *The World of Piers Plowman.* Philadelphia: University of Pennsylvania Press, 1975.

Kuskin, William. "Reading Caxton: Transformations in Capital, Authority, Print, and Persona in the Late Fifteenth Century." *NML* 3 (1999): 149–83.

————, ed. *Caxton's Trace: Studies in the History of English Printing.* Notre Dame, IN: University of Notre Dame Press, 2006.

Laclau, Ernesto, and Chantal Mouffe. *Hegemony and Socialist Strategy.* Trans. Winston Moore and Paul Cammack. London: Verso, 1985.

Laidlaw, J. C. "Christine de Pizan, the Earl of Salisbury and Henry IV." *French Studies* 36 (1982): 129–43.

Lambdin, Laura C., and Robert T. Lambdin, eds. *Chaucer's Pilgrims: An Historical Guide to the Pilgrims in "The Canterbury Tales."* Westport and London: Greenwood Press, 1996.

Lambert, John James, ed. *Records of the Skinners of London, Edward I to James I.* London: Allen & Unwin, 1934.

Lambert, Malcolm. *Medieval Heresy: Popular Movements from Bogomil to Hus.* New York: Holmes & Meier, 1977.

Lampe, David. "The Satiric Strategy of *Peres the Ploughmans Crede.*" *The Alliterative Tradition in the Fourteenth Century.* Ed. Bernard S. Levy and Paul E. Szarmach. Kent, OH: Kent State University Press, 1981. 69–80.

Lander, J. R. *Conflict and Stability in Fifteenth-Century England.* London: Hutchinson, 1969.

Larsen, Andrew E. "Are All Lollards Lollards?" *Lollards and Their Influence.* Ed. Somerset, Havens, and Pitard. 59–72.

Lavezzo, Kathy, ed. *Imagining a Medieval English Nation.* Minneapolis and London: University of Minnesota Press, 2004.

Lawton, David A. "Chaucer's Two Ways: The Pilgrimage Frame of *The Canterbury Tales.*" *SAC* 9 (1987): 3–40.

———. "Dullness in the Fifteenth Century." *ELH* 54 (1987): 761–99.

———. "English Poetry and English Society." *The Radical Reader.* Ed. Stephen Knight and Michael Wilding. Sydney: Wild & Woolley, 1977. 145–68.

———. "Englishing the Bible, 1066–1549." *Cambridge History of Medieval English Literature.* Ed. Wallace. 545–82.

———. "The Idea of Alliterative Poetry: Alliterative Meter and *Piers Plowman.*" *Suche Werkis to Werche.* Ed. Vaughan. 147–68.

———. "Lollardy and the 'Piers Plowman' Tradition." *MLR* 76 (1981): 780–93.

———. "The Unity of Middle English Alliterative Poetry." *Speculum* 58 (1983): 72–94.

———, ed. *Middle English Alliterative Poetry and Its Literary Background.* Cambridge: D. S. Brewer, 1982.

Leff, Gordon. *Heresy in the Later Middle Ages.* 2 vols. Manchester: Manchester University Press, 1967.

Lenaghan, R. T. "Chaucer's Circle of Gentlemen and Clerks." *ChauR* 18 (1983): 155–60.

———. "Chaucer's *Envoy to Scogan*: The Uses of Literary Conventions." *ChauR* 10 (1975–76): 46–61.

Lentricchia, Frank. *Ariel and the Police: Michel Foucault, William James, Wallace Stevens.* Madison: University of Wisconsin Press, 1988.

Lerer, Seth. *Chaucer and His Readers.* Princeton: Princeton University Press, 1993.

———. *Courtly Letters in the Age of Henry VIII: Literary Culture and the Arts of Deceit.* Cambridge: Cambridge University Press, 1997.

———. "William Caxton." *Cambridge History of Medieval English Literature.* Ed. Wallace. 720–38.

———, ed. *Literary History and the Challenge of Philology: The Legacy of Erich Auerbach.* Stanford: Stanford University Press, 1996.

———, ed. *Reading from the Margins: Textual Studies, Chaucer, and Medieval Culture.* San Marino: Huntington Library, 1996.

Lewis, P. S. "War Propaganda and Historiography in Fifteenth-Century France and England." *TRHS* 5th ser., 15 (1965): 1–21.

Lewis, Robert E., and Angus McIntosh. *A Descriptive Guide to the Manuscripts of the "Prick of Conscience."* Oxford: Medium Ævum Monographs, n.s. 12, 1982.

Lightsey, Scott. "Chaucer's Secular Marvels and the Medieval Economy of Wonder." *SAC* 23 (2001): 289–316.

Lindberg, Conrad. "The Manuscripts and Versions of the Wycliffite Bible: A Preliminary Survey." *Studia Neophilologica* 42 (1970): 333–47.

Little, Katherine. "Chaucer's Parson and the Specter of Wycliffism." *SAC* 23 (2001): 225–53.

Littlehales, Henry. *Some Notes on the Road from London to Canterbury in the Middle Ages.* London: Chaucer Society, ser. 2, no. 30, 1898.

Loach, Jennifer. *Edward VI.* Ed. George Bernard and Penry Williams. New Haven and London: Yale University Press, 1999.

Logan, F. Donald. "Archbishop Thomas Bourgchier Revisited." *Church in Pre-Reformation Society.* Ed. Barron and Harper-Bill. 170–88.

Loomis, Laura Hibbard. "The Auchinleck Manuscript and a Possible London Bookshop of 1330–1340." *PMLA* 57 (1942): 595–627.

———. "Chaucer and the Breton Lays of the Auchinleck MS." *SP* 38 (1941): 14–33.

Lucas, Peter J. "The Growth and Development of English Literary Patronage in the Later Middle Ages and Early Renaissance." *The Library* 6th ser., 4 (1982): 219–48.

Lucraft, Jeannette. "Missing from History." *History Today* 52/5 (2002): 11–17.

Lumiansky, Robert M. *Of Sundry Folk: The Dramatic Principle in the "Canterbury Tales."* Austin: University of Texas Press, 1955.

Lutton, Rob. "Connections between Lollards, Townsfolk and Gentry in Tenterden in the Late Fifteenth and Early Sixteen Centuries." *Lollardy and the Gentry.* Ed. Aston and Richmond. 198–228.

Lyall, R. J. "Materials: The Paper Revolution." *Book Production.* Ed. Griffiths and Pearsall. 11–29.

Lyon, Earl D. "Roger de Ware, Cook." *MLN* 52 (1937): 491–94.

Lyotard, Jean-François. *The Postmodern Condition: A Report on Knowledge.* Trans. Geoff Bennington and Brian Massumi. Minneapolis: University of Minnesota Press, 1984.

MacCracken, Henry Noble. "An English Friend of Charles of Orleans." *PMLA* 26 (1911): 142–80.

———. "More Odd Texts of Chaucer's *Troilus.*" *MLN* 25 (1910): 126–27.

McFarlane, K. B. *England in the Fifteenth Century.* Intro. G. L. Harriss. London: Hambledon, 1981.

———. "England: The Lancastrian Kings, 1399–1461." *The Cambridge Medieval History.* Cambridge: Cambridge University Press, 1936. 8:362–417.

———. *John Wycliffe and the Beginnings of English Nonconformity.* London: English Universities Press, 1952.

———. *Lancastrian Kings and Lollard Knights.* Oxford: Clarendon, 1972.

———. *Nobility of Later Medieval England.* Oxford: Clarendon, 1973.

McGann, Jerome J., ed. *Textual Criticism and Literary Interpretation.* Chicago: University of Chicago Press, 1985.

McGerr, Rosemarie. *Chaucer's Open Books: Resistance to Closure in Medieval Discourse.* Gainesville: University Press of Florida, 1998.

McGinnis, Myrta Ethel. *"Piers the Plowman* in England, 1362–1625." Ph.D. diss., Yale University, 1932.

McGregor, James H. "The Iconography of Chaucer in Hoccleve's *Regiment Principum* and in the *Troilus* Frontispiece." *ChauR* 11 (1976–77): 338–50.

Machan, Tim William. *English in the Middle Ages.* Oxford: Oxford University Press, 2003.

———. "Late Middle English Texts and the Higher and Lower Criticisms." *Medieval Literature.* Ed. Machan. 3–15.

———. "Middle English Text Production and Modern Textual Criticism." *Crux and Controversy.* Ed. Minnis and Brewer. 1–18.

———. "Texts." *Companion to Chaucer.* Ed. Brown. 428–42.

———. "Textual Authority and the Works of Hoccleve, Lydgate and Henryson." *Viator* 23 (1992): 281–99.

———. "Thomas Berthelette and Gower's *Confessio.*" *SAC* 18 (1996): 143–66.

———, ed. *Medieval Literature: Texts and Interpretation.* Binghamton: Medieval & Renaissance Texts & Studies, 1991.

McHardy, Alison. K. "Bishop Buckingham and the Lollards of Lincoln Diocese." *SCH* 9 (1972): 131–45.

———. "Careers and Disappointments in the Late-Medieval Church: Some English Evidence." *SCH* 26 (1989): 111–30.

———. *"De Heretico Comburendo,* 1401." *Lollardy and the Gentry.* Ed. Aston and Richmond. 112–26.

———. "Ecclesiastics and Economics: Poor Priests, Prosperous Laymen, and Proud Prelates in the Reign of Richard II." *The Church and Wealth.* Ed. Sheils and Wood. 129–37.

———. "Liturgy and Propaganda in the Diocese of Lincoln during the Hundred Years War." *SCH* 18 (1982): 215–27.

McKenna, J. W. "Henry VI of England and the Dual Monarchy: Aspects of Royal Political Propaganda, 1422–1432." *Journal of the Warburg and Courtauld Institutes* 28 (1965): 145–62.

McKisack, May. *The Fourteenth Century, 1307–1399.* Oxford: Clarendon, 1959.

MacMichael, N. H. "Sanctuary at Westminster." *Westminster Abbey Occasional Papers* 27 (1971): 9–14.

McMillan, Douglas J. "The Single Most Popular of Thomas Hoccleve's Poems: *The Regement of Princes.*" *NM* 89 (1988): 63–71.

McNiven, Peter. *Heresy and Politics in the Reign of Henry IV: The Burning of John Badby.* Woodbridge: Boydell, 1987.

———. "Prince Henry and the Political Crisis of 1412." *History* 65 (1980): 1–16.

———. "Rebellion, Sedition, and the Legend of Richard II's Survival." *BJRL* 76 (1994): 93–117.

McSheffrey, Shannon. *Gender and Heresy: Women and Men in Lollard Communities, 1420–1530.* Philadelphia: University of Pennsylvania Press, 1995.

Madden, J. E. "Business Monks, Banker Monks, Bankrupt Monks: The English Cistercians in the Thirteenth Century." *Catholic Historical Review* 49 (1963): 341–64.

Malone, Ed. "Doubting Thomas and John the Carpenter's Oaths in the *Miller's Tale*." *ELN* 29 (1991): 15–17.

Manly, John M. "The Lost Leaf of *Piers the Plowman*." *MP* 3 (1906): 359–66.

———. "*Piers Plowman* and Its Sequence." *The Cambridge History of English Literature*, vol. 2: *The End of the Middle Ages*. Cambridge: Cambridge University Press, 1908. 1–42.

———. "Tales of the Homeward Journey." *SP* 28 (1931): 613–17.

Mann, Jill. *Chaucer and Medieval Estate Satire*. Cambridge: Cambridge University Press, 1973.

———. "The Power of the Alphabet: A Reassessment of the Relation between the A and the B Versions of *Piers Plowman*." *YLS* 8 (1994): 21–50.

Marks, Diane R. "Poems from Prison: James I of Scotland and Charles d'Orléans." *FCS* 15 (1989): 245–58.

Marotti, Arthur F. *Religious Ideology and Cultural Fantasy: Catholic and Anti-Catholic Discourses in Early Modern England*. Notre Dame, IN: University of Notre Dame Press, 2005.

Martin, Geoffrey. "Knighton's Lollards." *Lollardy and the Gentry*. Ed. Aston and Richmond. 28–40.

———. "Wyclif, Lollards, and Historians, 1384–1984." *Lollards and Their Influence*. Ed. Somerset, Havens, and Pitard. 237–50.

Martin, J. W. "The Publishing Career of Robert Crowley." *Publishing History* 14 (1983): 85–98.

Marzec, Marcia Smith. "The Latin Marginalia of the *Regiment of Princes* as an Aid to Stemmatic Analysis." *Text* 3 (1987): 269–84.

Matheson, Lister M. "Chaucer's Ancestry: Historical and Philological Re-assessments." *ChauR* 25 (1991): 171–89.

———. "The Middle English Prose *Brut*: A Location List of the Manuscripts and Early Printed Editions." *Analytical and Enumerative Bibliography* 3 (1979): 254–66.

———. Review of Hanna's *William Langland. YLS* 8 (1994): 192–94.

Matthew, F. D. "Trial of Richard Wyche." *EHR* 5 (1890): 530–44.

Matthews, David. *The Making of Middle English, 1765–1910*. Minneapolis: University of Minnesota Press, 1999.

Meale, Carol M. "Patrons, Buyers and Owners: Book Production and Social Status." *Book Production*. Ed. Griffiths and Pearsall. 201–38.

———. "Reading Women's Culture in Fifteenth-Century England: The Case of Alice Chaucer." *Mediaevalitas: Reading in the Middle Ages*. Ed. Piero Boitani and Anna Torti Cambridge: D. S. Brewer, 1996. 81–101.

Medcalf, Stephen. "Motives for Pilgrimage: *The Tale of Beryn*." *England in the Fourteenth Century: Proceedings of the 1991 Harlaxton Symposium*. Ed. Nicholas Rogers. Stamford, CT: Paul Watkins, 1993. 97–108.

Meecham-Jones, Simon. "The Invisible Siege—The Depiction of Warfare in the Poetry of Chaucer." *Writing War: Medieval Literary Responses to Warfare*. Ed. Corinne

Saunders, Françoise Le Saux, and Neil Thomas. Cambridge: D. S. Brewer, 2004. 147–67.

Meroney, Howard. "The Life and Death of Longe Will." *ELH* 17 (1950): 1–35.

Meyer-Lee, Robert. "The Allure of the Phantom Popet." *The Chaucer Newsletter* 22/2 (Fall 2000): 6.

Meyvaert, Paul. "'Rainaldus est malus scriptor Francigenus' — Voicing National Antipathy in the Middle Ages." *Speculum* 66 (1991): 743–63.

Middleton, Anne. "Acts of Vagrancy: The C Version 'Autobiography' and the Statute of 1388." *Written Work.* Ed. Justice and Kerby-Fulton. 208–317.

———. "The Audience and Public of *Piers Plowman.*" *Middle English Alliterative Poetry.* Ed. Lawton. 101–23 and notes 147–54.

———. "Chaucer's 'New Men' and the Good of Poetry." *Literature and Society.* Ed. Edward Said. Baltimore: Johns Hopkins University Press, 1980. 15–56.

———. "Introduction: The Critical Heritage." *Companion to "Piers Plowman."* Ed. Alford. 1–25.

———. "Langland's Lives: Reflections on Late-Medieval Religious and Literary Vocabulary." *The Idea of Medieval Literature: New Essays on Chaucer and Medieval Culture in Honor of Donald R. Howard.* Ed. James M. Dean and Christian K. Zacher. Newark: University of Delaware Press, 1992. 227–42.

———. "Narration and the Invention of Experience: Episodic Form in *Piers Plowman.*" *Wisdom of Poetry.* Ed. Benson and Wenzel. 91–122.

———. "*Piers Plowman.*" *A Manual of the Writings in Middle English, 1050–1500.* Gen. ed. Albert E. Hartung. Vol. 7. New Haven: Connecticut Academy of Arts and Sciences, 1986. 2211–34 and 2419–48.

———. Review of John M. Bowers, *Crisis of Will in "Piers Plowman." Speculum* 64 (1989): 130–34.

———. "William Langland's 'Kynde Name': Authorial Signature and Social Identity in Late Fourteenth-Century England." *Literary Practice and Social Change.* Ed. Patterson. 15–82.

Millar, Bonnie. *"The Siege of Jerusalem" in Its Physical, Literary and Historical Contexts.* Dublin: Four Courts Press, 2000.

Miller, B. D. H. "The Early History of Bodleian MS Digby 86." *Annuale Medievale* 4 (1963): 23–56.

Minnis, A. J. "Chaucer and the Queering Eunuch." *NML* 6 (2003): 107–28.

———. "The Influence of Academic Prologues on the Prologues and Literary Attitudes of Late Medieval English Writers." *MS* 43 (1981): 342–83.

———. *Medieval Theory of Authorship.* 2nd ed. Philadelphia: University of Pennsylvania Press, 1988.

———. "Reclaiming the Pardoners." *JMEMS* 33 (2003): 311–34.

———. "'Respondet Waltherus Bryth...': Walter Brut in Debate on Women Priests." *Text and Controversy from Wyclif to Bale.* Ed. Barr and Hutchison. 229–49.

———, V. J. Scattergood, and J. J. Smith. *Oxford Guides to Chaucer: The Shorter Poems.* Oxford: Clarendon, 1995.

———, ed. *Late-Medieval Religious Texts and Their Transmission: Essays in Honour of A. I. Doyle.* Cambridge: D. S. Brewer, 1994.

————, ed. *Middle English Poetry: Texts and Traditions: Essays in Honour of Derek Pearsall.* Woodbridge: York Medieval Press with Boydell Press, 2001.

————, and Charlotte Brewer, eds. *Crux and Controversy in Middle English Textual Criticism.* Woodbridge and Rochester: Boydell & Brewer, 1992.

————, and A. B. Scott, with David Wallace, eds. *Medieval Literary Theory and Criticism c. 1100–c. 1375.* Rev. ed. Oxford: Clarendon, 1991.

Miskimin, Alice. *The Renaissance Chaucer.* New Haven: Yale University Press, 1975.

Mitchell, Jerome. "Hoccleve Studies, 1965–1981." *Fifteenth-Century Studies.* Ed. Yeager. 49–63.

————. "Hoccleve's Supposed Friendship with Chaucer." *ELN* 4 (1966): 9–12.

Montrose, Louis A. "Professing the Renaissance: The Poetics and Politics of Culture." *The New Historicism.* Ed. Veeser. 15–36.

Mooney, Linne. "Chaucer's Scribe." *Speculum* 81 (2006): 97–138.

————. "John Shirley's Heirs." *YES* 33 (2003): 182–98.

————, and Lister M. Matheson. "The Beryn Scribe and His Texts: Evidence for Multiple-Copy Production of Manuscripts in Fifteenth-Century England." *The Library* ser. 7, 4 (2003): 347–70.

————, and Mary-Jo Arn, eds. *"The Kingis Quair" and Other Prison Poems.* Kalamazoo: Medieval Institute Publications, 2005.

Moore, Arthur K. *"Sir Thopas* as Criticism of Fourteenth-Century Minstrelsy." *JEGP* 53 (1954): 532–45.

Morgan, Philip. "Henry IV and the Shadow of Richard II." *Crown, Government, and People in the Fifteenth Century.* Ed. Rowena E. Archer. New York: St. Martin's, 1995. 1–31.

Morganstern, Anne McGee. *Gothic Tombs of Kinship in France, the Low Countries, and England.* University Park: Pennsylvania State University Press, 2000.

Morris, Colin, and Peter Roberts, eds. *Pilgrimage: The English Experience from Becket to Bunyan.* Cambridge: Cambridge University Press, 2002.

Morse, Ruth, and Barry Windeatt, eds. *Chaucer Traditions: Studies in Honour of Derek Brewer.* Cambridge: Cambridge University Press, 1990.

Mullett, Charles F. "John Lydgate: A Mirror of Medieval Medicine." *Bulletin of the History of Medicine* 22 (1948): 403–15.

Neilson, George. *Caudatus Anglicus: A Mediaeval Slander.* Edinburgh: George P. Johnson, 1896.

Neville-Sington, Pamela. "Press, Politics and Religion." *Cambridge History of the Book in Britain,* vol. 3. Ed. Hellinga and Trapp. 576–607.

Newhall, Richard Ager. *The English Conquest of Normandy, 1416–1424.* New Haven: Yale University Press, 1924.

Nicholson, Peter. "Chaucer Borrows from Gower: The Sources of the *Man of Law's Tale.*" *Chaucer and Gower.* Ed. Yeager. 85–99.

————. "The Dedications of Gower's *Confessio Amantis.*" *Mediaevalia* 10 (1984): 159–80.

————. "Gower's Revisions in the *Confessio Amantis.*" *ChauR* 19 (1984): 123–43.

Nightingale, Pamela. "Capitalists, Crafts and Constitutional Change in Late Fourteenth-Century London." *P&P* 124 (1989): 3–35.

Nissé, Ruth. "Grace under Pressure: Conduct and Representation in the Norwich Heresy Trials." *Medieval Conduct*. Ed. Ashley and Clark. 207–25.

———. "'Oure Fadres Olde and Modres': Gender, Heresy, and Hoccleve's Literary Politics." *SAC* 21 (1999): 275–99.

Nolan, Maura B. "The Art of History Writing: Lydgate's *Serpent of Division*." *Speculum* 78 (2003): 99–127.

Oakden, J. P. *Alliterative Poetry in Middle English*. 2 vols. Manchester: Manchester University Press, 1930–35.

Oates, J. C. T. "Richard Pynson and the Holy Blood of Hayles." *The Library* 5th ser., 13 (1958): 269–77.

O'Keeffe, Katherine O'Brien. "Texts and Works: Some Historical Questions on the Editing of Old English Verse." *New Historical Literary Study*. Ed. Cox and Reynolds. 54–68.

Olmert, Michael. "Troilus in *Piers Plowman*: A Contemporary View of Chaucer's *Troilus and Criseyde*." *Chaucer Newsletter* 2 (1980): 13–14.

Olson, Glending. *Literature as Recreation in the Middle Ages*. Ithaca and London: Cornell University Press, 1982.

———. "The Misreadings of the *Beryn* Prologue." *Mediaevalia* 18 (1993): 201–19.

Orme, Nicholas. "Medieval Hunting: Fact and Fancy." *Chaucer's England*. Ed. Hanawalt. 133–53.

Ormrod, W. M. "The Use of English: Language, Law, and Political Culture in Fourteenth-Century England." *Speculum* 78 (2003): 750–87.

Orsten, Elizabeth M. "'Heaven on Earth': Langland's Vision of Life within the Cloister." *American Benedictine Review* 21 (1970): 526–34.

O'Shea, Stephen. *The Perfect Heresy: The Revolutionary Life and Death of the Cathars*. New York: Walker & Co., 2000.

Owen, Charles A., Jr. "The Alternative Reading of *The Canterbury Tales*: Chaucer's Text and the Early Manuscripts." *PMLA* 97 (1982): 237–50.

———. *Pilgrimage and Storytelling in the "Canterbury Tales."* Norman: University of Oklahoma Press, 1977.

Owst, G. R. *Literature and Pulpit in Medieval England*. 1933; rpt. Oxford: Blackwell, 1966.

Palmer, J. J. N. *England, France and Christendom, 1377–99*. London: Routledge & Kegan Paul, 1972.

———. "The War Aims of the Protagonists and Negotiations for Peace." *Hundred Years War*. Ed. Fowler. 51–74.

Parkes, Malcolm B. "Patterns of Scribal Activity and Revisions of the Text in Early Copies of Works by John Gower." *New Science out of Old Books*. Ed. Beadle and Piper. 81–104.

———. "The Provision of Books." *History of the University of Oxford*, vol. 2: *Late Medieval Oxford*. Ed. J. I. Catto and Ralph Evans. Oxford: Clarendon, 1992. 407–83.

———. *Scribes, Scripts and Readers: Studies in the Communication, Presentation and Dissemination of Medieval Texts*. London: Hambledon Press, 1991.

Parr, Johnstone. "Astronomical Dating for Some of Lydgate's Poems." *PMLA* 67 (1952): 251–58.

Partridge, Stephen. "Minding the Gap: Interpreting the Manuscript Evidence of the Cook's Tale and the Squire's Tale." *English Medieval Book*. Ed. Edwards, Gillespie, and Hanna. 51–85.

Patterson, Annabel M. *Censorship and Interpretation: The Conditions of Writing and Reading in Early Modern England*. Madison: University of Wisconsin Press, 1984.

Patterson, Lee. *Chaucer and the Subject of History*. Madison: University of Wisconsin Press, 1991.

———. "Court Politics and the Invention of Literature: The Case of Sir John Clanvowe." *Culture and History, 1350–1600*. Ed. David Aers. Detroit: Wayne State University Press, 1992. 7–41.

———. "Making Identities in Fifteenth-Century England: Henry V and John Lydgate." *New Historical Literary Studies*. Ed. Cox and Reynolds. 69–107.

———. *Negotiating the Past: The Historical Understanding of Medieval Literature*. Madison: University of Wisconsin Press, 1987.

———. " 'What Is Me?' Self and Society in the Poetry of Thomas Hoccleve." *SAC* 23 (2001): 437–70.

———. " 'What Man Artow?' Authorial Self-Definition in *The Tale of Sir Thopas* and *The Tale of Melibee*." *SAC* 11 (1989): 117–75.

———, ed. *Literary Practice and Social Change in Britain, 1380–1530*. Berkeley and Los Angeles: University of California Press, 1990.

Pearsall, Derek. "Authorial Revision in Some Late-Medieval English Texts." *Crux and Controversy*. Ed. Minnis and Brewer. 39–48.

———. "Chaucer's Tomb: The Politics of Reburial." *MÆ* 64 (1995): 51–73.

———. "Editing Medieval Texts: Some Developments and Some Problems." *Textual Criticism and Literary Interpretation*. Ed. McGann. 92–106.

———. "The English Chaucerians." *Chaucer and Chaucerians*. Ed. D. S. Brewer. University: University of Alabama Press, 1966. 201–39.

———. "Hoccleve's *Regement of Princes*: The Poetics of Royal Self-Representation." *Speculum* 69 (1994): 386–410.

———. "The Idea of Englishness in the Fifteenth Century." *Nation, Court and Culture*. Ed. Cooney. 15–27.

———. "The 'Ilchester' Manuscript of *Piers Plowman*." *NM* 82 (1981): 181–93.

———. "Interpretative Models for the Peasants' Revolt." *Hermeneutics and Medieval Culture*. Ed. Patrick J. Gallacher and Helen Damico. Albany: State University of New York Press, 1989. 63–70.

———. *John Lydgate*. Charlottesville: University Press of Virginia, 1970.

———. *John Lydgate (1371–1449): A Bio-bibliography*. Victoria: University of Victoria English Literary Studies, no. 71, 1997.

———. "Langland and Lollardy: From B to C." *YLS* 17 (2003): 7–23.

———. "Langland's London." *Written Work*. Ed. Justice and Kerby-Fulton. 185–207.

———. *The Life of Geoffrey Chaucer: A Critical Biography*. Oxford: Blackwell, 1992.

———. "The Literary Milieu of Charles of Orléans and the Duke of Suffolk, and the Authorship of the Fairfax Sequence." *Charles d'Orléans in England*. Ed. Arn. 145–56.

———. "'Lunatyk Lollares' in *Piers Plowman*." *Religion in the Poetry and Drama of the Late Middle Ages in England*. Ed. Piero Boitani and Anna Torti. Cambridge: D. S. Brewer, 1990. 163–78.

———. "Lydgate as Innovator." *MLQ* 53 (1992): 5–22.

———. "Manuscript Illustration of Late Middle English Literary Texts, with Special Reference to the Illustration of *Piers Plowman* in Bodleian Library MS Douce 104." *Suche Werkis to Werche*. Ed. Vaughan. 191–210.

———. "The Manuscripts and Illustrations of Gower's Works." *Companion to Gower*. Ed. Echard. 73–97.

———. *Old English and Middle English Poetry*. London: Routledge & Kegan Paul, 1977.

———. "Texts, Textual Criticism, and Fifteenth Century Manuscript Production." *Fifteenth-Century Studies*. Ed. Yeager. 121–36.

———. "Theory and Practice in Middle English Editing." *Text* 7 (1994): 107–26.

———. "Thomas Speght (c. 1550– ?)." *Editing Chaucer*. Ed. Ruggiers. 71–92.

———. "The *Troilus* Frontispiece and Chaucer's Audience." *YES* 7 (1977): 68–74.

———, ed. *New Directions in Later Medieval Manuscript Studies*. Woodbridge: Boydell for York Medieval Press, 2000.

———, ed. *Studies in the Vernon Manuscript*. Cambridge: D. S. Brewer, 1990.

Peikola, Matti. "'And after all, myn Aue-Marie almost to the ende': *Pierce the Ploughman's Crede* and Lollard Expositions of the Ave Maria." *ES* 81 (2000): 273–92.

———. "'Whom Clepist Þou Trewe Pilgrimes?' Lollard Discourse on Pilgrimages in *The Testimony of William Thorpe*." *Essayes and Explorations: A "Freundschrift" for Liisa Dahl*. Ed. Marita Gustafsson. Turku, Finland: University of Turku, Anglicana Turkuensia, 15, 1996. 73–84.

Pelikan, Jaroslav. *The Vindication of Tradition*. New Haven and London: Yale University Press, 1984.

Perkins, Nicholas. *Hoccleve's "Regiment of Princes": Counsel and Constraint*. Cambridge: D. S. Brewer, 2001.

Perroy, Edouard. *The Hundred Years War*. Trans. David C. Douglas. Bloomington: Indiana University Press, 1959.

Phillips, Helen. "Register, Politics, and the *Legend of Good Women*." *ChauR* 37 (2002): 101–28.

Pigg, Daniel F. "With Hym Ther Was a Plowman, Was His Brother." *Chaucer's Pilgrims*. Ed. Lambdin and Lambdin. 263–70.

Pinti, Daniel J. "Governing the Cook's Tale in Bodley 686." *ChauR* 30 (1996): 379–88.

Piper, Edwin Ford. "The Royal Boar and the Ellesmere Chaucer." *PQ* 5 (1926): 330–40.

Pitard, Derrick G. "A Selected Bibliography for Lollard Studies." *Lollards and Their Influence*. Ed. Somerset, Havens, and Pitard. 251–319.

————. "Sowing Difficulty: *The Parson's Tale,* Vernacular Commentary, and the Nature of Chaucerian Dissent." *SAC* 26 (2004): 299–330.

Pollard, A. J. "The Lancastrian Constitutional Experiment Revisited: Henry IV, Sir John Tiptoft and the Parliament of 1406." *Parliamentary History* 14 (1995): 103–19.

Pollard, Graham. "The Company of Stationers before 1557." *The Library* 4th ser., 18 (1937): 1–37.

Porter, Elizabeth. "Chaucer's Knight, the Alliterative *Morte Arthure,* and Medieval Laws of War: A Reconsideration." *Nottingham Medieval Studies* 27 (1983): 56–78.

Postan, M. M. "The Costs of the Hundred Years' War." *P&P* 27 (1964): 34–53.

Powell, Edward. *Kingship, Law, and Society: Criminal Justice in the Reign of Henry V.* Oxford: Oxford University Press, 1989.

————. "The Restoration of Law and Order." *Henry V: Practice of Kingship.* Ed. Harriss. 53–74.

Powell, Susan. "A New Dating of John Mirk's *Festial.*" *N&Q* n.s. 29 (1982): 487–89.

————. "The Transmission and Circulation of *The Lay Folks' Catechism.*" *Late-Medieval Religious Texts and Their Transmission.* Ed. Minnis. 67–84.

Powicke, Michael. "The English Aristocracy and the War." *The Hundred Years War.* Ed. Fowler. 122–34.

Prendergast, Thomas A. *Chaucer's Dead Body: From Corpse to Corpus.* New York and London: Routledge, 2004.

Prescott, Andrew. "London in the Peasants' Revolt: A Portrait Gallery." *London Journal* 7 (1981): 125–43.

————. "Writing about Rebellion: Using the Records of the Peasants' Revolt of 1381." *History Workshop Journal* 45 (1998): 1–27.

Provost, William. "Chaucer's Endings." *New Readings of Chaucer's Poetry.* Ed. Robert G. Benson and Susan J. Ridyard. Cambridge: D. S. Brewer, 2003. 91–105.

Pugh, T. B. *Henry V and the Southampton Plot of 1415.* Southampton: Southampton University Press, 1988.

Putnam, Bertha H. "Maximum Wage-Laws for Priests after the Black Death, 1348–1381." *AHR* 21 (1915): 12–32.

Quain, E. A. "The Medieval *Accessus ad Auctores.*" *Traditio* 3 (1945): 228–42.

Quinn, William A. "Chaucer's Problematic *Priere: An ABC* as Artifact and Critical Issue." *SAC* 23 (2001): 109–41.

Rand, E. K. "Chaucer in Error." *Speculum* 1 (1926): 222–25.

Reddaway, T. F. *The Early History of the Goldsmiths' Company 1327–1509.* London: Edward Arnold, 1975.

Reeves, A. Compton. "The World of Thomas Hoccleve." *FCS* 2 (1979): 187–201.

Renan, Ernest. "What Is a Nation?" Trans. Martin Thom. *Nation and Narration.* Ed. Homi K. Bhabha. London and New York: Routledge, 1991. 8–22.

Rex, Richard. "Blessed Adrian Fortescue: A Martyr without a Cause?" *Analecta Bollandiana* 115 (1997): 307–53.

————. *The Lollards.* New York: Palgrave, 2002.

Richards, Jeffrey. *Sex, Dissidence and Damnation: Minority Groups in the Middle Ages*. London and New York: Routledge, 1991.

Richardson, H. G. "Heresy and the Lay Power under Richard II." *EHR* 51 (1936): 1–28.

Richardson, Malcolm. "The Earliest Known Owners of *Canterbury Tales* MSS and Chaucer's Secondary Audience." *ChauR* 25 (1990): 17–32.

———. "Henry V, the English Chancery, and Chancery English." *Speculum* 55 (1980): 726–50.

———. "Hoccleve in His Social Context." *ChauR* 20 (1986): 313–22.

Rickert, Edith. "Chaucer's 'Hodge of Ware.'" *TLS* (20 October 1932): 761.

———. *Chaucer's World*. Ed. Clair C. Olson and Martin M. Crow. New York: Columbia University Press, 1948.

———. "King Richard II's Books." *The Library* 4th ser., 13 (1933): 144–47.

———. "Thou Vache." *MP* 11 (1913–14): 209–25.

Riddy, Felicity, ed. *Prestige, Authority and Power in Late Medieval Manuscripts and Texts*. Woodbridge: Boydell & Brewer for York Medieval Press, 2000.

Rigg, A. G. *A History of Anglo-Latin Literature 1066–1422*. Cambridge: Cambridge University Press, 1992.

Robbins, Rossell Hope, "Dissent in Middle English Literature: The Spirit of (Thirteen) Seventy-Six." *M&H* n.s. 9 (1979): 25–51.

Roberts, Phyllis B. "The Unmaking of a Saint: The Suppression of the Cult of St. Thomas of Canterbury." *Hagiographica* 7 (2000): 35–46.

Robertson, Anne Walters. *Guillaume de Machaut and Reims*. Cambridge: Cambridge University Press, 2002.

Robertson, D. W., Jr. "Chaucer and the 'Commune Profit': The Manor." *Mediaevalia* 6 (1980): 239–59.

———. *A Preface to Chaucer*. Princeton: Princeton University Press, 1962.

Robertson, Kellie. "Laboring in the God of Love's Garden: Chaucer's Prologue to *The Legend of Good Women*." *SAC* 24 (2002): 115–47.

Robinson, Ian. *Chaucer and the English Tradition*. Cambridge: Cambridge University Press, 1972.

Robinson, Pamela R. *Catalogue of Dated and Datable Manuscripts c. 737–1600 in Cambridge Libraries*. 2 vols. Cambridge: D. S. Brewer, 1988.

———, and Rivkah Zim, eds. *Of the Making of Books: Medieval Manuscripts, Their Scribes and Readers: Essays Presented to M. B. Parkes*. Aldershot: Scolar Press, 1997.

Rogers, A. "The Political Crisis of 1401." *Nottingham Mediaeval Studies* 12 (1968): 85–96.

Rogers, Nicholas J. "Fitzwilliam Museum MS 3–1979: A Bury St. Edmunds Book of Hours and the Origins of the Bury Style." *England in the Fifteenth Century*. Ed. Williams. 229–43.

Rogers, William Elford. *Interpretation in "Piers Plowman."* Washington, DC: Catholic University of America Press, 2002.

Ronan, Nick. "1381: Writing in Revolt—Signs of Confederacy in the Chronicle Accounts of the English Rising." *Forum for Modern Language Studies* 25 (1989): 304–14.

Root, Robert Kilburn. "The Manciple's Prologue." *MLN* 44 (1929): 493–96.

Rosenwein, Barbara H., Thomas Head, and Sharon Farmer. "Monks and Their Enemies: A Comparative Approach." *Speculum* 66 (1991): 764–96.

Roskell, J. S. *The Commons and Their Speakers in English Parliaments, 1376–1523.* Manchester: Manchester University Press, 1965.

———, Linda Clark, and Carole Rawcliffe. *The History of Parliament: The House of Commons 1386–1421,* vol. 2: *Members A–D.* Stroud: Alan Sutton, 1992.

Ross, Thomas W. "Thomas Wright (1810–1877)." *Editing Chaucer.* Ed. Ruggiers. 145–56.

Ross, Trevor. "Dissolution and the Making of the English Literary Canon: The Catalogues of Leland and Bale." *Renaissance and Reformation* n.s. 15 (1991): 57–80.

———. *The Making of the English Literary Canon: From the Middle Ages to the Late Eighteenth Century.* Montreal: McGill–Queen's University Press, 1998.

Rosser, Gervase. *Medieval Westminster, 1200–1540.* Oxford: Clarendon, 1989.

Rothwell, W. "Chaucer and Stratford atte Bowe." *BJRL* 74 (1992): 3–28.

———. "Stratford atte Bowe and Paris." *MLR* 80 (1985): 39–54.

Rubin, Miri. "Small Groups, Identity and Solidarity in the Late Middle Ages." *Enterprise and Individuals in Fifteenth-Century England.* Ed. Jennifer Kermode. Wolfeboro Falls, NH: Sutton, 1991. 132–50.

Ruggiers, Paul G., ed. *Editing Chaucer: The Great Tradition.* Norman, OK: Pilgrim Books, 1984.

Russell, George H. "'As They Read It': Some Notes on Early Responses to the C-Version of *Piers Plowman.*" *LSE* n.s. 20 (1989): 173–89.

———. "The Evolution of a Poem: Some Reflections on the Textual Tradition of *Piers Plowman.*" *Arts* 2 (1962): 33–46.

———. "The Imperative of Revision in the C Version of *Piers Plowman.*" *Medieval English Studies Presented to George Kane.* Ed. Kennedy et al. 233–42.

———. "Poet as Reviser: The Metamorphosis of the Confession of the Seven Deadly Sins in *Piers Plowman.*" *Acts of Interpretation.* Ed. Carruthers and Kirk. 53–65.

———. "Some Aspects of the Process of Revision in *Piers Plowman.*" *"Piers Plowman": Critical Approaches.* Ed. Hussey. 27–49.

———. "Some Early Responses to the C-Version of Piers Plowman." *Viator* 15 (1984): 275–303.

———, and Venetia Nathan. "A *Piers Plowman* Manuscript at the Huntington Library." *HLQ* 26 (1963): 119–30.

Ruud, Martin B. *Thomas Chaucer.* Minneapolis: University of Minnesota Studies in Language and Literature, no. 9, 1926.

Said, Edward W. *Beginnings: Intention and Method.* New York: Basic Books, 1975.

Salter, Elizabeth. "Langland and the Contexts of *Piers Plowman.*" *E&S* n.s. 32 (1979): 19–25.

Samuels, M. L. "Dialect and Grammar." *A Companion to "Piers Plowman."* Ed. Alford. 201–21.

———. "Langland's Dialect." *MÆ* 54 (1985): 232–47.

———. "The Scribe of the Hengwrt and Ellesmere Manuscripts of the *Canterbury Tales*." *SAC* 5 (1983): 49–65.

———. "Scribes and Manuscript Traditions." *Regionalism in Late Medieval Manuscripts and Texts*. Ed. Felicity Riddy. Cambridge: D. S. Brewer, 1991. 1–7.

Sandler, Lucy Freeman. "Lancastrian Heraldry in the Bohun Manuscripts." *The Lancastrian Court*. Ed. Jenny Stratford. *Harlaxton Medieval Studies* n.s. 13 (2003): 221–32.

———. *The Lichtenthal Psalter and the Manuscript Patronage of the Bohun Family*. London and Turnhout: Harvey Miller Publishers, 2004.

———. "*Omne Bonum*: Compilatio and Ordinatio in an English Illustrated Encyclopedia of the Fourteenth Century." *Medieval Book Production: Assessing the Evidence*. Ed. Linda L. Brownrigg. Los Altos Hills, CA: Anderson-Lovelace, 1990. 183–200.

———. "Political Imagery in the Bohun Manuscripts." *Decorations and Illustration in Medieval English Manuscripts*. *English Manuscript Studies* 10 (2002): 114–53.

Sandquist, T. A. "The Holy Oil of St. Thomas of Canterbury." *Essays in Medieval History Presented to Bertie Wilkinson*. Ed. T. A. Sandquist and M. R. Powicke. Toronto: University of Toronto Press, 1969. 330–44.

Saul, Nigel. "Richard II and Westminster Abbey." *The Cloister and the World: Essays in Medieval History in Honour of Barbara Harvey*. Ed. John Blair and Brian Golding. Oxford: Clarendon, 1996. 196–218.

Sayce, Olive. "Chaucer's 'Retractions': The Conclusion of the *Canterbury Tales* and Its Place in Literary Tradition." *MÆ* 40 (1971): 230–48.

Saygin, Susanne. *Humphrey, Duke of Gloucester (1390–1447) and the Italian Humanists*. Leiden, Boston, and Cologne: Brill, 2002.

Scanlon, Larry. "King, Commons, and Kind Wit: Langland's National Vision and the Rising of 1381." *Imagining a Medieval English Nation*. Ed. Lavezzo. 191–233.

———. "The King's Two Voices: Narrative and Power in Hoccleve's *Regement of Princes*." *Literary Practice and Social Change*. Ed. Patterson. 216–47.

———. *Narrative, Authority, and Power: The Medieval Exemplum and the Chaucerian Tradition*. Cambridge: Cambridge University Press, 1994.

Scase, Wendy. "The Audience and Framers of the *Twelve Conclusions of the Lollards*." *Text and Controversy from Wyclif to Bale*. Ed. Barr and Hutchison. 283–301.

———. "'First to Reckon Richard': John But's *Piers Plowman*." *YLS* 11 (1997): 49–66.

———. "'Heu! Quanta Desolatio Angliae Praestatur': A Wycliffite Libel and the Naming of Heretics, Oxford 1382." *Lollards and Their Influence*. Ed. Somerset, Havens, and Pitard. 19–36.

———. "*Piers Plowman*" and the New Anticlericalism. Cambridge: Cambridge University Press, 1989.

———. *Reginald Pecock*. Aldershot: Variorum Authors of the Middle Ages, vol. 3, no. 8, 1996.

———. "Reginald Pecock, John Carpenter and John Colop's 'Common-Profit' Books: Aspects of Book Ownership and Circulation in Fifteenth-Century London." *MÆ* 61 (1992): 261–74.

————. "'Strange and Wonderful Bills': Bill-Casting and Political Discourse in Late Medieval England." *NML* 2 (1998): 225–47.

————. "Two *Piers Plowman* C-Text Interpolations: Evidence for a Second Textual Tradition." *N&Q* n.s. 34 (1987): 456–63.

Scattergood, V. J. "Chaucer and the French War: *Sir Thopas* and *Melibee.*" *Court and Poet.* Ed. Glyn S. Burgess et al. Liverpool: Cairns, 1981. 287–96.

————. "Literary Culture at the Court of Richard II." *English Court Culture in the Later Middle Ages.* Ed. Scattergood and Sherborne. 29–43.

————. *The Lost Tradition: Essays on Middle English Alliterative Poetry.* Dublin: Four Courts Press, 2000.

————. "Perkyn Revelour and the *Cook's Tale.*" *ChauR* 19 (1984): 14–23.

————. "*Pierce the Ploughman's Crede*: Lollardy and Texts." *Lollardy and the Gentry.* Ed. Aston and Richmond. 77–94.

————. "*The Tale of Gamelyn*: The Noble Robber as Provincial Hero." *Reading the Past: Essays on Medieval and Renaissance Literature.* Dublin: Four Courts Press, 1996. 80–113.

————. "Two Medieval Book Lists." *The Library* 5th ser., 23 (1968): 236–39.

————, and J. W. Sherborne, eds. *English Court Culture in the Later Middle Ages.* New York: St. Martin's, 1983.

Schaap, Tanya. "From Professional to Private Readership: A Discussion and Transcription of the Fifteenth- and Sixteenth-Century Marginalia in *Piers Plowman* C-Text, Oxford, Bodleian Library, MS Digby 102." *The Medieval Reader: Reception and Cultural History in the Late Medieval Manuscript.* Ed. Kathryn Kerby-Fulton and Maidie Hilmo. New York: AMS Press, 2001. 81–116.

Schirmer, Walter F. *John Lydgate: A Study in the Culture of the XVth Century.* Trans. Ann E. Keep. London: Methuen, 1961.

Schmidt, A. V. C. "*Ars* or *Scientia*? Reflections on Editing *Piers Plowman.*" *YLS* 18 (2004): 31–54.

————. "The Authenticity of the Z-text of *Piers Plowman*: A Metrical Examination." *MÆ* 53 (1984): 295–300.

————. "Langland's Visions and Revisions." *YLS* 14 (2000): 5–27.

Scott, Kathleen L. *Dated and Datable English Manuscript Borders, c. 1395–1499.* London: British Library for the Bibliographical Society, 2002.

————. "An Hours and Psalter by Two Ellesmere Illuminators." *Ellesmere Chaucer.* Ed. Stevens and Woodward. 87–119.

————. "The Illustrations of *Piers Plowman* in Bodleian Library MS Douce 104." *YLS* 4 (1990): 1–86.

————. "Limner-Power: A Book Artist in England c. 1420." *Prestige, Authority and Power.* Ed. Riddy. 55–75.

————. "Lydgate's Lives of Saints Edmund and Fremund: A Newly-Located Manuscript in Arundel Castle." *Viator* 13 (1982): 335–66.

————. *A Survey of Manuscripts Illuminated in the British Isles.* Gen. ed. J. J. G. Alexander. Vol. 6: *Later Gothic Manuscripts, 1390–1490.* 2 vols. London: Harvey Miller, 1996.

Seaman, David. "'The Wordes of the Frankeleyn to the Squier': An Interruption?" *ELN* 24 (1986): 12–18.

Selzer, John L. "Topical Allegory in *Piers Plowman*: Lady Mede's B-Text Debate with Conscience." *PQ* 59 (1980): 257–67.

Serjeantson, Mary S. "The Index of the Vernon Manuscript." *MLR* 32 (1937): 222–61.

Seward, Desmond. *The Hundred Years War*. New York: Atheneum, 1978.

Seymour, Michael. *A Catalogue of Chaucer Manuscripts,* vol. 1: *Works before the "Canterbury Tales."* Aldershot: Scolar Press, 1995.

———. *A Catalogue of Chaucer Manuscripts,* vol. 2: *"The Canterbury Tales."* Aldershot: Scolar Press, 1997.

———. "Hypothesis, Hyperbole, and the Hengwrt Manuscript of the *Canterbury Tales.*" *ES* 68 (1987): 214–19.

———. "Of This Cokes Tale." *ChauR* 24 (1990): 259–62.

———. "Manuscript Portraits of Chaucer and Hoccleve." *Burlington Magazine* 124 (1982): 618–23.

———. "Manuscripts of Hoccleve's *Regiment of Princes.*" *Edinburgh Bibliographical Society Transactions* 4/7 (1974): 253–97.

———. "The Origin of the Egerton Version of *Mandeville's Travels.*" *MÆ* 30 (1961): 159–69.

———. "The Scribe of Huntington Library MS HM 114." *MÆ* 43 (1974): 139–43.

———. *Sir John Mandeville*. Aldershot: Variorum Authors of the Middle Ages, vol. 1, no. 1, 1994.

Sheils, W. J., and Diana Wood, eds. *The Church and Wealth*. Oxford: Blackwell, 1987.

Shikii, Kumiko. "Chaucer's Anti-clericalism as Seen in the Monk." *The Fleur-de-Lis Review* (25 December 1980): 25–54.

Shippey, T. A. *J. R. R. Tolkien: Author of the Century*. Boston: Houghton Mifflin, 2001.

Shoaf, R. A. "'Noon Englissh Digne': Dante in Late Medieval England." *Dante Now: Current Trends in Dante Studies*. Ed. Theodore J. Cachey, Jr. Notre Dame, IN: University of Notre Dame Press, 1995. 189–203.

Shonk, Timothy A. "A Study of the Auchinleck Manuscript: Bookmen and Bookmaking in the Early Fourteenth Century." *Speculum* 60 (1985): 71–91.

Shrader, Charles R. "A Handlist of Extant Manuscripts Containing the *De Re Militari* of Flavius Vegetius Renatus." *Scriptorium* 33 (1979): 280–305.

Shuffelton, George. "*Piers Plowman* and the Case of the Missing Book." *YLS* 18 (2004): 55–72.

Simon, Hugo. "Chaucer a Wicliffite: An Essay on Chaucer's Parson and Parson's Tale." *Essays on Chaucer*. London: Chaucer Society, 2nd ser., no. 16, 1876. 227–92.

Simpson, James. "The Constraints of Satire in *Piers Plowman* and *Mum and the Sothsegger.*" *Langland, the Mystics and the Medieval English Religious Tradition: Essays in Honour of S. S. Hussey*. Ed. Helen Phillips. Cambridge: D. S. Brewer, 1990. 11–30.

———. "Contemporary English Writers." *Companion to Chaucer*. Ed. Brown. 114–32.

———. "'Dysemol Daies and Fatal Houres': Lydgate's *Destruction of Thebes* and Chaucer's *Knight's Tale.*" *The Long Fifteenth Century*. Ed. Cooper and Mapstone. 15–33.

————. "Grace Abounding: Evangelical Centralization and the End of *Piers Plow-man*." *YLS* 14 (2000): 49–73.

————. "Madness and Texts: Hoccleve's *Series*." *Chaucer and Fifteenth-Century Poetry*. Ed. Boffey and Cowen. 15–29.

————. "Nobody's Man: Thomas Hoccleve's *Regement of Princes*." *London and Europe in the Later Middle Ages*. Ed. Julia Boffey and Pamela King. London: Westfield Publications in Medieval Studies, no. 9, 1995. 149–80.

————. "The Power of Impropriety: Authorial Naming in *Piers Plowman*." *William Langland's "Piers Plowman."* Ed. Hewett-Smith. 145–65.

————. *Reform and Cultural Revolution, 1350–1547*. Oxford: Oxford University Press, 2002.

————. "Spirituality and Economics in Passus 1–7 of the B-text." *YLS* 1 (1987): 83–103.

Skeat, Walter W. *The Chaucer Canon*. Oxford: Clarendon, 1900.

————. *The Evolution of the "Canterbury Tales."* London: Chaucer Society, 2nd ser., no. 38, 1907.

Šmahel, František. "Literacy and Heresy in Hussite Bohemia." *Heresy and Literacy*. Ed. Biller and Hudson. 237–54.

Smeeton, Donald Dean. *Lollard Themes in the Reformation Theology of William Tyndale*. Kirkville, MO: Sixteenth Century Journal Publishers, 1986.

Smith, D. Vance. *The Book of Incipit: Beginnings in the Fourteenth Century*. Minneapolis: University of Minnesota Press, 2001.

Smith, Jeremy J. "John Gower and London English." *Companion to Gower*. Ed. Echard. 61–72.

————. "The Trinity Gower D-Scribe and His Work on Two Early *Canterbury Tales* Manuscripts." *The English of Chaucer and His Contemporaries*. Ed. M. L. Samuels and J. J. Smith. Aberdeen: Aberdeen University Press, 1988. 51–69.

Somerset, Fiona. *Clerical Discourse and Lay Audience in Late Medieval England*. Cambridge: Cambridge University Press, 1998.

————. "Expanding the Langlandian Canon: Radical Latin and the Stylistics of Reform." *YLS* 17 (2003): 73–92.

————. "Here, There, and Everywhere? Wycliffite Conceptions of the Eucharist and Chaucer's 'Other' Lollard Joke." *Lollards and Their Influence*. Ed. Somerset, Havens, and Pitard. 127–38.

————. "Professionalizing Translation at the Turn of the Fifteenth Century: Ullerston's *Determinacio,* Arundel's *Constitutiones*." *The Vulgar Tongue: Medieval and Postmedieval Vernacularity*. Ed. Fiona Somerset and Nicolas Watson. University Park: Pennsylvania State University Press, 2003. 145–57.

————, Jill C. Havens, and Derrick G. Pitard, eds. *Lollards and Their Influence in Late Medieval England*. Woodbridge: Boydell, 2003.

Spearing, A. C. "Lydgate's Canterbury Tale: *The Siege of Thebes* and Fifteenth-Century Chaucerianism." *Fifteenth-Century Studies*. Ed. Yeager. 333–64.

————. *Medieval to Renaissance in English Poetry*. Cambridge: Cambridge University Press, 1985.

————. "Prison, Writing, Absence: Representing the Subject in the English Poems of Charles d'Orléans." *MLQ* 53 (1992): 83–99.

Spiegel, Gabrielle M. "History, Historicism, and the Social Logic of the Text in the Middle Ages." *Speculum* 65 (1990): 59–86.

Spielmann, M. H. *The Portraits of Geoffrey Chaucer.* London: Chaucer Society, ser. 2, no. 31, 1900.

Sponsler, Claire. "The Captivity of Henry Chrystede: Froissart's *Chroniques,* Ireland, and Fourteenth-Century Nationalism." *Imagining a Medieval English Nation.* Ed. Lavezzo. 304–39.

————. "Eating Lessons: Lydgate's 'Dietary' and Consumer Conduct." *Medieval Conduct.* Ed. Ashley and Clark. 1–22.

Staley [Johnson], Lynn. "Chaucer's Tale of the Second Nun and the Strategies of Dissent." *SP* 89 (1992): 314–33.

————. "Personal Identity." *Companion to Chaucer.* Ed. Brown. 360–77.

Stanley, E. G. "Of This Cokes Tale Maked Chaucer Na Moore." *Poetica* 5 (1976): 36–59.

Steiner, Emily. *Documentary Culture and the Making of Medieval English Literature.* Cambridge: Cambridge University Press, 2003.

————. "Langland's Documents." *YLS* 14 (2000): 95–115.

————. "Lollardy and the Legal Document." *Lollards and Their Influence.* Ed. Somerset, Havens, and Pitard. 155–74.

Stevens, Martin, and Daniel Woodward, eds. *The Ellesmere Chaucer: Essays in Interpretation.* San Marino: Huntington Library, 1997.

Stillwell, Gardiner. "Chaucer's Plowman and the Contemporary English Peasant." *ELH* 6 (1939): 285–90.

Stock, Lorraine Kochanske. "Parable, Allegory, History, and *Piers Plowman*." *YLS* 5 (1991): 143–64.

Storm, Melvin. "The Pardoner's Invitation: Quaestor's Bag or Becket's Shrine." *PMLA* 97 (1982): 810–18.

Straker, Scott-Morgan. "Rivalry and Reciprocity in Lydgate's *Troy Book.*" *NML* 3 (1999): 119–47.

Stratford, Jenny. *The Bedford Inventories: The Worldly Goods of John, Duke of Bedford, Regent of France (1389–1435).* London: Society of Antiquaries, 1993.

————. "The Early Royal Collections and the Royal Library to 1461." *Cambridge History of the Book in Britain,* vol. 3. Ed. Hellinga and Trapp. 255–66.

————. "The Manuscripts of John, Duke of Bedford: Library and Chapel." *England in the Fifteenth Century.* Ed. Williams. 329–50.

Strohm, Paul. "Chaucer's Fifteenth-Century Audience and the Narrowing of the 'Chaucer Tradition.'" *SAC* 4 (1982): 3–32.

————. "Chaucer's Lollard Joke: History and the Textual Unconscious." *SAC* 17 (1995): 23–42.

————. *England's Empty Throne: Usurpation and the Language of Legitimation, 1399–1422.* New Haven: Yale University Press, 1998.

————. "Fourteenth- and Fifteenth-Century Writers as Readers of Chaucer." *Genres, Themes, and Images in English Literature from the Fourteenth to the Fifteenth Century*. Ed. Piero Boitani and Anna Torti. Tübingen: Gunter Narr Verlag, 1988. 90–104.

————. "Hoccleve, Lydgate and the Lancastrian Court." *Cambridge History of Medieval English Literature*. Ed. Wallace. 640–61.

————. *Hochon's Arrow: The Social Imagination of Fourteenth-Century Texts*. Princeton: Princeton University Press, 1992.

————. "Jean of Angoulême: A Fifteenth-Century Reader of Chaucer." *NM* 72 (1971): 69–76.

————. "Politics and Poetics: Usk and Chaucer in the 1380s." *Literary Practice and Social Change*. Ed. Patterson. 83–112.

————. *Social Chaucer*. Cambridge, MA: Harvard University Press, 1989.

————. *Theory and the Premodern Text*. Minneapolis and London: University of Minnesota Press, 2000.

————. "The Trouble with Richard: The Reburial of Richard II and Lancastrian Symbolic Strategy." *Speculum* 71 (1996): 87–111.

Strong, Patrick, and Felicity Strong. "The Last Will and Codicils of Henry V." *EHR* 96 (1981): 79–102.

Stubbs, Estelle. "Clare Priory, the London Austin Friars and Manuscripts of Chaucer's *Canterbury Tales*." *Middle English Poetry*. Ed. Minnis. 17–26.

————. "A New Manuscript by the Hengwrt/Ellesmere Scribe? Aberystwyth, National Library of Wales, MS. Peniarth 393D." *Journal of the Early Book Society* 5 (2002): 161–68.

Suggett, Helen. "A Letter Describing Richard II's Reconciliation with the City of London, 1392." *EHR* 62 (1947): 209–13.

Summers, Joanna. *Late-Medieval Prison Writing and the Politics of Autobiography*. Oxford: Clarendon, 2004.

Sumption, Jonathan. *The Hundred Years War*, vol. 2: *Trial by Fire*. Philadelphia: University of Pennsylvania Press, 1999.

————. *Pilgrimage: An Image of Mediaeval Religion*. Totowa: Rowman and Littlefield, 1975.

Sutherland, Annie. "*The Chastising of God's Children*: A Neglected Text." *Text and Controversy from Wyclif to Bale*. Ed. Barr and Hutchison. 353–73.

Swanson, Robert N. "Chaucer's Parson and Other Priests." *SAC* 13 (1991): 41–80.

————. *Church and Society in Late Medieval England*. Oxford: Blackwell, 1989.

————. "Literacy, Heresy, History and Orthodoxy: Perspectives and Permutations for the Later Middle Ages." *Heresy and Literacy*. Ed. Biller and Hudson. 279–93.

————. "The Origins of *The Lay Folks' Catechism*." *MÆ* 60 (1991): 92–100.

Szittya, Penn R. *The Antifraternal Tradition in Medieval Literature*. Princeton: Princeton University Press, 1986.

————. "The Antifraternal Tradition in Middle English Literature." *Speculum* 52 (1977): 287–313.

Tanner, Norman P., ed. *Heresy Trials in the Diocese of Norwich, 1428–31*. London: Camden 4th ser., vol. 20, 1977.

Tatlock, J. S. P. "The *Canterbury Tales* in 1400." *PMLA* 50 (1935): 100–139.

Taylor, Andrew. "Anne of Bohemia and the Making of Chaucer." *SAC* 19 (1997): 95–119.

Taylor, Charles. *Sources of the Self: The Making of Modern Identity.* Cambridge: Harvard University Press, 1989.

Taylor, John. *English Historical Literature in the Fourteenth Century.* Oxford: Clarendon, 1987.

Taylor, Sean. "The Lost Revision of *Piers Plowman* B." *YLS* 11 (1997): 97–134.

Theilmann, John M. "Political Canonization and Political Symbolism in Medieval England." *Journal of British Studies* 29 (1990): 241–66.

Thomas, Alfred. *Anne's Bohemia: Czech Literature and Society, 1310–1420.* Minneapolis: University of Minnesota Press, 1998.

Thompson, John J. "After Chaucer: Resituating Middle English Poetry in the Late Medieval and Early Modern Period." *New Directions in Later Medieval Manuscript Studies.* Ed. Pearsall. 183–99.

———. "Chaucer's *An ABC* in and out of Context." *Poetica* 37 (1993): 38–48.

———. "A Poet's Contacts with the Great and the Good: Further Consideration of Thomas Hoccleve's Texts and Manuscripts." *Prestige, Authority and Power.* Ed. Riddy. 77–101.

———. "Thomas Hoccleve and Manuscript Culture." *Nation, Court and Culture.* Ed. Cooney. 81–94.

Thomson, John A. F. "John Foxe and Some Sources for Lollard History: Notes for a Critical Appraisal." *Studies in Church History* 2 (1965): 251–57.

———. "Knightly Piety and the Margins of Lollardy." *Lollardy and the Gentry.* Ed. Aston and Richmond. 95–111.

———. *The Later Lollards, 1414–1520.* Oxford: Oxford University Press, 1965.

———. "Orthodox Religion and the Origins of Lollardy." *History* 74 (1989): 39–55.

Thomson, Rodney M. "The Library of Bury St. Edmunds Abbey in the Eleventh and Twelfth Centuries." *Speculum* 47 (1972): 617–45.

Thomson, Williel R. *The Latin Writings of John Wyclif: An Annotated Catalog.* Toronto: Pontifical Institute of Medieval Studies, Subsidia Mediaevalia, no. 14, 1983.

Thorne, J. R., and Marie-Claire Uhart. "Robert Crowley's *Piers Plowman.*" *MÆ* 55 (1986): 248–54.

Thornley, Eva M. "The ME Penitential Lyric and Hoccleve's Autobiographical Poetry." *NM* 68 (1967): 295–321.

Thrupp, Sylvia L. *The Merchant Class of Medieval London.* Ann Arbor: University of Michigan Press, 1948.

Tilly, Charles. *Coercion, Capital and European States, AD 990–1990.* Oxford: Blackwell, 1990.

Tinkle, Theresa. "The Imagined Chaucerian Community of Bodleian MS Fairfax 16." *Chaucer and the Challenges of Medievalism: Studies in Honor of H. A. Kelly.* Ed. Donka Minkova and Theresa Tinkle. Frankfurt am Main: Peter Lang, 2003. 157–74.

Tolmie, Sarah. "The *Prive Scilence* of Thomas Hoccleve." *SAC* 22 (2000): 281–309.

Torfing, Jacob. *New Theories of Discourse: Laclau, Mouffe and Žižek*. Oxford: Blackwell, 1999.

Torti, Anna. "Hoccleve's Attitude toward Women." *A Wyf Ther Was: Essays in Honour of Paule Mertens-Fonck*. Ed. Juliette Dor. Liège: Université de Liège, 1992. 264–74.

Tout, T. F. "The Beginnings of a Modern Capital: London and Westminster in the Fourteenth Century." *PBA* 10 (1923): 487–511.

———. "Literature and Learning in the English Civil Service in the Fourteenth Century." *Speculum* 4 (1929): 365–89.

Trigg, Stephanie. *Congenial Souls: Reading Chaucer from Medieval to Modern*. Minneapolis: University of Minnesota Press, 2002.

Tuck, Anthony. "The Cambridge Parliament, 1388." *EHR* 84 (1969): 225–43.

———. "Carthusian Monks and Lollard Knights: Religious Attitude at the Court of Richard II." *Studies in the Age of Chaucer, Proceedings, No. 1, 1984: Reconstructing Chaucer*. Ed. Paul Strohm and Thomas J. Heffernan. Knoxville: New Chaucer Society, 1985. 149–61.

———. "Henry IV and Chivalry." *Henry IV*. Ed. Dodd and Biggs. 55–71.

———. "Henry IV and Europe: A Dynasty's Search for Recognition." *McFarlane Legacy*. Ed. Britnell and Pollard. 107–25.

———. "Nobles, Commons and the Great Revolt of 1381." *The English Rising*. Ed. Hilton and Aston. 194–212.

———. "Why Men Fought in the 100 Years War." *History Today* 33 (April 1983): 35–40.

Turville-Petre, Thorlac. *The Alliterative Revival*. Cambridge: D. S. Brewer, 1977.

———. "The Author of *The Destruction of Troy*." *MÆ* 57 (1988): 264–69.

———. *England the Nation: Language, Literature, and National Identity, 1290–1340*. Oxford: Clarendon, 1996.

———. "Poems by Chaucer in John Harpur's Psalter." *SAC* 21 (1999): 301–13.

———. "Putting It Right: The Corrections of Huntington Library MS Hm 128 and BL Additional MS 35287." *YLS* 16 (2002): 41–65.

———. "Sir Adrian Fortescue and His Copy of *Piers Plowman*." *YLS* 14 (2000): 29–48.

Tzanaki, Rosemary. *Mandeville's Medieval Audiences: A Study on the Reception of the "Book" of Sir John Mandeville (1371–1550)*. Aldershot, England/Burlington, VT: Ashgate Publishing, 2003.

Uhart, Marie-Claire. "The Early Reception of *Piers Plowman*." Ph.D. diss., University of Leicester, 1986.

Ullmann, Walter. "Thomas Becket's Miraculous Oil." *Journal of Theological Studies* 8 (1957): 129–33.

Unwin, George. *The Gilds and Companies of London*. 4th ed. London: Frank Cass, 1963.

Utley, Francis Lee. "How Judicare Came in the Creed." *MS* 8 (1946): 303–9.

van Engen, John H. *Rupert of Deutz.* Berkeley and Los Angeles: University of California Press, 1983.

Vaughan, Míceál F., ed. *Suche Werkis to Werche: Essays on "Piers Plowman" in Honor of David C. Fowler.* East Lansing: Colleagues Press, 1993.

Veeser, H. Aram, ed. *The New Historicism.* New York and London: Routledge, 1989.

Von Nolcken, Christina. *"Piers Plowman,* the Wycliffites, and *Pierce the Plowman's Creed." YLS* 2 (1988): 71–102.

———. "Richard Wyche, a Certain Knight, and the Beginning of the End." *Lollardy and the Gentry.* Ed. Aston and Richmond. 127–54.

Wakelin, Martyn F. "The Manuscripts of John Mirk's *Festial." LSE* n.s. 1 (1967): 93–118.

Waldron, Ronald. "John Trevisa and the Use of English." *PBA* 74 (1988): 171–202.

Walker, Simon. "Political Saints in Later Medieval England." *McFarlane Legacy.* Ed. Britnell and Pollard. 77–106.

Wallace, David. *Chaucerian Polity: Absolutist Lineages and Associational Forms in England and Italy.* Stanford: Stanford University Press, 1997.

———. "Dante in Somerset: Ghosts, Historiography, Periodization." *NML* 3 (1999): 9–38.

———. "Italy." *Companion to Chaucer.* Ed. Brown. 218–34.

———. "Pilgrim Signs and the Ellesmere Chaucer." *Chaucer Newsletter* 11.2 (1989): 1–3.

———. *Premodern Places: Calais to Surinam, Chaucer to Aphra Behn.* Oxford: Blackwell, 2004.

———, ed. *Cambridge History of Medieval English Literature.* Cambridge: Cambridge University Press, 1999.

Warner, Lawrence. "Becket and the Hopping Bishops." *YLS* 17 (2003): 107–34.

———. "Jesus the Jouster: The Christ-Knight and Medieval Theories of the Atonement in *Piers Plowman* and the 'Round Table' Sermons." *YLS* 10 (1996): 129–43.

———. "John But and Other Works That Will Wrought (*Piers Plowman* A XII 101–02)." *N&Q* n.s. 52 (2005): 13–18.

———. "Langland and the Problem of *William of Palerne." Viator* 37 (2006): 397-415.

———. "The Ur-B *Piers Plowman* and the Earliest Production of C and B." *YLS* 16 (2002): 3–39.

Watkins, John. "'Wrastling for This World': Wyatt and the Tudor Canonization of Chaucer." *Refiguring Chaucer in the Renaissance.* Ed. Krier. 21–39.

Watson, Nicholas. "Censorship and Cultural Change in Late-Medieval England: Vernacular Theology, the Oxford Translation Debate, and Arundel's Constitutions of 1409." *Speculum* 70 (1995): 822–64.

———. "Desire for the Past." *SAC* 21 (1999): 59–97.

———. "Outdoing Chaucer: Lydgate's *Troy Book* and Henryson's *Testament of Cresseid* as Competitive Imitations of *Troilus and Criseyde." Shifts and Transpositions in Medieval Narrative.* Ed. Karen Pratt. Cambridge: D. S. Brewer, 1994. 89–108.

————. *Richard Rolle and the Invention of Authority*. Cambridge: Cambridge University Press, 1991.

Wawn, Andrew N. "Chaucer, *The Plowman's Tale* and Reformation Propaganda: The Testimonies of Thomas Godfray and *I Playne Piers*." *BJRL* 56 (1973): 174–92.

————. "Chaucer, Wyclif and the Court of Apollo." *ELN* 10 (1972): 15–20.

————. "The Genesis of *The Plowman's Tale*." *YES* 2 (1972): 21–40.

————. "Truth-telling and the Tradition of *Mum and the Sothsegger*." *YES* 13 (1983): 270–87.

Weis, René. *The Yellow Cross: The Story of the Last Cathars, 1290–1329*. New York: Knopf, 2001.

Wenzel, Siegfried. "Chaucer's Pardoner and His Relics." *SAC* 11 (1989): 37–41.

————. *Preachers, Poets, and the Early English Lyric*. Princeton: Princeton University Press, 1986.

White, Hayden. *The Content of the Form: Narrative Discourse and Historical Representation*. Baltimore and London: Johns Hopkins University Press, 1987.

White, Helen C. *Social Criticism in Popular Literature of the Sixteenth Century*. New York: Macmillan, 1944.

Wilks, Michael. "Chaucer and the Mystical Marriage in Medieval Political Thought." *BJRL* 44 (1962): 489–530.

————. "'Reformatio Regni': Wyclif and Hus as Leaders of Religious Protest Movements." *SCH* 9 (1972): 109–30.

————. "*Thesaurus Ecclesiae* (Presidential Address)." *Church and Wealth*. Ed. Sheils and Wood. xv–xlv.

Williams, Daniel, ed. *England in the Fifteenth Century: Proceedings of the 1986 Harlaxton Symposium*. Woodbridge: Boydell Press, 1987.

Williams, Raymond. *Keywords: A Vocabulary of Culture and Society*. Oxford: Oxford University Press, 1976.

————. *Marxism and Literature*. Oxford: Oxford University Press, 1977.

Wilson, Christopher. "The Tomb of Henry IV and the Holy Oil of St. Thomas of Canterbury." *Medieval Architecture and Its Intellectual Context*. Ed. Eric Fernie and Paul Crossley. London: Hambledon, 1990. 181–90.

Wilson, Edward. "*Sir Gawain and the Green Knight* and the Stanley Family of Stanley, Storeton, and Hooton." *RES* n.s. 30 (1979): 308–16.

Wilson, R. M. *The Lost Literature of Medieval England*. 2nd ed. London: Methuen, 1970.

Wimsatt, James I. *Chaucer and His French Contemporaries*. Toronto: University of Toronto Press, 1991.

Windeatt, B. A. "The Scribes as Chaucer's Early Critics." *SAC* 1 (1979): 119–41.

————. "Thomas Tyrwhitt (1730–1786)." *Editing Chaucer*. Ed. Ruggiers. 117–43.

Winstead, Karen A. "The *Beryn*-Writer as a Reader of Chaucer." *ChauR* 22 (1988): 225–33.

————. "'I Am Al Other to Yow Than Yee Weene': Hoccleve, Women and the *Series*." *PQ* 72 (1993): 143–55.

Wittig, Joseph S. "'Culture Wars' and the Persona in *Piers Plowman*." *YLS* 15 (2001): 167–95.

Wogan-Browne, Jocelyn, Nicholas Watson, Andrew Taylor, and Ruth Evans, eds. *The Idea of the Vernacular: An Anthology of Middle English Literary Theory, 1280–1520.* University Park: Pennsylvania State University Press, 1999.

Wood, Chauncey. "Chaucer's Most 'Gowerian' Tale." *Chaucer and Gower.* Ed. Yeager. 75–84.

Wood, Robert A. "A Fourteenth-Century London Owner of *Piers Plowman*." *MÆ* 53 (1984): 83–90.

Woodmansee, Martha, and Peter Jaszi, eds. *The Construction of Authorship: Textual Appropriation in Law and Literature.* Durham, NC: Duke University Press, 1994.

Woolf, Rosemary. *The English Religious Lyric in the Middle Ages.* Oxford: Clarendon, 1968.

———. "The Tearing of the Pardon." *"Piers Plowman": Critical Approaches.* Ed. Hussey. 50–75.

———. "The Theme of Christ the Lover-Knight in Medieval English Literature." *RES* 13 (1962): 1–16.

Wright, C. E. "The Dispersal of the Libraries in the Sixteenth Century." *The English Library before 1700: Studies in Its History.* Ed. Francis Wormald and C. E. Wright. London: Athlone, 1958. 148–75.

———. "The Dispersal of the Monastic Libraries and the Beginnings of Anglo-Saxon Studies." *Transactions of the Cambridge Bibliographical Society* 1 (1949–53): 208–37.

Wright, Nicholas. *Knights and Peasants: The Hundred Years' War in the French Countryside.* Woodbridge: Boydell Press, 1998.

Wright, Sylvia. "The Author Portraits in the Bedford Psalter-Hours: Gower, Chaucer and Hoccleve." *British Library Journal* 18 (1992): 190–201.

Wurtele, Douglas J. "The Anti-Lollardry of Chaucer's Parson." *Mediaevalia* 11 (1989 for 1985): 151–68.

Yeager, R. F. "*Pax Poetica*: On the Pacifism of Chaucer and Gower." *SAC* 9 (1987): 97–121.

———, ed. *Chaucer and Gower: Difference, Mutuality, Exchange.* Victoria, BC: University of Victoria English Literary Studies, no. 51, 1991.

———, ed. *Fifteenth-Century Studies.* Hamden, CT: Archon Books, 1984.

———, and Charlotte C. Morse, eds. *Speaking Images: Essays in Honor of V. A. Kolve.* Asheville: Pegasus Press, 2001.

Zeeman, Nicolette. "'Studying' in the Middle Ages—and in *Piers Plowman*." *NML* 3 (1999): 185–212.

Žižek, Slavoj. "Beyond Discourse Analysis." *New Reflections on the Revolution of Our Time.* Ed. Ernesto Laclau. London: Verso, 1990. 249–60.

———. *The Sublime Object of Ideology.* London and New York: Verso, 1989.

General Index

Abbey of the Holy Ghost, 131, 239
Adams, Jenny, 309
Aers, David, 278, 281, 283, 295
Agincourt, 97, 160, 194, 205, 301
Alexander, J. J. G., 246
Alford, John A., 239
Alfred the Great, 132–33
Alington, William, 124–25
Allen, Hope Emily, 141, 274, 279
Allen, Judson Boyce, 239
Allen, Rosamund, 322
alliterative poetry, 13, 15, 18, 20, 30, 127,
    136–37, 144, 150, 159, 166–67, 169,
    217, 218
Allmand, C. T., 252, 254, 258, 315
Ancrene Wisse, 19, 113, 131, 279
Anderson, Judith, 250
Anne of Bohemia, Queen of England, 24,
    99, 132–33, 185, 187
Anonimalle Chronicle, 44, 83, 112
anonymity, x, 8, 19, 22–24, 26, 36, 55, 62,
    63, 68, 72, 78, 85, 91, 94, 102, 104,
    108, 127, 128, 144, 145, 147, 148, 156,
    160, 166, 172, 178, 179, 214. *See also*
    namelessness
antagonism, 3, 9, 10, 26, 29, 40–41, 53, 93,
    110, 122, 137, 155, 193, 214, 225
antimendicant (antifraternal), 120, 139, 145,
    149, 150–51, 154, 156
Aquinas, Thomas, 45

Aristotle, 10–12, 37, 201, 219
Arn, Mary-Jo, 269, 273, 312
Arnold, John H., 284
Arnold, Matthew, 67
Arundel, Thomas, Archbishop of
    Canterbury, 27, 42, 91, 109, 123, 124,
    132, 149, 156, 168, 171, 176, 179, 185;
    Constitutions, 117, 122, 125, 127, 133,
    140, 178, 192, 201, 206, 217, 223
Aston, John, 61, 107, 120
Aston, Margaret, 113, 243nn147, 152, 252,
    275n14, 281n94, 317n89
Athlone *Piers Plowman* editions, 57, 60,
    73–74, 77–79, 117, 262n104
Auchinleck Manuscript, 19, 238nn97, 101
Audelay, John, 152
Auerbach, Erich, 10, 39, 250
Augustine of Hippo, 48, 175, 220, 223
Austen, Jane, 68

Badby, John, 122–23, 134, 192, 258n40
Baker, Denise, 45, 46
Baldwin, Anna, 47
Baldwin, Ralph, 175, 178
Bale, John, 37, 40, 41, 63, 64, 70, 108, 109,
    138, 149, 220, 223–24
Ball, John, 23, 26, 36, 57, 59, 76, 103–6, 108,
    110, 112, 115, 132, 169, 171, 221
Banckett of Iohan the Reve vnto Pers Ploughman,
    23, 220

Manuscripts Index

JOHN M. BOWERS is professor of English at the University of Nevada, Las Vegas.